A TREATISE ON MIND

VOLUME 3

The Buddha-Womb

and the Way to Liberation

Other Titles in the Series

The I Concept

Volume 1: The 'Self' or 'Non-self' in Buddhism

Volume 2: Considerations of Mind - A Buddhist Enquiry

Cellular Consciousness

Volume 4: Maṇḍalas - Their Nature and Development

Volume 5: An Esoteric Exposition of the Bardo Thödol (Part A)

Volume 5: An Esoteric Exposition of the Bardo Thödol (Part B)

The Way to Shambhala

Volume 6: Meditation and the Initiation Process

Volume 7: The Constitution of Shambhala

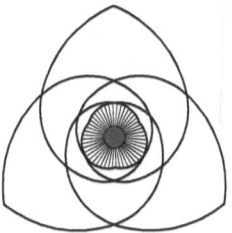

VOLUME THREE

The Buddha-Womb

and the Way to Liberation

BODO BALSYS

UNIVERSAL DHARMA
PUBLICATIONS
SYDNEY, AUSTRALIA

ISBN 978-0-9923568-2-8

Revised Edition, 2025

Āḥ!

Homage to the Lord of Shambhala.
Inconceivable, inconceivable, beyond thought
Is the bejewelled crown of this most excelled Jina.
He whose Eye has taught many Buddhas.
And who will anoint the myriad,
that in the future lives will come.
As I bow to His Feet my Heart's afire.
Oh, this bliss, this Love for my Lord
can barely be borne on my part.
It takes flight as the might of the Dove.
The flight of serene *nirvāṇic* embrace.
The flight of Light so bright.
The flight of Love so active tonight.
The flight of enlightenment for all to come to
their mind's Heart's attire.

Obeisance to the Gurus!
To the Buddhas of the three times.
To the Council of Bodhisattvas, *mahāsattvas*.
To them I pledge allegiance.

Oṁ Hūṁ! Hūṁ! Hūṁ!

Dedication

Thanks to my students, past, present and future, and in particular to those that have helped in the production of this Treatise.

Oṁ

Acknowledgments

Special thanks to Angie O'Sullivan, Kylie Smith,
and Ruth Fitzpatrick
for their efforts in making this
series possible.

Oṁ

Contents

Preface xi

1. The Great Gates of Diamond Liberation
   Part 1: Māra, Secret Mantra and Dependent Origination 1
   - The dark or evil forces 1
   - The Māra legend 6
   - The 'secret folk' of Vajrapāṇi 12
   - Verse two of the text, and Secret Mantra 15
   - The third paragraph of the text 22
   - The fourth paragraph and Dependent Origination 31
   - The sixteen petals of the Throat centre 39

2. The Great Gates of Diamond Liberation
   Part 2: Zodiacal Considerations of the Heart Centre 45
   - The twelve statements of the *samādhi* 45
   - Astrological considerations of the reversed wheel 48
   - The zodiac and *pratītyasamutpāda* 52
   - The great Mother, Origination, and the Eightfold Path 59
   - The reversed wheel and the twelve signs 66
   - The rectified wheel 88
   - The Bodhisattva *bhūmis* 124
   - Further astrological considerations 138
   - The sacred petals of the Heart centre 144
   - Consideration of the Head lotus 151

3. The Great Gates of Diamond Liberation
   Part 3: The Centres below the Diaphragm, and Voidness 162
   - The Middle Path 162
   - Discerning what is real 165
   - The governing signs of the Middle Path 170
   - The eight-armed cross 180
   - The Splenic centres 183
   - Liberation and the Diaphragm centre 186
   - Splenic centre II 197
   - Forms of enlightenment and the Rays 211
   - The *chakras* of the four directions 215
   - The three Buddha bodies 220
   - The six *pāramitās* 228

4. A Note on Emptiness 253
   - Not empty of light 253

Blind spots and the *dharmakāya* 255
The characteristics of *śūnyatā* 259
Thought-bubbles and cosmos 263
The relativity of truth 268
5. The Buddha and the Soul-Concept 276
Vacchagotta's query 276
Characteristics of the Sambhogakāya Flower 280
The Sambhogakāya Flower 288
The Śūnyatā Eye and the Dhyāni Buddhas 292
Sukhāvati and mantra 295
The seven Patriarchs and the sixteen Arhats 297
Further characteristics of the Sambhogakāya Flower 307
The Rays of light 314
The Śūnyatā Eye and the Bodhisattva path 317
The concept of no soul 324
6. The Sambhogakāya Flower and Dharmakāya 332
The Dharmakāya Flower 332
The Bodhisattva *bhūmis* 339
Considerations of the Dharmakāya Flower continued 341
Pratyekabuddhas 348
Further considerations of the Dharmakāya Flower 352
The dimensions of perception 354
7. The Ratnagotravibhāga Śāstra and the Sambhogakāya Flower
PART A. The Buddha Element 366
The Buddha nature 366
The result and function of the purification process 373
The functions of the *tathāgatagarbha* 376
The relations of the *tathāgatagarbha* 378
The general manifestation of the Buddha germ 381
The *tathāgatagarbha's* evolution and its all-pervading character 383
The unalterable character of the *tathāgatagarbha* 384
The indivisible character of the *tathāgatagarbha* 392
The Bodhisattva, the *tathāgatagarbha* and the Heart lotus 394
The *dharmakāya* and the *tathāgatagarbha* 400
The Parable of the Painting 407
7. The Ratnagotravibhāga Śāstra and the Sambhogakāya Flower
PART B. Nine illustrations characterising the *tathāgatagarbha* 411
The levels of perception 411
Rūpa, kāma and *arūpalokas* 412
The Six Realms and planetary evolution 416

The nine major petals of the Sambhogakāya Flower....419
The Sambhogakāya Flower and the Ratnagotravibhāga....426
The Sacrifice-Will—Sacrifice-Will petal....428
The Sacrifice-Will—Love-Wisdom petal....439
The five Sacrifice-Will, Love-Wisdom, and Knowledge petals....444
The Sacrifice-Will—Knowledge petal....449
The Love-Wisdom—Sacrifice-Will petal....458
The Love-Wisdom—Love-Wisdom petal....463
The Love-Wisdom—Knowledge petal....467
The Knowledge—Sacrifice-Will Petal....472
The Knowledge—Love-Wisdom petal....477
The Knowledge—Knowledge petal....485
The meaning of the examples....491
The *dharmakāya* and the *tathāgatagarbha*....501
Reasons for presenting the *tathāgatagarbha* doctrine....507
Bibliography....513
Index....516

Figures

Figure 1. The Throat centre....40
Figure 2. The Heart centre and the Zodiac....50
Figure 3. Thusness and Aquarius....89
Figure 4. The Ram's horns....114
Figure 5. The bonded Fishes....121
Figure 6. The ten Bhūmis and the Zodiac....125
Figure 7. The Chakras as the Wheel of Dharma....164
Figure 8. Splenic centre I, 'The Middle Path'....171
Figure 9. The Diaphragm centre....187
Figure 10. The Diaphragm centre as a distributor of Energies....196
Figure 11. Splenic centre II....202
Figure 12: The Solar Plexus centre....224
Figure 13. The Sambhogakāya Flower....290

Tables

Table 1. The Eightfold Path and the Zodiac....60
Table 2. The five Senses....313

Preface

This treatise investigates Buddhist ideas concerning what mind is and how it relates to a concept of a 'self'. It is principally a study of the complex interrelationship between mind and phenomena, from the gross to the subtle—the physical, psychic, supersensory and supernal. This entails an explanation of how mind incorporates all phenomena in its *modus operandi,* and how eventually that mind is liberated from it, thereby becoming awakened. Thus the treatise explores the manner in which the corporeally orientated, concretised, intellectual mind eventually becomes transformed into the Clear Light of the abstracted Mind; a super-mind, a Buddha-Mind.

A Treatise on Mind is arranged in seven volumes, divided into three subsections. These are as follows:

The I Concept
Volume 1. *The 'Self' or 'Non-self' in Buddhism.*
Volume 2. *Considerations of Mind–A Buddhist Enquiry.*
Volume 3. *The Buddha-Womb and the Way to Liberation.*

Cellular Consciousness
Volume 4. *Maṇḍalas - Their Nature and Development.*
Volume 5. *An Esoteric Exposition of the Bardo Thödol.*
(This volume is published in two parts)

The Way to Shambhala
Volume 6. *Meditation and the Initiation Process.*
Volume 7. *The Constitution of Shambhala.*

The I Concept represents a necessary extensive revision[1] of a large work formerly published in one volume. Together the three volumes investigate the question of what a 'self' is and is not. This involves an analysis of the nature of consciousness, and the consciousness-stream of a human unit developing as a continuum through time. It will illustrate exactly what directs such a stream and how its *karma* is arranged so that enlightenment is the eventual outcome.

The first volume analyses Prāsaṅgika lines of reasoning, such as the 'Refutation of Partless Particles', and 'The Sevenfold Reasoning' in order to derive a clear deduction as to whether a 'self' exists, and if so what its limitations are, and if not, then what the alternative may be. The analysis resolves the historically vexing question of how—if there is no 'self'—can there be a continuity of mind that is coherently connected in an evolutionary manner through multiple rebirths.[2] In order to arrive at this explanation, many of the basic assumptions of Mahāyāna Buddhism, such as Dependent Origination and the Two Truths, are critically analysed.

The second volume provides an in-depth analysis of what mind is, how it relates to the concept of the Void *(śūnyatā)* and the evolution of consciousness. The analysis utilises Yogācāra-Vijñānavādin philosophy in order to comprehend the major attributes of mind, the *saṃskāras* that condition it, and the laws by means of which it operates.

The enquiry into the nature of what an 'I' is requires comprehension of the properties of the dual nature of mind, which consists of an empirical and abstract, enlightened part. As a means of doing this, the *ālayavijñāna* (the store of consciousness-attributes) is explored, alongside the entire philosophy of the 'eight consciousnesses' of this School.

Volume three focuses on the I-Consciousness and the subtle body, by first utilising a minor Tantra, *The Great Gates of Diamond Liberation,* to investigate the nature of the Heart centre and its functions, then the

---

1 The book was inadequately edited hence contains many errors and grammatical mistakes that have been corrected in this treatise.

2 My earlier work *Karma and the Rebirth of Consciousness* (Munshiram Manoharlal, Delhi, 2006) lays the background for this basic question.

chakras below the diaphragm. This is necessary to lay the foundation for the topics that will be the subject of the later volumes of this treatise concerning the nature of meditation, the construction of *maṇḍalas,* and the yoga of the *Bardo Thödol.*

The focus then shifts to investigate where the idea of a self-sustaining I-concept or 'Soul-form' may be found in Buddhist philosophy, given the denial of substantial self-existence prioritised in the philosophy of Emptiness. Following this, the pertinent chapters of the *Ratnagotravibhāga Śastra* are examined in detail so that a proper conclusion to the investigation can be obtained via the *buddhadharma.* This concerns an analysis of how the *ālayavijñāna* is organised, such that the rebirth process is possible for each human consciousness-stream, taking into account the *karma* that will eventually make each human unit a Buddha. In relation to this the ontological nature of the *tathāgatagarbha* (the Buddha-Womb) must be carefully analysed, as well as the organising principle of consciousness represented by the *chakras.* I thus establish that there is a form that appears upon the domain of the abstract Mind. I call this the Sambhogakāya Flower. The final two chapters of this volume principally define its characteristics.

The second subsection, *Cellular Consciousness,* is divided into two parts. Volume four deals with the question of what exactly constitutes a 'cell', metaphysically. The cell is viewed as a unit of consciousness that interrelates with other cells to form *maṇḍalas* of expression. Each such cell can be considered a form of 'self' that has a limited, though valid, body of expression. It is born, sustains a form of activity, and consequently dies when it outlives its usefulness. This mode of analysis is extended to include the myriad forms manifest in the world of phenomena known as *saṃsāra,* including the existence and functioning of *chakras.*

Volume five deals with the formative forces and evolutionary processes governing the prime cells (that is, *maṇḍalas* of expression), and the phenomenon that governs an entire world-sphere of evolutionary attainment. This is explored via an in-depth exposition of the *Bardo Thödol* and its 42 Peaceful and 58 Wrathful Deities. The text also incorporates a detailed exposition concerning the transformation of *saṃskāras* (consciousness-attributes developed through all past forms of activity) into enlightenment. The entire path of liberation enacted by a *yogin* via the principles of meditation, forms of concentration, and related techniques *(tapas, dhāraṇīs)* is explained. In doing so, the soteriological purpose of the various wrathful and theriomorphic deities is revealed. This volume is published in two parts. Part A explores chapter 5 of the *Bardo Thödol* concerning the transformation of *saṃskāras* via meditating upon the Peaceful and Wrathful Deities. This necessitates sound knowledge of the force centres (*chakras*) and the way their powers (*siddhis*) awaken. Part B deals with the gain of such transformations and the consequence of conversion of the attributes of the empirical mind into the liberated abstract Mind.

The third subsection, *The Way to Shambhala,* is also in two parts. They present an eclectic revelation of esoteric information integrating the main Eastern and Western religions. Volume six is a treatise on meditation and the Initiation process.[3] The meditation practice is directed towards the needs of individuals living within the context of our modern societies.

Volume six also includes a discussion of the path of Initiation as the means of gaining liberation from *saṃsāra.* The teaching in Volume five concerning the conversion of *saṃskāras* is supplementary to this path. The path of Initiation *is* the way to Shambhala. As many will choose to consciously undergo the precepts needed to undertake Initiation in the future, this invokes the necessity of providing much more revelatory information concerning this kingdom than has been provided hitherto.

How Shambhala is organised is the subject of volume seven, which details the constitution of the Hierarchy of enlightened being[4] (the Council of Bodhisattvas). It illustrates how the presiding Lords who govern planetary evolution manifest. This detailed philosophy rests on the foundation of the information provided in all of the previous volumes, and necessitates a proper comprehension of the nature of the five Dhyāni Buddhas. To do so the awakening of the meditation-Mind, which is the objective of *A Treatise on Mind,* is essential.

---

3 The word Initiation is capitalised throughout the series of books to add emphasis to the fact that it is the process that makes one divine, liberated. It is the expression of divinity manifesting upon the planetary and cosmic landscape.

4 The word 'being' here is not pluralised because though this Hierarchy is constituted of a multiplicity of beings, together they represent one 'Being', one integral awakened Entity.

How to engage with this text

In this investigation many new ways of viewing conventional Buddhist arguments and rhetoric shall be pursued to develop the pure logic of the reader's mind, and to awaken revelations from their abstract Mind. New insights into the far-reaching light of the *dharma* will be revealed, which will form a basis for the illustration of an esoteric view that supersedes the bounds of conventionally accepted views. Readers should therefore analyse all arguments for themselves to discern the validity of what is presented. Such enquiry allows one to ascertain for oneself, what is logical and truthful, thus overcoming the blind acceptance of a certain dogma or line of reasoning that is otherwise universally accepted as correct. Only that which is discovered within each inquiring mind should be accepted. The remainder should, however, not be automatically discarded, but rather kept aside for later analysis when more data is available—unless the logic is obviously flawed, in which case it should be abandoned. There is no claim to infallibility in the information and arguments presented in this treatise, however, they are designed to offer scope for further meditation and enquiry by the earnest reader. If errors are found through impeccable logic, then the dialectical process may proceed. We can then accept or reject the new thesis and move forward, such that the evolution of human thought progresses, until we all stand enlightened.

This treatise hopes to assist that dialectical evolution by analysing major aspects of the *buddhadharma* as it exists and is taught today, to try to examine where errors may lie, or where the present modes of interpretation fall short of the true intended meaning. The aim is also to elaborate aspects of the *dharma* that could only be hinted at or cursorily explained by the wise ones of the past, because the basis for proper elaboration had not then been established. This analysis of *buddhadharma* will try to rectify some of the past inadequacies in order to explore and extend the *dharma* into arenas rarely investigated.

There will always be obstinate and dogmatic ones that staunchly cling to established views. This produces a reactive malaise in current Buddhist ontological and metaphysical thought. However, amongst the many practitioners of the *dharma* there are also those who have clarified their minds sufficiently to verify truth in whatever form it is presented, and will follow it at all costs to enlightenment. The Council of Bodhisattvas heartily seek such worthy ones. The signposts or guides upon the way to enlightenment have changed through the centuries, and contemporary practitioners of the *dharma* have yet to learn to clearly interpret the new directions. The guide books are now being written and many must come forth to understand and practice correctly.

If full comprehension of such guide books is achieved, those *dharma* practitioners yearning to become Bodhisattvas would rapidly become spiritually enlightened. Here is a rhyme and reason *for* Buddhism. The actual present dearth of enlightened beings informs us that little that is read is properly understood. The esoteric view presented in this treatise hopes to rectify this problem, so as to create better thinkers along the Bodhisattva way.

The numbers of Buddhists are growing in the world, thus Buddhism needs a true restorative flowering to rival that of the renaissance of debate and innovative thinkers of the early post-Nāgārjunian era. In order to achieve this it must synthesise the present wealth of scientific knowledge, alongside the best of the Western world's philosophical output.

Currently the *buddhadharma* is presented as an external body of knowledge held by the Buddha, Rinpoches, monks and lay teachers. This encourages practitioners to hero worship these figures and to heed many unenlightened utterances from such teachers, based on a belief system that encourages people to *uncritically* listen to them and adopt their views. When enlightened teachers *do appear* and find consolidated reasons for firing spiritual bullets for the cause of the enlightenment of humanity, then all truth can and will be known. The present lack of inwardly perceived knowledge from the fount of the *dharmakāya* on the part of many teachers blocks the production of an arsenal of weapons for solving the problems of suffering in the world. Few see little beyond the scope of vision in what they have been indoctrinated to believe, allowing for only rudimentary truths to be understood. While for the great majority this suffices, it is woefully inadequate for those genuinely seeking Bodhisattvahood and enlightenment. The cost to humanity in not being given an enlightened answer as to the nature of awakening, is profound.

We must go to the awakening of the Head lotus to find the most established reasoning powers. Without the 1,000 petals of the *sahasrāra padma* ablaze then there is little substance for proper understanding, little ability to hold the mind steady in the dynamic field of revelation that the *dharmakāya* represents. How can the unenlightened properly understand Buddhist scriptures, when there is little (revelation) coming from the Head centres of such beings? Much still needs to be taught concerning the way of awakening this lotus, and to help fill the lack is a major purpose of *A Treatise on Mind.*

Those who intend to reach enlightenment must go beyond the narrow sectarian allegiances promoted by many strands of contemporary Buddhism. Buddhism itself unfolded in a dialectical context with other heterodox Indian (and Chinese etc.) traditions, and prospered on account of those engagements. When one sees the unfolding of enlightened wisdom in such a fashion, the particular information from specific schools of thought may be synthesised into a greater whole. Each school has various qualities and types of argument to resolve weaknesses in the opposing stream of thought. This highlights that there are particular aspects in each that may be right or wrong, or neither wholly right or wrong. Through this process we can find better answers, or if need be, create a new lineage or religion which is expressive of a synthesis of the various schools of thought.

The Buddha did not categorically reject the orthodox Indian religio-philosophical ideas of his time, nor did he simply accept them—he reformed them. He preserved the elements that he found to be true, and rejected those 'wrong views' which lead to moral and spiritual impairment. If the existing system needs reformation it becomes part of a Bodhisattva's meditation. The way a reforming Buddha incarnates is dependent on how he must fit into such a system. Thus he is essentially an outsider incarnating into it to demonstrate the new type of ideas he chooses to elaborate. If there is a lot of dogmatic resistance to the presented doctrine of truth, then a new religion is founded. If there is some acceptance then we see reformation. There is always room for improvement, to march forward closer to enlightenment's goal, be it for an individual or for a wisdom-religion as a whole. There is a need for reform throughout the religious world today.

By way of a hermeneutical strategy fit for this task, we ought look no further than the Buddha himself. The Buddha proposed that all students of the *dharma* should make their investigations through the *Four Points of Refuge*. These are:

1. The doctrine is one's point of refuge, not a person.
2. The meaning is one's point of refuge, not the letter.
3. The sacred texts whose meaning is defined are one's point of refuge, to those whose meaning needs definition.
4. Direct awareness is one's point of refuge, not discursive awareness.[5]

These four points can be summarised or rephrased as: the doctrine (*dharma*), true or esoteric meaning, right definition, and direct awareness are one's point of refuge, not adherence to sectarian bias, semantics, the dialectics of non-fully enlightened commentaries, or to illogical assertions. What may be long held to be truthful, but is not, upon proper analytical dissection, needs rectifying. Also, in other cases, a doctrine or teaching may indeed be correct, but the current interpretation leaves much to be desired, and hence should be reinterpreted from the position of a more embracive or esoteric view.

Hopefully this presentation finds welcoming minds that will carefully analyse it in line with their own understandings of the issues, and as a consequence build up a better understanding of the nature of what constitutes the path to enlightenment. Their way of walking as Bodhisattvas should be enriched as a consequence.

For a guide to understanding the pronunciation of Sanskrit words, please visit our website.
http://universaldharma.com/resources/pronounce-sanskrit/

Our online esoteric glossary also provides definitions for most of the terms used in this treatise.
http://universaldharma.com/resources/esoteric-glossary/

---

5 Griffith, P.J., *On Being Buddha, The Classical Doctrine of Buddhahood*, (Sri Satguru Publications, New Delhi, 1995), 52.

My eyes do weep as I stare into this troubled world,
For I dare not place my Heart in my brother's keep.
He would grapple that Heart with hands so rough
So as to destroy the fabric of its delicate stuff.
Oh to give, to give, my Heart does yearn,
But humanity must its embracive,
Humbling, pervasive scene yet to learn.
To destroy and tear with avarice they know,
But little care to sensitive rapture they show.
How to give its blood is my constant fare,
For that Love to bestow upon their Hearts I bemoan.
But they hide their Hearts behind mental-emotional walls.
No matter how one prods these walls won't fall,
So much belittling emotional self-concern prop their bastions.
Oh, how my eyes do weep as I stare.
I stare at their fearsome malls and halls.
That lock Love out from all their abodes
And do keep them trapped in realms of woe.

Oṁ Maṇi Padme Hūṁ

1

The Great Gates of Diamond Liberation Part 1: Māra, Secret Mantra and Dependent Origination

The dark or evil forces

The subject of what constitutes evil, and the forces pertaining to it from a yogic perspective, is vast. Consequently, it will only be introduced here, but shall be further explained throughout this series. These forces constitute one's psychological attributes and *saṃskāras* as well as a diverse but highly organised hierarchy of beings. Upon the physical plane, however, beings appear as scattered predatory, exceedingly selfish and ruthlessly powerful individuals. They prey upon all of humanity through the power of money, false and lying propaganda spread through our mass media, the distorted legislative and legal systems governing us, and by occult methodology. They work via humanity's natural cupidity, selfishness, separative attitudes, self-centeredness and ignorance. They are much vaster in number and material power on the physical plane than the Bodhisattvas that oppose their activities in the world. This hierarchy is given the general appellations 'the forces of darkness', 'the forces of evil', or 'the dark brotherhood'. Their predatory effects must be taken into account by all serious students of meditation who are awakening higher perceptions. The Bodhisattva path consists of learning the techniques to counter their influences in the world. Without such activity enlightenment is not possible.

Esoterically, darkness is that which opposes the generation of light, rather than simply being that which light vanquishes. Consequently, darkness does not just merely relate to ignorance, or to one's negative *saṃskāras,* though they are manifestations of it. Lords of darkness oppose the perpetuators of the white *dharma*. The proponents of the white *dharma* manifest a liberating force, projecting the power of Love in service to all. Lords of darkness work to enslave all under the domination of their ruthless will and material might.

As well as the avaricious humans that bear malicious intent upon the general well-being of all upon the earth, there are also a host of psychic entities and manifestations of the mind that must be dealt with psychically and meditatively by a *yogin*. Such forces and entities are collectivised under the generic term Māra in Buddhism. However, there are also *yogins* that tread the path of the manifestation of the evil of darkness consciously, just as there are those that work to generate light. For the wilful manipulators of the forces of mind for personal gain and to manifest power over others, I shall generally use the appellation 'the dark brotherhood'. They are yogic brothers to those seeking enlightenment, but utilise diametrically opposite methodology. Their purpose is to perpetuate *saṃsāra* and to bind all to its conditionings. Such action is also conceived of in terms of black magic and sorcery. Others use yogic techniques learnt from former lives in an unconscious manner to amass vast sums of money which they wield as the power to control what they wish.

Looking to scripture with respect to this subject, an analysis of the first verse of a Mādyamika text, *The Samādhi 'Great Gate of Diamond Liberation'*, is helpful. This is the second scripture translated by Wayman in the chapter entitled 'About Voidness: Two Scriptures', from the book *Untying the Knots in Buddhism.*

> Then Vajrapāṇi master of the secret folk, emerged from that *samādhi* "Great Gate of Diamond Liberation". Whereupon, the venerable Śāradvatīputra spoke as follows to Vajrapāṇi, master of the secret folk: Son of the family, in what state were you, displaying this marvel of magical power? What is the name of the *samādhi* in which you induced the sinful Māras to generate the mind of Enlightenment; and also arranged all the evil spirits, ghosts, hindering demons, swerving spirits (*vināyaka*) to take pledges and generate the mind of Enlightenment?[1] [1, 2]

1 Alex Wayman, *Untying the Knots in Buddhism,* (Motilal Barnasidass, Delhi, 1997). Wayman states that 'this text was found in the Ārya-Mahāvajrameruśikharakūṭāgāra-dhāraṇī, among a group of Vajrapāṇi texts in the Kanjur, Rgydd 'bum division', 281.

2 Ibid., 287.

The fact that our instructor is Vajrapāṇi is important, as it informs us that the text we are concerned with is Tantric. He is the Bodhisattva who holds the dorje/*vajra* (the object of immutable power of the Tathāgatas) in his right hand and a skullcup in his left. He embodies the power and skill of all Buddhas, and in wrathful form is the ferocious emanation of Vajradhara. In peaceful form he is the Dhyāni-Bodhisattva of Akṣobhya. Vajrapāṇi is here styled 'master of the secret folk'. The term 'secret' means veiled, hidden, esoteric, not revealed to normal eyes, as well as being 'ear whispered', only conveyed as oral instructions from guru to *chela*. Secret folk are all of the subjective entities and beings that a *yogin* comes across in his meditative life as he develops the *siddhis*. Here they are depicted as the evil entities that oppose the *yogin's* quest for enlightenment, but they can also be taken to include such entities as *gandharvas, devas,* and *ḍākinīs.*

The word 'secret' immediately informs us that this Tantra conveys hidden intention, implicit also in the fact that it comes from the holder of the *vajra*. Thus it will also be seen to have non-literal and also definite meanings. As Dudjom Rinpoche states:

> Tantras are characterised by these six limits:
> There are those which employ the language of [hidden] intention
> And likewise those which do not
> Those which are literal and likewise those which are not,
> And those of provisional meaning and of definitive meaning.[3]

When a *yogin* embarks on a course of *dhāraṇīs* and austerities, he must work upon *saṃskāras* generated in former lives that oppose the accomplishment of enlightenment. Some modern commentators interpret a *yogin's* struggle in terms of psycho-somatic and psychological conditionings. While this is true to an extent, however, a *yogin's* meditative repertoire consists of considerations far broader than mere psychological or mundane ones. The *yogin* knows that all things are embodied Life, that forms of sentience permeate all beings. His universe is multidimensional and his consciousness permeates the reality of the multitudinous lives to determine the fundamentals of sound, colour,

3 Dudjom Rinpoche, Jikdrel Yeshe Dorje, *The Nyingma School of Tibetan Buddhism,* (Wisdom Publications, Boston, 1991), 290. He references 'the Root Tantra of the *Kālacakra (Kālacakramūlatantra)'* for this quotation.

and form. This knowledge is ascertained in meditation and he can utilise *mantras* and *dhāraṇīs* as forms of control of the elemental Life constituting all things. *Yogins* live in a hylozoistic universe, and this is the foundation of the *siddhis*, the transcendental powers attributed to the enlightened. Westerners specifically need a deeper understanding of the nature and reality of *siddhis,* as often a sceptical or disdainful attitude is evidenced when the terms magic, the occult, psychic powers, or thaumaturgy, are used.

Siddhis are wilfully developed by two main types of beings:

a. Those developed by the wise, as a consequence of the path of wisdom (gnosis/*prajñā*). The fundamental basis is love and wisdom working for the liberation of all beings. The *siddha* nearly always veils his/her abilities from the eyes of the profane. *Siddhis* wisely manifested for the benefit of all beings never feed the ego, nor are they demonstrated for mere show. The western terms used for such practitioners are 'white magicians', followers of the 'right hand path', or an 'occultist'.

b. Those developed by the self-centred ones desirous of psychic power. Yogic techniques are utilised to bind all forms of Life to the practitioner. Bondage, not liberation, is consequently produced for the all, with dire karmic consequences. Absolute power over others upon physical and psychic realms is the objective in any of the categories of selfish concern. The powers of the ego are exemplified, and hell-states follow the perpetuators of such action. The left hand path of the black magician is espoused. There are two categories:

    1. Those that generate black *prāṇas* (sometimes admixed with deep red, green, orange, browns, and violet). This is along the *iḍā* line, and concerns the intensification of the powers of the intellect to dominate no matter what the consequence or cost to another. Here we have the pure cunning of the adept of this path, who can use the most vile, manipulative, and cruel methods to achieve his ambitions. The above auric colourings denote the unabated hatred, avarice, psychic violence, devious scheming, and ruthless manipulation of lives and substance, that a sorcerer utilises to get his way in the fields of politics, religion, the worlds of finance, and of sex.

2. Those that generate all the shades of the grey. Their auras and thought processes are always dulled by a greyish hue, and in their most powerful form, are aberrations of daylight colourings. They are along the *piṇgalā* line, which generally concerns subtle distortions of the pure white *dharma*. Often the magician along this line masquerades as a philanthropic type, healer, or conscientious religionist, but always his true motives reveal his manipulative self-centred form of activity. When closely examined such activity will always be found to be antithetical to the enlightenment of all sentient beings. No true love for humanity is seen. Most 'psychics' fall into this category.

A whole cacophony of different types of psychic entities can be evoked that are coloured by the above hues. They will do the nefarious bidding of the black magician, once he has mastered the art of their control. Buddhists are often under the illusion that Bodhisattvas are free from the influence of such entities, but this is not the case, except when the Bodhisattva has gained liberation in that life. All have much *karma* of dabbling with such psychic forces in past lives of religious activity. Therefore a great deal of their meditative time is spent in cleansing the *saṃskāras* of such *karma* from their auras. A good example of a *yogin* who had to overcome such influences is Milarepa, who practiced the black arts when he was young. He spent seven years manifesting severe backbreaking labour, and other agonising tasks under instruction from his guru Marpa, to atone for his former activities. Thus he also psychically cleansed his *prāṇas*. It is well worth reading his biography from this perspective.[4] Even the attacks of the hosts of Māra upon the Buddha, which he had to fight off before gaining his enlightenment, is really the effect of the *karma* of erroneous psychic practices from former lifetimes. The *karma* was saved for that life as a final testing before liberation, and as an example for practitioners of what they must also conquer if enlightenment is to be gained.

Such influences can therefore be considered expressions of the dull or dark coloured *prāṇas* of one's *nāḍīs*, or else appear extraneously as real entities that attack the psychically inclined. Of the dark brotherhood,

4 For reference see W.Y. Evans-Wentz, *Tibet's Great Yogi, Milarepa,* (Oxford University Press, Oxford, 1972).

the most dangerous type are the grey-hued ones who whisper into the ear subtle thought-suggestions, or project strong thought-forms into the mind of the *chela* that is prone to listening to distortions of truth which lead away from the razor-edged path of liberating accomplishments. The grey ones are specialists in fostering what is desirous and appealing, the subtle forms of ego-clinging, prideful wishes, and the glamorous images appearing in the minds and desire bodies of their targets. Thus upon the path there is a stage when the practitioner realises that not all thoughts are their own, when the sum of the psyche is to be mastered.

When incarnate, the dark brotherhood are often those in power over the masses, and in control of vast stores of wealth. Theirs is a life of ruthless scheming and one-pointed focus upon materialistic incentives. Such may not consciously be sorcerers, but inwardly are the reincarnates of those that developed left hand attributes in former lives of yogic practice. No matter the outer seeming, much attendant *karma* follows such beings.

The Māra legend

Concerning Māra I shall first present some extracts of Khosla's chapter 'the Māra Legend', in order to put the symbolism and concept of Māra into proper perspective.

> Māra has been given many names. He is called *Kaṇha* (black or dark one), *Adhipati* (Chief); *Antāgu* (destroyer); *Maccu* (Killer), *Manuci,* Yakka or *Yakṣa, Pamattabandu* (a friend of the indolent or careless or passionate) and *Vāsavatti*[5]...In scholasticism, there are five Māras, which are of great hinderance in the attainment of Nirvāṇa. They are:
>
> (I) Khanda Māra (Māra of the elements of body)
> (II) Kleśo Māra (Māra as vices of passion or sin)
> (III) Maccu Māra (Māra as death)
> (IV) Abhisaṅkhara Māra (Māra of the Karma)
> (V) Devaputta Māra (The sinful Angel or temptor)
>
> Skandhas are Māra, because so long [as, *sic*] they exist, Nirvāṇa can not be attained. Kleśa or the original sin or passion or lust or the

5 Sarla Khosla, *The Historical Evolution of the Buddha Legend,* (Intellectual Publishing House, New Delhi, 1989), 72.

> Evil Principal is the Māra and a great hindrance to the attainment of Nirvāṇa. Death (Maccu māronam antaka) and Karma (Abhisaṅkharo) are the manifestation of the Evil Principal.
>
> Rebirth involves previous death. Whatever is continued existence there must be Karma and Kleśa. Which are the abiding cause[6]...Māra's main object was to prevent Buddha from attaining enlightenment. He, a personified supernatural enemy of the Buddha, had ten-fold mythological army (Daśabala), with which he unsuccessfully attacked Buddha.[7]

The five Māras embody the defiled qualities of the five types of *prāṇas*. The 'ten-fold army' will be seen to express the baser, untransmuted aspects of the five *prāṇas* (winds), and their subsidiary expressions (branch winds) of Tantric philosophy.[8] 'Māra of the elements of the body' represents the Earthy *prāṇas*. 'Vices of passion or sin' refer to the evocation of the Watery *prāṇas*. 'Death', or that which is responsible for death-like attributes, because of egotistic and *saṃsāra*-clinging attributes (which is perpetually changing and thus continually dying), is the concrete mind. This refers to the evocation of Fiery *prāṇas*. 'Māra of the Karma' refers to the basic *prāṇas* that circulate through the *nāḍī system,* and which will convey the consequent diseases and psychic sicknesses from past lives of erroneous action. They therefore represent the Airy Element. 'The tempter' refers specifically to the extraneous hosts that work to assail the mind or to attack the weak points of a *yogin's* spiritual armour. These entities are karmically linked to the awakening *saṃskāra*s of the person concerned. One must nullify their influences and consequently convert them to the way of the right as Vajrapāṇi did, so that they 'take pledges and generate the mind of Enlightenment'. (This simple statement in fact veils many lifetimes of accomplishment.) The process of conversion, one way or other, is the nature of this 'war' between the left and right hand paths. The Aetheric Element is here represented.

---

6 Ibid., 75-76.

7 Ibid., 80. He later states (Ibid., 81) 'mention of [the] ten-fold army of Māra and the legend, which has its origin in *Sutta Nipāta (Padāna Sutta),* is repeated in later Buddhist literature'.

8 Here viewed in terms of the *iḍā* and *piṅgalā* attributes of the *kleśas*.

Continuing with Khosla:

SN (IV. p. 152)[9] gives a vivid picture of Buddha's explanation to his disciples, about Māra's smoky and murky movements. 'Do you see Bhikkus! that smokiness going east, north, south, downward and in between?" "Yes Lord". "That, Bhikkus! is Māra, the evil one, who is seeing everywhere for the conscious of Godhika of the clansman." Godhika, with consciousness not reinstated, hath utterly ceased to live".[10]...In Pali tradition, Māra appears in the life of Bodhisattva quite soon. When Buddha was about to cross the city-gates of Kapilvastu, Māra appeared there and tempted him, saying "Go not forth, Sir! in seven days from now, the treasure-wheel will appear and will make you sovereign over the four continents and the two thousand adjacent isles. Stop, O Lord! I am Vāsvatti "-------" Bodhisattva replied, "it is not the sovereignty that I desire. I shall become Buddha and make the ten thousand world systems for joy."

From that time onwards, Māra followed Bodhisattva, "ever watching for a slip, as closely as a shadow, which never leaves an object."[11]...This defeat of Māra by Bodhisattva is quite natural, before attaining enlightenment. All the traditions record it. But in later literature (Nidānakatha, Lalitavistara, Mahavastu, *Buddhacarita* and Tibetan records), this brief narration of Padhānasutta has been stretched to the maximum extent of the imagination of the then writers. In Nidānakatha,[12] finding Bodhisattva's firm resolution Māra calls his hosts (Mārabalam). His army stretches 12 leagues to the right, left, front, behind, above and is nine leagues in height. His sound of cry is like an earthquake's noise. Māra's elephant is 250 leagues high, girdled with mountains. He creates thousand arms for himself, seizing in them all kinds of weapons. The battalion of Māra assumes various colours and forms and is equipped with various kinds of weapons.

The attack on Gautama was from all sides and of all kinds e.g. whirlwind, mighty rain, storm of rocks, storm of deadly weapons, ones two edged swords, spears and arrows, smoking and flaming through the sky, storm of charcoal embers, sand and mud. But when

---

9 *Samyutta Nikaya,* Tr. By Mrs Rhys Davids, assisted by Suryagoda Thera, (Pali Text Society, London, 1950), (IV. 152).

10 Khosla, 82.

11 Ibid.

12 Rhys Davids, Mrs. *Nidānakatha* (Buddhist Birth Stories). Tr. From the Fousboll's edition of the Pali Text, (Indological Book House, Varanasi, 1973), 190 *ff.*

> all these reached Bodhisattva, they became divine flowers. Then, to terrify the sage, Māra brought darkness, which also disappeared, as if before the bright sun. When all these efforts failed, Māra asked Bodhisattva to vacate the seat, which the devil claimed to be his. Bodhisattva claimed the seat, saying that Māra has neither perfected in ten perfections, nor in the five great acts [of, *sic*] renunciation, nor perfected the way of good in knowledge and understanding, so this seat belongs to him (Bodhisattva) and not to Māra. Being enraged, Māra threw his sceptre-javelin which is in the shape of a wheel.
>
> At this Māra's company shouted in joy and Māra claimed it as his victory and his host as the witness. But Bodhisattva, drawing his right hand from beneath his robe, stretched it before the earth and said "Art thou not witness of the seven hundred fold great gift I gave in my birth as Vassantra." The great earth said "I am your witness."
>
> At this Māra fled away. The gods praised Tathāgata for this victory.[13]

Clearly Māra personifies the hosts of darkness in general, viewed in psychosomatic and psychological terms, as well as psychic forces and embodied entities. He has a 'ten-fold mythological army', as well as being an external entity, and is a very cunning tempter, with extraordinary powers of delusion, subtle persuasive power, plus having the ability to directly psychically attack those working to gain enlightenment. He can appear in any terrifying aspect or forms that will feed one's desires, whilst his entourage, and aspects such as the daughters of Māra[14] can be very enticing.

The 'smoky and murky movements' described in the *Samyutta Nikāya* is quite illuminating. They represent the quality of the *prāṇas* generated by Godhika whilst he was incarnate. They must now seek his consciousness, wherever it goes, because they represent the inevitable apparel of that consciousness and will produce a hellish experience when Māra karmically connects. Not even an all-compassionate Buddha can prevent such an inevitability.

The twelve leagues that his army stretches 'to the right, left, front, behind, above' refers to the occupation of space, as is governed by the cycles of time. This involves the turning of the wheel of the twelve signs of the zodiac, which delineate the twelve houses categorising the various

---

13 Khosla, 83-84.

14 Depicted in Tibetan sources, the *Māra sutta*, the *Mahavastu* and Aśvagosha's *Buddhacarita*. (See Khosla, 77-9.)

groupings of this army, and indicates the nature and qualifications of the modes of attack. The zodiac can be interpreted in terms of turning clockwise ('to the right', representing evolutionary progression), and anticlockwise (the 'left', associated with *saṃsāric* identification). It can refer to the present epoch (the 'front'), the past ('behind'), directed towards enlightenment ('above'), or purely involved with mundane concerns, the great illusion. (The direction 'below', is not mentioned but also implied here.) Each sign qualifies a different category of dark forces and weaponry. The height of nine leagues refers to the principal 3 x 3 fold divisions of this army. This number was explained in relation to the nine headed Hydra that personifies the sum of the dark forces in *Karma and the Rebirth of Consciousness.*[15] The main body of this Hydra represents ignorance, which unites the nine into a ten-fold unity.[16] Thus we have another interpretation of the ten-fold army of Māra.

'An earthquake's noise' indicates the enormous destructive potency of the mantras that are uttered by Māra. The elephant he rides upon indicates the potency of the Earthy force that he can wield,[17] whilst his height (250 leagues) can be viewed in terms of the 5 x 5 x 10 greyish to black *prāṇas* that constitute that potency. This number is interpreted yogically as a grouping of five *prāṇas* conveyed by any *nāḍī (iḍā* or *piṇgalā)* which convey the attributes of the sense-consciousnesses, each of which have five subdivisions. This is multiplied by the ten petals of the Solar Plexus centre, which governs the expression of the entire Watery psychic domain, and the attributes of the emotional-mind, from which the potencies of Māra are derived. As the *prāṇas* embody the aspects that constitute consciousness, so the number five from this perspective also symbolises the Fires of mind. The multiplier 10 is also used as a device to indicate that these *nāḍīs* are multiplied manifold throughout

15 Bodo Balsys. *Karma and the Rebirth of Consciousness,* (Munshiram Manoharlal, Delhi, 2006) 194-217.

16 Three of the heads relate to overcoming physical plane appetites: sex, money and material comforts. Three relate to mastering the desire principle: fear, hate and ambition, and the final three are more specifically concerned with overcoming mental considerations, under the rubrics of pride, separateness and cruelty. The entire body of the Hydra is ignorance, making the ten-fold aspect.

17 The material domain and its psychic correlations being the focus of expression of the forces of Māra.

the macrocosmic body. The 'thousand arms' he creates for himself that seize 'in them all kinds of weapons' relates to the unfoldment of the 1,000 petalled lotus wherein the darkened, unregenerate *prāṇas* of Māra reside, and which need conversion in the meditation process.

The composite of all these forces is a powerful brute that a *yogin* must successfully battle and convert in order to finally be styled a *jina,* a victor.

We should also look to the symbolism of the *three daughters* of Māra.

> Then (just before enlightenment) his daughters, Taṅha, Ārati & Rāga (Craving, discontent & lust) come to his rescue. They assume various forms; each of them assumes the appearance of a hundred women, girls, women who have never had a child, or only once or only twice, middle aged women, older women—and six times they went to the Blessed one, and professed themselves his humble hand-maidens. But the blessed one paid no attention, as he had become free by the complete extinction of rebirth conditions.[18]

The daughters (who have different names in the various traditions) can be considered to generally embody the qualities of craving, desire or attachment (producing discontent) and lust (ambition or passion). They represent attributes that keep one firmly bound to the pleasurable aspects of *saṃsāra.* They can also be conceived of in terms of the central animals of the Tibetan Wheel of Life, the red cock symbolising desire-attachment, greed; the green snake representing aversion, enmity and hatred; and the ignorance or delusion associated with a black hog.

The daughters represent the most powerful of the weapons directed by Māra, apart from his sceptre-javelin which is in the shape of a wheel. (Which therefore embodies the power of a complete *chakra*, effectively the potency of any of the three main *chakras* below the diaphragm.) The power of these daughters rests esoterically in the fact that they represent the circulation of the debased *prāṇas* through the three central psychic channels, *iḍā, piṇgalā, and suṣumṇā.* They also manifest in the form of aberrations of the three *guṇas; sattva* (truth, rhythm, balance, that which must be attained), *rajas* (kingly mobility, the force that overcomes inertia) and *tamas* (inertia), in terms of all forms of energy that can be analysed.

18 Khosla, 77.

They are feminine because they are aspects of the goddess *kuṇḍalinī*, of the elemental Fires that have been forced by the will during yogic practices. They work to bind all aspects of consciousness inextricably to the form, via an (often overwhelming) intensification of the abovementioned characteristics. Here the *iḍā nāḍī* can convey the *saṃskāras* of intensified craving or thirst (for objects of *saṃsāra),* the *piṅgalā nāḍī* intensified lust or passion, and the *suṣumṇā nāḍī* the ramifications of ambition to attain whatever is desired.

Everyone upon the path to enlightenment must battle with the dual aspects of Māra, like the Buddha did, to vanquish all forms of ignorance, obstacles to the path, and the *saṃskāras* of evil-doing from past lives, which manifest in the form of personified entities. This will inevitably allow them to manifest the *bhumispraśamudra,* the earth touching gesture, for witness by the Mother of the World that *saṃsāra* and its karmic accounting system has been totally mastered. They can then be born outside Her womb into *śūnyatā* and thence cosmos.

The statement 'From that time onwards, Māra followed Bodhisattva, "ever watching for a slip, as closely as a shadow, which never leaves an object"' hints at Māra manifesting as a member of the dark brotherhood, continuously scheming how to prevent the Bodhisattva from achieving his goal. There is no mastery without an internal battle to overcome such entities. It betokens a 'war' between the white and dark brotherhoods that has been ongoing for aeons. The reason being that the enlightened one's presence and teachings spells the end to the dark one's power and domain, for all those that follow those teachings.

The 'secret folk' of Vajrapāṇi

The nature of the five types of entities that 'Vajrapāṇi, master of the secret folk', caused 'to take pledges and generate the Mind of enlightenment' can now be analysed.[19] They are 'secret' because those upon the active path of meditation at a certain stage of the path of yoga, come in contact with them psychically, and consequently such entities, forces, apparitions,

19 The reference here is to the passage earlier quoted: 'What is the name of the *samādhi* in which you induced the sinful Māras to generate the mind of Enlightenment; and also arranged all the evil spirits, ghosts, hindering demons, swerving spirits (*vināyaka*) to take pledges and generate the mind of Enlightenment?'

are not perceived by the ordinary person. They must however be dealt with by the meditator (thus taking the guise of Vajrapāṇi).

Vajrapāṇi (bearer of the *vajra)* is one of the eight Mahābodhisattvas that are explained in detail in Volume 4 of this series. He embodies the liberating power of all Bodhisattvas, and holds the northern position of the cross of direction in space, the way of ascension to the liberated domains *(dharmakāya).* His potency therefore incorporates the awakening of the *sahasrāra padma* (the 1,000 petalled lotus, the crown *chakra* on top of the head). He eliminates the last vestiges of hindrances in the mind of the *yogin*, hence he embodies the *vajrayāna* path. This role as psychic protector against all hindrances ('demons') to enlightenment is implied in the quote below from Getty:

> Besides being the protector of the Nāgas against the Garuḍas, Vajrapāṇi is the implacable enemy of the demons.[20]

The *nāgas* (serpents) in the above context refer to the serpents of desire in the *nāḍīs,* which can be intensified by the premature forces of the awakening of *kuṇḍalinī* ('serpent power'). Garuḍa is a bird-man who normally consumes the harmful psychic potencies *(nāgas).* He is the vehicle of Amoghasiddhi (as well as being associated with Vajrapāṇi and the wrathful forms of Padmasambhava). However when the liberating Fires of *kuṇḍalinī* are appropriately released (in the form of *nāgas)* Garuḍa's energy is not needed, because they are controlled by Vajrapāṇi. By such activity, Vajrapāṇi is well positioned to be our instructor in the art of safely assisting the flow of this energy so that no undue psychic problems arise.[21]

Yogically, 'the secret folk' represent the *prāṇas* that are to be converted by means of the process of *samādhi.* There are five types of *prāṇas*, relating also to the qualities of the five Elements. With respect to this we need to be aware that our concern is not just with the various forms of these winds within the body, but also with their actualised macrocosmic correspondences. Through former foul or erroneous magical or yogic practices they have karmic jurisprudence, allowing

20 Alice Getty, *Gods of Northern Buddhism,* (Oxford University Press, Oxford 1928), 51.

21 Volume 5A *(An Esoteric Exposition of the Bardo Thödol)* explains this yogic process and related problems concerning the control of psychic forces (*saṃskāras*) in detail.

them to attack the aspiring one psychically. The *yogin* must repulse or transmute the psychological factors of the accrued *saṃskāras,* and also develop skilful means in accomplished *siddhis* to convert or repel the externalised Māras, evil demonic entities, *rākśasas,* conjurations of sorcery, etc. The process necessitates the transmutation of the darker colourings, and the blacks or greys, into clear radiant auric hues, if the fully empowered *vajra* is to be held in the form of the consciousness of a new 'master of the secret folk'. We thus have:

1. *The sinful Māras.* As explained, they represent the sum of the psychic entities that afflict the consciousness of an individual. This includes various forces associated with the deceptions of all aspects of consciousness, and of the many types of extraneous entities aiming to prevent the enlightenment of the *yogin.* Collectively they represent the Earthy or grossest aspect of the Aetheric Element expressed in the form of any of the five *prāṇas* of mind.

2. *The evil spirits.* They represent psychic or mental forces, aspects of one's mental-emotional *saṃskāras,* that are the aggregate of one's base nature, such as hatreds, pride, fear, avarice that can be personified as entities. Such attributes can attract extraneous psychic entities, *karma* from past lives, that have the capacity to reinforce or engender the effects of the *saṃskāras.* They are thought-forms and images sent by sorcerers (or any other member of the dark brotherhood) to produce fearful reactions, or to psychically attack a *yogin.* The associated Element is that of the Air, which governs the *nāḍī* system via which such attacks come.

3. *Hindering demons.* These are the personification of scheming, malicious, lustful and desirous aspects of the human psyche. They represent *prāṇas* that need to be cleansed or transformed. They can be considered malevolent forces that work to stimulate pride for instance, or sexuality in general. Here the thought processes of the materialistic or empirical mind is intensified, represented as the aberration of Watery and Fiery *saṃskāras.* They are aspects of one's mental-emotional *prāṇas,* often brought up in meditation from the ancient past that directly hinder the flow of a quiet meditative mind, and consequently, must be dealt with appropriately. There are also meditation images taken to be real, but are often phantasms, mirages,

apparitions. They often waste the meditator's time in interpreting the streams of images, instead of doing worthwhile visualisations.

4. *Ghosts* can be apparitions, insubstantial phantasms, images that masquerade as real entities, to which the inexperienced may have fearful reactions. They can also be discarnate entities needing help and guidance to enter higher domains in the after-life.
5. *Swerving spirits.* They represent entities, or distracting energies hindering the bodily form from functioning properly. Aches, pains, and base types of energy effects are experienced in the body, forcing the meditative one to deal with these influences rather than being absorbed in *samādhi*. The 'swerving spirits' need to be disciplined, as indicated by the name *'vināyaka.'*[22] Their attribute is Earthy.

Many examples of the types of entities that *yogins* experience in all of these categories could be given, but this would be detrimental in view of people's creative imaginations, as they may invoke premature psychic attacks. The information is therefore wisely presented esoterically to those being trained to meditate via their karmic affiliation with an enlightened one. With respect to this, the descriptions in Buddhist texts are generally veiled in mythologising or symbolic gloss. This is wise, for it allows those that are being trained to consciously cleanse their psychic *karma* to access the truth. It also prevents access to those who may be inadvertently harmed by too much revealing information. All who aspire to gain enlightenment possess such *karma* (the Buddha for instance is an example), and consequently must learn the art of transforming or eliminating the *karma*. The highest forms of Tantra deal with this process.

Verse two of the text, and Secret Mantra

The second verse of the *samādhi 'Great Gate of Diamond Liberation'* from Wayman's book proceeds as follows:

> When he had so spoken, Vajrapāṇi, master of the secret folk, spoke as follows to āyuṣmat[23] Śāradvatīputra: Reverend Śāradvatīputra; This

22 *Vināyaka,* from the root *'vi-nī',* to instruct, educate, from which also is derived the term *vinaya,* referring to the schools of discipline in Buddhism.

23 *Āyuṣmat* (venerable one). Wayman in footnote 55 on page 35 states "the Buddha, by

> *samādhi* cannot be comprehended by name, letters, or words. Why so? It is because whether it be the name, the color, the shape, the place, and whether one is equipoised or has a straying mind, none of these are the natures of the *samādhi*. When it is without name, without color, without shape, without place, without equipoise, without straying, why should it occur to someone, Śāradvatīputra, to ask what is the name of the *samādhi?*[2][24]

From the first verse we saw that Śāradvatīputra addresses Vajrapāṇi as 'Son of the family', and logically we can deduce that this family was the Council of Bodhisattvas. (Of which Vajrapāṇi is a most senior member.) Now, as Vajrapāṇi had just emerged from *samādhi* and Śāradvatīputra clearly saw what had happened in that *samādhi,* how Vajrapāṇi had displayed 'this marvel of magical power', it is easy to deduce that Śāradvatīputra was also a Bodhisattva and was likewise engrossed in *samādhi.* He was also a monk, thus Vajrapāṇi addresses him as 'reverend Śāradvatīputra'.

We can also infer that he was initiated into the mode of fighting the forces of Māra and the dark brotherhood, and therefore did not need fuller explanation. However, the subtleties of the nature of this *samādhi*, which is expressive of the open gates of liberation, would prove useful, therefore Vajrapāṇi presented the discourse.

The first part of the discourse concerns the 'name, letters, or words' of anything. First, Vajrapāṇi describes the way the intellect functions. It is that which would try to comprehend, and its tool is precisely to segregate the qualities of a thing relative to another thing by means of naming. Once something has been named then its further descriptive qualifications are expressed by means of letters and words. He however tells us that this *samādhi* cannot be comprehended through such an analytical process, that it is beyond the mind's conceptualisations in terms of names, letters and words.

---

having 'destroyed birth' and also defeated the 'death Māra', this seems behind his repudiation of the title *'āyuṣmat'*, which means literally, 'possessed of life, i.e., long life"'. With reference to Śāradvatīputra therefore, we see that he is a venerable one that has not yet fully conquered Māra, hence is enquiring from Vajrapāṇi how to do so.

24 Alex Wayman, *Untying the Knots of Buddhism*, 287.

Such an elementary rationalisation would however have already been well understood by the brother *yogin* Śāradvatīputra, thus there is also an esoteric agenda. This concerns the power of Secret Mantra, which are specifically exemplified in the Nyingma tradition. According to Dudjom Rinpoche, the *mantrapiṭaka*[25]:

> Was taught by the Teacher, Vajradhara, observes that the ground and result are indivisible and spontaneously present, owing to which the natural expression of the truth of the origin [of saṃsāra] appears as the truth of the path, and the natural expression of the truth of suffering appears as the truth of cessation.[26]...It says in the *Kālacakra Tantra:*
>
>> The collection of vowels and consonants is not unchanging. The unchanging sound refers to Vajrasattva,[27] the pristine cognition of supreme, unchanging bliss. Similarly, since they are the reality which protects the mind, the mantras, too, are called the supreme, unchanging pristine cognition.[28]

We see therefore that when Vajrapāṇi stated 'This *samādhi* cannot be comprehended by name, letters, or words' he was really referring to the teaching of Secret Mantra, wherein Vajrasatva's 'unchanging sound' is experienced. This is the experience of a Mind that is 'equipoised'. That which can be comprehended by means of 'name, letters, or words', on the other hand, is constantly changing, being descriptive of attributes of *saṃsāra*. It is the view of a 'straying mind'.

---

25 The term *piṭaka* means 'basket', a category of learning. In general Buddhism there are three 'baskets', the *vinaya* (disciplines), the *abhidharma* (esoteric instructions), and the *sūtras* (the general discourses of the Buddha). *Mantrapiṭaka* therefore refers to a fourth 'basket', the secret lore of mantras, which can also be called *tantrayāna* or *vajrayāna*.

26 Dudjom Rinpoche, 257.

27 *Vajrasattva* (rdo rje sems dpa): the personification of the vehicle (*va*) of the immutable principle (*sat*) from which stems the adamantine or indestructible power sustaining all being (*vajra*). It is one of the titles given to the Ādi Buddha, the One who integrates or fuses the qualities of the five Dhyāni Buddhas into Oneness. Generally depicted as white in colour but can appear in any of the five colours of a Jina. He holds a *vajra* in the right hand and a bell against his thigh. Credited with the transmission of Ati yoga to humanity.

28 Ibid., 258.

The equipoised Mind sees the 'name' as the overall Word or Power, that emanatory sound that commands (substance). The letters are the seed syllables constituting the component aspects of what is moved, whilst the 'words' represent a mantric phrase that constitutes the sum total of the *maṇḍala* that must come into expression. This represents the downward thrust of the mantra to control aspects of *saṃsāra* (or the origination thereof). Here the generation of *siddhis,* psychic powers, are necessitated. Conversely a reverse process can be utilised in a mantra to produce liberation from form. The 'name' manifests a colour, signifying its embodied quality and its potency, according to the intensity of the hue. It also manifests a 'shape' (*maṇḍala*) that establishes its purpose and is also projected in a 'place', a time zone, the appearance of the form that can be experienced by others. (Signifying the accomplishment of its purpose.) The mantra must be held steady, unchanging, in the meditation-Mind for its purpose to be achieved without aberration.

More detail can now be given concerning this way of Secret Mantra:

> Now this [way of mantras] is also known as the vehicle of indestructible reality *(rdo-rje theg pa,* Skt. *Vajrayāna).* By definition, this term conveys the sense of "undivided" *(mi-phyed)* and "imperishable" *(mi-shigs).* That which is not divided into anything different never wavers from mind-as-such in the abiding nature of reality, despite the different apparitional modes of both saṃsāra and nirvāṇa. Therefore, as it is said [*Hevajra Tantra,* Pt. 1, Ch. 1, v. 4a]:
>
> > It is the undifferentiated nature that is expressed in the word *vajra.*
>
> The mind of all the buddhas is imperishable because it is the essence of reality which cannot be destroyed by any symbolic doctrine. Since it is similar to a *vajra,* the so-called indestructible mind of all buddhas abides, as previously explained, as the essence of mantra.[29]

Mantras express the essence of a thing, the power that supports the *maṇḍalic* structure within which, or of which, a thing is composed.[30]

---

29 Ibid., 260.

30 The word *mantra* is derived from the root *man,* to think, and the syllable *tra,* which represents the mechanism that carries the thought. Literally 'protection of mind'. It refers to the pure sound, which is the perfected speech of an enlightened being. A sacred verse or word of power. Mantras can be seen as the incantations

This 'essence' is the integral *Life* that sustains the duration of whatever is. Through correct undeviating intonation of a mantra (as taught by an enlightened preceptor), constituting of name, letters, and even words, whatever constitutes *saṃsāra* and *śūnyatā* can be revealed and controlled. Mantras act as mechanisms for the liberation of the integral Life, thus of human consciousness. Mantras reveal the nexus between *saṃsāra* and *śūnyatā,* uniting the two along any line of meditative investigation. All attributes of *saṃsāra* can be moulded by the energies coming via the domain of the Real (*śūnyatā*) and that manifests via the etheric body that houses the *nāḍīs.* These energies are controlled by the potency of sound, knowledge of which constitutes this, the most esoteric of sciences. Sound is the emanatory basis of all manifest being, thus when the nature of sound is truly comprehended then the 'basis' of whatever is meditated upon can be controlled or changed. When mantric words are utilised then work is conveyed in that meditation, phenomena is moved or altered according to the will of the *yogin,* and consequently *siddhis* are demonstrated.

The *'name'* constitutes knowledge of the overall characteristics of whatever the subject of meditation is. It is the emanatory demonstration of what sustains the overall *Life.* It is accordingly revealed by the interior wisdom of the *yogin* and unified into form as an emanation of Love. This involves the coming together of all the elements constituting that Life.

The *'letters'* constitute the internal characteristics of the name, each of which can be directed or modified by the will of the one who knows the name. They represent the *bījas* of inherent potentiality and incorporate the nascent Fires of the Clear Mind. If altered the entire *maṇḍalic* patterning emanating from that name alters accordingly.

The *'words'* constitute the combination of as many names as is needed in order to make the complete picture, the *maṇḍala* of the grouping observed as a nexus. They can be alchemically moved or transmogrified. If done so, the *yogin* demonstrates the nature of a *siddha.*

---

uttered by the religious to bring about specific objectives. They are forms of words or sacred syllables rhythmically expressed so that when sounded produce certain effects. They are used in all forms of magical and meditative practices and are given their potency according to the quality of the *deva* lives they attract, and which embody the related sound patterns. This is done according to the esoteric knowledge, directed will, and psychic purity of the person or group sending forth the sound.

The practice necessitates the defeat of the forces of Māra, which means the utter purification of all of the *prāṇas* that are to form the composition of the name, letters, and words. Any aberration or deviation of the unchanging meditation of the *vajra*-mind of the *yogin* would produce devastation to the life of the form under consideration and to the psyche of the *yogin*.

Having introduced the general characteristics of the subject of mantras Vajrapāṇi then provides the detail. He presents further information in the form of a listing headed by the word 'name'. This name is generalised as a second Ray aspect that manifests as an inherent triplicity. The first Ray quality of the Will (in various sub-Ray attributes) is represented by each of the letters, and the third Ray function manifests by the activity of the words. However, if name, letters, and words are to be part of a *maṇḍala* then there would also have to be a manifest colour, a quality of radiance, with various hues characterising the component parts of the pattern of words. Here is presented a fourth Ray quality of beauty or harmonious order.

This then introduces the next phase of the process, that gives the mantra an overall shape, whether spheroid, ovoid, square, etc. The manifestation of the shape and qualities of the mantra is governed generally by the scientific (fifth Ray) aptitude of Mind. The form and characteristics of the *maṇḍala* are now complete, and endowed with the energies of five *prāṇas*/Elements veiled by the five Rays mentioned below, and which are a natural expression of the *vajra*-mind. The view therefore is from the highest domain downwards.

- *Letters,* Ray I of Will or Power, Aetheric Element, the elementary *bījas* from which the structure springs.
- *Name,* Ray II of Love-Wisdom, Airy Element, the overall *prāṇic* characterisation of the *maṇḍalic* structure.
- *Words,* Ray III of Mathematically Exact Activity, the Fiery Element, the infusing of the *maṇḍala* with the major patterns of manasic concern.
- *Colour,* Ray IV of Harmony overcoming Conflict, the Watery Element, the general clothing of the form of the *maṇḍala* with its qualifications of emanatory hues.
- *Shape,* Ray V of Scientific Endeavour, Earthy Element. Its final

establishment as a 'thing' in the realm of mind. It now exists as a complete radiant thought-form.

In these five qualities we have a manifestation of characteristics within the *samādhi* that finds no lower expression than the Clear Light of the abstract Mind.[31] These five Rays can also be considered sub-Rays of the Fiery Ray of Mind. In the three remaining aspects of the list given by Vajrapāṇi (the place, equipoised or straying mind) we have a projection of these abstracted qualities into the three worlds of human livingness, when the order is reversed. Vajrapāṇi evokes the mirror-like wisdom of Akṣobhya to do so. This is seen from the fact that the 'straying mind' (referring to the actively engaged empirical mind) is last on the list.

Once the *maṇḍala* has been established then the *yogin* must do something with the construct. The final three aspects presented by the list concerns this. The *yogin* must seek out a *place* to direct the construct, as it must have a purpose or final resolution. This is done by means of a 'straying mind' that is equipoised. The mind is straying because it must seek out the right place in *saṃsāra* wherein the *karma* exists for its purpose to be resolved. We are therefore concerned with the process of concretising upon the physical domain what has been established in the domain of mind/Mind.

The term equipoise refers to the establishment of a balanced state, making a thing stable. It thus also has reference to the amount of energy put into a construct so that it does not fall apart. It must possess sufficient intensity to fulfil its purpose within the realms of form. It must be sustained for the duration of its karmic purpose by the poised *dhyāna* of the *yogin*. His Mind sees to it, that the purpose inevitably will bring all aspects and effects of the *maṇḍala* to the Void. The *maṇḍala* exists for the liberation of the all.

The *name* thus manifests its purpose (potency) via the empirical mind, evoking images therein that it can utilise. The mind can dissect and identify through the process of naming. Each name becomes a separate entity, a 'self'. *Saṃsāra* thus manifests.

---

31 Which from the above perspective is viewed as Earthy, but from the point of view of normal empirical considerations is Fiery.

Letters find expression in that which is equipoised—the emotional body, which is stilled, made mirror-like for the duration of the *samādhi,* so that the abstracted qualities of the *maṇḍalic* construct can find expression in the realms of form without aberration of any kind. The emotional body is governed by the sixth Ray of Devotion, which for the *yogin* represents the driving impetus to establish a physical presence of the *maṇḍala* in the material domain. The abovementioned intensity is but a higher, refined aspect of the one-pointed form of energisation associated with devotion.

Words find their externalisation in the dense form where everything has its 'place'. Here the images that were formulated in the mind and which named things are strung into 'sentences' for comprehension and articulate expression. They allow the 'I' to function in a world filled with complexity. Such activity is governed by the seventh Ray of Ritualistic Activity. Thus everything concerning the *maṇḍala* is grounded in the cycles of time and reappearing *karma* (which is ritualistic, cyclic, in nature). *Colour* and *form* become attributes of the form that finds its placing in *saṃsāra.*

With respect to the above process, Vajrapāṇi then states:

> When it is without name, without color, without shape, without place, without equipoise, without straying, why should it occur to someone, Śāradvatīputra, to ask what is the name of this *samādhi?*[32]

Here the *śūnyatā-saṃsāra* nexus is implied, that though one has been concerned with the appearance of phenomenological effects, ultimately all resides in the Void, where the mind that names does not exist, consequently 'names' are meaningless. The statement implies that after the thought-construct has served its purpose it must inevitably be resolved back into *śūnyatā* by the *yogin,* for the *karma* to be annulled.

The third paragraph of the text

The third paragraph of this *samādhi, 'Great Gate of Diamond Liberation',* presented by Wayman is:

> Besides, reverend Śāradvatīputra, this clarification is neither a

32 Wayman, 287.

> clarification to oneself, nor a clarification to another, and neither a clarification to both. Still, one imagines a clarification. Here, a clarification is void of being a clarification. Self is void of self, and the other is void of being another. Also, both are void of being both. This is because, they are an imagination of what is not the case. Whatever two syllables are composed, they are void of being a word; and the syllable is not a syllable.[3][33]

In analysing this verse one must understand that Vajrapāṇi is explaining the nature of the yoga (Tantrapiṭaka) that allowed him to thoroughly overcome 'the sinful Māras', etc. The 'clarification' in question therefore concerns the nature of the yoga practice, and what is perceived in the associated *samādhi.* Though succinct, the Tantra, however, presents much detailed information. One must carefully analyse the structural content of the words and the context to which they are put to comprehend the ontology. They manifest the patterns of the *maṇḍala* of Vajrapāṇi's meditation. From this can be derived the actual practice.

This extract starts with consideration of the ability of the mind to clarify (things). Because the things clarified are illusional, so also is the clarification. This is the Mādyamika doctrine, which has validity in the guise of ultimate truth verses relative truth, the comprehension of which this verse is structured around.

There are thirteen principal statements involving this teaching of clarification. First we must analyse the clarification itself (which is what makes clear, hence made comprehendible). This is done by means of a rational mind that asks questions. The analysis made is of any topic that is under meditative investigation. Here the subject explicated concerns Secret Mantra. With this in mind we can proceed.

There are four directions that the mind can go in its quest for clarification, to which the first four phrases refer.

- *The southern direction* of downward into materiality. The phrase 'the clarification' infers this direction, which relates to what one experiences via the phenomenological world of the senses. This refers to the place in the physical domain wherein the generated *maṇḍala* is to be grounded. The meditating one must have clarification in the

33 Ibid.

complete environment wherein it is to be expressed, if its purpose is to be achieved. The *yogin* must ascertain how much of *saṃsāra* the construct is to incorporate and interrelate with.

- *The northern direction* of upward to the divine. The reference here is the phrase 'neither a clarification to oneself'. The short answer is that it cannot be a clarification to oneself if there is no 'self' to consider. This is true with respect to the personal 'self', though many people look upward to such an imagined 'self' for clarification, for this is the base of their perceived identity. Looking upward, the *yogin* identifies either with the group awareness of the Sambhogakāya Flower, or else to *śūnyatā* or the *dharmakāya,* where no 'self' can be found. With respect to the Sambhogakāya Flower, it is true to say that clarification is not needed, because it already knows, having previously seeded the personality to live out its life in *saṃsāra.*
- *The western direction* of outward to the field of service to assist humanity. There can be no such assistance to others if no 'selves' exist. Clarification normally refers to one's predilection to relate to whatever is out there in the world of the senses in terms of individual entities that interrelate with one's own 'self'. But when no 'self' exists then such interrelation produces no such clarification. However, paradoxically, one needs to reside in a selfless state in order to perceive the nature of the clarification concerning Secret Mantra. This esoteric lore cannot be taught to 'selves'. Only those *(yogins)* striving to conquer the illusion of 'self' can thus learn the Tantra. Those that do not undertake the necessary yogic training have not the ability to understand the subtleties of mantras, or of the Void from which they stem. Aspirants must be induced to apply the path of purification, whence they can come to know. As such clarification is necessarily esoteric, so proper explication is withheld for safety's sake until the *chela* (spiritual student) has been properly prepared. A teacher is not interested in inadvertently producing black magicians out of avaricious or self-focussed individuals. Genuine humbleness of heart and compassionate motives are the keys to the approach to this subject.

Also, there is no need to elucidate in the realm of the Sambhogakāya Flower because therein such knowledge is commonly shared.

- *The eastern direction* of inward to the Heart of Life. The Heart centre veils the secrets of Life, for one goes therein to meditatively receive empowerment, and then to the Heart within the Head for the esoteric teachings of Secret Mantra. The Heart centre betokens the way to the experience of *śūnyatā.* It is the place of serene resolve from whence this *samādhi* of the 'Great Gate of Diamond Liberation' ensues. It envisions in all directions at once, to the field of service as well as to the domain of the Sambhogakāya Flower. It therefore needs no clarification, because it is the heart of the process whereby the *maṇḍala* to be generated is constructed.

Having analysed the four directions wherein one receives an elucidation of the *dharma,* we come to a general, integrating statement, 'still one imagines a clarification'. This phrase relates to the domain of the mind/Mind wherein such imagination is possible. The phrase does not just refer to the fact that the images in the mind are illusional, but also to the techniques of building the *maṇḍala* by utilising the creative imagination. Without the creative faculty of the mind, the thought-form building of 'letters, name, words, colour, and shape' would not be possible. Once the construct has been imaginatively created, then it must be moved in one of the four directions in the mind's eye. The 'one' who 'imagines' here is thus the *yogin,* and through such creativity the detail of the entire construct is 'clarified', seen via the all-seeing Eye.

If the *yogin* explicates method, quality, design and purpose to another, then that 'other' will also imaginatively receive a clarification and accordingly proceed with the imagery. Yogically, information is conveyed directly from Mind to Mind. Thought transference is the common mode of parlance amongst *siddhas* and their students (*chelas*).

The *cardinal cross* of resolute purpose is implied for the next four points presented, where the will is utilised to drive all to its ultimate conclusion. This cross manifests in the four directions of the fixed cross, however the end result of all activity is not just envisaged, but accomplished.

Note that the mutable cross of periodical changing activity is absent from this analysis because it concerns the controlling, refinement and transmuting of *saṃskāras.* This process lies in the background, or is implied to have been accomplished in this *samādhi.*

- The phrase 'a clarification is void of being a clarification' denotes the fact that such a *maṇḍalic* construct has its foundation in the Void. The direction east is therefore implied, whereby the *yogin* (or *yoginī)* has utilised his/her will to overcome all impediments so that *śūnyatā* could be realised and become the serene base for all future activity. When *śūnyatā* is the base of a thing then it is 'void of being a clarification'.
- We can now proceed to considerations of the Voidness of the 'self' and the concept of 'another'. Both are considered aspects of the imagination and hence are not real ('not the case'). However, the phrase 'Self is void of self' is curious, as it implies that there is a form of self, as is postulated in this book, but that it is void of the qualities that one would attribute to a 'self'.[34] The direction implied is south, wherein the *yogin* utilises the will to ensure that all vestiges of the 'self' concept is annihilated. This includes any perspective attacks from the forces of Māra, to which the *maṇḍalic* construct of the 'clarification' is directed. Nothing is allowed to impede the ensuing *samādhi*.

  The question hinted at here is 'what is it that builds the construct (the clarification) if the "self" is Void?' We can look to a) the Sambhogakāya Flower, b) a Mind that is not an 'I', c) a Tathāgata for the answer. In each case, though a 'self' does not exist, nevertheless an Identity does. Such an Identity (Monad) is difficult to conceive of by those ensconced as 'selves'. Answers b and c are well understood in Buddhism, hence need no commenting. Consideration of the Sambhogakāya Flower in this respect, however, needs elucidating. The fact that 'Self is void of self' is true when related to the lower personal 'self', but both true and not true when relegated to the Sambhogakāya Flower. In analysing such a Flower we can say:

  1. It is certainly void of what the lower concrete mind would identify with phenomena as a 'self', but it is not void of a form of distinctiveness from other similar Sambhogakāya Flowers,

34 I am of course disregarding the normal consideration of this phrase, which simply states that there is no self, other than what is conceived conventionally as a personality. My interpretation is, as usual, a more esoteric consideration that can also be found implied in enlightened statements through careful analysis.

i.e., we have the concept of individuation within the context of group evolution.

2. It is void of the 'I' or 'me' concept, but is not void of the qualifications of consciousness that allow it to pursue a path that promulgates a series of rebirths of the personal-I.
3. It is void of the taints of *saṃsāric* activities of itself and within itself, but it is not void of the *bījas* that can be seeded to activate *saṃskāras* of any evolving personal-I. It therefore seeds *saṃsāra* with the potentiality of future activity, and reaps the consequences, but is not part of its *māyā.*
4. It is void of any form of discursive thought structures, but it is not void of the accumulation of conscious awareness reaped through many incarnations of evolving personal-I's.
5. It is void of image-making tendencies in relation to conceptions of a separated 'self' but it is not void of the qualifications that are productive of enlightenment in *śūnyatā*'s guise.
6. It is part of a continuum of unfolding revelation that is neither void of the consciousness stream of *saṃsāra's* consequences or from *śūnyatā*'s embrace. Nor is it void of the emanatory instigations from the *dharmakāya.*
7. It is therefore 'void of self', but it is not void of the driving force that will propel the all to the 'other shore' of liberated being/non-being. This driving force in turn can be considered a 'self of the Void', for it can be considered the aspect of the Void that transforms all darkness into the form of lighted substance that accommodates the Void. It is then no longer dual, not one or many either, but the all and the other combined in no-thing.

- When the *yogin's* will is directed westward then he seeks residence at the *saṃsāra-śūnyatā* nexus. From here the Bodhisattva path of outward service to all can be accomplished, as both *saṃsāra* and *śūnyatā* are accommodated in the 'clarification'. The related phrase is 'The other is void of being another'. When the construct is a clarification, then its expression exists in the Clear Light of the substance of the abstract Mind and when it is void then it rests in *śūnyatā*. Both can therefore be considered Void of each other. The nexus is the mode of interrelation between the two, which establishes the *samādhi*. It is intrinsically empty, yet has the five-fold characteristics mentioned above. Each characteristic is founded upon one or other of the five Void Elements described in Volume 1. A clarification is therefore Void, but is replete with meaning when expanded in the field of consciousness. Then its meaning is the perfected expression of the *dharma* because its foundation is *śūnyatā*. Once established thus it can then be projected to *saṃsāra*, so that it can be experienced in terms of conventional truth (the appearances of things).

- The direction north causes the *yogin* or *yoginī* to utilise his/her will to penetrate into *dharmakāyic* domains. The *dharmakāya* establishes the pure pristine Reason which is the fount of the *dharma*, which in turn is Void of things. The phrase 'both are void of being both' then comes into perspective. Both *śūnyatā* and *saṃsāra* are integrated as aspects of *dharmakāya,* therefore there is neither *śūnyatā* nor *saṃsāra*. Rather there is one integral entity with cosmos, which is established at the nexus between these two aspects. This then is the essence of the Buddha-Mind, which is 'void of being a clarification', because the clarification itself is freed of any form of empirical discernment. (From whence comes the concept of clarification.)

We know that the mind is what composes two or more syllables to make words, and that it is the larynx in the throat in conjunction with the activity of the lungs and mouth that must articulate the words, to produce meaning in the realms of form. Here therefore is a reference to the inevitable concretisation of the mundane construct of the mantra by utilising the throat to sound the necessary words, and the mind to visualise name, colour, shape, and place. However, with respect to Secret Mantra the essence or heart of the construct is ultimately void of any sound pattern that would make it a word. Its potent base is *śūnyatā*.

Next we should consider each syllable or *bīja* constituting the mantra to trace the source of its potency. This allows us to pierce another veil of revelation, to realise that intrinsically each syllable is 'not a syllable'. This has reference to the *dharmakāya* level of interpretation, wherein the complete mantra is made potent as an expression of the Buddha-Mind. The syllable has been transmogrified into an expression of the wisdom sequence of a Dhyāni Buddha. The syllable is the *dhyāna* of a Buddha, as a pure unadulterated gnosis which can explode as liberating consciousness-revelation in the meditator's mind.

Having provided general teachings concerning this verse, further detail can be provided. There are thirteen main phrases (divided into three parts). The first five relate to the expression of conventional truth. (1. 'This clarification', 2. 'neither a clarification to oneself', 3. 'nor a clarification to another', 4. 'neither a clarification to both', 5. 'one imagines a clarification'.) The next five phrases relate to ultimate truth. (6. 'a clarification is void of being a clarification', 7. 'Self is void of self', 8. 'the other is void of being another', 9. 'both are void of being both', 10. 'they are an imagination of what is not the case'.) The final three phrases relate to the main subject being discussed in this exposition of Secret Mantra. (11. 'Whatever two syllables are composed', 12. 'they are void of being a word', 13. 'the syllable is not a syllable'.)

The first grouping can then be related to the five Elements, whilst the second grouping concerns their conversion into the Void Elements. Thus the phrase 'This clarification' is Earthy because it relates to the phenomenal world. A 'clarification to oneself' is Watery because it evokes an inherent emotional input, producing the concept of 'self'. When expressing 'clarification to another' then a mental (Fiery) input is needed. When there is 'neither a clarification to both' then the abstract Mind (here the Airy Element) is evoked to produce *samādhi,* where such clarification is not needed. The Aetheric Element is evoked in the imagining of the clarification in *samādhi,* to produce the complete *maṇḍalic* construct, the 'magical power' that allows the overcoming and conversion of the 'sinful Māras'.

The second pentad (numbers 6 to 10) concerns the process of converting the *saṃsāric* attributes of the first pentad into their corresponding Void Elements. Thus the sixth phrase corresponds to the first, the seventh phrase to the second, etc. The actual process of conversion utilises the type of teachings concerning the transformation of *saṃskāras,* as presented in Volume 5A. It also necessitates the use of *dhāraṇīs* (aids in mind fixation) and mantras. The last three statements come into play here. Indeed, the clarification is precisely the generation of Secret Mantra.

In the clarification, whenever two (or more) syllables are being composed in *dhyāna* for mantric purpose, their objective is not to feed concepts in oneself. Neither are they formed to explain things to others. There is no need for clarification to either. Instead mantric words must be expressed as needed to convert attributes of one's *saṃskāras* into Void Elements. Then the mantra is 'void of being a word'. By the use of the creative imagination an entire *maṇḍala* of expression can be constructed in the Mind, wherein syllables are linked together as part of a mantric sentence. Their meaning then becomes subservient to the entire construct.

The 'clarification' consequently is void of being a clarification because the *maṇḍala* is not an object of common speech or thought. Rather, it exists and must silently be projected to fulfil its purpose via the *samādhi* of a *yogin*. The *maṇḍala,* (integrally a 'self') is, however, also 'void of self', as all exists in the meditation-Mind and is constituted from the Void Elements that have accrued the substance of Mind. The eighth phrase, 'the other is void of being another' here relates to the identity of *saṃsāra* and *śūnyatā* in this thought-form construction. Both are incorporated in one nexus of expression. Neither can *saṃsāra* (the thought construct) and *śūnyatā* be considered to be identical. They are the same and yet not the same ('both are void of being both'). The construct has come into existence (e.g., as the necessary energised form to convert the forces of Māra) through the focussed potency of Mind (as an 'imagination'). It is empowered by the relevant mantric sentence that must eventually be integrated into the Void, hence it is 'an imagination of what is not the case'.

Finally, the Ray listing earlier presented can be incorporated in the present analysis, where 'Letters' (Ray one) refers to the expression of the abstract Mind wherein 'One imagines a clarification' (number 5). 'Name' (Ray two) constitutes the junction between letters and words. Thus the phrase 'neither a clarification to both' (number 4) applies here. It signifies the focussed (Airy) *dhyāna* that projects an *antaḥkaraṇa* (consciousness link) to create the Fiery 'Words' (Ray three), where the phrase 'nor a clarification to another' applies. Here the *maṇḍalic* construct formed in the mind necessitates the control of speech.

'Colour' (Ray four) details the *maṇḍala* with the Watery attributes that paint the expression with various hues. Here the *yogin* must remain one-pointed in his *dhyāna* and not allow the mind to wander, to chatter to itself, thus lose concentration. The final 'Shape' (Ray five) of the *maṇḍala* (utilising the Earthy Element) can be completed in all respects ('clarified') and projected on its errand to effect its purpose in *saṃsāra*. In doing so one must remain in 'Equipoise' (Ray six) because attributes of one's *saṃskāras* are to be mastered and the demons of 'self' and the forces of Māra conquered. In doing so the 'clarification' is 'void of being a clarification' until its effects have been empirically expressed. The result must then be brought to the Void through the meditation process. Finally we have the 'Discussion' (Ray seven), that allows the *yogin* to communicate his experiences to others. Such teaching centres around the premise that 'Self is void of self', which is the premise that the *yogin* begins with, and has now thoroughly comprehended the meaning.

Points 8, 9 and 10 of the later listing are extensions of the final three statements. Point 11 ('Whatever two syllables are composed') couples with point 8 ('the other is void of being another'), point 12 ('they are void of being a word') couples with point 9 ('both are void of being both'), and point 13 ('the syllable is not a syllable') couples with point 10 ('they are an imagination of what is not the case'). The reason being that once the purpose of the manifestation of the syllables, words and mantric sentences have been accomplished then all shall be resolved back into the Void. Also, the coupling demonstrates the relation between the two truths within the Tantra.

The fourth paragraph and Dependent Origination

Wayman's translation continues:

> That way one may understand the meaning of Dependent Origination. Even if that meaning is told, it comes from nowhere and goes nowhere; even so, because of dependency on another, it is also imagined as syllables. Because it is imagined, imagination is also void. Because of Dependent Origination, dependency on another is void. Because, arising from the cause and condition, Dependent Origination is also void. Because generated by cause and condition adventitiously, it is

> void of being an origination. Here, Dependent Origination is void of its own-character (*svalakṣaṇa*).[4][35]

This verse informs us that we may understand Dependent Origination from the previous verse, where we are told that 'Whatever two syllables are composed, they are void of being a word; and the syllable is not a syllable'. Our vision is immediately directed to the organs of speech, the throat and mouth, and esoterically, to the *chakra* that utilises speech and emanates mantras—the Throat centre *(viśuddha chakra).* This centre therefore establishes the basis for the formulation of Dependent Origination, as *saṃsāra* is now the focus of our concern. The Throat centre controls the emanation of the Fires of mind/Mind, and thus the entire thinking process, which must overcome the darkness of ignorance and conquer *saṃsāra*. The wheels of dependency exist essentially for this purpose. The energies of the Throat centre can be directed to the Head centre, that also accommodates the potency of the abstract Mind, and thus the capacity to gain enlightenment. The Throat centre activates the various little wheels of articulate streams of thought, whilst the Head Lotus holds the sum of the expression of consciousness wherein the multitude of smaller and greater wheels are turning.

The concept of two syllables indicates that we must analyse the reality of Dependent Origination in terms of differentiation. Each syllable concerns the setting in motion of a wheel of *manasic* activity, from whence Dependent Origination arises. Syllables are units of pronunciation, and when two or more are placed together they make a word, which normally needs a vowel sound. Words can then be strung together to make sentences. The implication here is that Dependent Origination depends upon the articulation of words, of mental activity. From the mind then comes the activity that makes us interrelate with the things that cause dependency.

From the point of view of ultimate truth however, they are void of constituting a word that impacts activity upon the mind, that even if there were meaning to the words 'it comes from nowhere and goes nowhere', because dependent upon each other, or imagined, and all is void. The simile the author uses here therefore is that just as the dependent relation

---

35 Ibid., 288.

of syllables are void, so also are the dependent forms of activity that are basic to Dependent Origination. Ultimately this may be so, but relatively not so; which is the point needing repeating (continuously recycling through the wheel of dependency). The ultimate is not possible to achieve without many steps of dependency along the way. Therefore while this process is happening it is not 'void of its own character' because that character persists for the duration of the dependency. Only when the ultimate is attained does 'its own character' lose its foundation. However by then this 'character' is no longer necessary because the goal has been achieved—the ultimate. Once that state has been reached the meditator can choose to abide in the ultimate state, or to articulate syllables to communicate with those ensnared by dependent activities. Once the syllables have been uttered then a sequence of dependencies have been established. Welcome to the *śūnyatā-saṃsāra* nexus where one or other exists (dependency or non-dependency), neither, or both together. All are possible in the enlightened Mind, depending upon how that Mind chooses to express itself.

Two syllables also hint at the nature of the wheel of dependency to turn either left or right, with two differing possible outcomes. We need not look to each of the twelve links of this wheel here,[36] but rather to the overall concept of what it is that sustains *saṃsāra.* When, therefore we analyse this fourth paragraph of the *samādhi 'Great Gate of Diamond Liberation',* then at first eight principal statements can be found, which can be placed upon the arms of the eight-spoked wheel of direction in space *(aṣṭadiśas).* We should also look to each spoke being dual, consisting of a positive and a negative aspect, similar to the statements in this paragraph, which generally start with a phrase relating to *saṃsāra,* followed by one related to *śūnyatā.* This is consistent with the expression of the *saṃsāra-śūnyatā* duality. This duality then can be applied to the wheel, which provides us with the necessary number sixteen that signify the number of petals to the Throat centre. Manifesting in the form of dualities, the statements effectively present sixteen characteristics to analyse (though the second part of each statement generally relates to the Void). The presented list shows the qualities that establish the gates to the experience of *śūnyatā* via the mind. There are also eight

36 See Volume 1, chapter 9, for detail.

implied corollaries to each statement that provide an opposing view to the presented ones and provide substantiation for *saṃsāra*. Thus we have the basis to the turning of the wheel of Dependent Origination.

The central place where the arms of the cross meet represents the *saṃsāra-śūnyatā* nexus. This position of the wheel is neither *śūnyatā* or *saṃsāra*, neither word or syllable, but partakes of both. It thus cannot be described in terms of one or the other. It is the gate to the Dharmakāya Way and therefore is established as the highest possible liberating truth. It is the emanative point of power for the expression of the Secret Mantra, which then becomes the *maṇḍala* of the wheel. The meanings of these directions of the eight-armed cross of direction in space *(aṣṭadiśas)* were explained previously with respect to Figure 1 in Volume 1. The interpretation of the 8 x 2 statements is in accord with the nature of the arms of the two crosses constituting the *aṣṭadiśas*. (The fixed and mutable crosses.) Each statement is in the form of a couplet (indicating the two ways that the wheel can turn, from left to right, or from right to left[37]), and also deals with polar opposites. The eight associated statements can now be considered.

1. The *western* direction of outward to the field of service. The related statement is that this is the 'way one may understand the meaning of Dependent Origination', which refers to the expression of Secret Mantra derived from *samādhi,* as was explained in paragraph four of this Tantra. This represents the esoteric doctrine and is self explanatory in the light of what has already been provided. Dependent Origination may be understood not just intellectually or by experience, but also perceptually by means of non-discursive direct awareness. This explanation then, for *chelas,* concerns the remainder of the seven statements. It follows however that such meaning may indeed not be comprehended, because 'the meaning comes from nowhere and goes nowhere'. One must then analyse what coming and going 'nowhere' represents, and for this they travel northwest.

37 Esoterically, the left to right direction relates to the way of establishing the liberation that *śūnyatā* offers, whilst the right to left direction, concerns the mode of travelling deeper into the trammels of *saṃsāra*.

2. The direction *northwest* concerns the expression of emanatory goodwill that projects the gain of the entire *maṇḍala* of activity to new domains of experience. The related phrase is that the meaning 'comes from nowhere and goes nowhere', and this is so 'Even if that meaning is told'. The superficial interpretation of this statement therefore is that such explanation is meaningless because its content cannot be understood. The more esoteric interpretation being that it comes and goes nowhere because it remains in the Void. Consequently, in order to understand its meaning one must refine one's perceptions so that they too are Void. What then can be explained?

   The opposing corollary being 'even if that meaning is not told' concerns remaining in ignorance. This is the obvious result of not knowing the true meaning or logical eventuation of the Tantra. Even so, relative ignorance prevails until the *samādhi* is actually undertaken by the *chela*. As this 'meaning' is being spoken, so it concerns intellectual discursion, effectively from the polar opposite of this northwest direction, the southeast arm of expression (into *saṃsāric* activity). Hence it comes from the great illusion, which is here likened to 'nowhere'. Similarly the exoteric teaching is going to elucidate others about what might be a more enlightened domain, nevertheless, it too similarly is going 'nowhere' because it remains where it has always been, in the Heart of Life.

   Alternatively, if a meditator does not think with the Heart then the impressions come from 'somewhere', because then the concept of time is involved. This is concerned with the movement of consciousness from here to there, which also involves the manifestation of *karma* because of the movement of something in space. (Thus supporting the wheel of Dependent Origination.) Inevitably this movement needs an opposing movement in order to produce eventual equilibrium. Thinking with the Heart is therefore a way of avoiding negative karmic repercussion, because it produces thoughtless Thought that has *śūnyatā* as its base.

3. The direction *north* represents the way upward towards enlightenment. As one aspires towards enlightened perception, the meaning of whatever one meditates upon is told and becomes well understood. This is a necessary part of the process of gaining

wisdom. The purpose seeds the mind with arenas of enlightened revelations where the way to helping sentient beings can be properly forged. Such meaning is important to possess, as it is the basis to the wisdom of Bodhisattvas. The related phrase being 'because of dependency on another, it is also imagined as syllables'. Here the domain of the Head centre is awakened, wherein all of the dependencies upon others is generated. (Specifically the spiritual preceptor, the *guru,* who can guide the way, is implied.) The creative imagination comes into play and symbols are strung together as words and sentences in order to explore the view of Secret Mantra. The Head centre is then made potent by empowerment via such Mantra, allowing the manifestation of the higher *siddhis*.

Effectively the explication is directed to those in the southern direction. When we look to 'another' then we are engrossed in the things appertainable in the realm of *māyā,* which we distinguish from ourselves. (The focus of consciousness here is downward into the realms of form.) Others are taught and their imaginative life manifests as they dissect words (the knowledge of things) into their syllables, into particulars. The potency of mantra is then cognised and utilised to travel north.

4. The phrase 'Because it is imagined, imagination is void' refers to the *northeast* direction, which implies unity of all forces needed to be brought together. Here it concerns the sum of whatever is stored as *bījas* in the *ālayavijñāna* environment. The syllables that are 'imagined' differ here from those explained above. In this direction the syllables are commands, intuitions, karmic impulses from the Sambhogakāya Flower, which the mind instantaneously translates into words, sentences, paragraphs, moving images. They are the ideas and impressions of what to do and the rationale for life's processes. The opposing corollary which manifests can be stated as: 'syllables and words are non imagined facts in the mind'. These seed syllables thus manifest as signs that can be recognised and acted upon by the mind. (From them, however, imaginings can arise.) After one has acted upon the images that formerly appeared in the mind, then the awareness from the resultant experiences and discovery of their transience are gained. Everything transient

is seen to be void, hence even that which has appeared from the liberated domains. However, such understanding takes much time to awaken, because the allurements of the objective reality from sense impressions have to be first overcome. On the path of return what is 'non-imagined' pertains to ascertaining the real as obtained through *samādhi,* and which produces the dissolution of all forms of imaginings, for they are seen to be void of substantiality.

The 'imaginings' from this northeast direction are projected into the southeast orientation (the next arm of the mutable cross), where forms in the mind appear to be empirically real, because validated with sense perception. Often many rigid belief systems appear where the individual takes something learnt as unalterable fact. Such a one effectively only looks within the direction chosen and can see no other view. They are the ramifications of reified syllables that have become words and images in the mind. Inevitably all forms of dogmatism must be overcome by generating the fluidity of concepts that is the hallmark of the enlightened. Being transient, all images and related actions inevitably become void.

5. The *eastern* direction refers to travelling inward to experience the way of the Heart. The Heart represents the open gate to liberation. It is the realm of no-thought, and the spaciousness of awareness obtained from it is directionless, vast and omnipresent. Here we have the phrase 'Because of Dependent Origination, dependency on another is void'. Here the two truths are exemplified, where Dependent Origination represents conventional truth and the Void ultimate truth. This pathway to the Heart centre (ultimate truth) via the platform of the Throat centre (conventional truth) represents the horizontal east-west arm of this cross. Dependent Origination is the mainstay of deductive reasoning and the growth of knowledge, as the individual travels from the west to the east, upwards and inwards to liberation, by mastering, refining and transmuting all *manasic saṃskāras.*
6. The phrase 'Because, arising from the cause and condition, Dependent Origination is also void' concerns the *southeast* direction, and thus the effect of the assimilation of what has been imagined and consequently seeded from the northeast turn of the mutable cross. The originating seed syllables from the *ālayavijñāna* have

grown into images in the mind and have been effectively planted in the fertile soil of *saṃsāra*. Consequently the causes of Dependent Origination are now observed in the way they have been conditioned from above. In this southeast arm of the mutable cross much action manifests in *saṃsāra* that allows later reaping the consequences of the planted impressions. The wheel of Dependent Origination thus continuously turns through its twelve houses whereby various new desirous pursuits can be experienced. Inevitably the factors of pain and suffering cause the individual to consciously tread the Eightfold Path (when the southwest arm is reached), thus to overcome ignorance. Inevitably thereby the individual learns that 'Dependent Origination is also void'.

7. The *southern* direction of downward into the field of the interdependent lives is implicated in the phrase 'Because generated by cause and condition adventitiously, it is void of being an origination'. Within *saṃsāra* the mind is consequently continuously distracted, leading one far from enlightenment. The term 'adventitious' refers to the impact of external influences from the environment one resides in, to the factor of external *karma* produced in this direction. The implication is that because these influences impact our decision making, so then true origination of (new) activity does not happen. There is an interdependent chain of causes and effects to analyse here, leading to an ontological search for the beginnings of things. This subject has been dealt with in Volume 1 and shall not be repeated here. That no effective beginning of events may thus be found is arguably true from this perspective, however from the perspective of a mind generating thoughts to act, with a consequent action engendered, then there is an origination, upon which individual *karma* is the consequence.

Leaving speculative concerns about the origin of things aside, from this southern direction one can make a conscious decision to turn about in one's seat of consciousness away from the cause-effect actions in *saṃsāra* and upwards to the domains of liberation. One can then leave the thraldom with the minutiae of one's personal life behind. When the 'turning about' transpires and the person commences upon the yogic path, then he/she will inevitably awaken the inherent forces of the Sacral and Base of Spine centres. This causes the ascent of the vital airs up the spinal column that sustains the *dhyāna* of the meditator, inevitably awakening *kuṇḍalinī.*

8. In the *southwest* position the dissertation of Dependent Origination is continued, by bringing consideration of the *prāṇas* gained from sense perception directly to the scrutiny of the mind's eye, the eye of knowledge and of reason. This is the 'eye' of the concrete mind, which co-ordinates and analyses what has been gained. The phrase being 'Here, Dependent Origination is void of its own-character (*svalakṣaṇa*)'. The corollary being 'because of such generation it is replete with the character of being a "self", and inevitably the nature of this "self" must be thoroughly analysed, to discover that it is void of 'its own-character'. At first the 'eye' acts to select from the world of material phenomena that which it desires for the empire building of knowledgeable factors of the mind. The mind prides itself with the gain of such empires in its chosen specialities. This accumulation of knowledge is based upon characteristics of self-identity and self-aggrandisement, which are confidently projected to similar selves for them to notice or gain something from. However, being built up from a cacophony of transience, such content is effectively void. Inevitably, empirical deduction is superseded by abstracted consciousness, which is not disposed to a 'self' concept, but rather to universality of thought, the enlightened Mind, which is replete with revelatory insight, but is void of concepts.

The sixteen petals of the Throat centre

The following information is based upon the structure of the Throat centre, which has sixteen main petals. Four of these are major and are orientated in the cardinal directions. They are derived from twelve smaller petals. Detailed information concerning this *chakra* is given in Volume 5B to which the reader should refer. Figure 1 from that volume is provided below, including the reference numbers, which I shall utilise for the present purpose. The numbers also relate to astrological signs, which will not be delved into here, however, because of the importance of the signs in interpreting the activity of the twelve petalled lotus, they will be elaborated on in the next chapter, where the Heart centre is explained.

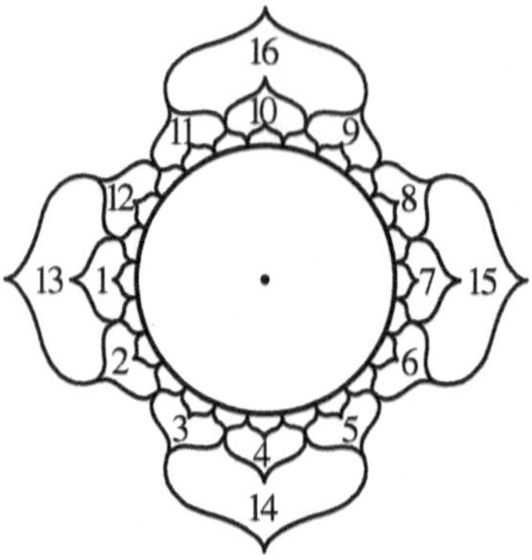

Figure 1. The Throat centre

The esotericism of *pratītyasamutpāda* (Dependent Origination) is provided in Volume 5A as part of the description of the Six Realms, which should be read in context with what is presented below.

The petal labelled 1, concerning the eastern direction, starts the cycle of dependency. The first of the links of this wheel is ignorance *(avidyā),* the result of being born into the illusion-filled realm, based upon reliance of an image of 'self'. The symbolism for this link is a blind woman trying to find her way with a stick. The related phrase in the *samādhi* is 'because of dependency on another'. Such dependency therefore is the cause for the generation of ignorance. Overcoming ignorance then represents the long, eventual journey to discover the inward way of the Heart.

Petal number 2 concerns the development of the image-making faculties and the factor of desire that comes with it, producing karmic formations *(saṃskāras)* that keep us tied to the wheel of birth and death. The image is that of a potter at his wheel, which signifies the creation of thought-forms. The associated phrase follows from the previous one 'it is also imagined as syllables'. This implies the use of speech to communicate one's thoughts and desires, producing the manifold interactions with people, from whence the *saṃskāras* originate.

The third petal is symbolised by the grasping tendencies of a monkey, thus developing the basic elements of consciousness (*vijñāna*). The associated phrase is 'Because it is imagined', which relates to the concepts and images of the mind that this monkey-minded individual continuously seeks in order to feed the idea of 'self' and self-worth in *saṃsāra*. The monkey-mind is emotionally based and a long way must yet be travelled in the field of consciousness before the monkey conceives the need to control the emotions, if liberation from pain and suffering is to ensue.

The fourth petal relates to the birthing and development of the mind proper, the ability to name things *(nāma-rūpa)* and to identify with what is thus named. The associated phrase is 'imagination is also void'. What is experienced produces images in the mind, and what is thus imagined is illusional, hence, void. The general symbolism for this *nidāna* (link) depicts a man in a boat steered by a ferryman. The boat signifies the containment of mind within the consciousness-stream that is developed via continuous rebirth.

The fifth petal consolidates the development of the intellect (*pravṛttivijñāna*), hence it represents the most intense involvement with materialistic observations. The associated phrase is 'Because of Dependent Origination', hence here the activity that sustains the cycles necessitating continuous rebirth is at its apogee. The symbolism provided in the thangkas for this *nidāna* is a house with six windows, which symbolises the six consciousnesses via which a normal person functions.

The sixth petal relates to the proper beginning of the process whereby the thinker begins to comprehend the nature of *saṃsāra* and takes the steps to master it. The associated phrase is 'dependency on another is void', and the symbolism relates to a pair of lovers, who have made contact *(sparsā),* but not yet in full union. Sexual interrelations are the mainstay of providing the material for rebirth, and inevitably a person will perceive that such interrelation is transient and void of true meaning. The quest for yogic union inwards to integrate male-female forces takes precedence.

The seventh petal deals with the more emotional (Watery) *saṃskāras* developed, which are the most difficult to master. The attribute of 'feeling' *(vedanā)* attributed to this link is symbolised by an arrow piercing a man's eye. Much karmic consequences from former materialistic and desirous pursuits now come to the fore to teach the consequences of attachment. Inevitably a meditative path is sought to try to understand why. The answer comes in the guise of the explanatory phrase presented in this verse 'Because, arising from the cause and condition'. Causes and conditions therefore must be mastered in one's meditative pursuit.

Petal eight concerns the many battles one has concerning mastering the emotional body, before the realisation comes that 'Dependent Origination is also void'. The symbolism concerns a woman serving a drink to a person, with the attribute being thirst or craving *(tṛṣṇā).* At the present level of interpretation the thirst is for more knowledge as to why so much suffering ensues from one's emotional entanglements. Yogic pursuits then produce the inevitable right conclusions.

The ninth petal is related to the *nidāna* that shows a man or else a monkey gathering fruit, and the related quality being 'clinging' *(upādhāna).* Here the path often becomes divergent, where a choice is made to continue the path of attachment to the allurements of *saṃsāra* or to one-pointed focus upon spiritual attainment. Consequently, the fruits of either enlightenment or pleasure seeking are further sought. (The concept of 'clinging'.) The associated phrase is 'generated by cause and condition adventitiously', which here refers to the effects of life's experiences, the processes conditioning consciousness from externalised *karma,* and whether the individual has learnt enough from such happenings to overcome clinging to materialism.

The tenth petal concerns the approach of mastery of thoughts and intellectual pursuits, the gain to many of life's experiences now being at hand. The symbol being that of sexual intercourse, or a pregnant woman, with the attribute being 'becoming' *(bhāva).* For materialistic thinkers the choice has been made to continue pursuing further knowledge and understanding, or phenomenal (sensual) activities, producing therefore further cycles of rebirth. For those that have gained spiritual insight, true union with the highest ideals is sought instead, the awakening of the Head centre and the enlightenment it brings is pursued. The associated phrase being 'it is void of being an origination', which reflects the process of the accomplishment of the mastery of mind so that Mind supplants it. The remaining two petals sum up the realisation gained through such accomplishment.

The phrase for the eleventh petal is 'Dependent Origination is void', the revelation of which is the gain of the development of the enlightened Mind. The image provided for this *nidāna* is that of a woman giving birth *(jātī),* signifying that all of life's experiences are now recycled, to be reborn upon a higher cycle of accomplishment. For the enlightened one this concerns treading the Bodhisattva path towards the highest levels *(bhūmis)*. The eighth phrase also stated that 'Dependent Origination is void'. The difference between that and this phrase is that with the earlier phrase it was discovered through much turmoil, whereas now it is simply perceived in the Mind's Eye.

The final petal represents the gain of all the experiences in *saṃsāra,* where hopefully the bitter lessons of life have been learnt. The mind reviews all that has transpired in the past, and accordingly grows in wisdom. It can then direct the next cycle of experiences at will. Consequently, the associated phrase for this petal is 'Dependent Origination is void of its own-character', which sums up the entire discourse, as it produces the void of all mental-formations concerning the character of dependent interrelationships, in the singleness of the Clear Light of Mind. Its naturalness simply is, not dependent upon any other existent. The image presented for this *nidāna* is a man bearing a corpse, which signifies death *(maraṇa)*. Everything material must inevitably cease to exist, eventually even the 'corpse' of the mind.

The four major petals of this *chakra* are symbolised by the opening statements of this fourth verse of the *samādhi*. These four petals relate to the mastery of the four main Elements, Air for the eastern petal, Water for the southern petal, Fire for the western one, and Earth for the northern petal. Consequently, they relate to the development of the attributes of the wisdoms of the four Dhyāni Buddhas that emanate from Vairocana. Each of the major petals incorporate the attributes of the three minor petals that represents its base. There are thus (1 + 3) x 4 = 16 petals implied, where the major petal develops the attribute of the related Dhyāni Buddha and the minor ones the supporting wisdoms of the other three Jinas.

Concerning the northern petal (number 16), the *prāṇas* are directed upwards to the Head centre wherein the Buddha-Mind can be comprehended. The 'syllable that is not a syllable' then represents the Buddha *vacana* (speech). The Earthy Element here is not viewed in terms of the illusional world of perception, but rather in terms of the descent of the *dharmakāya* via ever-increasing density, so that eventually the empirical mind can comprehend the import of such speech. The All-accomplishing Wisdom of Amoghasiddhi is consequently awakened.

The associated phrase is 'That way one may understand the meaning of Dependent Origination'.

The southern direction (number 14) is represented in the words 'Even if that meaning is told'. Here the Buddha-Word then manifests below the diaphragm via the Solar Plexus centre (governing the dispensation of the Watery Element), to produce thought-forms, images that are a reflection of the enlightened domains. They awaken the minor *siddhis* via which the *yogin* or seer can gain valid impressions of the real. We see therefore that this meaning is told not so much in terms of words, but rather via symbols and images of Secret Mantra that produce direct cognitive impression in the *yogin's* or seer's Mind. The Eye of vision (Ājñā centre) has awakened to perceive the real, and the Equalising Wisdom of Ratnasambhava is developed.

Next the eastern direction (number 13) is implicated in the words 'it comes from nowhere'. This 'nowhere' therefore represents the Void of which the Heart centre is the custodian. Residing in *śūnyatā* then the *yogin* utilises the Mirror-like Wisdom of Akṣobhya to reflect the experience of the Void into the phenomenal domains (via the western direction) in order to transform the recalcitrant *saṃskāras* of the 'hearers' into enlightenment-attributes. From this petal therefore emanates the *nāḍī* that leads to the Heart centre, within which such a one resides when communicating with those who have come for spiritual nourishment. It represents the compassionate Bodhisattva way. The associated Element is Air, the carrier of the *prāṇas* (of liberation).

Finally, the western petal (number 15) 'goes nowhere' as it represents the Throat centre itself and the organs of speech. It therefore empowers the emanation of the Creative Word, Secret Mantra as an expression of the Fires of Mind. Amitābha's Discriminating Wisdom draws the compassionate potency from the eastern direction and manifests it as liberating speech, where the Bodhisattva manifests in the guise of a *nirmāṇakāya* of a Buddha for the 'hearers'. The teachings may inspire minds, but are aimed at the Heart, so as to awaken perception of the Void ('nowhere') in those that are thus inspired.

2

The Great Gates of Diamond Liberation Part 2: Zodiacal Considerations of the Heart Centre

The twelve statements of the *samādhi*

Here I shall continue the detailed analysis of *'The Samādhi "Great Gate of Diamond Liberation"'* as presented by Wayman. The passage quoted follows from where we left off in the previous chapter:

> What is void of own-character lacks a character. What lacks a character is Thusness (*tathatā*). What is Thusness is error–free Thusness. What is error-free Thusness is not otherwise Thusness. What is not otherwise Thusness is the *samādhi*. What is the *samādhi* is comprehending it. What is the comprehension is voidness (*śūnyatā*). What is the voidness is discerning (the real). What is discerning (the real) is calming (the mind). What is calming (the mind) is liberation (*vimokṣa*). What is liberation is the Middle Path. [5]
>
> What is the Middle Path, is one without one extreme, is without two extremes, without apprehensible, without apprehender, without apprehension, without nihilism, without eternalism, without arising, without ceasing, without constructive thought, without discursive thought, not independent, not dependent on another, not going, not coming, without thorough defilement, without complete purification, without union, without separation. That is discerning (the real). [6]
>
> What is discerning (the real) is without personal aggregates (*skandha*), without realms (*dhātu*), without sense organs (*indriya*), without sense bases (*āyatana*), without objective realms, without attaching names to objective realms, without (destiny's) action, without

> the fruit of (destiny's) action. What is without (destiny's) action and without the fruit of (destiny's) action is the incomparable right-completed Enlightenment. What is the incomparable right-completed Enlightenment is the incomparable right-completed Buddha. What is the incomparable right-completed Buddha is the Dharma. What is the Dharma is not born, does not die. What is not born and does not die should be understood to be the same as the sky.[7][1]

There are eleven statements presented in paragraph 5. With the first statement of the sixth paragraph they represent qualities that constitute the type of *prāṇas* emanated by the twelve petals of the Heart *chakra,* once that centre has been awakened. This *chakra* governs the expression of the energy of compassion *(bodhicitta)* for each human unit. It also resolves the purpose of compassionate activity. Secret Mantra necessitates the evocation of the Heart's energies. One must think with the Heart if the *maṇḍala* that will produce the liberation of manifest space is to be empowered. Thinking with the Heart implicates awakening the petals of the Heart in the Head Lotus, which is also organised in terms of groups of twelve petals. All the *prāṇas* that are to vitalise the *maṇḍala* must be directed to the Heart if the *maṇḍala* is to be made potent with the qualities of *bodhicitta.* It then becomes the living *dharma.*

The twelve statements are:

1. What is void of own-character lacks a character.
2. What lacks a character is Thusness (*tathatā*).
3. What is Thusness is error–free Thusness.
4. What is error-free Thusness is not otherwise Thusness.
5. What is not otherwise Thusness is the *samādhi.*
6. What is the *samādhi* is comprehending it.
7. What is the comprehension is voidness (*śūnyatā*).
8. What is the voidness is discerning (the real).
9. What is discerning (the real) is calming (the mind).
10. What is calming (the mind) is liberation (*vimokṣa*).
11. What is liberation is the Middle Path.
12. What is the Middle Path, is without one extreme, is without two extremes.[2]

---

1 Alex Wayman, *Untying the Knots in Buddhism*, 288.

2 This is the first line of the sixth paragraph of the *samādhi.* It doubles up as the eastern petal of Splenic centre I.

The twelve petals of the Heart *chakra* can be divided into four triads of petals bearing the qualities of the cardinal directions. The petals have a relation to the twelve links of Dependent Origination. They are also catalogued by means of the attributes of the twelve signs of the zodiac, esoterically understood. The four cardinal directions are the four main gates pointing to *śūnyatā.*

The two ways the wheel can turn:

a. From left to right, the way of travel or generation of the *prāṇas* of enlightened beings. Here the twelve aspects associated with the Void of this list find their application. It details the steps needed to gain liberation.

b. From right to left. This way generates the *prāṇas* of the average person, of *karma* producing activities and consequent bondage to material forms. Attachment to *saṃsāra* is intensified. This is the way the wheel of Dependent Origination normally turns.

This twelve-fold listing is arranged in accordance with the spokes of the Heart *chakra's maṇḍalic* wheel, as depicted in figure 2. This wheel can turn in either direction, according to the type of *prāṇa* (coming from either below or above the diaphragm) that is conveyed. However, for the Heart centre the right to left motion occurs only in the most base of individuals. The reason being is that the function of the petals of this *chakra* are concerned with transforming the characteristics *(saṃskāras)* conveyed by the *prāṇas* into the twelve aspects relating to the attributes of the Void presented above.

Figure 2 elaborates the information presented by Figure 5 in Volume 1, entitled 'The Relationship of Śūnyatā to Saṃsāra'. Four of the twelve aspects listed express qualities of the innermost tier that stems from *śūnyatā,* as presented by Nāgārjuna's Four-Cornered Proof. They are: 'not self' (north), 'not both' (east), 'not caused' (south), and 'not other' (west). The eight other aspects of figure 5 find expression as the remainder of the petals of the Heart *chakra.*

Each petal can be considered to embody a miniature of the main wheel, with the aspect of the Void characteristic associated with it as the hub of the wheel. Each is a cleansing ground and transformative station for the *prāṇas* directed to it. (They are sub-hues of the basic quality attributed to the petal concerned.) We must remember here that our concern is the process happening in a *yogin's samādhi,* wherein he consciously works to transform base *saṃskāras* into the attributes of liberation. He must do this if he is to successfully build the needed *maṇḍala* of liberation according to the precepts of Secret Mantra.

The *prāṇas* circulate from the peripheral minor wheels of the petals to the heart of the entire *maṇḍala* via the three levels depicted in Volume 1, Figure 5. The central space represents the utterly pure space of *śūnyatā*, having been cleansed of all defilements by the time the *prāṇas* reach it.

The twelve links of Dependent Origination relate to the outer tier of the diagram, the place of karmic formations. The middle tier directly pertains to the abstracted consciousness that interrelates the Void to *saṃsāra*. It therefore concerns the method that allows the Void and *saṃsāra* to interrelate without mutual annihilation. This is done via the four pathways represented by Nāgārjuna's Four-Cornered Proof.

When the little wheels turn from left to right they reject the *prāṇas* that are incapable of expressing the qualities of enlightenment. These *prāṇas* are directed to the Splenic centre for further processing. We then have the causative impulse of Dependent Origination from a psychic perspective. It concerns returning to the trammels of *saṃsāra,* a recycling (rebirthing) of the defiling *prāṇas* into the general *prāṇic* flow to be experienced as re-emerging *karma*. The *karma* then manifests in a future time, hopefully to transmute the *saṃskāras* into a more vibrant *prāṇic* hue.

Astrological considerations of the reversed wheel

Each of the gates of the cardinal directions can be considered to be triune. In considering Dependent Origination, the focus is upon the southwest petal of the western triad because this direction represents the outwards expression of human perception. Much of the gain of awareness is developed here. Because the western triad of petals is involved with processing the *prāṇas* of the panoply of normal human relationships and social intercourse, so the southwest petal of the triad is concerned with the minutiae of the expression of people's thinking, emotions and actions in the world of the senses that is the physical domain. From this perspective the various forms of activity that generate ignorance through normal human interrelationships, and eventually the mode of conquering it, are grounded here.

In the reversed wheel (from right to left) these forms of activity deepen materialism and hence one's ignorance quotient. Such activities persist for a long time, as the participants are slow to learn from them. In its general manifestation we have the petty gossip of the ill-informed about their intense involvement and desire for consumerism, sexual matters, sport, and entertainment in general, etc. We thus have the production of individual mental-emotional constructs (*karma*) of all types within the society or nation. The purpose is for the person to eventually master the entire process of life regarding interrelation with general humanity. Gradually ignorance is overcome as the knowledge base increases, producing present day materialistic psychological and philosophic ideas, based upon a minute analysis of the physical basis of the human personality and psyche, utilising scientific methodology. The objective is to arrive at a complete understanding as to the true nature of the phenomena of human personal and social interactions and relations. It can then instigate a form of elimination of ignorance, concerning the nature of human interrelations. In this way the wheel is rectified. The discovery of how the emotions, selfishness, accumulation of material goods for the personal-I, intense self-identification, avarice, competitiveness, etc., produce the sum of human woes then proceeds. The path to liberation and its appearance for humanity as a whole, is a marker that a new era has begun.

Once Buddhists have taken on board a more esoteric view, as presented in this series, and generally promulgate the teachings then this new epoch will surely commence, with the rectification of the wheel being evident for humanity. People's eyes will then be lifted above the realm of the purely phenomenal into the subtle psychic domain of the *yogin* and then towards the *dharmakāya*. The wheel producing enlightenment turns from left to right and shall be called *the rectified wheel.*

The best way to explain the function of these petals is by utilising astrological considerations. Though the Tibetans have adopted Chinese Astrology for such purposes I shall present a Western approach that undertakes a complete comprehension of the nature of the liberated domains and the vicissitudes of the path to enlightenment. The entire order of cosmos needs to be explained, and for this purpose the information given in the book *Esoteric Astrology* by Alice A. Bailey shall be utilised.[3]

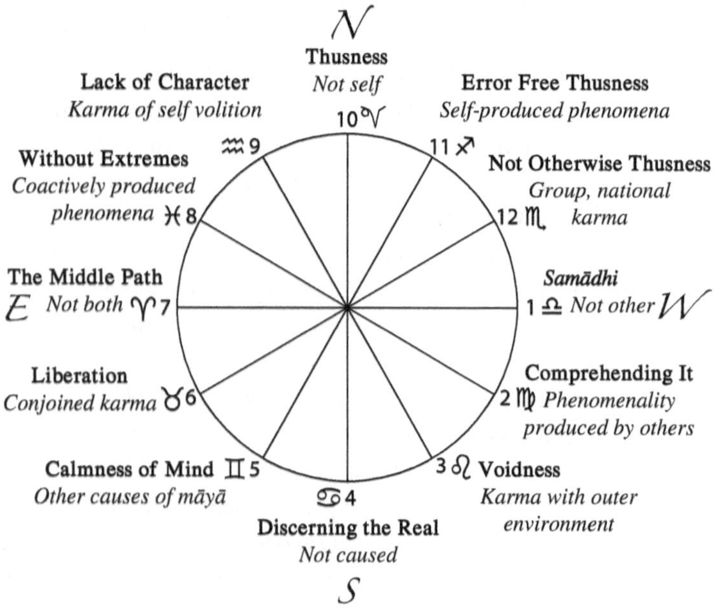

Figure 2. The Heart centre and the Zodiac[4]

♈ Aries	♎ Libra	♌ Leo
♉ Taurus	♏ Scorpio	♍ Virgo
♊ Gemini	♐ Sagittarius	♒ Aquarius
♋ Cancer	♑ Capricorn	♓ Pisces

3 Alice A. Bailey, *Esoteric Astrology*, (Lucis Press Ltd., London, 1968). Though written from a Western perspective, the book presents the most lucid revelatory explanation of the subject presently available. The book is undoubtedly the product of a fully enlightened mind, unlike most astrological treatises. This and most of the other books by Bailey were telepathically communicated by a very high level Bodhisattva, an enlightened Tibetan Rimpoche from the time of the 13th Dalai Lama. He utilised the content of Bailey's mind to present his purpose for Westerners under the pseudonym of D.K.

4 Note that the numbers 1–12 in figure 2 refer to the twelve steps of the wheel of Dependent Origination.

This form of astrology provides many important new esoteric perceptions not found in any orthodox presentation, therefore should be studied by those wishing deeper insights into the way of organisation of all manifesting phenomena; of all the forces conditioning Life. An exposition of the principles of esoteric astrology should help Buddhists to properly interpret many salient parts of their *sūtras* and *Tantras*. This is because much astrological information is presented in this way by the enlightened, and can be wrought from the texts by those possessing the right keys to comprehending the astrological symbolism. Sometimes the astrological cues are quite clear, and elsewhere veiled, and must be extrapolated, as in this case.

In this chapter concerning the astrological implications of the Heart centre, one needs to broaden one's vision away from just the considerations of an individual, and to view the treading of the path of humanity itself as being determined by the movement of an externalised Heart centre, which governs the process of the awakening of the enlightenment path for all. This Heart centre is effectively embodied by the Council of Bodhisattvas that processes and reflects the energies pouring in from twelve great constellations of stars to our earth, that similarly manifest as a Heart centre in cosmos. (Cosmos and the earth are linked as one integral body of expression, allowing subjective as well as mundane energies to impact upon it and consequently influence its evolution.) The interrelatedness of all these centres is what is being described in this astrological section, though travelling upon the reversed wheel is a mode of activity relegated to humanity alone. (The *māyā* they are evolving to master.)

Also much that is stated here concerning the Heart centre is in fact an expression of the Heart within the Head centre, wherein the final aspects of the transmutation of *saṃskāras* pertaining to enlightenment happens. This subject shall be fully explored in Volume 5A.

This information thus presents a new form of astrology for Buddhists, that provides them another exegetical tool, allowing better comprehension of the nature of the path to enlightenment. Later authors may expand upon some of the information given here to present new lines of investigation. Others who are not astrologically minded may cursorily read this chapter and focus upon the information on the Sambhogakāya Flower in the later chapters, however those that do persist in pursuing this astrological view will be well rewarded with a broadened comprehension concerning the causes of things.

The zodiac and *pratītyasamutpāda*

Astrologically, the southwest petal earlier considered is governed by the sign *Virgo the virgin*. The focus of what the Virgoan native produces and shares concerns the nature of life in the material world, of the resources, technology and implements that people use in their daily lives. The generation of enlightened *prāṇas* obtained through comprehension of this petal lays the foundation for later mastery of *saṃsāra,* when the turning of the wheel of the Heart centre progresses northwards. In many ways it embodies the general qualities of the entire cycle of Dependent Origination, because the virgin becomes the Mother that gives birth to the wheel of dependency through all forms of habit-forming propensities. At first one is born to materialistic consciousness, and the forms of ignorance it represents. Later, after much trial and tribulation upon the wheel, the first steps of engendering enlightenment are born. One's seat of consciousness then turns about when the eyes are no longer focussed upon the manifold lures of *saṃsāra*, but to the possibility of eventual liberation from the wheel of dependency. This necessitates the following of the middle way of the Buddha and treading the Bodhisattva *bhūmis*.

The actual turning about in consciousness is activated in the next petal, governed by the qualities of *Libra the balances*. Libra also governs the expression of the law of *karma* throughout the turning of the entire wheel. It therefore directs the way it manifests.

Dependent Origination can be said to constitute Virgo's womb. One is born out from it after the rectification of the wheel, whereby the stages of the Bodhisattva path to Buddhahood can be undertaken.

The 'gate of diamond liberation' assigned to the Virgoan petal is denoted as *'What is the samādhi is comprehending it'*. It is the sixth of the statements presented in the text, and the corresponding phrase from paragraph 4 of the text, related to the Throat centre's activity, is 'Depending upon another is void'. Right from the start of birthing into *saṃsāra* the injunction to all that enter the wheel is that ultimately it is fruitless to depend upon another for enlightenment, or to the world of the phenomena into which one is immersed, because it is inherently Void. One must achieve the goal heuristically. The *samādhi* presented in this Heart centre petal therefore relates to the direct yogic experience of this truth. Everything that one was previously ignorant of can then be comprehended. The specific focus being the field of human relationships. This stage can also be described as insight meditation *(vipassanā)* that assists the removal of the veil of obscuration from the discernment of the true nature of *śūnyatā*. Therefore by this stage (the sixth of the twelve presented above) a *yogin* has gained some proficiency or mastery of the attainment of *samādhi*. (It follows after the sign Libra, wherein contemplation and meditation is the focus.)

The directions indicated in this diagram can also be integrated with those depicted in Volume 1, Figure 5, allowing us to move from the *western* petal associated with group or national *karma*, shown in that figure to the innermost tier depicted as 'not others'. The process can also be viewed as the *prāṇas* being directed upwards towards Libra for processing in the westernmost petal indicated in Figure 2 above. Such *karma* is then directly converted into liberating action through lessening contact with the materialistic world and with those that are affiliated with it. This produces the contemplative life of the Bodhisattva.

With respect to this, there are five steps in the *yogin's* meditative life indicated in the qualities listed above that produce enlightenment, allowing unrelenting *samādhi* wherein Thusness is attained. Until then there is always a possibility of returning into *saṃsāric* activity. These steps are represented by travelling upon the rectified wheel from the southern to the western petals of the Heart centre:

1. First we have the question relating to calming the mind, thus overcoming the field of desire and its attachments (Taurus the bull). Everything concerning our reason for existence must be questioned, so that the wisdom which is a keynote of this sign can be evoked. Taurus is an Earth sign, but here the *prāṇa* that is its Aetheric connotation is implied.

2. The development of calmness of mind *(śamatha)*, Gemini the twins, where all dualities are resolved into a unity. All aspects of *māyā* are dealt with and must be controlled through pacification. It is therefore concerned with the general *prāṇic* flow in the *nāḍī* system. As a

consequence this petal specifically processes the Airy Element, which governs the *prāṇas* generally.

3. This allows the discernment of the real, Cancer the crab, producing birthing into new zones of experience. Here one's mental-emotional characteristics are processed with respect to what has been contacted (touched) in the material domain in order to ascertain the truth of such substantiality. This involves a specific analysis of desire and of clinging to *saṃsāric* attributes, then to the mode of release from such attachment. Watery *prāṇas* are thereby processed.
4. Voidness can then be experienced, Leo the lion, the sign of the self-centred prideful lion, where one must counter the 'self' image to produce voidness. Once concepts of Voidness have been established, then their attributes must be awakened via the abstract Mind by transforming all concepts of 'self' into forms of selflessness. All aspects of mind can then be analysed to see if each thought has any basis in fact. Fiery *prāṇas* are therefore specifically processed (as they govern the mind) and then refined into the liberating Fire.
5. Once experienced, the Void must be comprehended. This process is governed by Virgo the virgin, who represents the material domain, where the Earthy *prāṇas* are fully processed. The sum of the material domain wherein human livingness has its place must be fully comprehended by the meditation-Mind. All comprehension must be grounded upon the physical domain if all is to be thoroughly understood to be void, allowing enlightenment to ensue. Virgo rules this process as it enables our feet to be firmly planted on the ground so that the Eightfold Path can be trod.

All of this activity is consolidated in the sign Libra the balances, where the Thusness that is the *samādhi* can then be established through contemplative absorption. The abovementioned Western *prāṇic* qualifications can then be thoroughly analysed in context within this *samādhi*.

These petals process all aspects of *karma,* until even the subtlest obscuring *karma* has been rejected. The mind is being trained via these five petals to become meditative and serene. *Samādhi,* the serene ocean of mental quiescence, is produced and stabilised through habitual meditation. Eventually the Thusness becomes realisable when the motion of the mind becomes imperceptible.

These five petals are consequently considered non-sacred, with the remaining seven being sacred, an important distinction to be noted. Basically, the essences of the five *prāṇas* and the subtle *saṃskāras* needing processing, undergo the final process of refinement in the five non-sacred petals. The *prāṇas* that can't be included as attributes of the five wisdoms of a Tathāgata are rejected, or further refined. What remains is circulated into the serene liberating pool of the Heart.

The seven sacred petals process the seven Ray energies that qualify the sum of the space occupied by being/non-being, and which are described by the remaining seven parts of the listing, 'not otherwise Thusness', 'error-free Thusness', etc. Detail of the qualities indicated by the list will be considered when I deal with each astrological sign in turn.

The process of 'comprehending it' involves coming through the birthing canal of right comprehension into the Clear Light of being/non-being in Virgo.[5] The *samādhi* associated with the next (Libran[6]) petal helps accomplish this end. This necessitates overcoming all forms of ignorance, overcoming thereby the entire wheel of Dependent Origination. It concerns the process of a Bodhisattva's mastery of the awareness that reveals the Void. As a consequence, the Wheel is rectified and the five *prāṇas* are transformed into their wisdom attributes. This produces right comprehension of the nature of Voidness in Leo[7] through overcoming the predilections to the 'self' concept that dominates that sign. The *karma* with the outer environment is then fully resolved. The foundation for such resolution necessitates the complete discernment of the real in Cancer,[8] wherein all phenomena is seen to be 'not caused',

---

5 Virgo the virgin governs the corollaries in consciousness to all functions of womanhood, of birthing processes of all types.

6 Libra the balances governs the manifestation of *karma* and consequently the process (movements) associated with the wheels of the law, the zodiac, and thus also of Dependent Origination.

7 Leo the lion governs the development of the intellect and the *ahamkāra* principle (the ego, 'I-ness', concepts of 'self'), thus upon the rectified wheel we have the development of the opposing qualities that pertain to Voidness.

8 Those born in the sign Cancer the crab have a natural determination to cling on to all aspects of *saṃsāra* that are desired. (The symbolic use of the claws of the crab.)

within the Void. Thus it overcomes the main function of this sign as the place of periodic incarnation, producing the causing of 'things'.

Śamatha now becomes the natural state of the manifestation of mind. (This calmness of mind is mainly developed in Gemini the twins, where the polar opposites are resolved into a unity.) Here all other causes of *māyā,* of resolute aspects of dualism (the 'I' and 'not I') are similarly resolved into the natural state of abiding in the Clear Light. Wisdom is then attained in Taurus, with the awakening of the all-seeing Eye. (Esoterically, the Eye of the bull of wisdom.) Liberation (completion of a goal) is achieved for any cycle, and Aries the ram then projects a new cycle into activity. The true nature of the seven Rays that are the constituency of the Light of the liberated Mind are then inevitably revealed in their entirety. The rectified path (from left to right, Aries, Taurus to Pisces) that manifests can then set the entire wheel ablaze with light.

In *samādhi* the *yogin* that resides at the *saṃsāra-śūnyatā* nexus is also absorbed in the 'not otherwise Thusness' (Scorpio[9]) that represents the polar opposite of the Taurean petal of the Heart lotus. Here one experiences at need the various aspects of Thusness associated with the other sacred petals. The Scorpion has the ability to pierce the mysteries veiled by the other petals by mastering all of the tests concerning sex, attachments and the desire principle that occur in this sign. The cleansed non-sacred petals remain as the doorways to liberation to interrelate with that still trapped in the *māyā* of *saṃsāra*. The *yogin* moves from Libra to Scorpio following the way of the rectified wheel.

Having considered the overall schema concerning the nature of the reversed zodiacal wheel and the non-sacred petals, it should be noted that Aries governs the first of the Dependent Originations, setting the level of the ignorance quotient for each new outpouring of the wheel. (Libra, its polar opposite, however, governs the overall cycling of the wheel and the rectification of the karmic activity associated with it.) As before mentioned, ignorance is relative, whilst every cycle of the great wheel of *karma* (the law) is directed by Libra. The *karma* projected

---

This rigorous involvement with phenomena inevitably causes comprehension of the true nature of suffering, thus discernment of the real.

9 Governed by Scorpio the scorpion, who possesses the ability to sting to death everything that is 'otherwise'.

depends upon what *saṃskāras* need to be recycled and worked upon until Buddhahood is obtained.

The list of the Buddha's twelve-fold formula of Dependent Origination *(pratītyasamutpāda)* is generally given in the following sequence, to which I have added the conditioning astrological signs:

1. *Aries the ram.* First we have fundamental ignorance *(avidya)* and its continuous cycling through the reversed wheel until that wheel has been rectified. Aries starts the cycle of becoming impelled from the abstract domains of Mind.
2. *Taurus the bull.* With ignorance comes the *saṃskāras,* the habit forming *karmic* propensities, and the rebirth-producing volitions *(cetanā).* Taurus clothes the field of desire-attachment, the originating Thought to act (in Aries), thus causing *saṃskāras* to appear.
3. *Gemini the twins.* Consciousness *(vijñāna)* comes via past life karmic factors and *saṃskāras.* Attributes of the 'I' are therefore developed, reinforced, and then battled through. Gemini interrelates the various opposing and often warring forces in the zodiac *(saṃsāra),* until a balance is reached. The *nāḍīs* constituting the foundation of manifest life are here established and vitalised.
4. *Cancer the crab.* Through consciousness, the mental and physical phenomena are conditioned via the mind that names and the form that receives sensations *(nāma-rūpa).* This allows the establishment of one's identity in the physical environment. Cancer governs the process of birthing physical phenomena, mass consciousness and the Watery world most are immersed in, wherein all forms of sensations are experienced. The newly born entity begins the process of sense-contact, hence 'naming' things.
5. *Leo the lion.* Through mental and physical phenomena are conditioned the six bases *(ṣaḍāyatana),* the five sense organs through which impressions can come, and consciousness, which correlates those impressions. Leo governs the self-conscious personality wherein these 'six bases' are exemplified.
6. *Virgo the virgin.* Through the six bases the sensorial impressions that come through contact *(sparśa)* with the physical environment are conditioned. Virgo is the mother of the phenomenal universe, and of all attributes of consciousness derived from it.

7. *Libra the balances.* Through the impressions, feeling sensations *(vedanā)* are conditioned. Here the 'feeling sensations' are contemplated upon as to their worthiness for continuation, or else to find something other to take their place.
8. *Scorpio the scorpion.* Through feeling is conditioned craving *(tṛṣṇā).* In this sign one battles with these cravings and the sum of the emotions as part of the path towards enlightenment. The scorpion's sting produces many unwelcome attitudes of mind to master.
9. *Sagittarius the archer.* Through craving, clinging or grasping *(upādāna)* is conditioned. Either the archer fires strong arrows of attachment to aspects of desire; or else arrows of one-pointed aspiration to gain enlightenment.
10. *Capricorn the goat.* Through clinging is conditioned the process of becoming *(bhāva),* consisting in the active and passive life process leading towards rebirth. The materialistic goat climbs the mount of material plane accomplishment, which once attained sets the conditions for rebirth. For his spiritual brother, on the other hand, this mount is that of Initiation into the mysteries of being/non-being.
11. *Aquarius the water bearer.* We have a consequent rebirth *(jāti).* Aquarius represents the free-flowing energies that qualifies new ventures. For the average person, these ventures are generally fickle, with selfish incentive. For those on the path, the new venture represents the Bodhisattva path, or the next level of accomplishment, which these waters of Life energise.
12. *Pisces the fishes.* Thus we get grief, sorrow, despair, old age, death *(jaramaraṇa)* and the repetition of the cycle (in Libra). Pisces, the last sign of the zodiac, sums the attainment of the zodiacal wheel, representing the ending of things, the cycle of death, with a consequent rebirth.

It should be noted that though the motion of the zodiacal wheel is depicted in a clockwise motion, where its movement is in terms of the precession of the equinoxes, which is an illusional motion, due to the earth rotating around its axis. The true (esoteric) wheel is in the opposite direction, in accord with the sun's sweep of the heavens.

The great Mother, Origination, and the Eightfold Path

The activity associated with Dependent Origination happens via the Virgoan wheel of the Heart centre, which establishes the womb of the great Mother. Therein the entire Eightfold Path to liberation is trod. Once the role of the virgin-Mother is comprehended, then analysis of the processes of life is greatly facilitated, and the study of consciousness can be delineated with greater exactitude. Comprehension involves analysing the qualities accorded to the twelve dependencies in relation to the signs of the zodiac. The astrological considerations of the Buddha's listing of the twelve petals of the rectified wheel can then be clarified.[10]

Virgo the virgin is the southwest petal of the *western* triad of the zodiacal wheel and sets in motion the field whereby the sense-consciousnesses can evolve via contact with the material universe. From this foundation the 'habit forming *karmic* propensities' (the second of the dependencies, governed by Taurus) that arise out of ignorant actions eventually unfolds the 'process of becoming' the objective for a life, necessitating eventual rebirth. Such an objective will represent, at a higher turning of the wheel, the climbing up of the mount of Initiation and liberation. (Governed by the tenth of the dependencies, ruled by Capricorn.) The Earthy triplicity of the zodiac is here outlined in the signs Virgo, Taurus and Capricorn.[11] They represent the darkness of the substance of space that needs to be conquered (Virgo), penetrated by consciousness that evolves through wilful volitions (Taurus), and converted to light upon the path of mastery (Capricorn). This entire process of conversion of ignorance to light happens within the substance of the 'womb' embodied by the sign Virgo. Virgo is forever the mother of the child. This 'child' represents the *saṃskāras* of the consciousness-stream that evolve via the incarnation process. Virgo hides the light of Life, producing forms veiled by the ignorance that manifest the rebirth producing volitions. Eventually the light is revealed through the striving

10 Obviously such zodiacal interpretation of their scriptures will take time to be understood and accepted by mainstream Buddhists.

11 All three signs govern the expression of the Element Earth. Similarly, Cancer, Scorpio and Pisces are Water signs; Aries, Leo and Sagittarius are Fire signs; and Gemini, Libra and Aquarius are Air signs.

of an awakening consciousness, which represents the steps one takes to be born out of that 'womb' of the rebirth process.

On the reversed wheel there are nine signs from Virgo to Capricorn (including Virgo), which symbolise the nine 'months' of the gestation period preceding the birth of the enlightened attitudes that cause one to walk the path to liberation. From another perspective, we have the nine stages of the process of Initiation into the mysteries of being/non-being at whatever level of expression the seeker is at. These are experienced whenever aspects of any of the nine heads of the Hydra are effectively slain. Capricorn represents the summit or mount of such attainment. From every angle the symbolism of Virgo, though styled a 'virgin', is associated with gestation, birth, the prenatal life of the developing Bodhisattva. It is concerned with the gestation of consciousness in the fields of the earth, which we call evolution. This is but the process that inevitably conquers ignorance.

With respect to this, nine signs are related to the Buddha's Eightfold Path.[12] They produce the types of activity whereby the wheel of Life can be rectified, the gain being enlightenment.

Eightfold Path	Sign	Keynotes
Right understanding	Aries	Mental beginnings
Right aspiration	Taurus	Desire-aspiration
Right speech	Gemini	Relationships of all types
Right action	Cancer	Movement and incarnation
Right livelihood	Scorpio	Tests and trials on the path
Right effort	Sagittarius	One pointed direction
Right mindfulness	Aquarius	Service to others
Right absorption	Pisces	Salvation or liberation

Table 1. The Eightfold Path and the Zodiac

12 See also *Esoteric Astrology,* 278. I have rearranged, and related to the Eightfold Path, the listing of the signs related to Virgo through planetary affiliation, given by D.K.

Conditioning all of this is Virgo, the mother, the womb (the *saṃsāric* domains) wherein the process setting the stage for undertaking the Eightfold Path resides. This path, therefore, represents the stages of the process allowing one to be born out of that womb into the domains of light.[13]

1. *Right understanding,* Aries the ram, producing mental beginnings. This implies obtaining an intellectual grasp of the essence of all religious philosophies, the cause and result of the evolutionary process, of wrong actions and attitudes, of the mystery of being/non-being, and nowadays also of the basic laws and precepts discovered by scientific investigation. One obtains such understanding through contemplative reflection upon the nature of the Four Noble Truths, and the expansion of the philosophy into the remainder of the *buddhadharma.* The sign Aries the ram is the first sign in the zodiac, and therefore instigates the primary mental understanding of the nature of the path and the necessity of following it to enlightenment. Aries instigates the impetus of the will to carry through to conclusion one's initial decision. This is necessary if such understanding is not to remain a purely mental exercise.
2. *Right aspiration,* Taurus the bull, the keynote being desire-aspiration. This implies aspiration towards the development of compassion and thus enlightenment. It follows naturally from obtaining right understanding, and concerns setting one's feet on the path, producing liberation from suffering and cyclic rebirth. One thereby finds the portals of the Heart of Life wherein resides enlightenment. This sign introduces the desire principle, which is transformed into right aspiration and devotion to the *dharma* when one is no longer attached to *māyā.* Here understanding is clothed with images of enlightenment as a consequence of the development of wisdom, which such aspiration produces.
3. *Right speech,* Gemini the twins, where relationships of all types are espoused. Once right attitudes of mind are developed then the person necessarily curbs all idle chatter and cultivates silence, speaking only what will benefit others or that will produce right (magical)

13 My accounting of the Eightfold Path here shall be relatively brief, with the focus being their relation to the respective signs of the zodiac governing them. They are treated in greater detail in chapter 8 of Volume 4.

results. The effect of erroneous or zealously misdirected speech can produce serious consequences to the aspirant's endeavours to cultivate harmlessness. This is also applicable to one's writings (an extension of speech). The power of the written word for good or for bad is obvious to all. How one speaks and to whom is spoken defines one's social acquaintances and boundaries. The nature of that speech determines the outcome of the relationships. Speech must be skilfully presented to endeavour to unite the warring factions of ideas into an equable common embrace.

Speech must be made sacred, as a form of creativity brought to the precincts of the temple of the Heart (an activity ruled by Gemini), and then never allowed to leave that temple. It can then officiate in every expression of a Bodhisattva's service arena. The cultivation of silence is necessary if the person is to meditate and utilise sacred mantras with effectiveness.

4. *Right action,* Cancer the crab, signifying mass movement and incarnation. The nature of the Cancerian influence here is symbolised by the ability of the crab to scurry from one convenient place to another upon the rocky shoreline of *saṃsāra* to find sources of nourishment (the *dharma*) and shelter (from *māyā*). Being the most southerly of the signs, it is the place of incarnation of ideas and of the *maṇḍalas* developed by the meditation *(dhyāna).* Right action necessitates the ability to apply the ideas formulated in realms of the meditation-Mind into the *māyā,* to achieve the unfolding purpose of what was formulated. It incorporates impeccable timing for every coming event. This is symbolised by the quick and precise movements of the crab along the shoreline, by its ability to not be affected by the vicissitudes of the waves. (The *saṃsāric* interrelationships as dictated by *karma.*)

Right action must be applied in thought and speech, as well as in the world of forms. Inevitably, a meditative rhythm is produced that conquers the 'I' concept (associated with the next sign, Leo the lion, who governs the activity of the personal-I). The *dhyāna* produced is intensified in Libra the balances, and brought to its conclusion in the sign Capricorn the goat. (As explained previously, these three signs are not part of the list of the Eightfold Path.) Such action then automatically determines the outcome of all aspects of life. Skilful means will then be utilised via compassionate meditation to help all sentient beings. This becomes the keynote of the Eightfold Path, where action rather than mere belief is emphasised. Only direct (experimental) action produces the manifest expression of the other aspects of the path. It concerns what we do and refrain from doing, thus also necessitates deep self-analysis of the real motives for all actions.

5. *Right livelihood,* Scorpio the scorpion, governing tests and trials on the path to light. Right action carries naturally through into right livelihood, which takes naught from others that is not given, nor harms the development of any other being. It therefore implies following the Bodhisattva path of harmlessness and right service.

The tests upon this path involve overcoming all negative and hindering *saṃskāras* that have been carried forth from past lives and which must be transmuted, specifically with respect to the field of strong desire, sensuality and accompanying emotions. The *yogin* also must counter the accompanying attacks from the dark foes who continuously look for signs of weakness in the meditative armour. The continuously recurring *saṃskāras* of desire, plus unwholesome psychic effects, are symbolised by the ability of the scorpion to sting with venomous jabs. The scorpion lives in the symbolic deserts of materiality, symbolising the general tenor of *saṃsāric* activity. Tests for worthiness of shouldering the burdens of enlightenment must be undertaken within the material world, and the Watery context of the venom projected by others and of one's own psyche. The tests are designed to provide the necessary fruits of accomplishment that exalt the skilful aspirant in chosen arenas of service work. The purpose lifts the aspirant into levels of revelation not hitherto possible.

Such service is the result of a life-long contemplation upon need in relation to the developed characteristics one possesses. It causes one to robe oneself in qualifications determined by Ray type, befitting one to be a scientist, artist, etc. It gleans the best of past life experiences, plus that developed in this life, as conditioned by the various mental, emotional and socio-political environments in which one resides. The service necessitates the ability to vision the direction that the course of events of a chosen field may take, in order to develop qualities that will be of greatest benefit to those being served.

Right livelihood also concerns a sincere, heartfelt, ritualistic devotion to the bounty of Mother Nature and to the karmic opportunities of life, which provides one with the resources that are the mainstay of one's livelihood.

6. *Right effort,* Sagittarius the archer, firing arrows of one-pointed direction. These arrows are of ambition or aspiration towards a distant goal to which one steadfastly strives to reach. Inevitably, one learns to strive for enlightenment with persevering one-pointed aspiration. *Bodhicitta* then becomes the driving energy, the taut bow string that fires the arrows. Enlightenment is thus acquired, necessitating a persistent striving that with certainty will overcome all the obstacles to obtaining the goal, through production of the qualities needed to meet all needs.

   Such effort underlies the five previous precepts, manifesting in each of them to differing degrees of intensity at various stages of the path. In the final two precepts, the person must be so imbued with the qualities accrued that the effort is automatic, spontaneous. To all intents, therefore, it becomes effortless, below the threshold of consciousness. When related to meditative development, the initial effort of striving or working to concentrate is later superseded, because complete relaxation of all cognitive processes is needed. The initial momentum is then effortlessness. The act of effort prevents concentration in its final stages.

7. *Right mindfulness,* Aquarius the water bearer, the keynote being service to others. The water bearer pours the waters of life, a free-flowing field of energy, outwards to all who are willing to find succour in the plenitude of the *dharma* so offered. The *dharma* flows from the zone of meditative intention to the field of need, wherein the little ones reside who have succumbed to the turmoil of *māyā.* They need to be rightly nourished to have the strength to find their way out from confusing illusions. The water bearer's qualities and actions are the prototype for all forms of Bodhisattvic activity.

   If the other precepts are followed, then whatever prevents release from suffering falls away. One is left with concentrated energies that are assimilated and projected towards the goal. It produces perfect mindfulness of all things, concentrating upon the production of meditative development and the demonstration of the *dharma*. The *dharma* here concerns following the Bodhisattva path. Its purpose necessitates the elimination of *karma* that ties all sentient beings to material existence. Not only is the Bodhisattva's *karma* thus cleansed, but for all that such a one serves. The entire effect of group karmic affiliations and associated *saṃskāras* becoming cleansed produces the progress of group enlightenment. All beings that such a one spiritually interrelates with therefore move toward liberation together, each at their respective level of development.

The Bodhisattva develops a specific, effortless intensity in meditation in which the mind is held steady, unwavering in light, focussed upon the plan to assist the all. It is effortless because it is the outcome of long periods of meditation that have become a spontaneous and intense state of transcendence, there being naught there to resist the realisation of the most potent energies or revelations. The mind is centred around the thought that there can be no true liberation for one if all are not also brought to such freedom (from suffering). This then defines the parameters of right mindfulness of purpose and of liberation for all. It is the Bodhisattva way. When focussed (upon a form or idea) the Bodhisattva's intention becomes the seed that can effectively explode into that which empowers a complete stream of realisation for many beings, and can direct others to realms beyond thought.

8. *Right absorption,* Pisces the fishes, with salvation, or liberation, being the keynote. Such salvation concerns an absorption into that which is void of all discernible characteristics, but which is the fount of all liberating insight. This can also be seen as an absorption into the heart of the Hierarchy of Enlightened Being.

Being the last of the signs of the zodiac, Pisces signifies termination or completion of a cycle. It is consequently also the sign of a world saviour (a Buddha or Avatar), who has sacrificed his state of abstraction in *nirvāṇic bliss* in order to incarnate into the Waters of *saṃsāra* for the sake of liberating the (human) 'fishes' swimming therein. They are bonded to all aspects of their Watery world.

Excluding Virgo, there are three signs not included in this list, because these signs play different roles, being signs of crises:

a. *Capricorn* the goat, who scales mountainous heights, represents the goal, the summit of achievement. This is the place where enlightenment is gained. A crisis is produced upon every stage of proceeding up this mountain, as cherished ideas and idealisms must be superseded by loftier, more truthful expressions of thought.
b. *Libra* governs the turning of the wheel of the Law. It therefore governs all factors of an aspirant's life by directing the related *karma* to cleanse *saṃskāras* via the cycles and rate of motion of the wheel of the vicissitudes of life. The crises associated with all of the major changes in life's expression are thus controlled by this sign.
c. *Leo* represents the qualities of the ego, of the personal-I that undergoes the process of mastering this Eightfold Path. Here every crises manifests associated with the battlefield between the concept of an 'I' and the elimination of that concept. Such battles happen all along the path of liberation.

Once mastery has been achieved, then the liberated one sows the seeds for the harvest of life in Virgo. 'Seeds' refer to the qualities that bestow enlightenment amongst worthy aspirants, which later bear fruit as Buddhahood. These seeds of light are sown according to the degree of darkness that must be overcome.

The reversed wheel and the twelve signs

This section, which endeavours to explain the more generalised conditionings governing the adventitious activities of the average person, shall be summarised in terms of the nature of the four groups of petals that organise the Heart centre. The Heart is the Life of all living emanatory or vital being.

1. The *northern triad* of petals is ultimately concerned with the direction of *prāṇas* to the Head centre, where the qualities of the *dharmakāya* can be evoked.
2. The *western triad* incorporates the attributes that will eventually develop the abstract Mind associated with the Throat centre's awakening.

3. The *eastern triad* relates to the generation and the empowerment of the attributes of the Void into all aspects of the Heart centre.
4. The *southern triad* concerns the projection of transforming energies so that eventually the *prāṇas* from the centres below the diaphragm can be absorbed into the Heart centre. The Void Elements are consequently achieved.

For each direction, the general influence of their polar opposites must also be taken into account. On the reversed wheel, however, the more mundane considerations concerning the average person are developed. I shall explain them very briefly because this treatise is focussed upon the path to enlightenment. All of these attributes are in reality generated in the centres below the diaphragm, with the *prāṇas* passing through the respective petals of the Heart centre on the way to be stored as consciousness attributes of the Head lotus.

We saw that the first two petals of the reversed wheel relate to the qualities of Libra and Virgo, and that Virgo embodies the womb of space-time. It represents the substance wherein ignorance is generated, and which therefore must be mastered. The next petal, part of the southern triad, is governed by *Leo the lion,* associated with the egotistical individual that resides in ignorance, and who must eventually battle with it and materialism.

With respect to Dependent Origination, the Leonine petal generates the developing consciousness stemming from the experiences afforded by the expression of the *karma* of self-focussed interrelationships. The focus is upon the minutiae of human interactions in all matters concerning the form. Leo, the self-conscious individual, then reaps this experience. He is the lord of the earthy domain, similar to the lion who is proffered as the proud lord of the jungle. The jungle symbolises the complex emotio-mental reactions, tensions, violence, avarice, etc., associated with all forms of social interactions in our civilisations. These attributes express the sum of the animal-like propensities of one's persona. They are an expression of the desire-mind. Here, whatever is 'caused' must eventually be critically analysed and identified with by the individuals captivated by *saṃsāra*. Desire-forms of all types abound with respect to the 'self' and its ability to self-identify with these things. This produces the developed *saṃskāras* attributed to this petal, of the *karma* with the outer environment.

In this reversed petal the consciousness of the personal-I finds its natural home, for Leo governs the development and assertion of the 'I'-concept (the 'self') in all of its disguises. It is fitting, therefore, that here the third of the dependencies finds its full expression, where the *karmic* effect of what was spawned by ignorance develops consciousness.

The natural separative attitude of the mind is the foundation of intelligence, which views everything in terms of the 'I' and 'not I'. This distinction in its multifarious plenitude, where each 'I' vies for domination, is the jungle that the lion rules. The seeming supremacy of its 'I' over the realm it purveys is the basic expression of pride. Everything involving individuation, and thus attachment to the 'self' concept, is exemplified here. This pride is the mainstay of the personal-I that undergoes the challenges of life in *saṃsāra*. One must eventually learn to overcome the allurements to the concept of 'self' in this sign. This necessitates comprehension of the true nature of the vicissitudes of life. The attachment to the 'self' and its relation to other selves teaches one the transitory nature of everything, because nothing related to 'self' lasts. Inevitably one learns to not act in self-focussed ways.

In this petal, therefore, the Fires of mind are generated (Leo being a Fire sign) that ignite the substance of ignorance. The light of one's internal sun becomes increasingly illumined and radiatory through mental activity. Later, the complete blaze of the I-consciousness is brought to bear upon the field of darkness. All aspects of the Earthy domain will be revealed by that light. The victorious one in this sign consequently becomes the light of Life. Such 'lighted substance' is therefore the nature of the *prāṇas* projected by this petal of the southern triad. This triad is principally concerned with discerning the minutiae of physical plane phenomena. In this Leonine petal, however, the focus is the intricate analysis and detail that deals with the *karma* derived from interrelation with external phenomena.

The fourth of the petals of the Heart Lotus as a reversed wheel is ruled by the sign *Cancer the crab,* which is the major Watery sign in the zodiac. This, the most southern of the signs (signifying downwards into incarnate life), rules massed psychic sensitivity and reaction. Such sensitivity is lunar in nature, the Moon being the conditioning planetary ruler of Cancer. The moon highlights psychic receptivity, emotional awareness, sensitivity to other's opinions and impacts from all sides of the human form, for the moon is the mother of transitory forms and of illusions. This sign thus typifies an embryonic, emotional type of consciousness.

The fourth of the Dependent Originations now comes to the fore, the interrelation between the mind that names and the form that receives sensations *(nāma-rūpa)*. One's identity in the physical environment can then be established because this downward focus necessitates the mind to categorise and to delineate the things named in terms of the attributes possessed by their forms.

In its highest level it produces the types of activity manifested by present day materialistic science, with its minute dissection and analysis of physical phenomena. Forms of ignorance are eliminated as light is spread to comprehend phenomena by the empirical minds of the scientific community. Our technological age is the product of this form of generation of light. (Governed principally by the three southern signs in the zodiac.) It does not directly produce liberation, but is one of the markers upon that way for humanity as a whole. The upward way to liberation is trod once this intellectual activity is fused with the esoteric sciences.

Lacking proper insight, the human-crab is ruled by many fearsome images. It scurries backwards or sideways into the nearest hiding place to anything appearing dangerous. A hermit crab lives in its own specially selected shell of protective guise. In a similar manner, the average person builds shells of protectiveness, the houses and rooms (of the empirical mind) full of every material encumbrance desired. There are shells of emotionality and fearful reactions to other's intention and societal impositions. Such shells can become very concretised.

The Waters rule, because when looking at the material domain people generally do so emotionally, or with much gross desire for its allurements. They are glamoured by the things they can accrue for themselves, symbolised by the use of the claws of the crab to fasten on to something. The crab is tenacious, very possessive, fond of all pretty things and comforts of home. It lives both on the land and in the sea (the Watery emotional realm) and carries its habitat (all its possessions and earthly desires) with it wherever it goes. It would rather lose its claws than let go of what it has grasped. Being extremely sensitive to all forms of impressions that continually inundate him, imaginarily or in actual fact, the Cancerian almost immediately reacts, or else hides in his shell. These qualities define the nature of the Waters dispensed in Cancer. The *prāṇas* generated are therefore a type of Watery-Earthy mix (sometimes quite muddy), the colourings depending upon the nature and quality of the desire for murky allurements in *saṃsāra*.

Cancer rules the chest, to which there are twelve pairs of ribs, the significance of which is that they help cause the assimilation of external energies (e.g., of the zodiacal *prāṇas*). They help the lungs to breathe, and form the outer boundary of the central reservoir of life and light (the heart/Heart centre), protecting it from harmful extraneous influences. Being the sign of mass incarnation and mass consciousness, so all entities first physically manifest through this sign. It embodies the Watery substance of the great womb of Nature. Primarily it represents the containment of the energies below the diaphragm that have been directed there from the 'chest cavity' above.

It is said that Cancer 'visions the life in Leo'.[14] It does this because the Leonine subject offers a sense of emotional stability and security without the need to carry protective armour. The mind that is developed in Leo produces this. Leo fears no one, is strong, independent and self-reliant, quite unlike the hypersensitive, ever fearful crab as he scampers from hiding place to hiding place. Cancer is thus the sign of the mass instinctual consciousness which must eventually give way to the dominant self-consciousness of Leo.

Cancer is a dual sign, where the glyph of its claws expressed in opposite direction and in mutual embrace symbolises the masculine and feminine polarities in life (yin-yang). They have the capacity to cling to all attributes of life. One claw can also represent the embracing consciousness and the other the tenacious sense-perceptions that gain experience in manifest life. The claws are also quite capable of expressing emotional aggression.

Upon the enlightenment path (after battles with the field of desire in the sign Scorpio) the Cancerian becomes a dispeller of the Waters. He/she is the light bringer for all the watery lives, helping them to overcome ignorance concerning possessiveness. This necessitates overcoming

14 *Esoteric Astrology*, 332.

attachments to all forms of transience. A true equanimous detachment to all things *saṃsāric* must manifest.

It can be said that:

- Capricorn is the place of mastery of the Fiery mind, of consciousness.
- Scorpio is the place of mastery of the Watery emotions.
- Virgo is the place of mastery of the physical (Earthy) mechanism of response.
- Cancer represents the conditioning environment (the Watery-Earthy mix) wherein these forms of mastery can be accomplished. Its polar opposite is Capricorn, hence Cancer represents the base from which the mount of aspiration can be climbed.

The quality attributed to the southern (Cancerian) direction from Figure 2 is styled 'not caused' and is one of the four cardinal directions that are the open gates leading to *śūnyatā*. All things that are 'caused' must manifest via the etheric body (the *nāḍī* system) and be directed by the mind, normally united with the emotions, to manifest phenomena. That which is 'not caused' is thus not directed, and stays entirely in the field of consciousness (the *ālayavijñāna).* On the rectified wheel we would also look to *śūnyatā.* Therefore, *śūnyatā* is the ultimate or absolute interpretation of the term 'not caused'. The potential is not activated. Relatively, in terms of the stream of phenomenon, the term relates to what exists etherically in the *nāḍīs,* as this is the reality from which all appearing phenomena springs. What could appear physically as phenomena may or may not happen, but the potential exists subjectively. The dense physical appearance is the great illusion, an automaton of whatever forces come via the *nāḍīs.*

The four points of the *cardinal cross* of the dynamic, progressive Will are doorways of movement from one level of expression to the next higher, closer level to liberation. The concern, therefore, is with the elimination of *karma*. In the southern direction, the focus of one upon this cross is upon elevating physical activity to the higher domains, utilising phenomena (of the lesser kingdoms of Nature) that is therefore 'not caused' by human interrelationships. In this direction people are swayed by mass emotional tides and moods, consequently massed *karma* sweeps the individual in its embrace. Such activity represents the lowest point of human consciousness, where individuation slowly emerges from massed opinions and social activity. From here, therefore, one can only move upwards toward forms of self-identity, hence generating the *karma* of self-expression. The focus of the eastern direction is toward the Heart, and thus to the *dharma* that inevitably spells freedom from karmic constraints. The northern direction concerns breaking out of the bonds that tie one to form, through looking upwards toward liberation. The western direction produces a contemplative life wherein the processes of life are put into proper perspective.

Four of the signs of the zodiac constitute a *mutable cross,* of constant changing activity with respect to the external environment. They are the four signs wherein interaction with phenomena and other causes of *māyā* are principally expressed. They are Virgo, Gemini, Pisces, and Sagittarius.

The remaining four signs, Leo, Taurus, Aquarius, and Scorpio, express a *fixed cross* of a determined and then steadfast purpose. They are the principal signs wherein compassionate or loving attributes of human interrelations manifest, which inevitably are geared to obtaining enlightened perceptions with each turning of the wheel.

Cancer forms the Watery triplicity together with Scorpio and Pisces, which is the cause of humanity's mass emotional conditionings. We can look at the effect of this triplicity from two angles:

1. With regard to the world of sensation.
2. As that which purifies and cleanses.

1. One enters incarnation in Cancer to be immersed in the Waters of mass instinctual currents and emotional receptivity. Therein one is buffeted this way and that, according to the mood of those currents. In Pisces, the consciousness is firmly yoked to the personality and the 'fish' learns to swim wherever he wills within the confines of that conditioning. One can thus attain individualised character traits and become self reliant. In Scorpio one develops the power to sting, hurt, and bring death (through continuous affiliation with *saṃsāra).* Having emerged from the waters, yet still needing to master the experiences on land, one suffers much, causes much suffering, and undergoes many trials through the sense of isolation and enmity to all around. Thus the will is developed, which concerns one's ability to break free from the sensations and conditionings of the masses.

2. In Cancer the purificatory Watery Element begins its action. It conditions the masses, who cause radical changes in the environment and habitat of the crab. We also have periodical, cyclic, racial, and seasonal changes that effect the kingdoms of Nature as a whole, causing the cleansing or changing of attributes of their evolutionary development towards perfection.

In Pisces, which is part of the mutable cross of continuous and oft periodic activity (the swastika), it is the individual who is karmically purified in all his actions through the process of incarnation. Here the fish learns to swim free and in company with his fellow beings, it develops its life and finds sustenance in the Waters of being. That to which it was formerly bonded and later found to be unnecessary or hindering is eliminated, or purified and transmuted.

When the necessary purification of the grossest aspects of life have been accomplished, then the person can mount the fixed cross. In its earlier stages this cross (composed of Taurus, Aquarius, Scorpio, and Leo) is concerned with the expression of the various forms of human *karma,* and then their expiation via steadfast compassionate concern. Therefore, here one is fixed in conscious enlightening purpose, allowing *karma* to finally be resolved. Scorpio is the arm of this cross wherein the karmic battles with desire occurs. There are many agonising trials and tests of discipleship that will eventually allow the second Initiation, concerned with mastery of the Waters, to be undertaken. Purified Airy-Watery substance then clothes the creative *maṇḍala* of the one in *samādhi*, which is liberating in effect, eliminating all forms of bondage.

The rectification of the wheel has taken place and the person stands again in Cancer in a body of light, able to disperse and dispel the emotional ails and glamours of the world. By the time the wheel has placed one in Pisces, then a world saviour appears, a high degree Bodhisattva that has learnt to compassionately direct the massed Waters. Such a one is the embodied repository of the energies that affect whole kingdoms of Nature and planetary evolutions.

The southeast petal of the southern triad is governed by the qualities of the sign *Gemini the twins.* Gemini is concerned with fluidic, oft unstable relationships. The twins must learn to cooperate, to work together, to link their hands (which are ruled by Gemini) to creatively build and share. However, in the early stages there is often friction, strife, reproving, even warfare between them. The hands are the prime organs for sense contact and creativity, but are often used for unsavoury actions. (Gemini can also stand for two differing groups of people, or even nations.) The hands indicate the service which the immortal and mortal brother must render to each other if the separative relationship between them is to be annulled. Service is a major theme of the relationship between them in the latter stages of their development. It is this relation that eventually produces the appearance of the Bodhisattva and engenders all of the Bodhisattva stages *(bhūmis).* For each of these levels the Bodhisattva must again find himself in Gemini, learning how to balance all opposing forces concerning the new manifesting field of service.

The polar opposite of Gemini, Sagittarius, manifests the directing power that fires the aspiring Bodhisattva on the upward way, once the necessary calmness of mind has been generated in Gemini, and the issues then plainly seen can be resolved. The fluid interplay and instability of the Gemini subject, plus the one-pointedness of the personality focus of the Sagittarian, eventually produces a balancing of the pairs of opposites in Gemini, and then the directive effort of the Bodhisattva in Sagittarius. The power of the enlightenment-principle waxes greatly in glory, whilst the self-willed personality no longer shines.

The mercurial mind of the Gemini subject (Mercury being the exoteric planetary ruler) allows quick, automatic analysis of any situation at hand. It is always keen to ascertain new opportunities for personal gain, or to build the knowledge bank of information needed to sustain whatever field of activity (desire or emotionally focussed) in which the person is involved, or that is shared with others. (The 'brother' can also be thought of in terms of a community or society, or even of attributes of Nature's kingdoms.) The awareness developed is the basis for the manifestation of the fourth and fifth of the Dependent Originations, where through mental and physical phenomena ('name and form', *nāma-rūpa)* are conditioned the six bases, the organs of the senses.

The interrelation between the consciousness that names and the form that stimulates the mind to do so, signifies the twins in the Temple of Life. The mind needs the input from sense contact to grow and develop wisdom. At first it cooperates with the sum of what *saṃsāra* offers in order to build its empire of 'self'. Later, upon the enlightenment path, it makes war with these same attributes to ultimately gain *śūnyatā's* domain. *Śūnyatā* is the central precinct of the Holy of Holies of the Temple of Life governed by Gemini. Eventually, *saṃsāra* and *śūnyatā* are at-oned, producing the *saṃsāra-śūnyatā* nexus, symbolised by the ability of the twins to hold hands.

Our senses continuously seek out new sources of sensation, as well as the renewal of what is pleasurable. Via the senses, such activity generally becomes quite ritualised, though often unconsciously so. Ritualised habits (like having breakfast every morning, or the blood flowing in the veins) in all fields of undertaking is governed by Gemini. It engenders the strength or length of all *karma*-producing processes. The eventual purpose being the resolution of the pairs of opposites. All must be brought to the heart of life in Gemini, wherein the non-dual awareness of the Void is realised. Libra governs the outpouring of these cycles, to ensure that the *karma* is resolved. The manifested duration of the cyclic ebbs and flows of the generated *saṃskāras,* via the myriad forms of activity one incurs, are carried through to future lives to manifest appropriately via the *nāḍīs.* Longstanding ritualistic activity eventually produces an inner sense of timing or knowingness, of when and where to act for any situation to be. It produces the *sādhana* of the *yogin,* his meditative work and visualisations via the *chakras.* It is then the heartbeat of life pushing all onwards through their course of evolutionary being and final liberation.

From Figure 2 we see that the corresponding aspect for Gemini is designated 'other causes of *māyā'. Māyā* needs to be interpreted as more than simply being 'illusion'. Its true reference is to the substance or energy field, the qualifications of *prāṇa,* coupled with the effects of the wrongly discerning mind that produces illusion. It signifies what is incorporated within the etheric field of the internal and external *nāḍīs,* which are governed by Gemini. (As is also the blood that courses in our veins, which is a lower correspondence of the qualities and functions of the *prāṇas.*) Within this vital energy body is found the seven major *chakras,* hence all the fields of energy interplay with which the science of Astrology deals. (Gemini thus subtly relates all of the signs together.)

These forces are dual. The two pillars at the entrance of the temple of Gemini symbolise the *iḍā* and *piṅgalā nāḍīs,* and the adytum holds the Heart centre, which is the repository of *śūnyatā*. Within this energy field either the light of the mortal brother (the personality) or relative immortal brother (the Sambhogakāya Flower) is dominant and therefore the focus of all activity, or else the energies are fused, consummating a goal of evolution. For long ages, however, there is a fluid, mutual, yet also conflicting interplay between the brothers. At first, much strife and friction are produced and then harmony and heights of revelation when the integration dominates. The control of all such energies in the body also necessitates calmness of mind *(śamatha),* and without such control of the entire energy body the accomplished *yogin* can do nothing, *samādhi* is not possible.

We all live in energy fields. These 'other causes' refer to the way that such fields convey people's emotional responses and reactions conditioned by the mind, when externalised by means of the senses. These are causes of *māyā* that are not directly the result of normal human interrelationships (governed by the Leonine petal), but with the general environment in which people live.

The *southeast* petal of the *eastern triad* is governed by the qualities of *Taurus the bull.* At first the Taurian rushes with blind desire to contact or to achieve its objective. In the polar opposite of this sign (Scorpio) desire becomes a battlefield, but in Taurus it is definite and fixated upon the objective of 'home building'—building a comfortable environment of pleasurable experiences. The desires generated are comprehended via the *sixth* of the Dependent Originations, where the six bases establish sensorial impressions that come through contact with the physical environment, making what has been named 'real' in the mind.

After the battle with desire has been successfully fought in Scorpio, then by the time that Taurus is reached, the 'house' has become the Heart's Mind with its 'window' representing the all-seeing Eye, which Taurus embodies. It directs all Life processes, the inner vision of the *yogin* or enlightened being. It visions the future, the road, wheel, or process ahead, allowing one to manifest the appropriate actions with respect to the rebirth process. However, the 'eye'[15] of the average person functions to envision what is to be contacted, so as to clothe the thoughts generated in the mind with the sensations derived from experience of

15 An extension of the mind, the sixth of the bases.

such contact. This is done by activating the remainder of the senses. People generally build the images of things desired before they strive to get them. This works for those that seek sensual pleasure, money, or material power. In its highest connotation we also have the monk or *yogin* doing visualisations for Deity Yoga, meditation, *mantrayāna*, *mudrās*, etc., where there is a desired outcome. (Only in the highest stages of yoga does one transcend this process by residing in 'non-abiding *samādhi*'.)

This clothing process via the senses, where a repertoire of sensations pleasing to the mind is built, represents the *saṃskāras* generated by this Taurean petal of the reversed wheel.

Both Aries the ram and Taurus the bull have similar characteristics, and are often found living and working together on the fertile and grassy plains of *saṃsāra*. They are both headstrong, dominating, ambitious, and wilful. One is ram headed and the other bull headed. Both exemplify the energies of the first Ray of Will or Power. The difference is that Taurus clothes this Ray with emotional or desire substance and Aries more specifically with mental substance. Taurus represents the energy that drives to fulfilment the initial impulse engendered by Aries. Taurus expresses the march of desire through the ages, which sustains all action. (From another angle, such a desire is for the appearance of a Buddha on the world stage.) Desire is found in every field of application. In the gross sensual person it drives his physical urges to fulfilment. It becomes the aspiration of the disciple, and then transmuted into the illumined will of the Initiate. The Taurean is fond of good living, the comforts and security of the 'grassy fields' of his work environment and home, and is hard working.

Taurus provides the substance to the emanation of thoughts, and thus gives life to the varying images found in the realm of illusion, of people's conceptions of the heavenly or hell realms.

It is an Earth sign, which expresses the concreted energies projected to the dense physical domain from which one must ultimately become liberated. The pointed horns of the bull symbolise strife and also desire, the ability to pierce and project. They are the points of the dual *nāḍī* stream through which the strength and power of the bull are focussed. We also see in the bull the ability to trample upon and destroy the life incarnated into the form.

People rarely think just in terms of themselves when manifesting thoughts achieved through sense contact (though this is their focus). They generally share activities with family, friends, lovers, and socially. This is the basis to the conjoined *karma* assigned to this petal in Figure 2. Such *karma* is also the foundation of Love (transmuted desire), where the person actively thinks in terms of the broader community. It thereby produces a sense of comradeship, of belonging with them. Thoughts of shared activities that are possible are thus generated.

The *eastern petal* of the reversed wheel is governed by *Aries the ram*. Once Taurus establishes the home environment for the sense bases, wherein what is desirous can find a place, then Aries strengthens desire with strong will to acquire what is desired. Together they generate the *vedanā* (feeling-perception) contemplated on in Libra, utilising the sum of one's sensory data, feelings and general emotionality with respect to the material world. The foundation of the force that sustains the wheel of *saṃsāra* is thus established. The next petal (Pisces) then produces the swamps of *māyā* via the intense craving for incessant sensory stimuli that were established by the two previous petals of the reversed wheel. This consequently produces the rebirth impetus after the end of the zodiacal cycle.

It is easy to see how the Arian personality is considered to be the innovator, the originator instigating mental beginnings, especially when ruled by Mars, the god of war. Mars governs personal vigour, psychic energy (*prāṇa*), and in the form of self will, it governs all the energies conditioning the outer incarnate form.

The use of the ram's head to batter and buck comes to the fore, thus the Arian subject is said to be headstrong, determined, and impatient. The ram is ruled by his head and lives on the grassy plains, and sometimes rocky slopes of the earth. There the nourishment for everyday living is easily obtained, and the activities of his herd are also easily regulated. The herd can be viewed in terms of the massed internal (emotional) constitution of a person, as well as his outer responsibility and associations in the world when viewed in terms of group conditionings and affiliations. The major activities of the ram are concerned with manifesting a dominant personality, or with maintaining the coherency of the group by controlling and developing the herd or group activity and social harmony. The Arian battles, or strives, towards group unity.

When true equanimity is reached with all forces of Life, when *śūnyatā* and *saṃsāra* are integrated as a point of power in consciousness, the Arian then follows *the Middle Path* between extremes.

Directed personality effort, reactionary activity and strife; forceful action, wilfulness, impetuosity, and also instinctual urgings, are all the keywords of the undeveloped Arian disposition. Also, feeling-perceptions are naturally engendered in this the most easterly petal of the Heart for the reversed wheel. These perceptions are the foundation for later development of devotion to noble ideals and zealous aspiration when the wheel is reversing. Once the wheel is rectified, then Aries drives *bodhicitta* to fulfilment. It should be noted that Aries is the polar opposite of Libra, which is the sign where reversal takes place. Esoterically, polar opposites do not mean that they stand opposed to each other, but that they stand as open gates for the flow of energy impressions or qualities from one sign to the other. This can be likened to an inbreathing in one petal and an outbreathing in the other of the associated *prāṇas*, after they have been modified by the *prāṇic* circulation within the innermost sanctum of the wheel.

Taurus manifests contact with phenomena through which *saṃsāric* experience becomes possible under the instigation of the Earthy Element. Aries engenders a Fiery expression of general feeling-perceptions for things desired by the mind, and Pisces intensifies a Watery craving for the pleasurable pursuits of the senses. Thus are generated the *saṃskāras* of the three major Elements governing *saṃsāra*.

Nobody can gain liberation before all aspects of *saṃsāra* have been mastered and have been firmly eschewed as no longer useful or worthy. Repetitive forages with the forms of activity that generate the *prāṇas* of this eastern triad, to produce empirical understanding through feeling perceptions, eventually awakens the wisdom petals of the Heart. (In their elementary stages.) A form of repugnance then sets in because of the transitory nature of all things desired of a material nature. (Because of the pain of attachment thereto.) Hence the impressions generate desire to be liberated from such ceaseless activity. *Bodhicitta* is then generated.

Strong religious feelings and ideas can produce the fanatic, or fiery warrior fighting for his/her version of the *dharma,* because of the nature of the zealous force (Aries being a martial and a Fire sign) used to sustain the religious drive. Here the quick, often fanatical impulsive thoughts and actions of the ram must be transmuted into the meek and gentle qualities of the lamb. Impulsiveness must become gentle, serene action, producing carefully meditated and weighed out responses to any of life's situations. The new *saṃskāric* cycle must begin with the *prāṇas* of the lamb and gradually develop in full maturity and strength into a ram that will quickly overcome all obstacles to complete liberation. Impulsive action thereby becomes divine *Will,* steadfastly projecting the mantric power and *mudrās* for the purpose ahead. All become infused with Love. *Saṃskāras* will then be transformed, former base qualities cleansed of all lower *saṃsāric* considerations and then transmuted.

Aries embodies one of the four cardinal positions that lead directly to *śūnyatā,* and from Figure 2 we see that the consciousness aspect concerning this petal is designated 'not both'. This refers to the fact that experience of the fusion of *saṃsāra* with *śūnyatā* ultimately happens through the Arian imposition of the will in meditation. Upon the rectified wheel all dualities are blended through the power of the spiritual will into a unity. The mind/Mind becomes focussed to pierce the deepest veils preventing revelation of the mysteries of being/non-being. The *yogin* uses the will in *dhyāna* to awaken the *maṇḍala* of Love-Wisdom. Love conquers and absorbs all into its unifying embrace.

On the reversed wheel, the impetus of the Arian petal drives both conjoined *karma* and co-actively produced phenomena in turn, allowing the mind to assimilate each new phase of experience. Being one of the cardinal points, Aries drives awareness inwards to awaken the subtle impressions that constitute the psyche, thereby conquering ignorance.

The *northeast* petal of this eastern triad is governed by the sign *Pisces the fishes*, a Water sign. Here the *saṃskāras* generated through cyclic incarnation often intensify craving *(tṛṣṇā)* for things material and sensual. Craving (the eighth Dependent Origination, governed by Scorpio - another Water sign) is a strong yearning, inward desire or longing to possess something. The person inevitably develops a deep dissatisfaction with whatever is possessed and wants more, one way or the other. One craves for things not possessed, or to intensify former sensual, pleasurable or enjoyable experiences. Craving for something new often ends a cycle of attachment ('death') to something earlier craved for, but no longer satisfies. Thus a new cycle of activity starts. Craving-desire produces the deepest forms of bondage, thus this is the sign of the 'imprisoned soul', of bonded activity and of mediumistic tendencies (when that bondage is to forms of psychicism). The glyph for Pisces thus represents two fishes yoked together and swimming in the waters of *saṃsāra*. This bond signifies: a) the mind and what it desires, b) the personal-I and its relation to the Sambhogakāya Flower.

Normally, Pisces represents the ending of one cycle of the zodiac, with the next sign on the rectified wheel, Aries, representing a new beginning. On the reversed wheel, however, Virgo (the womb of time and space and the polar opposite of Pisces) can represent the beginning of any new cycle and Libra the ending of that cycle. In Pisces is engendered a satiation of emotional entanglements and often murky experiences (likened to being swampy), producing dissatisfaction, fomenting the beginning of the process of washing the *saṃskāras* clean in the next sign (Aquarius), or else a new cycle of indulgence in another arena of sensation. The enlightenment process necessitates satiation of any form of experience before it can be renounced via thorough comprehension, and a new cycle propagated. The propelling force *(vāsanā)* that keeps the wheel in motion is thereby enacted and we learn and evolve upon it. *Saṃskāras* of right comprehension are thus developed upon the reversed wheel, which in a round-about way progresses all forward. In a similar manner, the Buddha needed to completely experience his youthful pleasure garden, if he was to sufficiently comprehend its nature and transience, allowing renunciation of it and the entire phenomenal world. Mastery was then ensured.

What is experienced here is *the co-actively produced phenomena* that becomes the muddied Watery environment that the Piscean shares with his neighbours. People's psychic sensitivity to others is increased in this environment and the undeveloped Piscean is often mediumistic. All forms of relationships, desires for lovers, family life, and for any of the associated material encumbrances established in Taurus are then intensified. There is an innate love for 'the other', to which the Piscean bonds. A keynote being bondage to forms of desire and craving, which also intensifies affectionate *saṃskāras*. This develops into sacrificial Love on the rectified wheel, thus the drive of the Bodhisattva to never cease striving until all have been liberated in the three worlds. The Bodhisattva thus becomes the world saviour in Pisces.

Pisces rules the liver and the lymphatic system, which constitute some of the physical body's major protective mechanisms against diseases. (Basically, the liver produces bile and plays an essential role in the metabolism of carbohydrates, proteins, and fats, as well as helping to ward off antagonistic entities.) This exemplifies the higher aspects of the governing Rays of Pisces, of Love-Wisdom, and Will to help protect and nurture the principle of life, so that consciousness can grow towards enlightenment.

The *northeast* petal of the *northern triad* is governed by the sign *Aquarius the water bearer,* who dispenses the waters of life to all needy ones. In the lower turn of the wheel these 'waters' feed selfishness and conceit, producing many experiences which inevitably necessitate rebirth (the *eleventh* of the Dependent Originations). Aquarius constitutes a way out of the swamp depicted in Pisces, through attachment to any attribute of *saṃsāra* (e.g., wealth and prosperity) that seems to offer relief from pain-engendering proclivities. Inevitably comes perceptions and awareness that may shed light as to what is actually happening, and how to stay clear from proclivities to suffering. If the way out is not sought, then the Aquarian moves from one form of craving to the next, towards avaricious, ephemeral, self-focussed forms of activity. If liberation is sought, then inevitably he/she learns to detach from craving to produce the mutable enlightened thinking that is the hallmark of the Aquarian disposition.

The *karma* of self-volition is based upon the self-centredness that avaricious clinging produces. If the objective is release from suffering, then the native learns to defocus from self-centred activity, to actively mitigate and finally eliminate concepts of the ego-centric world view. The *saṃskāras* developed are loving in nature, with free-flowing ideas and open-minded religious or scientific enquiry. Consciousness shifts towards more inclusive group interrelationships. This lays the foundation for the group consciousness associated with this sign, and which is fully developed in the rectified wheel as one pursues the Bodhisattva path. The average Aquarian, however, tends to be shallow in the pursuit of meaningful spiritual or empirical knowledge. There is outer pretensions of knowing, but with no real depth of understanding.

A form of spiritual window shopping manifests where the person flitters from one glamorous expression to the next.

The *northernmost* petal is ruled by *Capricorn the goat,* climbing the rough, rugged path to the mountaintop of experiences. The intellect becomes fully developed and either makes a further step to link itself to the higher consciousness, or is focussed downwards to intensify its materialistic ambitions and attachments. The *saṃskāras* produced can therefore make one hard, cruel, and mentalistic. Our present materialistic civilisation is at this general stage of development. The worst types of *karma* is generated by such mental types who have divorced love from their world-view, except in terms of the type of passion that the mind conceives as right. This is one reason why the planetary ruler attributed to this sign is Saturn, the lord of *karma.*

The tenth of the Dependencies states that clinging conditions the process of becoming. This incorporates the sum of the *karma*-formations that the development of the mind produces. Much *karma* is accumulated through the self-focussed, often ruthless, materialistic ones who selfishly amass resources in *saṃsāra.* The cupidity of the little 'self' and its empire building, where all resources (political, monetary and mental-emotional) are used to manipulate everything desired, is a disaster for the general good of all. Thus the mount of *karma* is firmly established.

If the Capricornian can focus his vision upwards to enlightenment, to climb the great mountainous heights of accomplishment, then great service work to help all sentient beings is possible. Great are the mental resources that can be brought to bear for this task. The mount of *karma* must be vanquished as one climbs to the summit of revelation. Self-focussed materialism reorients to aspirations of liberation and eventual Buddhahood. All then is possible, because in this most northern of signs the awakening Mind controls all thought and related activities.

The quality assigned to this petal is *'not self'*, as it is one of the four cardinal positions that express the four gates of entry into *śūnyatā,* by mastering the four major types of *saṃskāras* concerned with 'self'. In Capricorn, the I-concept is most developed and the self-assertion of the personality finds its most concrete form. Here major transformations occur to overcome mental *saṃskāras* for each cycle of the wheel. The personal-I must die, and the dying process constitutes the goat's ability to tread the hard, rocky path to the summit and become transfigured in light. Much *karma* consequently must be cleansed. Upon the rectified wheel the all-seeing Eye of accomplished wisdom opens. Those who master the illusions of the 'I' then become group-conscious as they enter the next sign (Aquarius), which is the sign of the group-conscious disciple and of the world server. (In its higher attributes, the Aquarian dispensation personifies the qualities that constitute a Bodhisattva.)

The *prāṇas* generated by the Capricornian petal convey either the Earthy attributes of the personal will of *manasic* types, or else the Fiery energy of the aspirational mind that has set its sights to the revelations and liberation that the mountaintop of attainment accords.

The *northwest* petal of the *northern triad,* ruled by *Sagittarius the archer,* governs all forms of ambition and aspiration, be this toward the field of enlightenment, community projects and occupations, or for purely selfish or sensual endeavour. Sagittarius fires the arrows of thoughts, or desire-forms, of one-pointed ambition or aspiration of whatever is to be achieved. The personal will is thus exemplified, and later the Will-to-Good. Then the appropriate actions can manifest to achieve this aim.

A height of materialistic thinking was reached in the previous sign, so Sagittarius represents further grasping, ambitious schemes to get what the mind wants to further establish its power base. This concerns the *ninth* of the Dependent Originations. Here the archer fires the arrow of a former consciousness stream into new *saṃsāric* ventures. The individual purveys the world around and manipulates matter and the objects found in Nature for his own desires and ambitions. This substance is utilised to further build the emotional-mental personality.

How the will is used to manipulate and change the environment around one is collectively styled 'self-produced phenomena' at this petal of the Heart *chakra*. This concerns the various forms of destruction, construction and creative artistry that people manifest in order to feel comfortable and secure within the framework of a civilisation. (The hands governed by the polar opposite, Gemini, are fully utilised here, coupled with the Sagittarian will to produce and effect changes in the material world.) *Saṃsāra* is dominated, and its resources are procured to suit one's ambitious needs.

Once *saṃskāras* are mastered in this sign one becomes a Bodhisattva mounted upon the white steed of Love (*bodhicitta*). The unstoppable

Bodhisattva surmounts all obstacles blocking the vow to serve all. Ambition to serve the little self has been turned into a fervent aspiration to give all that has been acquired (the mental-emotional phenomena that was formerly produced) to enlighten all beings.

This sign and the next two are a summary of the qualities of the nine previous ones, starting with renewal in Sagittarius, to the complete expression of the vicissitudes of life in Scorpio. Scorpio appropriates the tests provided to the seemingly never-ending repetitive births and deaths cycled through each turn of the wheel (Libra). Sagittarius focuses upon projecting the forces, wherein things are manipulated and procured for the life sustaining process. Libra focuses upon contemplation of the life's processes, of feeling sensations, wherein the gain of all former activity is harvested, relinquishing what is no longer viable.

The *northwest* petal of the *western triad* is governed by the sign *Scorpio the scorpion,* the key to the processes associated with the dependencies via its battle with craving. It summarises the entire gamut of life coming as a consequence of rebirth that inevitably produces misery and grief. This necessitates a repetition of the wheel of birth and death, which the next sign (Libra) helps determine in either direction. In Scorpio the world of the personal-I is at its height and all complexities of *saṃsāric* involvement are active. Eventually such interactions rebound upon the personality and the consequent pain produces a non-attachment to *saṃsāra.* Thus a period of personal conflict ensues as the person transits from an attached to an unattached state. This petal of the Heart lotus thus concerns the battlefield of desire for an increasingly diverse number of sensations and things, the wish for this transiency to last forever, verses the unassailable edicts of *karma.* There is a consequent reorientation of focus away from *saṃsāra,* which produces the testings in this sign.

This battlefield is ruled by Mars, the god of war, the orthodox planetary ruler of Scorpio. The strength of the *saṃskāras* involved produce the forms of intensities in this battle, via opposing views and the conflict between desire and aspiration. Many of the unpleasant and nasty qualities of people, expressive of the legendary sting of the scorpion, manifest. The *prāṇas* generated are generally strongly coloured through all types of emotions, according to the nature of the desire-field generated, or of the processes being mastered.

Group or national *karma* is engendered in the western orientation because all fields of interrelationships with people are produced. One's active involvement in family and society must be mastered before one can properly tackle the illusion of selfhood. This then is the task set before the disciple in Scorpio. When the rectified wheel is attained, *karma* must be cleansed, producing many purifying stings upon the upward way to the Initiation experienced in Capricorn. Every test in the field of life is thus enacted here until a person emerges triumphant, having overcome all personal obstacles. Thus this is the sign of the triumphant one that eventually masters the sum of the Waters. The two-edged sword of light (of Mañjuśrī) can then be wielded to cut away all forms of glamour, illusions and ignorance.

Probably the most difficult activity for most aspirants at this stage of testings relates to eliminating or amending philosophies or concepts not conducive to attaining enlightenment. They generally have their foundation in a past life, where a certain religious ethos will have been zealously followed, hence the *saṃskāras* are strong and produce powerful dispositional tendencies, hard to overcome. Another example is that a *saṃskāra* may have been produced in a past life of unabated sexual licentiousness. In a future life, such *saṃskāric* energies generated may appear as an aversion, even fanatical self-righteous repugnance for such activities, producing criticism of those that commit them. (The educative value of karmic repercussions will by then have been experienced.) The new *saṃskāras* must also be cleansed and transmuted, similar to the way the earlier ones were. The *saṃskāras* are created in the same mould. In both cases it produces crusading ones. In the first, it is a crusade for manifold sexual experiences and in the second case it is against those who find pleasure in disapproved forms of sexuality. All types of fanaticism of mind and emotions produce evil doing.

Finally, we have the *western* petal governed by *Libra the balances,* representing the wheel of the law of *karma* turning. Where the *seventh* of the Dependent Originations relating to feeling perceptions manifests, there can be intensified cravings in Scorpio, or produce further contact with experienceable sensations in Virgo. The antidote is right knowledge and application of the *dharma,* which at first rectifies the reversed wheel, and finally produces liberation from the wheel. All happens within the adjudicating, and finally meditative embrace governed by Libra.

With each turn of the wheel, a bank of right knowledge is gradually built that eventually halts the process of karmic accumulation, which is finally consciously annulled. Libra thus adjudicates life's processes with the resolution of surfacing *karma*. The present karmic propensities are put on the scales and consciously weighed for their real worth. If the motivation for activity is selfish, then the wheel continues in a reversed mode, if unselfish or aspirational then the momentum for its reversal gathers apace. A characteristic of Libra is that of the meditative interlude between breaths, or forms of activity of either the right or the left.

Libra is thus the major synthesising petal of all forms of karmic interrelations with humanity, for it is the key petal of the western direction. Here is observed the overall co-actively produced karmic patterns; group, national, and international *karma*. Venus, the orthodox ruler of Libra, represents the conditioning mind that actively partakes in the *karma*-formations and assimilates the experiences gained through social intercourse. We also have the formulation of material plane law and social etiquette governing the way that people ought to behave.

As the major aspect of this petal reveals the hidden *karma* (forms of ignorance) from the past in such a way that the person has to deal with it appropriately, so it sets the tone of the nature of the *saṃskāras* to be mastered in any cycle. They are the main support of the wheel of rebirth. The *saṃskāras* flow from this western triad of petals, affecting the sum total of human social intercourse of the person concerned.

- The Airy *saṃskāras* manifest via the Libran petal, incorporating, therefore, the three main Elements governing body, speech and mind. Thus, the entire theme of ignorance is adjudicated here because the ignorance relating to all aspects of the personal-I must be overcome through cyclic activity.

- The more emotionally and sensually based *saṃskāras* are experienced and mastered via the Scorpio petal.

- The *saṃskāras* that purport to physicality, to form-oriented activities, are fully generated in the Virgoan petal and must be mastered as the entire wheel is trod.

These qualities become a mental resolution in the sign Leo, where the personal-I's ego is honed. Self-consciousness then becomes the dominant theme, until the battlefields of life manifest in Scorpio are meditatively assessed in Libra, and upon the rectified wheel the *yogin* can then climb the mount of *dhyāna* to great heights and liberation, in Capricorn.

Libra is a cardinal sign, and the quality attributed to it is 'not other'. This is the attitude to be developed with respect to the expression of the western form of karmic interrelations if the wheel is to be rectified. The individual must relinquish ties to normal human concourse with others in society and focus inwards through training the mind to develop the *samādhi* that is the interlude between breaths.

The rectified wheel

With respect to the rectified wheel, the list given in order of appearance is:
The northern triad

1. What is void of own-character lacks a character—Aquarius the water bearer.
2. What lacks a character is Thusness (*tathatā*)—Capricorn the goat.
3. What is Thusness is error–free Thusness—Sagittarius the archer.

The western triad

4. What is error-free Thusness is not otherwise Thusness—Scorpio the scorpion.
5. What is not otherwise Thusness is the *samādhi*—Libra the balances.
6. What is the *samādhi* is comprehending it—Virgo the virgin.

The southern triad

7. What is the comprehension is voidness (*śūnyatā*)—Leo the lion.
8. What is the voidness is discerning (the real)—Cancer the crab.
9. What is discerning (the real) is calming (the mind)—Gemini the twins.

The eastern triad

10. What is calming (the mind) is liberation (*vimokṣa*)—Taurus the bull.
11. What is liberation is the Middle Path—Aries the ram.
12. What is seen as the Middle Path is without one extreme—Pisces the fishes.

It should be noted that though we are examining the rectified wheel, the order presented is in the same direction as that of the reversed wheel. This is in keeping with the order of the presented list, which is not so much concerned with the turning of a wheel, but with quadrants of energy. (Which is consistent with the serenity achieved, associated with Thusness, which does not move as does a wheel.) Normally this wheel starts with Aries and travels round the zodiac to Pisces via Taurus.

1. *The northeast* petal of the *northern triad*—'what is void of own-character lacks a character'—Aquarius the water bearer.

Aquarius is a dual sign denoting the mutual embrace of two parallel streams of free-flowing energy. The upper band signifies the principle of enlightenment, and the lower band the formed realms whereupon that principle impacts. The sign is fluid, one of constant movement, periodic cyclic activity and recurrent mutations. (Aquarius is the sign where the various cycles of Life are consequently acknowledged and worked with.) This is seen nowadays in humanity's intensely active and sometimes chaotic mass transportation systems, communications, and rapid efflux and interchange of ideas.[16] This mutability gives this sign the attribute denoted as that which *'lacks a character'.*

The Buddhist interpretation of 'lack of character' has reference to the quality of Thusness, which is free of all nameable attributes. Clearly, the free-flowing energy attributed to Aquarius is a form of Thusness. However, when the symbol is examined, we see that this Thusness is represented by the space between the wavy lines.

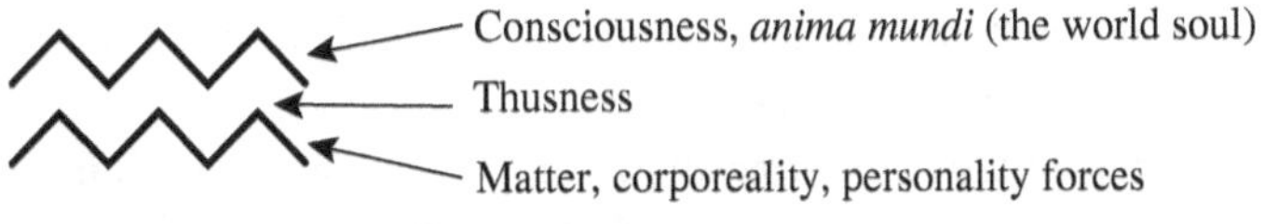

Figure 3. Thusness and Aquarius

Anima mundi is effectively a Western term for the *ālayavijñāna,* and corporeality stands for *saṃsāra.*

The lack of character of Thusness cleanses the *saṃskāras* of the *karma* of self-volition (generated principally upon the reversed wheel in

16 This is indicative of the transition process from the age governed by Pisces that has ruled us for over 2,000 years, to the Aquarian epoch.

the polar opposite sign, Leo the lion). The 'self' manifests such *karma* when it characterises things in terms of itself, consequently, upon the rectified path it eliminates its attachment to such things in this sign. It thus cuts attachment to the aspects characterising each appearing phenomena. Consciousness transforms itself by its redefinition, where characteristics that were identified as one thing with respect to its appearance in *saṃsāra,* are now viewed as forms of transience through knowing the truth of its phenomena. Phenomena is no longer identified with being substantial in itself, or attached to a 'self'. All definitions become fluid and mutable in consciousness, with things perpetually changing and interrelating ceaselessly around a non-characterised Thusness. That supporting changeability does not change, thus it holds all component parts together, like a stable mountain. (Symbolised by the next sign, Capricorn, the Thusness itself.)

2. *The northern* petal of the *northern triad*—'what lacks a character is Thusness (tathatā)'—Capricorn the goat.

Capricorn is the tenth sign of the zodiac. Ten is the number of perfection and of completion, corresponding to Capricorn's significance as the end point of evolution in the material world, specifically with respect to the development of the patterns of one's concrete mind. The end point of such development is Thusness. Capricorn consummates the cycles of testings manifested in Scorpio, hence Capricorn represents the mount of attainment, whereon Initiation is undertaken. Consciousness has been completely transformed, as all desire forms have been changed into aspects of enlightenment.

Passing the tests in Scorpio allows one to focus upon the termination of *karma* in Capricorn by means of the rightly focussed mind. It ends the tendency of consciousness to identify with things, binding people to cycles of birth and death. Consequently Saturn, the lord of *karma* governing the three worlds of human livingness, is the orthodox ruler of Capricorn, allowing *karma* to be appropriately rectified. Saturn utilises the activities of the past to wield the future.

Having attained the *ālayavijñāna,* and later the *dharmakāya* enlightenment in Capricorn, the Initiate stands upon the material domain and can see all, embracing cosmos with the Eye of the Mind ablaze. Material life and its *karma* is mastered, over which such a one rules in Saturn's guise. By being freed from karmic activity, and by discovering Thusness at the *saṃsāra-śūnyatā* nexus, the rebirth process is conquered, allowing the Initiate to enter at will into *dharmakāyic* space, or into rebirth at the open gate of the polar opposite of this sign, Cancer the crab. The Initiate in Capricorn can then adjudicate *karma* via Libra (another arm of the cardinal cross) so as to produce the 'not self' in the arenas where human consciousness dwells.

Karma moulds the individual (the 'self' concept), as well as the planetary dweller on the threshold. This 'dweller' represents the sum total of the collectivised selves linked in consciousness, whereby similar illusional and separative attitudes abide, producing a massed concept of self-hood. Such concepts constitute the processes making our civilisation what it is: the identity of nations, groups, and associated subsets of society. There are also individualised 'dwellers' constituting the collectivised *saṃskāras* of any succession of lives, the sum of the personal attributes gleaned from those lives. The Sambhogakāya Flower must meditate upon this aspect prior to sending a new personal-I into incarnation. This 'dweller' is symbolised by the crocodile (another image representing Capricorn at a certain stage of development). The 'dweller' is completely objectivised in Capricorn, but the battles that finally free the person from all karmic impositions (from the 'dweller') are waged from Cancer onwards (through 'discerning the real'), giving free reign to scale the mountainside of achievement as this entity is being overcome.

The path of illumination and enlightenment that results in the experience of Thusness represents the gain of the transfiguration upon the summit of earthly experience. Capricorn consequently expresses the way to open the door to complete participation in the domain of the Bodhisattva-Mind. It involves a process of initiation into mysteries that reveal the ability to control and direct *karma* so that it will cleanse what is qualified by the vibratory emanations (the *manasic* residue) of past evolutionary attainments. This process necessitates the transmutation of substance by way of the Heart's Mind (the potency of this petal) so that substance no longer offers resistance to potent subjective energies. The impact of the various Rays of light upon dense substance is thus wisely directed by the enlightened Capricornian Mind (established in Thusness) to produce this transmutation. It represents a process of dematerialisation, which is another term for the unveiling of the 'not self', Thusness.

3. *The northwest* petal of the *northern triad*—'what is Thusness is error–free Thusness'—Sagittarius the archer.

Sagittarius governs or directs the activities of the other signs of the zodiac, because upon the rectified wheel they move according to the way the Sagittarian arrows are fired. The 'error–free Thusness' is a product of the directive power of Sagittarius, because in order to be error-free one must be able to rightly discern, thus to rightly direct thoughts to enlightenment, and ultimately whole segments of the zodiac, or the entire wheel.

Sagittarius governs the hips in human anatomy, which symbolises the central supporting position for movement of the zodiacal signs. It represents the strength to make and to accomplish things. Direction is one of the keynotes of this sign, for the activities of the Sagittarian first directs the person towards Scorpio, where his ambition for material power leads to deepened sensuality and death, as well as to heightened materiality and selfishness (in Virgo). Then later, the mountainous heights associated with Capricorn must be climbed so that the process of the rectification of *karma* opens the gate to the experience of Thusness via the *dharmakāya*.

In Sagittarius, a person's aspirational zeal or personality ambition find their central source of power. The consciousness of humanity has gradually evolved from the mass instinctual type of awareness, as symbolised by the sign Cancer, to that of the self-conscious individual in Leo. In Scorpio, the desire-mind is at the height of its powers, and one must emerge from the battlefields in the swamps of *māyā* (represented by the testings in Scorpio) by being directed by the potency of the next sign, Sagittarius. In the following sign, Capricorn, the empirical mind is at its peak and must be mastered.

On the rectified wheel, the illumined Mind has been awakened, which is highly perceptive, veridically analytical, and has become integrated with the *ālayavijñāna, bodhicitta,* and later with the *dharmakāya.* Sagittarius directs the transition of mind into Mind so that the Clear Light, the Light of Life, is triumphant. The arrows fired by the archer represent the intuition, the flashes of Light incorporating vision of the attainment to be accomplished in Capricorn and residence in Thusness. The past is well known, as one now lives fully in revelatory

Light. The present is served in Clear Light, with the added faculty to vision the future by shooting the arrows of Mind from point to point upon the liberating way. This is the way of the awakening path at various stages of accomplishment, as directed by the vision evidenced by the symbolism of this sign. Sagittarius fires the arrows of wisdom (governed by Jupiter, its orthodox ruler) to enlighten all upon earth. The Initiate can figuratively 'dismount constantly from a white horse (the developed and purified personality) and find where the arrows of intuitional aspiration will take him'.[17]

The arrow, a strait and pointed line of direction, leads to liberation, and is able to pierce all the veils and cloaks of illusion and glamour. It is also an attribute of the directive thought of the archer. The arrow is quick, direct to the point, and piercing. (Qualities associated with the intuition, the liberated Mind.) The archer is able to quickly penetrate the heart of any matter. He can thus receive an understanding of the related properties, or qualities, or of any other subject or meditation that he may be pursuing, long before the information becomes evident in the world of form.[18] To be able to fire arrows into cosmos, however, the process will need to take many revolutions of the wheel of Initiation and attainment of the heights of Capricorn.

---

17 See page 181 of *Esoteric Astrology* for further detail.

18 This is part of the meaning of the symbolism of Saraha, the teacher of Nāgārjuna, being purported to be an arrow maker. When he first met his future Consort she was making arrows, and he asked her if she was a professional arrow maker. She said: '"My dear young man, the Buddha's meaning can be known through symbols and actions, not through words and books."...The reed is the symbol for the uncreated; the three joints, that of the necessity to realize the three existential norms; the straightening of the shaft, that of straightening the path of spiritual growth; cutting the shaft at the bottom, that of the necessity to uproot Saṃsāra, and at the top, that of eradicating the belief in a self or an essence; the splitting of the bottom into four sections, that of "memory," "nonmemory," "unorigination," and "transcendence"; inserting the arrowhead, that of the necessity to use one's intelligence; tying it with a tendon, that of being fixed by the seal of unity; splitting the upper into two, that of action and intelligence; inserting four feathers, that of looking, attending to the seen, acting on the basis of what has been seen and attended to, and their combination of fruition; opening one eye and closing the other, that of shutting the eye of discursiveness and opening that of the a priori awareness; the posture of aiming at a target, that of the necessity to shoot the arrow of nonduality into the heart of the belief in duality'. Herbert V. Guenther, *The Royal Song of Saraha,* (Shambala, Berkeley, 1973), 5-6.

We should also note the symbolism of the bow and arrow, poised in tension and ready to be fired in a given direction towards a target. The word *tension* is of significance when related to the meditative process. It produces the calmness of mind demonstrated in the polar opposite of Sagittarius, Gemini. Tension provides the clue to the mode of operation of the Sagittarian, esoterically considered. The meaning of this word should thus be further analysed. The tension referred to does not relate to emotionality, but rather an accumulation of intensified energy that is held in potential for future action.

Tension can be considered as the central point in the circle of the *maṇḍala*, a storehouse of power, of focussed immovable will, a state of dynamic poise. Wherever a point of tension exists, there energy is being generated, held in potential, and focussed for future use so that its force can be directed to the needed direction. It is an energetic expression of the will, thus governs the way to Shambhala. Tension is the heart, or foundation, of manifest being. It coheres all into unity. Without tension in its various gradations no form could exist, without such a cohesive force all would be chaos. Tension is thus the mode of holding *saṃsāra in situ* so that the entire world play can unfold to conclusion.

Tension exists where there is no subject-object duality, when subject and object have been resolved into a single point of fusion. It exists where there is perfect understanding, where one's consciousness is poised or focussed in such a way in relation to some principle or concept, so as to allow the light of that principle to instantaneously illumine the sum of one's consciousness. It is the potency of Secret Mantra, and at the appropriate time the Sagittarian Mind will fire this arrow of mantra to achieve its purpose, thus it is 'error-free'. Tension lies outside the realms of concern of temporal reality. It is an intensity of purpose involving an inner orientation and organisation of energies directed towards service and sacrifice. It is an inner, constantly cyclic attitude of determined and planned abstraction. On the other hand, it can also represent the focal point of creative activity. In tension, therefore, the mantra of being/non-being is held in serene absorption.

The application of the will manifests from this serene reservoir of potential to dynamically project the purpose of the mantra unerringly to its goal. To hold such a poised tension in the meditation-Mind therefore represents the dynamic fruition of the person's long drive to liberation.

(It is also the impetus sustaining that drive.) When focussed (upon a form or idea) it becomes the seed or germ *(bīja)* which can effectively explode into that which empowers complete expression of any stream of realisation, or else it can direct one to realms beyond all thought. It is 'effortless' because it is the outcome of long periods of meditative unfoldment that has become a spontaneous state of transcendence manifesting through the person, there being naught there to resist the realisation of the most potent energies or revelations. This then produces the last of the Eightfold Paths, perfect bliss or absorption. Such a state of tension is the diamond-Mind of liberated consciousness.

The aspirational zeal allowing one to tread the entire Eightfold Path is thus governed by Sagittarius. The path is trod in the zodiacal womb of Virgo, wherein the Watery substance governed by Pisces is slowly converted into the Airy essence to be contained in the Temple of Life (Gemini), whilst Sagittarius projects the potency that will convert it all into Thusness. This is the story of the mutable cross from the perspective of the rectified wheel. Aquarius (the northern arm of the fixed cross) energises the process because the purpose (or result) of right concentration of energies is the Bodhisattvic service work that is the leitmotiv of the Aquarian. Aquarius embodies the first of the characteristics relating to *śūnyatā* ('lack of character') given in the above list. Emptiness consequently lies at the heart of the mutable cross.

The production of a point of tension, and its manifest expression (the arrows of the consciousness-links, *antaḥkaraṇas*), allows building the bridge connecting enlightened consciousness to the formed realms. This tension also integrates the two wavy lines of the Aquarian symbol. Therefore, it delineates the nexus between *śūnyatā* and *saṃsāra.* The three main components of such a tensed sphere are: *the Will* to reach beyond, *the Love* to extend outwards and magnetically draw all into a unified sphere, and *the Skill* to rightly direct the two upon the battlefield of Life.

Tension constitutes eternal vigilance, implying watchfulness when another would normally be asleep. It is produced through the ardour of striving and salutary toil, through adaptability to the cycles of change and the ability to handle incoming forces. The forces constantly change because of the differing points of focus of the lower sheaths of the personal-I. It allows one to project the purpose of the *buddhadharma* within. Tension expresses the jewel in the heart of the lotus of each *chakra.*

From the mundane perspective, tension is seen in terms of being stressed out to the point of producing crises. Esoterically, however, points of tension and points of crises can be considered as cause-effect, for tension shatters boundaries of present possibilities, overcoming their limitations. The effect of tension produces a rapid expansion and explosion of the potential of the auric qualities of an individual, throwing off everything negative hindering the true expression of the divine. This produces points of crises. Tension empowers and reveals the good in that which is still imperfect and evolving. Points of crises mastered produce revelatory expansions of consciousness. They are in the nature of the tests needing passing as the steps to enlightenment are undertaken.

Tension produces bliss, the universality of consciousness. Its effects transform the fields of *māyā* into arenas of light. It produces the ability to build *antaḥkaraṇas* to the *dharmakāya*, effecting changes in consciousness. To sustain a point of tension, the mind must be infused with *bodhicitta* as the energy input. The consequent blissful experience is expressed through one-pointed service work. Eventually, the death of the Sambhogakāya Flower upon its own level of rarefied consciousness is produced.

The arrows (sparks of tension) can also be called moving lines of incandescent Love, or *antaḥkaraṇas* of enlightened purpose. The sparks of tension produce points of crisis, because they instigate the destruction that must come before building the new forms (even of civilisations) that bring one closer to the final liberation of whatever is. They can also be viewed as flashes of illumination or intuition (directed from the realm of enlightened Being) that pierce the Heart, making it Bleed in Love for all. This produces the consequent actions of service and sacrifice that distinguishes the enlightened one.

4. *The northwest* petal of the *western triad.* 'What is error-free Thusness is not otherwise Thusness'—Scorpio the scorpion.

This 'not-otherwise Thusness' concerns the end result of the nature of the tests upon the battlefield of desire that is accomplished in the sign Scorpio. The sum of one's Watery (emotional, desire based) attachment to *saṃsāra* must die in this sign. Right understanding must be established in regards to all aspects of phenomena. The process requires elimination of subtle and gross attachments, where the person can definitely say 'not this', 'not that' in terms of the attainment of enlightenment.

The martial energy utilised in this sign, when directed inwards via aspiration towards liberation, facilitates the proclivities of this sign to 'sting' open the gates of the cosmic Waters[19] (of *dharmakāya).* Intense energies then pour in from cosmos through the thoroughly stilled emotional body of a *yogin* to affect the entire physical life. Such energy is utilised via this petal to transform all of the forces of the *chakras* below the diaphragm.[20] All illusions are thus completely eliminated via the outpouring of energies from this petal, until only the Thusness remains. Elimination of the changing nature of *saṃskāras* is not easy, as *saṃskāras* must be converted into enlightenment-characteristics, refined and transmuted, so as to be 'not otherwise' than Thusness. Here we can also see that Thusness is void of being void. It is not this, not that, therefore 'not otherwise'.

The enlightened one working via this petal of the Heart *chakra* works to compassionately 'sting' to death all forms of evil caused by groupings of people, their aberrant doctrines and dogmas, of all the things that limit or mar human freedom and that trap the spirit within. They work thus regardless of what people, or those in power, think of them, it cannot be 'otherwise'. Ignorance, the substance of the darkness, is wisely countered at all costs. Inevitably nothing otherwise but the Thusness can stand. When viewing the dispelling of societal group ignorance (producing the testings), we see that standing firm in Thusness works to counter and eliminate the types of phenomena produced by others. This happens via the *prāṇas* engendered by the general western triad now being analysed.

5. *The western* petal of the *western triad.* 'What is not otherwise Thusness is the *samādhi*'—Libra the balances.

Samādhi here involves holding steady in meditative equipoise the Thusness that allows the liberated one to focus continuously upon the field of humanity. This 'field' involves the sum total of all their activities and of how to best help them in the various departments of life, according to the right cycles for the expression of characteristics to be evolved. This is the true function of the qualities of the sign Libra the balances. *Samādhi* concerns the interlude between the various breaths

19 The cosmic astral plane, the source of the potency of *bodhicitta* to all upon our planet.

20 Via the Diaphragm centre, represented by the Taurean petal.

of manifest activity. We have the inbreathing of information needing contemplation in relation to the service work at hand, the *samādhi* or revelatory experience of what is or needs to be done, and the outbreathing of the active expression of the results of the meditation. Such meditation qualifies this sign as being the judge, the adjudicator of the law, of the *dharma*. It is the keynote of the energy qualification of this petal.

Libra is said to govern the lower back, allowing for greater flexibility of movement for the entire torso, to bend downwards, upwards, sideways, and backwards. This flexibility and extension in all directions of consciousness and its ability to view a thing from all angles, is a major quality of the judge. He needs to be able to see things from all points of view and uphold great mutability of thought before pronouncing his opinion or judgement. Libra is consequently the sign of legislation, the upholder of the law from every angle:

1. In the personality life of common humanity, we first have the great religious codes of ethics imposed from above, via the agency of priests, prophets, sages, sagacious kings and rulers.

   Next are the laws formulated by humanity, which govern every aspect of our family and social life. Much beneficence has yet to be achieved by our judicial systems, especially in the fields of international legislation of all aspects of human livingness and right human relationships. Presently, the world's legislative system is like a green apple, of apparently nice appearance, but rotten at the core.
2. In the life of the acolyte to the mysteries of being/non-being we find the various rules governing Bodhisattvic activity, gained from interrelation with the subjective world. The acolyte has to deal with the potent energies obtained from his/her meditative life, plus instructions relating to the law of Love and the mastery of form derived from the Council of Bodhisattvas.
3. The Laws of Life to which the enlightened automatically acquiesce, and which are expressed during the outbreathing process of any meditative cycle. They govern the appearance of all phenomena, and sustain the activity of the subjective and manifest universe. Science is learning the basics of these Laws.

   The in and outbreathing process can be related to the activity of the two hands, or twins, in Gemini, which Libra can be said to direct.

The major part of the work of the judge is to help protect the environment in which the divine child (of our civilisation) must be nurtured. In our societies he must work to overcome the negative effects of:

a. The tenacity, greedy desires, and emotionality of the crab (Cancer). Nefarious effects of these qualities are often whipped up *en masse* by politicians and others in power via media outlets, to establish unjust laws that all are encumbered by.

b. The ravages of the prideful beast of the self-concept (Leo) to undeservedly take from others what the 'self' desires for itself. Thus we have, for instance, the forms of monetary compensation legally demanded from people that *never* took any form of resources from the demanding ones. The law of *karma* will unfailingly work to ensure that those that have been stolen from in this manner, through legal thievery, will be compensated, in this or a future life.

c. The deathlike sting (vengeful and separative in quality) of the scorpion (Scorpio) in the deserts of life. We thus have laws enacted on the behalf of the narrow-minded, self-righteous crusading ones, such as the programs against Jews in Nazi Germany, Communists in the 1950's U.S.A, homosexuals (and every other form of so-called sexual deviance), marijuana smokers, etc.

d. The selfishly ambitious and avaricious ones (Sagittarius). We have, for instance, the developing of and utilising unjust laws that exist for the maturation of the empire building plans of both individuals and nations. Great monetary resources are also unjustly extracted from the masses, despite the destructive effects upon society and the environment.

e. The hard, rocky, often cruel (Capricornian) policies of those in power. We thus have laws instigated by those who have amassed great monetary wealth (generally by bribing corrupt officials, or who have used their monetary power to considerably influence legislators), aimed at disempowering the weak and under-resourced. We thus have the manifestation of cruel laws that cause great hardship in the poorest sectors of society so that others can live in great opulence. We also have the establishment of capital punishment in some societies, and the use of state power to incarcerate or torture people.

The judge or legislator must not work through the attitude of imposed fear and penalty imposition, but by the improvement of social inequalities, of truly equable wealth distribution, and the wise utilisation of a proper understanding of human psychology (as born from *samādhi)* so that wrong doers can be rightly educated on what not to do. This new form of psychology will be based on the knowingness of the nature of all aspects of the subjective human psyche, plus of the law of *karma* and of the rebirth of consciousness. The judge must become the wise Bodhisattva.

It should be noted that the poor are unjustly penalised for being poor in our iniquitous societies. They suffer the greatest burden of the laws that overwhelmingly favour the rich, who do not have to struggle to make ends meet in their daily life, and who can afford good lawyers. A poor person, for instance, who robs paltry sums from another using whatever means is available, is universally treated far more harshly in the eyes of the law than the rich person who may steal (through legalised thievery) hundreds of millions, and often billions, from all sectors of society. Clearly such insidious thievery is enormously more destructive upon society than crimes caused out of economic hardship. Such crimes would not occur if massive wealth inequities were eliminated. Much legislative change needs to occur with the above in mind. Legislators are karmically tied to the types of laws they vote in. They should carefully think about the karmic debt they accrue, and must pay in future lives.

Also, 'crimes' that hurt no person (other than maybe the perpetuator), should never be called crimes, and thus be legislated against. The smoking of marijuana, for instance, fits in this category. The prohibition against all forms of drugs does massively more harm in our societies than ever could happen through full legalisation, drug purity control, with proper anti-use counselling and educational methods utilised. It is bewildering to see why this insane war against the freedom of choice of generations (specifically the youth) of our societies persists throughout the world, when the misery, pain, suffering and hardships it causes to billions of people is so overwhelmingly evident. The laws of prohibition only benefit organised criminals, law enforcement officers, legal people that profit financially from their resultant professions, and those that profit from the prison system and the confiscation of goods from the convicted. Everyone else in our societies suffer and pay enormously in every possible way for the monetary gains of the relatively few abovementioned people.

The family unit (wherein the crucial years of the child's development are nurtured) must be protected. The environmental conditions wherein people live must be greatly improved by distributing the wealth of nation's more equably, thus causing the disappearance of urban slums. An educational system must also be introduced based on sound spiritual values, where children are taught selflessness, brotherhood, the Love for all of Nature and for each other. It concerns awakening their innate creative and loving faculties, facilitating intuitive insights into the nature of reality. Education focussed upon a desire to amass wealth by selfish, avaricious means, and avowed materialism, should become a thing of the past. All forms of competitiveness, that breeder of foul disposition, war-like ambition, aggressive and separative tendencies, must vanish. Competitiveness must be replaced with the spirit of oneness, of sharing resources and developed altruistic and cooperative endeavour in all undertakings. This would greatly help to prevent what is now known as 'crime'.

In this western direction, therefore, the judiciary and (divine) legislators must truly build a shield of protection against all forms of evil based upon selfish and avaricious empire building, for those in their care. They must work for the dignity of people, safeguarding all hard-wrought human freedoms, allowing people to live out all aspects of life as they will, so long as it does not intrude upon the rights of others to act similarly.

A skilful meditation *(samādhi)* concerning the mechanism of eliminating the most woeful karmic formations caused by many in our societies needs to be conducted by the compassionate ones amongst us. The separative tendencies of others must be brought into a state of congenial selflessness. Everyone must come to the realisation that there is no true 'self' (wherewith they base their many forms of separateness). They must thus become liberated. Therefore, this petal is given the characteristic of *'not other'* in Figure 2. Co-operative unity must be sought upon every step of the way of the Libran disposition, allowing a true balance between opposites to be wrought.

Libra governs the hub of the Wheel of Life, of the Law determining the various cycles of being. It conditions the moment of the reversal of the wheel, when the aspirant on the mutable cross is able to mount the fixed cross and no longer retrogress through the zodiac. The hub manifests the energies of the jewel in the heart of the lotus, and projects the will to achieve. It is a place of dynamic peace (*samādhi*), and yet embodies the potential of all mutable activity.

Libra rules the narrow, razor-edged path of the middle way leading to liberation. Here the agile and analytical mental faculty has complete reign. The Libran, therefore, wisely balances and rightly judges the difference between the elements that compose the path to liberation and those that lead to illusion and glamour in all walks of life in the vales of experience. Humanity must be wisely led to renounce attachments to *saṃsāra* if they are to walk the eightfold path. In this sign, therefore, the intuition first sensed in Virgo fully manifests, enabling the person to choose what will rightly tip the balances, enabling one to climb the long road to liberation.

In Libra the entire question of material evolution (the third, or Mother aspect) is brought to justice. Here the evolutionary process finds its judgement day, and therefore the process that will eventually allow the enlightened one to rule the domain of *karma* is accomplished. The matter that is the residue of the past for all aspects of our civilisations (viewed in terms of *saṃskāras)* is thus uplifted and cleansed. This is the product of the *samādhi* that is not otherwise Thusness.

6. *The southwest* petal of the *western triad*—'What is the *samādhi* is comprehending it'—Virgo the virgin.

The term 'it' in the statement 'comprehending it' refers not just to the *samādhi,* but also to the background conditioning that has assisted the *samādhi* to arise, and generally what the *samādhi* is to rectify, as well as to the *dharmakāya* (veiled by *śūnyatā)* into which the *yogin* is absorbed. The interrelation, therefore, between our human societies and their *karma* (the focus of the Libran petal), and the relation of *saṃsāra* to the *samādhi,* is comprehended. The *samādhi* extends into the minutiae of all human interrelations and *karma* formations, because the average Virgoan is deeply enmeshed in the forms of phenomena produced by others. The *prāṇas* generated thus concern the true genesis of all karmic patterns in our societies, specifically of the foundation for the manifestation of group or national *karma.*

Virgo is the womb within which time evolves. With Cancer, it is one of the most ancient signs, as it embodies the sum of countless cycles of the material evolution of past aeons and incarnations of solar systems. This concerns the substance *(prakṛti)* in which the third, or activity aspect, gains its ascendancy, which eventually allows the birth of self-consciousness. In this sign, therefore, the third Ray of Mathematically exact Activity can find scope for right evolutionary expression. It manifests in the form of a first Ray potency via the Mercurial mind. (Mercury being the exoteric governor of this sign.) With this energy then the symbolic rocks of the earth (minds) can be appropriately carved to produce the forms needed. Virgo governs the period when the evolving personality is blind and completely lost in a world of mass psychic receptivity, until the time when the Clear Light of the spiritual day on the event horizon can be perceived. The light of Life must thereby evolve from out of the earth (the material world). The Bodhisattva that has consequently appeared will then elevate in light the essential Life of the earth itself to the Buddha throne.

In Virgo the comprehension of Life concerns rectifying the twelve links of Dependent Origination for humanity, and taught so that people can understand. The *samādhi* of Libra then becomes practical, an in-breathing of what was rightly formulated. Virgo is the sign in which the duality associated with Gemini is blended and fashioned into the unity represented by her 'Son' (the principle of enlightenment). It therefore forms an ideal matrix in which the *tathāgatagarbha* (the Buddha nature) within us, the hidden spiritual reality, can grow and mature.

Counting from Aries, it is the sixth sign in the zodiac, thus here is veiled the qualities of the hexagram which incorporates the attributes of the *tathāgatagarbha* into matter. There is a triad of qualities pointing upwards, embodying attributes of the abstract Mind, or the *tathāgatagarbha,* interlaced with a downward pointing triangle embodying the attributes of the threefold personality (of body, speech and mind). From every angle of vision the hexagram governs the evolution of all aspects of the form, of the womb of space-time. This Virgoan petal thus represents the means whereby 'it' (be this the form, or the *mātṛpadma,* the mother lotus that is the thought construct) is constructed and imbued with divine energy to sustain the duration of its existence (assisted by the Libran potency), so that a certain task can be accomplished. Such forms can be considered the 'child' or 'son' of the Mother. (Mother because it is the builder of the embodied form.) If the orientation is toward *dharmakāya* then the symbolism would pertain to the aspiration of the Son to the Father.

Along with Scorpio, Virgo is a triune sign, where life-consciousness-appearance (the *trikāya*) are interrelated. Indeed, the task of Virgo is to build the forms that precisely allow such interrelation, that become the medium that allows the *tathāgatagarbha* to utilise matter as a vehicle of expression, and to set about the task of its transmutation and elevation into the realms of Mind. Being part of the western triad such interrelation incorporates the phenomena produced by others.

Virgo 'hides the light which irradiates the world in Aquarius',[21] for therein enlightenment is nurtured. Once developed, it is utilised by Aquarians to flood the entire field of activity of humanity with light. The worst aspects of the *karma* of self-volition can thereby be overcome so that people can produce the garden cities of the earth. Virgoan energy must be rightly appropriated to fertilise and nurture the earth so that its greenery and salutary beneficence is produced in abundance. The present near disastrous, widespread rape of the earth Mother can thereby be countered. The *samādhi* is thus appropriately focussed to rightly comprehend the material domain via this Virgoan petal of the Heart centre. Thus the *prāṇas* rectifying the imbalances created by humanity upon the earth can be generated.

Much evil has been amassed by humanity, necessitating atonement, before the hidden light in Virgo can properly serve us. The Mother (the various aspects and forms of Tārā) cares for her callous and unthinking delinquent children. She must necessarily educate them through the denial of that which they greedily desire most, producing tribulation, if they are ever to learn from their folly and grow in light to mature as spiritual adults. Consequently, cataclysms (war, famines, etc.) manifest upon the face of the earth as the Mother convulses to overcome their rapine. Cataclysms are translated as crises of change, birthing new qualities, aspects of the *dharma* needing comprehension, then conversion to Thusness. Continuous crises force people to learn the basic teachings of the Four Noble Truths, to change attitudes by overcoming attraction to phenomena.

---

21 A.A. Bailey, *Esoteric Astrology*, 332.

7. *The southwest* petal of the *southern triad*. 'What is the comprehension is voidness *(śūnyatā)*'–Leo the lion.

The major theme of the Leonine subject is the development of self-awareness. The personality shines supreme and is dominant in this sign. Leo is consequently the most individualistic of the signs, wherein the self concept and its separative attitude dominates life. Consequently, here the greatest sacrifices must be achieved, to completely master and transcend the 'self', allowing the higher way to be followed whereby Voidness (*śūnyatā*) can be fully experienced. (Voidness referring to being void of the 'self' concept.) Out of necessity the place of generation becomes the place of mastery. Forms of light are generated as varying degrees of ignorance are conquered by the self-absorbed person. The appearance of light indicates that self-consciousness has been gained. Self-awareness later becomes illumination, which concerns generating the solar light that represents the Heart of Life. (The energies of the *tathāgatagarbha* are then consciously acceded to.) This petal therefore embodies the qualities of the sun-like attributes of the Heart centre. It expresses the *prāṇas* of the *iḍā nāḍī* that embodies the Fiery attributes of Leo. This petal consequently represents the conduit for the *iḍā nāḍī* that emanates from the Sacral centre, the source of vitality in the body. The process of the evolution of consciousness is the major objective of the physical manifestation of a sun, a process ruled by Leo.

In many ways Leo is the dominant Fire sign in the zodiac, especially in this materialistic age. Leo stabilises on the material domain the creative and transmutative ability of the Fire (via the self-conscious individual) that was originally projected in Aries. It then finds its major expression of focus in Sagittarius. (Aries and Sagittarius being the two other Fire signs.) On the path of return,[22] Fire purifies the mind and the entire threefold body.

In Leo's case the focus is solar Fire, as symbolised by the Sun. It is the fire of consciousness. Leo is consequently esoterically identified with the *tathāgatagarbha* (I-consciousness), the inner spiritual Sun, which can be considered to be the lion that seeks out his prey. In the latter stages of evolution the prey is the lower threefold personality (and its activities), complete with its animal desire body. The lion takes

22 The Bodhisattva path.

this to its lair after it has metaphorically caused its death, through the transmutation of animal-like *saṃskāras*. The radiant spiritual Sun *(tathāgatagarbha)* then occultly[23] engulfs the light of the personality. However, for the major part of the evolutionary period, the lion can also be considered to be the personality and his beastly passion. This produces the type of *karma* gained through interrelating with the outer environment that must later be sought by the stalking lion that is the Bodhisattva. Such action eventually allows an enlightened being to project a 'lion's roar' as a sign of sure victory over the vicissitudes of *saṃsāra*. The sun is the source of *prāṇa*, of the strength of the lion and of its vitality, of all evolutionary growth. It finds its direct correspondence, and is of supreme importance, on the three major levels of awareness (associated with the three bodies of a Buddha). For this reason the sun rules Leo exoterically, from the domain of the *tathāgatagarbha*, and also from the realm of liberated Being *(dharmakāya)*.

A Bodhisattva has developed sensitivity to impressions from the Heart of the Sun, (the Heart centre's links to the *tathāgatagarbha*), the central reservoir of light in his being. The liberated person is responsive to the light from the central Spiritual Sun (the Heart in the Head lotus, which manifests links to the *dharmakāya*) that irradiates the all with the light of Life. The self aware personality, the illumined being, and the Bodhisattva of the higher *bhūmis*, act to differing degrees as powerhouses of light, becoming sources of energy of the radiant sun to all around them. The personality generates the light of the physical sun (Sacral light), the Bodhisattva the light from the Heart of the Sun (the Sambhogakāya Flower), and the Bodhisattva of the higher degrees, the Light from the central Spiritual Sun (the *dharmakāya*).

It should be noted, therefore, the Voidness that is achieved in this sign is not void of light, but rather, void the 'self' concept, which to the stalker of the 'self' the light reveals to be fundamentally an illusion.

Internally, Leo rules the heart, the central reservoir of life, and the source of the factor of pride of the beast (when united with Solar Plexus energies and directed by mind). In Leo the diverse energies associated with the personality are regulated so that the light of the personal sun shines before people, allowing the Leonine subject to attract them to

---

23 This term has reference to the enlightening process of the liberating Fire enacted via meditation by a *yogin* or *yoginī*.

him. On the higher turn of the wheel, under the auspices of this sign, the guru or Bodhisattva is a central luminary that attracts disciples, manifesting as a group devouring the light-filled teachings.

8. *The southern* petal of the *southern triad.* 'What is the voidness is discerning (the real)'—Cancer the crab.

The Cancerian subject lives in the shell of emotions and moods that he has built, or else as an *ācārya* (spiritual teacher) in a body of light, which is needed to dispel the glamours of the emotional world of humanity. The psychic mental-emotional darkness created by humanity as its aura must be dispelled by the combined actions of the light bearers, the world's Bodhisattvas. Psychic murk has become the planetary 'dweller on the threshold',[24] which is ruled by Cancer-Capricorn, and which must be fought in the forthcoming Aquarian epoch if direct perception of the mysteries of the *dharma* is to happen upon a planetary scale. This epoch is that of Maitreya, who must appear to coordinate this battle and to be a focus for the liberating forces. The focal point for this cleansing is the combined Splenic centres that act as a sewer system for the human body and the planetary entity. Consequently, this petal of the Heart centre represents the cleansing potency that is directed to Splenic centre I to produce the necessary refinement and transmutation of *prāṇas*.

The objective of Cancer is to emerge from the waves and to enter life on dry land. This is done in order to master the Waters. There it is effectively transformed into a scorpion, to overcome the Watery deserts of illusion after the lessons learned in the sign Leo have been passed. In Pisces it re-enters the Waters upon a higher cycle (as an Avatar) to direct the potency of the flood of Love to all in need. Planetary transformation of the earth's astral swamp can then happen upon a large scale. In the story of these three Watery signs we have the vision of the need to dry out in Cancer, the application of transmutative energies in Scorpio, via the god of war, and the utilisation of the transmogrifying cosmic Waters[25] *(bodhicitta)* in Pisces to produce the liberation of all that are bonded in the spheres of sensation.

---

24 *Esoteric Astrology*, 207.

25 The difference between the cosmic Waters *(bodhicitta)* and those from the spheres of sensation is that one represents the transmutative energies of intensified Light, and the other the murk of mental-emotional and desire based *saṃskāras*. Both types of the Watery Element however, evidence a form of fluidity of expression, hence the designation 'Water'.

The continuous addiction to desire lays the foundation of the Cancerian's ability to later discern the real, because everything that is desired and latched onto by the claws of the crab is thoroughly experienced. The experiences intensify, until eventually the illusionality of their nature is discovered, and the crab scampers off into a new direction, a new field of desire.

The quality of *'discerning the real'* thus concerns mastery of the entire process continuously happening in the southern direction (the centres below the diaphragm), so that the sum of the materiality one incarnates into can be known for what it really is. This form of enlightenment allows one to visualise clearly the nature of *saṃsāra* and its correlation with the *dharmakāya* (via the polar opposite of Cancer, Capricorn). The Solar Plexus centre dominates the arena below the diaphragm, which is deeply conditioned by the massed emotional or desire currents (*saṃskāras*) of the human kingdom. This centre almost immediately precipitates them into objectivity as our emotions, moods, and feelings, greatly colouring the entire tonality of the human aura, individual or massed. An objective of the path to enlightenment in Cancer is to free oneself from psychic receptivity and the energies afflicting the unevolved masses which are ruled by Cancer.

By ruling the chest cavity, Cancer assists with the in and outbreathing of the laws and *prāṇas* that govern the incarnation process. As such, it is part of the cardinal cross, consisting of Aries, Capricorn, Libra and Cancer. They are the four main gates, or approaches, to *śūnyatā*. The directions in and out are esoterically a product of the nexus interrelating *śūnyatā* to *saṃsāra*. We can also relate this nexus to the Sambhogakāya Flower. Our focus then is on the processes that allow it to cause the appearance of each successive personal-I (in Cancer) and then to direct the *karma* (a Libran function) to its inevitable conclusion (the Capricornian purpose), causing an outbreathing of the inherent life (the result of the Arian will).

This cross, or throne, constituting these four rulers is technically 'not caused', in that it is the foundation of all that exists. Cancer represents the place of outpouring of its expression. Libra the balances governs the interrelation between all points of the cross. Capricorn represents the place of abstraction to the *dharmakāya*, whilst Aries manifests the motivating power that causes each door to open in turn. Because it is the place (door) from where causative *saṃskāras* flow, Cancer can also represent the way of approach to abstraction by means of identifying with cyclic law and the Dharmakāya Way. This is an important development of the symbolism of the yin-yang (of which Cancer's glyph is a modified version). From the yin-yang emanates the geometrical and energetic outlay governing the *vajra/*dorje.

In this disguise, Cancer conditions the manifestation of the energies of the four Mahārājas, (guardians of the 'four corners' of the universe), and the Lipikas (the karmic Scribes), who circumscribe these four corners and delineate all lines of definition, producing the boundaries of a Throne upon which a Buddha sits. The Throne represents the sum of his Buddha-field, the full extent of his power and influence in the realms of being/non-being. It signifies His ability to manifest into objectivity.

The polar opposite of Cancer is Capricorn, the gateway to liberation from the stranglehold of cyclic life. It is the door of Life looming ahead of the person that undertakes the Bodhisattva *bhūmis*. (Being the gateway to the physical plane expression, Cancer is thus the sign of recurring death.) The continual rounds of experience, and its emotional conditionings (Cancer), leads eventually to crystallisation and extensive materialism, symbolised by the jagged rocks and boulders that the *yogin*-goat must eventually climb. When doing so to attain the lofty heights in Capricorn, he is then able to enter both gates at will and choose to serve in the realms of death for the salvation of the world.

9. *The southeast* petal of the *southern triad.* 'What is discerning (the real) is calming (the mind)'— Gemini the twins.

Gemini governs all of the pairs of opposites in the zodiac (and thus in the life of the evolving person), subtly relating all of the signs together. For many ages the Gemini subject serves only himself, finally he compassionately perceives the needs of his brother and serves him. When the brothers have banded together in service, then their service is to subjugate their personal wills to revelatory purpose, so that all of Nature benefits from the resultant salutary action. Their interplay is thus kept in a fluid mutual response to one another in order to help produce fusion.

Mercury (signifying the intuition, and governing the fourth Ray of Beautifying Harmony overcoming Strife), the orthodox ruler of Gemini, helps the interplay of all categories of relationships, be they zodiacal or planetary. Mercury is the divine intermediary on all levels of perception and relates the higher and lower minds, the Sambhogakāya Flower and personality, as well as consciousness to the *dharmakāya*. It is the cause of the mental agility and fluidity so often found in the Gemini subject and helps foster his latent sense of duality. Exoterically, Mercury makes the Gemini native fluid, analytical, able to reason well in all types of situations and circumstances. He is versatile, apt to wander through many fields of expression, is constantly active, sensitive, and quick to react to his own or to other's needs.

Calmness of mind/Mind facilitates this process, as it is the steady base whereby things can be seen for what they are. Also, those things that are integrally opposed or different (which is what the 'twins' connote) can be interrelated into a fusion or unity. All things are brought together in the serenity and quietude that such calmness implicates. Another pair of opposites that is fused here is that of *saṃsāra* and *śūnyatā*. Depending upon one's viewpoint, they are then neither one or the other, but both, neither both, or a fusion that makes them 'other', where the serene Mind can discern all aspects in its meditative embrace. As it is for this prime duality, so it also becomes for all the other forms of duality in the zodiac. The *dharmakāya* also comes into the view of the calm Mind.

The manifestation of desire in Taurus results in the complete interplay and pull of the sexual forces in Gemini, wherein the primal cause of the suffering associated with the sex relationship is hidden. Through a wise use of the developed, fluid Mercury-Venus mind in Gemini,[26] the sexual and/or spiritual struggles of the person become understood and integrated. They inevitably find a point of balance in Libra, and are finally resolved in terms of their mutually beneficent service potential in Aquarius. (Gemini, Libra and Aquarius being the three Air signs.) These three signs govern the flow of the *piṇgalā nāḍī* stream in the body (the compassionate aspect of consciousness, rather than mind per se). We first have the generation of cooperative activity between the twins in Gemini, the meditative adjudication of the forces of life so that the balances are heavily weighed in favour of compassion in Libra, and the active service arena of the Bodhisattva dispensing the Waters of Life in Aquarius.

---

26 The esoteric ruler of Gemini is Venus, who also governs the fifth Ray of Scientific Aptitude, of the energies of the mind. Mercury is the exoteric ruler.

The concept of the union of the pairs of opposites ultimately produces the highest forms of Tantra, necessitating the meditative unfoldment symbolised by Libra and the Bodhisattvic activity of the Aquarian. The *mahāmudrā* philosophy is implied, applied through the veil of ritualistic observance. Inevitably the Unsurpassed Yoga Tantra *(anuttarayogatantra)* is practiced, which concerns the 'union of father and mother deities'.[27]

The Gemini subject is said to move 'towards Libra'[28], because the calmness of mind developed in Gemini is the prerequisite for the *samādhi* that is the natural expression of the awakened Libran. This allows the interplay of the pairs of opposites to become evenly balanced, thus the platform from which one's climb upon the high mount of Bodhisattvahood can be accomplished. We see also that in the integration of the energies of Mercury and Venus an objective of evolution is achieved. Then the light of the mind (governed by the qualities of Venus) and that of the Sambhogakāya Flower (being Mercurial in nature) are united to function perfectly in accord. The 'messenger of the Gods', the intuitive flashes of Light dispensed by Mercury, can then illumine the calm receptive mind.

10. *The southeast* petal of the *eastern triad.* What is calming (the mind) is liberation *(vimokṣa)*–Taurus the bull.

Taurus embodies the neck and throat that supports the head, and is the foundation or sustaining principle underlying the entire cycle of being/non-being. The vocal chords in the throat are the emanating source for the externalisation of mantric power (the divine Word) into manifestation. The neck also symbolises the constructed *antaḥkaraṇa* that relates the will of the person to the ideas and thoughts that have been created (symbolised by the remainder of the body to which the neck is attached).

We also have the Throat centre, which is responsible for the control of the Fiery *prāṇas* in the *nāḍī* system. These *prāṇas* vivify the eyes and eventually the third Eye, once *kuṇḍalinī* has been liberated. Consequently, Taurus is the sign of illumination and of the powers of

27 Dudjom Rinpoche, 274.

28 *Esoteric Astrology*, 332.

the directive Eye. The all-seeing Eye sees the goal in order to liberate. It envisions all of the parameters of the meditation-Mind, the vast vistas of cosmos, of the lines of direction *(nāḍīs)* from here to there in the realms of enlightened being. Inevitably, this Fiery substance will be able to control the desire principle which is rampant in the undeveloped Taurean subject. (The 'bull of desire'.) Consequently, this petal of the Heart centre projects liberating, transforming energies to below the diaphragm, wherein the principle of desire must be converted into compassionate action. The Taurean must learn to control speech and endeavour to explain the *dharma* in such a way that the self-willed rampaging bulls in the field of desire follow the path of the ageless wisdom that is the vehicle of enlightenment.

Esoterically, Vulcan, governed by the first Ray of Will or Power, rules this sign (the orthodox ruler being Venus). Vulcan works at the forge to fashion all beautiful, psychic, as well as material things, for he is the deity who can manipulate the Fire found at the heart of every atom. He works to transmute all base metals into spiritual gold, and empowers the forces of creation *(siddhis),* forging the necessary weapons in his underground furnace. This transmutation process is the basis of the qualification *liberation* given to this petal of the Heart Lotus, because here everything is thereby liberated from the imprisoning limitations of the form that trapped it.

Vulcan is the bringer of death (as also does a Volcano, which Vulcan rules exoterically) and aids the destructiveness of the bull. It helps destroy the form so that the inherent hidden Life can be set free. Vulcan works in darkness so that therein may be engendered light, which manifests through the Eye of the bull (the Ājñā centre). It produces the illumination of the path that is to be trod, and also of the plan of enlightened Being. He goes into the depths (the Sacral and Base of Spine centres) to fashion what is most beautiful and useful to the evolving Life within all. The Fires that are liberated can then be lifted to great heights. Vulcan then awakens the Śūnyatā Eye and embodies the transmutative purpose of this Eye in the realms of form.

Vulcan embodies the flux that allows the various trials and transmutations in the life of humanity (symbolised by Mercury in alchemical lore) that are sublimated in the crucible of experience, in conjunction with the various minerals (the salts and acids of mental-emotionalism) that come from the earth. Thus, as it establishes a relation between the two (the mineral and the human kingdoms), it causes the powers of the Philosopher's Stone that is said to give all knowledge to its possessor. It is therefore also related to the attainment that produces complete liberation from *saṃsāra*.

It is said that Taurus 'rushes blindly until Sagittarius directs'.[29] The archer pierces the Eye of the bull, awakening it. The blind onrushing desire of the unevolved Taurean that seeks sexual gratification and all forms of emotional relations produces the *conjoined karma* attributed to this direction. Eventually the Taurean evolves the ability to see in the realms of death (for by then Vulcan also rules the native) and aspires to the source of light, to become a perfected vehicle of light. He then illumines others, as did the Buddha, whose life exemplified the nature of this sign.

Light, desire, creation (fertility), illumination, the all-seeing Eye, have always been the properties of the divine cow Goddesses and Gods, such as Apis, Hathor, the bull in the Mithraic religion, and why the cow is considered sacred in India today. Illumination, and on the lower arc of evolution, desire, are therefore the keywords of this sign.

The difficulty of the Taurean subject can be seen in the first Ray of Will or Power (Vulcan) that governs him via the impetus of the mind (Venus, its exoteric ruler). This enhances his self-will, determination, and destructiveness. He must learn to offset and transmute them, for instance, to change self will into the Will-to-Good, and to mould the results of the destruction of aspects of the personality life into necessary constructiveness, by fashioning the tools and vehicles of future enlightenment. He must develop the Eye of wisdom instead of critical assertiveness. Knowledge (the 'eye doctrine') must be transmuted into wisdom (the Heart's awareness). Therein lies the difficulty, yet the ability to penetrate and perceive the causes and results of any line of action and of the plan, will, or purpose for any incarnation, is great. When the information gained is constructively expressed then there is a vast potential to benefit humanity and the lesser kingdoms.

The *polar opposite* of Taurus is Scorpio. At first in Taurus the lower nature triumphs because of the overpowering desire and satiation of the senses, producing eventually the death that the form nature symbolises

---

29 *Esoteric Astrology*, 322.

in Scorpio. Eventually, through the trials of the acolyte in the desert of materiality, desire gives way to aspiration, death to liberation, darkness to light, and the person stands illumined, enlightened, and liberated in Taurus. Taurus represents the field of application of the liberated one, whereas Capricorn (also an Earth sign) represents the place of attainment of that liberation. The other Earth sign (Virgo) is where the quest for liberation is born.

11. *The eastern* petal of the *eastern triad.* What is liberation is the Middle Path—Aries the ram.

Aries the ram embodies the thinking and directive capabilities, the head and brain, incorporating the Head lotus *(sahasrāra padma).* It concerns the domain from where abstract ideation, the Will-to-Liberate emanates, and is that *(śūnyatā)* into which everything will eventually be resolved. The *yogin* can then awaken all power in the quest for enlightenment.

Aries connotes the first differentiation of manifestation, the creative ideation, or Will-to-Be that seeds the instigating *bīja* of the *maṇḍala* and carries the construct through to completion. This process, enacted consciously or unconsciously, leads inevitably to the formation of all that we see around us. In Aries the impulse of the ram is always to be the conscious director. In the glyph for Aries is symbolised the achievement of a former spiral of evolution that becomes the seed germ, or father aspect for a new field of expression.

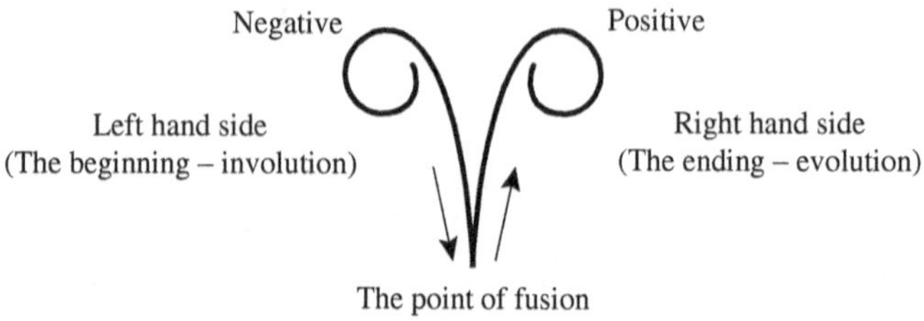

Figure 4. The Ram's horns

At the point of fusion, the achieved balance produces a Ray of dynamically qualified energy which reaches the lowest aspect of manifestation, and then on the path of return, the highest. The spirals of the horns emanate to and from *śūnyatā*. They are cause and effect of the focal point of the application of the will in *saṃsāra*. They indicate the mode of interrelation between *śūnyatā-saṃsāra*, and can be applied to any of the entry and exit points of the four cardinal directions. As depicted in Figure 2, it is 'not both' because it is the point of fusion of both directions, the true Middle Path or focal point of the Heart centre. Therefore, the zodiacal wheel starts here.

The downturned horns of the ram principally signify descent into incarnation of primordial causative energy (meaning the death of the spiritual). Later, at the point of fusion within the *samādhi* of the accomplished *yogin* (which happens at the polar opposite sign of Aries, Libra the balances), the will can be utilised to cause the death of the restrictive aspects of the form. *Śūnyatā* can then be revealed for what it is. The left hand spiral also symbolises the qualities of the *iḍā nāḍī* (the form building attribute of the mind). The right hand spiral represents the *piṇgalā nāḍī* (the liberating aspects of the awakening consciousness) and the point of fusion, the *suṣumṇā*.

The creative potency of seeding the *maṇḍala* to be gives Aries the status of being the originating thinker of the divine thought that dispels the darkness of ignorance. It also will have earlier caused the interrelation of the Buddha-germ (*tathāgatagarbha*) with the *māyā* of the substance constituting the form. Thus intelligence is seeded and developed. Being the reasoning, conditioning function of humanity, intelligence signifies the expression of self will, which fully flowers in the sign Leo the lion. At first the will drives the petty desires or ambitions of the personality, later it transforms human thought to produce liberation. It then becomes Divine Will, and is not an aspect of the 'self', but rather of the *tathāgatagarbha*, which stimulates and directs the awakening transmutative Fires that spirals consciousness beyond all restricted forms.

Esoterically, Aries is ruled by Mercury, standing for the fluid, quick, intuitive, highly perceptive Mind governing the path of return. This path necessitates the development of the Arian Divine Will. Here the mind becomes the mechanism wherein enlightenment can be revealed through the Mercurian process of building the links *(antaḥkaraṇas)* to the Sambhogakāya Flower and beyond. This eastern direction concerns the projection of the *prāṇas* of enlightenment inward and upward towards the field of expression I term cosmos. It concerns an outbreathing to the Buddha fields of 'thus gone' ones (Logoi). The Arian impulse governs the rhythmic breathing of the meditation enacted by the symbolism of its polar opposite, Libra the balances. The martial energy governing the desires of the undeveloped person (the Arian warlike activity) is then transmuted. The individual becomes an agent of the focussed will that enables one to travel the liberating, narrow, razor-edged path between all forms of extremes. This is 'the Middle Path' as governed by Mercury.

Mercury symbolises the Caduceus staff. It is a central rod (the *suṣumṇā nāḍī*) with the two other main *nāḍīs* (in the form of serpents) spiralling around and crossing over it (symbolising the entire *nāḍī* and *chakra* system), leading to a sphere with two wings sprouting from it. These wings symbolise the dual lobes of the Ājñā centre (the all-seeing Eye), which when awakened allows the person to esoterically fly in all domains of consciousness and beyond.

In Libra, the *saṃskāras* conveyed by the two main *nāḍīs* are weighed in the pans of the balance, where one pan represents *iḍā* and the other *piṇgalā,* while the central stand and mechanism of weighing represents *suṣumṇā.*

Both Mars and Mercury relate to the principle of conflict and help engender points of crises in a person's life. At first one struggles with the blows that the hammer of *karma* inflicts (Mars ruling the sixth Ray) as a consequence of self-willed activities in former cycles. Later, upon the path of return and the rectified wheel, the entire process of using the will to sever the ties to *saṃsāra* and establishing the fourth Ray Mercurial links to *śūnyatā* produces crises in consciousness. Eventually the peace relating to the resolution of conflict is obtained (the *samādhi* developed in Libra). The crises refer to the way an arena of *dhyāna* is eventually established within fields of effulgent conscious activity. Whenever something formerly cherished, such as a strongly held belief, is to be eliminated, then there is a point of crisis. Mercury produces crises through establishing the links to the abstracted domains wherein revelation is acceded for the necessity of change.

Mars is associated with the strife, struggle and war that is the result of the personality's various ambitions, fanaticism, or desires. When influenced by Mercury, these qualities are refined and transmuted into the qualities that enable the *yogin* to overcome all obstacles to enlightenment. The martial zeal is then utilised to fearlessly overcome the demons of Māra's horde, to destroy passions and forms of attachment to *māyā*. The major part of this struggle is undertaken in Scorpio (ruled both exoterically and esoterically by Mars, and therefore related to Aries). The *yogin* in Aries is, however, able to most effectively wield Mañjuśrī's two-edged sword to cut away all obscurations of mind and to generate *bodhicitta* in the pursuit of the Bodhisattva path.

Ruling the fourth Ray, Mercury mediates between the higher and lower mind, the *tathāgatagarbha* and personality, and the conflict associated with the resolution of all pairs of opposites. Such resolution is an objective of the life of the aspirant. This establishes the basis of the quality attributed to this petal of the Heart lotus as *'not both'*. The duality is externalised in Gemini, where a person deals with the vicissitudes of manifest life, and internalised in Aries, where the *yogin* strives to control his psychic constitution. Before this work can begin one must first gain illumination from the first stages of the resolution of duality, which takes place in the womb of Virgo (where Mercury is the orthodox ruler). Scorpio then produces the testings that propels the process to the higher levels of Mind wherein the major conflict between concepts of self and not-self must be resolved. Such resolution allows the *yogin* to control all dual forces in the meditation-Mind. The foundation of the *mahāmudrā* that is the union between a Buddha and his Consort can then be firmly established in the place of the Heart and fully expressed as the awakened Head lotus in Capricorn.

Analysing the polar opposites in the zodiac, it can be said that the cleansing process that produces the tests in Scorpio ultimately leads to the death of the personality. We then have the achievement of liberation in Taurus as a consequence of the *yogin's* path in Aries via the *samādhi* developed in Libra. One then manifests unfettered enlightenment in Capricorn as a consequence of mastering the process of rebirth in Cancer. The Clear Light is generated in Gemini because one-pointed aspiration in Sagittarius has conquered the ego in Leo and demonstrated the Bodhisattva virtues in Aquarius. New consciousness states and altered perceptions are born in Virgo and the *siddhis* of psychic receptivity are mastered in Pisces, to become a world conqueror roaring out the Leonine lion's roar of achievement. All can then hear the truths concerning the necessity of mastering *saṃskāras*.

Aries is a purveyor of the Element Fire, as it is part of the Fiery triplicity, Aries-Leo-Sagittarius. Aries channels that type of Fiery Will that emanates from the *dharmakāya*. From Leo emanates solar Fire, which relates to the development of an enlightened consciousness. From Sagittarius emanates planetary Fire, which relates to the developed personal will used for the manipulation of things desired in the formed realms. Fire is the substance of the mind, and is the major purificatory and transmutative agency. It clears the way by burning the dross left after the action of Water has taken its toll and has prepared the person to master the emotional and physical *saṃskāras*. Such mastery constitutes the first two levels of gaining enlightenment.

Sagittarius is one of the conditioning signs of the mutable cross of repeated incarnations and the constant changing attitudes and experiences of the personality. In Sagittarius the Fire of self will eventually develops into a one-pointed determination, fixed upon the way of Love that is so characteristic of the aspirant to enlightenment.

Leo is one of the conditioning signs of the fixed cross and is the dominant Fire sign at this time. The energies of Leo facilitate the development of self-consciousness in humanity, the ability to reason out what is right and wrong. Later, proper use of this faculty of mind under the auspices of Leo enables one to tread the burning ground to gain illumination, and then complete freedom from the dominance of the form. Its energies are embodied by the *tathāgatagarbha,* which becomes a stalking lion at this stage of the path, and is therefore of supreme importance to the life of the aspiring one. Leo draws upon Aries to fulfil the function of producing liberation from the 'self' concept.

The significance of Aries as the purveyor of Fire becomes clear in the life of an enlightened being, for Aries is one of the conditioning signs of the cardinal cross, the cross of Life. It conveys the dynamic electric Fire that predominantly conditions the meditation-Mind of the accomplished *yogin.* Here Aries projects all cycles into a consummating one and initiates a person into the higher Mysteries in which time and space no longer veil. It thus represents the beginning and ending of manifest being. Electric Fire is the energy of the enlightened Will of the liberated Bodhisattva.

The initial beginnings, desires, and schemes of the Arian find their point of equilibrium, or 'judgement day', in Libra, and consummation in Capricorn. There the ram becomes the scapegoat, and shoulders the burden of the *karma* of his group (or herd) to endeavour to relieve their sufferings and help them achieve liberation. So the mountainside of Initiation into the mysteries of the *dharmakāya* can be scaled. In the transformation of the ram into the goat lies the esoteric basis of the concept of the atonement described by Christian Theologians. It is the basis of the Bodhisattva's work with the higher *bhūmis*.

The Arian desire to manifest (which causes his myriad personality incarnations) achieves a point of balance and equilibrium in Libra. The resultant mental integration allows one to aspire to liberate the many and to tread the path of active return, with the testings then manifesting in Scorpio.

12. *The northeast* petal of the *eastern triad.* 'The Middle Path', is without extremes—Pisces the fishes.

Finally, we have *Pisces the fishes,* who rules the feet, and thus the ability to progress along the path of enlightenment. The feet are directed by the eyes, and the entire cognitive faculties of the person. It implies the ability to think of where to go and what to do on the journey, thus to conclusively reason out one's entire path or progress in life from beginning to end. It relates to the entire thought-form making ability in life, to demonstrate any cosmological process, or to circumscribe and project a *maṇḍala* as a complete body of manifestation.

The feet enable one to find the food one consumes. (The energies needed for the maintenance of all bodily functions.) The feet are also used to escape from the many types of dangers that lurk in the symbolic jungle, or stony desert paths upon which one may have to travel. The role of Pisces to survey (with the feet) the sum of the body of manifestation is also characteristic of the work of a world-saviour, the future Buddha who must descend and walk upon the earth for the benefit of all.

Pisces is the last sign of the zodiac, and is therefore the sign of conclusion of the entire gamut of the evolutionary process. It thus signifies the deep sleep (*pralaya)* state before the commencement of a new cycle of evolution (using 'the feet' to walk a new evolutionary path). This gives it the quality of *without extremes* in the listing of qualities of the Void, because from this perspective it absorbs the extreme of evolutionary attainment into *śūnyatā.* Then a new cycle of incarnate activity begins, wherein *śūnyatā* is veiled, effectively non-existent. Inevitably, the path producing liberation from the wheel of birth and death can be travelled.

Pisces is also the sign of sacrifice and death, not just of the personality nature, but also of the principle that causes the rebirth process. The Sambhogakāya Flower at first detaches itself in *samādhi* from self-absorbed contemplation within the abstract realms of Mind, or upon *śūnyatā,* and looks to the ocean of sensation in the world of form. If it is to sacrificially produce the appearance of a new personal-I then it must work with other Sambhogakāya Flowers to *co-actively* produce the phenomenological conditions within a world situation wherein the incarnate personalities can interrelate and share *karma*. It contemplates what mutable incarnation has to offer and becomes bonded or yoked to the life of the personality aspect by means of the *sūtrātmā* (thread of life). The death of its former freedom of Mind ensues and a personal-I appears. Its evolution comes thus under the general beneficence of the planetary Bodhisattva, which instigates Love and Wisdom as the qualities which must be evolved. Jupiter (governing the second Ray of Love-Wisdom), therefore, is the exoteric ruler of the person in Pisces, as such energy is needed to guide the person's path in life.

The personality undergoes many acts of renunciation under the influence of Pisces that eventually lead to the termination of that life. For a *yogin,* such renunciation may even go as far as the ending of the Sambhogakāya Flower's existence and entrance into *śūnyatā*. For most, however, the onset of the process of death allows the Flower to eventually cut the cord, abstracting the gain into itself.

As Pisces is the first sign on the reversed wheel after Aries, and being the polar opposite of Virgo (the womb of the reversed wheel) so here the personality will be seen to be at the elementary stages of its evolution and thus in the most unevolved, negative, and fluidly psychically sensitive state. At this stage one will be completely instinctive, receptive to the mass emotional life and its psychic currents and attitudes. The mind is dormant, and the germ of enlightenment is unawakened, hidden deep within the activity of this psychic receptivity. Consciousness is definitely bonded to the form and held captive to the experiences and sensations accrued by the person in the ocean of antagonistic, as well as beneficent, forces engendered by countless beings. Deep within the turbulence of the ocean of these forces the 'fish' of the enlightenment principle (*bodhicitta*) swims. Mediumship, personality inhibition, and receptivity to (massed) emotional agitations and moods, are thus some of the major qualities of the unevolved person in this sign. The influence of Jupiter however always pulls one towards one's evolutionary goal by bringing the Sambhogakāya Flower and form together in a functioning relationship. The symbol of this sign (the bonded fishes) indicates this:

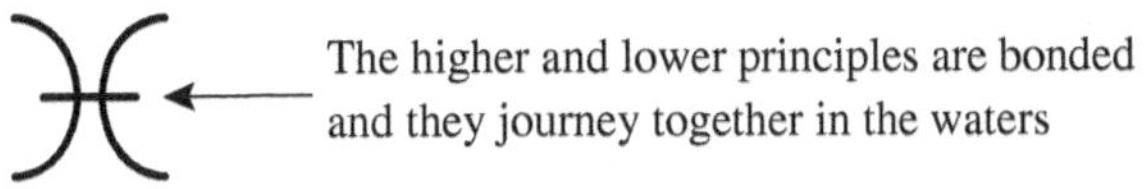

The higher and lower principles are bonded
and they journey together in the waters

Figure 5. The bonded Fishes

Jupiter always brings consciousness into new and fresh relationships with all aspects of the form, from which the Sambhogakāya Flower-personality can glean the qualities it needs. Cataclysms, civilisations and many cycles of racial evolution come and go, yet this bond persists from life to life until liberation is achieved by the accomplished *yogin*. The bond is seen in terms of the intricate *nāḍī* system which must be unknotted and its *prāṇas* integrated in the central channel (*suṣumṇā*). The *yogin* then directs his consciousness up the Life-line (*sūtrātmā*) to the *tathāgatagarbha* and then to the Śūnyatā Eye, from where higher revelation is experienced.

The objective of the experiences in this sign under the general stimulus of its planetary rulers allows the personality (and the Sambhogakāya Flower) to enter upon the liberating process. The concreted aspects of consciousness will be transmuted into their abstracted correspondences and the lower psychic attributes transformed into the higher *siddhis*. The process of transformation is described by Bailey as:

a. Negativity into positive soul control.

b. Mediumship into mediatorship.

c. Clairvoyance into spiritual perception.

d. Clairaudience into mental telepathy and finally inspiration.

e. Instinct into intellect.

f. Selfishness into divine selflessness.

g. Acquisitiveness into renunciation.
h. Self-preservation into selfless world service.
i. Self pity into compassion, sympathy and divine understanding.[30]

Here are represented some of the opposing aspects upon the path of life. For Pisces to represent the Middle Path, the *yogin* must discover the Life line that relates the opposites and travel thereby to dynamically integrate *saṃsāra* with *śūnyatā*. Thus the Dharmakāya Way is followed. The negative aspects of this list are transcended, whilst the positive aspects remain, yet the insights derived from the past are never lost upon the Bodhisattva path. *Śūnyatā* is not void of the Mind of compassion.

The higher form of sacrifice manifests when the *yogin,* identified with the Sambhogakāya Flower, is totally detached from the form nature and is focussed entirely upon *śūnyatā* via the Śūnyatā Eye. The resultant experience produces an intense energisation whose potency the Flower cannot contain, and it literally explodes in the Clear Light that is the expression of unfettered enlightenment. A bond, however, persists in the *yogin's samādhi*, because a link *(antaḥkaraṇa)* is established between his abstract Mind and the *dharmakāya,* as well as to the personality vehicle. This link is composed of living conscious light. All lesser attachments and unions have been severed, effected through the agency of Pluto (bearing the first Ray of Will, that brings death to limiting forms), the esoteric ruler of Pisces. This final death of all *saṃsāric* conditionings allows one to become an attendant of the court at Shambhala, the planetary Head Lotus. Shambhala is governed by a primordial Buddha acting as the Lord of this world. In this series, his attendant Bodhisattvas are denoted as the Hierarchy (or Council) of Bodhisattvas.

Pluto, the regent of death, is lord of the underworld, of the Bardo intermediate state between births.[31] The energy of Will or Power along

---

30 A.A. Bailey, *Esoteric Astrology*, 123-124.

31 The Bardo states are explained in Volume 5. The Tibetan term Bardo means 'between the two', especially the state between births. According to the *Bardo Thödol* six such intervals exist: the Bardo of birth, the Bardo of dreams, the Bardo of *samādhi,* the Bardo signifying the moment before death, the Bardo of *dharmatā,* and the Bardo of becoming. The *Bardo Thödol* is recited in the presence of the deceased for a total period of 49 days. It is said that the teachings can enable the deceased to attain liberation while in the Bardo states, or the best possible rebirth. When mentioned in this series, the state prior to rebirth is implicated.

its destroyer line produces the detachments, renunciations and deaths throughout the cyclic activity until liberation is attained. All forms of clinging associated with desire, of the material possessions that the personality finds so hard to let go are terminated, as well as limiting consciousness-attributes preventing the attainment of liberation. Eventually the life of the Sambhogakāya form is also terminated and the quality denoted as 'without extremes' *(śūnyatā)* is gained.

Most Bodhisattvas consummate their work in the sign Aquarius after a full cycle as servers of the world. They enter into *nirvāṇa* and find an approach to other world systems, or out of the solar system altogether on one of the cosmic Paths. (These Paths are *nāḍīs* in cosmos and the liberated one travels as a *bīja* within such a *nāḍī* that links *chakra* to *chakra,* star system to star system.) Some, however, continue their work in Pisces, to become Avatars, bearing cosmic forces under direct Logoic impress to produce great cyclic changes. Hence a higher form of bonding associated with the glyph for Pisces is achieved.

The energy of Pisces is essentially that of the first Ray, which of necessity must utilise the second Ray (Jupiter) as a vehicle in the realms of form. This Ray combination has a profound effect upon the life of the aspirant, producing the lure that leads to the path of Initiation into the mysteries of being/non-being. It is the consequence of the transmutative process, producing eventual escape through the type of death associated with liberation. For the unevolved masses this Ray combination instigates psychic sensitivity and mediumistic tendencies. Its penetrating and attractive qualities enable people to contact the radiatory emanation from sentient lives and from the subjective world. Rarely, however, do they comprehend the true nature of what they are experiencing, and are generally bewildered by the effects of such unconscious psychic receptivity.

Humanity's acute susceptibility to such impression is one of their major problems, for it enables people to be sensitively influenced by mischievous disincarnate entities, thought-forms, and currents of feeling-perceptions of all types from the emotional realm. Also experienced are the well planned streams of manipulative thoughts directed by the dark brotherhood to world leaders, disciples, and others of influence.

Pisces is said to 'take from all the signs',[32] because the results of

32 A.A. Bailey, *Esoteric Astrology*, 333.

the experiences in those signs are needed before the spiritual death of the Sambhogakāya Flower can be eventuated. This allows mediation between the one and the other. The Bodhisattva must undergo every possible experience and pass the tests in all the signs before being able to pass through the Śūnyatā Eye to the unfettered bliss of the Void.

The Bodhisattva *bhūmis*

It is not my intention in this series to iterate the exoteric teachings concerning the Bodhisattvas, as that information can be found in any orthodox text on the subject. Rather, I wish to explain their actual disposition and some of what subjectively influences them. The ten *bhūmis*[33] are progressive levels of realisation, the stages of perfection of a Bodhisattva. Bodhisattvas develop the *bhūmis* over a series of lives and this development is associated with ten signs starting with Cancer. Cancer represents the incarnation of new cycles of endeavour, and its liberating endeavour concerns the ability to discern the real. The minutiae of the problem at hand must be analysed, producing a graded series of revelations that unveil what the reality is.

The Bodhisattva stages are generally depicted in terms of: 1, the great joy of the stream enterer. 2, stainless purity as *saṃskāras* are mastered. 3, the illuminated one. 4, great wisdom. 5, invincible strength upon the path. 6, the presence of the awakened Mind. 7, the far-reaching stage of awakening. 8, steadfastness of the Bodhisattva virtue. 9, meritorious Buddha-like wisdom. 10, the *dharma* cloud of revelation that liberates.

The description of the *bhūmis* presented below will be an outline only. More information will be found scattered throughout this series. There is a need for a fresh explanation in Buddhism of the nature of Bodhisattvas and how they work, as what has been given in the available texts is often mythologised and inaccurate.

Generally a number of lives of are needed for development between one *bhūmi* and the next. There is no even development and often a Bodhisattva is unfolding a major portion of one *bhūmi* whilst simultaneously developing qualities related to others.

33 *Bhūmi*, from the verbal root *bhū*, to become, grow into.

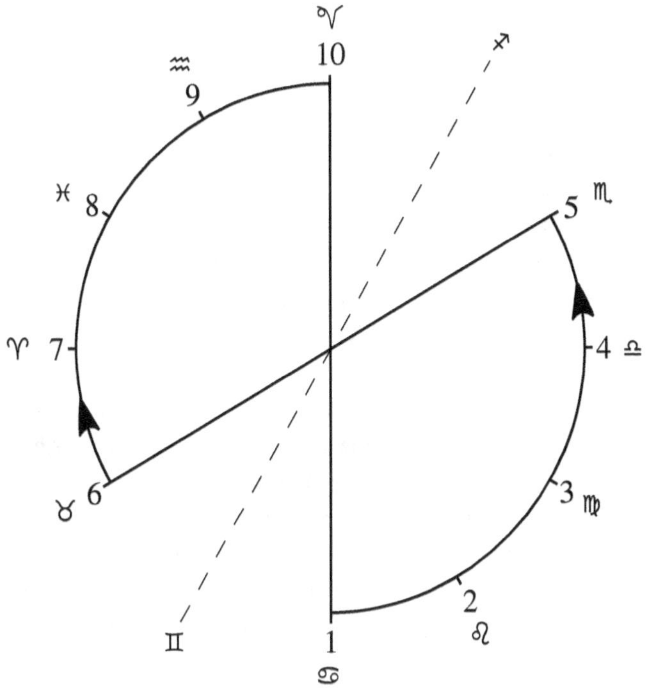

Figure 6. The ten Bhūmis and the Zodiac

Cancer, the sign of incarnation, represents the first Bodhisattva stage, the great joy of the stream enterer. Here one enters the stream of enlightenment through the ability to discern the real from the general miasma of *māyā,* the emotion-based Waters one has incarnated into. The aspiration to overcome the factors of the rebirthing process conditioned by Cancer is then evidenced. By realising the need to master the Watery emotions as a major challenge, this path of aspiration causes one to find a teacher that can reveal the higher way. The Watery Element constitutes one's entire psychic and emotional disposition, as well as veiling dark *karma* of erroneous magical (left hand) and yogic practices of the past. Many evil weeds in the *nāḍīs* need to be yogically eradicated.

The second Bodhisattva stage occurs in Leo, wherein *bodhicitta* is fanned, providing the Bodhisattva insights in to the nature of Voidness via the process of eliminating concepts of 'self'. Consequently, the novice Bodhisattva begins to counter the effects of humanity's involvement with the outer environment through educating them as to appropriate ways to think. The 'stainless purity' developed via rectified *saṃskāras* is an objective which necessitate embarking upon the path of yoga-meditation. Breathing exercises and the transformation of base substance eventually produces a radiant aura, similar to what is depicted around the great ones in Buddhist art. Such an aura is by nature healing in its effect upon the general environment. The process of transforming and transmuting *saṃskāras* is not quickly achieved, and neither is the development of the accompanying radiance. Some lives are generally needed to achieve this transformation. Layers of substance must be refined and transmogrified throughout the process, requiring the passing of many testings along the path to enlightenment, concerning the generation of the various *bhūmis*. A Bodhisattva does not magically appear, but must be developed by recapitulating what has been gained in past lives, then consolidating these gains and finally superseding them. Many virtuous characteristics need to be developed, and as the requirements for each stage are met by passing the necessary testings the Bodhisattva is consequently Initiated into the related mysteries.[34]

The first genuine steps in overcoming the allurements of the physical appetites to sex, money and material comforts, and battling with the egotism of the 'self' concept in Cancer and the next sign produces attainment of the first Initiation, governed by the Element Earth. The Leonine proclivity to develop a radiant aura (symbolised by the lion's mane) comes to the fore as these Earthy *saṃskāras* are overcome through utilisation of the Fiery attributes of the Leonine mind. Many more lives of Bodhisattvic activity are needed before the aura is completely radiant from the transmutation of *saṃskāras* into enlightenment attributes. The 'stainless purity' depicted in this second Bodhisattva *bhūmi* is fully attained only in the highest *bhūmis,* but a genuine start is made in Leo, and continues throughout the path.

The third Bodhisattva *bhūmi* is established in the sign Virgo the virgin, wherein the phenomena produced by others is comprehended by

34 The teachings associated with the esoteric version of *guruparamparā* (lineage tradition of a guru), is implicated here and explained in Volume 6, as well as the subject of Initiation.

the Bodhisattva and the appropriate service arena is then chosen. An adequate alleviation of the burden of suffering upon the planet can then begin. Cooperative endeavour is needed if the work of assisting others is to proceed, though a heuristic approach is demonstrated for all stages of the Bodhisattva path. This is the essential keynote of the Bodhisattva's entire path to liberation. Virgo, being the matrix of the substance that is the Womb of Life, gives birth to the Initiated one as the darkness of ignorance is overcome. The illumined Mind begins to stand in its place. The Bodhisattva becomes the illumined one by generating the wisdom gained from attaining the first to the higher Initiations that signifies that such a one is a light bearer in the world. The process related to transforming substance into the Void Elements has thus begun. The related *samādhi* shows the necessity for such transformation, the goal being accomplished in the later *bhūmis*.

The fourth Bodhisattva *bhūmi* is generated in Libra the balances, producing a focus upon yogic discipline and meditation. Here the intricacies concerning developing *samādhi* is mastered. Only through the art of applied meditation can great wisdom be developed. However, this also requires a complete comprehension of the law of *karma* and the vicissitudes of the way it manifests by having lived through and mastered its judgements in former lives. Causes and conditions are thoroughly analysed and the wisdom earlier generated is built upon as the Bodhisattva evolves through one *bhūmi* after another, until eventually 'great wisdom' is attained. Such wisdom comes from the proceeds of *samādhi* upon the nature of appearing phenomena and the *saṃskāras* that are the 'causes and conditions'. Their basic Watery nature is comprehended, and the Bodhisattva-*yogin* then works to eliminate them as conditioning factors in his/her psyche. The unruly nature of *saṃskāras* distort consciousness, preventing clear thought and therefore must be calmed, controlled and transformed, if the intended service work is to be accomplished. This is crucial, and such meditations are key to the Bodhisattva's future success.

In a sense, Libra represents the meditative interlude for all Bodhisattvas before further testing is applied in Scorpio (depending upon the Bodhisattva *bhūmi* they have achieved), with wisdom the consequent gain, symbolically achieved in the polar opposite of Scorpio, Taurus the bull.

The Bodhisattva can now penetrate the veils preventing the higher revelations and pacify the Wrathful Deities, the Heruka guardians of the *dharma,* as the Watery Element is mastered,[35] producing compassionate insight in the field of service. Compassion rides upon Watery empowerment and its mastery constitutes attaining the second Initiation.

The fifth Bodhisattva *bhūmi* is developed in Scorpio, by mastering major testings through the application of the arenas of service discovered. 'Invincible strength upon the path' is consequently gained. Such strength is gradually developed, built upon and intensified from having attained the first Initiation onwards. At every step of the way, however, testings are met and the related obstacles to the development of the Bodhisattva virtues must be overcome. All attributes of Dependent Origination are analysed for all levels of its expression, so that the challenges concerning overcoming its conditionings can be met at whatever level the Bodhisattva is at. The arena of service work can then manifest to mitigate the evil effects of group and national forms of *karma.* In doing so more obstacles to assisting humanity are met, and so the wheel turns as they are overcome through the wise action of the Bodhisattva, thereby laying the foundation for attaining the higher Initiations.

The eventual purpose is to make void the conditionings that generate the various originations. The gains of former meditative absorption are applied in the rigours of practice via the skilful means of the Bodhisattva. The resultant *samādhi* is now 'not otherwise' than what must be done with respect to humanity's true needs.

Here the Bodhisattva is impaled upon the fixed cross of steadfast serene intent, with arms outstretched in an attitude of giving. He/she takes the guise of Avalokiteśvara as the testings are mastered. Many 'hands' are psychically generated to awaken all of the potencies in the *nāḍīs* and Head lotus,[36] producing enlightenment. Corresponding with this internal effort is the outer field of service work, where the 'hands' represent the forces and skills generated needed to rightly educate humanity in the chosen service arena. Thus the 'invincible strength upon the path' is generated.

After passing the tests in this *bhūmi* the wheel turns to its polar opposite, Taurus. This produces a consequent liberation from the field of

35 This process is the principal topic of the fifth Volume of this series, *An Esoteric Interpretation of the Bardo Thödol.*

36 The symbolism of Avalokiteśvara and the significance of these 'hands' is thoroughly explored in Volumes 4 and 5.

desire, at whatever subtle level of expression it may exist. The wheel then moves towards Capricorn, where complete mastery of rebirth is achieved. The 'invincible strength' therefore comes as a consequence of being desireless, other than that which relates to the liberation of all beings.

Upon the eastern arm of the fixed cross in the sign Taurus, wherein the type of liberation accessible to the sixth Bodhisattva *bhūmi* is attained, the entire field of desire is conquered. This produces 'the presence of the awakened Mind'. Consequently the second Initiation is attained, signifying mastery of the entire Watery domain. The all-seeing Eye is awakened, allowing the Bodhisattva to see via the activities of the Solar Plexus centre. This brings into manifestation the lower *siddhis* at this stage of his/her evolution, or the transmundane *siddhis* via the Head lotus upon attaining the higher *bhūmis*. The Bodhisattva can then see far into the future and deep into the past, allowing the conscious comprehension of the *karma* of those served, so that the *karma* can be appropriately rectified.

The victory over desire-attachment has produced mastery of all the fruits of the earth via the awakening of the Mind. The Bodhisattva becomes a fully integrated and accepted member of the Council of Bodhisattvas, joining in the combined meditative effort for the liberation of all. The lore of Secret Mantra is now accessible, as the attributes of the Fiery, Airy and Aetheric Elements become fully expressed, producing liberation via calming the mind. This happens in the signs Aries through to Capricorn, which govern the qualities developed in the highest Bodhisattva stages.

Aries governs the development of the seventh *bhūmi* wherein the Middle Path *(madhyamaka)* of the intricacies of the Heart's Mind are explored. The *samādhi* developed allows one to eventually be absorbed in the revelations of the way of compassionate unfoldment manifesting throughout space via the emptiness of Mind, producing the realisation of *śūnyatā*. For those still unfolding the first six *bhūmis*, however, the Fiery focussed mental intent towards abstract thinking in this sign produces the gaining of the *ālayavijñāna* enlightenment (the third Initiation), implying conscious identification with the Sambhogakāya Flower. This Flower (the *tathāgatagarbha)* represents the middle between the extremes of *śūnyatā* and *saṃsāra*. *Antaḥkaraṇas* can then be consequently directed to Shambhala, via the development of the abstract Mind, as the Bodhisattva contemplates great vistas of service work via the various outlets available. The Arian energies instigate every new Bodhisattvic venture in the domain of Mind. The Clear Light of Mind is established, producing 'the far-reaching stage of awakening' that will eventually allow the type of perception accorded to a Tathāgata to be realised.

Pisces, being the sign of death and the resultant severance of ties to all forms of *saṃsāric* affiliations, subjective and refined, as well as empirical and obvious, so that vaster vistas of compassionate service can be attained, establishes the eighth of the Bodhisattva *bhūmis*, 'the steadfastness of the Bodhisattva virtue'. Old bonds are sacrificially broken so that *antaḥkaraṇas* can be projected towards the vision of a greater, more beneficent future for all. The Watery dispensation of our earth sphere is eliminated, and new vistas of cosmos are established, as the approach of Buddhahood now awakens in the Bodhisattva's Mind. The time for breaking the bond to all upon earth hence manifests upon the event horizon. Prior to this, however, the detachments leading to the death of the Sambhogakāya Flower are accomplished as a consequence of the steadfast efforts of the Bodhisattva path. The Bodhisattva is so absorbed in compassionate thought and activity that the intermediate vehicle acting as a consciousness-store and liberating mechanism is no longer needed. The compassionate rhythm is self-sustaining and all encompassing, with the driving *vāsanā* to Buddhahood being the motor for all action.

Absorption into the *śūnyatā* revelation (being 'without extremes')[37] now looms, having mastered all forms of co-actively produced phenomena. (Symbolised by breaking the bonds that unites the two fishes composing the glyph of Pisces.) The Airy Element becomes the focus of development, and the *dharmakāya* is part of the Initiate's ken. The *śūnyatā* experience produces the 'steadfastness of the Bodhisattva virtue', where 'no extremes' are possible, there being no bounds to the Bodhisattva's compassionate expression, or to the experience of *śūnyatā*.

Aquarius represents the free-flowing freedom of expression that is the gain of the attainment of *śūnyatā,* which is coupled to the expression of the ninth *bhūmi,* 'meritorious Buddha-like wisdom'. The Bodhisattva now meditates upon the remaining *karma* of self-volition he/she possesses, whilst preparing for Buddhahood. The *karma* must

37 This relates to undertaking the fourth Initiation, which represents the epitome of the Bodhisattva virtue and vow.

be skilfully resolved in a way that allows those that possess positive consciousness-links to the Bodhisattva to be carried to the 'other shore', to the destined arena in cosmos. There the *nirvāṇee*[38] prepares for their coming. The vow to never cease striving until all have been liberated continues no matter where the Initiate exists. The vastness and duration of this vow demonstrates the 'meritorious Buddha-like wisdom'. Aquarius affords the unobstructed movement of energies in all arenas of being/non-being that the Bodhisattva now embraces. This allows the function of being the water bearer, pouring forth the Waters of Life to adequately quench the spiritual thirst of all needy supplicants. The prototype Bodhisattva has appeared and nothing can stop the shedding of symbolic tears of compassion for all who suffer. The fluid meditation-Mind ('without character'), spontaneously and instantly analyses the way of cleansing and eliminating group *karma,* to which the Bodhisattva is still bonded and which becomes the Bodhisattva's way. Everyone must be delivered to 'the other shore'. There being no bounds to the extent of such meditation.

Finally we have the Thusness expressed in Capricorn at the tenth *bhūmi* and the pinnacle of earthly attainment. The Bodhisattva's *karma* with the earth sphere is well-nigh exhausted, as it presents a limitation of what can be done to relieve suffering wherever it exists in cosmos. The mode of karmic rectification of sentient beings in cosmos is now an inclusive part of the meditation of the Bodhisattva as he/she stands upon the great heights of the mountain of achievement. Cosmic Mind *(dharmakāya)* is appropriately accessed and represents 'the *dharma* cloud of revelation that liberates' all. The Bodhisattva is now a Master of Wisdom (a fifth degree Initiate). Vast is the meditative insight and inexplicable is the perception when the mantle of Buddhahood falls upon the Bodhisattva's shoulders as the next step of the path advances that will inevitably lead such a one away from earth service upon any of the cosmic Paths.

The type of movement of this wheel of ten signs can be viewed in terms of spiral-eights, implying cycle after cycle of progressively

38 The term *nirvāṇee* is utilised to denote one who has entered the state of *nirvāṇa,* signifying 'extinguished', the state beyond sorrow, residence in *śūnyatā.* The alternate rendering is *nirvāṇī.*

spiralling forms of enlightened activity. When the spirals are placed one on top of another, they effectively form a backbone that houses the main *nāḍīs* in their ascension to the 1,000 petalled lotus. Here, however, we observe the activities of the sum of the Bodhisattvas upon this planet, who draw all sentient beings to enlightenment (literally to Shambhala being the planetary Head centre). From this perspective, a Master of Wisdom can be considered to be one who is responsive to energies and attributes from Shambhala via an awakened Head centre.

There is always a dynamic, fluid mutability and instantaneous perception at all times in enlightened beings, hence we see that each Bodhisattva effectively progresses through a version of each of these ten stages whilst passing the Initiation level for a particular *bhūmi* before the next stage is reached. One level merges into the next in the form of the abovementioned spiral. Bodhisattvas enter into the next respective *bhūmi* for them after they have completed the requisite work, when the associated sign rules or is significantly aspected in their natal chart.

Gemini and Sagittarius are not part of this exposé because Gemini represents the place of residence of the Bodhisattva (the temple), within which his/her compassion is generated and from which it emanates. It is the temple of worship, be this the temple of the body, of consciousness, or that expressive of *śūnyatā* or beyond. Sagittarius fires the arrows of conscious direction in the arenas of service work in all of the Bodhisattva stages. The two signs also represent two arms of the mutable cross, of constantly recurring mutable activity, which is diminished upon the Bodhisattva path. Bodhisattvas instead manifest steadfast, poised purpose upon the fixed cross. All mutable form of action is governed by this cross, or by the cardinal cross of resolute dynamic Will.

The arm of the wheel represented by the Scorpio-Taurus polarity signifies the nature of the major work of all Bodhisattvas upon the fixed cross of compassionate intent. The arm representing the Cancer-Capricorn polarity indicates the cardinal cross's empowerment of enlightenment when the *karma* for liberation repeats itself prior to any Initiation. The remaining six signs (Leo, Virgo, Libra, Aries, Pisces and Aquarius) represent forms of activity of Bodhisattvas in their fields of service, and what is effectively a left to right or right to left movement for them. The Bodhisattva plunges into the depths of *saṃsāra* in the five lower signs in order to inspire and to liberate, producing the symbolism of an associated retrograde motion of the wheel. This is a right to left motion, figuratively speaking[39] (the mirror image of the motion that is perceived when looking at Figure 6), which occurs with respect to the Bodhisattva's life in the signs from Cancer to Libra. It concerns the Bodhisattva's activity amongst those needing to reverse their mode of travel in *saṃsāra* so that they can progress upon the rectified wheel. In Libra, the need for a contemplative lifestyle is taught, whereby serenity can be developed, consequently producing insights into all of the causes of *māyā* and self-produced phenomena. In a Virgoan cycle, avarice, vanity, and materialistic tendencies in humanity are specifically tackled. In a Leonine cycle, the difficult task ensues related to converting all forms of self-focussed, selfish, mentalistic and prideful activity into their opposites. The Cancerian meditation tackles the major forms of emotionality. Scorpio sums up all of this activity in the form of the major testings needed to be passed in order to attain Initiation. Hence, all of the previous transformative battles accomplished in the other signs are brought to a final resolution so that they can be mastered.

From Scorpio the wheel moves to Capricorn via Taurus, to cleanse human foibles. Another cycle then starts moving from Capricorn to Taurus. This a figurative left to right motion of the spiral-eight referring to the Bodhisattva's inner life. Initiation occurs in Capricorn allowing the Bodhisattva access to a higher strata of revelation than ever before. Capricorn represents the Door of cosmic Mind providing the Bodhisattva/Initiate access to all Minds that have similarly attained the summit of achievement and have earlier gained liberation upon higher turns of the wheel. The Bodhisattva can then evoke the compassionate Waters of Life *(bodhicitta)* that can be dispensed to humanity in Aquarius.

Aquarius represents an active, selfless striving for greater enlightened status, enabling the Bodhisattva to emulate the qualities of the subjective archetype of all Bodhisattvas, Avalokiteśvara. The Bodhisattva esoterically looks from above, from a great height, and evokes a wise compassionate stance for the suffering ones below, formulating the plan of how best to assist (utilising the symbolic thousand arms of his/her

39 Astrologically, however, the movement from Aries through Taurus to Capricorn represents the right hand path, the rectified wheel; whereas that from Aries through Pisces represents the left hand path, the reversed wheel. It is also the way of the precession of the equinoxes.

Head lotus to do so). In Pisces the process producing the death of the last vestiges of ego manifests in the Bodhisattva's Mind, facilitating a greater capability to serve. In Aries there is the generation of the higher or Divine Will that overcomes all impediments preventing the elimination of the planetary woe (according to the limitations of the available *karma),* as well as being able to pierce the veils concerning the ability to travel upon any of the cosmic Paths. There is a consequent strengthening of the will in the instigation of all new beginnings in the fields of service. Taurus then generates greater wisdom and spiritual insight as to the present need. The all-seeing Eye penetrates deep into the mysteries of being-nonbeing *(dharmakāya)* so that the new service construct can be rightly built. This is necessary if the Bodhisattva is to gain the continuous insights needed to clothe the *maṇḍalas* that will educate the increasingly enlightened ones being served.

Aries-Pisces produce the will to achieve (Aries) and the sacrificial intent (Pisces) to overcome all barriers preventing the good of the all from manifesting. Taurus-Cancer builds the house of the construct whereby the new forms of service can incarnate to integrate the needy into its protective embrace. Until such activity has happened within the Bodhisattva's psyche and cogently applied, the wheel turns from right to left to serve those with emotional minds. The wheel rectifies when wise decisions have been made contemplatively by them in Libra producing the testings in Scorpio, and eventual Initiation in Capricorn.

The list of the petals of the Heart centre given in the *'Samādhi "Great Gate of Diamond Liberation"'* is in the order of the reversed wheel, rather than that of the rectified one.[40] This is because the view is in terms of the meditation of a high level Bodhisattva manifesting in Aquarius (the sign of group interrelations and Bodhisattvic service), who contemplates the mode of future service work via the polar opposite of Aquarius, Leo. Leo represents the vehicle of appearance, the *nirmāṇakāya* of the Bodhisattva, through which humanity is served. Leo is the focal point activating the fixed cross of the Bodhisattva's compassionate career.

The meditation of a Bodhisattva depends upon the level of attainment achieved via any of the three forms of Thusness:

40 It moves from Aquarius to Pisces via Capricorn.

a. That related to the *dharmakāya,* here simply denoted 'Thusness'. It needs no descriptive qualification because it is the Buddha-Mind. Bodhisattvas of the eighth, ninth and tenth *bhūmis* are focussed upon the attainment and demonstration of its qualities. The eighth and ninth *bhūmis* relate to the stages of mastering the ability to reside in *dharmakāya,* which is only properly achieved at the tenth. After this one can conceive an effective reversal of the wheel, with some further Bodhisattvic activity manifesting in Aquarius, relating to cleansing *karma* of a subtle nature, and finally severing ties to the earth and entering the freedom of cosmos as a Buddha in the sign Pisces.

b. That related to *śūnyatā.* For those developing calmness of mind and are seeking to tread the 'Middle Path' between extremes, the true goal is the liberation that *śūnyatā* provides. *Śūnyatā* becomes the target to which the one-pointed archer fires his arrows of clear reason to pierce all veils. The one-pointed focus of the meditation-Mind of the Sagittarian has eliminated all forms of the discursive mind, leaving only an 'Error-free Thusness' as the ultimate gain. In the Void there is nothing to relate to phenomena or to consciousness that can make an error. As this is the mode of travel for all Bodhisattvas, so the Sagittarian focus provides their target. The seventh, eighth and ninth *bhūmis* concerns the ability of the Bodhisattva to reside continuously in *śūnyatā.*

First needed is calmness of mind (via Gemini, the polar opposite of Sagittarius), which is refined in *samādhi* (Libra). Then all of the tests and trials that will inevitably produce 'error-free' insights of the nature of the Void in Scorpio must be mastered. The Sagittarian focussed intent generates the *dhāraṇīs* to overcome such obstacles. The generated wisdom attained in Taurus as each testing is mastered facilitates the attainment of varying degrees of liberation, allowing the higher *bhūmis* to be trod until Voidness is achieved. The will to transmute base *saṃskāras* is generated in Aries, until the aperture of the Eye of the Sambhogakāya Flower is so broadened in Pisces that it can no longer withstand the potency and its death ensues. (This aperture allows all directions in space to be accessed, with no possibility of *mayāvirūpic* allurement distorting the view.) The experience of the Void is stabilised in Aquarius, and its Waters *(bodhicitta)* can pour forth to quench the needy via the embodied vehicle, Leo, Aquarius' polar opposite.

c. That related to the Sambhogakāya Flower. The testings in Scorpio lay the groundwork for the experiences of all the *bhūmis* at each level of expression that need to be successfully mastered. Such testings become vaster in scope and more subtle as the higher *bhūmis* are trod. The characteristic finally developed is the 'not otherwise Thusness'. For the major part of the process (the first seven *bhūmis* wherein 'the Middle Path' is sought) the testings relate to abstraction into the Sambhogakāya Flower. This form of Thusness is 'not otherwise' because it is relegated to the precincts of the abstract Mind. Consciousness is abstracted, cleansed of defilements, and poised in the Clear Light, being the medium of expression for revelations from the *dharmakāya*. The revelations received are consequently conveyed via Thusness. They are 'not otherwise'.

    The Sambhogakāya Flower is the middle between the Monadic presence *(dharmakāya)* and the incarnate personality. Bodhisattvas of the first seven *bhūmis* work to continuously reside in its Light, allowing the ability to see through the Śūnyatā Eye to discern the real. To do so they must pass all the tests in Scorpio concerning the elimination of concepts of a personal 'self'. In these levels they attain the ability to identify with the Sambhogakāya Flower wherein Thusness can be experienced via the Śūnyatā Eye.

The significance of Gemini the twins (one of whom is immortal and the other mortal) in this process should be noted. The centres below the diaphragm (the Solar Plexus, Sacral, and Base of Spine centres) constitute the mortal brother. They govern the sensual person, who is principally fed by emotional and physical energies. Later, as the person becomes more mentally and spiritually polarised, the centres above the diaphragm (the immortal brother) are increasingly vivified by energies from the higher realms and the sublimated energies from the lower *chakras*. This makes the Gemini subject ever responsive to the dominant subjective forces that energise and cause the crystallisation of the motives for all his actions.

The *prāṇas* associated with both groupings of *chakras* can be considered 'other causes of *māyā'* that the Gemini subject must learn to properly interrelate through the development of calmness of mind *(śamatha). Māyā* can be considered to be the forces *(saṃskāra)* or energies that produce deceptive images to the mind that flow through the etheric body, the true human form.

Because it rules the etheric body and the associated *nāḍī* system, so Gemini also governs the nervous and blood systems, the dense externalisations of the *nāḍīs*. Gemini therefore conditions the sensitivity of the person's reaction to external stimuli and the development of consciousness in such a way that fluid interactions and exchanges of information between all around becomes possible. From this perspective, Gemini is the Temple of Life consciously accessed by the *yogin* in his meditation, who takes the guise of the one-pointed archer (Sagittarius) firing arrows of directed contemplative will to awaken the major and minor target *chakras* in the *nāḍīs*.

The immortal brother signifies the *chakras* above the diaphragm (the Heart, Throat, Ājñā and Head centres) that govern the planes of reality. Here enlightenment is gained, where the *prāṇas* awakening the Heart of Life produce liberation from all forms of bondage.

In Libra all the issues concerning the innate duality of the twins (both internal and external) are brought to equilibrium, a field of resolution. The law of the good can then dominate all relationships and activities. The mortal brother can also signify humanity, and the immortal one the Council of Bodhisattvas. The externalisation process of this Council represents an eventual successful linking of the hands of the Brothers on a planetary scale. This process will allow Maitreya to appear and to irradiate all with his light and wisdom, facilitating the liberation for all that is the Taurean field of service. The Initiation path will then be appropriately revealed so that the higher *bhūmis* can be undertaken by all.

Much that has so far been provided concerning the spiry Bodhisattva Way can be expanded upon by the earnest student.

Further astrological considerations

In considering further Astrological implications, it should be reiterated that the wheel of the Heart is divided into seven sacred and five non-sacred petals. The five non-sacred petals process the *prāṇas* derived from the five sense-perceptions. This incorporates experiences gained from the formed realms via the twelve stages of Dependent Origination whereby consciousness evolves. The non-sacred *prāṇas* are absorbed from the southern portion of the *maṇḍala*[41] of the Heart lotus. They transform sense perceptions into higher, more embracive qualities, so that eventually the wisdoms of the five Dhyāni Buddhas are evoked. Briefly speaking we have:

1. The sense of *smell–Taurus* the bull, concerns the liberation produced through calming the mind. Being the highest or most subtle of senses, it is appropriate that smell relates to the most refined types of human activity. The subtlest aromas or perfumes of enlightenment are only experienced in the rarefied spaces of the meditation-Mind. Taurus normally embodies the Earthy Element, but in this connotation we have the Aetheric reflex of the Earth.
2. The sense of *Taste—Gemini* the twins and the expression of *'calmness of mind'*. Only through calmness can one develop the ability to literally 'taste' the *dharma* as experiential truth so as to distinguish it from untruth. All of the 'other causes of *māyā'* can likewise be tasted, to be able to unequivocally distinguish each for what they truly are. The general *prāṇic* flow in the *nāḍīs* can therefore be digested and integrated into consciousness.
3. The sense of *Touch—Cancer* the crab and the process of *'discerning the real'*. The touch in this southernmost position is not just concerned with material things, but also with the sum of the Watery emotional world. Only through the sense of touch can one properly discern the real, the true validity of things; as sight is prone to illusions, whilst smell and taste deal with subtleties, and hearing responds to sounds, which can come from any direction. The crab lives in the dual Watery-Earthy realm that allows this

41 It should be noted that the twelve pairs of ribs in the chest cavity, ruled by Cancer, are physiologically divided into seven pairs, called 'true pairs' in the texts (symbolised by the seven sacred planets or petals), and five 'false pairs' (symbolised by the five non-sacred planets, or petals of the Heart centre).

sense to properly express itself in all *saṃsāric* arenas. From a higher perspective, an enlightened person can touch the sublime levels of the *dharmakāya* and so experience the truth of the *dharma*.

4. The sense of *Sight–Leo* the lion and the quality of *Voidness*. Leo governs the development of the Fiery attributes of the mind of self-conscious individuals and therefore the ability to visualise and to perceive. Leo is the ruler of the jungle of animal-like passions developed by the 'I' that views all things in relation to itself. It is the stalking lion seeking to pounce upon anything it wishes. The higher 'lion' (the Sambhogakāya Flower) stalks the prey of the enlightenment that causes a *yogin* to eliminate the *saṃskāras* of 'self'. The Void comes into view when the 'I' ceases to be empowered in any way.
5. The sense of *Hearing—Virgo* the virgin and the quality of *'comprehending it'*. Hearing is the most limiting of the senses and demands sound which comes from the interrelation of things concrete, the Earthy Element governed by Virgo. When one hears something it immediately produces a response in the mind towards its comprehension. Otherwise, meaningless sounds and noises are heard producing a destructive intent in consciousness. Later, the inner hearing of a *yogin* is developed, enabling hearing of mantra from sublime levels of being.

The polar opposites of these five signs are responsible for transmuting the essences of the five Elements. Thus the heightened subliminal perceptions associated with the sense of taste in Gemini, that are expressed via calmness of mind, become transformed into error-free Thusness via the focussed application of the cleansing Fires in Sagittarius. The mental calmness developed in Gemini, that heightens the ability of one to perceive what is, becomes focussed and applied one-pointedly in Sagittarius to pierce the veils to the experience that *śūnyatā* affords. The *prāṇas* that enter via the Gemini gate are stripped of their unessential characteristics via the technique of *śamatha* and are further refined when they pass through the centre of the *maṇḍala* of the Heart *chakra* (the most sacred shrine, the adytum within the temple governed by Gemini), along the axis towards the polar opposite of Gemini. Sagittarius burns the dross with the most rarefied Fire, and the resultant *prāṇas,* which are now void of characteristics, are projected as error-free arrows into the Thusness that is the Void. The Airy Void Element is consequently produced.

The Watery material substance that is 'touched' and discerned to be not real in Cancer is transformed into Thusness, once one has manifested the continuous cyclic transformative effort via the Bodhisattva *bhūmis.* This is esoterically termed 'scaling the heights' in Capricorn. The Bodhisattva continuously refines and clarifies the substance of his/her mind so that unessentials become extinguished. The mind is then moulded upon the pattern of the paradigm of the *dharmakāya* and once the veil of *śūnyatā* is penetrated then the paradigm holds the Thusness. The pinnacle of earthly attainment has been reached. The Watery Void Element is created by means of being dried out by the Fiery intensity of Capricorn.

In order to ascertain that something truly exists it must be touched, as the other sense-perceptors offer possibilities of being deceived. The concern is not just of the phenomena experienced upon the earth, depicted as *saṃsāra* (which the enlightened one knows to be illusional), but with its transmuted correspondence in cosmos. The realms of *dharmakāya* are immeasurably vast and their nature has never been more than briefly depicted in any scripture. This domain, the cosmic astral ocean, is at first explored via its corresponding Void Element. The liberated one esoterically touches the new that becomes established in the bliss-aura of the 'beyond', surpassing all earthly considerations. What has formerly been perceived existent is now thoroughly experienced, with much detail of the new revealed, but there is no exact way of depicting such information utilising present terminology. Volumes 6, 7 and later books shall, however, provide some detail, as Shambhala represents one *chakra* existing in *dharmakāya* that thereby has the ability to communicate with other such centres.

The ability to enlighteningly vision, though in terms of a subtly pervasive notion of the sense of 'I', manifests in Leo during the earlier Bodhisattva *bhūmis.* Such perception is transformed into universality, oneness, termed 'lack of character', as expressed by the ideal Bodhisattva of the higher *bhūmis,* in Aquarius. The entire field of service upon the earth is then clearly seen by the Bodhisattva, allowing the dispensation of the Waters of Life to all needy ones. The Bodhisattva consciously becomes part of an enlightened group meditation working for planetary transformation and the liberation of everyone from the thraldom of *māyā.*

The *prāṇas* flowing from the Leonine to the Aquarian petal of the Heart lotus become cleansed of all *samskāras* that bind consciousness to the limitations associated with the conceptions of 'self'. The Airy attributes of Aquarius fans and refine the Fires of Leo until only the most rarefied Fire remains as its Void Element.

The sense of hearing in Virgo allows clear comprehension of all the sounds in Nature and of one's physical plane living. When this sense-perception is transmuted by the enlightened one in Pisces then all *mantric* sounds governing manifest being can be heard. The co-actively produced phenomena of those swimming in the waters of sensation *(saṃsāra)* can then be directed to produce eventual enlightenment for all. The enlightened one therefore resides at the bridge between the extremes of both *saṃsāra* and *nirvāṇa*. The Watery attributes of Pisces washes clean the most defiling dross of the Earthy Element, so that only the most purified aspect remains as the Earthy Void Element. The ability to hear and convey all forms of mantric sound then expresses the potency governing the All-accomplishing Wisdom of Amoghasiddhi, where Virgo embodies the sum of all types of Earthy substance[42] that can be controlled by sound. Pisces, having washed clean the dross of substance producing the Earthy Void, then helps produce the clarified resonance of the mantric sound.

Similarly, the Discriminating Wisdom of Amitābha is the expression of the universal Mind gained through the elimination of the concept of 'self' in Leo, where Voidness is produced by the Airy Aquarian petal ('Lack of Character') that intensifies the Leonine Fires.

As one climbs up the spiral-cyclic ladder created by the successive turning of the twelve petals of this wheel of Love, starting (at every new level) from the base of 'Discerning the Real', established in Cancer, the Watery, emotional-desire dross is eventually dried away. This is accomplished by the Fiery blaze from the Capricornian petal (Thusness). The eventual gain is the Equalising Wisdom of Ratnasambhava.

---

42 See Volume 1, chapter 6, for the reasons for my assignment of the Elements to the Jinas, which differ somewhat from the normal assignments derived from *The Bardo Thödol.*

The Sagittarian petal (error-free Thusness) conveys the *prāṇas* of the Mirror-like Wisdom of Akṣobhya once calmness of mind has been achieved in Gemini. The liberated Archer fires the arrows of directed purpose for all beings to achieve the *śūnyatā* goal. (These arrows are like rays of the sun reflected by a mirror.) Once the base has been established in *śūnyatā* then the *will* can be directed either towards the *dharmakāya* (Thusness) or towards the *ālayavijñāna* ('not otherwise Thusness') in order to accomplish Bodhisattvic purpose. This is the basis of Akṣobhya's wisdom, for he mirrors the qualities of one into the other.

The Earthy (esoterically Aetheric) aspect of Taurus represents the combined *prāṇas* of the four above Elements, viewed in their most refined attributes (stimulating the sense of smell). They are melded together to produce the Dharmadhātu Wisdom of Vairocana and brought to their essences by means of the transmutative process represented by the polar opposite of Taurus, Scorpio. Scorpio consequently is the general place of tribulation, condensation, distillation, refinement, and sublimation of these Elements. This process necessitates the use of the Watery Element to wash clean the sum of the stains of the Earth. The entire field of desire, originally sown in Taurus, is transformed into selfless compassion. Compassion (viewed as the force of *bodhicitta)* helps produce liberation.

The abstracted Watery *prāṇas* of Love are exemplified in this entire schema because Love-Wisdom is the major quality to be developed by humanity as they tread the Bodhisattva *bhūmis*. Esoterically, they consequently evolve out of the confines of the cosmic Earthy domain,[43] and into the Watery cosmic astral ocean, which relates to the second level of *dharmakāya*. Herein the various Logoi of the general population of stars in our local galaxy manifest compassionate interrelations. This then signifies the 'liberation' attributed to the Taurean petal. It is the ultimate gain of the activity that awakens the twelve petals of the Heart centre.

Taurus and Scorpio therefore admix and process the general *prāṇas* of the Heart lotus. In the elementary stages, the field of desire in Taurus establishes the pleasurable loving interrelationships, and forms of union with 'the other', constituting the basis for the manifestation of conjoined

43 This domain constitutes the 'womb' of our evolution on earth.

karma. (Such desirous activity is at that stage intensified in Scorpio.) Concern for one's lovers, family, and friends generates the basic *prāṇas* that are then accommodated by the Heart centre. Much attachment to the object of one's affectionate and loving activities, however, occurs via the centres below the diaphragm, hence eventual suffering.

After the path to liberation is sought and the aspirant enters Scorpio (the polar opposite of Taurus), he/she battles to be freed from all forms of attachment. The objective being the ability to Love dispassionately and universally, via right knowledge, to evoke wisdom. The aspirant has learnt that the only true method of release from suffering concerns treading the Bodhisattva path. Therefore he/she undergoes the trials and testings upon that path in Scorpio to fully awaken the qualities of the Heart lotus, engendering its *prāṇas*. All of the petals of this *chakra* are consequently awakened and further developed as the Bodhisattva *bhūmis* are trod. Liberation (the unfettered expression of the qualities of the Heart lotus) occurs when one finally re-enters the sign Taurus.

The Taurus-Scorpio polarity therefore acts as a medium of transformation of the five *prāṇas* derived from loving *saṃsāric* interrelationships (as engendered by the lower, southern petals of the Heart lotus) into the *prāṇas* of the five Tathāgata Wisdoms associated with the five northern petals. The tests in Scorpio also cause many types of *prāṇas* to be rejected as not worthy of being expressed as aspects of the Heart. They are then directed to the Splenic centre for further processing. Taurus principally processes the most refined Earthy-Watery *prāṇas* from the Solar Plexus centre. Scorpio deals with the Watery-Earthy *prāṇas*. The focus of these two signs is the refining of the *piṇgalā nāḍī prāṇas* by further cleansing their Earthy impediments. They can then be utilised in the northern portion of the Heart centre's *maṇḍala* to awaken the all-seeing Eye.

The horizontal line of the Heart *maṇḍala*, represented by Aries and Libra, concerns the mechanism of a mirror that reflects one hemisphere of the *maṇḍala* into the other. This is accomplished by the *samādhi* that is the hallmark of Libra, assisted by Aries, which represents the mind's focussing power projecting the seed *bījas* that will flower into inevitable enlightenment. The 'not otherwise Thusness' then manifests upon the compassionate path of the Bodhisattva. Thus the 'Middle Path' is followed in all forms of activity through ever-subtler turnings of the wheel, as signified by the Arian petal. These two signs continuously recycle the *karma* of the transmutative process so that all of the other signs can produce the Void Elements.

The sacred petals of the Heart centre

It should be noted that the Heart centre is the serene ocean of absorption of the *piṇgalā* stream. In a similar manner, the Throat centre absorbs *iḍā nāḍī prāṇas,* though they are generated by the centres below the diaphragm. The 1,000 Petalled Lotus integrates both streams and anchors the potency of *suṣumṇā* when it is released.

The seven *sacred petals* are qualified by the seven Rays of light, as well as incorporating the transmuted correspondences of the five senses. They qualify the sum of the space occupied by being/non-being, and are depicted by the remaining seven parts of the listing of this *samādhi,* 'not otherwise Thusness', 'error-free Thusness', etc.

- First Ray of Will or Power, Aries the Ram—'the Middle Path'.
- Second Ray of Love-Wisdom, Libra the balances—the *samādhī* that awakens the Middle Path.
- Third Ray of Mathematically Exact Activity, Capricorn the goat—Thusness.
- Fourth Ray of Beautifying Harmony overcoming Strife, Sagittarius the archer—'error-free Thusness'.
- Fifth Ray of Scientific Reasoning, Aquarius the water bearer—the Thusness *(śūnyatā)* lacking character.
- Sixth Ray of Devotion, Scorpio the scorpion—'not otherwise Thusness'.
- Seventh Ray of Cyclic, Ceremonial Activity, Pisces the fishes—that which is 'without one extreme'.

The Aries-Libra interrelation generates the attributes of the first and second Rays for this entire wheel of the Heart centre, despite the fact that none of their planetary rulers are upon this Ray. The first Ray concerns abstraction and Initiation, producing the death of all types of forms, whilst the second Ray is the major synthesising Ray, absorbing the refined qualities of all the others. The first and second Rays govern the east-west orientation of the zodiac attuned to the Heart centre. They concern the abstraction of empirical thought into the domain of Mind that is the way of the Heart (Aries), and the activity of the wheel that will inevitably produce this abstraction (Libra). The will to initiate the movement of the wheel, and of any new cycle, is projected via Aries, whilst Libra regulates the duration of the related cycles of activity. At first the developed Libran individual oscillates between the material domain and the liberated, making choices along the way. The law of *karma* intercedes and helps in the decision making, so that later upon the path the balances swing to choosing a contemplative life wherein Love-Wisdom is gained. This becomes the keynote for the law that is dispensed in this sign. The second Ray of Love-Wisdom governs the manifesting purpose of the *karma* that conditions the path of liberation. It is the beneficial result of karmic involvement with *saṃsāra*. The lord of *karma*, however, is Saturn, which is governed by the third Ray of Mathematically Exact Activity because it rules the *karma* forming attachments with *saṃsāra* that is the output of the empirical mind. This Saturnian influence, plus the law of cycles governed by Libra, gives Libra exoterically a general third Ray attribute. Within this context it controls the world of human affairs, with the additional influence of its exoteric ruler, Venus,[44] which governs the expression of the mind/Mind. For the Bodhisattva (the Initiate), however, 'Divine Love'[45] and understanding is the governing influence because the objective of the cycles of activity is to bring all to the Heart of Life.

Once the meditative balance is achieved then 'the Middle Path' associated with the sign Aries can be trod. This Middle Path is the

44 Three sets of rulers to the signs are presented in *Esoteric Astrology*, 68. First we have the orthodox ruler governing the average person, next is that pertaining to the aspirant to enlightenment, and finally that which conditions enlightened beings and the domain they reside in (the Hierarchical ruler). We thus have: *Aries* (Mars, Mercury, Uranus); *Taurus* (Venus, Vulcan, Vulcan); *Gemini* (Mercury, Venus, the Earth); *Cancer* (the Moon, Neptune, Neptune); *Leo* (the Sun, the Sun, the Sun); *Virgo* (Mercury, the Moon, Jupiter); *Libra* (Venus, Uranus, Saturn); *Scorpio* (Mars, Mars, Mercury); *Sagittarius* (Jupiter, the Earth, Mars); *Capricorn* (Saturn, Saturn, Venus); *Aquarius* (Uranus, Jupiter, the Moon); *Pisces* (Jupiter, Pluto, Pluto).

45 *Esoteric Astrology*, 333.

keynote for travelling the way of all the petals of the Heart centre upon the rectified path. The cycles are ritualised by means of the esoteric ruler of Libra, Uranus (ruler of the seventh Ray of Ceremonial Activity), which externalises the subjective directives of the third Ray.

The third Ray garners the *karma* generated and mathematically directs its manifestation, whereas the second Ray works to convert the effects of all karmic action into Love and Wisdom. The first Ray (from Aries) cuts the roots of all karmic action. The empirical mind (Venus) wedded to the desire-emotional body generates *karma*. Hence the story of *karma* is told in movement from the sign Libra to Aries. It necessitates travelling up the mountainous path (Capricorn, the mount of *karma),* via the Bodhisattva *bhūmis*. In Capricorn we again find Saturn and Venus as the rulers, their purpose being the conversion of the Fires of mind into Mind via the Initiation process. (All three signs are also linked by the arms of the cardinal cross.)

The third to the seventh Rays are Rays of Mind, because they are directly concerned with phenomena and the wisdoms arising through transmutation of experiences from the five sense-perceptors. The Rays of Mind are represented via the different emanations of the Jina wisdoms, whilst the second Ray integrates these wisdoms in terms of the principle of Love. The Will, however, must be utilised to overcome *saṃsāra* if wisdom is to be generated.

The east-west line of the zodiac/Heart centre therefore veils the expression of the three major Rays from which the others are derived. This line of interrelation is ruled by the Ādi Buddha, Samantabhadra and his Consort, Krodeśvarī. They govern the turning of the entire wheel of the Heart centre wherein the process of converting the defiled Elements into their Void attributes via the activity of the Bodhisattva path happens.

The first Ray attributed to Aries is literally the refraction of all the seven sub-Rays of the second Ray into manifestation (via the seventh Ray potency of the Hierarchical ruler of Aries). This starts the activity of the wheel of the Heart centre, wherein the signs governing the remaining sub-Rays of this one fundamental Ray manifest their various forms of activity. These energies first impact upon the abstract levels of the Mind. Libra then sows the *karma* of former cycles of activity in such a way that Love-Wisdom is generated, or further refined, and its power broadened. This power manifests via its esoteric ruler, Uranus (whose seventh Ray attribute integrates with that of Aries), that projects the objectives of the sub-Rays of Love-Wisdom by sowing the *karma* of what is to be via Saturn, its Hierarchical ruler. Saturn is then the reaper of the Love that is the gain of it all.

The vertical Cancer-Capricorn line represents the way of ascent of the *bhūmis* up the mount of Initiation and service, from incarnation in Cancer to their conclusion in Capricorn. The third Ray expression dominates the Capricornian purpose. Under its auspices the Fires of Mind ruled by Saturn works to convert the Watery dispensation of Cancer into rarefied Mind as the path of Initiation is trod. Hence Capricorn empowers the transmutative furnace. It is ruled by Saturn esoterically and exoterically. Saturn is the Lord of *karma* and the objective is to turn the Bodhisattva into a Master of Wisdom (of the tenth *bhūmi).* The ascent concerns mastering *saṃskāras* and transforming *karma*. The Equalising Wisdom of Ratnasambhava is first generated as the vicissitudes of life are conquered as one ascends from incarnation in Cancer. The remaining Jina wisdoms are generated as one traverses the path around the zodiac upon this upward way.

The orientation towards cosmos is governed by the *cardinal cross*, where Capricorn represents the open gate away from earth involvement. It is the place of ascent to the higher levels of *dharmakāya,* though Capricorn is governed by the Earthy Element. This Element here actually represents the crystallised Fire *(dharmakāya)* from cosmic sources that has been reified as the mountain of Mind, which the aspiring one seeks to access in order to gain enlightenment. Such is the vision from above-down, but from below-up this mountain is that of the liberating cosmic Mind, the *dharmakāya,* integrated in its lower strata with the substance of mind that is a product of the 'earth' that is *saṃsāra.*

The associated sense-perceptor to the Element Earth is hearing, which indicates that the way to *nirvāṇa* is through the ability to hear and respond to Secret Mantra from the most sublime sources in cosmos. The Element Water governing the polar opposite sign, Cancer, with its corresponding sense-perception of touch, allows one who can knowingly sound Secret Mantra to 'touch' and experience, to mould, the substance of the *dharmakāyic* domains.

Note with respect to Secret Mantra that the way of approach to liberation in the case of Capricorn is via reception to cosmic Mind, whereas that via Taurus liberates one via reception to the cosmic Waters of Love-Wisdom. The northern approach represents the *vajrayāna* path, and the eastern approach the *mahāmudrā*. However, there is very little distinction as one travels the path of Initiation, as both aspects *(iḍā* and *piṅgalā)* are trod simultaneously, but there is a differentiated emphasis according to the Ray equipment of the Bodhisattva concerned. The *vajrayāna* develops all five Jina wisdoms as a unity. The *mahāmudrā* is focussed via the mirror of Akṣobhya-Vajrasattva that manifests as Vairocana's vision. The *iḍā vajrayāna* line awakens the Head lotus and the *piṅgalā mahāmudrā* line the all-seeing Eye. They function as a unity to produce the complete awakening of the Bodhisattva.[46]

The densest aspect of the impacting cosmic Waters upon the higher strata of earth evolution manifests via the sub-Ray aspects of the seventh Ray. Their potency reflects into the lower strata of Mind (via *śūnyatā)* in terms of the first Ray via Pluto, the esoteric and Hierarchical ruler of Pisces. This Ray combination facilitates the transformation of all aspects of the Earthy substance contained in Virgo's womb for those evolving through our planetary manifestation. Consequently, the method of awakening the Piscean petal of the Heart centre is via the seventh Ray. All aspects of the Earthy domain must be conquered, needing the ritualistic aspect of the seventh Ray, however, the second Ray represents the energy of conversion into enlightenment-attributes. (This energy is also conveyed by the orthodox planetary ruler, Jupiter.) This work manifests via Amoghasiddhi's All-accomplishing Wisdom, allowing the entire material domain to be mastered and transformed by the will of the *yogin*. The cycles of rebirth consequently end. The first Ray aspect of Pluto, the esoteric ruler of Pisces, helps to produce this transformation, working via the esoteric ruler of Virgo, the Moon (here veiling the first Ray potency). For the transmutation of base substance the use of the will, backed by Love-Wisdom and focussed via cyclic activity, governed by the seventh Ray, are precisely the energies needed to be wielded by the *yogin*. Mercury, the intuitional Mind, the exoteric ruler of Virgo, represents the crucible whereby this transmutative process happens.

---

46 Accordingly, in some *maṇḍalas* of the Jinas, Akṣobhya is at the heart of the *maṇḍala* and in others it is Vairocana. Also, Akṣobhya appears with a blue body and a radiant white aura, whereas Vairocana has a radiant white body with a blue aura.

Aquarius is the head of the *fixed cross* aspect of the *maṇḍala* of the Heart. It represents the universal Mind governing steadfast Bodhisattvic activity. Consequently, it is the directive agency for the activity of all Bodhisattvas as they travel along their respective *bhūmis.* The fifth Ray of Scientific Reason regulates the mode of expression of their compassionate service. Fanned by the Air, the Fires of the self-focussed empirical mind of Leo (Aquarius' polar opposite) is converted into the mutable, Clear Light of Mind as the Bodhisattva path is trodden. By overcoming the illusion of 'self', the Void is gradually awakened and the Discriminating Inner Wisdom of Amitābha is evoked. The planetary rulers of Aquarius (Jupiter, governing the second Ray of Love-Wisdom, and Uranus, the seventh Ray of Ceremonial Activity) are well disposed to assist in the transformation of mundane thought into wisdom vectors (the second Ray), by means of the ritualistic, transformative abilities of the seventh Ray.

It was shown earlier that the Scorpio-Taurus axis empowers the turning of the spiral-eights of Bodhisattvic activity. Ray six of Devotion (via Mars, the esoteric and orthodox ruler of Scorpio) governs the process of stepping upon this path. Under the auspices of this Ray, the entire Watery disposition of the person must be mastered as desire-emotions are converted to devotion-aspiration to follow the path. The Bodhisattva devotes him/herself to the service of others and aspires to climb the mount to bring all thereto. To do so, the sixth Ray martial energy battles to overcome the various forms of desire-attachment generated in *saṃsāra.* It draws upon the first Ray energy of the Will of Vulcan, the esoteric ruler of Taurus, to convert and transmute the *saṃskāras* into enlightenment-attributes. There is also a fourth Ray energy of Harmony overcoming Strife flowing via Mercury, the Hierarchical ruler of Scorpio,[47] which is the energy governing humanity in general. This energy allows the Bodhisattva to influence all aspects of human affairs, to help produce the transformative challenges converting *kāma-manas* into intuition and eventual enlightenment.

The first and sixth Ray potencies that dominate the expression of these two signs esoterically produce the ability to overcome all allurements of the path so that eventually the Dharmadhātu wisdom of Vairocana can be attained. The general Watery attributes (governed

47 In fact via both Taurus and Scorpio. (See *Esoteric Astrology,* 489-90.)

by Mars) must be converted into the highest compassionate Love by the use of Vulcan's will during the entire path.

The *mutable cross* concerns the method for gaining the experiences in *saṃsāra,* which must eventually be mastered before the attainment of *śūnyatā* is possible. It begins with learning the *dharma* through hearing it in Virgo, then gaining a taste of enlightenment in Gemini. Touching the subtler dimensions of perception follows next in Pisces. This allows firing mantric arrows in Sagittarius to pierce the subtlest veils of perception. This activity increasingly awakens the inner vision, allowing Thusness to be perceived in order to ascertain its 'error-free' status. Inevitably the process becomes automatic, spontaneous, until there is nothing further left to envision in the pristine stillness of the calmness of mind developed in Gemini. The Mirror-like Wisdom of Akṣobhya is thereby attained to end the cycles of mutable activity.

The mode of activity of the fixed cross, the cross of renunciation and compassion, is common to all Mahāyāna schools. However, the south-north arm, the way of ascension by means of Mind, is exemplified by the Yogācāra doctrine, and the Mādhyamika exemplify the east-west arm concerning the development of *bodhicitta.* In general, the consequentialist Prāsaṅgika-Mādhyamika school exemplify the activity of the mutable cross to produce 'the error-free Thusness' of Sagittarius. The Tantric practices of the Nyingma (the Yogācāra-Mādhyamika) exemplify the way of the cardinal cross (ritualistic Tantric meditation), producing the Thusness *(dharmatā)* associated with Capricorn. The Sautrāntika-Mādhyamika integrate these two crosses via the fixed cross, producing the Aquarian 'void of own-character'. These three signs represent the northern triad of the wheel of the Heart centre, signifying ways of liberation from *saṃsāra.*

The petals of the Heart lotus are the paradigm for the expression of the twelve main petals of the 1,000 petalled Lotus *(sahasrāra padma),* wherein detailed unfoldment associated with any particular petal is enacted. What has been depicted above can therefore also be applied to this lotus. The higher correspondences of the projected *prāṇas* are directly processed there. When properly assimilated and expressed, we have the awakening of the *prajñāpāramitā*, the boundless virtue of wisdom, esoterically considered. These signs can also be analysed from this perspective.

Consideration of the Head lotus

The attributes of Vajrasattva, the Dhyāni Buddhas and the *dharmakāya* are awakened in the petals of the Head lotus (*sahasrāra padma*). The Heart centre on the other hand embodies the Mirror-like Wisdom of Akṣobhya that reflects *dharmakāya* into *saṃsāra*. It is thereby the place of experience of *śūnyatā* (or 'error-free Thusness'). The appellation Vajrasattva-Akṣobhya, the 'All-Creating King' described in Volume 2, chapter 7 (and also in the *Bardo Thödol*), therefore depicts the esoteric relationship between these two centres (each of which contain twelve main petals) when viewed as a working relationship.

Astrologically, the Rays that govern the twelve main petals of the Head lotus are the same as with the Heart centre. The Heart centre embodies the principle of Life, whereas the Head centre embodies the ordering of consciousness and the Mind that expresses that Life. Life sustains the expression of consciousness and consciousness delineates a progression of experience that eventually reveals what Life is. *Śūnyatā* incorporates Life, but Life is itself a containment of attributes of cosmos in the form of Vajrasattva-Akṣobhya, which is Monadic. It is an indivisible form (the true Buddha within, to which the designation *nirmalā-tathatā* can apply) upon which the Śūnyatā Eye within the *tathāgatagarbha* focuses to receive the energies in order to transform *saṃsāra*. This is but one way of rendering the gnosis of the two truths, and veils much esotericism.

The Rays govern the Head lotus in the following manner:

Sagittarius – the Fourth Ray

Sagittarius directs the way of escape from *saṃsāric* involvement. This concerns the mechanism of awakening the Heart in the Head Lotus[48] by firing arrows of abstracted 'error free' logic to progressively vivify each petal. The arrows pierce the veils of the various forms of ignorance, and redirect or transform defiled *prāṇas* that are not 'error free'. This implicates the use of the fourth Ray of Harmony overcoming Strife, to produce harmony (the Mirror-like Wisdom) in the midst of strife (the

48 The detail of the process of this awakening shall be provided in Volume 5A, chapter 7. A *yogin* uses the Sagittarian persona to do so.

saṃskāras that fetter consciousness). Inevitably pathways to the Void are clarified, which continues until *saṃskāras* no longer need refinement.

In the higher *bhūmis* the Bodhisattva's focus has shifted from awakening the individual petals of the Heart centre to the petals of the Heart in the Head centre. Simultaneously the externalised Heart, being the group of which he/she is the central dynamo, is awakened. The *maṇḍala* that exists for the service of all sentient beings is consequently vivified. Eventually the arrows *(antaḥkaraṇas)* fired are directed towards cosmic links that must be travelled upon when Buddhahood has been attained. Arrows are also directed backwards to the constituency of the Bodhisattva's target group *maṇḍala*, to help abstract them onto the Bodhisattva path prepared for them.

Capricorn – the Third Ray

Capricorn represents the ability to climb the mountain of Mind that is the *dharmakāya,* allowing identification with its sources at various domains in cosmos, which is the fruit of the Dharmakāya Way. Thusness becomes the ground that the liberated one walks upon along that Way. This necessitates the complete awakening of the Head centre, which is structured in such a way that all attributes of *dharmakāya* can be registered in consciousness. The twelve main and subsidiary petals are able to process all *saṃskāras* of mind/Mind developed through experience of being/non-being. They are awakened in sequence, as detailed in Volume 5, chapter 7, allowing a Tathāgata to eventually appear. The awakening of the 1,056 petals of this centre is by means of firing Sagittarian arrows of thought constructs, or 'error-free Thusness', to any of the target petals. Revelation of the mysteries of whatever petal of the Head centre is being awakened is then accomplished.

The awakening of these petals first produces impressions of the knowledgeable things of empirical thought, and later a capacity for abstract thought, signifying the instantaneous, inclusive, detailed analysis of things, which becomes the hallmark of enlightened perception. This is a function of the third Ray of Mathematically Exact Activity. This perception eventually evolves into the cosmic or transcendental Mind of a Jina.

When all twelve major petal groups of the Head centre stand awakened then the attributes of Thusness manifest in their pristine expression, applied to any of the directions of the zodiac, according to the form of activity pursued by the enlightened One. Inconceivably vast is the cosmic Mind veiled by the 'Thusness' in the form of the *svabhāvikakāya,*[49] yet its nature is held steady in the Clear Light and its attributes are imprinted in the petals of the Head Lotus. There the omniscience of cosmos can be viewed in the clear screen of the Mind's Eye.

There is nothing to distinguish *saṃsāra* from *nirvāṇa* and *nirvāṇa* from *saṃsāra,*[50] the two are thus indelibly integrated in the vast panorama of this Mind-Space that is our goal. Every *yogin* must eventually stand at the pinnacle of this mount of attainment, upon whichever petal he has subjectively climbed, no matter the personality attributes and Ray background. The multifarious experiences of touching all aspects of *saṃsāra* to discern the real via repeated incarnations through the open gate of Cancer (Capricorn's opposite pole) has also served him well.

Technically, each incarnation of a consciousness-stream lays the foundation for experiencing the qualities needed to awaken but one small petal of the Head Lotus. If not properly mastered in one incarnation then a repeat incarnation (or even a repeat cycle of incarnations) is necessary. Thus the power of the mind unfolds, laying the foundation for enlightenment. The attributes of this mind are then abstracted into *dharmakāya*.

Aquarius – the Fifth Ray

Esoterically, Aquarius directs the *iḍā nāḍī* flow (governed by the fifth Ray of Scientific Reason), awakening the left lobe of the Ājñā centre. Consequently, the Discriminating Inner Wisdom of Amitābha, representing the *padma* family of deities, is evoked. The right lobe of this centre is awakened by the *piṇgalā prāṇas* of the fourth Ray Sagittarian impetus. This happens under the auspices of the Mirror-like Wisdom of Akṣobhya and the *vajra* family of deities. Together both lobes of the all-seeing Eye are fully awakened by appropriately energised *prāṇas*, allowing the complete vision accessible via Capricorn to be pursued. The Bodhisattva can then envision whatever field of service is considered most valuable. The vision takes the three times into account within the eternal Now. To enlighteningly serve necessitates observing

---

49 Self-born body, the (controversial) fourth body of a Buddha, synthesising the other three.

50 So states Chapter 25:19 of the *Mūlmadhymakakārikā of Nāgārjuna*.

the *karma* of the chosen subject to see how the *saṃskāras* developed in the past can be modified or transformed by the subject so as to be more applicable for gaining enlightenment.

The Throat centre (*viśuddha chakra*) governs the *iḍā nāḍī* flow because it controls the activity of the vicissitudes of the mind/Mind. It is the primary directive centre assisting one to rightly discriminate. This centre evokes and articulates the mantras discerned in Pisces, thus starting a new cycle of expression when the mantric purpose is externalised. A higher form of telepathy is here indicated wherein the liberated ones in cosmos can be contacted. Contact allows unfathomed reception of the bliss of unbridled Love. Telepathy binds the universe in one vast undertaking of multifarious Unity.

Each petal of the Ājñā centre is an extension of the major petals of the main *chakras* below the head, there being two lobes of 48 petals each to this centre, and we have the sum of 48 major petals to the major *chakras* below the head: the Base of Spine (4), Sacral (6), Solar Plexus (10), Heart (12) and Throat (16).[51] They must also be viewed in terms of the generation of *iḍā* and *piṇgalā nāḍīs*. Thus 2 x 48 petals[52] are necessary to awaken all of the petals of the Ājñā centre. This gives one the ability to integrate and work with all the related *prāṇas,* thus to vision the nature of the unfolding *saṃskāras* and the approaching *karma* associated with each petal. The major petals of each *chakra* and the corresponding petals of the Ājñā *chakra* must be purified by the energies of the Error-free Thusness, if the *yogin* is to clearly vision in the arenas of activity veiled by the *chakra*s. This necessitates attaining an undeviating one-pointed yogic *samādhi* that awakens the third Eye. The calmness of mind that is developed via the Gemini influence lays the foundation for this eventuation.

The way that the Ājñā centre is constituted, with its right-hand lobe (or 'wing') responsive to the circulation of *piṇgalā prāṇas,* and the

51 See Lama Anagarika Govinda, *Foundations of Tibetan Mysticism,* (Dutton, 1960), 140-146. The number of petals presented may differ to the traditional exoteric Buddhist accounts, but the reasons for the use of the account derived from Hindu yoga tradition is made abundantly clear in Volumes 4 and 5, where considerable detail is provided concerning the nature of the *nāḍī* system and the *chakras.*

52 This makes 96 petals, which is the base number for the tiers of petals of all major *chakras.*

left-hand lobe to the *iḍā prāṇas,* allows it to interrelate, integrate, or to vision the nature of the unfoldment of the major petals of the Head lotus. In turn, the Head centre is attuned to the constituency of the *tathāgatagarbha* and then to the *dharmakāya.*

The *iḍā prāṇas* from the Solar Plexus centre are the basis to the development of the minor *siddhis* associated with the three worlds of human livingness. For those upon the left hand path, these *siddhis* intensify the concept of an 'I' and the control by that 'I' of the empirical world, producing intense separativeness and self-centred power. Those upon the right hand path subvert the 'I' to compassionate activity, producing universality, inner hearing and enlightened vision.

When the *piṅgalā prāṇas* from the Heart centre are dominant then the vision that ensues includes all aspects of the inherent life associated with the group of which the seer is a part, and its integration with all related groups. Esoteric streams of revelation from the Council of Bodhisattvas becomes accessible. *Bodhicitta* can then be directed to everyone (governed by Leo, the polar opposite of Aquarius). The revealed teachings become increasingly more esoteric and vast as the Bodhisattva unfolds the higher *bhūmis.*

The activity of awakening the petals of the *chakras* is generated by the seventh Ray of Ceremonial Activity, as this Ray integrates the others, and its potency is needed to awaken the complete vision of the Eye. This Ray (of Uranus, the exoteric ruler of Aquarius) empowers the practicalities of the ritual or rhythm engendering the demonstration of enlightenment.

We saw that Aquarius connotes free flowing energies and a constant mutability of all aspects of being. When relegated to *śūnyatā* and divorced from all forms of ephemera (from space-time concepts), it produces a fundamental 'lack of character' concerning the reality of these aspects. What is experienced is not divorced from beingness or unified harmony in action, but the experience is of the Heart's immutable wisdom to unify, rather than that of the mind (which segregates and thus 'characterises'). The initial experience of the Void by the accomplished person in Leo (technically the experience of the *arhat*) becomes the mutable and equanimous activity of the serving Bodhisattva in Aquarius.

Pisces – the Seventh Ray

Pisces represents the process whereby the hearing of Secret Mantra is derived from two directions ('extremes'), cosmos (the *dharmakāya*) and *saṃsāra*. It binds them into unity (hence the phrase 'without extremes'). Its specific forte is the direction of the flow and control of the Waters (cosmic and those within our earth sphere), which is the foundation of all work by the accomplished *siddha*. Water is the Element in which the 'fishes' swim. The cosmic Watery substance is denoted as *bodhicitta* when expressed via the Heart centre, but its purpose is to produce phenomenological effects within the womb of the great Mother (Virgo) wherein it awakens the principle of compassion. It is the energy field wherein the divine child (humanity) is sustained and within which it develops. The Heart centre (or the Heart in the Head) is the chalice or 'skull cup' contained in the hands of Wrathful Deities for the containment of this energy.

All substance is constituted of energy and integrated in terms of energy fields. The ebb and flow of such energy fields concretise or congeal all activity associated with *saṃsāra*. Thus also is expressed the streams of manifesting *karma*. The fields are coloured by Rays of variegated hues and controlled by means of sound. Collectively, the substance of such fields is here termed the Waters, and their control is the basis of the art that is mastered by a *siddha,* whose training comes under the auspices of this sign if all seven Ray aspects governing life are to be mastered. In Pisces the seventh Ray manifests by way of the first (via Pluto, its esoteric ruler).[53] It is also utilised by Aries, which incorporates the seventh Ray potency via the will to instigate any aspect of a new cycle of activity that is but a variegation of Love-Wisdom.

The subject of sound and its relation to manifestation is obviously esoteric ('ear whispered') and little can be revealed in an exoteric publication. The *chakra* concerned is the Solar Plexus centre (*maṇipūra chakra*), which controls the expression of emotion-desire-feeling in the average human, hence with *kliṣṭamanas* (defiled mind). When *kliṣṭamanas* becomes undefiled by following the austerities and the precepts of the *yogins,* the *maṇipūra chakra* then directs the potency of mantra in the form of *bodhicitta*, which manifests via the magical activity of a *siddha*. This is necessary if the All-accomplishing power

53 Here the seventh Ray is viewed as the reflex of the first Ray.

of Amoghasiddhi is to manifest. The Ray producing concretising energy via the Solar Plexus centre is the sixth Ray of Devotion, but its expression is ruled by the seventh Ray of Ceremonial Endeavour, to which it is closely allied, if the magical powers are to manifest.

Inner hearing concerns recognising all sounds at every level of being/non-being. It can involve listening to the clashing noises emanated by the selfish, avaricious and separative ones who suffer and cause suffering in *saṃsāra*. The objective is to assist them to attune to the harmonious delight of Nature's overall melody. Such 'melody' integrates with consciousness and cleanses aberrant noises by means of *mantras* of liberation from the *dharmakāya*.[54] One group of petals after another in the Head lotus will awaken as each arena of concern is harmonised in accord with the overall pattern found as the divine archetype (Shambhala). The petals, however, need to be vivified with *iḍā, piṅgalā,* and finally *suṣumṇā prāṇas* along all the Ray lines. The process continues until eventually one is liberated from *saṃsāra. Bodhicitta* is utilised as the liberating, cleansing energy, and as a consequence we have the manifestation of the compassionate activity of the Bodhisattva.

The glyph of Pisces analysed at this level symbolises the link of mantric sound that unites two zones of influence. One represents the zone of the Sambhogakāya Flower (the *tathāgatagarbha*) and the other the vast *dharmakāyic* expanse. Such comprehensive fusion of both *saṃsāra* and *nirvāṇa* manifests as a free abiding of both sides at once in Pisces, but bound by the link of sound to the degree that the Flower can hold the potency of the *dharmakāya*. This fusion is symbolised by the conjoined fishes, with the bond signifying a state of 'without extremes'. However, at one stage the bond is broken, death ensues, be this physical death with respect to the inhabiting consciousness, or subjective death, the experience of *śūnyatā,* then the condition 'without extremes' manifests without conditions. Having attained a form of liberation by integrating with the Sambhogakāya Flower, the Bodhisattva increasingly attunes to the *dharmakāya,* producing such an inclusive, expansive activity that awareness can no longer be contained in the *tathāgatagarbha,* producing the Flower's esoteric death. The cycle of the *tathāgatagarbha* has ended, but the *tathatā,* 'Life', which is

54 Here viewed in terms of cosmic Waters.

'without extremes' endures.

Aries – the first Ray

In *Aries* the *samādhi* developed in Libra lays the foundation for the highest meditative impressions. Aries directs the *samādhi* into new fields and areas, as it instigates all new cycles of meditative unfoldment. Eventually the mind is awakened to become a reflection of cosmos by being receptive to the *dharmakāya*. Groups of petals of the Head lotus are awakened at once. The experience opens the doors to the zones of residence of the Buddha Fields within the plenitude of cosmos. The Clear Light of the meditation-Mind must be held steady and acutely focussed by means of the first Ray of Will, of which Aries is the custodian, to be able to discern clearly the aspects of the *dharmakāya* needing to be expressed.

There are three levels associated with awakening the Head lotus. Any of these levels can be the focus at a particular time, or can happen simultaneously. Individual petals, as well as tiers of petals can awaken according to the stage of development of the *sādhana* (devotional practice) of the *yogin,* as well as the level of Initiation attained. Such awakening necessitates tests passed in Scorpio. The information here is a broad generalisation. In Volume 5 detail shall be provided in terms of the Peaceful and Wrathful Deities of the *Bardo Thödol.*

- The *iḍā* level directed by the Arian insight, that awakens smaller groups of petals of the Head lotus governed by the Aquarian disposition. This is the basis to all degrees of Bodhisattvic activity, happening specifically via its polar opposite, the self conscious personality in Leo.
- The *piṇgalā* level directed by the Sagittarian focus, awakening larger petals (or tiers thereof) in the Head lotus. (Literally a target with concentric rings, that the Archer fires his arrows at.)
- The *suṣumṇā* level absorbed by the Capricornian governance of mind/Mind, vivifies with living Fire this entire organ of enlightened expression. One of the twelve major petals of the Head lotus is awakened under Capricornian impetus for each turning of the wheel until all is a consummating blaze of Fire.

The awakening of these Head lotus petals via Sagittarius, Aries and Scorpio is driven by Mars (the god of war), who is at least one of their planetary rulers. Mars provides the driving *prāṇic* energy or incentive *(vāsanā,* the driving force of consciousness), awakening the petals. Scorpio represents the will to overcome limiting *saṃskāras* so that Sagittarius can fire the arrows to gain Initiation. Sagittarius represents the will to envision and to awaken, to open the gates (of the major petals) to liberation. Aries represents the will to initiate the Bodhisattivic activity that is finally accomplished in Aquarius. It instigates the plan for any cycle of achievement.

In relation to this, Pisces represents the inflow of cosmic Waters to the Sambhogakāya Flower, and Sagittarius represents the direction of the accomplishment of cleansing *saṃsāric* murk by means of the Waters, so that Initiation can be gained in Capricorn. This is the energy utilised by Amoghasiddhi to overcome *saṃsāra* by being yogically directed to control all aspects of phenomena that governs the womb of Nature in Virgo (the polar opposite of Pisces). Aquarius represents the influx of impressions from cosmic Mind (the highest levels of *dharmakāya),* which is perceived via the intuition and meditative activities of the Bodhisattva. These impressions become the leitmotiv of the Bodhisattva's activities.

Aries lays the foundation that allows the true expression of the Heart's Mind to manifest, as it causes the turning of the cycles of activity producing unfoldment of the Bodhisattva *bhūmis,* impelled by ever higher receptivity to the sublime strata of the *dharmakāya,* to which the Bodhisattva becomes increasingly attuned. Each new cycle causes the Bodhisattva to follow increasingly subtler expressions of 'the Middle Path'. The ram thus manifests the impetus for every drive to liberation. The old cycles of *karma* and associated *saṃskāras* become rectified in the major petal governed by the polar opposite of this sign, Libra the balances.

Taurus and Scorpio – the Sixth, Fourth and Second Rays

Taurus and Scorpio together manifest as a dual Splenic centre, the qualities of which will be detailed later. They are concerned with the elimination of sickly *prāṇas* and recycle that which is vital. Scorpio processes the *prāṇas* via Mars, its exoteric and esoteric ruler, causing the testings concerning the elimination of desire-attachment. The Scorpion esoterically stings to death (here a sixth Ray function) all aspects that would interfere with the eventual manifestation of Thusness, and which would make it 'otherwise'. Therefore, the major transmutative testings that eliminate everything *saṃsāric* from the persona of the personal-I are accomplished in this sign. It thus lays the foundation for all possible accomplishments associated with the sacred petals by purifying the *prāṇas* engendered by the non-sacred petals. This necessitates the function of the superimposed Splenic centre that rejects the *prāṇas* that are no longer viable to the system. As this is accomplished, the second Ray of Love-Wisdom is generated and the related qualities *(prāṇas)* are passed on to the northern quadrant via the *piṅgalā nāḍī* and the directive will of Sagittarius. The remaining *prāṇas* are reprocessed in the southern quadrant via Taurus and the effects of the fourth Ray. Consequently, these three signs have a strong esoteric relationship concerning the transmutation of the entire field of desire, and its conversion into *bodhicitta.*

This entire process is a major task of humanity, and is esoterically the reason for human existence, because it involves more than just the individual consciousness, but also the transformation and transmutation of the substance of the sheaths people incarnate through. This concept implicates the nature of Bodhisattvic activity upon a far subtler level than is normally cognised. This is one reason why these three signs convey the fourth Ray of Beautifying Harmony overcoming Strife.[55] When the second Ray of Love-Wisdom assigned to Gemini (the polar opposite of Sagittarius) is included, then the symbolic nature of the *piṅgalā* flow to and from the Heart centre is completed.

Similarly, *Taurus* exemplifies the wisdom aspect of the second Ray of Love-Wisdom. Through it, and its pivotal juncture between the two quadrants, the all-seeing Eye can be awakened and an enlightened being can arise. It is the sign of illumination that comes as a consequence of 'calming the mind'. The Eye can then be utilised to rightly discern what is needed to attain Thusness and to liberate others. The Eye peers into all domains, *chakras*, and planes of phenomenal activity. It allows one to walk upon the earth and yet to keep one's head in the spaciousness

55 *Esoteric Astrology*, 489.

of the sky that the Thusness represents. After the battle has been won concerning the nine-headed Hydra in Scorpio, then the victorious one in Taurus can demonstrate any of the ways associated with the five signs of the abstracted aspects of Mind. Love-Wisdom then utilises aspects of the Buddha-Mind associated with any particular sign. Everything must however be interpreted in accordance with the Bodhisattva level that an accomplished one is at.

Cycle after cycle of liberating activity ensues under the auspices of Libra, whereby the evolving divine Love of the Bodhisattva generates Love-Wisdom, cleansing and transmuting available *karma,* not only for him/herself, but for the entire group the Bodhisattva actively works to serve. Liberation in this case means liberation from the *karma* that bonds one to *saṃsāra.* The five petals of the southern direction can be considered to channel the transforming *prāṇas* from their polar opposites, as well as generating *iḍā, piṅgalā* and *suṣumṇa* energies.

Aries starts the cycle, Taurus governs the awakening of the *siddhis* associated with the Solar Plexus centre after desire-attachments have been conquered. Gemini embodies the 'house' of the *nāḍī* system, hence the activity of the *iḍā* and *piṅgalā prāṇas.* Cancer governs the energies expressed by the Sacral centre. Leo is concerned with awakening *kuṇḍalinī* via the Base of Spine centre. Virgo opens the doors of mastery of the *prāṇas* from the minor *chakras* (called the Inner Round). Libra governs the generation of *suṣumṇa prāṇas* once the *yogin's* path is consciously trod. Scorpio stages the testings. Sagittarius directs the Fires, and Capricorn contains them as all-embracive Mind. The liberation of *kuṇḍalinī* produces the universal Mind of the enlightened Bodhisattva in Aquarius after the mount has been yogically climbed in Capricorn. All beings can be consequently served and brought to enlightenment. Pisces achieves the final severance of bondage to it all.

3

The Great Gates of Diamond Liberation Part 3: The Centres below the Diaphragm, and Voidness

The Middle Path

In continuing the analysis of the opening paragraphs of '*The Samādhi—"Great Gate of Diamond Liberation"*', translated by Wayman, we next have:

> What is the Middle Path, is without one extreme, is without two extremes, without apprehensible, without apprehender, without apprehension, without nihilism, without eternalism, without arising, without ceasing, without constructive thought, without discursive thought, not independent, not dependent on another, not going, not coming, without thorough defilement, without complete purification, without union, without separation. That is discerning (the real). [6]
>
> What is discerning (the real) is without personal aggregates *(skandha),* without realms *(dhātu),* without sense organs *(indriya),* without sense bases *(āyatana),* without objective realms, without attaching names to objective realms, without (destiny's) action, without the fruit of (destiny's) action. What is without (destiny's) action and without the fruit of (destiny's) action is the incomparable right-completed Enlightenment. What is the incomparable right-completed Enlightenment is the incomparable right-completed Buddha. What is the incomparable right-completed Buddha is the Dharma. What is the Dharma is not born, does not die. What is not born and does not die should be understood to be the same as the sky.[7][1]

---

1 Alex Wayman, *Untying the Knots in Buddhism,* 288.

The Middle Path is the heart of the *buddhadharma* and astrologically involves the process of walking the way of the twelve signs of the zodiac so that Voidness can be experienced throughout. Here 'Voidness' refers to the characteristics of the wheel remaining after all *saṃsāric* attributes have been excluded. The Middle Path can be considered to be the production of Voidness by first engendering calmness of mind. Without this calm abiding (*śamatha*), whereby all external distractions in meditation are eliminated, there can be no Void. This produces a comprehension of Voidness[2] on all levels of perception, being the ground for the experience of Thusness. The wheel of the Middle Path has Voidness (see Figure 8) as the central factor because it is the heart of the liberation to be gained. The attainment of calmness of mind produces the experience of 'Comprehending it' (in Virgo, signifying the material domain) whereby the 'real' can be discerned. Such comprehension produces a birth of the new, revealing the 'child' that perpetually is. This *tathāgata*-child, the *tathāgatagarbha,* exists in her womb and becomes progressively known until it is finally consciously born as a consequence of one's *samādhi* (in Libra).

The purpose of the wheel that will now be analysed relates to this womb experience and concerns the production of the Middle Path via the *prāṇas* of *the five non-sacred petals* of the Heart centre needing further processing. The Wheel of the Middle Path is an expression of the Splenic centre. The Splenic centre is a dual centre, with one larger wheel of twelve petals (Splenic centre I) superimposed upon a smaller one of eight petals (Splenic centre II).

The petals to each *chakra* are arranged in tiers, where smaller ones are integrated to make the major petals. Their function is to receive the *prāṇas* of the Elements of the *saṃskāras* that they are designed to process and then to redirect them to other centres. There are also internal tiers of lesser petals that process *prāṇas* from the minor centres of the Inner Round. Counting the Splenic centres as a unit, which acts as a major *chakra,* there are eight major *chakras* that can manifest as the wheel of the *dharma* (via the eight directions of space), as shown in Figure 7.

---

2 Such comprehension cannot be accomplished by the empirical mind.

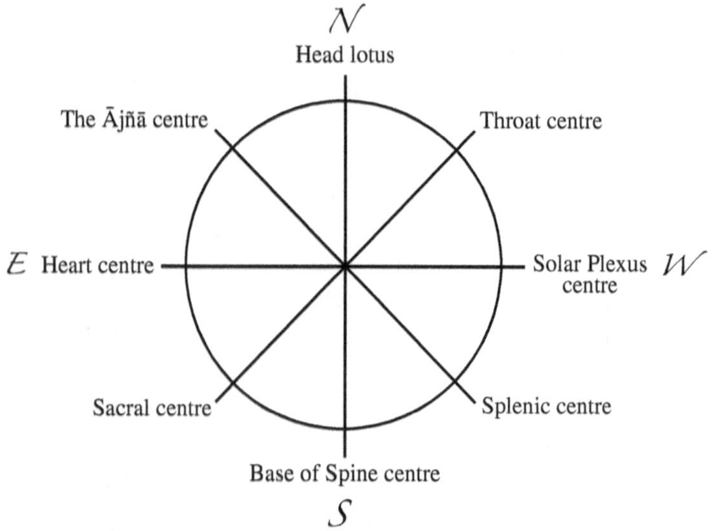

Figure 7. The Chakras as the Wheel of Dharma

Armed with the information presented earlier concerning the nature of the various directions in space, the qualities of the *chakras* can be better comprehended. Much can then be correlated concerning the relationships between the *chakras* and the mode of experiencing the *dharma*.

The Head lotus stands at the northern direction because it constitutes the summation of all attributes developed by the other centres. The Ājñā centre is at the northeast direction of 'unity' because this direction facilitates its multidimensional focus. The Heart centre embodies the eastern direction of inwards towards the Heart of Life (here representing *śūnyatā*). The Sacral centre embodies the southeast direction of 'expression' (into the field of desire-attachment). The Base of Spine centre embodies the southern direction of downwards to the elemental lives because it supports all the other *chakras*. The dual Splenic centre embodies the southwest direction of 'understanding' because it is concerned with the refining and transmutation process that produces comprehension of all that is processed. The Solar Plexus centre represents the western direction of outwards to humanity because it processes the personal will and desire-mind attributes that are the mainstay of interrelations between people. The Throat centre represents the northwest direction of 'goodwill' because it embodies the characteristics of *manas* and the mode of transformation of mind, hence the organs of speech from which such goodwill emanates.

The explanation of *the Middle Path* to be presented is an extension of the Arian petal of the Heart centre because its main function is to refine *saṃskāras* and disseminate *bodhicitta.* Aries also projects all new cycles of activity, such as this new wheel turning. The first twelve phrases from the quotation have a direct relationship to the twelve signs of the zodiac according to the manner of walking the rectified path. Now, however, this path is depicted in terms of the qualities of the twelve-petalled Splenic centre's petals, so that the associated *prāṇas* can be absorbed in the Heart centre. They then sponsor a new cycle of activity, as instigated by Aries.

Discerning what is real

There are eight phrases following the initial twelve that manifest an eight-spoked wheel of direction and right orientation in space. At their heart is the *samādhi* that allows the meditator to 'discern the real', producing 'right completed Enlightenment' via the apprehension of the *dharma.* (This *dharma* is the *dharmakāya* expressed into the realms of consciousness.)

This *samādhi,* which is an expression of the western petal of the Heart centre, will inevitably direct the properly qualified *prāṇas* to the 'Middle Path' (the eastern Arian petal) to make the *prāṇas* truly sacred.

The eight petals associated with this wheel, that discerns the Real, represent the expression of the *Diaphragm centre.* The first twenty phrases of verse six of this *samādhi, 'Great Gate of Diamond Liberation',* are therefore concerned with the relation of the twelve-petalled Splenic centre to the Diaphragm centre and of the approach of their *prāṇas* to the Heart centre. The last phrase of verse 6 of the quote provides the title of the wheel we are analysing, or rather, its central qualifying point. The succeeding eight phrases of verse seven are concerned with the qualities of the superimposed eight-petalled Splenic centre and of the approach to it, as processed by the Solar Plexus centre.

The diaphragm acts as a type of motor for the movement of the lungs, that breathes in and out the life supporting air for the body. Similarly the function of the *Diaphragm centre* is to move *prāṇas* that cross over from the portions of the *nāḍī* system above and below the diaphragm. That below the diaphragm generates desire, which produces attachment to things. Consequently, the five sense-consciousnesses evolve. Those above the diaphragm direct the various attributes of consciousness, producing states of rarefied awareness and enlightenment. The Diaphragm centre projects the vital *prāṇas* of Life channelled from the Heart centre to the Splenic, Solar Plexus and Sacral centres. Life sustaining airs can then be conveyed to all aspects of the form via the major and minor *chakras* that embody the functioning of the organs and glands.

Earlier, the meaning of *The Middle Path* in relation to the sign Aries was explained, but now shall be investigated in relation to the progression of the wheel of Splenic centre I, that starts from the direction east (the Arian position) and goes to Pisces via Taurus. The hub of this wheel is Voidness and the purpose of the functioning of the petals is to ultimately produce this quality. Each petal of this wheel describes one or other aspect of what constitutes the Middle Path. We should also remember that this path is the way the Heart centre (the middle *chakra*) unfolds to open the doors to *śūnyatā* for each sign. There is consequently a direct relation between the Heart centre and Splenic centre I in that the Heart centre pours vitalising *prāṇas* to Splenic centre I so that the *prāṇic* dross from the centres below the diaphragm can be cleansed. Splenic centre I therefore prepares *prāṇas* for reception by the Heart centre. In a liberated being the two centres are but mirrors of each other. The twelve links of Dependent Origination are effectively based upon the paradigm of the functions of Splenic centre I.

The Heart centre, Splenic centre I and the Diaphragm centres, form a functioning unity. The Heart centre embodies the most abstracted (Will) level of the *prāṇas* for this triad, producing Thusness. Splenic centre I manifests the activity of conversion of the *prāṇas* from below the diaphragm. This centre, therefore, properly awakens insight meditation *(vipassanā)*. The Diaphragm centre represents the qualities of love by directing the *prāṇas* to where they must go in either direction without qualifying them in any way, except via their admixture, which redirects some misplaced *prāṇas* back to the centres below the diaphragm for further processing.

The opening of the doors to enlightened perceptions necessitates using the dynamic and positive *will* (the assertive force of Aries the ram). Such a will can manifest in the form of an ineffable *patience* to see others pass through the gates towards enlightenment before one takes the final steps to complete liberation. It necessitates the *yogin's persistence* to rent veil after veil of illusion upon the upward way. It will mean *perseverance* in the face of individual hardship and strife. There is also a necessary *preservation* of all liberating forces and their concentration upon the meditation at hand to *produce* the tension of Mind that becomes the ritualistic *power* behind mantra and *mudrā*. All this allows the *yogin* to finally *pierce* the last veil, or door to *śūnyatā*.

In the above we have the methodology of the seven Ray attributes when applied to the process of liberation.

1. The dynamic Will that pierces veils—the first Ray of Will or spiritual Power.
2. Ineffable patience—the second Ray of Love-Wisdom.
3. Persistence to see the task accomplished—the third Ray of Mathematically Exact Activity.
4. Perseverance to overcome hardships—the fourth Ray of Beautifying Harmony overcoming Strife.
5. Preservation of liberating forces—the fifth Ray of Scientific Reason.
6. Production of focussed tension—the sixth Ray of Devotion.
7. The power of ritual and mantra—the seventh Ray of Ceremonial activity, concretising Power.

It should also be noted that Thusness and Voidness can be distinguished in that:

- *Voidness* is that which is void or empty of something or of things. It refers to that lacking *saṃsāric* qualifications. It is effectively a state 'in between' *saṃsāra* and the *dharmakāya*. It therefore acts as a mirror that reflects one to the other.

- *Thusness* refers to a state of being that has the Void as its foundation and which expresses that which abides once *saṃsāric* qualifications have been removed, and which is organised by the patterns relegated by the *dharmakāya*.

In terms of the *chakra* system, the 'Middle Path' consists of the integral combination of the Heart, Diaphragm, and Splenic centres. This triplicity stands midway between the Heart in the Head lotus (the *sahasrāra padma*), and the Sacral and Base of Spine centres in the lower part of the body. This makes it the 'middle', that can effectively express and process all associated *prāṇas*. When connected to the Solar Plexus and Sacral centres we then have a group of five *chakras*: the Heart, Diaphragm, Splenic centre I, Solar Plexus, and Sacral centres. The Sacral centre is the foundational centre for generating and circulating the base *prāṇas* of desire and attachment that sustain the activity of all centres in their early stages. Later, this centre circulates the vital liberating *prāṇas* that help to cleanse the entire *nāḍī* system. These five *chakras* generate the qualities of the *piṇgalā* path within the Dharmakāya Way.

When the associated *piṇgalā prāṇas* have been appropriately purified they will facilitate the generation of the qualities of Love-Wisdom—the mirror-like serene space of the Heart's quietude governed by Akṣobhya. Vairocana's qualities express the Diaphragm centre's ability to channel *prāṇas,* interrelating all centres above and below the diaphragm. Amitābha's attributes governs the ability of Splenic centre I to rightly discriminate wholesome from unwholesome *prāṇas.* Ratnasambhava's quality is generated by harmonising the often turbulent Watery *prāṇas* to control the Solar Plexus centre. It directs all *saṃskāras* generated below the diaphragm to fulfil their rightful (enlightening) mission. Amoghasiddhi's qualities are generated through the ability of the Sacral centre to control the potency of desire and the sum of the *prāṇas* in the body, allowing the awakening of the liberating all-accomplishing Fires from the Base centre.

The appropriate evocation of the *prāṇas* of the Splenic, Diaphragm and Heart centres represent the way to *śūnyatā,* and when integrated with the Sacral and Ājñā centres, they become the driving dynamo of the compassionate zeal of all Bodhisattvas, allowing them to see far. When the focus upon the Diaphragm centre (a minor centre) becomes superseded by the Throat centre that is brought into expression, then it evokes the creative Fires that vitalise their service work. Effectively, the field of service represents all of the forces impacting upon the Solar Plexus centre of humanity. Also, the Heart centre must dominate the evocation of all *prāṇas* if *prajñā* (wisdom) is to be evolved and liberation attained. Otherwise the dark path manifests, focussed upon the Throat centre, wherein the Fires of mind are prostituted to serve the aggrandisement of the powers of the separative 'I'. The development of the Heart centre is thus common to all who follow the right hand path. Those who follow the left hand path disdainfully eschew its qualities, utilising only the *prāṇas* from the non-sacred petals to do their bidding.

The *iḍā* path within the Dharmakāya Way is represented by the alignment of the Ājñā, Throat, Solar Plexus, Splenic centre II, and Sacral centres.[3] These centres are embodied by the characteristics of the Consorts of the Dhyāni Buddhas. They effectively generate the creative or destructive Fires of the mind/Mind. They eventually give birth to the *prāṇas* of the wisdom principle outlined above (their 'son') when the Middle Path of the Heart centre is included and appropriately followed. The ability to vision in all domains of consciousness via the Ājñā centre is awakened by developing mastery over both lobes of this centre through the control of the substance of the *saṃskāras* under the auspices of Akṣobhya's Consort. The direction of the phenomena of the powers of mind/Mind is gained by developing the attributes of Vairocana's Consort. Amoghasiddhi's Consort assists in the mastery of Solar Plexus energies to help produce the minor *siddhis*. Working with the energies from Amitābha's Consort assists in *manasic* evolution via refining and redirecting *prāṇas* within Splenic centre II. The energies of Ratnasambhava's Consort helps one to master the substance of desire, to eliminate attachments other than those directed to developing attributes that harmonise the aura and produce enlightenment.

The *suṣumṇā* path within the Dharmakāya Way is represented by the qualities of the Ājñā/Head, Throat, Heart, Solar Plexus, and Sacral/Base of the Spine centres. Here the characteristics of the complete *maṇḍala* of the Dhyāni Buddhas are expressed.[4] All paths are integrated into the

---

3 The concern here is with the major *chakras,* hence omitted is the role of the Stomach centre as a generator and store of *iḍā prāṇas,* and similarly for the Liver centre with respect to *piṅgalā prāṇas.*

4 This grouping of five *chakras* is consequently espoused in Buddhist Tantra, however, one can see that it is but one facet of a complicated science regarding the awakening of perceptions and the evolution of consciousness.

Head lotus via the two lobes of the Ājñā centre and its central sphere. The awakening of the five tiers of petals of the Head lotus manifests in accordance with the complete development of the attributes of the Dhyāni Buddhas, as will be detailed in Volume 5A. These tiers (wheels of petals of the Head lotus) absorb all of the *manasic* and wisdom conveying *prāṇas* generated by the individual.

This fivefold internal structure allows the five Elements to be inevitably transformed into the wisdoms of the Dhyāni Buddhas, and thereby rule and control all that is. The outermost tier processes mainly the *kāma-manasic* (desire or emotional mind) *prāṇas*. Consequently, it can be considered the Solar Plexus in the Head. The associated Element is Earth and the Jina attribute developed through its mastery is the All-accomplishing Wisdom of Amoghasiddhi. The next inner tier of petals processes the development of Love-Wisdom attributes and establishes the links to the Sambhogakāya Flower. It is consequently called the Heart in the Head, and the associated Element is Water. The Equalising Wisdom of Ratnasambhava is developed through its mastery. The third tier governs the process of the awakening of Mind. The associated Element is Fire, and the Discriminating Wisdom of Amitābha is developed through its mastery. The third tier is termed the Throat in the Head. The next innermost tier concerns the development of the Mirror-like Wisdom of Akṣobhya, the mastery of the Element Air, and awakening to *śūnyatā*. The central tier concerns mastery of the Element Aether, conveying the *dharmakāya,* hence complete mastery of all phenomena. The governing Jina is Vairocana.

The governing signs of the Middle Path

Figure 8 depicts the qualities of the Middle Path as part of the twelve petals of Splenic centre I, to which the zodiacal signs are assigned to provide a more detailed comprehension of the processes involved. When the information below is integrated with what is provided in Volume 5A, chapter 4, in relation to the Herukas and Consorts, it should be noted that the differences in the two accounts stem from the fact that in the account in the *Bardo Thödol* the focus is upon the integration of the *prāṇas* of Splenic centre I into the Heart centre. Accordingly, the energies of the Herukas need to be generated for the respective petals to transform the remaining impurities before being passed on to the Heart centre via the Arian petal. The Heruka's energies are therefore paramount. In the present account the focus is upon the initial conversion of *saṃskāras,* hence the effect of the energies from the Consorts of the Herukas takes precedence. Here the substance of the *saṃskāras* must be refined. This is accomplished via the work of the minor centres, as briefly described below.

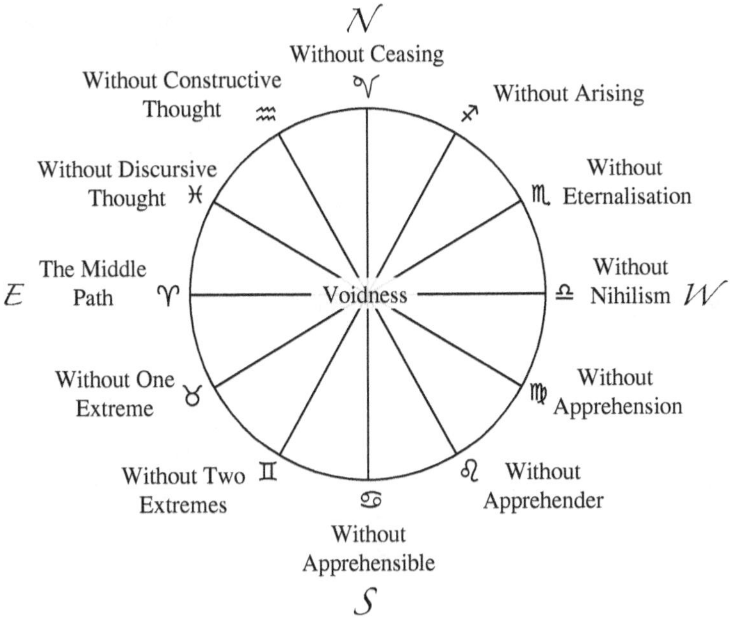

Figure 8. Splenic centre I, 'The Middle Path'

Aries, Fiery prāṇas to and from the Heart centre.

The 'Middle Path' relegated to Aries concerns the *nāḍī* that leads from Splenic centre I to and from the Heart centre. It channels the *prāṇas* that can be absorbed in the Heart centre, or that are to be projected from it into the Splenic centres to help transform the associated *saṃskāras.* Ultimately, they must become Void Elements.

The door relegated to the sign *Taurus the bull* is designated *'without one extreme'.* The Earthy aspect of Aetheric *prāṇas* to and from Splenic centre II are channelled from this petal. Being the gain of the transformation process they represent the most refined of the *prāṇas* gained through physical plane interactions. Also, the downpour of cleansing, transformative energies from the Heart and Throat centres pour into manifestation via the Arian petal to this and the Airy Gemini petal. Together the Taurean and Gemini petals represent the downward thrust of the *piṅgalā* stream from this centre to Splenic centre II. These energies are the main cleansing potencies used by Splenic centre II to refine defiled *prāṇas.*

Taurus, Aetheric-Earthy prāṇas of the piṅgalā stream to and from Splenic centre II.

The tendency of the blind onrushing path of the bull is to be extreme in each field of desire. Clearly, therefore, the candidate on the road to *śūnyatā* must control the *saṃskāras* generated by such activity so that no fanaticism is possible, and then to transform and project this force towards the quest for enlightenment. In terms of *prāṇic* vitalisation from the Heart, the bull represents the (onrushing) force of the transmogrifying *prāṇas* causing *saṃskāras* to become transmuted into the quality allowing experience of Voidness. All forms of energies are integrated so that only 'the Middle Path' is produced. The Void generated concerns that which remains when desire is eliminated. Then there is no rush in any direction to experience anything, there is simply that equanimous calmness (of mind) that allows the Eye to vision the real. The *prāṇas* projected to the Heart energise its corresponding Taurean-Scorpio interrelation, which was stated to represent the key interrelation of that wheel. All energies are here blended, thus being 'without one extreme'.

Gemini, Airy-Fiery prāṇas of the piṅgalā stream to and from Splenic centre II.

The designation relegated to the sign *Gemini the twins* is *'without two extremes',* which implicates the activities of the twins. Here one twin (the immortal brother) represents the ability of this petal to receive the transmogrifying energy from the Heart centre. The other twin (the mortal brother) is focussed upon the processes manifesting in Splenic centre II, to which these energies are directed to process *saṃskāras* with a *piṅgalā* flavouring. The objective being to equalise the attributes of the *prāṇas* so that those from the Heart centre and those derived from *saṃsāric* activity are at-oned. Consequently, the extremes have been annulled. The 'two extremes' of this quotation can refer here to the *prāṇic* vitalisation in the body, and the extremes viewed in terms of consciousness. Both must be harmonised into Void attributes.

Technically, Gemini admixes the two in the Temple of Life, leaving only the most refined attributes in the inner sanctum. They are to be blended by means of the techniques associated with *śamatha,* to be absorbed into the corresponding petal of the Heart lotus and projected by the Sagittarian impetus to the target of liberation. All *saṃskāras* created in relation to the various forms of *māyā* must be cleansed in this way.

The 'two extremes' can also relate to the *saṃsāra-śūnyatā* interrelation. The Middle Path is then the way to enlightenment that fuses both into a oneness, where there is neither a form of nihilism (which the term Void can implicate), nor forms of attachment to transient, ephemeral, corruptible things, ideas and idealisms. It should be noted that the *saṃsāra-śūnyatā* fusion establishes Akṣobhya's Mirror-like Wisdom and the Dharmakāya Way. This process of interrelating the 'extremes' is a paradigm for the nature of the commingling of *prāṇas* of the polar opposites of all of the petals, but is governed by the Gemini petal, as Gemini rules the *nāḍī* system.

Cancer, mainly Watery prāṇas to and from Splenic centre II.

The *prāṇas* processed at the *Cancerian* petal are denoted as *'without apprehensible'.* The southern direction associated with Cancer concerns the sum of the material phenomena into which people are born and that can be apprehended by means of the senses. Therefore, the *saṃskāras* to be cleansed relate to things that people identify with and take as the real. Such things are, however, not truly apprehendable in this way because they are illusional. Inevitably, people will know the true nature of the ephemera, that ultimately there is nothing to be apprehended other than the process of change itself. Cancer's southern orientation signifies processing the most base (murky) Watery *saṃskāras,* needing constant recycling. They are the major *prāṇas* to be processed in people's psyche, where the 'murky' designation signifies a commingling with the Earthy Element (symbolised by the crab's ability to live both on land and water). This is the main petal overlapped with Splenic centre I, indicating the identity between the two Splenic centres at this juncture.

Splenic centre II processes mainly Watery-Earthy *prāṇas* and Splenic centre I Fiery-Watery ones. It converts them into Airy attributes so that they can be absorbed into the Heart centre's circulation.

The *prāṇas* derived from interrelating with phenomena are channelled to the reciprocal petal of the Heart lotus, denoted 'discerning the real', once the basic attribute of what will be experienced as Thusness is ascertained in consciousness.

Leo, channels Fiery-Airy prāṇas of the iḍā stream to and from Splenic centre II.

The statement given for *Leo the lion* is *'without apprehender'.* Leo refers to the dominant, assertive 'self', the personal-I, which is the apprehender of the phenomena into which one is born in the sign Cancer. The *saṃskāras* to be transmuted therefore concern the elimination of concepts wherein one places oneself at the centre of one's universe, in relation to which all things are viewed. The I-concept must be eliminated in one's entire emotional-mental apparatus and not just conceptually. Self-involvement must be transmuted into a Will-to-Good for all. This is the gist of what the entire wheel of the Middle Path produces. The process of transforming one's 'self' concept in this way constitutes the Fiery *iḍā prāṇas* that are directed from this petal to Splenic centre II.

For a great deal of human history this downward focus of Fiery *prāṇas* reinforces the I-concept, intensifying attachment to phenomena and interrelation with the world of 'I's'. Only upon the yogic path is there a direction of the Fiery Will (utilising Capricornian impetus), to overcome the concept of ego. The entire path producing the enlightened status of dispassionate awareness then begins, until no apprehender can be found. From this perspective, this sign is the crux of the wheel, because it is the apprehender that must undertake all of the transformations associated with the rest of the signs. They are stages of the way upon the wheel that produce the true Middle Path.

Virgo, channels Earthy-Watery prāṇas of the iḍā stream to and from Splenic centre II.

The next sign, *Virgo the virgin,* sets the stage for all that is to follow, because first the apprehender undergoes the process of apprehension. Effectively, Virgo is fused with the sign Leo here. (Mythologically, the two signs were united in the form of the sphinx, which has a woman's head and a lion's body.) Virgo-Leo, governing the flow of the *iḍā* stream (the consciousness bearing factors) to and from Splenic centre II, thus also governs the faculties of mind allowing the apprehender to perceive things, and to anticipate things to come. Such anticipation deepens as *saṃsāra* becomes largely comprehended. In time, the individual intuits that there must be something more to what is understood. Projections are made to comprehend the subjective domains and the fields of consciousness. The *saṃskāras* of anxiety and worry are eliminated, as well as erroneous ideas. Inevitably, an unwavering faith in the dictates of *karma* develops as deep insights into the meaning of life are realised and the gnosis of the Clear Light of Mind is awakened. Consequently, the state of perception attributed to Virgo in Figure 8 ('without apprehension') manifests, as the empirical mind no longer rules to apprehend anything. The Fiery energies producing the conversion of the *saṃskāras* of apprehension are thus conveyed by this petal of Splenic centre I to Splenic centre II. Concretions of mental-emotions are consequently transformed into clarified perception and enlightened vision.

Libra, channels the admix of prāṇas via the Airy Element to and from the Solar Plexus centre.

The sign *Libra the balances* carries the logic of the self-concept to a conclusion, where the presumption is that only phenomena exists, as experienced by the 'self'. Thus when the 'self' ceases to exist everything else ceases with it, which is the conceptualisation of the philosophy of *nihilism*. Libra connotes the wheel of the Law, of that which judges what must be. From the viewpoint of the personal-I such judgement concerns the consequential nature of the processes of life and death. The nihilistic view of those that are intensely self-focussed is the reckoning that there is no further activity after death, that life's judgement allows no continuation of consciousness after the 'I' has died. To a nihilist, considerations of life devoid of such an 'I' is deemed unthinkable and therefore impossible.

The veil to be removed in this sign thus concerns the elimination of such tendencies via what is experienced through meditative insight. The sum total of emotional (Watery) based thought is challenged as the Libran undergoes cycles of contemplation and meditation. Deep analysis shows that such Watery thought is the source of much pain and steps are made to master the forces of the Solar Plexus centre, to which the *prāṇas* from this petal of Splenic centre I are directed. Specifically the transmogrifying *prāṇas* from the Heart centre via Aries (the polar opposite of Libra) are brought to bear to calm the often turbulent Waters of the Solar Plexus centre. A placid mirror can then be generated that reflects the reality of Life via the developed Wisdom of the Heart centre. All forms of nihilism consequently vanish.

The *saṃskāras* to be overcome in this sign therefore concern all forms of nihilism or the futility of life, by presenting examples of the livingness of life after death. Physical death is seen as an interlude between one state of existence and another. Through recognising that something other than a materialistic universe exists, concepts of karmic consequences arise to account for the laws that would govern such an extended universe. The meditation develops forms of clairvoyance and intuitional thought that transcend the boundaries of the 'self' concept. The *prāṇas* generated then become further refined in the *samādhi* associated with the corresponding petal of the Heart lotus. The way of compassion is consequently trod.

Scorpio, channels Watery-Earthy prāṇas of the piṇgalā stream to and from the Liver centre.

The intensity of the martial and devotional qualities of the *Scorpio* subject tends to produce fanatics and those that consider an eternal life in heaven as the reward for their activities upon earth by following the dictates of their religious scriptures. Others wish to extend pleasurable experiences of life in *saṃsāra* for as long as possible. Such 'eternalism' meets its doom in the battlefield of desire that besets the life of the aspirant in this sign. In Scorpio, the *saṃskāras* developed by *yogins* concern overcoming fanaticism of all types. Whatever misaligned intensities arise in the body of desires, emotions and mind, must be controlled and transformed if one is to walk the middle way to enlightenment. Thus, aspirants are tested in this sign. The *piṇgalā prāṇas* relating to conquering misplaced religious idealism and zealous attitudes generated in this petal are directed to the Liver centre. Both the Scorpionic and Sagittarian petals receive the cleansing *piṇgalā nāḍī* flow coming via their polar opposites (Gemini and Taurus) after the successful washing and refining process has occurred in Splenic centre II. The *prāṇas* are projected to the Liver centre (a minor centre that is the right hand extension of the Solar Plexus centre) wherein the general loving dispositions of the individual are stored and processed.

Sagittarius, channels Fiery-Airy prāṇas of the piṇgalā stream to and from the Liver centre.

The *saṃskāras* mastered in Sagittarius are those that arise as a consequence of lifetimes of wrongly directed thoughts in any arena of activity in the three worlds of human livingness. Such thoughts arise like arrows being targeted to an object of desire to conquer material ambition. It should be obvious that the appellation given to each of the signs are the opposing transformed aspects of what is normally engendered. In Sagittarius's case the phrase is *'without arising'*, therefore arising thoughts must be prevented at their source. The archer must learn not to create or fire such 'arrows'. Also, what does not arise is technically 'the Middle Path'. This path simply exists and must be revealed by eliminating the veils of substance and of concepts to each point of the wheel of the zodiac. The one-pointed arrows of 'right-completed'[5] thought of the *dharma* in Sagittarius, directed toward the targets of enlightenment and liberation, quickly eliminates illusional and glamoured forms of thinking. It prevents the arising of the extremes, the cause of the fighting between the 'brothers' represented by the polar opposite sign, Gemini. The *prāṇas* engendered are targeted to produce Voidness.

Capricorn, channels prāṇas to and from the Diaphragm centre.

With respect to the *Capricornian* petal, the quality to be achieved is designated *'without ceasing'*. Here one must ceaselessly strive to climb the mountain of attainment as the wheel that cleanses the substance of veil after veil obscuring the Middle Path of life, cyclically turns. The *saṃskāras* to be transmuted here consequently represent those that qualify all aspects of mind, to be replaced with attributes of Mind. With each turn of the wheel and milestone passed upon the upward way, consciousness becomes increasingly subtler and refined in nature. Thus the person eventually stands in the Clear Light allowing *dharmakāya* to be experienced. There is no ceasing of striving to climb up the mount of

5 Wayman, 288.

mind/Mind for that goal to be achieved. At first such activity is arduous because there are many rough rocks and crags of mind to master, but later the activity becomes effortless and spontaneous. Inevitably, the reinforced habits of striving become so ingrained that they are automatic, similar to having forgotten the effort required to learn to walk as a child. Having attained the goal, effortless striving persists.

The *prāṇas* engendered are those coming as a consequence of striving to lift all veils of the planes of perception *(lokas).* Yogically, the symbolism concerns mastering all of the *chakras* as one travels up the spinal column *(suṣumṇā nāḍī)* to the Head lotus. This Capricornian petal assists in raising *prāṇas* from below the diaphragm to those above it via the Diaphragm centre.

Aquarius channels Airy-Fiery prāṇas of the iḍā stream to and from the Stomach centre.

The sign Aquarius the water bearer is designated as *'without constructive thought'*. The Aquarian normally produces shallow and quite fleeting thoughts relating to everyday desires and wishes. Superficial attitudes is a keynote of the average Aquarian, contrary to the type of concretising materialistic thinking that typifies the Capricornian. Thoughts are generally constructed around keynote ideas and acceptance of an established ideology. The *saṃskāras* to be mastered thus concern overcoming superficial acceptance of teachings and forms of propaganda. The Aquarian must become more focussed, to seek out the heart or truth of any matter, to thereby deepen understanding of the *dharma*. The mutability of the Aquarian produces thought-constructs that are more embracive of the whole picture, but to access the 'Middle Path' ideas must become truly universal in nature, to include all things. All aspects relating to the twelve petals of the Heart centre concerning truth must be discerned. The universal Mind that is a keynote of the developed Bodhisattva is thereby engendered. The way of approach is through developing the intuitive perception that *bodhicitta* accedes. In this way the enlightenment that clearly sees everything in one moment of time is assured. Revelatory thoughts and images then spontaneously arise as needed.

The *prāṇas* generated are the refined attributes of the *manasic iḍā nāḍī* stream (of the Leonine-Aquarian line) after they have been refined by the Splenic centre II circulation. The general Airy *manasic prāṇas* are directed by the Leo petal to Aquarius, which then incorporates them into the Stomach centre to help pacify some of the more turbulent or erroneous thoughts there. (This centre processes all mentalistic *saṃskāras* below the diaphragm, though at first they are mundane and often of irritation, hatred and dogmatic or shallow-minded opinions.) Fiery aspects of that centres *prāṇas* may also pass through the Aquarian gate to Leo for further processing in Splenic centre II. The generation of *bodhicitta* becomes foremost in the Aquarian mind when the Bodhisattva path is espoused.

Pisces channels iḍā prāṇas (mainly of a Watery-Earthy nature) to and from the Stomach centre.

Finally we are given the quality *'without discursive thought'* attributed to *Pisces the fishes*. The concept of discursive thought involves moving from topic to topic in a rambling manner with relatively little analysis. For the average person such activity is most marked in Pisces. Consequently, the mediumistic tendencies wherein such (Watery) thought activity dominates must be overcome. Here the mind is influenced by any thought or impression that appears in the psychic environment. Once such impressions appear in consciousness, they are shallowly and emotionally interpreted, producing bonded activity. The *saṃskāras* to be transmuted therefore concern the emotional bonds that persist from life to life, from which a meditator must learn to unyoke him/herself. Attachment must first be made to higher discursive thought, allowing deep analysis concerning all ideas in the world's thought strata, specifically those relating to enlightenment. A *yogin* later learns to detach from all conceptual thoughts and to *saṃsāric* allurements, causing all bonds to ephemera to be broken by developing the Clear Light of Mind, whereby non-discursive thought manifests.

The *prāṇas* of this Piscean petal flow to and from the Stomach centre, wherein the *kamā-manasic* results of a past cycle of endeavour (a past life, or lives) are gleaned, and which can be accessed in the reciprocal process in the new cycle, when discursive thoughts are again expressed. From this perspective, Pisces governs experiences in the psychic domains in the afterlife.

The eight-armed cross

The remaining eight phrases presented in the sixth verse of this text are concerned with the discernment of the real. This involves the process that orients the moving *prāṇas* according to the directions of the eight points of the compass. Yogically, one then envisions the *Diaphragm centre,* the organ that directs *prāṇas* to the polarities of the *nāḍī* system. Positioned midway between the upper and lower portions of the body, this centre effectively manifests as a mirror, projecting *prāṇas* from above to below the diaphragm, and *vice versa.* The mutable interplay between the two types of energies forces out the coarser types of *prāṇas* that are not refined enough to be appropriated by the higher centres. They are then directed to Splenic centre I for processing.

The wheel of the zodiac is constituted from properties of the interrelated cardinal, fixed and mutable crosses,[6] and has the propensity to move from right to left, left to right, and also fourth dimensionally. Energy also moves from within-without, without-within, above down, and below up, along the spokes of the wheel, as well as between polar opposites, and between any of the points (petals) of the wheel. The three types of motion: rotary, spiral-cyclic, and forward progressive, should also be taken into account.

The direction *north* of the eight-spoked cross represents aspiration to the domains of liberation, the awakening of the Head lotus and the experience of *dharmakāya.* Yogically it signifies travelling up the spinal column, awakening *chakra* systems as it proceeds. Inevitably, we have the release of *kuṇḍalinī* that moves from the Base of Spine centre to the Head centre.

The direction *northeast* represents *unity.* This concerns being attuned to all forms of Life, subjectively, objectively, or transcendentally, and with humanity in particular. It necessitates receptivity to the incoming energies from one's family, or group of which one is a part. It can also include the membership of the Council of Bodhisattvas. It concerns receptivity to streams of energies, and blending together the factors, with which a causative agent must work. (The word 'causative' here relates to

---

6 The various volumes of this treatise shall detail the qualities of these crosses, as they are utilised by all causative agents, human or superhuman.

the conscious, self-willed production of phenomena that exists for some duration of expression.) It concerns the information coming from any aspect of human civilisation, or from the Sambhogakāya Flowers in the *ālayavijñāna* environment. From another perspective, it represents the input of the *bījas* from the Sambhogakāya Flower into the personality.

The direction *east* represents travelling inward to the Heart of Life by manifesting compassionate activity, and ultimately to the *śūnyatā* experience, which is the fruit of the middle way between extremes. It therefore represents the direction the Bodhisattva travels internally whilst he/she is actively serving via the western activity.

The direction *southeast* represents *expression* and concerns the process associated with the battlefield of desire. Here all is unfolded in the field of Life. On a higher turn of the spiral this battlefield involves overcoming the major *saṃsāric* impediments associated with the desire-mind. It necessitates the process of assimilating the outgoing energies that are directed to the formed realms from the northeast direction. At first, desire and the concrete mind of general humanity is stimulated, then their fields of aspirational activity. The causative agent must rightly direct quantified streams of energy and absorb impressions from *saṃsāra*. The process necessitates activating mental *bījas* (or for average humanity, mental-emotional ones) so that future experiences will benefit from past awareness and impressions. They can then be assimilated into consciousness. Perceptions evolve as actions happen through time. Without drawing upon the past experiences, there can be no reference point to the present, thus there would be no sequence of *bījas* activated for the manifestation of any activity. Expression also involves considerations of right timing or of cyclic activity.

The direction *south* represents incorporating the little lives embodying one's body of manifestation into consciousness. It is the field of service to the lesser kingdoms in Nature and to the sum of the conditioning of *saṃsāra*. Yogically, it concerns awakening the types of perception associated with the minor *chakras* (the Inner Round), or those below the diaphragm.

The direction *southwest* concerns making all experiences an essential part of the unit of consciousness. This necessitates an identification with the experiences, producing *understanding*, so that new *bījas* are created for the future activities of that ego, to be recalled when needed. The experiences become assimilated into consciousness and consequently become the past, part of one's own personal identification, producing the ability to progress to the future, to new categories of impressions that influence consciousness. Eventually the complete flowering of the *tathāgatagarbha* is experienced. What is assimilated then becomes the note, a new quality or colouring of *prāṇa* to be channelled into the *nāḍīs*.

Once the experiences have been assimilated, a person normally shares this with others. This represents the direction *west,* of outwards expression into the field representing humanity. Mass education, cultural exchange and communication, mutually beneficent social interactions, the concourse of nation states and civilisations is the result, as well as the many wars and social evils that victimise all of us in one way or other. Consequently, this is the arena of service for all Bodhisattvas and people of goodwill.

The direction *northwest* concerns the process of *outward expansion* of the entire sphere of identification into the future, the forward progression of the individual towards enlightenment. Once the energies of Life have been expressed on the plains of the earth and the battles of desire have been fought, then comprehension of the entire Life process proceeds with certainty. This produces entry into the path of Initiation into Life's mysteries. Eventually, the evocation of the emanatory goodwill *(bodhicitta)* that directs the person off the mutable cross and away from manifestation takes place. The work of the causative agent thus finds its fruition. The purpose of the long, aeonic cycles of endeavour comes to light.

The emanatory auric quality sent out ahead (denoted as a goodwill or *mantric* beneficence) is replete with future patterns of what is to be. It can also represent what conscious units in the external environment define as a Deity, viewed as a unique Individuality. The emanatory energy produces the projection of *antaḥkaraṇas* out of the physical domain into the higher spheres, and thence cosmos. Creative or causative activity is projected from a limited field of application to another more embracive one. The energy or quality of the singular unit or group then merges into the whole, producing ever-expanding scenarios of activity. Having fulfilled this task, the causative agent attracts the gain of former activity, so that the related qualities can be utilised for even vaster work.

The Splenic centres

Viewing the *Splenic centre* as a dual superimposed *chakra* we see that its function is to process *prāṇas,* refining what is possible, rejecting those that debase consciousness and recirculating what is needed. It processes the vitalising *prāṇas* from breath and the food ingested, which refers also to the intake of new ideas. The *prāṇas* are first directed from minor centres at the breasts to the Heart centre, where they are combined with the intrinsic energy of Life obtained via the Heart's link to the Śūnyatā Eye of the Sambhogakāya Flower. The integrated *prāṇas* of the personal-I are then collectively known as *jīva,* an individual's life energy. They are then directed to Splenic centre I, which incorporates them into the entire body. The *jīva* then combines with *prāṇas* that are recycling through *nāḍīs*. The reject *prāṇas* (often of greyish greens or brownish colours) are projected out of the system via the superimposed eight petalled Splenic centre II. This happens through the smaller *chakras* that represent the next level of *prāṇic* circulation (the Inner Round). This level of *chakras* absorb some of these *prāṇas* before directing the dross to the level of the acupuncture points, which does likewise before passing them out of the body via myriads of tiny pores, producing a radiatory health aura. Its nature depends upon the quality of the *prāṇas* leaving the body. When people are sick the lines of energy are not aligned, but are more skewed and lack vitality.

These lines of energy eventually develop into the dynamically radiant aura of a Bodhisattva or Buddha. The fine lines of energy radiating from the body change from vibrant lines of small length to intense radiations occupying a large space around the body. Also, jewels of accomplishment are developed, as well as the beauty of apparel seen aurically around the Bodhisattva, as depicted in Buddhist art.

A dynamic, radiatory aura is not easily developed, but once developed indicates the mastery of *siddhis* and the power to heal. The aura must be built anew in each life. Accomplished beings manifesting such auric fields are rare; only a few incarnate during any epoch, except in exceptional circumstances, such as the appearance of a high level Bodhisattva or Buddha, when an entire *maṇḍala* of great ones manifests with him. Such appearances happen when a major cycle of human evolution is to be instigated and aspects of civilisation are to be profoundly stimulated. It signifies the dynamic vivification and awakening of a major *chakra* composed of many human units.

Much yet needs to be revealed concerning the method of appearance of great ones and why they do so at a particular time. The epochs of history are governed by such appearances, producing the evolutionary progression of humanity and all orders of evolving Life. Enlightenment necessitates a proper understanding of the science of the *chakras*. Knowledge of the externalised *chakras* lay the foundation for many revelations concerning how the course of history is structured. Understanding the nature of the awakening Heart centre is essential. The middle way is the way of compassion because the process releases a materialistically addicted person from the dross of attachments. It produces the radiatory healing aura of Bodhisattvas (according to the stages of the turning of the wheels) as a side effect.

The processes manifesting on a tiny scale in the human *nāḍīs* are mirrored in the broader scenarios of Life. One can go inward via contemplation to ascertain the outward process of the way of treading the great Wheel.

The twelve-spoked wheel (Splenic centre I) is superimposed upon the eight-spoked wheel (Splenic centre II), which generates *'destiny's action'* (the rectification of the substance of *karma*). Splenic centre II is concerned with the process of transmuting *saṃskāras* or rejecting those no longer necessary for the healthy maintenance of the body.

Note that the petals of *chakras* manifest energetically in the form of wheels turning, according to either of the three types of motion previously described. It is not possible to adequately depict this motion, as some petals of the major *chakras* are practically dormant waiting for the appropriate response from the individual concerned, whilst others are acutely active because of the nature of the *saṃskāras* then being expressed by the individual. The nature of the energy flow from one petal to another is also virtually instantaneous, however, the general pattern of flow can be visualised at any one time. The relationship of *prāṇic* flow and petal movements between the three *chakras* (Splenic centres I and II and the Heart centre) manifest in a similar manner to the movements of the cogs of the wheels driving the internal mechanism of a clock.

The rate of motion of the wheels of the twelve and eight-spoked Splenic centres turn like the minute and second hands of a clock in relation to each other and to the Heart centre. The motion causes the petals to move in and out of alignment with each other. The petals of the wheel of the major *chakras* manifest analogous to the form of the hour hands of the clock. This 'hand' is concerned with the overall life pattern of *saṃskāras*. The 'minute hand' is concerned with the expression of a major stream of *saṃskāras* coming into play. The 'second hand' channels the vicissitudes of each moment of individual life and *saṃsāric* activity.

From a higher perspective, the 'second hand' can refer to the general processing of a *saṃskāra* in the individual within a particular life. The 'minute hand' will then refer to processing a specific type of *saṃskāra* for a group of generally seven lives, where the qualities of the *saṃskāra* is developed and mastered. The 'hour hand' represents the process of the transmutation of that *saṃskāra* into enlightenment attributes so that it can be accommodated in a particular petal of the Heart centre. This generally takes many cycles of seven lives to accomplish. Thus the Wheels of Life pertaining to *saṃsāra* and of perpetual rebirth of *saṃskāras* continuously revolve, until the rectified qualities associated with the twelve petals of the Heart centre are fully expressed. The Heart's motion represents the middle way of turning, where the 'middle way' represents the essence of what has transpired.

The Dharmakāya Way is expressed in the form of wheels turning within wheels of increasingly greater size of magnitude and order of duration within the Head lotus. Eventually the wheels of the *nirmāṇakāya* of a Buddha evolve and turn with respect to greater Wheels of certain stellar spheres in cosmos.

The entire process producing the complete awakening of the twelve petals of the Heart lotus presents a view as to the magnitude of *śūnyatā* and the middle way not normally considered. Hence the term 'Void' does not do it justice, as it is the essence of many lives of accomplishment whereby *saṃsāric* dross is eliminated.

When these *prāṇas* are combined with the transformed and refined *manasic prāṇas* from the Throat centre then we have what I term the 'Heart's Mind', meaning that the corresponding petals in the Head lotus have been awakened, a consequence of travelling the Dharmakāya Way. Of necessity, this takes a large number of lives to accomplish.[7]

---

7 The number of lives generally necessitated before a person obtains liberation is symbolised by the number 777. See Volume 4 of this *Treatise on Mind* for further detail.

Thus it is not possible to become a Buddha in merely one life, as the foundation for such an attainment is arduous in the making, involving much evolutionary time.

Liberation and the Diaphragm centre

The energies producing liberation are the major qualifying *prāṇas* generating *bodhicitta,* pouring from the Taurean petal of the Heart centre to the Diaphragm centre, and consequently the centres below the diaphragm. These *prāṇas* will also contain attributes that were rejected from Heart centre circulation and consequently need further refining. Liberation also involves the projection of refined *prāṇas* upward to the Heart centre,[8] so that attributes of *bodhicitta* can be further developed, as well as directing the rejected *prāṇas*[9] from the centres above the diaphragm downwards to the Splenic centre for processing. The *prāṇas* directed towards the Heart centre will be further processed in the petal that empathises with the qualities they carry. This pertains to 'the real', whilst *saṃsārically* focussed *prāṇas* (the 'unreal'), are rejected.

The Diaphragm centre is the central mechanism of energising the *nāḍī* system with vitality from the general environment. This represents the psychic in and out-breathing process of the individual. The other centres concerned in this process are the minor centres located centrally between the shoulder blades and at the right and left lungs, as well as Splenic centre I, which fully integrates the incorporated *prāṇas* into the general system. The Heart centre plays the role, as previously mentioned, of establishing the integral *jīva* of the individual.

To comprehend the nature of Diaphragm centre circulation we shall first analyse its *northern* petal, labelled 'not independent'. It conveys *prāṇas* originating from the centre Between the Shoulder Blades, and the energies from the Head lotus via the Throat centre. More specifically, it is the place of rejection of *prāṇas* above the diaphragm (from the centres in the chest cavity), and is the place of exit and entry

8 *Prāṇas* are also sent to the Lung and Shoulder Blade centres, which are minor centres concerned with *prāṇic* vitalisation, the in and out-breathing of *prāṇas*. Consequently, they are directly linked to the Heart centre.

9 Such *prāṇas* convey *saṃskāras* whose attributes consciousness no longer deems worthy of expression.

of consciousness into and out of the form at the moment of death and at birth. It therefore represents the start of the building and vitalisation of the *nāḍī* system. Consequently, it is the highest of the five centres concerned with *prāṇic* vitalisation of the body.

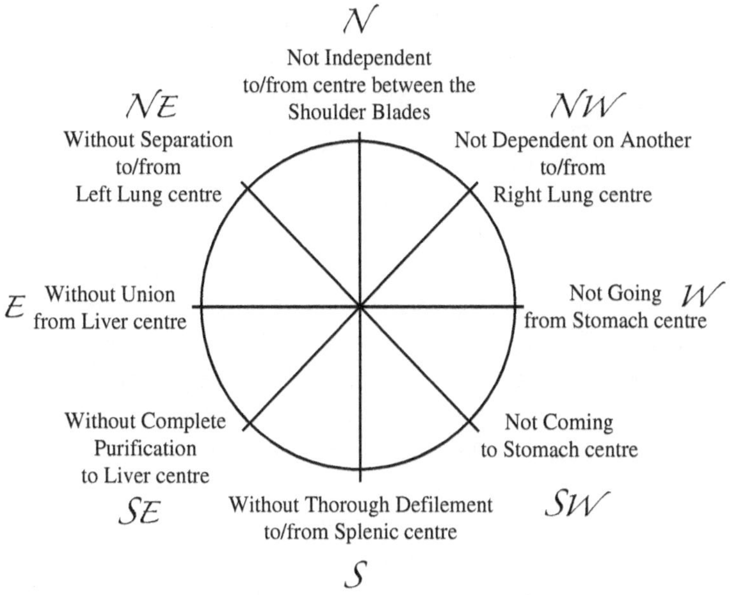

Figure 9. The Diaphragm centre

The interrelation between the Diaphragm and Shoulder Blade centres happens via the Taurean petal of the Heart *chakra* ('liberation'). The Diaphragm centre then passes them to the general *prāṇic* pool of Splenic centre I (via its Capricornian petal), which then passes the modified *prāṇas* via its Taurean petal ('without one extreme') to Splenic centre II. This energy stream helps wash clean the *prāṇas* of both Splenic centres that have an empathy with the quality of the incoming *prāṇas*. In this way their *saṃskāras* are refined or transmuted according to the degree that consciousness can utilise the Heart centre as a base of expression of the life process. Effectively, therefore, these energies are 'not independent' from those of the Heart centre (which they convey), and they are the most refined *prāṇas* that can be handled below the diaphragm. They are the attributes needing developing over the long run so that liberation can eventually ensue.

Overall, the energy of *bodhicitta* is generated by the cleansing process, otherwise *saṃskāras* are recirculated and expressed for further *karma* formations. The *prāṇas* from Splenic centre I enter the northern petals of Splenic centre II (entitled 'without destiny's action'), to cleanse the desire-mind dispensation processed by this centre. It should be noted, however, that this centre is mainly concerned with purifying Watery-Earthy *prāṇas*. Once these *prāṇas* have been appropriately cleansed then Watery-Fiery energies will flow from Splenic centre I to vitalise the southern petal of Splenic centre II, and then the Inner Round. This is the major route for the Heart's energies to influence the minor centres in the *nāḍī* system.

Described above is a downward motion for the *prāṇas,* which manifest 'without thorough defilement' via the southern petal of the Diaphragm centre. An upwards focus also produces a state of being 'not independent' because this direction produces integration with all that is real. The 'real' being that which expresses the functions of the Head and Heart lotuses. Following this path to its conclusion facilitates enlightenment, allowing a person to become meditatively awakened. The development of enlightened qualities are dependent upon the transformative process that drives *prāṇas* upwards. The northern petal introduces the type of energies from the realm of enlightenment that will unify the part with the all, thus with the demonstration of oneness. This can be symbolised by the absorption of the rivulet of consciousness into the ocean of being/non-being, once the *prāṇas* of the minor centres have been thoroughly energised from the Heart centre.

The *northeast* petal is characterised by the quality *'without separation'.* This centre breathes in *prāṇas* to be incorporated into the system via the Left Lung centre. This petal therefore expresses what is not separate from the rest of the environment concerning all the factors that cause one to exist. The external *manasic prāṇas* from this centre entering the Diaphragm centre mix with the energies from the Heart centre (coming from the eastern petal) and the resultant qualified *jīva* energises the Stomach centre via the southwest petal. There they are properly digested. As previously stated, the Stomach centre processes all *manasic* propensities, the gain of sense-consciousnesses as derived from contact with the external environment. The effect for the average person is to intensify the *manasic prāṇas* therein (producing strong ideas, forceful mental attitudes).

The Stomach centre *prāṇas* generally enter the Solar Plexus centre, which processes all Watery activity associated with consciousness. Inevitably, the more Earthy attributes enter the Splenic centre II circulation, which will over time wash clean the *karma* of all forms of attachment and the worst aspects of materially oriented emotionality. In this manner, all of the lower centres will inevitably become energised from the Heart.[10] The Heart produces a communality, a unity of purpose, through engendering the factor of *bodhicitta* throughout the diversity of forces associated with the lower centres.

Inevitably, the enlightenment-path is trodden and the *prāṇas* from the left Lung centre help refine thoughts, producing more enlightened mental attitudes. When consciousness finally focuses via this northeast direction then there is a harmonious flow, no separation of the *prāṇic* consciousness-stream coming via the Stomach centre to the Left Lung centre. The *iḍā prāṇic* orientation from the Stomach centre towards the Heart lotus, produces a spaciousness known as the Clear Mind, which is subtly unified with all other such Minds.

The esoteric subject under consideration in relation to the Lung centres concerns yogic breathing, where the originating *prāṇas* come from the right and left nostrils (via two minor *chakras)* via the Shoulder Blade centre. It should be noted that forceful breathing practices can be dangerous because the resultant *prāṇas* can overly stimulate the Stomach or Liver centres, as well as the Sacral centre. Any mind fixation practices, *dhāraṇīs,* related to counting breaths and holding them in consciousness with wilful intent should not be attempted unless one has an enlightened preceptor. The compassionate refining and transforming energies from the Heart centre must first be invoked and brought to the lower centres if the practice is to be safely accomplished. The main objective of such practices is to assist in the cleansing and refinement of *saṃskāras* so that the all-seeing Eye can be awakened, and consequently the rapid expansion and movement of the petals of the Head lotus.

---

10 This brief outline shall be significantly elaborated in Volume 5A.

The *eastern* direction of progressing inwards to the Heart of Life is designated as *'without union'*. It concerns the way of directing the *prāṇas (bodhicitta)* from the Heart centre to the minor *chakras* constituting the Inner Round after the Life energy has been integrated with the proceeds of the breathing process. The objective is to cause the cleansing or transmutation of the more base, animal-like *saṃskāras* (emotions, desires, and materialistic aspirations) that they generate. There consequently can be no union with them until all defilements have been thoroughly dispelled. There is also an incoming flow of *prāṇas* from those centres that have been thus cleansed and which can manifest the most intense form of *bodhicitta* that they are capable of expressing. The objective of the *prāṇas* entering the Heart centre is not union with its attributes, but rather the development of *śūnyatā,* which is considered to be Void of attributes.

The *east to west* arm of the Diaphragm centre interrelates the *prāṇas* of the Heart and Solar Plexus centres via intermediaries, the Liver and Stomach centres. These two centres are but extensions of the Solar Plexus centre. The refined *kāma-manasic prāṇas* from the Stomach centre and those from the Liver centre *(kliṣṭamanas)* are integrated in the Diaphragm centre, manifesting a form of cross-over, mixing these *prāṇas.* The purpose concerns making the general *manasic (iḍā) prāṇas* of the Stomach centre more compassionate *(piṇgalā)* in nature by an admixture with the Liver centre flow, and vice versa. This produces a more balanced thought process, if the Diaphragm centre is not overwhelmed by the energies flowing through it from the lower centres because of a strong emotional will of the person concerned. Normally, what cannot be mixed is recycled back to the respective centres for reprocessing.

It should be noted that the concern here is with the *prāṇic* circulation that is subsidiary to the *iḍā* and *piṇgalā* flow up the spinal column between the major *chakras.* The main objective of this subsidiary circulation is to refine, purify and ultimately transform the associated *saṃskāras.* The Diaphragm centre therefore acts as a type of cleansing house, or gate, partially blocking the way upwards of unrefined *prāṇas* to the higher centres, allowing those centres to be empowered with qualities applicable to the qualities they were designed to convey. It does this by being central to the breathing process, where the incoming vital energy assists in the conversion of the qualities of the lower centres.

This vitality rejects the unregenerate *prāṇas* that find their way to this centre. In the earlier stages of human evolution these energies intensify the activity of the lower centres.

For those upon a yogic path where the input of the energies from the Stomach and Liver centres are strongly clashing then the Diaphragm centre will be unsettled, overwhelmed, producing unpleasant sensations therein. The remedy concerns controlling the Watery input from both minor centres, allowing the Diaphragm centre to appropriately mix the opposing energies, so that they can be received by the Lung centres and then the Throat centre, or else the Heart centre.

Note that because of the differing spiritual ages of practitioners, as well as the attributes of average humanity, it is difficult to properly explain the nature of *prāṇic* circulation. Everything depends upon the state of advancement of the individual, thus the *prānas* can flow to or from the respective centres. The more refined the psyche the greater the sensitivity to the flow of coarse *prāṇas*. They produce negative effects in the centre they lodge in until they are refined, eliminated or transmuted, and projected to higher centres. This process converts the base qualities of *saṃsāra* into those that generate enlightenment. This *prāṇic* turning about in consciousness rectifies the wheel of the zodiac. (Including the motion of the lesser wheels of the *chakras.)* Average humanity do not feel the effects of coarse energies, as that is their normal psychic constitution, but they often succumb to sicknesses and diseases as a consequence.

The *southeast* direction of 'outward expression' is designated *'without complete purification'*. The *prāṇas* from the Diaphragm centre enter the Liver centre, which acts as a storage facility specifically along the *piṇgalā* line of loving, affectionate, cooperative attributes, allowing proper assimilation of these *saṃskāras*. As such, they have not been sufficiently purified to adequately engender the compassionate attributes of the Heart. The engendering of such attributes is the purpose of the circulatory system below the diaphragm and has its proper genesis in the attributes of the Liver centre. The purification process necessitates an influx of *prāṇas* from the Heart centre, which find receptivity in Liver centre activity when consciousness is sensitively attuned to other's needs. In the early stages, impressions from the Heart centre are generally completely swamped by the desire-filled emotive life of the normal day to day experiences of the individual. *Bodhicitta* needs to be gradually developed to transform the desire base into higher aspirational thoughts and impulses.

When the *prāṇas* of desire and attachment are directed upwards, they are expressed in the Diaphragm centre in a form needing further purification before they can enter the Heart's circulation. A considerable portion finds their way to the Splenic centre for refinement before they are of the required quality. The remainder passes either to the Heart centre, or to the right Lung centre, where their effects are 'breathed' out through compassionate activity. As long as there is a desire-filled contact with the material world it is not possible to purify the associated *saṃskāras*. There is a needed input of heart-based *prāṇas* for the purposes of right understanding of people's true needs so that one can rightly give. Many bitter experiences must be digested and assimilated before the need to travel the Bodhisattva path becomes clear. The experience of what is pleasurable generally reinforces desire for further intoxicating stimulants. Such *prāṇas* are recycled through the lower centres and will inevitably produce sickness and diseases through lack of empathy with the evolutionary push of the entire organism. The *prāṇas* from the Heart centre will always work to project such *saṃskāras* to the surface so they can be properly processed. The *prāṇic* circulation for a human unit manifests in a similar fashion to that of humanity in general, thus humanity experiences *karmic* rectifying factors such as droughts, earthquakes, famines, wars, etc. They are the effects of massed *saṃskāras* evoked by the activities of those concerned, to experience the effects of the *prāṇas* they generated in the past.

The phrase *'without thorough defilement'* of the *southern* direction projects *prāṇas* downwards to Splenic centre I, allowing interaction with the substance of *saṃsāric* life. This petal therefore integrates all the energies associated with *prāṇic* flow below the diaphragm and which have been sufficiently refined in order to pass to the higher centres. Here is expressed the *karma*-forming *saṃskāras* dealt with at any moment of life, and which spiritually defile if not properly cleansed. By the time such energies pass upwards to be directed by the Diaphragm centre many of their gross attributes have been washed away, hence the nature of the *prāṇas* found at this petal are 'without thorough defilement'. They can pass through the Heart centre via the non-sacred petals relatively unaltered, towards the Throat centre via the Shoulder Blade centre. Or else they can enter into the Heart centre's circulation if sufficiently refined. The liberated being interacts with such substance to help liberate others, but is not defiled by it, because it is non-attached to it in any way.

The *southwest* direction (of understanding) is designated *'not coming'*. Here the *prāṇas* are directed to the Stomach centre to be assimilated into consciousness after having been 'digested' via this centre's activities. It produces the quality of consciousness that sustains the now, being the main *saṃskāric* expression for any cycle of undertaking. Thoughts and desires are processed to produce understanding of what is and shall be. Therefore, there is effectively nothing in this direction that is 'coming', as the *prāṇic* field is already *in situ,* and consciousness must comprehend what is expressed there. This field, however, is continually being modified as per the mood of consciousness at any time. (There is thus a coming and going of *prāṇas,* as for all the *chakras.)* Depending upon the nature of the comprehension (which is often quick and impulsive), so one immersed in the Stomach centre awareness can manifest in a forceful, reactionary or explosive manner. Thus we have the expression of anger, hatred, irritation, contempt, heavily opinionated and prejudicial attitudes. (Such qualities manifest because this centre is the store of *iḍā prāṇas* below the diaphragm and is energised by the weight of the force of the Solar Plexus centre.)

The process producing right understanding must gradually occur internally before people recognise the need to awaken higher perceptions. Much psychic realignment and adjustment of energies is needed to transform consciousness.

We can see that this exposé concerning the minor centres posits, contrary to popular belief, that consciousness is not just centred in the brain, but that its qualities are developed in the minor centres, and when the *saṃskāras* travel to the Head lotus the experiences can then be cognised. There is consequently a direct interrelation between the neurons of the physical brain and the Head lotus, which must be intact for perceptions to become an integral part of the persona. Without the *chakras* the physical organism would not be aware of anything, except maybe elementary sensations; neither could there be any possibility of rebirth. If the connections between the Head lotus and the physical apparatus is severed, we would have an imbecile, with the consciousness attached, but hovering external to the form, unable to utilise its instrument.

The scientific community must yet ascertain what the emotions actually are, how they arise, their true purpose and how they differ from consciousness. Certainly the neurons do not convey these attributes, as they do not pertain to physical plane sensations, but rather to a subjective domain. Scientists must correlate the fact that though animals have brains and neurons, they do not have human emotions, or imagination. Therefore, what is it that makes humans different? They presume it is in a larger, more complex brain in humans, but in fact it is in the nature of the type of *chakras* utilised, some of which animals do not possess. The highest centre for domesticated animals is the Solar Plexus centre, which allows elementary emotional and affectionate identification with humans to occur, but little else. However, they possess a form of telepathy and certain psychic capabilities associated with that centre little understood by our modern materialistic scientists. In time they will learn to communicate with our animal brethren from an awakened Solar Plexus to Solar Plexus interaction. This will revolutionise the study of the entire evolutionary process.

The physical sense-consciousnesses manifest first through the *chakras* that exist to process them. (Effectively, for instance, many people think with their 'stomachs', for others their thought life is heavily dominated by impressions from their sex-organs.) An awakened being can directly perceive via any of the *chakras,* whilst psychics and clairvoyants normally perceive via minor centres. Once the sensations of the lower centres are stilled, then higher perceptions develop and the Clear Light of Mind that perceives *dharmakāya* is possible. The brain consciousness is consequently transcended and the higher dimensional perceptions of the awakened *chakras* take their place.

The appellation 'not coming' can also refer to the effects of the Heart's compassionate stance, which rarely, if ever at first, find expression in the Stomach centre. (Which, being the custodian of the *saṃskāras* of mind, is most separative and self-focussed.) Only upon the enlightenment path does the Heart's energy (the subjective sun's rays) begin to transform self-centredness into selflessness.

The *western* direction of outward interrelation with humanity concerns the quality *'not going'*. It was stated previously that the east-west axis of this eight-spoked wheel projects *prāṇas* to the Heart centre (the east) and the Solar Plexus centre (the west) through intermediaries (the Stomach centre in this case). Technically therefore the *prāṇas* from this direction are 'not going' outwards to the field of service.

There is a problem for the energies of the Stomach centre to directly access the Heart's embrace, as was earlier explained in relation to the east-west axis. Mostly, the energies are redirected to Splenic centre I for reprocessing. Only at the latter stages of development, when the Waters have been dried, can the transformed energies of mind (i.e., of Mind) enter into union with the Heart centre. (Consequently transforming the eastern petal's appellation of 'without union', into a oneness.) Here lies the basis to the consideration of the appellation 'not going'—to the Heart centre via the polar opposite eastern direction. Rather, the Solar Plexus energies come to it for processing (and in the stages of aspiration they are mixed with *prāṇas* from the Heart centre). Coming from the Stomach centre, the energies are generally directed to the centres associated with any other of the spokes of this wheel.

We should also note that the *prāṇas* of all minor centres are synthesised by the Solar Plexus. It is the abdominal brain that exemplifies the western direction and integrates all of the associated animal-like qualities. In a sense the Diaphragm centre is the pump for the entire Inner Round circulation, thus there is both 'coming and going' of all *prāṇas,* but because this centre occupies the central position of the entire system there is literally no coming or going of its own intrinsic quality. This has been described here as 'discerning the real', which means *prāṇically* that it redirects admixed *prāṇas* to their appropriate destinations according to their attributes. They go upwards if they pertain to the real (the awakening of higher perceptions), or downwards if the *saṃskāras* are sensually inclined. These *prāṇas* are predominantly Watery, controlled by the Solar Plexus, which is the prime directing agency here. The Diaphragm centre receives these *prāṇas* and redirects them to the upper or lower torso, but not to the Solar Plexus centre, except indirectly through intermediaries.

For the *northwest* petal (the path of return), manifesting the cleansing mantra of emanatory goodwill to all, the mode of action is given as *'not dependent on another'*. The *prāṇas* from this petal are directed from the right Lung centre, involving the breathing out of the emanatory *prāṇic* note from below the diaphragm, which is then incorporated into the circulation of the Head centre via the right lobe of the Ājñā centre. Petals within these centres are accordingly awakened depending upon the attribute of 'the real' that the *prāṇas* possess. Being *piṇgalā* they are of a compassionate nature, awakening enlightening attributes (of the Heart in the Head lotus) in the realms of thought. The *prāṇas* will be immediately absorbed in the appropriate subsidiary petals of that lotus, being only dependent upon what has already been achieved in the centres below the diaphragm. The innate act of discernment of the Diaphragm centre has already eliminated all dross *saṃskāras* not capable of being utilised by the higher centres. (Also the Lung centres can project Airy *prāṇas* out of the system via the centre Between the Shoulder Blades.)

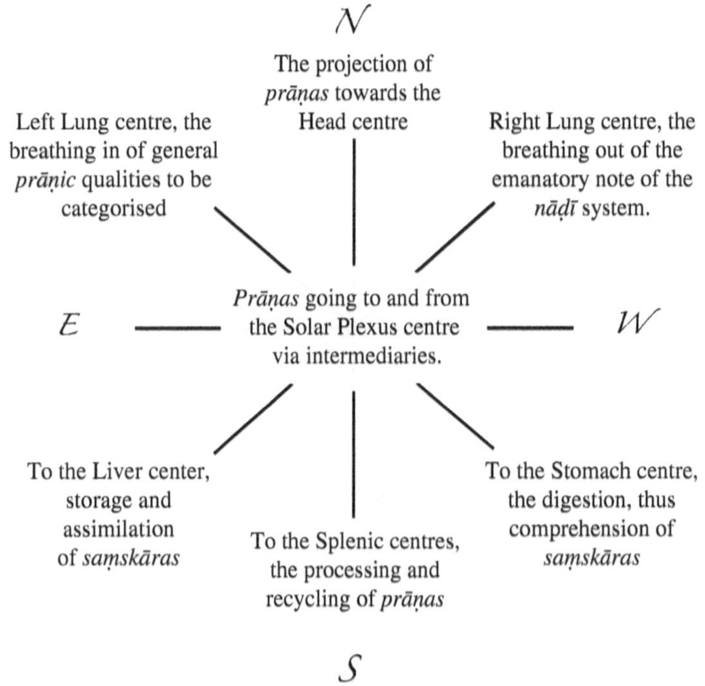

Figure 10. The Diaphragm centre as a distributor of Energies

One should note that the *nāḍīs* are an integrated system where all factors are dependent upon each other. The *prāṇas* from below the diaphragm will be absorbed into the appropriate centre and petal in the upper torso that resonates at the right frequency to do so. That petal will then be stimulated with the associated *saṃskāras.* Though all such petals are part of a grouping, affecting each other as the *prāṇas* are processed, all related petals also act as self-contained unities ('not dependent').

One becomes awakened and liberated through non dependency upon others from the perspective that enlightenment proceeds through mastery of one's own *saṃskāras.* The concept of goodwill incorporates the most refined qualities one possesses, directed to another. The evolved quality automatically identifies with all that is producing a union of one with the all. Being the real, it exists of its own accord and is not dependent upon extraneous forces or entities. The emanatory quality is a note of recognition that instantaneously feeds the all with the qualities integral to it.

Splenic centre II

Splenic centre II is concerned principally with the effects of 'destiny's action' (the dispensation of *karma).* Splenic centre I is partly superimposed upon it. This means that these two wheels function as an integral unity. Rejected Watery-Fiery *prāṇas* pass from Solar Plexus centre activity and from the circulation above the diaphragm into Splenic centre I and the Watery-Earthy *prāṇas* into Splenic centre II. This centre then processes and redirects the *prāṇas* back to the higher centres, throughout the *nāḍīs* of the Inner Round, or else out of the body altogether.

We saw above that Splenic centre II represents the activity aspect of a triplicity, with Splenic centre I manifesting as the Will aspect. It converts *kāma-manasic saṃskāras* into the more refined attributes necessary for enlightenment by washing them with the *prāṇas (bodhicitta)* from the Heart centre.

The second point of this triplicity is the Diaphragm centre, which acts as a steady director of *prāṇas* from one portion of the body to the other. It is therefore mirror-like in its functioning. This concerns the wisdom attribute that discerns the real in terms of which way to direct the *prāṇas.* It is passive with respect to the actual transmutation of *prāṇic* qualifications. Splenic centre II, on the other hand, is mutable, dealing with a rapid influx and efflux of the *prāṇas* engendered by a person, wherein *karma*-formations based upon attachment, desire and emotions and their relation to physical activity are expressed. It is the crucible or field of application wherein the various aspects of the life process are mixed with vitality to refine murky substance, producing a less volatile emotionality and subtler perceptions. Inevitably, the *prāṇas* can be directed to the higher centres wherein liberation from one's base nature is eventually attained. *Saṃskāras* that surface in the life process must be experienced, and when vivified with the cleansing *prāṇas* from Splenic centre I, we have the battlefield transforming people's normally turbulent emotions. If the person is receptive to the push from potent subtler *prāṇas,* then progression by cleansing *karma* and transmuting *saṃskāras* happens. Consciousness then focuses upon expressing the qualities of the higher centres. Otherwise, further *karma* is produced. Thus evolution proceeds.

Because the person has moved into higher fields of activity, *prāṇas* are rejected and return to general *saṃsāra,* represented by the wheel of the Six Realms. (The field of desire and of clinging to ephemera.) From a *prāṇic* perspective, these realms can be viewed thus:

a. The *human realm* is the place of generation of *prāṇas* conditioning all human relationships. Self-centred concepts and pride rules, but inevitably loving attitudes appear and once attachment to the attributes of *saṃsāra* are eliminated through the development of wisdom, then the evocation of *bodhicitta* is possible.

b. The *animal realm* concerns *prāṇas* generated via the Inner Round circulation carrying general emotions that are animal-like, hence delusional.

c. The *hell realms* are constituted of *prāṇas* generated by the most avaricious or violent human emotions of hateful or malicious intent, especially those engendered by sorcery.

d. The *preta realm* is generated by Watery *prāṇas* of pure desire or selfish emotional intensities.

e. The *asura realm* is generated by the *prāṇas* of intensified mental-desire, of thoughts that perpetuate love for aspects of *saṃsāra.* This produces a jealousy or envy of those that possess superior ethics, virtuous 'god-like skills', positions of authority or wealth, or who have developed enlightened attributes.

f. The *god realm*[11] in its lowest expression is generated by the *prāṇas* of lofty and even altruistic thoughts and idealisms (associated with the centres above the diaphragm), but which are still tainted by sentimentality, the 'self' concept, or loving-mind, hence demonstrate subtle illusions and forms of ignorance about the nature of phenomena. The more esoteric connotation is that it represents the liberated domains, wherein all such considerations have been eliminated.

Being no longer useful to the incarnate individual, the *prāṇas* that are completely rejected during any stage of *prāṇic* circulation enter a zone of containment called *the Eighth Sphere.* It is styled the 'eighth' because it contains what can no longer be sustained by the seven major *chakras.* It is a hell zone when consciously experienced because of the *prāṇas* that consciousness has eliminated and which would sicken or stifle its growth if perpetuated in. They rebound as future *karma*, however, in the after death state when experienced the *prāṇas* manifest a hell state. Its conditions were created by consciousness and need to be transmuted into a higher form of expression if they are to be incorporated into the Sambhogakāya Flower. The hell sphere (of potential conscious receptivity) consists of the most concreted aspects of the substance (the most Earthy mix of the Elements) of the Six Realms. Ultimately, all substance is resurrected through later cycles of outpouring and transmuted through illumined yogic activity.

In the relation of the Six Realms to Splenic centre II circulation it should be noted that all of the Watery *prāṇas* that produce aberrations in human consciousness are animal-like, which are the focus of the refining process associated with both Splenic centres. This Watery aspect is found in all of these realms, helping to produce the main qualities needing rectifying. The processing of aberrant Fiery *prāṇas* happens in the 'god' realm (the Head centre), and rejection of Watery conditionings begins in the

11 Note that the term 'god' here is a translation of the Sanskrit word *deva* (Tib. lha), which means 'shining one'. Though this word is generally interpreted as gods or deities it should not be confused with my rendering of the term, which refers to the feminine parallel kingdom in Nature to humanity.

preta realm (the Diaphragm centre). Problematic Fiery-Watery and Earthy *prāṇas* are dealt with in Splenic centre I (governing the *asura* realm).[12] Watery-Earthy *prāṇas* are processed in Splenic centre II, governing the animal realm, and subtly aberrant Airy *prāṇas* for those awakening the Heart centre in the human realm. These Airy *prāṇas* are the highest presented and carry the subtlest attributes of the others. Rejected *prāṇas* that pass into the Eighth Sphere, represents the hell realms.

The *preta* realm is generated by all of the factors of human emotional interrelations below the diaphragm. Consequently, the bulk of these *prāṇas* are processed in Splenic centre II, thus from this perspective it can be considered to embody the general environment wherein the *pretas* reside. However, the Diaphragm centre acts as a final arbiter of these *prāṇas* (a rejection of Watery substance with vitality from the breathing process) before they pass through to the centres above the diaphragm. (For average humanity this function is overwhelmed by the sheer force of Watery *prāṇas*, hence such *prāṇas* are factored in the petals of the higher centres.) The *pretas* have been relegated to being residents of this centre because therein they receive no nourishment sustaining their former avaricious forms of activity. Thus is the story of the Six Realms told *prāṇically.*[13]

Everyone has the capacity to experience all of the Six Realms during their unfolding life. One thus experiences god-like and pleasurable sensations (generally in one's love life), animal-like emotional propensities at another stage, hell-like emotional reactions and vitriol during another part of the life experience, etc. Sometimes these states are experienced in rapid succession in the volatile emotional body according to the metre of the way the blows of *karma* affect the individual.

---

12 *Asuras*, in Buddhism, are viewed as anti-gods that are hostile and jealous to the gods. They are residents in the realm between humans and gods, and are constantly at war with the gods over the tree of wish-fulfilment. *Pretas* are literally hungry ghosts. Those whose greed whilst incarnate led them to be born with an extended belly and tiny necks. They are said to exist on a diet of excrement, which turns to fire in the mouth, leaving them perpetually hungry and thirsty. They symbolise the forms of those who have incarnated in the lower strata of the inner realms after a life of pronounced avarice and selfishness. Being but aberrant forms of a human entity the depictions of *asuras* and *pretas* need to be viewed metaphorically rather than literally, similarly with the depiction of those in the hell states.

13 See Volume 5A, chapter 3, for further detail concerning this subject.

The Gonad centres, the field of sexual orientation and expression that will inevitably produce the birthing of a child, embody the *manasic* (creative) function of Splenic centre II at the level of Watery-Earthy *saṃskāras.* They need to convey the most Fiery aspect of these Elements at this level to produce the potency of the creative process, and to handle the 'heat' of the sexual function. The northern direction of Splenic centre II circulation must convey both the Fiery and Watery Element from Splenic centre I circulation, hence the attribute of *kliṣṭamanas* is processed here. These attributes are the most potent *prāṇas* directed to Splenic centre II from Splenic centre I. Generally in Splenic centre II the Fiery Element is missing and needs to be generated from the lower centres concerning the sexual function (the Gonad, Sacral and Base of Spine centres) and from physical plane interrelationships (relegated to the Earth Element). This represents the pure vitality from the Sacral centre, supplemented by the *kuṇḍalinī* from the Base of Spine centre at the various levels of its generation. *(Kuṇḍalinī* is seven layered.)

The southern direction therefore introduces the Fiery Element, up to the time when the energies from the Heart can pour through Splenic centre I. Then this sun-like Fire en-flames all directions of Splenic centre II, producing a transforming crucible for the substance of the sheaths. *Kuṇḍalinī* then awakens to produce the furnace, or Fire, for rapid transmutation of substance. Consequently a *siddha* is born, able to work multidimensionally.

There are eight spokes to the wheel of Splenic centre II which process the animal-like characteristics of the Six Realms. They are viewed in terms of the attributes of the eight consciousnesses needing refining. These petals in effect concern the processes that help to process the attributes (hence *karma)* that once cleansed from defilements will allow one to escape the conditions of the Six Realms. What passes through them via the *chakras* related to these petals have direct relation to the degree the *prāṇas* have been converted, transformed, or simply intensified by the time of death. They condition the type of experiences the deceased will have in the afterlife. This is because when a life ends all that happens is that a person severs ties to the physical body. The vital body still remains (controlled by Splenic centre activity) and consciousness is still incarnate within the *chakra* system. The predominant *prāṇic (saṃsāric)* qualifications therefore determine the eventual fate of the person concerned.

The southernmost petal sinks *prāṇas* into the physical spleen which then concretises the effects of one's daily psychic activities. The subjective and physical spleens represent the place of moving out of the subjectivity of various Bardo[14] experiences into incarnation. It signifies the focus of consciousness into the minutiae of everyday bodily experiences, with its forms of healthy vitality or of disease, as the function of the spleen is the cleansing of the blood system, and subjectively of *prāṇas*.

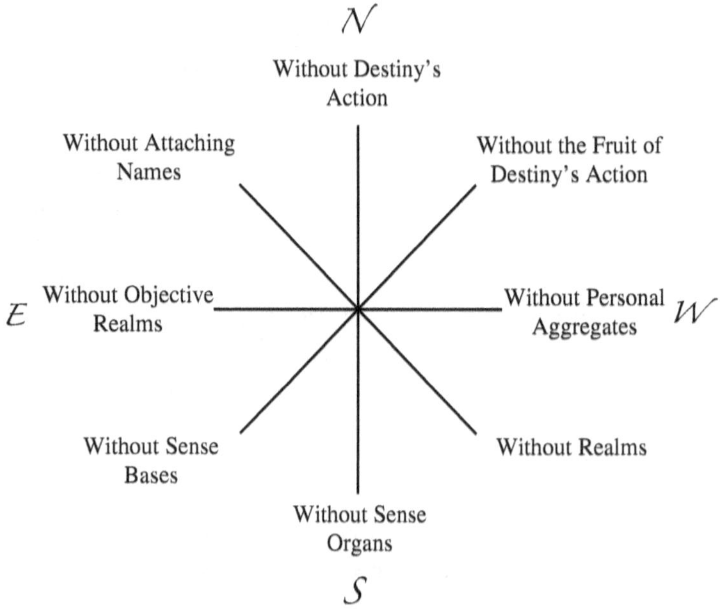

Figure 11. Splenic centre II

14 Govinda states: 'At every moment something within us dies and something is reborn. The different *bardos,* therefore, represent different states of consciousness of our life: the state of waking consciousness, the normal consciousness of being born into our human world, known in Tibetan as the *skyes-nas bardo;* the state of dream-consciousness *(rmi-lam bar-do);* the state of *dhyāna,* or trance-consciousness, in profound meditation *(bsam-gtan bar-do);* the state of the experiencing of death *(hchhi-kha bar-do);* the state of experiencing of Reality *(chhos-nyid bar-do);* the state of rebirth-consciousness *(srid-pa bar-do)'.* From the Introductory Forward by Lama Anagarika Govinda in *The Tibetan Book of the Dead,* by W.Y. Evans-Wentz (Oxford University Press, London, 1957), lx-lxi.

The empowerment of Splenic centre II sets the tenor of the type of experiences to manifest during any new incarnation and also conditions the karmic play that manifests once one disincarnates. It is therefore an effective distributer of the *karma* conditioning the life experience of an individual.

The qualities given to each of the petals of Splenic centre II start with the word 'without'. This means that each of these petals are involved in channelling the *prāṇas* of the associated quality in such a way that eventually that quality will be transmogrified into a corresponding enlightened function. They will then no longer manifest the *saṃskāras* of the associated *saṃsāric* aspect of the petal, and are thus 'without' their original qualifications. Splenic centre II therefore transforms base *prāṇas* and redirects those associated with 'destiny's action', 'attachment', etc., expelling those that are no longer viable to the system, or projects those *prāṇas* that approximate the qualities indicated to be 'without' for further processing in the higher centres. Their purpose is to eventually express the qualities of the petals of the Heart centre in their rectified aspects. They then lack the associated qualities that epitomise *saṃsāra*. This eight petalled lotus is therefore the dynamo that moves the base *prāṇas* that will eventually find their expression in the twelve petals of the Heart centre.

The *western direction* of outward to the field of service is denoted 'without personal aggregates *(skandhas)'*. This direction manifests outward to the field of service. Here this field represents the left Gonad centre where the most Earthy attributes of the Fiery Element are processed. This represents the most physical and sensual aspects of the 'sixth sense', the intellect *(manas)*. Hence at this level of expression this petal processes the sum of what may be considered 'personal aggregates', desire driven activities. The objective inevitably is to transform desire and the sexual function so that the external sexual function is sublimated into the inner forms of *prāṇic* union accomplished by a yogin as attachment to the form is transcended.

The east-west direction concerns the creative function of this centre so that the *saṃskāras* generated are in accord to the *yogin's* will, producing the required type of *siddhi*.

Being below the diaphragm and the major organ of elimination in the body, Splenic centre II is specifically concerned with processing concreting substance rather than the consciousness factors of the *saṃskāras*. (They are better described as attributes of consciousness-volitions.) *Saṃskāras* producing personal aggregates to be expressed in the life processes are directed to the Sacral centre. This centre then incorporates these *prāṇas* for distribution to all minor centres constituting the Inner Round, wherein the *chakras* can manifest the characteristics to be conveyed. It also projects aspects of the aggregates to the major centres as a driving vitality.

If enlightenment is the goal, then these predominantly Watery *skandhas* have to be transmuted and directed upwards from Splenic centre II to Splenic centre I ('destiny's action'). The qualities attributed to the eight petals of Splenic centre II describe the processes needed to eventually transmute the sexual and desire function, and that which attaches itself to things. The attributes must be without desire-attachment if enlightenment is to be achieved. All eight directions must be mastered. The related *saṃskāras* must be stripped of their baser characteristics and directed upwards for further refining.

The *southwest direction* of 'understanding' is denoted 'without realms *(dhātu)*'. The inference here is to that which has no boundaries with respect to containing *prāṇas*. Here the most Fiery-Aetheric *prāṇas* that can be developed via this Watery-Earthy processing are directed to Splenic centre I, which then further refines them with view of incorporating them in the Throat centre and the Head lotus. (Producing an infinite expansion, 'no boundaries', of consciousness.) This upward motion of the Fires of mind through the *lokas* is here designated 'without realms'. The attributes of the highest and subtlest of the senses, the smell sense-consciousness, is specifically processed.

The direction *south* of downward to the little ones is designated 'without sense organs *(indriya)*'. This direction relates to channelling *prāṇas* to the physical body via the minor *chakras* and the externalised organs they embody. It is obvious that no interrelation with the material world can occur without these organs, and therefore no opportunity for experiential growth. This petal sinks *prāṇas* into the physical spleen which then experiences the concretised effects of one's daily activities. It is also concerned with the sewer-like elimination of *prāṇas* to the Eighth Sphere. Depending upon the nature of these *prāṇas,* so we have sickness as a means of cleansing *karma*, or we can have good health. The *prāṇas* cleansed are an Earthy version of Fire. The sense-consciousness associated is that of sight, allowing one to see into the sum of the activities of the minor *chakras* right through to the hell zones of human experience. Consequently, attachment to the sum of one's physical apparatus is produced, which must be transcended upon the yogic path. The subjective organs *(chakras)* replace the sense organs in the yogin's Mind, hence the appellation 'without sense organs'. Control of these internal sense organs must then be accomplished.

The *chakras* are expressions of the real, the true meters for the conveyance of energies from the grossest to the most enlightened state of being. They deal with both phenomena and the qualities of the liberated states. They relate one to the other and therefore are mechanisms of the *śūnyatā-saṃsāra* interchange. They manifest interfaces where the interrelation is possible.

In an enlightened being the sense organs still exist and function, but they are no longer the focus of attention because the *chakras* are used directly rather than unconsciously. They act as instruments of pure cognition and allow contact without attachment to the objects of *saṃsāra*. Effectively, when nothing new can intrinsically be apprehended by the senses and consciousness shifts inwards, then the 'solidity' of things become non-substantial, ephemeral, unreal.

The direction *southeast* of 'expression' is designated 'without sense bases *(āyatana)*'. These sense bases are the fields of activity for the senses from where sensory input arises that are categorised by the mind. All interrelationships with the material world and with others are implied, wherein people derive the basis for the development of their minds. This is the outcome of attachment to the world of desire, as controlled by the qualities of the Sacral centre.

This southeast direction projects the expression into the physical domain of the energies from the northeast direction via this centre. Here, therefore, one experiences physical sensations via the sense-perceptors, as these sense bases express the sum of the *manasic* qualities the apprehender has gleaned from material things. The most Earthy *prāṇas* are processed, coming to and from Splenic centre I (which here stands in the northeast). The associated sense-perceptor is hearing.

From this direction the *yogin* turns inward to the source of the impressions coming through this petal, rather than outward to the sense bases. In doing so, the importance of the physical world recedes and the mantric sound heard ('without attaching names') that controls the *prāṇic* flow from the northeast direction ('unity'). This represents the way of escape to the Heart centre. The effect of the sense bases are then increasingly mitigated as the door is opened that will inevitably allow one to experience the Void.

The direction *east* is styled 'without objective realms'. The direction of the *prāṇas* here is inward to and from the right Gonad centre, which acts as a store for the energy of desire as a creative energy. Thus the more emotional (affectionate) aspects are exemplified. This 'store' can be considered the *ālayavijñāna* for this level of Watery-Earthy *prāṇic* expression concerning the sensuous sphere *(kāmaloka).* It represents the foetus in the womb of consciousness, of all the forces (Sacral, Base of Spine and minor centres) that have produced the desire world. It refers to the state of existence that humans evolve through upon the road to enlightenment, from the sensuous domains to the formless realms. The *yogin* must therefore transform the layered structure of *kāmaloka* (and *rūpaloka,* the formed realms) so that no 'objective realms' whereby to experience the desire principle remains. The substance of desire must be transformed into desirelessness and the *bodhicitta* that is an expression of *śūnyatā.*

The *northeast* direction of 'unity' is relegated the attribute 'without attaching names'. That which attaches names is the mind when it organises itself to know things. Here, therefore, we must first view the functioning of the mind that brings all knowable things (the concept of 'unity') into its ken, via the polar opposite southwest direction. Ultimately our view shifts to that form of *prāṇic* vitalisation that overcomes the directives of the empirical mind. This manifests via this northeast petal, which processes the most refined (Airy) of the Watery-Earthy *prāṇas* associated with the taste sense-consciousness. The *prāṇas* are then directed to Splenic centre I for further refinement.

Refined *piṇgalā* energies that originated in the Heart centre can also pour through this petal, producing the concept of unity as they wash clean the more muddied aspects of the other petals of Splenic centre II. As this is done, so the attributes of self-identification, which attaches names to things contacted via the sense-consciousnesses, is weakened. As a consequence of the *yogin* focussing impressions from the Heart centre upon the 'I' concept, the 'I' is then found to be lacking in substantiality. The process necessitates a conscious inbreathing of transmutative *prāṇas* by stabilising and holding consciousness steady. Secret Mantra is utilised to clear away the debris in the mind caused by identifying with things named, allowing all realms to be mastered (the southwest direction) as one ascends to the Heart and Heart in the Head centres. This process is effected by the seed syllable Oṁ assisting in the mastery of consciousness.

The three northern petals of Splenic centre II are mainly concerned with processing Watery *prāṇas* in their interrelation with Splenic centre I. The remaining five petals are mostly concerned with Earthy-Fiery *prāṇas* and have interrelations with the lower centres, specifically the generative organs and the Sacral centre. They therefore process some problematic *prāṇas* that are often productive of *preta*-like or hellish states, when many of their base *saṃskāras* generated are either recycled or rejected via the minor centres. One can see here the absolute necessity for yogic control of this centre before *kuṇḍalinī* can safely arise.

These northern petals are superimposed upon by Splenic centre I. This means that they also act as petals of that centre, effectively making fifteen petals in all. This number is important because it connotes a triplicity of five petals each, allowing the complete processing of three groups of sets of five *prāṇas*. They manifest what can be considered the Will group, which processes forceful mental-emotional (Fire-Water) *prāṇas*, the *piṅgalā prāṇas* that are mostly Watery and the *iḍā prāṇas* that are mostly Earthy. All are aspects of consciousness, generating *karma*-formations, whose power needs to be lessened. Eventually the yogic process begins, wherein the effects of *karma* are eliminated by means of yogic *tapas* and the *sādhana* controlling all the forces instigating consciousness.

The remaining five petals of Splenic centre II are concerned with channelling the Inner Round circulation of all the *prāṇas* reticulating through the minor and major centres below the diaphragm.

In the case of the *northern* direction of upwards to the higher domains, we have the appellation *'without (destiny's) action'*. 'Destiny's action' refers to the action of *karma*. What is implied, therefore, is activity without *karma* formations. We saw previously that *karma* is the effect of wilful volition by consciousness. The Throat centre is implicated because it controls the Fires of mind; the consciousness that envisions what it wishes to do, and that manifests the activity to produce the desired outcome. To do so it clothes the initial image with desire, the various forms of Watery substance. Thus 'destiny's action' is produced.

The *prāṇas* coming to Splenic centre II via this petal are from the Throat centre coupled with those from the Solar Plexus centre. They direct the expression of *karmic* volition, and will be utilised to produce a new seed-thought for a future action. Also, the most Fiery *prāṇas* that Splenic centre II can express are often directed northwards to assist in this thought-form production. They are generally the most refined, but can also be tinged with much emotion or sensual imagery. Overall, this petal therefore processes the *kliṣṭamanas* generated by the individual, which conveys 'destiny's action' at this level of expression, and its fruit is projected northwest in terms of purified Watery (devotional, aspirational or affectionate) *prāṇas*.

The process of refining *kliṣṭamanas* involves manifold incidents that karmically propel the person to climb the mountain of attainment, to achieve whatever is the focal point of aspiration. This petal helps to determine whatever the *karma* is to fulfil at any stage of one's life. Eventually, through yogic practices, the forms of *karma* that attach consciousness to *saṃsāra* will be annulled. The generation of the associated *saṃskāras* then cease, either through transmutation and upwards direction to the Heart, or higher centres, or else being projected out of the system altogether by preventing their future occurrence.

The elimination of *karma* necessitates the Waters being dried up so that only pure Airy-Fire remains, which is automatically directed to the Heart centre. It can then continue to the Throat or Head centres. This happens through elevating the meditation to the highest centre or level of Mind possible. Here the utilisation of the seed syllable Āḥ is effected to delineate the right usage of the energy of Mind.

The *northwest* direction of outward emanatory purpose is designated 'without the fruit of (destiny's) action'. The fruit of destiny's action is the gain from the expression of *karma* via the development of consciousness. Normally, desire based (Watery) activity is implicated, but at the higher stages of human development there are also the gains of aspiration and right devotion. The sense-consciousness associated is touch. To achieve the complete drying of the Watery Element the *prāṇas* must be directed to the Heart centre, via processing by Splenic centre I. This process eventually produces the experience of the Void. This direction therefore concerns the way that the emotions are transcended. Desire-affection and aspiration become compassion. Thus the wheel of the Heart centre is rectified, as subtle emotions are generally the most difficult aspects of consciousness to master. They produce many tribulations upon the path of yogic austerity.

The *prāṇas* from this direction empower the seed syllable *Hūṁ* through activating the *'vajra* of the Heart'.[15] The three northern petals represent the three main downward pointing prongs of this *vajra,* that convey the energies of the Lords of the three main Elements concerned with this exposé of Splenic centre II. These prongs are effectively a ritual dagger (phur ba, *vajrakīla)*[16] held in the hand and wielded in the meditation-mind of a *yogin.* They express the energies of Ratnasambhava for mastery of the Watery Element ('without the fruit of destiny's action'); Amoghasiddhi for mastery of the Fiery-Watery-Earthy mix ('without destiny's action'); and Amitābha, a Fiery-Airy mix ('without attaching names') to conquer the Earth Element. In doing so these three prongs of energy transform the types of substance associated with the polar opposites of the directions via which these energies enter Splenic centre II.

With respect to the three seed syllables Oṁ, Āḥ, Hūṁ, Govinda has this to say:

> In the ordinary human being the psychic Centres are filled only with the elementary forces of the body and of mundane consciousness. In the spiritually developed, i.e., in those who strive beyond themselves,

15 This esoteric statement has reference to the potency of the awakened Heart centre, and to the effect of drawing its energies to thoroughly transform and transmute all *prāṇas* pertaining to *samsāra.* It is the potency of the Heart's Mind, which is the wisdom of the Dhyāni Buddhas. As well as the quote given from Govinda's book, see also Evans-Wentz's rendition in *Tibetan Yoga and Secret Doctrines* (Oxford University Press, London, 1958), 341, where it appears as the concluding statement of 'The Path of the Five Wisdoms: the Yoga of the Long Hūṃ' (page 339).

16 The symbolism of the *vajrakīla* is explained in Volume 5A, chapter 6.

the forces of these Centres are influenced and sublimated by the guiding principles of the *Dhyāni-Buddhas,* whose symbols are placed into these Centres. But only perfect spiritual unification can bring about their complete transformation. Therefore we find on Tibetan temple-banners *(thaṅ-ka)* that, only in representations of Buddhas, Bodhisattvas and saints, the seed-syllables of Body, Speech, and Mind, namely, OṀ-ĀḤ-HŪṀ, are written on the reverse side of the painting on the places corresponding to the three higher psychic Centres.

The meaning of these three seed-syllables, therefore, goes beyond that of individual symbolic figures like *Vairocana, Amoghasiddhi,* or *Akṣobhya;* in other words, they are applied to the highest plane of experience, in which all separate aspects of *Dhyāni-Buddhas* are fused and disappear. In the same way the three higher Centres take over the psychic functions of the remaining Centres: *Amoghasiddhi's* functions are fused (as we saw) with those of *Amitābha* in the Throat Centre, so that the seed-syllable ĀḤ, which now takes the place of HRĪḤ, becomes the exponent of the whole *maṇḍala* of the Knowledge-Holding Deities. The HŪṀ, however, comprises all the aspects of integration, from *Ratnasambhava's* synthetic 'Wisdom of the Oneness of all Beings' (which otherwise would be associated with the Naval Centre) and *Akṣobhya's* 'Wisdom of the Great Mirror', in which the formless as well as the forms of all things are contained, up to *Vajrasattva's* integration of all *Dhyāni-Buddhas* in the adamantine reality and activity of his spontaneous way...[17]

After this 'breaking-through' towards unification and universality (OṀ) has been achieved, the consciousness flows back upon the human plane and turns into action in the HŪṀ of the Heart Centre. Thus HŪṀ unites both sides of reality: the living, pulsating presence of individual existence and the supra-individual timelessness beyond all dualities. It is the highest principle, the highest experience-form of inner reality, immanent in all beings. Therefore it has been said: 'The Mind of all the Buddhas of the three times, which is from origin pure and spontaneous, and which goes beyond word, thought, and speech, rises as the indestructible, empty, radiating body of the Five Wisdoms in the form of HŪṀ, clear and perfect in all its organs and fields of activity.

'The five poisons transform themselves into the imperishable, self-luminous Wisdoms through the practice of the creative and reabsorptive process of meditation in the Yoga of the Inner Fire.

17 Govinda, *Foundations of Tibetan Mysticism,* 206-7.

> With the maturing of the Four Bodies and the Five Wisdoms, may the Vajra of the Heart be realized even in this life.'[18]

Whenever one achieves the fruits of one's striving the *saṃskāras* must then be cleansed from the system. This is because what becomes the crowning glory of attainment later becomes a base for further upward aspiration. It can then be rejected, having no purpose in the future cycle. What is rejected is not necessarily wasted, because one person's rejected *prāṇas* may become another's next step to enlightenment. Under the impetus of *bodhicitta* the Bodhisattva also works like this, because teachings will be presented to others of qualities to be developed useful to them but which the Bodhisattva has superseded, having moved on to a higher level of realisation.

Everything that prevents or mars complete enlightenment must be cleansed, thus all former fruits of attainment become stepping stones for what is to come. The process continues until consciousness mirrors the real *in toto.* Self-reliance and right focus are keywords for this liberating stance. However, the concept of 'self' (derived from the fields of activity for the senses associated with the southeast direction) becomes selflessness once a proper union with the rectified qualities of the Heart centre become established via a northwest aspiration. This necessitates eliminating self-focussed constructive and discursive forms of thought.

Forms of enlightenment and the Rays

Next we are presented with seven statements that express the nature of the seven Rays.

> What is the incomparable right-completed Enlightenment is the incomparable right-completed Buddha. What is the incomparable right-completed Buddha is the Dharma. What is the Dharma is not born, does not die. What is not born and does not die should be understood to be the same as the sky. [19]

The statements depict the outcome of pursuing the process of transforming *prāṇas* from their base qualities to their enlightened

18 Ibid., 208-209.

19 Alex Wayman, 288.

expressions, according to the basic energy qualification of the person. The inference, in terms of the theme of energy of what transpires after consciousness has been transcended ('what is without the fruit of [destiny's] action'[20]), are forms of Light, as veiled by the term 'enlightenment'. There are seven outcomes, as there are seven sub-Rays to the Light that conveys the liberation process.

1. The *'incomparable right-completed enlightenment'.* Here the first Ray of Will or Power is indicated. Enlightenment is the product of the liberating Will that drives all *chakras* to completion. Without the use of the Will to transform the *prāṇas* in the *nāḍīs* enlightenment would not be possible. The *yogin* needs the Will to sustain his meditation. This enlightenment is 'incomparable' because it awakens all petals of the *sahasrāra padma.* Nothing in Nature can compare to this fully awakened crown of accomplishment upon a Buddha's head. It is 'right-completed' because all lesser and major wheels are fully vivified with various forms of living vibrant Light. Nothing is left to awaken, the motion of the wheels being not just spiral-cyclic but also fourth dimensional, in terms of turning in upon themselves to universal integration, as well as outwards to encompass all space.
2. The *'incomparable right-completed Buddha'.* Here the second Ray of Love-Wisdom is implicated, of which the Buddha is the most obvious expression and example for all to follow. The term 'incomparable' refers to the quality of Love, which is the cosmic magnet that draws all beings into one interdependent unified expression. Love is not comparable to anything; it simply IS. It can be conceived as the 'glue' that sustains the all and integrates all into the One. In the form known as *bodhicitta* (the Will-of-Love[21]) it manifests the way of release from *saṃsāra.*

   The phrase 'right-completed' refers to the wisdom aspect of this dual Ray of Love-Wisdom. Wisdom is that which must be rightly 'completed' or developed as a consequence of the evolutionary journey upon the wheel of Life. It is not attainable without Love.

20 Ibid.

21 This and the other forms of will (strong desire, selfish will, free will, goodwill, Will-to-Love, Will-of-Love and Divine Will) are explained in Volume 4, chapter 7.

Wisdom can also be defined as active Love. Thus the Will-of-Love drives all forward to great heights of bliss. Love sustains all that is and is not, whilst wisdom is actively applied Love gained through *saṃsāric* turmoil, whereby Bodhisattvic activity is developed. The first and second Rays always work as a functioning unity, producing the 'right-completed enlightenment' of the 'right-completed Buddha'. The other Rays are eventually abstracted into them.

3. The third Ray of Mathematically Exact Activity synthesises the qualities of the remaining five Rays, and this synthesising emanatory quality is here termed *'the dharma'*. These five Rays are exemplified by the differing attributes of the five Dhyāni Buddhas. (Whilst Will and Love-Wisdom are common to all.) They are the wisdoms derived via sense contact in *saṃsāra* whereby the attributes of the five Elements in the form of *prāṇas* are refined. By means of these Rays the entire cycle of manifestation is energised, the qualities of which are synthesised by the Jinas. The *dharma* is the active, exacting expression of the teachings of the Buddha, or of anyone that has attained 'right-completed wisdom'. It is the means of dissemination of the 'right-completed enlightenment' into manifestation with precision so that those bound to the various fields of activity can eventually abide in serene Thusness. The Dharmadhātu Wisdom of Vairocana corresponds to this Ray, as this wisdom manifests in a precise mathematical manner with respect to *saṃsāra*. It relates to the organisational aspect of *dharmakāya*.

4. The phrase *'the dharma is not born'* relates to the fourth Ray of Beautifying Harmony overcoming Strife. Its middle position acts as a mirror reflecting the three higher abstracted Rays into the lower three (which govern the three worlds of human livingness). From this perspective, as an expression of the *dharma*, this Ray can be considered to be 'not born' because it bears the activities of the others. It does, however, produce an equalising or harmonising effect, as consistent with the entire mode of operation of 'the Middle Path', of which the Buddha *dharma* is a fundamental expression.

   The Mirror-like Wisdom of Akṣobhya is its expression, where the attributes of the higher Rays manifest their reflected (inverted) power to overcome the impediments of body, speech and mind; of the physical, emotional and mental domains.

5. *'The dharma...does not die'*, relates to the fifth Ray of Scientific Reasoning. This reasoning governs the development of consciousness, the Fires (*saṃskāras*) of which are born with each new perception that is assimilated. What has been assimilated does not die, but is transformed from life to life until it becomes clarified and liberating, transformed into the living *dharma*. The transmuted Fires ultimately become the field of revelation entitled the Dharmakāya Way. Here the Discriminating Inner Wisdom of Amitābha governs its rulership over the entire domain of mind/Mind.
6. *'The dharma....is not born and does not die'*, relates to the way *dharma* manifests via the sixth Ray of Devotion. This Ray is the force *(vāsanā)* that drives all to fulfilment. This driving energy sustains the entire quest for knowledge, causing perpetual rebirths, and then the quest for enlightenment. Inevitably it even drives a Buddha onwards into cosmos after his *parinirvāṇa*. First strong desire for sensual pursuits and for comforting material allurements manifests. Later this energy translates into devotion for noble ideals and spiritual quests, as well as aspiration upon the path of enlightenment. Devotion then transforms into a fervent liberating one-pointedness that pierces the veils of even the most subtle forms of ignorance until the *dharmakāya* stands revealed. This energy consequently is the basis for the Equalising Wisdom of Ratnasambhava because it represents the means whereby *saṃsāra* is incorporated ('equalised') into *dharmakāya*.
7. *'The dharma....should be understood the same as the sky'*, refers to the seventh Ray of Ritualised Activity, demonstrative Power, which is a compilation of all the Rays, hence the sum of the manifestation of the *dharma*. Their colours manifest like the rainbow (which arcs so splendidly in the sky). This implies that the way to establish the All-accomplishing Wisdom of Amoghasiddhi that manifests as the spaciousness of cosmos is to ground all attributes of the other Rays into *saṃsāra*.[22] It manifests as one pierces the uppermost veils of

22 Each of the Rays embody one or other of the planes of perception *(lokas)*, signifying, therefore, that Amoghasiddhi's rulership is that of the physical domain. Here even the process of rebirth can be considered to be ritualised, emanating from the precincts of the *tathāgatagarbha*.

being/non-being through ritualised meditative activity and the proper sequencing of the life processes within a physical body. All aspects of the form must be mastered by means of its *prāṇic* integration with the spacious manifestation of the Clear Light of Mind. Such a Mind being equated with the vast expanse of space, here equated with the sky.

The integration by means of Amoghasiddhi's wisdom of all Ray attributes into *saṃsāra* via the ritualistic activity by a *yogin* generates the might of the Rays to convert *saṃsāra*. Its attributes are consequently vanquished (transmuted), as cycle after cycle of refinement of consciousness (the cleansing of *saṃskāras*) produce the spaciousness of the enlightened Mind. All the Rays manifest their radiance as the brilliance of the aura of a Buddha, filling all space with his accomplishment.

The *chakras* of the four directions

There are four main sections in the main passage quoted from Wayman, namely: 'the Middle Path', 'discerning the real', 'right completed enlightenment', and 'the Dharma'. They represent the open gates or modes of experience of the Thusness produced by the Dharmakāya Way, via the four cardinal directions. Thus:

1. *The Middle Path* represents the approach via the eastern direction of the form of activity manifested by the Heart centre.
2. *Discerning the real* represents the southern method of gaining the enlightened Mind through a proper 'right completed' analysis of the sum of the nature of phenomena, and its relation to *śūnyatā*. It produces the *śūnyatā-saṃsāra* interchange.
3. *Right completed enlightenment* refers to the western method of thorough interchange with the sum of human interrelationships, and of human activity via the forms of Bodhisattvic interplay with humanity through the manifestation of skilful means. Thus Buddhahood is eventually obtained.
4. *The dharma* refers to the downpour of revelatory information from the northern direction consisting of the realms of those that have gained Buddhahood in past epochs. This is the direct, pure *dharmakāya* experience.

The text then continues with a response from reverend Śāradvatīputra stating that 'This Dharma passage is a hard thing to know for all those who have not generated virtuous roots or who have meagre faith. The objective domain of the Tathāgata's eye does not belong elsewhere. That eye of the Tathāgata is without aim and without place'.[23] This quote has obvious reference to an explanation of the nature of the Ājñā centre whereby the way a Tathāgata views things is established. The four directions in space are implicated. The 'domain of a Tathāgata' refers to the northern direction *(dharmakāya),* to which a Tathāgata no longer needs to aspire. That which 'does not belong elsewhere' refers to the western direction of outward expression to humanity, which represents the field of compassionate service. That which is 'without aim' refers to the eastern direction, which is the way of the Heart and the *śūnyatā* experience. The phrase 'without place' refers to the southern direction of the formed realms, wherein a Tathāgata no longer resides.

Answering Śāradvatīputra, Vajrapāṇi states:

> Reverend Śāradvatīputra, a 'Tathāgata' has the character of Thusness. What is the character of Thusness is voidness. What is voidness is without a Tathāgata, and a Tathāgata is without a character.[24]

As the dialogue concerns the nature of the Ājñā centre with respect to a Tathāgata, Vajrapāṇi's comment is by way of elucidation.

The northern direction *(dharmakāya)*—the 'domain of a Tathāgata', is further qualified as that which 'has the character of Thusness'. This refers to an upwards vision to the Head lotus.

The eastern direction—That which is 'without aim' is coupled to the phrase 'What is the character of Thusness is voidness'. This refers to visioning through the Heart centre which views all via this voidness.

The western direction—that which 'does not belong elsewhere', is coupled with the statement 'What is voidness is without a Tathāgata'. This refers to the two truths characterising the development of human consciousness. 'What is voidness' refers to absolute truth, and 'without a Tathāgata' refers to the conventional truth that conditions the minds of most people. The awakening of the Throat centre is here implied,

23 Alex Wayman, 289.

24 Ibid.

allowing people to discern the difference between these truths.

The southern direction—the phrase 'without place' is coupled with the explanation: 'a Tathāgata is without a character'. This refers to the fact that a Tathāgata has no residence in *saṃsāra,* consequently has no character, or 'I' concept therein. The Solar Plexus centre, which rules the domain below the diaphragm, is here implicated, wherein this 'I' concept originates via its inherent self will.

Śāradvatīputra then queries: 'if a Tathāgata is without a character, then why is it taught that a Tathāgata possesses the thirty-two characters of a great person, and why is his body adorned with the eighty minor marks? How can we make a place for the three bodies of a Tathāgata? How did the Tathāgata become manifestly and fully awakened to the incomparable, right-completed Enlightenment?'[25] Continuing along the lines of these four directions we then can conclude that 'the thirty-two characters of a great person' relates to the western direction and the attributes of the Throat centre. The question 'why is his body adorned with the eighty minor marks?' then refers to the southern direction, the attributes of the Solar Plexus centre and the sum of the Inner Round that it governs. The question 'How can we make a place for the three bodies of a Tathāgata?' relates to the eastern direction and the attributes of the Heart centre. Finally, the question relating to obtaining the 'incomparable, right-completed Enlightenment' refers to awakening the Head lotus.

In answering these questions, Vajrapāṇi states in paragraph 10 of this *samādhi:*

> Vajrapāṇi, master of the secret folk, explained: Reverend Śāradvatīputra, 'thirty-two characters of the great person' as a term of convention *(saṃvṛti).* 'Adorned' means elaborated letters and speech. 'Minor mark' means the character of illusory and dream formations. 'Right-completed Enlightenment' means the character of sky-formation. 'Making a place for the three bodies' is the character magically manifested by the two collections (of merit and knowledge).[10][26]

We see here that Vajrapāṇi hints at the esoteric interpretation of the 32 marks. The exoteric idea relates to the Buddhist concept of

25 Ibid.

26 Ibid.

a perfected form, such as inward curling body hairs, wheels of the *dharma* on the soles of the feet, webbed fingers and toes, blue eyes, etc. These are mind concepts, based upon a conception of perfected *karma* but do not pertain to physical plane reality. Gautama may indeed have been a handsome gentleman, but such exhibitionalism concerning the illusional form is not any enlightened being's consideration. Rather, these marks veil the inner beauty and perfected expression of the *nāḍī* and *chakra* system. Indeed the teachings of Vajrapāṇi bears this out, where he states that such marks are simply a 'convention *(saṃvṛti)'*. The term *saṃvṛti* means holding a false conception (from the Sanskrit root *vṛt,* 'to enclose'). Hence it is that which covers up, the origin of illusion, *māyā.*

A enlightening quote from Dudjom Rinpoche should be added, who correctly explains the nature of these marks in terms of attributes of the *nāḍī* system.

> The twofold bliss is that of the sixteen vowels which symbolise discriminative awareness (*shes-rab,* Skt. *prajñā*) and the sixteen consonants which symbolise skilful means (*thabs,* Skt. *upāya*). During the perfection stage of contemplation (*rdzogs-rim,* Skt. *sampannakrama*) these seed-syllables of light occupy the right and left channels in the body respectively, but they intermingle in the central channel. (Our text here reads *phan-tshun ma-'dres...*instead of *phan-tshun 'dres-shing...*) Then, generating the coalescent bliss of discriminating awareness, or emptiness, and skilful means, or compassion, they give rise to the sixteen delights (*dga'ba bcu-drug*). This experience is duplicated in accordance with the upward and downward movement of the vital energy (*rlung,* Skt. *vāyu*), and so these sixteen delights come to possess the thirty-two major marks of the buddha-body of perfect rapture. Each of the sixteen delights experienced in series by the male consort is also endowed with the five pristine cognitions, making a total of eighty minor marks. This is the resultant and primordial buddha-body, which is not created by an accumulation of causes and provisions. The feeling of receptiveness, which this surpasses, is an experience belonging to the path of connection (*sbyor-lam,* Skt. *prayogamārga*) in the causal phase of the vehicle."[27]

---

27 Dudjom Rinpoche, *The Nyingma School of Tibetan Buddhism, Its Fundamentals and History,* footnote 124, pages 10-11 of Notes.

Here is indicated the intricate teaching concerning the nature of the subtle body and the movement of the *prāṇas*[28] in the *nāḍīs*. The process conveys the 'pristine cognitions' and 'delights' of the consciousness-stream for those that have the eyes to see the nature of this substantial phenomena based upon the patterns of the real. In continuing with the quote and placing Vajrapāṇi's elucidation upon the arms of the already established fixed cross line of reasoning, we have the phrase '"Adorned" means elaborated letters and speech', which substantiating convention, implicates the western direction of the mode of activity of the Throat centre (governing the expression of the Fiery Element). This centre has sixteen (12 + 4) main petals,[29] which processes the 'sixteen delights'. When 'duplicated in accordance with the upward and downward movement of the vital energy (*rlung,* Skt. *vāyu*)', then the 'sixteen delights come to possess the thirty-two major marks of the buddha-body of perfect rapture'.

The minor marks that possess 'the character of illusory and dream formations', can be placed at the southern direction, governed by the Solar Plexus centre, which controls the dissemination of the Watery Element in the body. The enlightenment that 'means the character of sky-formation' can be placed at the northern direction and the awakened Head centre, governing the synthesis of all the Elements under the auspices of Aether. The concept of making 'a place for the three bodies' relates to the eastern position and the Heart centre's expanse. Whilst the phrase 'the character magically manifested by the two collections (of merit and knowledge)' relates to the east-west orientation, where 'merit' is the Heart's expression, and 'knowledge' is that of the Throat centre.

In the juxtaposition between these orientations the major pathways of the *nāḍī* system are expressed. Esoterically, we have the flow of the *iḍā nāḍī,* producing the 'knowledge' (wisdom) of the Throat centre's awakening, and the *piṅgalā nāḍī* producing the 'merit' that is the Heart centre's custodianship of the path of compassion. The south-north alignment relates to the awakening of *suṣumṇā* as the *kuṇḍalinī* rises from the centres below the diaphragm to awaken the Head lotus, producing 'the character of sky-formation', i.e., unfettered enlightenment.

---

28 The term *vāyu* that Wayman uses incorporates the five *prāṇas*.

29 See Volume 5B, chapter 1, where the attributes of the sixteen main petals of the Throat centre are explained in detail.

The elaboration of 'letters and speech' relates to the sum of the discursive intellectual functions governed by the Throat centre. Esoterically, this includes the evocation of Secret Mantra. The 'character of illusory and dream formations' relates to the sum of the activities associated with the Watery Element, the emotional and imaginative faculty of humans, incorporating also *skyes-nas bardo* (dream consciousness), wherein revelatory information can be derived.

It can now be added that the main petals of the important *chakras* below the diaphragm, and which are detailed in Volume 5A, provide the number 80 for the minor marks. We have 8 petals for the Diaphragm centre, 20 petals for the Splenic centres, 10 petals for the Solar Plexus centre, 10 petals each for the Liver and Stomach centres, 6 petals for the Sacral centre, 4 petals for the Base of Spine centre, and 6 each for the two Gonad centres.

The 32 major marks relate to the combination of the 12 petals of the Heart centre with the 16 petals of the Throat centre, coupled with the 4 petals of the Base of the Spine centre, as it is the foundation for the rest and the cause of the *kuṇḍalinī* that awakens their potencies. Consequently, the major and minor marks relate to the sum of the *prāṇas* evoked from the main petals of the important *chakras* below the Head centre. When mastered, these petals produce the *siddhis* of the awakened one.

The three Buddha bodies

The 'three bodies' refers to the three bodies of a Buddha: the *dharmakāya, sambhogakāya,* and *nirmāṇakāya.* We are told that their place is 'magically manifested'. The means thereto is by awakening the *iḍā, piṇgalā* and *suṣumṇā nāḍīs.* Perfecting the attributes of the *manasic iḍā nāḍī* to develop wisdom produces the *nirmāṇakāya,* the outward appearance of a Buddha that can communicate with humans by means of the elaboration of 'letters and speech'. The evocation of the loving and compassionate attributes of the *piṇgalā nāḍī* to conclusion produces the subjective *sambhogakāya* aspect of a Buddha (as represented in Buddhist art). The *suṣumṇā* path up the central *nāḍī* produces the liberated spaciousness of the *dharmakāya.* In all cases *kuṇḍalinī* is needed to produce an awakened one, but the modes of expression of the three bodies come to their final resolution via the perfected expression of these *nāḍīs*. Having introduced the topic of the three bodies, Vajrapāṇi elaborates:

> Reverend Śāradvatīputra, besides, there is the objective realm for the body secret of the Tathāgata. Here 'body secret' is the character which is the natural result of great merit. What is the natural result of merit is the Sambhogakāya of the Tathāgata. Besides, it is the body secret and the marvelous action of the body of the Tathāgata. Reverend Śāradvatīputra, 'speech' is the character of both convention *(saṃvṛti)* and absolute *(paramārtha)*. What is the character of both convention and absolute, that is the Nirmāṇakāya of the Tathāgata.[11][30]

This paragraph possesses two parts. The first relates to the nature of the manifestation of a Buddha. In fact, here is veiled the attributes of the five Dhyāni Buddhas. The second part relates to the expression of speech. Concerning the Dhyāni Buddhas we have:

1. The 'objective realm for the body secret of a Tathāgata' refers to the All-accomplishing Wisdom of Amoghasiddhi. He governs the appearance of the Buddha's wisdom in the objective realms, which his activity has conquered. The 'body secret' here includes the *nāḍīs* of an enlightened being, as well as to the subjective domains, which are mastered and the related revelations garnered.
2. The 'character which is the natural result of great merit' relates to the Equalising Wisdom of Ratnasambhava. His character of compassionate understanding integrates *śūnyatā* with *saṃsāra* ('equalising' the two), thereby offering the aspiring ones the means to gain liberation. This relates to treading the Bodhisattva path (and later Tantric practices) whereby 'great merit' is obtained. 'Merit' in this context referring to that which causes the liberation of others.
3. The 'Sambhogakāya of the Tathāgata' refers to the Discriminating Inner Wisdom of Amitābha, who governs activities upon all domains of mind/Mind. The 'Sambhogakāya' implied here is an emanation of the Mind, existing upon its abstract levels. When related to humans, then it is the *tathāgatagarbha,* the Sambhogakāya Flower, the attributes of which is part of 'the body secret' discovered as part of the meditation path. Its qualities shall be revealed in chapter 6.

30 Wayman, 289.

4. The 'body secret and marvellous action' of a Tathāgata refers to the Mirror-like Wisdom of Akṣobhya, which reflects the qualities of the 'body secret' into manifestation. As this is done, so accordingly the miraculous or 'marvellous action' of a Tathāgata (or enlightened being) manifests.
5. The 'body of the Tathāgata' then relates to the *dharmakāya,* which embodies the sum of the 'Body, Speech and Mind' of the enlightened, liberated one.

Speech is sacred and must be carefully controlled if liberation is to ensue. According to this Tantra its conventions manifest upon three levels, related to the three bodies of a Buddha. First to the *dharmakāya,* which relates to the 'absolute *(paramārtha)'.* This is the most esoteric level of a Buddha's speech *(vacana),* which is heard in silence through one having developed the inner organs and transcendental perception to be able to hear. That which integrates both 'convention *(saṃvṛti)* and absolute *(paramārtha)'* is the Sambhogakāya of the Tathāgata. It interrelates the *dharmakāya* to the *nirmāṇakāya.* Telepathic thoughts are projected from Mind to Mind (or from Mind to minds) at this level of expression. A perceiver need only still the chattering of the empirical mind to hear this subtle voice of insight speak. All forms of speech outwardly manifest in the 'convention' that is 'the Nirmāṇakāya of the Tathāgata'.

Continuing upon this line of thought Vajrapāṇi elucidates further, now presenting the way that the three Buddha bodies can be obtained:

> Comprehending that Dependent Origination is without nihilism and without eternalism is a comprehension by way of understanding proper to mental perception *(manovijñāna).* One may know it by repeated practice of meditation *(dhyāna),* that is, without aim, without any defilement, and void of purification. It is not the objective realm of body, not the scope of speech. What is not an objective realm for the natural presence of the mind is the Dharmakāya of a Tathāgata, rightly united in the realm of sky. That is how a place is made for the three bodies of the Tathāgata [12].[31]

This paragraph has three parts, again relating to the three bodies of a Buddha, but now our perception has been brought to the level of attainment

31 Ibid, 289-90.

of the normal aspirant. Aspirants must develop the attributes of these three bodies over time. Consequently, we begin with the subject of Dependent Origination (and hence the *nirmāṇakāya* level of interpretation), which relates to the world of everyday experience. Being comprehended by *manovijñāna* and being without nihilism and eternalism, Dependent Origination (here the discriminating consciousness) therefore represents the middle way of this level of experience.

The second part of this phrase relates to the *sambhogakāya* aspect, which deals with the subtle, 'secret' aspects of consciousness that are primarily Watery in nature. There are seven phrases concerned with this level of interpretation. They are: 'One may know it', 'by repeated practice of meditation *(dhyāna)*', 'without aim', 'without any defilement', 'void of purification', 'not the objective realm of the body', and 'not the scope of speech'. These seven statements, plus the earlier three relate to the attributes of the petals of the Solar Plexus centre, once the associated *prāṇas* have come under control by means of the *dhyāna* of the *yogin*.

The driving force of Dependent Origination *(pratītyasamutpāda)* is the Solar Plexus circulation, though the actual process of cleansing the related *prāṇas,* whereby one may come to 'know it', is Splenic centre I.[32] This relationship of the links of *pratītyasamutpāda* to the twelve petals of Splenic centre I is explained in Volume 5A. What shall be elaborated here is the necessity of the mastery of the petals of the Solar Plexus centre if the wheel of rebirth is to be overcome. I shall not deal with this subject at length here because it is adequately treated in that Volume in relation to the Īśvarī of Emanation and Pacification of the *Bardo Thödol*.[33] Consequently, the phrases related to the petals shall be briefly explained, allowing the interested reader to make the correlations with what is later presented in Volume 5A.

This *chakra* has ten main petals, whose activities are of extreme importance in the life of the average person. It processes the Watery desire-emotional output, producing the ubiquitous desire or emotional-mind *(kāma-manas)* of humanity. To break free from Dependent Origination is to dry the Waters conditioning *saṃsāric* life by means of the mastery of the Fires of the Mind.

---

32 See Volume 5A, 163-69.

33 See Volume 5A, 288-308.

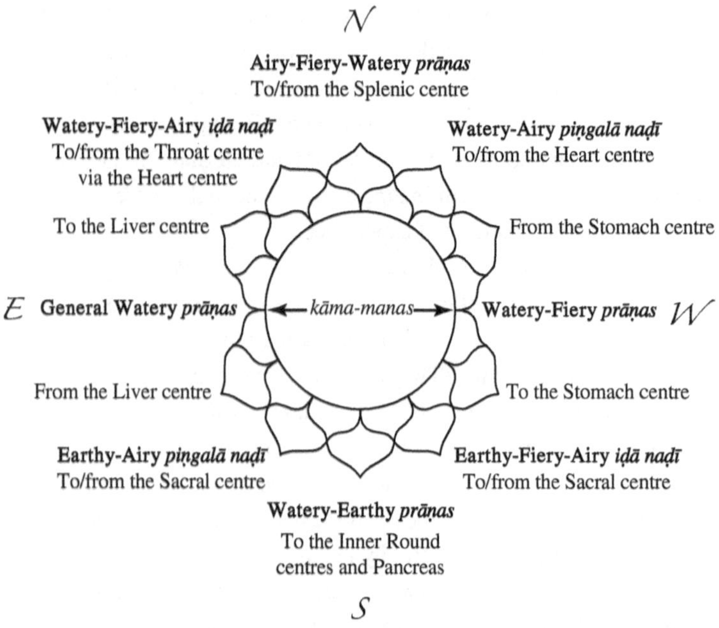

Figure 12: The Solar Plexus centre[34]

The first three statements relating to the *nirmāṇakāya* level of interpretation generate the process of the *iḍā (manasic)* attributes of the Solar Plexus centre, which are eventually directed to the Throat centre via the *iḍā nāḍī.* This is signified by the phrase 'Being comprehended by *manovijñāna'*, where *manovijñāna* relates to ordinary intellectual discursion. The statements 'without eternalism' and 'without nihilism' project *prāṇas* to and from the Stomach centre (the western direction), wherein all types of extreme and fanatical mental attributes are stored and processed. The objective of the *yogin* here is to overcome all tendencies to strong mental-emotionality by cultivating the middle way of the *dharma.* Neither the doctrines of the adherents of other religions (promoting concepts of eternalism), or of the materialists (promoting nihilism) is of any concern to the *yogin.* The other statement given associated with the *iḍā* stream is 'void of purification', which relates to the *iḍā nāḍī* coming from the Sacral centre (the centre governing the manifestation of the

34 See Volume 2, pages 101-115 for a detailed explanation of Figure 12, and Volume 5A, pages 288-294.

field of desire). This relates to the fact that the entire *iḍā nāḍī* stream must be thoroughly purified if the *nirmāṇakāya* of a Buddha is to appear and to eloquently teach disciples. All subtle forms of desire-attachment consequently must be thoroughly comprehended and transformed.

The phrase 'One may know it', referring to *pratītyasamutpāda,* relates to the petal of the Solar Plexus centre whose *nāḍī* leads to Splenic centre I, wherein the twelve links of the wheel of birth and death are experienced and purified, as explained in Volume 5A. Through the continual cyclic processing and refinement of the *prāṇas* generated below the diaphragm one inevitably thoroughly learns the meaning of life in *saṃsāra,* and eventually the method of escape.

There are three petals associated with the generation of the *piṇgalā nāḍī* stream signified by the phrases 'without aim' and 'without defilement', which relate to the *nāḍīs* going to and from the Liver centre, as well as the statement 'nor the scope of speech', which relates to the *piṇgalā nāḍī* going to and from the Sacral centre. The *prāṇas* in this *nāḍī* generally do not process the aspects of speech, because at first they are almost purely concerned with the expression of the desire element, which is a subjective force, not a mentalistic attitude (whereby speech is generated). Eventually this desire force is transformed into the energy of high devotion and aspiration to overcome materialistic impediments, being the energy that drives the *yogin* to master phenomena.

With respect to the attributes designated as 'without aim' and 'without defilement', the Liver centre stores *prāṇas* from the generally loving and emotional interrelations between people. They must eventually be transformed into Love-Wisdom and the compassionate aspects of the Bodhisattva ideal. The types of self-will, selfishness and ambitious scheming that often accompanies social interrelationships is consequently annulled ('without aim'). Also, the types of *saṃskāras* bearing the attributes of *kliṣṭamanas* (the general quality of these *piṇgalā prāṇas)* are converted into the Heart's pure essence ('without defilement').

The phrase 'repeated practice of meditation' conveys the *piṇgalā nāḍī* to the Heart centre. This phrase refers to the need to repeatedly recycle *prāṇas* via Splenic centre I (governing the wheel of Dependent Origination) via meditation until *piṇgalā* attributes arise that are sufficiently refined to allow passage to the Heart centre. For much of the yogic process, the Solar Plexus centre is the focus of repeated meditation to pacify its Watery disposition and to refine its *prāṇas* via Splenic centre I. The arising *saṃskāras* must be carefully monitored and converted into enlightenment attributes. The Head centre cannot awaken until the Watery Solar Plexus has been transformed into a quiescent lake.

The phrase 'not the objective realm of body' relates to the *nāḍī* going to the Inner Round and the physical form via the pancreas. This is the externalisation of the energies from the Solar Plexus centre, and care must be taken that the pancreas and related digestive juices are not overly stimulated through the excessive use of the will or forceful energisation. The entire digestive process is at stake. (Not only of food, but also of the thought process.) If the refinement of *prāṇas* happen via the repeated meditation of the *yogin,* then the body's secretions will rightly take care of themselves. They are therefore not an objective of the meditative focus, but rather the pathways to the Heart and Head centres.

Thus through control of the forces of the entire driving dynamo of the (Watery) subtle body, and its transformation into a type of Fire-mist, the *sambhogakāya* form, the radiant aura and inner ornaments of a *yogin* is created.

The next phrase given is:

> Reverend Śāradvatīputra, besides, what be the body secret of the Tathāgata, that is the Dharmakāya. What be the Dharmakāya, observe as the Middle Path of natures *(dharma).* What be the Middle Path, that is not born, does not die. Whether Tathāgatas arise, or do not arise, this Dharmakāya remains[13].[35]

Using the phrase 'mind secret' in the text rather than 'body secret' (as Wayman suggests[36]) we see that the phrase 'what be the [mind] secret

35 Wayman, 290.

36 Wayman states that 'There may be a corruption in the text where in para 13 the Dharmakāya is declared "the body secret of the Tathāgata," rather than, as expected, the "mind secret" because in para 11, it is the Sambhogakāya which is attributed the "body secret" and which "is the natural result of great merit"—in fact, the first four perfections, as is also mentioned in para 20. In para 11, the Nirmāṇakāya is attributed the speech (secret). Then, in para 13, the Dharmakāya is said to be what remains as the Middle Path of natures *(dharma),* hence not the result of merit. It appears from para 21 that the last two Perfections, of Meditation and of Insight constituting the collection of knowledge, is how one reaches the Dharmakāya'. (Ibid., 282)

of the Tathāgata, that is the Dharmakāya' refers to the awakening of the attributes of the Head lotus, conferring enlightenment. The phrase 'What be the Dharmakāya, observe as the Middle Path of natures *(dharma)*' refers to the awakening of the Ājñā centre that actually 'observes' multidimensionally. The term 'natures *(dharma)*' here refers to the factors of existence of Buddhism (the *dharmas*[37]). The Ājñā centre integrates these factors that are said to constitute the sum of phenomena (as emanating in the mind), with the *dharmakāya,* in such a way that one can 'observe', to envision what transpires in either. Being of the mind they here represent 'the Middle Path' between the enlightened Mind and the actual appearance of things. The Splenic centres process these appearances so that they can eventually be incorporated as the *dharmakāya.* 'The Middle Path, that is not born' has already been established to represent the way of the Heart centre unfolding. It is 'not born' because it is the custodian of the experience of *śūnyatā.* The 'Middle Path, that...does not die' refers to the path of the central *nāḍī, suṣumṇā.* It channels the Fiery Element, that is directed by the Throat centre. It does 'not die' because it incorporates the Clear Light of Mind, that overcomes the processes of birth and death. Inevitably, it is the *dharmakāya.* The phrase 'Whether Tathāgatas arise' relates to the Base of Spine/Sacral centre interrelation, from which *kuṇḍalinī* arises. The phrase 'Whether Tathāgatas...do not arise', refers to the Solar Plexus centre, whose Watery environment must be completely mastered and pacified, hence is not the place of arousal of the *dharmakāya,* though many upon the path of yoga may at first confuse the minor *siddhis* that arise from it as the *dharmakāya.* Thus is the path of the attainment of enlightenment, via 'the body secret' (to use the actual text), referring to the *nāḍī* system, told. Via it 'this Dharmakāya remains'.

37 *Dharmas,* factors of existence, a doctrine found in the *Abhidharma* of Theravāda Buddhism. The elements of mind. For a summary of their properties see Theodore Stcherbatsky, *The Central Conception of Buddhism,* (Motilal Baranasidass, Delhi, 1994), pp. 74-75. Briefly, each *dharma* (element) is a separate entity or force, there is no substance apart from the qualities of a *dharma,* they have no duration, but flash as new appearances with each moment. The *dharmas* cooperate with each other. (There are 72 of these *saṃskṛta-dharmas.)* Thus they stem from causes and proceed to extinction when influenced by wisdom, but when influenced by ignorance they are continuously generated. The gaining of liberation therefore produces their extinction.

The six *pāramitās*

The fourteenth verse of the text states:

> Reverend Śāradvatīputra, 'natural result of merit' belongs to the terminology of 'the perfections' *(pāramitā)*. Here, also regard a 'perfection' as a natural result of merit. Who so? Reverend Śāradvatīputra, the Perfection of Giving *(dāna-pāramitā)* is allowed to have two kinds—outer and inner things. Among them, the 'outer' is a term of convention *(samvṛti)* and 'inner' is a term of the absolute *(paramārtha)*.[14][38]

Having analysed the 'body secret' (subtle body), Vajrapāṇi now moves the dialogue to the essential ingredient of the practice, namely the cultivation of the perfections *(pāramitā),* of which there are two types. The first ('the outer') relates to the dissolution of the ego by means of following the Bodhisattva path, thus the observation of the *pāramitās.* 'Perfection' then is 'a natural result of merit'. This outer giving is the convention known and understood in *saṃsāra,* and has obvious benefits therein. The inner form of giving (the purification of *saṃskāras)* is the yogic practice outlined above, which in conjunction with the outer produces *paramārtha.*

The fifteenth verse states:

> Among them the 'outer' is the giving of food to whoever desires food; the giving of drink to whoever desires drink; likewise, the giving of male servant, female servant, workman, wage earner, elephant, horse, chariot, earth, head, arm, leg, eye, flesh, blood, marrow, fat, and so on, up to bone. Besides, when used with the perfection of (skillful) means *(upāya-pāramitā)* the giving of maturation, (fulfilling of) human hopes, abundance, magnificence, and the paying of respect. All these are 'outer' giving.[15][39]

The concept of giving the body parts here refers to the service provided to others by means of the functioning of these parts. It is an archaic method of reckoning, incorporating the fact that the body is perishable, and even at death provides nourishment to entities that

38 Wayman, 290.

39 Ibid.

consume the corpse. Also, 'food' and 'drink' refer to the two main types of *prāṇas: manasic* 'food', the ideas that feed people's minds, and 'drink', referring to the emotional input of loving, affectionate and devotional teachings. From this perspective the 'female servant' refers to the *iḍā nāḍī* and the 'male servant' to the *piṅgalā nāḍī.* They assist in providing the food and drink. The sixteen remaining statements refer to the attributes of the sixteen main petals of the Throat centre. This is the organ of the creative voice whereby the spiritual discourses, conveying the food and drink, is conveyed to people by the teacher. The use of this centre consequently is the major way that an enlightened one gives outwardly to those that come to him/her for advice. The first four statements refer to the four major petals of this centre.[40]

The 'workman' refers to the major eastern petal (13) depicted in Figure 1 (chapter 1), representing the Airy mainstay or heart of the sixteen statements. Wages *(manas)* signify the Fiery energies of the major western petal (15). The strength of the elephant upholds the weight of the mastery of accomplishment (here viewed as the *dharmakāya),*[41] representing the Element Earth, the major northern petal (16). The horse represents the general Watery dispensation of the animal kingdom, the major southern petal (14). The remaining statements veil aspects of the twelve smaller petals (numbers 1-12), where the phrase 'and so on' refers to qualities generated from the Inner Round.[42]

The energies of the Throat centre (intelligence) are then used to help perfect skilful means in the art of giving. The examples of 'outer giving' have a relation to the five Elements, and by extension the associated sense-perceptions. The 'giving of maturation' relates to the Aetheric Element (and smell sense-consciousness), the summation or completion of life's experience in any field of expression. The fulfilling of 'human hopes' relates to the Watery Element (and touch sense-consciousness),

40 See Figure 1 in chapter 1, as well as chapter 1 of Volume 5B for detail concerning the attributes of these petals.

41 If it was supporting the aspects of *saṃsāra* it would then manifest as the southern petal. The Elements here represented are governed by the orientation of the Jinas.

42 I shall not labour to correlate the statements here with the petals of the Throat centre, as a detailed explanation of the functions of the petals would have to be given, and this is provided in Volume 5B. Interested readers can endeavour to do this if desired, by utilising the information in that Volume.

as these 'hopes' are expressions of people's desires, aspirations and ambitions. 'Abundance' relates to the Earthy Element (and hearing sense-consciousness), as therein is expressed the material wealth and things that makes life easier. 'Magnificence' is an expression of the Fiery Element (and sight sense-consciousness) which develops the mind and consequently comprehends the magnificence of the *dharma*. The 'paying of respect' relates to the Airy Element, evoking the Heart's compassion (and hence the taste sense-consciousness).

Skilfully assisting individuals to refine their approach to life and to prosper in that above way lays the foundation for following the *dharma*, and eventually the yogic path leading to liberation. This then is the mode of activity constituting the 'outer giving'.

Verse sixteen states:

> By the 'inner (is meant) the giving of the doctrine *(dharma)*, And it is of two kinds: While understanding and absorbed in Dependent Origination, to resort to the Perfection of (Skillful) Means controlled by compassion with tales of giving, tales of morality, tales of forbearance, and tales of (the other perfections) striving, meditation, insight, means, power, aspiration, and knowledge. Moreover, inner giving might resort to the Perfection of Power controlled by sympathetic joy at (anybody's) elimination of the positing of extremes (such as eternalism or nihilism), of the constructive thought and discursive thought of birth and cessation, and of the (dualistic) knowing and knowable. These (two) are gifts of the Doctrine.[16][43]

Continuing with the theme of the first of the *pāramitās,* related to generosity *(dāna),* the perfection of giving, we now look to the inner meaning of this approach to enlightenment via the Bodhisattva path ('the giving of the doctrine of the *dharma')*. We are told that it is of two kinds. The first kind presented concerns being 'absorbed in Dependent Origination'. By understanding its conditionings, therefore being awakened, one can 'resort to the Perfection of (Skillful) Means'. Because the awakened *yogin* is focussed compassionately upon those evolving through this wheel, we see that the energies utilised for the twelve statements that follow are projected via the associated petals of Splenic centre I. Having thoroughly cleansed the *prāṇas* flowing

---

43 Wayman, 290.

through these petals the *yogin* can utilise their resultant purity to help transform the corresponding defilements of those he is striving to help.

When related to the twelve petals of Splenic centre I, as depicted in Figure 8, we have the statements:

1. The Arian petal, 'the Middle Path' is 'controlled by compassion', as it leads to awakening the attributes of the Heart lotus. Here the first *nidāna* (links) of the wheel of Dependent Origination is implied, that of ignorance, and the means of overcoming it is by following this 'Middle Path', thereby awakening the attributes of the Heart centre.
2. The Piscean petal, 'without discursive thought', relates to the transformed attributes of this petal. At first, however, discursive thought is utilised to present 'tales of giving' concerning the way of compassionate undertaking so that the person can wisely travel through the zodiac, or wheel of Dependent Origination. This relates to the final *nidāna* of this wheel, associated with death, and the consequent need for rebirth. As one learns to be compassionate, so one cleanses the forms of selfish and materialistic *karma* that binds one to *saṃsāra*.
3. The Aquarian petal, denoted 'without constructive thought'. In relation to Dependent Origination, however, we have the manifestation of constructive concepts producing 'tales of morality'. Ethical discipline *(śīla)* is the natural disposition of the water bearer, as well as being the fount of all Bodhisattvic activity. The tales provided relate to providing an understanding to others for the need to establish an ethical basis in all undertakings, so that the Bodhisattva path can be trod. Inevitably, the free-flowing mutability of the thought energies conveyed by this sign produces the enlightened Mind that instantaneously receives impressions without the mind having to 'construct' and formulate the thoughts.
4. The Capricornian petal ('without ceasing') translates in terms of the Wheel of Life as continuous striving for the Bodhisattva and to develop ineffable patience *(kṣānti)* with respect to the mental-emotional foibles of others. The Bodhisattva does not prejudge, but rather is compassionate as to where people are really at and to what they need. Patience (forbearance) is also needed by all perspective *yogins* as they learn to discipline themselves to learn this inner

dharma. The teacher must assist the student to overcome every challenge in life, especially those relating to mastery of *saṃskāras*. 'Tales' are provided, giving many examples in relation to this process. The mount of Initiation into the mysteries of enlightenment takes a long time to climb. The related *nidāna* is 'becoming', gaining the fruit of all life's processes.

5. The Sagittarian petal, 'without arising', is here coupled with the symbolism of the ninth Dependent Origination of a man or frivolous monkey gathering fruit, symbolising seeking after new knowledge. The attribute is 'clinging' *(upādāna)* to any desirable aspect of *saṃsāra*. One-pointed arrows of thoughtful skill demonstrating various other perfections are needed to assist people to overcome attachments to ephemera. Because strong desire is evoked by people to cling onto ephemera, so 'the other perfections', and the *pāramitās* in general, are needed to help them overcome their rebirth causing proclivities. By utilising the liberating Sagittarian will, the 'frivolous monkey' must desire to pluck the fruit of the *dharma* with the same ardour formerly directed to forming attachments.

Omitting Aries, but including Scorpio, these petals that concern the *pāramitās* expressed by an enlightened one relate to the five non-sacred petals of the Heart centre. Together they engender the wisdom attributes of the Throat centre when the Mind is awakened. Effectively, however, they are petals of transformation of *saṃskāras* rather than petals of reception, which relates to the southern portion of the zodiac, from Taurus to Virgo. For this reason the Fiery Element dominates, conveyed by Aries, Aquarius and Capricorn and directed by Sagittarius to Scorpio, where this energy impacts with Watery substance to effect refinement and transformation of *saṃskāras*. Scorpio represents the battlefield for the conversion of the characteristics of mind into those of Mind, in turn evoking the attributes of the Dhyāni Buddhas.

The expression of these Rays of Mind produce the 'tales', the moral stories supporting the *pāramitās*. They will inevitably produce the demonstration of the *prajñāpāramitā* via the evocation of the Jina wisdoms when the processed and refined *prāṇas* find their placing in the Heart centre. The Arian petal produces the perfection of skilful means (the Middle Path) as the wheel is turned from life to life. Eventually the Dharmadhātu Wisdom is produced in Capricorn. 'Tales of giving' are an expression of the sum of life's experiences, hence Amoghasiddhi's Wisdom manifests in Pisces. 'Tales of morality' express the attributes of the universal Mind wielded by Aquarius, then manifesting as Amitābha's Discriminating Wisdom. 'Tales of forbearance' are the gain of overcoming the hard-ships as one climbs the mount of Initiation under Vairocana's auspiciousness. The 'Tales of the other perfections' are perfected via the testing ground in Scorpio and Ratnasambhava's Equalising Wisdom. Consequently, first and second Ray attributes are wrought from the matrix of Life.

6. The weight of these accomplishments manifest in Scorpio to evoke Mind in the form of 'striving' (a sixth Ray function), when coupled to the attribute 'without eternalisation'. Carrying forth the Fiery impetus from the previous signs via this striving produces the will to master *saṃsāra.* A considerable amount of determined aspiration must be engendered to overcome attachment or clinging to sensual pursuits. Many trials and tribulations follow, as associated with Scorpio, before real mastery is attained. From the Splenic centre's perspective, this is accomplished via the five lower petals. The imagery for this *nidāna* is that of a woman serving a drink to a person, signifying thirst, craving *(tṛṣṇā).* The concept here being that those that crave want the objective of their craving to last for ever ('eternalisation'), and the revelation acceded with the help of the Bodhisattva is that this is simply not possible, that it is best to 'crave' and strive for enlightenment, which is 'eternal'. Mastering such craving, however, is a difficult tribulation filled process, because the urges to attachment appear again and again, though often upon subtler levels of expression. Each time, the aspirant must generate a resolute determination to overcome and to transform the characteristics into enlightenment vectors.

The 'other perfections' signify the Ray characteristics needing to be expressed and mastered if the Clear Light of Mind is to rule. They relate to the way that the Rays dominate the formed realms.

7. The Libran petal, designated 'without nihilism' is here coupled with the appellation 'meditation', which concerns the development of the first Ray Will to pierce the higher domains so that enlightenment can be gained. The meditation calls forth the compassionate energies *(bodhicitta)* from the Heart centre via the Arian petal (the polar opposite of Libra) so that the entire Solar Plexus circulation (to which the *nāḍī* from this petal is directed) can be flooded with and controlled by these *prāṇas.* Solar Plexus purpose must thereby continue (not be annihilated) so that the compassionate one can interrelate with general humanity that are governed by this Watery disposition.

   The associated *nidāna* is 'feeling' *(vedanā),* symbolised by an arrow piercing a man's eye. This signifies the discovery of impermanence through grief (the blows of *karma,* governed by Libra), which inevitably cause the person to contemplate what caused this painful partial blindness, and how to rectify the underlying conditionings. Wisdom and compassion is the eventual gain, overcoming the nihilistic attitudes that many people take when confronted with the painful effects of *karma's* hand. The Bodhisattva teaches them that rather than nihilism and self-pity they should seek liberation from the woes of *saṃsāra.*

8. The Virgoan petal is signified by the appellation 'without apprehension'. The associated *nidāna* is a pair of lovers, they have made contact (*sparsā),* but are not yet in full union. One's mind (symbolising one lover) must comprehend the vicissitudes of *saṃsāra* (the other lover). All phenomena must be apprehended in the material domain (governed by Virgo) through 'contact' and viewed to have no substantial basis. This introduces the term provided in the text 'insight', which is gained as a consequence. The enlightening intelligence of the third Ray utilises the five Rays of Mind to process sense perception via the five sense-perceptors[44] to awaken the abstract Mind, as Virgo governs the substance of the material domain. This and the remaining four petals of Splenic centre I interrelate *prāṇas* with Splenic centre II, which

---

44 The third Ray relates to the mastery of the sense of smell, the fourth Ray to taste, the fifth Ray to sight, the sixth Ray to touch and the seventh Ray to hearing.

directly processes the gain of contact with phenomena. The 'tales of giving' directed from the polar opposite sign help engender the compassionate insights needed to tread the path to liberation upon the physical domain.

9. The Leonine petal, designated 'without apprehender'. Here we have the imagery of a house with six windows, which symbolises the six senses *(ṣaḍāyatana)* wherein consciousness resides. The intellect is the focus, where the powers of the mind develop via the concept of an 'I', which apprehends the things around it. The associated quality given is 'means', referring to providing the ability to overcome attachment to the phenomena apprehended via the concept of 'self', the cause of much suffering. The mind must be used as a means to find a proper proportion to balance the forces of life, hence to master them. Here the fifth Ray of Scientific Reason is implicated. The strife caused by the conflicting interrelations between different 'selves', of opinions and ideologies, politics and relationships, must be eliminated through the development of Mind. The means thereto is via right (yogic) perception, listening to the 'tales of morality' from the polar opposite sign and working to develop group consciousness.
10. The tenth, Cancerian petal, is denoted 'without apprehensible', and the *nidāna* is depicted as a man in a boat steered by a ferryman, signifying the journey the mind makes in the path of life. The associated quality is *nāma-rūpa,* relating to the tendency of consciousness to name the things it perceives or desires. The water the boat is on relates to the consciousness-stream that takes new birth each life, as symbolised by the sign Cancer, which governs the rebirthing process. The associated Ray is the seventh of Cyclic Activity, materialising Power, governing rebirth. Here the Bodhisattva must lead the aspirant to higher states of consciousness, away from the desire-mind that apprehends phenomena by empowering habit patterns. Rather, the ability to master the *saṃskāras* must be gained so that the dependent chains producing rebirth are broken. The Temple of Life (in Gemini) must be sought. 'Tales of forbearance' to master all of the aspects of incarnate life are listened to and the 'power' (the quality given in the text for this petal) developed to be

able to travel the long mountainous road to liberation. Eventually the Void that is not apprehensible by mind will be experienced.

11. For the Gemini petal, denoted 'without two extremes', the corresponding *nidāna* is depicted as the grasping tendencies of a monkey, who develops elementary logic (*vijñāna*). The monkey swings through branches grasping for object after object in its search for knowledge of what is desirable. The 'twins' here represent the monkey and its environment. The associated term provided in the text is 'aspiration', which here betokens the desire to attain more pleasing, harmonious fruits in life, signifying the attributes of the fourth Ray of Harmony overcoming Strife. Aspiration drives the path to enlightenment, which eventually integrates all into unity by overcoming all conflicts. The inner sanctum of Life is found and in that Temple one hears all of the 'tales' relating to the *pāramitās* to help engender aspiration towards liberation. All of the *saṃskāras* in the *nāḍīs* can be consequently transformed as one aspires to do so. The 'power' of the previous sign can then be utilised to produce eventual liberation. The 'extremes' of the *iḍā* and *piṇgalā nāḍīs* can thereby be fused into oneness in *suṣumṇā* and the inner Fires awakened.
12. The Taurean petal presents the image of a potter, signifying the creation of thought-forms, ideas clothing the mind with images of what is desired. Volitions are produced to act out according to desire impulses. *Saṃskāras* are therefore formed keeping us bound to Dependent Origination. The associated petal of Splenic centre I is designated 'without one extreme', which implies that eventually the potter produces the attributes of the Clear Light of Mind. The corresponding term in the text for this petal is 'knowledge' (of the *dharma*). Wisdom is thus obtained through overcoming desire-attachment and evoking the second Ray of Love-Wisdom. The higher esoteric knowledge *(prajñāpāramitā)* comes through striving and mastering what was seeded in Taurus via the polar opposite sign Scorpio, as 'the Middle Path' is traversed with each turning of the wheel.

After presenting this list Vajrapāṇi continues his thesis of inner giving, i.e., the attributes needed to be developed in order to cleanse, refine and transform *saṃskāras*. The *saṃskāras* being the consequence of the last Taurean petal of the list presented above. He consequently summarises the six *pāramitās* as they affect the Bodhisattva. They are the natural consequence of having mastered the wheel of Dependent Origination and the expression of the Bodhisattva vows. These *pāramitās* are elaborated in the subsidiary verses (to verse 22). As the verse presently considered comes under the context of the 'perfection of Giving *(dāna-pāramitā)',* so also all of the *pāramitās* come under its rubric. Without such compassionate thought as a foundation the other virtues lose their potency.

First needed for the inner *pāramitās* is 'the Perfection of Power'. This relates to the (spiritual) power of meditative concentration *(dhyāna).* For the awakened one all charitable action happens as a consequence of meditation. All interrelations produce karmic consequences, and the Bodhisattva views such consequences in terms of the elimination of *karma* for all concerned. Also, only within the field of the meditation-Mind can all actions be truly seen in perspective and the far-reaching consequences be made known. We are then told that this power is 'controlled by sympathetic joy at (anybody's) elimination of the positing of extremes (such as eternalism and nihilism)'. This quote relates to the fourth and third of the external *pāramitās (vīrya,* striving and *kṣānti,* forbearance). We see therefore the entire focus of a Bodhisattva's meditation is upon the liberation of others and to generate the power to do so. Such power involves developed *siddhis* as well as exoteric capabilities.

'Constructive thought' relates to *dāna-pāramitā,* the 'Perfection of Giving'. 'Discursive thought of birth and causation' relates to the 'Perfection of Morality' *(śīla-pāramitā),* whilst thoughts concerning the dualism of 'knowing and knowable' relates to the projection of wisdom by the Bodhisattva *(prajñāpāramitā).* Such wisdom relating to the 'knowing and knowable' are then 'gifts of the Doctrine'. The ordering of the *pāramitās* in this list differs from that presented in the general explanation, because once the primacy of *dāna-pāramitā* is established then the inner form of giving must be awakened, the mode of manifestation of the *pāramitās* presently concerning us. This is followed by the outer expression of the *pāramitās.*

Phrase 17 (and literally the remaining text) continues with an explanation of *prajñāpāramitā. Prajñāpāramitā* being defined as the great ocean of virtue, the perfection of wisdom. It also refers to the vast literature presenting the essential aspects of the path to *śūnyatā* that is fundamental to Mahāyāna Buddhism.

> The one which controlled by Perfection of Insight *(prajñāpāramitā)*, while there is neither lassitude nor over-excitement of body, speech and mind; and while there is no straying (to improper objects) of body, speech and mind; or, solely, resorts to the Perfection of (Skillful) means controlled by equanimity *(upekṣā)* while one remains without defilement *(kleśa)*—is the Perfection of Morality *(śīla-pāramitā)*.[17][45]

Relating to the outer *pāramitās,* this statement is easy enough to comprehend, as it is meant as a clarification to the average practitioner. Referring to the 'body, speech and mind' it should be noted that in Buddhism the term 'body' normally relates to the five Elements, plus the aggregates *(skandhas)* that are constituted from them. The term 'speech' refers to the subtle constitution of a person, consisting of the ten winds and central *nāḍīs*. These are the subtle factors supporting the faculty of mind to utter words, and inevitably mantras. The term 'mind' relates to the five sense-consciousnesses plus the collating intellect, coupled with the organs of action.[46]

This accounting is archaic and does not allow proper esoteric correspondences, or for the true properties of the constituents categorised under these headings. While it is true, for instance, that the Elements constitute the substance of the forms of whatever manifests, these forms must be comprehended from a multidimensional perspective. The dense physical body, the emotions, mind/Mind, *śūnyatā*, and *dharmakāya* all manifest via expressions of one or other of the Elements. The body is constituted of the Earth Element, the emotions embody the Water Element, Fire manifests as mind/Mind, *śūnyatā* is an aspect of the Element Air, and the vehicle of *dharmakāya* is Aether.[47]

The five aggregates utilise the Elements, but are really vectors of the mind/Mind. They were explained in Volume 1, chapter 2, where the five *skandhas* are given as: 1. form, or body, the sense organs, sense objects and interrelationships (*rūpa*), 2. perception or sensation, feelings and emotions (*vedanā*), 3. aggregates of action, or the motives to thus

45 Wayman, 290-91.

46 See Tenzin Gyatso and Jeffrey Hopkins, *Kālachakra Tantra: Rite of Initiation* (Wisdom Publications, 1991, Boston), 72-74 for detail.

47 See Volume 1, Figure 2, for the way the Elements interrelate.

act (*saṃskāras*), 4. the faculty of discrimination (*samjñā*), 5. revelatory knowledge (*vijñāna*). We see clearly that to list the *skandhas* under the rubric of 'body' is problematic, even if, as suggested in Volume 1, the term *skandha* is relegated more purely to consideration of form *(rūpa)* and of the mental substance *(manas)* that incorporates the body of expression of the material world. The *saṃskāras* are then differentiated from the *skandhas,* because all interrelations with phenomena by means of the faculty of discrimination is carried by them. *Saṃskāras* are the *prāṇic* attributes that convey the proceeds of all aspects of consciousness; be they emotional-mental or purely mental *(manasic).*

The attributes of mind include *vedanā, saṃskāras, samjñā* and *vijñāna,* but the sense organs, such as 'mouth', 'nose', 'ears' or of the facilities of action, such as the arms and legs are but means of developing attributes of consciousness whilst incarnate. They are not the elements of mind, and are not carried through as the mental continuum from life to life. Consequently, throughout this series when I use the term 'body, speech and mind', the reference for 'body' is to the sum of the physical form *(rūpa),* the sense organs, the tangible internal constitution, flesh, bones, etc. It is simply the mechanism of response into which one has incarnated, and via which the external material world can be contacted and experienced, allowing the manifestation of consciousness. For 'speech', the emotional body *(vedanā),* conveyed by the subtle internal constitution is meant. (This includes the mental-emotions that are the normal driving force behind people's speech.) By 'mind' is meant *manas,* constituting the intellect that collates the five sense-consciousnesses, the faculty of discrimination *(samjñā),* plus revelatory knowledge *(vijñāna)* via higher thought processes.[48]

Verse eighteen states:

> The one which, disregarding one's own body and life, resorts to the Perfection of Insight controlled by friendship (or, love, *maitrī),* while avoiding (judgement of) merit or demerit, virtue or vice, truth or falsehood, moving or motionless entities—that is here the Perfection of Forbearance *(kṣānti-pāramitā).*[18][49]

---

48 There is also the distinction between empirical mind and the abstract, enlightened Mind (the Clear Light of Mind), the faculty of pure insight, that expresses revelatory knowledge.

49 Wayman, 291.

This verse focuses upon the demonstration of insight meditation *(vipassanā)* directed via the four arms of the fixed cross, where perfection of this meditation represents the northern arm. 'Disregarding one's own body and life', thereby generating egolessness and selflessness, is the southern focus. Producing compassionate insight *(maitrī)* represents the eastern direction. Eliminating the critical mind by seeing things as they truly are, thereby avoiding judgement of 'merit or demerit', 'virtue or vice', etc., relates to the western direction of observing the character traits of humanity.

As the western direction relates to the main compassionate focus of the Bodhisattva, so this perception can also be characterised by these four directions. People's 'merit or demerit', of whether they are rightly focussed in the *dharma* or involved in meditative pursuits, then represents the northern focus of the meditation. The phrase 'virtue or vice', relating to the level of their ability to generate compassionate activities, represents the eastern orientation of the meditation. The production of 'truth or falsehood' relates to the western direction, as to how people use their minds. Finally, the phrase 'moving or motionless' refers to the southern direction, as to the forms of action (and hence *karma)* people produce. Viewing thus, the Bodhisattva can then make the appropriate decision of how best to assist.

All forms of action associated with these four directions are analysed so as to skilfully help individuals, according to the next step of development for them. Skilful means is evoked and considerable time and patience must be allocated to seeing the fruits of the meditation and resultant action bearing fruit, because all human foibles and the strength of their desires, attachments and wrongly directed minds, must be accounted for. Thus 'the Perfection of Forbearance' is generated.

Verse nineteen states:

> The one enthusiastically enterprising without discouragement for achieving (the perfection of) giving, morality, forbearance, and *samādhi,* while resorting to the Perfection of Insight controlled by friendliness, continual placelessness, and non-aiming at that (goal)—that is here the Perfection of Striving *(vīrya-pāramitā).*[19][50]

50 Ibid.

This list of worthy characteristics to be developed as one attains the perfection of striving can be analysed according to the attributes of the eight-armed cross of direction in space. We start with the western direction of outwards to the field of service representing humanity. Here one enthusiastically strives to be enterprising 'without discouragement for achieving (the perfection of) giving'. It is not easy to rightly give, as wisdom demands that the gift of *dharma* be appropriate, to serve the right need at the right time to produce the right effect.

Often such gifts are wrongly timed or inappropriate, considering the often skewed level of attainment, character, lack of sustaining power, or veiled aspects of the psyche that many possess and which the serving one may not see. The effort of giving can then be squandered and good intentions abused, when resources in time etc., are limited. Thus caution is often the better part of valour, as much needs observing to ascertain what is to be rightly given and when, or if at all, because many would be recipients are 'blind and deaf', i.e., have not the capacity to use what is given. Much can go wrong, producing the wrong effects in the recipient, *adharma* rather than *dharma* can be the consequence.

The expression of this western direction, therefore, is crucial, and many are the testings accorded to the Bodhisattvas of the first three *bhūmis* concerning the perfection of this art of right giving. It is easy to be discouraged at the results, as many failures litter the path of would be Bodhisattvas at first, and *forbearance* (the northern direction of upwards to the *dharmakāya)* is needed to see the tasks through, often over many decades, and even lifetimes. This term also incorporates a persistent striving for further enlightenment and meditation upon the task at hand.

The term 'morality' relates to the northwest direction of emanatory goodwill. Here it signifies the living ethics that a Bodhisattva follows, by which others will recognise his/her fundamental character. Such morality at first generally follows the conventions of the society, altruism, philanthropy, etc., which can be considered the outer morality. Later, unconventional (inner) morality will manifest for the most advanced Bodhisattvas, because 'gift giving' will involve eliminating the available *karma* blocking further awakening or enlightenment of those the Bodhisattva seeks to help. Such *karma* will often be some of the worst the individual possesses, which must be followed through according to what was sown, producing many problematic results. The unfolding *karma* produces many twists upon the path to liberation, providing much testing for all. Following the inner morality generally produces abstraction from the outer world of seeming by the *yogin*/Bodhisattva, and misunderstanding by those served as to the 'character' of the Bodhisattva that generates unconventional deeds and teachings. The Bodhisattva can then be, and often is, vilified, sometimes hated or crucified in the minds and actions of those around.

The cleansing of past misdeeds is a subject that few that seek enlightenment seriously contemplate. It, however, is a crucial component taken into account by the enlightened, and many evil actions from former lives of the aspiring ones need to be accounted for. Much forbearance is needed with respect to possible outcomes once the disciple is tested with the appearing *karma*.

In order to perceive such *karma* the *yogin*/Bodhisattva must enter into *samādhi* (meditative concentration), here signifying the northeast direction concerning the unification of all forces and images in meditation. The appropriate teachings can then be provided to aspirants and practitioners, taking their *karma,* relative spiritual age and Ray disposition into account. Right teachings must be provided at the correct time.

The *samādhi* thus produces perfection of insight *(vipassanā),* here associated with the eastern direction of travelling towards the Heart centre. Correct insights as to the nature of liberation and of the way to experiencing *śūnyatā* must be timed when the students are ready to perceive.

The southeast direction of expression into the world of experience (wherein the supplicants to the guru's beneficence may be found) is denoted as 'controlled by friendliness'. This friendliness comes naturally for all who have awakened the Heart centre's expression, as directed below the diaphragm (south) via the Solar Plexus centre where the supplicants are polarised.

The concept of 'placelessness' (the southern direction of material involvement), implies that the Bodhisattva will be found wherever he/she is needed most. There are no roots in *saṃsāra* that ground such a one.

Finally, for the southwest direction of 'understanding' we have the phrase 'non-aiming at that (goal)', where the 'goal' nominally refers to Buddhahood, but practically relates to the outer expression of the service work to be done. The entire process becomes automatic, spontaneous, with no effort required to assist. Such activity is but the emanation of the Heart's efflorescence in giving. *Bodhicitta* need no longer be sought, it is a fully established fundamental in the Bodhisattva's life.

Thus via these eight directions of accomplishment the 'perfection of striving *(vīrya-pāramitā)'* is mastered. Vajrapāṇi then states to Śāradvatīputra 'this is the collection of merit which accomplishes the secret of the Tathāgata's Sambhogakāya'.[51] The inner radiance, or luminosity of the resplendent aura of the Bodhisattva or Buddha is thereby established, which of itself acts as a mechanism to help cleanse people's subtle bodies. The intensity of the radiance brings imperfections to the surface of those close to the awakened one, which must be appropriately dealt with.

Verse twenty-one states:

> Reverend Śāradvatīputra, besides, the collection of knowledge is what understands those four Perfections; analyses, explains and clarifies the Perfections; and while absorbed in that (pursuit), rightly teaches impermanence, non-self, and voidness; that feeding and collection are non-given things, that all given things are non-given things. In short, what rightly teaches the dispelling of lust, hatred, and delusion, defilements and associated defilements; and is equal to the Dharmadhātu, the base of infinite space; this, aimless, is the Perfection of Meditation *(dhyāna-pāramitā)*. What is the self-presence of thusness, voidness, transcendent voidness *(atyanta-śūnyatā),* voidness at the latter end (*aparāntaśūnyatā*), and of the Dharmadhātu, that is here, the Perfection of Insight (*prajñāpāramitā*). Reverend Śāradvatīputra, this is the collection of knowledge.[21][52]

By informing us that so far we have been analysing the *sambhogakāya* aspect in the paragraphs dealing with the *pāramitās*, then the present verse, which concludes the discussion of the *pāramitās,* will logically explicate the *nirmāṇakāya* and *dharmakāya* aspects.

The focus of the *sambhogakāya* teachings is the *piṇgalā nāḍī* stream, and consequently the Heart and Solar Plexus centres. (The engendering

---

51 Verse 20, Wayman, 291.

52 Wayman, 291.

of compassion.) That of the *nirmāṇakāya* will be the *iḍā nāḍī* stream (the *manasic* focus, the expression of wisdom) and consequently the Throat centre, which controls the expression of these *prāṇas*. Hence verse 21 starts with the phrase 'besides, the collection of knowledge which is what understands those four Perfections'. This is then followed by a series of twelve plus four statements, associated with the attributes of the major petals of the Throat centre. We then have five statements defining Voidness and Thusness related to the *dharmakāya*. They also signify the expression of the five main tiers of the petals of the Head centre. This relates to the *suṣumṇā* level of interpretation that produces, when awakened in the Head centre, the completed wisdom of a Tathāgata. This then reveals the secrets concerning following the path of the *pāramitās*.

What was earlier stated concerning the petals of the Throat centre can now be added to, starting with the Libran petal (number 7 of Figure 1). Here the mind is used as an analytical tool, and in the later stages such analysis happens via meditation. The next statement given is that it 'explains and clarifies', which relates to the Virgoan function (petal number 6), who governs the dissemination of the mind as far as mundane empirical facts are concerned. (Virgo being an Earthy sign, governing the material domain.) The following statement 'rightly teaches impermanence' relates to the Leonine function (petal number 9), who governs the self-focussed individual, that discovers such impermanence in all his/her proceedings, and then educates others concerning it. This process leads to the eventual elimination of the concept of an 'I', that is likewise impermanent. The following sign, Cancer (petal number 10), is the sign of rebirth of incarnation into a transitory body, which is, contrary to general opinion, a 'non-self'. Following this pattern of investigation, Voidness is discovered in the inner sanctum of the Temple of Life (Gemini, petal 11).

'Feeding and collection' are governed by desire and attachment to things (ruled by the qualities of Taurus the bull, petal 2). They are 'non-given' because the individual grasps these things for him/herself, thereby producing *karma*. Desire-attachments provide volatile actions and responses, which must eventually be tempered by wisdom (another Taurean trait) and mastered through the use of the will until steadfast reality remains as the Thusness of things. The qualities to be mastered via petal 1 (Aries), is denoted as 'all given things'. Aries represents the start of the zodiacal wheel, thus of the emanation of everything. The Arian will must be developed upon the yogic path so that eventually the related *karma* is cleansed, making things 'non-given'. This is the way to the Heart centre (the eastern direction), wherein emptiness rules.

The next three attributes mentioned, lust, hatred and delusion are the three poisons depicted at the centre of the wheel of the Six Realms. They are symbolised by a red cock (lust, here associated with the Watery attribute ruled by petal 12, Pisces the fishes); a green snake (hatred, the use of the critical mind to attack things it detests, ruled by petal 10, Capricorn who governs the mount of mind/Mind); and ignorance, delusion, symbolised by a black hog. (Here ruled by petal 11, Aquarius the water bearer, and the lack of clear empirical thinking that qualifies the average Aquarian.) The last two points of this list 'defilements and associated defilements' are governed by the attributes of petals 9 and 8 of the Throat centre. The mechanism to cleanse these unwanted characteristics manifest via the one-pointed aptitude of Sagittarius and the many tests upon the path to liberation governed by the attributes of Scorpio the scorpion. The last five points hint also to the evocation of the antidotes to these poisons via the development of the wisdoms of the five Dhyāni Buddhas.

The next four points of this verse relate to the qualities of the four major petals of the Throat centre. Their interrelation with the other major *chakras* represents the equipment utilised by the *nirmāṇakāya* to serve others, primarily through the use of speech and the written word. The phrase 'is equal to the Dharmadhātu' relates to the northern petal, the *nāḍī* from which leads to the Head centre wherein the *dharmadhātu* is experienced. The phrase 'the base of infinite space' relates to the eastern petal, whose *nāḍī* leads to the Heart centre, wherein the spaciousness of consciousness is experienced. The southern petal conveys the *prāṇas* towards the Solar Plexus centre, to which the term 'aimless' applies, as the enlightened one has no foundation there, except that its expression is controlled by the *dharmadhātu.* The western petal of the Throat centre produces 'the Perfection of Meditation' because via this petal all of the attributes of mind/Mind are directed via Secret Mantra (the Mouth centre) or via the other directions to control the associated *siddhis,* or the visioning of the all-seeing Eye.

The final statements denote the gain of this meditation via the demonstration of the wisdoms of the Jinas. Vajrapāṇi informs us that their qualities, plus the perfection of the attributes associated with the abovementioned petals, is 'the collection of knowledge'. First we have 'the self-presence of thusness', which relates to the All-accomplishing Wisdom of Amoghasiddhi. Through him Thusness manifests throughout the vehicle that was formerly designated as a 'self', and through the sum of the form via which experiences manifest. Here 'Voidness' is an expression of Ratnasambhava's Equalising Wisdom, which integrates *śūnyatā* with *saṃsāra.* 'Transcendent voidness (*atyanta-śūnyatā*)' then is an expression of the Discriminating Inner Wisdom of Amitābha wherein the attributes of mind are transformed into Mind, hence the experience of *dharmakāya.* 'Voidness at the latter end *(aparāntaśūnyatā)'* is an expression of Akṣobhya's Mirror-like Wisdom, which reflects the 'two ends' of being/non-being, *śūnyatā* and *saṃsāra,* into each other. Finally we have the integrating Dharmadhātu Wisdom of Vairocana. Together they manifest as 'the Perfection of Insight *(prajñāpāramitā)*'.

It should be noted that *prajñāpāramitā* is considered feminine because it is the Mother of all wisdom. Esoterically, however, it also relates to the fact that the expression of the wisdoms conveyed by the Jinas exist within the Womb of the Consort of the Ādi Buddha.

Though six perfections are the main subject of this section, two others are also mentioned in the text: 'the perfection of (skillful) means *(upāya-pāramitā)'* and 'the Perfection of Power'.[53] The perfection of skilful means is applicable to both the outer and inner forms of the perfection of giving, whilst the inner giving also includes the perfection of power. They are considered 'gifts of the doctrine'. Effectively, this makes eight *pāramitās* from this reckoning, but this duality of skilful means and power really underlie the expression of all the other *pāramitās,* and all are effectively but emanations of the 'Perfection of Insight (*prajñāpāramitā*)'.

Verse twenty-two states:

> Since Nirvāṇa is blissful, the absolute, calm, untroubled, wholesome, without sickness—enroll in the Dharma-text! Get placed on the path with every station (of success)! The Buddha Bhagavat's introspective

53 Wayman, 290.

knowledge realm is equal to the unequalled by reason of equality, (the Tathāgata) adds the omniscient wisdom possessed of all the best aspects (i.e., the Perfections). Hence, one should rightly embrace, rightly extol, rightly rejoice (in that path); and should enrol upon the stage which is delightful, pure, and gladdening. One should not transgress the time and right measure for maturing the sentient beings by distinguished expression (conveying) understanding of the Dharma, and taming them like the great ocean. Thus one acts in obedience to the cause (i.e., the path, etc.) for those (results, i.e., Nirvāṇa, or omniscience).[22 (sic)][54]

The last verse ended with the 'collection of knowledge' *(prajñāpāramitā),* and here we start with *nirvāṇa.* Both themes relate to the awakening of the Head centre, which is now the focus of the analysis. Proper explanation of the complexity of the 1,000 petalled lotus is beyond the scope of this text, hence shall be the subject of Volume 5A, chapter 7, to which the reader should refer. Only an outline is here indicated, and that only briefly in relation to the twelve major petals and some of the types of energies that pour through them.

First we have the seven Ray characteristics of *nirvāṇa. Nirvāṇa* here is not simply equated with the Void, but rather to the effects of the experience of it. These effects are contained in the Head lotus, which is constituted in such a way that this is possible. It represents the pool of energies contained in the Mind of an awakened one, which when expressed in terms of wisdom is *prajñāpāramitā.*

The first Ray attribute of Will or Power represents the most refined and intense of all energy effects, which with respect to *nirvāṇa* is experienced as bliss, the emptiness of the Clear Light of Mind.[55]

'The absolute' then relates to the mode of expression of the second Ray of Love-Wisdom, as far as the depth of compassionate understanding is concerned. The fount of expressed wisdom is absolute, adamantine, like the manifestation of the rays from the *vajra.*

---

54 Ibid., 291-92. Wayman has 25 here, but as this verse follows verse 21, and there is no indication of a hiatus, one can presume that verse 22 is meant. Similarly for verses 23 and 24, where Wayman has 26 and 27 respectively.

55 The Clear Light is best considered an integration of the most abstract aspects of the first three Rays.

The word 'calm' relates to the expression of Mind manifesting as the third Ray of Mathematically Exact Activity. It is an ever-present ocean of the clear calm embrace of *dharma*.

The term 'untroubled' refers to the gain of the fourth Ray of Harmony overcoming Strife, producing an untroubled expanse of revelations.

The word 'wholesome' refers to the way that the Scientific Reason of the Mind (the fifth Ray) can speak words of power and of the *dharma* to acolytes or to a wide audience.

There is no 'sickness' or tainted *prāṇas (saṃskāras)*–the cause of sicknesses of any kind, nor emotional defilements in an awakened one. Pure health and accompanying healing radiance is the gain of the expression of the sixth Ray of Devotion-Aspiration. This energy projects the dynamic radiatory aura of an awakened one. It is the consequence of the yogic path utilising this Ray to purify the entire *nāḍī* system from its obscurations.

The seventh Ray of Ceremonial, Cyclic Activity is veiled in the phrase 'enroll in the Dharma-text!'. It implies cyclic reading, revising, pondering and meditation upon the texts until the esoteric intent of the meaning is comprehended. The *vajrayāna* is followed until all petals of the Head lotus are fully awakened. Cycle after cycle (astrologically considered) are trodden, generating the necessary qualifications to do so. The remainder of the verse, consisting of twelve main statements, are concerned with this path.

The phrase 'Get placed on the path with every station (of success)!' relates to the (wilful) Arian petal, representing the beginning of the wheel of the *dharma* turning, wherein incoming *prāṇas* expressing the *dharma* are processed so that they can be appropriately directed to the right petal ('station') to produce successful outcomes.

The Taurean petal represents clothing the images obtained via the Arian petal with the general ideas and images contained within the corpus of the Head lotus (the 'introspective knowledge realm') so that the *dharma* can be better idealised and expounded. This relates to the phrase 'The Buddha Bhagavat's introspective knowledge realm is equal to the unequalled by reason of equality'. 'The unequalled' here can refer to the *dharmakāya,* which the Head centre has the capacity to bear once the petals have been fully awakened, 'clothed' with enlightenment-attributes.

The phrase that '(the Tathāgata) adds the omniscient wisdom possessed of all the best aspects (i.e., Perfections)' indicates that these general ideas and images are further refined with the detail needed for complete comprehension. (Which is needed before they can be projected into manifestation, via the petal ruled by Cancer, the sign of incarnation.) Here the attributes of Gemini the twins is evoked, which interrelates the polar opposites in the zodiacal wheel of the Head lotus, incorporating the results of the inner sanctum of realisation. The heart, or kernel, of the truth of whatever is can then be realised. The series of short statements that follow implicate the contribution of the remaining petals to this refining and detailing process, so that the output, conveyed in speech *(vacana)* or writing, is as perfect as possible, worthy of being denoted *prajñāpāramitā,* in line with the way the perfections manifest. From this Cancerian petal onwards the focus moves from the Head lotus *per se* to its activity in the outer world of seeming.

To rightly embrace means to make something yours, to include it as part of your repertoire. Esoterically, the thoughts formerly processed are now thoroughly integrated into a *maṇḍalic* thought structure and are consequently ready to be enthusiastically expounded. They are rightly extolled by the egoless 'I', the *nirmāṇakāya,* embodying the sun-like attributes of Leo the lion, who is famed for basking in the sun. (At first in the light of self-focussed activity and later in the radiance of the Clear Light, or in the luminosity of the Sambhogakāya Flower.) This sign is also ruled by the sun exoterically and esoterically. The next phrase given is 'rightly rejoice (in that path)', which concerns a mastery of the *pāramitās* shown in the outward stage of public opinion. Here the attributes of Virgo the virgin is implied, who governs the material domain, and the birthing of new ideas, and the process of Initiation into the mysteries taught by the seer.

The teachings consequently given is for those taught to 'enroll upon the stage which is delightful, pure, and gladdening', which then incorporates the art of meditation, as followed by the seer, and governed by the sign Libra the balances. The admonishment that 'One should not transgress the time and right measure for maturing the sentient beings' relates to the phase of testings (governed by Scorpio the scorpion) for the teacher to manifest right timing and exactly the appropriate teachings for the students at hand. It also governs the cycles of testings that determine the breadth of their accomplishments. The phrase 'by distinguished expression' relates to firing the Sagittarian arrows of perception to the goal, which conveys 'understanding of the Dharma' (embodied by Capricorn, here embodying the mount of Mind, thus the *dharmakāya).* They are then to be 'tamed like the great ocean' of wisdom (an expression of the fountain of Life poured by Aquarius the water bearer). This verse concludes with the phrase 'Thus one acts in obedience to the cause (i.e., the path, etc.) for those (results, i.e., Nirvāṇa, or omniscience)'. The symbolism of Pisces the fishes is here veiled, which bonds the path ('the cause') to the results *(nirvāṇa).* Pisces then terminates the cycle of expression, allowing a new cycle of activity to begin.

Verse twenty-three states:

> For the sake of the great assemblage of persons, their benefit and happiness; for the sake of gods and men, one should place them in the series one after another of the incomparable Dharma method of the Mahāyāna. One should confer the scriptures one after another so there is no interruption in the stream of (consciousness) for the (three) insights, consisting of hearing (the scripture), pondering it, and cultivating it; or in the mental continuum becoming the *yogi* through repeated exercise of wisdom. When there is a fortunate person, but not yet matured, on account of his being worthy of getting matured, I have put forward a single gate of just a side, but have barely explained the entrance.[56]

The verse summarises by presenting general teachings concerning helping the lay public and aspirants, 'assemblages of people', to learn the verities of the *dharma.* The first three statements concern the 'body, speech and mind' of these people viewed as a unit. The 'body' referring to the entire corpus of people that have assembled for the teachings. 'Speech' referring to succouring their emotional needs and fanning their aspirations. 'Mind' implies providing loftier more exalted teachings for 'gods', effectively here the residents of the inner realms, and men, referring to incarnate thinking humans. The next phrase: 'one should place them in the series one after another of the incomparable Dharma method of Mahāyāna' brings our vision back to the yogic path and the nature of the flow of *prāṇas.* Such a progression of a

56 Wayman, 292.

'series' can also refer to the progression of 'moments' of time, or of the progress of the *dharmas*. The people are placed thus according to their various dispositions and capabilities, as they are not just dealt with as a group, but also individually over a measure of time. Each person bears unique qualities and consequently have different needs, thus educating them accordingly constitutes 'the incomparable Dharma method of Mahāyāna', which refers to a *piṅgalā nāḍī* stream. The 'method' here therefore relates to the demonstration of great compassion. The Bodhisattva path is here espoused.

The phrase 'One should confer the scriptures one after another so there is no interruption in the stream of (consciousness) for the (three) insights, consisting of hearing (the scripture), pondering it, and cultivating it' refers to the expression of the *iḍā nāḍī* stream. Here the attributes of the Mind are utilised in the form of wisdom to provide the insights to those that are receptive to them. Sūtrayāna is here implied.

The reference to the 'mental continuum', whereby one becomes 'the *yogi* through repeated exercise of wisdom' refers to the *suṣumṇā* path developed by the *yogin* via his austerities and *dhyāna*. Vajrayāna is here implicated.

The final statement 'When there is a fortunate person, but not yet matured, on account of his being worthy of getting matured, I have put forward a single gate of just a side, but have barely explained the entrance', relates to the fact that the teachings manifest in the form of a *maṇḍala*. Indeed, this '*Great Gate of Diamond Liberation*' can consequently be entered via any of the four cardinal directions of the gates of a typical Buddhist *maṇḍala,* depending upon where one stands upon the ladder of enlightenment. There are five tiers or levels to the *maṇḍalic* structure, and Vajrapāṇi here implies that these teachings have barely sufficed to bring a worthy one to the third level of the *maṇḍala* where the 'gates' exist.[57]

Verse twenty-four states:

> When he had so spoken, *āyuṣmat* Śāradvatīputra was full of surprise and wonder followed by joy, and said this to Vajrapāṇi, master of the

---

57 See Volume 4, pages 160-71 for detail of these levels, which is further developed esoterically in relation to the constitution of a Head centre in Volume 5A. (See Figure 22, 'The Throat tier in the Head centre as a *maṇḍala*'.)

> secret folk: Son of the family, excellent, excellent! It is just because such as us have (sorely) limited knowledge, and because you have clarified such a meaning of the profound words to the *śrāvakas* who follow the sermons by others that also you, son of the family, are excellent. Vajrapāṇi replied: Reverend Śāradvatīputra, so it is: as you said it, it is exactly so. Reverend Śāradvatīputra, as to what this *samādhi* is called, it is said that this *samādhi* has the name, "Great Gate of the Diamond Liberation."[58]

This verse concludes the text, which we have seen encrypts the nature of the yogic process needed to be undertaken to gain enlightenment. The 'Great Gate' therefore refers to any of the four gates of the implied *maṇḍala,* whilst the term 'diamond' is usually a translation of the *vajra,* the symbol of indestructible power. It is held in the hands, Heart and Head of the *yogin,* and its five Rays project the ineffable wisdoms of the Dhyāni Buddhas. The *samādhi* then is the means of expressing such wisdom.

Oṁ

58 Wayman, 292.

4

A Note on Emptiness

Not empty of light

Emptiness is not empty on the basis that one is unaware of the bumps of consciousness by being closed-eyed. Such 'bumps' hold facts about things in the outside universe that are special to consciousness because they lead to obtaining a better handling of life's processes. Emptiness appears from the inside, not the outside of consciousness. The concept of emptiness exists as part of a containment of all things undefinable that consciousness endeavours to sort out later in the sequence of time. It exists within the sphere of consciousness because that which can be considered 'the outside' is the progress of consciousness, i.e., of all things that it can define. This includes the yet to be fully discovered cosmos. We also have apperception of feelings, touch sensations, etc., of things that consciousness is aware of and also what it must know. The internal universe is what consciousness has already met, experienced, and catalogued. The past is held in *bīja* form and retrievable by memory, and includes even the undefinable that is hidden, as is 'the middle way' of the Heart centre. The pathways to liberating revelation are 'there' (in the *nāḍī* system), but the means to experience the subtler revelations are yet to be unravelled from the maze of the life process.

The mind represents a visioning process that often begins to close its eyes as soon as it starts to inspect detail, because it must focus upon specifics and thus loses sight of the broad panorama. When engrossed in the larger perspective in the process of embracing space then consciousness starts to emulate the process of being empty. It begins to negate the appearances of detail in our world; form, colour, and lines. Yet consciousness is internally aware of their existence.

In its own way consciousness creates this external universe, the 'outside', for it pervades the space of the vision that it sees before it. It creates its many realities and also its own form of emptiness for its peace of mind when it seeks solace from the arenas of continuous activity. This outside world is symbolised by a desert, with sandstorms being created as the focus of vision disturbs the elements, because the object of focus in the mind's eye can be viewed as a wind in the desert landscape of the mind. The desert indicates the intrinsic emptiness of phenomena, with the true meaning of objects appearing mirage-like and obscured by the 'sandstorms' we actually perceive.

The focus of vision is a singular point of emptiness, because the winds of *saṃsāra* swirl around it. The focal point is the place of calm in the eye of the storm. It is at rest, everything else moves, forming into images and thence dissolving again into nothingness, or memories. The vision is similarly expressed once the eye moves because everywhere one looks, the symbolic sand and dust settles somewhere upon the object of vision, obscuring the resulting images. The details are obscured in a haze of memory loss as new images are formed to capture the attention of the eye. Consciousness then takes the images that are ordinarily perceived by the eye and creates its composite pictures. All images are focussed upon the screen of a singular point of emptiness, but the essence or the real of what is perceived is quickly obscured by the dust. *Śūnyatā* is obscured by the moving pictures.

Consciousness needs clear light in order to visualise the images. The light itself signifies emptiness and sustains the active expression of deriving knowledge from what is viewed and inevitably, wisdom. The light acts like the silvered surface of a mirror reflecting into consciousness knowledgeable vistas of images for a necessary duration of time that allows consciousness to analyse and deduce the context of what has been observed. Without this reflective ability the images would immediately disband or not form at all. The Void, however, represents a potent force that would annihilate the images, thus consciousness must be contained in a form that can withstand this force. Inevitably, the expression of emptiness must shine through to claim every strata of conscious image-making, yet for the major part of its evolution consciousness knows not this emptiness. Viewing *śūnyatā* from the focal point of the eye is like looking into the sun, and knowing one is observing the heart of matter at a wide angle.

It is natural for the *winds* of time in space to act as a mechanism to form the appearance of things when consciousness faces any object in any direction. The eye looks upon the object of its perception with the freedom to view all spaces, angles, and perspectives, but when 'dust' settles upon the mechanism of the eye it obscures the vision, thus the approach of ignorance. The eye then sees through its impediment dimly and this establishes modes for attachment.

Śūnyatā is a mechanism for vanquishing the appearing panorama of landscapes that are set like the banquet of manifesting illusional games: the bustling activity of personalities, of colour, vivid sounds, life in general, and the processes of death. This is the usual way all appears before our eyes and is similar to the way most images appear formed before the smaller eyes of the minor *chakras* in relation to the qualities of the various sense perceptors. Each eye contains the pupil that is the veil of the Void.

Blind spots and the *dharmakāya*

In time, that which will work through each Eye is the pure light of the unfathomable *dharmakāya*. Knowing the essence of all being, this fount of life is the true perceiver and can focus into and through the Mind's Eye, as a mechanism for freeing the mind from considerations of form and incarnation in general. It is not bound by the appearance of any phenomena, and can choose to perceive what it wills, but the law of *karma* is its *modus operandi*. It works to cleanse the accumulated layers of 'dust and sand' from the Eye and seeds necessary images needing to be beheld and sustained by that Eye as part of the liberation process. Consciousness thus learns to detach from what is no longer viewed as real.

The process of nonattachment is similar to looking at the sunrise. The experience of attachment is pleasant at first, but as the sun rises it forces one to close one's eyes, or to turn away. The vision is obscured, offering solace to the blinding light. The person has not learnt to stand in the full light of the day of enlightenment. Blind spots have effectively appeared in the form of darkened spaces wherein consciousness resides. It has become attached to objects displaying lesser forms of (reflected) light. This allows consciousness to evolve along paths that allow it to slowly accustom to various forms of intense light, wherewith it can formulate the nature of the progress so far attained. The size of the blind spot denotes, therefore, the extent of the form of ignorance.

Refocussing the eyes using yogic processes allows one to visualise the source of the light and thus to detach from former sources of revelry, but the magnitude of the light is too intense at first, so one learns to squint. In continuing an interrupted gaze with often sideways glances the multifarious facets of vision enlarge, thus consciousness has not lost anything for its interruptions. The facets of clarified consciousness obliterate the formed spaces of mind into forms of substancelessness. The *prāṇas* generated allow the Eye to see in the Clear Light without squinting. In time the facets manifest the diamond-like nature of the enlightened consciousness.

The retina of the physical eyes would be burnt out if one actually stared at the sun in this manner. However, the process symbolises the nature of gaining enlightenment, for the former way of seeing what transpired in the past must be destroyed. This sheds light where once there were blind spots, but one now stands effectively blind to the actions that caused them. This 'blindness' expresses the fact that the illusionality of *saṃsāra* can no longer become an object of attentive, attached focus, rather the reality behind all phenomena will be seen in the Mind's Eye from many angles of perception at once. New forms of internal visioning take the place of blind spots.

Those that lack esoteric vision see but a mirage containing as much of the experiences of the landscape; the storm of volatility, the blizzard of images, that their minds can contain at any moment in time. The blizzard subsides and the mind retains only things of value to the personality concerned. The minds of most people, however, retain little of real worth because their focus is askew or obscured.

When the intensity of what the inner sun veils is experienced, then one knows ineffably more than previously, because from this position all images are instantaneously directed back along the pathways from whence they emanated, and also forwards to their ultimate conclusion. All phenomenological processes become instantaneously observable via a serene, dispassionate *samādhi* of comprehension, and the Void is experienced unsullied by the movement of 'coming and going'.

Volatility does not exist in the serene state of an enlightened Mind. Intrinsically such a Mind is aware of the smaller (atomic) unities within the broader panorama, and of the greater forms that exist outside of the normal consciousness or awareness zone. But such forms, and the overview of its common particles, are generally not of major concern. That form and every other in the mental landscape are incorporated as part of the integral being of the enlightened one, and are automatically experienceable, but a higher selectivity is in place. The illusionality of the changing forms within the overall *saṃsāric* play is noted with respect to how each form of transience may serve the purpose of engendering liberation (of the all). If presently no such purpose is served by the mutable forms then those forms are discarded as irrelevant. The enlightened are not attached to what they observe, and purposefully lead the unenlightened to a similar view. Selectively, therefore, aspects of any panorama are found that skilfully befits the task at hand. Such non-identity is rarely identified by the common eye, nor the nature of the subtle fingers people possess that mould and grasp, trying to claim substance for the little self. The task, therefore, is to reveal to such eyes what they cannot see or do not want to view, because of obscuring delusional self-focussed activities.

The world-view of an enlightened one is in terms of that which is in accord with the Thusness that is 'error-free' and 'not otherwise', where the essence of everything is experienced, and even of specifics, if the focus is thus. The vision is not attached to any individual or to the facets of sentience they portray, though responding to the effects of selfishly grasping, avariciously orientated humanity necessitates great compassion. The view relates to the perspective given in the picture concerning sand and the desert-scape.

When viewing from the *dharmakāya* to the 'outside' then the vision is downwards, of descent through the higher strata of vibrant images, to the vast brewing, perturbed, purulent cloud of thoughts circulating the earth, created by human minds. This also incorporates rivers and torrents of desirous, avaricious, reactionary, and fear-based emotions. Within the thought-streams one can find complexes consisting of many *nāḍīs* manifesting as tunnels of time and space that have collectively attracted to them subjective dust clouds, mists, and veils of pleasurably intoxicating and non-pleasant types of substance. One can also view the awareness-states of streams of non-human lives, and the reality behind the phenomena of substance.

To look in perfect detail at this world the enlightened being must choose what to observe, the time, history, era, people, place, landscape, earth-globe and the type of *karma* that created a 'bubble' around the appearing phenomena, or any related circumstances associated with it.

These auric bubbles of *karma* and consciousness-limitation, of *saṃskāric* involvement, surround all beings caught up in *saṃsāra*. The smallest bubble sustaining a person is the seed of the immediate action to manifest and which can grow to be incorporated into the sum of one's activities (one's consciousness-sphere). The immediate thought in a sphere of action can be considered the smallest atom in relation to everything else associated with the 'bubble of the now'. In fact there are smaller atomic realities yet to become actualised. They are the seeds (*bījas*) that are potentials in consciousness. The seeds can flash into and out of objectivity in a mere millisecond of mentation, or else grow to large size and sustainability, according to the amount of energy put into their purpose. The fusion of will and energy, focussed by conscious direction, creates and propels the associated *vāsanā*. Thus the smallest atom in consciousness can grow to become the size of a God, or Logos of a universe, the activity of which can evaporate to reveal emptiness, or to flower into the vastness of the *dharmakāya*.

An enlightened being first visualises the biggest bubbles that surround people, groupings, or nations, showing the overall *karmic* propensities, then the lesser vortices of energies. The propensities observed allow envisioning the way all actions will progress in the foreseeable future. He/she will also automatically vision that which is freshly propagated. This completes the detail needed to ascertain the need, which is revealed by the Eye of the consciousness-void, wherewith the truth of all things are viewed with their deceptive coverings of *māyā*. Every auric quiver is then noticed and recorded with exactitude in the calligraphic process of the Clear Light of the abstract Mind. Within the *auric fields*[1] of the sum of human interrelations, *karma* can be interpreted and worked out

---

1 These auric fields are characterised by the mental-emotional energies that colour the psychic domains of humanity.

to a liberated resolution, for all auras interpenetrate and interrelate with colourings and forces of various intensities.

The consciousness-void of the enlightened (in *samādhi*) works to bring all volitions in the auric environment of humanity into harmonious resolution. This necessitates a reversal of the auric currents of those that manifest the human *saṃskāras*, a turning around of the Wheel of Life.

The smallest *saṃskāric* transgression must become one's object of focus, for every time one makes and creates negative impressions, or even when manifesting a new positive step in thinking and action, it changes the state of the aura. Where the point of change starts to influence the auric state is what the individual must notice. He must learn to take the right decisive action towards liberation. To see effectively, the Eye must open properly and the obscuring dust cleansed. Cleansing such volitions through annulling the intensity of the *vāsanā* (by 'discerning the real') is a battle that constitutes experiencing heavenly or hell states for the participants. The intensity of the craving, feeling, and clinging with which one had formerly seeded the emotions must be experienced in the reversing wheel when the knot of the quagmire is unravelled. All thought processes must eventually harmonise into the Middle Path.

The characteristics of *śūnyatā*

There are five aspects of *śūnyatā* that one should consider:

1. It is empty of all forms of conceptualisation. All conceptualisations revolve around thoughts of 'I', and in *śūnyatā* there are no such thoughts. In fact, it can be conceived of being created, in the sense that it is the expression of having so refined the Elements that all that remains is their Void aspects. The Void Elements then exist as the pristine substance of *śūnyatā*. All enlightened beings therefore reside in the Void of their own creativity. This Void substance, however, commingles with the universality of the substance similarly created over the aeons by 'thus gone' ones. The Void Elements are vectors for the principle of Life that sustains the activity of 'thus gone' ones in *nirvāṇa*. Such activities embrace the Mind-states of all that have proceeded and the continuation of the *vāsanā* of liberation into the far reaches of space. It should be noted that *nirvāṇa* is defined as the ultimate state of residing in *śūnyatā*, achieved at the death of the

form, but it is best conceived of as an awakening to *dharmakāya.*

2. It is empty of emptiness, thus it is not a nihilistic state. It cannot be obtained by simply eliminating concepts of mind. Instead, the mind must become fully developed, strengthened, and intensified through generation of *bodhicitta* (the compassionate Mind, a one-pointed drive to serve without resort to an 'I' at the centre of things) and then made to rest in its own naturalness. Its emanation then is the Clear Light. The 'I' cannot exist in the intensity of energy that is expressed as this naturalness. It is too weak a construct to sustain its form in the dynamic force of the real.
3. It is characterised by its own natural luminosity (radiant emanatory being/non-being, denoted above as Clear Light). Though no mental formations *(saṃskāras)* exist there, they can, however, dynamically arise when there is need (to help sentient beings) through activating their *bījas* from the consciousness-store *(ālayavijñāna).* The Void Elements are consequently clothed in *manasic* substance.
4. It acts as a mirror reflecting the all-pervading bounty of the *dharmakāya* into *saṃsāra,* and the refined, transmuted aspect of *saṃsāra* into the *dharmakāya,* without altering or qualifying it in any way.
5. It is spontaneously replete with inclusive wisdom. Lightning-like, it reveals the truth about any subject. This is an expression of its function as a 'mirror', becoming the zone of the genesis of insights associated with *bodhicitta.* The emptiness of the generated wisdom is *dharmatā,* where *dharmatā* is but the focal point of the Eye of *dharmakāya.* The 'mirror' therefore reflects *dharmakāya* into *saṃsāra* in the form of *bodhicitta,* and the mode of expression is *dharmatā,* the fount of the Dharmadhātu Wisdom. The background to the 'zone of genesis' of *dharmatā* was presented in the consideration of the Heart centre.

These five aspects are viewed in terms of the cogent wisdoms of the Dhyāni Buddhas. They can be viewed as stages of the experience of *śūnyatā.* Without them *śūnyatā* has not been experienced, but rather a nihilistic state of mind where the mind has tricked itself that it resides in the void. That 'void' is, however, mind-constructed and sustains the

I-concept because it has the thought of its non-existence, or the non-existence of thoughts at the very centre of itself. The Hīnayāna *śūnyatā* is often considered thus, as a state of mind self-absorbed in concepts of 'no-mind', hence is a form of blindness, centred around a concept of nothingness. It does not represent the wisdom that characterises the truly liberated, as the complete development of the awakened state in the all, for the all is not demonstrated, hence is subtly separative in its nature, exclusive rather than inclusive. Inclusivity, however, is a hallmark of the wisdom obtained from residence in *śūnyatā*. The Hīnayāna *śūnyatā* can also manifest as the first (and sometimes the second or third) of the above stages, but this necessitates further rebirth in order to eventuate the Dharmadhātu Wisdom.

The Buddha-Mind is replete with wisdom that excludes nothing external to or from within itself. It takes all phenomenological aspects of *saṃsāra* in its ken and speaks the truth. Truth is the natural outpouring of *śūnyatā*. Wisdom is inherent in the principle of *light* (luminosity), and with respect to *śūnyatā*, it stems from *śūnyatā's* function as a 'mirror'. Here it is of value to consider the Nyingma tradition, as explained by Pettit:

> The Nyingma tradition does not emphasize śūnyatā as a principle unifying the views of sūtra and tantra, because śūnyatā is implicit in the realization of luminosity. Moreover, śūnyatā in the context of luminosity is not merely an absolute negation *(prasajyapratiṣedha, med dgag),* as the Gelug system maintains, but the coalescence of form and emptiness, referred to as "the emptiness endowed with all characteristics" *(stong nyid rnam pa kun ldan).* For Mipham, to say that the emphasis of absolute negation is the meditational "object" of fundamental luminosity is contradictory at worst, and redundant at best. An absolute negation is a conceptual image exclusive of appearance and is not free of the elaboration of non-existence. Luminosity is nonconceptual wisdom that understands emptiness as the coalescence of relative and absolute truths, which means "emptiness endowed with all characteristics".[2]

The function of the *śūnyatā*-mirror manifesting in the form of 'emptiness endowed with all characteristics' is what should be

2 John W. Pettit, *Mipham's Beacon of Certainty* (Wisdom, Boston, 1999), 67.

emphasised whenever the nature of enlightenment is considered.

Two further characteristics of *śūnyatā* are:

1. It functions as a 'diamond-cutter' of illusions throughout the life of the individual capable of realising *śūnyatā*. *Śūnyatā* acts as the transmogrifying force for *saṃskāras* when the energies of the Heart centre are incorporated in the centres below the diaphragm at the appropriate time to cleanse characteristics no longer needed. The *karma* is rectified according to the exigencies of Ratnasambhava's Equalising Wisdom, and the higher transmuted *saṃskāra* comes into play in the life of the individual. The process continues until eventually only the pure, unsullied aspects of the five Dhyāni Buddhas remain. Thus the process underlying the compassionate activity of Bodhisattvas is made clear with respect to the functioning of the *nāḍī* system in relation to the awakening Heart centre.
2. It acts as a stable base for the existence of *saṃsāra*. Without *śūnyatā*, an ordered, regulated *saṃsāra* could not exist, and chaos would reign instead. This is based upon the fact that *śūnyatā* is the 'real'; it is unchanging, everlasting (so to speak). As it is stable, so it supports that which is constantly changing *(saṃsāra)*, holding its duration together in a coherent and non-chaotic way. If the stability provided by *śūnyatā* did not exist, then *saṃsāra* would be a nihilistic expression. Changes would be haphazard, unregulated and meaningless. Mental *saṃskāras* would be intensely segregated, separative, and predatory with respect to other mind structures. One mind structure (personal-I) would thus tend to prey on another, to dominate in the quest 'to know'. Aggressive competitiveness would be the result, and again, this would be chaotic.[3] There could be no possibility of units of *bodhicitta* evolving to help bring order to the fray. *Karma* could not exist because it could not be bound to anything to work with to bring

3 Such consideration actually describes the type of world-view that the dark brotherhood try to impose via their methodology, which in many ways governs our present civilisation. Predatory selfishness is 'evil' because it is destructive to the entire process of evolving life, for the stability of any manifesting form. Sickness, death, and disintegration of the life process is the *modus operandi* of such activity. Therefore, the concept of the middle way of the Heart and *śūnyatā* is anathema to the dark brotherhood. In contrast, though *śūnyatā* does bring death to the form, it signifies expansive liberation into wisdom vectors, not separative warring forces.

about final resolution (into *śūnyatā*). Hence it could not equalise the warring parties to bring order to chaos.

From the perspective of *saṃsāra, śūnyatā* becomes a base for something 'beyond'. *Śūnyatā* thus represents the end attainment of *saṃsāric* existence, but is also the beginning of a vast undertaking in a Domain wherein consciousness is transcended, but if utilised functions similar to the instinct of self-preservation.

Śūnyatā-saṃsāra are the natural components of the yin-yang (*yab-yum*) symbol, or of the Buddha naturally fecundating the womb of his Consort. Emptiness may be the underlying quality of the outer seeming, the truth that *karmic* activity will inevitably reveal, but emptiness by itself will not bring about the evolution of *bodhicitta.* This necessitates something working via it to produce eventual Buddhahood via transforming *saṃsāra* into wisdom attributes. Thus a focus upon emptiness alone will produce the Hīnayāna *śūnyatā*, the Arhat experience, but not the Mahāyāna ideal, the *dharmatā* of things, which necessitates the evocation of *bodhicitta. Bodhicitta* is not derived from the sense consciousnesses, or from empirical deduction, nor is it an instinct. Yet it is the gain of the evolutionary process, the purpose of *karma* to awaken. Its manifestation consequently is caused by a higher directing principle, the *tathāgatagarbha* manifesting attributes of the Mind that is *dharmakāya,* and steeped in the principle of Love that uses the Heart *chakra,* or the Heart in the Head, as its means of expression.

Thought-bubbles and cosmos

It was previously shown that a consciousness-stream represents the stream of *saṃskāras* moving through time, conditioning consciousness. In relation to this, a thought-bubble represents a sphere of containment of any portion of such streams concerning any subject, such as the concept of an 'I' that a personality builds in relation to the perceived image of what is considered real in relation to the life process. The smaller types of awareness-bubbles (related to the individual human units) in the Eye of an enlightened one are thus described, but not the vaster ones. The vast ones are the big life events that incorporate the integration of many aspects of a national identity, of a civilisation, or even of the evolutionary process of kingdoms other than the human. This means that the vast thought-bubbles incorporate the smaller individualised units as part of their containment. One may ask 'How vast?'

The answer is that there simply is no (apparent) ending to the progressively larger spheres of containment in our universe. They grow in size, complexity, and disappear into fields of sublimity beyond the ken of even the most advanced Bodhisattva upon our earth sphere. In this idea lies that which have been termed Buddha-Fields in Buddhist texts. Each such sphere is a vast domain of experience and integrated *karmic* interrelation that has a set duration of sustaining power, providing scope for evolutionary purpose for those traversing through them. However, they also possess their own transience with respect to those that have a vaster Vision and who have transcended the related qualities.

Everything is relative, and such relativity also concerns the limitation of a Buddha's attainment. Thus, contrary to what Buddhists believe, there are bounds to a Buddha's Mind, which he must also aspire to transcend. There is really no end to striving in this universe, as long as there is a (multidimensional) cosmos wherein one resides and travels through. Whilst a universe exists, a Buddha must grow and evolve to incorporate the sum of its boundaries, which leads him far, far away from what the earth contains. Its limitations as a school of learning endeavour have been passed. The Buddha consequently takes his *parinirvāṇa*, and simply enters a higher classroom for experience, a vaster realm of Being wherein he must find his place. This realm transcends the conceptualised awareness of those still conditioned by the consciousness-bubble of the earth sphere. Every transcendental level of expression represents a sublimely supernal realm or plane of reality in relation to that which has been transcended. (What was transcended consequently had a transient but useful validity.)

Emptiness can be considered an expression of the aura of the serene Mind of a Logos (a contemplative 'thus gone' Buddha that embodies a world-sphere). The mental landscape in which humans live is then normally below the field of awareness and threshold of activity of such Buddhas. The expression of human empirical consciousness can be considered the earthy material substance of their world. The Logoi thus view the human bubbles of consciousness as existing in the form of 'sand and stones', which delineate the comparative nature of the sluggishness of normal human consciousness. It is weighed down and concretised by *saṃsāric* considerations when compared to a Buddha-Mind. However, the Void that is the Buddha's aura is found at the core of each such bubble, and from this also emanates the *tathāgatagarbha*. It is the 'seed' guaranteeing future liberation that will inevitably turn a conscious unit into a Buddha once the defilements have been removed by transmogrifying its concretion. In this way the relatively inert is transformed into the expansive Fire that exists as part of the Conscious embrace of the contemplative Logoic One.

When the Buddha-Mind envisions the level of human thought, it observes the domains of Mind where the particles of light emanating from the Landscape of the *dharmakāya* can flow to. These domains represent the Bodhisattvas whose consciousnesses have been expanded to an extent where they offer no resistance to the flow of the Thusness. Their aura also has grown to include the needs of myriad human and sentient units. They are points of a *maṇḍala* that integrate them all into a unity, allowing the Buddha-Mind to see into the miasma of the world sphere. The aspiring human unit within the *maṇḍala* can then also peer into the Buddha-Mind. The *dharmakāya* landscape is therefore not unknowable to unenlightened humans, it can be comprehended by their consciousness every time they become receptive to the down-flow of a Buddha's gaze in their meditations. It becomes part of their inner experiences that drives them on to gain access to higher levels of the Bodhisattva *bhūmis*.

At first consciousness has great resistance to such an energy flow. It would be instantly destroyed if the energy was not transformed and toned down to a usable level of experiential expression for the bubbles of human consciousness. The transforming agent is the Sambhogakāya Flower, which softens the potency from the *dharmakāya* universe for each human unit. The *dharmakāya* can hence be perceived via the Flower's Eye.

The 'bubbles' represent the basic building blocks, the foundation, or most lethargic energy state, of the environment wherein a Buddha finds himself after *parinirvāṇa*. Relative to everything else in the cosmic environment these 'bubbles' are the basic, concreted *manasic* forms of images, upon which a Buddha literally 'stands'. They are relatively inert in the expanded time zone of the cosmos. As the ages pass only incremental changes will be observed in this collective substance. Its clarification proceeds according to the nature and strength of the Bodhisattvic activity working through it. Collective self focus, selfishness and darkened low grade thoughts predominate for untold millennia. Much is recycled from one aeon to the next.

New human units evolve to continue the matrix to replace that substance that has been refined by those units that have moved to the higher strata of Mind, and beyond. Everything reincarnates, and as the entire mass is uplifted so the newly evolved ones create more for the Logoi and their entourage to transmute. Cycles come and go in such undertaking, and the Life of an incarnate Logos in a Thought bubble, representing an earth sphere, depends upon the time the collective *saṃskāras* of one unit of evolving substance, characterised by a particular Ray quality of a humanity, can be refined into the attributes of Mind.

The consideration of time has changed, and in *dharmakāya* one year of earth time can be but a minute of cosmic time. The way we reckon time has speeded up exponentially. Cycles of accomplishment *(yugas)* are, however, the reckoning of time as a *manvantara* (evolutionary period) proceeds. Therefore, when vast Beings, the Logoi, move to do something in the *dharmakāya* cosmos, many millennia of earth time may have occurred.

Each cycle concerns a set of transformations to be accomplished in the matrix. The *nāḍīs* and *chakras* are primed with the forces *(prāṇas)* that are the streams of Life from former evolutionary attainments. There is always an admix of the new gained from that incarnation with the old *saṃskāras,* karmic streams, that can be considered the failures of the past. The plants from a former globe have become animals and the animals from that former system will now Individualise into a human kingdom through the formation of their collective *tathāgatagarbhas* upon the domain of the abstract Mind. They then evolve through cycles of evolution through set stages. The first of these, as far as physical manifestation is concerned, is known esoterically as 'Lemurian', wherein the attributes of the physical form and its sense-consciousnesses focussed upon the desire principle dominates. Then comes the cycles of the development of emotional considerations, of the imagination and the psychic domains of the heaven and hell states. This stage of evolution is labelled 'Atlantean'. The next main cycle, which is esoterically labelled 'Aryan', relates to the evolution of mind and its transformation into Mind.

We are presently at the end of the Aryan cycle, and at the beginning of a new age or era associated with the awakening of the principles of the Heart centre for humanity. Compassionate idealism will then begin to rule the course of civilisation, and many will become Bodhisattvas. The ending of each major cycle is always preceded by a period of major crisis and turmoil, such as that related to the sinking of Atlantis in the former Watery cycle. We are now at the threshold of a similar crisis, with the Fires of mind being the determinant symbol.

Vast is the undertaking via the unfolding cycles, as the evolution of each racial cycle for humanity is similar to the processes an individual *yogin* undertakes in trying to transform base *saṃskāras* below the diaphragm so that they can accommodate the petals of the *chakras* above the diaphragm. Lemurian development in human evolution corresponds to the attributes of the Base of Spine and Sacral centre development. The Atlantean cycle relates to the activities of the Liver centre's interrelation with the Solar Plexus centre. The Aryan cycle corresponds to the corresponding Stomach centre interrelation with the Solar Plexus centre, wherein Throat centre attributes are developed. The new era fast approaching concerns the transformation of these *kāma-manasic prāṇas* so that they can be accommodated in the Heart centre.

One can intuit the enormity of such considerations as the planetary *yogin* arises out of humanity to produce such an accomplishment. The efforts of the Council of Bodhisattvas presently is to incarnate en-masse to give birth to such an entity. Hence the Hierarchy of Light is to externalise as an incarnate expression, to produce a new planetary civilisation. This will be the result of a major crisis period affecting humanity, wherein many present members of humanity will disincarnate and enter into an Eighth Sphere zone awaiting to incarnate upon a new globe that is forming to accommodate them. They will represent the 'failures' of the present evolutionary epoch. The present animal kingdom will later incarnate upon that globe and become humans by appropriating 'Soul-forms', the *tathāgatagarbha,* that can accommodate the evolution of the mental substance they will incorporate into their disposition. The two groupings of human units, those from the present earth, and the new humanity will then evolve together, and incorporate conjoined *karma* as they slowly evolve enlightenment-attributes.[4]

4 What is hinted at here is a vast subject that will be explained in my future series entitled *The Astrological and Numerological Keys to the Secret Doctrine.*

The remainder upon earth will march on to incorporate the attributes of the ascending *prāṇas* to the Heart centre for the planet, and hence the forthcoming Aquarian age will be brought into maturation.

The above is a prelude to the final three chapters of this volume, that describe the attributes of the Sambhogakāya Flower, as it should be noted that such Flowers do not appear out of nowhere. They are products of the past and arise out of necessity (as part of the meditation process of the embodying Logos, the Ādi Buddha) so that the principle of mind can evolve by means of containers of mind in such a way that elementary substance *(prakṛti)* can be converted into mind, and thence evolve to Buddhahood.

Humans are deluded when they try to view the causation of cosmic 'things' via the concretion of their consciousnesses and dull auras. They view with too dull a light to identify the intensity of exalted states of being. The bright light cannot be seen because of the many veils of substance between the human viewer and the liberated luminary. Those that have refined and transformed consciousness may see the subjective sun and not be dazzled by its luminosity. Therein one may not actually 'see' emptiness as a fact, but rather, as such a refined expression within the cosmic landscape that the mind must be empty to conceptualisations (being in fact the effect of the removal of the veils). The reality then is crystal clear, but many lack appropriate definitions to describe what is viewed. The term 'emptiness' hence is used to describe the nature of such a mind. It is 'empty', but not of the ability to Vision what is seen, though what is visualised is empty of mind, yet embodies attributes of Mind. Buddhas and Logoi would certainly say there was something there and identify with it. The ability to develop such Vision consummates the yogic process.

The Spaces *(maṇḍalic palaces)* occupied by Logoi and their immediate minions are exquisitely established in the vast Deep of the Thusness. In the ineffable silence of meditation deep is the *dharmatā* of cosmic Beingness revealed.

The relativity of truth

What can be actualised as truth can only be formulated thus as relative. It ascertains a certain viewpoint of fact or of situations, or else it would not be truth. Even the ultimate truth is considered so in relation to relative truth. Truth permeates aspects of relativities with other things that cannot exist without each other. We have parables, myths, and observations, and all dependent structures that exist to explain truth. Even Nāgārjuna's logic of the *catuṣkoṭikā:* 'is, is not, neither is and is not, and both is and is not', is perfectly sound from the point of view of relativity. It is a method of inquiry that can be used for all terms that delineate anything. There would be no purpose for truth if there were no relationships. (Like the concept of Dependent Origination, which can be considered a method for identification when related to the truth of *śūnyatā.*)

There are three categories of thought that Buddhists must thoroughly analyse in their ontological and philosophical doctrines: relativity, order, and uniting separates (individualities). If they can accept the theory of relation between manifesting individualities to eventually produce a proper (hierarchical) ordering throughout space, through and beyond *śūnyatā,* then my books will be accepted. Buddhists will then have a better understanding of truth and how truth is relative, dependent upon certain factors existing in the mind for comprehension. Individualities, for instance, manifest in cosmos as Logoi, and Logoi work to evolve all that is their bodies of manifestation into *śūnyatā. Karma* governs the interrelation between Logoi, as well as that evolving within their forms. No Buddha is freed from such relationships. Buddhas are, however, freed from the 'seed', the *tathāgatagarbha* and its environment, that spawned them.

It should also be noted that *karma* is dependent upon relationships. The theory of relationships doesn't end with just mind-conditioned understandings, because a law of dependency to relationships is exemplified in *karma* as a definition of its form of expression.

Many Buddhists have made the philosophy of the organism of whatever sect they belong to represent one holistic truth for them, and beneath this in heuristic value are many little separate truths, discernments, and points of discussion. There are barriers, knots of reason, between such versions of truth and others. This creates an imbalance between various versions of 'truth' whereby a claustrophobic atmosphere can be noted, disallowing higher energies and perceptions to be expressed via the sieve of the structure. Concepts can become too clogged with the rocks and stones of opinion, with the particulate matter being too ingrained and compacted with concretised thought structures.

The highest order, or topmost aspect of this sieve structure (and the laws pertaining to it) is the holistic scenario. In this arena Buddhists have produced many middle ground theories, but proper overall view is often lacking, except those that are elementary in nature, as are the four Noble Truths, as well as the concept of liberation. In one's thinking it is best to start from the top down, with the broadest visioning possible, and then to analyse the detail, the minutiae. If the abstruse higher laws are properly instated and managed in a philosophical system then that system will be more refined and sophisticated, presenting accurate detailed analysis, even in its smallest truths and separations of concepts. When the high order of revelatory discoveries become properly assimilated then even higher separations of vast revelation streams, beyond the attitudes presently known or expressed as truth, can be discovered.

Such discovery will bring the higher sub-planes of *nirvāṇa* into view, transforming the understanding of such things as the Six Realms, Tantra and the detail of cosmos. Buddhists will then possess a more sophisticated understanding of *karma*, the domains of the Bodhisattva, the view of *dharmakāya,* and all related ontological and eschatological constructs of thought. This will project this religion into the New Age, upgrading it in the manner that the Buddha intended.

Humanity puts concepts of their own individuality into their definitions of things. Because a Buddha is the final outcome, the last step of the wheel for humanity on this earth, Buddhists have put the concepts of their own identity into the definition of what a Buddha is. It is their idea of the transfigured, transmuted, transcendent form of being a human. He is the higher correspondence of what the wheel, a reincarnating principle, represented, and also does not represent. This is important, for their definitions of a Buddha shapes the concepts and awareness of themselves as Buddhists, what they can achieve, what is the Law and the final outcome, the final steps of the purpose of being born upon the wheel.

These concepts then shape what they think humanity is, what it knows of itself. These ideas incorporate all of the laws that go into the making of a Buddha, as well as syllogisms or logic as to whether he has *karma* or not, what a Buddha means to humanity, how his essence evolves in the three realms before he takes enlightenment and the types of conditionings he is subject to. They are framed by the human mind and include what such a mind conceives what freedom from mental constraints of all types means. This then presents the concepts of *śūnyatā*. Details of definition of a Buddha's life identify purpose, especially when compared with the circumstances of the average person on the wheel.

If we properly define the law of *karma* then the definition of the nature of a Buddha will change. A Buddha will then be seen to exist outside the earthly law of *karma*, but he does not exist outside the Law *per se*. The earthly law will be seen to be a bubble within a larger, more comprehensive Law.

A question then arises, 'What if we were to try to eliminate the concept of smaller and larger, of all polar opposites and divergences, according to the principles of 'no-mind', thus of *śūnyatā*, because smaller and larger are here viewed to be illusional?'

With respect to such a query we can state that smaller and larger are expressions of the truth of the divergences and separations found in Nature. They, in fact, exist if *śūnyatā* is considered to be truly freed from such phenomenological considerations, for then one has separated *śūnyatā* from something 'other', and that this 'other' is not homogeneous. Thus, if there is negation of separations, then one who thinks this way will be caught up in illusion. Conventionally such an argument can be wrought because 'smaller' is a divergence or separation from 'larger', and the mind categorises thus. There is no illusion there, as the concept of illusion concerns the separation between different transient categories of being/non-being. However, what is viewed as 'non-being' is relative to how a mind conceives 'being'. Life persists in *nirvāṇa*, thus manifests in a form not perceptible to those minds that identify bodily forms with 'being'. Life can also be considered in terms of the concept of the *sambhogakāya* form of a Buddha. But the *dharmakāya* also manifests its own form of beingness, Buddha-Fields, the Monadic (or Logoic) Eye, and the like. There also we find separations. The entire paradigm of being/non-being has simply shifted from one limited arena of the livingness of Life to another, vaster one.

Thus divergences cannot be negated, as they can exist within ganglia and complexions of great unity. They may exist as opposites, but together they form a manifesting unity, and in some ways don't exist, when a particular divergence is applied in some areas to one thing and at the same time an Identity into unity of transcendental subtlety is considered.

The divergence of opposites can also make some logical assumptions seem untruthful. This is because if the distance between the number of dots and dashes (indicating things) separating the clauses at either end of the sentence of the entire construct considered is too great, then the process becomes too unwieldy for the imagination to keep track of. In fact, *saṃsāra* and *śūnyatā* exist in a *cul-de-sac* intertwined with each other. There is only one outlet, and that is *dharmakāya*.

When one endeavours to view smaller and larger as being illusional, then one must also look to the case of the separation between the smaller aura of an average human and that of the larger one of a Buddha. If the absolute truth relating to the nature of *śūnyatā* is true then this separation is illusional, thus making the smaller aura and the larger one to be one integral unity. (There is no separation in fact, for *śūnyatā* as the all will not allow such.) Then why is the one with the smaller aura not enlightened whilst a Buddha is? The answer is that both exist in the other, whilst applied laws cause the concept of separation in time. The *tathāgatagarbha* encapsulated in the smaller aura cannot yet shine as the aura of a Buddha because of obscuring defilements that limit the extent of the intensity of the auric structure, plus the lack of characteristics developed that will expand to encompass a Buddha's Mind in stature. A Buddha automatically incorporates the smaller (consciousness) in his awareness if he wills it so, but will not sanction the 'taste' of the smaller one's attachments.

Thus smaller and larger, therefore, cannot be an amorphous whole with no relativity. The relativity here concerns the concept of growth in evolutionary time, the factors therein make the entire holistic structure through relationships. Such concepts can be negated by the imaginative factor of consciousness looking at a whole, or at unities within the whole. The imagination can create or disregard what it wills, thus it has the capacity to negate truth. It can selectively look at one factor and focus upon one time sequence only by disregarding the rest, thus can distort any factor to produce whatever it conceives of as the best. It can be a guide to clear deductive logic, but invariably is used by the majority to destroy or distort images of the real appearing in the mind's eye. Thereby it is the creator of illusion.

All entities manifest in terms of degrees of smaller unities of separations in relation to the largest unity, representing the whole.

The manifestation of diversity and the process of unity are not mutually exclusive. They cannot simply cancel each other out, both exist as part of a functional *maṇḍala*. However, the separateness inherent in the minds of unthinking humanity needs reforming because of the inherently destructive intent or effect upon the general unity of the whole of Nature. Humanity needs the vision obtained through access to the higher strata of livingness, wherein concepts of unity have overcome destructive intent. The nature of truth destroys separative attitudes and integrates diversity into the Oneness of the cosmic whole.

The answer to the question concerning the separation between smaller and larger, therefore, is that all is one, diversity is *māyā* and expresses itself in forms of strife, and yet *māyā* has its rightful place, to produce harmony in the midst of strife. Out of that harmony arises the truth of the cause of it all, and why, which demonstrates as the march of wisdom.

The fact that the whole exists as a compilation of smaller, separate entities enables us to detail the different states of consciousness between being human and a Buddha. The detail helps us comprehend the relativity of each set of conditionings, as well as the type of environmental factors they are or will be in. We can then predict a reasonable outcome for the lifestyle of such individuals, or of the components of any higher system of law. And so, like clockwork, we set up the relative mechanisms so as to envision the functions of the whole. (This then provides the differences between a Buddha, human, or a frog, in consciousness or sentient states.) The concept of the 'whole' can then be transported to another system, another's faculty of awareness, where we can readily divulge the secrets of the future and contact a better notion of the detail that relativity requires. If such a transposition can be made then we will be happy, and can then service humanity as Bodhisattvas must.

Each such effort upon humanity must be sustained in the laws governing the partial and the whole as a coherent organism. All individualities are governed by group laws as they travel up the ladder of revelation in the process of their rise to (spiritual) fame via the wheel of *karma* (the zodiac). The wheel consists of the set steps required to make each human aware, awakened to the possibility of Buddhahood. Each such step manifests a set of new *karmic* circumstances, allowing the subsequent outcome to be predicted in relative detail. From the overview of the whole one can see the set of circumstances in the process of marching to the future. This allows the demonstration of wisdom, and the preview of such things as people's rebirths.

All manifestations via *karmic* law generally propel the all to higher levels of freedom within *saṃsāra*. Upon its wheel all individuals are directly or indirectly interrelated, allowing an integral *maṇḍala* of future potentiality that drives them all forward to the higher strata of life to be constructed.

To become enlightened involves transforming consciousness, transiting images from one state to a more refined one, and *karma* works to assist the transition.

When thinking rationally, you can use two methods of deduction, one where you find your truth in the beginning (the past), to view the genesis of particulars, or you can branch your thinking to concern the future, thus to view universals. If you think with universals then intuitively you are thinking for the future, to create new understandings and innovations. This prevents a *rigor mortis* of fixed ideas to set in (a philosophic senility) and continues the process of observation and deduction of the way everything evolves, and how time progresses.

Logical deductions presenting rational thought on that which is inclusive, the aetiology of the past, the present, and the future is then possible. The future contains the sum of all past experiences, whose truth has become known. Here everything is possible. Logic has expanded to become inclusive of the all, and this is the best. Therefore, continuously strive to achieve the truth that the future will resolve.

Many separations are valuable because they explain reasons or need for change from one state to another. Buddhism thus represents a method to travel from level to level of visioning. Method implies an action to get somewhere; it concerns the separating line between where one wants to go and where one is. It also separates the past from the now, to eliminate old unbecoming traits or diseases of mind, thereby facilitating various states of health. One must thus choose the proper line of demarcation between all states of conscious involvement with things.

People's thoughts are drawn to the past because of attachments thereto by consciousness and reinforced by habitual *saṃskāras*. These habits are therefore easily invigorated. This produces repetitious, sluggish thought which tends to avert the effort of forming the new. Effort is needed to produce changes, and the tendency is to resist the needed expenditure of energy. A non-willingness to change past viewpoints curtails all forms of enlightened activity. The past is limited, whereas the future implicates all possibilities requiring effort. The use of the will to change limitations creates new and maybe difficult possibilities, but also certainty of expansion of consciousness.

To be attached comes through making conscious separation between 'it' (or the type of behaviour) and oneself. To be non-attached is to become dispassionate to the concept of 'self' and its relation to a separate object, therefore the 'it' merges into the unity of the consciousness-space. If there is no concept of 'self' then there is no way to attach this selflessness with what one can label as things. Identity then manifests in place of separations. Consciousness still categorises, but in terms of unities of *maṇḍalas* of expression.

When there is no attachment to the transience of all things, where then can there be suffering? This is the view of traditional Buddhism, and stands true. If honesty counts at all, then be honest with your own thinking processes and trace your thoughts back to veiled, lethargic, reinforced habits of forms of attachments and change them through right effort. In the future, aspirants and scholars alike must more efficiently eliminate obstacles to enlightened growth, thus efficaciously expand their auras to something akin to a Buddha's. To do so one must produce the conditions that will allow the *tathāgatagarbha* to expand within. By attaching the mind to its embrace, one lessens attachment to causes of suffering through karmic volition of continuous cyclic activity. Beyond that is the Void and the *dharmakāya's* ineffable embrace.

Oṁ

5

The Buddha and the Soul-Concept

Vacchagotta's query

The *sūtra* to be analysed here is from the *Saṃyutta-Nikāya IV*, as translated by Snellgrove. It starts with a wandering monk coming and sitting beside Gautama.

> Seated thus at his side, the wandering monk Vacchagotta asked the Blessed One:
>
> "How is it, noble Gotama, is there an ātman?"
>
> When he spoke thus, the Blessed One remained silent.
>
> "How is it, noble Gotama, is there then no ātman?"
>
> Again the Blessed One remained silent, so the wandering monk Vacchagotta rose from his seat and went away.
>
> Not long after he had gone away the worthy Ānanda asked the Blessed One: "How come's it, Lord, that the Blessed One failed to reply to the question asked by the wandering monk Vacchagotta?"
>
> "If I had replied to him, Ānanda, when he asked the question: "Is there an ātman?" by saying that there is, then I would have been supporting the teachings of those ascetics and brahmans, who speak of permanence. If I had replied to him, when he asked the question: "Is there no ātman?" by saying that there is not, that would have been supporting the teachings of those ascetics and brahmans, who speak of annihilation. If I had replied to him when he asked the question: 'Is there an ātman?' by saying that there is, would that have served the purpose of awakening him the realization that all the elements *(dharmas)* are non-self?"
>
> "It would not, Lord."

> "If I, Ānanda, had replied to him, when he asked: 'Is there no ātman?' by saying that there is not, that would have resulted in his falling from one delusion into a still greater one: 'Alas, the ātman that I once had, that is no more.'"[1]

On face value, the teachings provided in this story are quite straightforward. There are, however, some questions to be asked: 'Considering that the Buddha was silent to Vacchagotta and not to Ānanda, why was Ānanda's mind considered worthy enough to be clarified but not Vacchagotta's?' The Buddha could have taken the time to skilfully explain to Vacchagotta, as he did to Ānanda, but did not because the silence was also a necessary teaching to the assembled monks. We therefore should ask 'Are there any further esoteric ramifications to be deduced concerning why the Buddha saw the need to be silent?' Being impeccably wise, it should be obvious that he had many ways to teach his audience, and not just by means of his mouth. The silence itself was a major teaching for those with their inner Eyes awakened. It actually provided a certain seminal instruction as to what a soul *(ātman*[2]*)* may or may not be when put into context with the information presented in this story, subjective and objective. He thus indirectly gave teachings on the nature of the soul. This is a point overlooked by Buddhists in their rush to deny the existence of a soul. Ānanda was told directly, and also indirectly, that a 'soul' could be conceived of in these terms:

a. It could not be thought of in terms of the extremes of philosophical thought, it was neither *ātman* ('self' or soul) or *nairātmya* (not-self). A 'soul' concept cannot be conceived of in terms of annihilation or permanence. Something in between, however, is not discussed, hence could be an option.
b. It therefore can partake of both *ātman* and *nairātmya.*
c. It does not exist, and at the same time does exist.

---

1 David Snellgrove, *Indo-Tibetan Buddhism*, (Shambhala, Boston. 2002), 21-22. He quotes from the Saṃyutta-Nikāya IV. 400ff, and also refers to Guenther, H.V., *Buddhist Philosophy in Theory and Practice,* (Shambhala, Berkeley, 1971), 25-6.

2 The Brahmanical term *ātman* implies a permanent, indestructible soul-form or higher principle of man.

d. It was something (or 'no-thing') different to anything that was conceivable at that time. Thus the time for revelation of its nature had not yet come as no basis was then provided for grounding the concepts.

e. Thus there was not the terminology available to rightly explain what the soul was or was not. Therefore, so as to not confuse (thereby causing *karma*) the Buddha had to keep silent.

f. Also, the silence was itself the teaching as to what the soul was, that its mode of communication to human consciousnesses was in silence, for in that meditative stance, in the calm-abiding of Mind, its voice could be heard.

g. The silence could be broken in the case of a pure or rightful questioner, such as Ānanda, who could reside in the sphere of consciousness implied by the Buddha's answer. This questioner is one who had the ability to comprehend directly beyond words what was veiled behind the face value meaning of what Buddha said, or rather did not say.

Hence an answer as to why the Buddha discriminated so was because Ānanda had the capability to realise what 'soul' was in that life, and hence to comprehend what the Buddha had to say privately, and Vacchagotta did not. Obviously both the silence to Vacchagotta and the non-silence to Ānanda were the teaching as to what the 'soul' is or is not.

There are actually five principal aspects to the dialogue presented:

1. The two questions of Vacchagotta, representing the foundations of the path of enquiry, 'Is there a soul?', and 'Is there no soul?'
2. Vacchagotta himself, representing the desire or chatting-mind, as symbolised by the 'talking pleasantly'.[3]
3. Ānanda's question, representing the interpretative, meditative Mind.
4. The community of monks listening, representing the accumulation of mind/Mind.
5. The Buddha, as the enlightenment-principle.

---

3 Brahmchari Sital Prashad's version states: 'Once a Bachchhagotta Paribrajaka went to Buddha, met Him and after talking pleasantly, sat aside and asked the question, "Gotam, Is there a soul?"'. *A Comparative Study of Jainism and Buddhism* (Sri Satguru Publications. Delhi. Second Edition, 1982), 45-47.

From this, two further points can be deduced:

6. The perspective that the community of monks and the Buddha together represent a sphere of activity that can be considered to represent the functions of a soul, and the central co-ordinating point within the sphere. Ānanda represents the moving vortices of energy, or mind, that interrelates the point at the centre (the Buddha) to the circumference. The 'soul' here represents the enlightening principle composed of a number of factors (manifesting as an organism or *maṇḍala)* that are liberating in nature.
7. That which approaches the circumference from outside its periphery (Vacchagotta) comes to extract information from it in order to ascertain the foundations of the path. But this information is given in silence, indicating that the foundation can only be gained thereby, not by pleasant chattering or the desire-mind. The approach of Vacchagotta thus represents the way of approach of factors found in *saṃsāra* to that which is represented as a 'soul'. Vacchagotta symbolises the incarnate personality endeavouring to quickly gain answers to perplexing questions. No answers are forthcoming unless one is prepared to spend the time and the appropriate methodology, represented by the monks accompanying Gautama.

In the above interpretation we see that the interrelated consciousnesses of the Buddha and his disciples are enclosed within the subjective circumference of a sphere of activity. This constitutes a *maṇḍala* that indicates the nature of the constitution of a 'soul'. From such a sphere, or organism of enlightened activity, answers can be forthcoming, as was given to Ānanda because he was a facet of consciousness therein. Such a *maṇḍala* can be depicted as a sphere or ovoid, a *garbha* or womb of the Tathāgata. Within this community of monks (the *garbha* of their future Buddhahood) the Tathāgata resides and fulfils his function. The community of monks are the *tathāgatagarbha* (in the varying stages of its development), from which the progress of enlightenment is sustained. The Buddha represents the *dharmakāya*, which is yet to be evolved by the component members of the embryo. Like the cells of an embryo, each individual monk is eventually born out from the sphere of *saṃsāra* and evolves into the spiritual entity that the Buddha represents.

Characteristics of the Sambhogakāya Flower

The subjective form, the *'garba'* of conscious being which en-Souls, thus can be defined as an enlightening principle that works from the highest domain of consciousness that incorporates, stores, and directs the collective awareness of a grouping of lives. It can also refer to an entity that functions similarly with respect to the development of a singular consciousness-stream that incarnates through successive vehicles in *saṃsāra* so that wisdom and eventual liberation from *saṃsāra* is gained. In the first definition we have the conception of a group or world-soul, and in the second definition we have the concept of an individual soul, the *tathāgatagarbha*-Sambhogakāya Flower.

We can also conclude that information from this 'soul' can be accessed only in silence by someone seeking enlightenment. When the non-enlightened mind is stilled, quietened, functioning only as an interpretative device, then impressions are possible. This posits the processes associated with *vipassanā* and the state of *dhyāna*. The revelations appearing in an unawakened consciousness therefore work to produce its awakening. This process transpires in a sphere of consciousness (the *ālayavijñāna*), but the enlightenment-principle is not necessarily bound by the conditionings of that *ālaya*. This sphere of consciousness is also defined by a hierarchical structure; as are the organised disciples of the Buddha. There is an inner group of advanced, exemplary disciples, such as Śāriputra, Maudgalyāyana and Ānanda; a middle group of trained, developed monks (elders), and an outer group of novices.

We thus have three major tiers or spheres of different densities (or intensities) of consciousness represented by these three groups. The densities refer to the weight of mental energy (substance) compared to the potency of its clarity, as possessed by these three groups. The relative states of awakened perceptions are thereby categorised.

Those with the largest amount of unawakened substance, where the darkness of ignorance is greatest, are found in the outermost tier of this soul-form. There the *saṃskāras* of base sensorial attachments and worldliness abound to a far greater extent than for those of the inner tiers representing the enlightenment-principle. This outer tier is represented by the indolent and novice monks.

The middle tier of this soul-form consists of the bulk of the community of monks, who have already eliminated many of the grosser mental *saṃskāras* from their consciousnesses. The density of their mental substance is lessened because their thoughts are more refined through constant meditative practices. The intensity of their minds are therefore stronger, being more focussed to the path of enlightenment.

The innermost tier consists of those that are closest to the Buddha, who are already reckoned *arhats*, the most awakened, possessing wisdom almost equal to his. The density of their minds, comprising the essence of mind, is most refined and rarefied, with the intensity being correspondingly great. This intensity means that their Will-to-enlightenment quickly overcomes obstacles. They are the least likely to falter upon the path, and will always act as the examples for all the others to follow.

The middle tier consists of those that embody the general loving aspirations of the *saṇgha*.

The outermost tier consists of those who are knowledgeable in the ways of the world and have still not eliminated many of the mental concepts and attachments to it.

The innermost tier can thus be characterised by the quality of *spiritual Power*, and consists of the least number of disciples. They have awakened *prajñā*, transcendental wisdom, in its various forms of expression.

The middle tier can be characterised by the quality of *spiritual Love*, and consists of a larger number of disciples. They express *bodhicitta* as the base to their activities.

The outermost tier can be characterised by the quality of *spiritual Knowledge*, consisting of the greatest number of disciples. Here also is represented the general community that support the *saṇgha*, from which the novices are drawn. Their immediate purpose consists of awakening gnosis for the requirements of the path.

We can surmise another point here, in relation to the fact that the Buddha is generally represented as sitting upon the opened petals of a lotus flower. The *chakras* are thus implicated, whereby consciousness is conveyed. Logically, therefore, this soul-form, which embodies the qualities of many units of consciousness, can also be viewed in terms of the petals of such a flower. It is the true power base from which a Buddha arises.

The opened petals of the lotus thus represents the foundation of the Buddha's enlightenment. He sits upon it as it supports his activities in the material world. From this perspective his disciples represent those petals, as they are precisely the support for his activities in the world. The lotus symbolism is also used because it represents the way of the path to light. Its roots are anchored in the mud of the swamp representing *saṃsāra* in its entirety, the murky substance of people's desires and materialistic endeavour. The water represents the emotional nature, which is fluid, ever changing, the basis for people's lives. The sunshine giving life to all, towards which the flower grows, represents the enlightenment principle.

Three tiers of petals can thus be broadly considered. Furthermore, each tier must also be represented as a trinity, as each group can also be viewed in terms of 'most advanced', 'general population', and 'novices'. Thus *nine main petals* to this soul-form are expressed, tied together by a central Buddha-like enlightenment principle.

We should also consider three of the main disciples of the Buddha, each of whom are the acknowledged specialists in one of the three main arenas of his teachings.[4]

- Śāriputra, noted for his great wisdom, anchors the most esoteric teachings, that then was viewed as the Abhidharma, but which in time would flower to express the nature of the *dharmakāya*. This finds its analogue in the general characteristics of Love-Wisdom of the Sambhogakāya Flower, with all the petals exemplified.

- Ānanda, the personal attendant of the Buddha, who was famed for his prodigious memory. He memorised the *sūtras*, the main body of teachings, which are the heart of what is needed for the adherents of Buddhism. The analogue is expressed as the Knowledge petals of the Sambhogakāya Flower. This Flower abstracts life's processes into a *sambhogakāya* form. This tier of petals projects images to the Head lotus and receives the resultant wisdom gained from the disciplines related to the conversion of *saṃskāras* from *saṃsāric* activity by the personal-I via *prāṇas* coming from the Head lotus.

4 They are known as the *tipiṭaka* (Skt. *tripiṭaka),* the baskets of wisdom, consisting of the *vinaya piṭaka, sutta piṭaka* and the *abhidhamma piṭaka* of the Theravāda Pali canon.

Those of a knowledgeable context are retained in the Knowledge petals and those that are compassionately based are passed to the Love-Wisdom petals. The purpose of the Knowledge petals relates to the development of the abstract Mind.

- Upāli who recorded the *vinaya*, the monastic disciplines, anchors the regulations governing the arena of conduct for the monks who wish to gain the experiences needed to comprehend the higher revelations. The analogue being the discipline needed to master one's *saṃskāras* by means of controlling attributes of mind in the Head lotus, allowing the absorption of the most refined knowledge-attributes, compassion and wisdom by the Sambhogakāya Flower. The Head lotus expresses the attributes of the *nirmāṇakāya* aspect of a Buddha to be.

Other major disciples of Gautama also need to be introduced. First, Mahākāśyapa, who was known to be the supreme ascetic and foremost disciple, who thus succeeded the Buddha to rule the *saṇgha* after the Buddha's *parinirvāṇa*. Mahākāśyapa was said to have exchanged his robe made of fine Benares cotton with the Buddha's tattered one that was found at a rubbish dump and later headed the first Buddhist council at Rāgagṛha. There he recited the Abhidharma, thus taking the role of Śāriputra, who had died by then. We also have Maudgalyāyana, who was known for his expertise in the expression of subjective powers. Then there is Subhūti, who became an expert on the teachings on emptiness (*śūnyatā*). Finally we have Śāṇavāsika, who was very learned in the Tripiṭaka, and who succeeded Ānanda to become the third Patriarch.[5]

These disciples are those whose names:

> Appear most often in the Sūtras, associated with specific aspects of the teachings: Śāriputra, noted for his comprehension of the Abhidharma teachings: Upāli, who was the authority on the Vinaya teachings; Ānanda, the Buddha's personal attendant, who heard every word the Blessed One spoke; Maudgalyāyana, known for his psychic powers;

---

5 Disciples such as Aniruddha (Pali: Anuruddha), who was said to be foremost in divine vision could also be added, but they manifest lesser attributes to the disciples herein explained. 'Divine vision', for instance, is but a category of Maudgalyāyana's subjective powers.

> Mahākāśyapa, the great ascetic; and Subhūti, who fully comprehended the Prajñāpāramitā teachings.
>
> Both Śāriputra and Maudgalyāyana passed away before the Buddha's Parinirvāṇa. When the Buddha was about to take his final departure, he entrusted the care of the teachings to Mahākāśyapa, predicting that a series of seven patriarchs would maintain the purity of the Dharma and serve as reminders to the Sangha of the Buddha's presence and blessing. Mahākāśyapa thus became the first Patriarch, succeeded, as the Buddha requested, by Ānanda. Ānanda was followed by Śānavāsika, Upagupta, Dhītika, Kṛṣṇa, and Mahāsudarśaṇa. All seven Patriarchs inspired the Sangha and propagated the Dharma in India and in other lands.[6]

The six manifest in the form of two triads of disciples, with Śāriputra, Maudgalyāyana, and Subhūti demonstrating the more esoteric upward pointing triangle that expresses the type of doctrine that later became the Mahāyāna. Mahākāśyapa, Ānanda, and Upāli therefore represent the more exoteric downward pointing triangle expressing principally the type of doctrine that became the mainstay of the Theravāda School.

The major characteristics attributed to all of these disciples offer clues as to their esoteric placing in the *maṇḍala* surrounding the Buddha for this early Buddhist dispensation. We thus have their relation to the form of externalisation of the qualities of the *tathāgatagarbha.* There are seven disciples to whom can be assigned the seven Ray characteristics.

1. Mahākāśyapa's exemplary asceticism signifies the first Ray quality of Will or Power governing the yogic prowess needing to be demonstrated if one is to gain liberation. (Which is a driving force sustaining the *saṇgha.)* This is also signified by his taking the tattered robe of the Buddha as an example of the direct accession of spiritual power from the Buddha to him. Being the directly appointed successor, he thus took the role of the leadership of the *saṇgha* via a first Ray function. The tattered robe signifies the relative difference in wisdom-attributes between Mahākāśyapa and Gautama, that Mahākāśyapa's level was akin to Gautama's at the time after he began his ascetic career and finding the robe. Mahākāśyapa's asceticism also enabled him to

6 Tarthang Tulku (ed.), 'The Great Arhats', *Crystal Mirror, Vol. VI,* (Dharma Publishing, Berkeley, 1984), 193.

manifest the function of an Ājñā centre for this Buddhist dispensation. It established the link between the subjective domain Gautama entered at his *parinirvāṇa* and the community of monks.

2. Śāriputra's vast esoteric knowledge is an expression of the qualities of the second Ray of Love-Wisdom that characterises Buddhism as a whole. This command of the esoteric wisdom tradition indicates the function of the attributes of the Heart centre for early Buddhism.

3. Maudgalyāyana, whose subjective powers *(siddhis)* are an effect of the ability of the abstract Mind (an expression of the Mathematical exactitude of the third Ray) to control the forces governing the *nāḍī* system. The *siddhis* indicate a command of the power of *mantras* associated with the Throat centre's function.

4. Subhūti's grasp of the nature of emptiness, which later became the basis of the teachings of the *prajñāpāramitā,* expresses the qualities of the middle between extremes. Here we have the fourth Ray of Beautifying Harmony overcoming Strife acting as a mirror to reflect the qualities of the *dharmakāya* into *saṃsāra.* The *chakra* implicated is the dual Splenic centre, whose function is to transform all *saṃskāras* into the qualities accessible by the Heart centre by unveiling their intrinsic emptiness.

5. Ānanda's prodigious memory sustained the main corpus of Buddhism in a way that could be recited and made accessible to the minds of the novice monks and lay people. He thus expresses the qualities of the fifth Ray of Scientific Reason. This ability, plus being the personal attendant of the Buddha, was the basis of being chosen as the second Patriarch. Here we have the quality that governed the general interplay of the main community of monks via the purified, controlled Solar Plexus expression for the early *saṇgha.* (Such memory can be considered to be one of the minor *siddhis* governed by this centre.)

6. Śāṇavāsika. As the third Patriarch, he upheld and helped propitiate the Tripiṭaka so that it could be comprehended by a wide, ever-growing audience. He thus expresses the function of the sixth Ray of Devotion in the way that these teachings became propagated and were received by the new Buddhist converts. The *chakra* implicated

here is the Sacral. Its energy helped invigorate the order to reach out to convert and interrelate an ever increasing number of lay people into the structure of the Buddhist community.

7. Upāli. As the one responsible for upholding the monastic discipline and rules to be followed, the ritualistic observances of the monks, so he manifests the functions of the seventh Ray of Ceremonial aptitude or Ritual, materialising Power. Such discipline represents the basic quality that sustains the activities of the community of monks, and therefore is an expression of the most basic major centre, the Base of Spine centre.

When Śākyamuni is added to this list, then is implicated what all of the Ray expressions abstract into, here represented as the general function of a Head lotus. It manifests the Mind that is the *dharmakāya*.

Concerning the constitution of the Sambhogakāya Flower, it should be noted that as well as the three main tiers of petals there is also a central triune bud surrounding the jewel in the heart of the lotus (which expresses the potency of *śūnyatā*). Each of these bud petals of sacrificial intent direct qualified energies from the central jewel to the general arena of the petals, as well as synthesising the most refined of the qualities of one or other of the three major tiers of petals. These bud petals therefore represent the 'containment' of *śūnyatā*, the 'jewel', and they expand when an individual develops the ability to access the Void. They represent the iris part of the mechanism of the Śūnyatā Eye explained below.

These petals relate to the overall evolution of the *buddhadharma*. The effect of the period of the seven Patriarchs relates to the general development of the Knowledge petals of the Soul form of Buddhism. The generated *prāṇas* are abstracted into the third of these bud petals, awakening its activity. The ramifications of the advent of the general Mahāyāna doctrines awakens the central of these bud-petals signifying the perfection of the Love-Wisdom petals. Tantricism relates to the development of the Will-Sacrifice *prāṇas* of Buddhism, and hence awakens the first of these bud petals, allowing the veiled potency of the central Śūnyatā Eye to irradiate the entire Flower with its potency. This is a process still unfolding, as indicated in this series of books. As practitioners continue to awaken the higher Will petals of this Flower, providing further revelations along the Dharmakāya Way that integrates the *vajrayāna* and *mahāmudrā* methodology via a new esoteric doctrine, then the Soul-form of Buddhism will transmogrify. An explosion of glory and radiant bliss into a completely liberated field of expression will be produced, transcending the old forms of thought. The *dharmakāya* teachings now expounded will become the new norm as more great Ones incarnate to provide further revelations illuminating that Way.

Another important factor that should be noted here refers to the early deaths of key members of the *saṇgha*. First we have Maudgalyāyana, who died just before Gautama's *parinirvāṇa*. Upon hearing of the death of his friend, Śāriputra was said to be so distraught that he also died. Just after the first Council, Mahākāśyapa, being quite elderly, also died.

As well as representing the abovementioned *chakras,* it can also be stated that Mahākāśyapa, Maudgalyāyana and Śāriputra represent the functioning of the main lobes of the Ājñā centre that process all the *prāṇas* of Buddhism before passing them on to the Head lotus, embodied by the *dharmakāya* of the Buddha-Mind. Maudgalyāyana thus processes the general *iḍā nāḍī prāṇas* (the left lobe), Śāriputra the *piṇgalā nāḍī prāṇas* (the right lobe) and Mahākāśyapa the central sphere of this *chakra*, which integrates the two streams into a unity before passing them on to the Head lotus for further processing and storing. This is but a way of describing the normal relation between the Throat and Heart centres to the two lobes of the Ājñā centre.

The symbolism of this esoteric trinity vacating their forms at about the same time is important. It paved the way for Ānanda, who represented the main corpus of the *buddhadharma,* to take control of the *saṇgha,* to carry the weight of the dispensation of the flowering doctrine (its Knowledge base and Love-Wisdom principle) to all future Buddhists. He first had to prove himself to be an *arhat* before the first Council at Rājagṛha would accept him as such. This symbolises the necessity of the *saṇgha* to properly control the often unruly and unwieldy energies of the Solar Plexus centre before Buddhism could come of age as a growing organism.

All of the *chakras* above the diaphragm centre (including the Head lotus with the *parinirvāṇa* of Gautama) were effectively removed as objectively functioning entities. The *chakras* below the diaphragm remained, centred upon the Solar Plexus centre with the Inner Round in control. This signified that after its initial impetus from the higher guiding principle, Buddhism had to evolve from below up as a manifesting personality, and begin to master all of the conundrums of such a vehicle. It had to evolve the capacity to develop the qualities of the higher centres, and thus appropriately come of age from first principles, like any maturing adolescent.

We thus have the appearance of the many divergent sects, the 'eighteen schools' of early Buddhism, then the development of the Mahāyāna and finally Tantricism. The period of these eighteen schools to the time of around the third Council, said to have been convened by Aśoka around 250 B.C., refers directly to the *prāṇic* circulation of the corpus of Buddhism associated with the *chakras* below the diaphragm (mainly the Base of Spine centre and Sacral centre awakening). From about the fourth Council onwards, which happened around the year 100 A.D. and the onset of the Mahāyāna, the petals of the Solar Plexus centre and the associated minor centres were awakened. The *prāṇas* then began to seek out and develop the Heart centre via the *prajñāpāramitā* doctrines and the brilliant logic of Nāgārjuna. With the onset of the Yogācāra tradition (about 400 A.D.) we have the awakening of the Throat centre. Tantricism introduced the period when the Buddhist *prāṇas* sought to awaken the Ājñā centre, which needed the prior establishing of the Heart and Throat centre activity.

The Sambhogakāya Flower

When the bud petals are added to the three major tiers of petals of this Flower, then there are four groups of three petals making the necessary number twelve that allow the complete energisation of a Heart *chakra*. Life can then be 'breathed' into a personal-I and the entire journey to enlightenment monitored, sustained, and progressed. The Heart is Life, from where emanates the *bodhicitta* that is the mainstay of the Bodhisattva path. Meditation upon it facilitates the experience of *śūnyatā*.

The Sambhogakāya Flower can be considered the first or Will point (the *dharmakāya* aspect) of a triad where the Heart *chakra* is a second or Love-Wisdom point (the *sambhogakāya),* and the Head lotus, the third or Activity point (the *nirmāṇakāya).* All of these flowers are based upon a paradigm of twelve main petals. Because of this the way to identification with the Sambhogakāya Flower is via the Heart or Heart in the Head *chakras* whilst in meditation *(dhyāna)*. It cannot be accessed by the empirical mind or the emotions. At the same time it must be capable of absorbing the experiences and accumulations of cognitive sense-contacts from the material domain. It must also have *śūnyatā* at the heart, or foundation of its expression. Indeed, acting as *the nexus* it facilitates the medium of approach to *śūnyatā* via *saṃsāra*. It is the zone of interrelation between the two and contains the one whilst sustaining the other. It functions so that only clarified awareness can remain at the level of expression of the bud petals, and the intensity of this clarified Mind can then contain *śūnyatā*.

We know that *śūnyatā* does not represent final extinction of everything, but is simply 'empty' of *saṃsāric* conditionings. Being a middle principle, a mirror-like state, *śūnyatā* allows aspects of the *dharmakāya* to be reflected into the Sambhogakāya Flower so that clear impressions derived from *saṃsāra* are enlightendly organised. The impressions gained clothes the consciousness of one absorbed in *dhyāna* to assist the further drive to liberation, without that consciousnesses being overwhelmed by the potency of the energy from the *dharmakāya*.

The Sambhogakāya Flower thus exists as a refined form of consciousness not defiled by the conditionings of the material domain, yet it processes the store *(ālayavijñāna)* of the sum total of what has been derived from material involvement by embodied units of consciousness. It directs the accumulated streams of *saṃskāras* and *skandhas* of all past incarnations of the consciousness-stream it incorporates as a unity. All is stored in *bīja* form in the *ālaya,* which it embodies. This is possible because it is a container in the field of refined consciousness that it organises so as to direct the forward progression of each incarnating *jīva* (personal-I) towards gaining the perfumes and nectars of enlightenment. The process is achieved through the mechanism of three major whorls of consciousness-energy that take the form of petals. They consist of the substance of the higher abstract Mind, and each of these whorls are also triune, making nine whorls altogether.

The qualities of these three whorls of petals are provided in the terms *spiritual Will or Sacrifice, Love-Wisdom,* and *spiritual Knowledge.* The 3 x 3 petals can thus be described as below, where the dominant energy or quality is given first and the subsidiary one is given second. Sacrifice-Will, however, is more correctly denoted as Sacrificial Will, meaning the will that sacrifices attachments to produce liberation, or an enlightened goal. It is the energy that evokes the potency of *dharmakāya* and produces great spiritual power in *saṃsāra*.

1. Sacrifice-Will—Sacrifice-Will
2. Sacrifice-Will—Love-Wisdom
3. Sacrifice-Will—Knowledge

4. Love-Wisdom—Sacrifice-Will
5. Love-Wisdom—Love-Wisdom
6. Love-Wisdom—Knowledge

7. Knowledge— Sacrifice-Will
8. Knowledge—Love-Wisdom
9. Knowledge—Knowledge

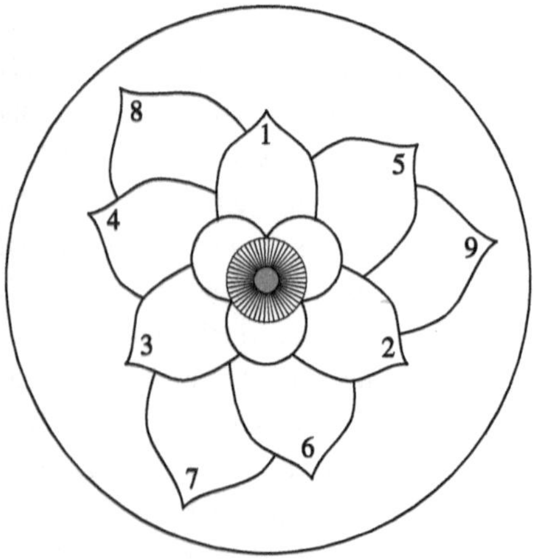

Figure 13. The Sambhogakāya Flower[7]

7 This diagram and attributes of the petals are derived from Alice A. Bailey, *A Treatise on Cosmic Fire,* (Lucis Publishing Company, New York, 1973), 823, where the related information is presented from a different perspective.

Note that the petals do not unfold at an even rate, and therefore the depiction of the Flower here is idealised, representing one that is fully awakened. There is also considerable internal motion, as each petal is revolving at its own rate, as is also the Flower as a whole. In a similar manner, the disciples of the Buddha are not static, each has his own field of activity, as well as internal meditative awakening. The Buddha at the centre is in the dynamic form of equipoise we call serenity.

What is described above as Sacrifice-Will, Love-Wisdom, and Knowledge also has a direct correlation in 'the *trividhasvabhāva* of the Tathāgata-embryo', explained by Brown:

> Being pure always, absolutely and innately, the *svabhāva* ("self-nature") of the Tathāgata-embryo is undefiled by nature *(prakritya-saṃkliṣṭa)*. This initial purity, initially asserted simply and directly, is then translated in a rather forced and recondite style, as powerful, universally non-differentiated, and compassionate. Since the Absolute Body *(Dharmakāya)*, Absolute Suchness *(Tathatā)*, and the germ *(gotra)* have already been identified as the *trividhasvabhāva* of the Tathāgata-embryo *(garbha)*, their respective peculiar characteristics of power, unilateral identity, and mercy are here the illuminants through which fundamental purity becomes expressive.[8]

Here we see that the characteristics of 'power, unilateral identity, and mercy' are synonymous with what I term Will or Sacrifice (power); Love-Wisdom (unilateral identity), because Love is that which unilaterally identifies with the all and makes of it a unity; and spiritual Knowledge (mercy), because this Knowledge is what allows *bodhicitta* to function, producing compassion, and hence mercy for all sentient beings. Compassionate activity is the overall qualification of the Sambhogakāya Flower. Detail concerning these petals and the Tathāgata-embryo shall be provided in chapter 7A and 7B, on the *Uttaratantra of Maitreya.*

It should also be noted that 'the *svabhāva* ('self-nature') of the Tathāgata-embryo is undefiled by nature' relates to the *nirmalā tathatā* of the *tathāgatagarbha,* the *samalā* aspect however is tainted,[9] but

---

8 Brown, Brian Edward, *The Buddha Nature,* (Motilal Banarsidass, New Delhi, 1991), 69.

9 *Samalā tathatā,* Suchness (here the *tathāgatagarbha*) covered over or concealed with impurities. *Nirmalā tathatā* is Suchness apart from pollution (*saṃsāric* defilements).

only what is a purified essence can be contained in the Sambhogakāya Flower. It carries the refined fruits of the evolutionary experiences of the manifested personal-I's, plus what is rayed into it from the *dharmakāya.*[10] Existing upon the abstracted realms of Mind it consequently lies beyond considerations of the dense form. We can, however, describe the way it contains ideations of quantified energy and the *bījas* holding the potential of the thought-constructs to later eventuate.

The central jewel at the heart of the Sambhogakāya Flower embodies the link of the *dharmakāya* and 'contains' the potency of *śūnyatā* (which is a dynamic energy). Thus it is the fount of all knowledge and the guarantee of eventual liberation from even what consciousness represents. This jewel can then help awaken the 1,000 petalled lotus in a person's head.

The Śūnyatā Eye and the Dhyāni Buddhas

The central expression of the Sambhogakāya Flower, which holds *śūnyatā* in its embrace, and which allows an inward and outward progress of energies and related impressions, is here called the Śūnyatā Eye. There are lines of energy to and from the *dharmakāya* and the Flower, which makes it the true *garbha* (womb) of the Buddha, the *tathāgatagarbha,* that allows the *dharmakāya* to impress *saṃsāra* via the *śūnyatā-saṃsāra* nexus. The lines depicted (48 in all, equal to the number of petals to a lobe of the Ājñā centre) represent the way of escape from *saṃsāra.* They are also the mechanism via which an enlightened one can peer into the phenomenal realms at will.

Those in *saṃsāra* need the Śūnyatā Eye (the Eye of the *dharma)* to obtain impressions from *śūnyatā.* The bridge between *saṃsāra* and *śūnyatā* needs to be built in the field of consciousness via the moderating influence of the *tathāgatagarbha.* As one learns to build, so consciousness must be refined to be able to access the rarefied strata of the abstract Mind. From there one can learn to peer through the Eye and access the intensity of the Will-Sacrifice energies pouring through. As such ability is stabilised, then it is possible to build links to the *dharmakāya* internal and external to the Sambhogakāya Flower's form.

---

10 Unregenerate qualities developed by the personal-I's are also accommodated as *bījas,* but are not included as part of the actual form of the *tathāgatagarbha.*

These links are anchored within an even greater Eye, the Dharmakāya Eye of the Monadic form, literally that aspect which is a cosmic vehicle, a Tathāgata that allows one to 'move beyond' the bounds of the earth and its *karma*. The intensity of energies pouring through destroys the long-standing intermediary, the Sambhogakāya Flower, and one is liberated, but still to fully access the potency of the Monadic form. This takes the three higher Bodhisattva *bhūmis* to accomplish, and then Buddhahood, signifying complete integration with the Monad.

There are five levels of expression of the Sambhogakāya Flower, relating to the esoteric grouping of five main *chakras*, the five Elements, the five sense consciousnesses, and their transmutation into the wisdom qualities of the five Dhyāni Buddhas. These wisdom-attributes can be found to be reflected in the Bodhisattva qualities assigned to the most important of the Buddha's disciples. The conception here is that of viewing Gautama's *saṇgha* taking the form of such a Flower. In this schema, the Buddha manifests in the form of an Ādi (primordial) Buddha.

- Vairocana, the Dharmadhātu Wisdom, the central jewel of this lotus. This jewel is represented by the attributes of *Mahākāśyapa,* who wore the discarded tattered robe of Gautama, the most precious symbol of Gautama's enlightenment. The characteristics of this enlightenment then energised the entire flower. The stern yogic prowess of the Tantric path is here implied, to produce the tattered attachments to *saṃsāra* in relation to the revelations coming via *śūnyatā.*

- Akṣobhya, the Mirror-like Wisdom governing the functions of the three surrounding bud-like petals. Here we have *Subhūti,* who was considered a foremost disciple of Gautama. His main teachings were the *prajñāpāramitā,* hence meditation upon *śūnyatā* (via which this wisdom expresses itself). *Subhūti* effectively subjectivises the three main streams of *saṃskāras* generated by the *saṇgha* so that they can enter into the domain that *śūnyatā* represents.

- Amitābha, the Discriminating Inner Wisdom, expressed by the three Knowledge petals. Here we have the general function of *Ānanda* represented, who knowledgeably upheld the doctrines to be remembered and comprehended. The main body of the monkish community were thereby fed with the *dharma*. The overall structural form of this Flower for Buddhism was then sustained by the mnemonic abilities of the early monks to retain all of the main teachings *(dharma)* derived by means of the *saṅgha.* This *dharma* emanates from the abstracted domains of Mind, via which all truth can be comprehended.

- Ratnasambhava, the Equalising Wisdom, expressed by the three Love-Wisdom petals. Here the attributes of *Śāriputra,* master of the esoteric wisdom, become evident. Love-Wisdom is also the overall characteristic of the entire Flower. At first, such wisdom is viewed similar to the Abhidharma, but later becomes the corpus of the Mahāyāna doctrines.
- Amoghasiddhi, the All-Accomplishing Wisdom, the three Sacrifice-Will petals. This wisdom is implicated by the development of the yogic insight and psychic powers of *Maudgalyāyana.* Mastery of all aspects of the incarnate form is necessitated if the attributes of mind are to be transformed into Mind via sacrificial Will focussed upon compassionate activity. This all-accomplishing effort continues to refine the *saṃskāras* of mind until only the Clear Light remains and the bud petals awaken, revealing the central jewel of the Flower.

Continuing along this vein, Upāli represented the mechanism of conveyance of the instruction into the symbolic Head lotus of the incarnate personal-I of the *saṅgha.* He symbolises the mechanism of incarnation via which the Flower functions and which must obey various rules for the manifestation of the conditions that will make liberation possible. This relates to the consciousness of the personal-I that acts as a vehicle for the expression of this Flower. Śāṇavāsika, and the general evolution of the corpus of Buddhism from the third Council on, represents the development of the Head lotus and the other *chakras* of the body to which the energies from this Floral form could flow. The principle doctrine of the *prajñāpāramitā* that is the 'mother of all the Buddhas' could then evolve, producing the objective of it all. Such *prajñā* needs to be developed if *samalā tathatā* is to be converted to *nirmalā tathatā,* and the *tathāgatagarbha* liberated from its bondage to form.

Sukhāvati and mantra

Because the Sambhogakāya Flower *(tathāgatagarbha)* exists upon the abstract domain of the Mind, so the Discriminating Inner Wisdom of Amitābha governs the qualities of the structure of the petals as a whole. Here the *tathāgatagarbha* processes the abstraction and refinement of consciousness. *Samalā tathatā* is thereby transformed into its *nirmalā* form and a liberated being eventually appears. This is one major esoteric reason why Amitābha's Pure Land, the Western Paradise realm (Sukhāvati), was promoted as an attractive goal for Buddhists. Thus the development of such sects as the Pure Land School was facilitated. The focus of their practice consists of continually reciting the holy name of Amitābha (Amida) to obtain birth in this realm. Mainly the teachings of the smaller and larger *Sukhāvati-vyūha sūtras* are utilised for scriptural validation. The descriptions therein of this Paradise Realm are really an idealisation of the nature of the collective consciousnesses of all human Sambhogakāya Flowers.

The reality of the practice is that in so reciting the mantras, many could effectively achieve an exhilarating down-flow of energies from this Buddha within. The practice also assists in obtaining a qualified visualisation of the nature of this *sambhogakāya* realm. An eventual goal ('liberation') would be achieved if conscious mergence with the *tathāgatagarbha* could be achieved. The practitioners were guaranteed success, as such becomes a truism after the devotee dies. Those of pure *manasic* intent (i.e., having the Watery *saṃskāras* stripped from them during their bardo experiences) will automatically find their way to this realm prior to rebirth. This is part of the normal process of all human units possessing developed minds and is therefore the factual basis for the symbolic truth presented in the teachings concerning Sukhāvati. Thus after a blissful sojourn, there is a necessary rebirth into *saṃsāra* to continue the long spiralling journey to Buddhahood.

It is indeed a realm to aspire to, because it is the domain of enlightened being wherein the Buddha-womb can be found and which is beyond *saṃsāra*. However, liberation necessitates the transformation of *saṃskāras*. It is therefore not possible to get there simply by chanting the holy name of Amitābha, no matter how much the wishful desire body wants it. Mantras of this nature can however condition the mind for such an eventuality in the future.

The only way for conscious identification with this paradise realm whilst incarnate is by developing the type of compassionate consciousness that is synonymous with the Discriminating Inner Wisdom of Amitābha. This necessitates rightly discriminating between all alluring aspects of phenomena so that only what leads to enlightenment is utilised. Consciousness must be refined until it is so purified from defilements that nothing is left that can attach itself to *saṃsāric* conditions. The higher abstract Mind must also be developed, which is a reflection of the Dharmadhātu Wisdom of Vairocana.

Also hinted at in the description of the Sambhogakāya Flower is the more esoteric meaning of the often repeated mantra (Oṁ Maṇi Padme Hūṁ) attributed to Alaya Avalokiteśvara (Chenrizigs Padmapani), the Lord of Compassion. He holds the lotus blossom (symbolising this Flower), is said to cry tears of compassion for the suffering ones in *saṃsāra*, and has vowed never to cease striving to achieve their liberation. It is interesting to note that to achieve this compassionate goal he actually needs to travel down no further than to the domain of the Sambhogakāya Flower. By impressing this kingdom with an overall *maṇḍalic* plan for the eventual liberation of all beings he can direct them to appropriately influence the incarnate personalities they embody. Vast must be the meditation upon this schema because of the nature of the massed *karma* to be mitigated and annulled, and of the vacillating, tenacious nature of the *manasic* substance to be converted and transmogrified.

Govinda's book, *Foundations of Tibetan Mysticism,*[11] gives an excellent explanation of the meaning of this mantra and of the way that it relates to the wisdom associated with the five Dhyāni Buddhas. To add a further dimension to what he has written it can now be said that:

- The Oṁ represents the awakening to the Clear Light of the consciousness of the Sambhogakāya Flower.
- The Maṇi represents the jewel in the heart of the lotus, expressed by the mechanism of the lines of energy of the Śūnyatā Eye.

---

11 Lama Anagarika Govinda, *Foundations of Tibetan Mysticism,* (E.P. Dutton, New York, 1960), 228-34. The book is styled around the import of this mantra.

- The Padme expresses the process associated with awakening the qualities of each of the petals of the entire Flower.
- The Hūṁ concerns the enlightened down-flow of this entire expression into the *vajra* of the Heart centre of the meditating one.

The seven Patriarchs and the sixteen Arhats

It might be opportune here to endeavour to trace the qualities associated with the development of the early historical period of Buddhism as ruled by the seven Patriarchs via the associated *chakras* governing them. Our focus therefore is upon the period from the time of Gautama to the end of Aśoka's rule.

The *first Patriarch,* Mahākāśyapa, established the foundation for the development of the future of Buddhism. He helped to ground the *saṇgha* in the material domain. This, coupled with demonstrating yogic prowess, indicates that the period over which he presides constitutes the manifestation of the attributes of the Base of Spine *chakra* for Buddhism. The implication here is also that only through yogic austerities (also significantly demonstrated by Gautama) could there be an arousal of the *kuṇḍalinī* needed to produce complete enlightenment. The established religion thus transcends mere knowledge, as it also kindles the Fires of sure revelation that awakens all to the Thusness.

It can be said that the four great Ones that died by the time Ānanda became the second Patriarch represent the petals of this Base *chakra.* It manifested for a sufficient time to instigate the foundational purpose of what was to proceed. The *kuṇḍalinī* Fire needed to sustain the entire movement was projected. (In its lowest aspect *kuṇḍalinī* provides the internal heat and integrating power to cohere the form into unity and to sustain its existence.)

The purpose of Ānanda, the *second Patriarch,* was to help establish the functioning Head lotus (the *sahasrāra padma)* of the *saṇgha,* to which the awakened Fires could flow. Though, as earlier stated, this process had to be established from the centres below the diaphragm, nevertheless Ānanda was the custodian of the knowledge of the *sūtras,* that when properly expounded would help awaken the Head lotus. They represent the introductory Fires of right knowledge needed to awaken these petals, when carried through in the aspirations of the monks that meditated upon them. Hence the four who disincarnated represented the Base of Spine, or foundation of Buddhism, whereas Ānanda represented the continuation of these *prāṇas* in such a way that eventually the 1,000 petalled lotus of the *buddhadharma* could be awakened.

Observation of the *tripiṭaka* (the three baskets of teachings) was the first outpouring of the process that would eventually flower into the vast wisdom store contained in the collected texts of later generations of Buddhists. The mechanism for the consciousness expansion of all aspects of the unfolding Head centre of Buddhism was thus established by the initial disciples of the Buddha. The *tripiṭaka* relates to awakening of the outermost tier (the Solar Plexus tier) of the Head lotus for Buddhism. The Mahāyāna *sūtras* assisted in that development, plus facilitated the awakening of the middle (Heart) tier of that lotus, and the *vajrayāna,* the innermost tier (the Throat in the head).

As the Head centre of the Buddhist dispensation expanded by the development and awakening of each of its petals and then groups of them in turn, so it determined the timing of the incarnation of significant exponents of the *buddhadharma* in the foreseeable future. Compassionate grounds and the movement of the awakening *chakra* determined the need and the type of *prāṇa* (teaching dispensation) that had to be provided. Such *'prāṇas'* relate to the Ray line of the exponent, plus the intensity of the force (intrinsic level of enlightenment) that could be brought into expression by the incarnating ones. The *maṇḍala* for the future expansion of the entire evolving religion was thereby established.

There is thus a planned incarnation of great Ones to further the evolutionary growth of all aspects of Buddhism (or any other aspect of civilisation) according to the nature of the manifestation of planetary *chakras.* All happens as a consequence of the meditative design of the enlightened Ones that guide the process. Nothing happens by chance, consequently the entire Buddhist organism evolves towards its liberation as a unit.

Another key aspect of the life of Ānanda was to plea with the Buddha to allow the ordination of women, allowing them to become nuns. After an initial hesitation, this was granted. The symbolism here is important because the women represent the *iḍā nāḍī* and the men the *piṇgalā nāḍī* flow. Both are needed if the Head lotus (and indeed any *chakra)* is to be appropriately awakened. The four great Ones embodying the petals of the Base centre, plus Ānanda, then represent the foundation of the conduit for the expression of the five sense-consciousnesses of Buddhism, of the way of awakening of the five tiers of petals of the Head lotus, with Gautama embodying the central sphere, and Ānanda the outermost tier. (The qualities of which are explained in Volume 5A).

Having established the foundational base, as well as the highest centre for the development of the corpus of Buddhism (thus birthing its 'personal-I') as the fruit of the action of the first two Patriarchs, the remainder of the body of manifestation could then be incorporated through the purpose of the next five Patriarchs. This groundwork allowed the *prāṇas (saṃskāras)* developed by the entire corpus of Buddhism to be expressed. Thus by the time of the activity of the seventh Patriarch the total body of the religion had fully incarnated, and was properly organised. It could then grow from the youthful expression presided over by the Patriarchs to a mature wise being by the time of the establishment of Buddhism in Tibet.

The *third Patriarch,* Śāṇavāsika, was said to have first guided a group of a thousand, and later another two thousand people, to become *arhats.* He was also noted for battling the *yakṣas* of Magadha:

> Engaging in a contest of miraculous powers. When they realised they could not outdo him, they accepted his direction: hearing him teach the Dharma, they soon attained the first stages of realization. The epidemic came to an end.[12]

Such a 'contest of miraculous powers' necessitates the utilisation of the Ājñā centre to accomplish. This *chakra* is an extension of the *sahasrāra padma.* Working in close affinity with Ānanda, this Patriarch thus establishes the ability to vision into the future of what needs to be incorporated into the corporeal body of the religion, for it to gain enlightenment as a unit. It was necessary to establish the Eye of the *dharma,* which this patriarch was skilful at propagating, if the growth of the entire organism was to be envisioned and all associated *prāṇas* (units of consciousness) to be rightly directed in accord with the way inspired

12 *Crystal Mirror, VI.,* 206.

by its eminent progenitor. The multiples of a thousand mentioned above refer to the nature of the integration of the *prāṇas* directed by the Ājñā centre into the thousand petals of the Head lotus, which was consequently awakened. The number 2,000 refers to the expression of the second Ray of Love-Wisdom as the necessary accomplishment, which sets the keynote for Śāṇavāsika.

Before this wisdom could manifest all of the demons of Magadha (the symbolic lower corporeal nature) had to be defeated. First, however, the psychic organs need to be awakened to achieve this marvel of conquering 'the epidemic' (of malevolent ignorance) of those the religion was established to educate. The sealing of the task necessitated the appearance of the later Patriarchs and further development of the religion, as directed by the all-seeing Eye.

The *fourth Patriarch,* Upagupta, was known for 'His compassion for living beings [which] mirrored the Great Compassion of the Tathāgata'.[13] He thus embodied the qualities and functions of the Heart centre. The Heart is Life, therefore by his time the *saṇgha* came to be fully vitalised with the prime energies of its true dispensation, which centred around concepts of the Void. The teachings of the Bodhisattva path and those related to the *prajñāpāramitā* via the evocation of *bodhicitta* could then be formulated and later established as the base for all future expansion of the religion. With the Heart of the religion now functioning as a major, rather than a minor centre, Buddhism would no longer be in danger of falling into obscurity, a form of death where it would be considered little more than a minor offshoot of Hinduism. Its progressive development was ensured by the work of the remaining Patriarchs. (The abovementioned centres were also not functioning at their full capacity in the young *saṇgha,* and needed the awakening of the Heart centre to 'breathe' Life into them. This process happening over the course of many centuries.)

The *fifth Patriarch,* Dhītika, came from a rich Brahman family, who gave up his wealth to follow the *dharma,* as the leader of five hundred Brahmans. He:

> propagated the Buddha's teachings widely and brought many to realization. In distant lands and cultures, he appeared in miraculous ways

13 Ibid., 208.

> to gain the respect of the people and to open their hearts to the meanings of the teachings. The people of Tukhāra, far to the north worshipped the sky gods, making burnt offerings of grains, jewels, and fragrant wood. To them he appeared flying through the sky together with his five hundred followers[14]...developed the understanding of thousands.[15]

The symbolism of the 500 Brahmans that went with him wherever he went symbolises the forces (Fires) of the mind (the five sense-consciousnesses and related wisdoms), governed by the directive potency of the Throat centre. The appearance 'in miraculous ways' from the sky has a reference to the fact that he came from 'above', i.e., from the centres above the diaphragm to those ensconced in those below. Directive mantras from the awakened Throat centre empowered this miracle making.

Activity relating to the expansion of mental comprehension of thousands, i.e., the fanning of *manasic* Fires, is also a function of the Throat centre, which rules the direction of these Fires. It can project the *prāṇas* downward to the centres below the diaphragm, or upward towards the Head lotus. (Thus the utilisation of the keyword 'thousands'.) During his time we have the outpouring of a large collection of new texts, leading the *saṇgha* to investigate many fields of meditative enquiry upon unique variations of the *dharma*. This corresponds to the formation of the various organelles in the corporeal body (the symbolic sense-perceptors) associated with the development of the eighteen schools of early Buddhism and their forms of controversy. It was a natural by-product of the empirical expansion of membership and the evolution of consciousness-attributes.

The *sixth Patriarch,* Kṛṣṇa was a successful merchant and travelled the seas to distant lands. On his seventh voyage 'Kṛṣṇa's companions were captured by a sea monster as they stopped at a small island. Kṛṣṇa prayed to Dhītika for help; hearing him, Dhītika appeared and rescued Kṛṣṇa's companions. Upon their return the merchants showed their gratitude by supporting the Sangha with the wealth they had gained. Later they sought ordination from Dhītika, and eventually became Arhats'.[16]

---

14 Ibid., 210.

15 Ibid.

16 Ibid., 212.

The symbolism relating to the Watery Element and sailing ships upon it to collect goods (all types of *saṃskāras*) implies that Kṛṣṇa embodied the qualities of the Solar Plexus centre for Buddhism. The period he presided over now bears considerable disputation ('a sea monster') amongst the sects, as the mental-emotional *saṃskāras* become more intensified and defined. This happened in conjunction with the vitalisation of the Inner Round (the minor *chakras* governed by the Solar Plexus centre) of the Buddhist dispensation. Many new pathways of thought could be explored, with cul-de-sacs of reasoning appearing centred around the qualities of a particular minor *chakra*. This produced many schisms in the religion because of the nature of the emotional currents associated with the Solar Plexus centre, and because it governs the personal will.

The *seventh Patriarch,* Mahāsudarśaṇa, who served during the reign of Aśoka, was the subduer of 'the yakṣinī Hiṅgalācī, who, when aroused, caused epidemics among the people and demanded the sacrifice of animals and human beings in order to cease these afflictions. Seeking out Hiṅgalācī, he turned the force of her anger against her; when she realized the power of his meditation, she abandoned her ways and took refuge in the Dharma. Thus Mahāsudarśaṇa converted her and other powerful beings into protectors of the Dharma. Later, he travelled extensively in the south, where he established Saṅghas and built monasteries'.[17]

From this we can gather that he embodied the functions of the Sacral centre for Buddhism, as this *chakra* (the *svādhiṣṭhāna*) regulates the vital airs of the *nāḍī* system and therefore the *prāṇas* of sickness and disease. The violence associated with blood antonement, the demanding of 'the sacrifice of animals and human beings', is also a Sacral centre function. It is the basic centre governing all material aggressive forces, those of animal instincts, such as the primal urges associated with sex.

Vital *prāṇa* from the Heart centre must be directed to the arena of disease if a cure is to be psychically effected. When brought to the sacral arena it becomes the most potent subduer of the emanations of all *yakṣas* and *yakṣinīs* affected through the meditation process. Mahāsudarśaṇa was obviously able to achieve this work quite successfully, thus demonstrating his power as a Buddhist *yogin*. His missionary work in the southern direction also relates to the fact that the Sacral and Base of

17 Ibid., 214.

Spine centres are an integral unity. His ability to build monasteries thus symbolises the proper grounding of the Buddhist religion on earth via this Base centre. Therefore the *nāḍī* system of the Buddhist dispensation was now complete, with all elements and *chakras* functioning, allowing the major flowering of the religion to henceforth occur. This allowed the onset of the Mahāyāna dispensation and the later Tantric outpouring of the Mahāsiddhas.

The power of this Sacral centre/Base of Spine combination was also subjectively utilised by Aśoka to conquer most of India. After his conversion to Buddhism and consequent contrition he worked to spread the *dharma* over the vast extent of his empire. This is also a function of the Sacral centre, which governs the sexual function and birthing process. Thus the Buddhist religion could manifest the complete potential of its birthing. Aśoka ensured its survival, by effectively fostering this religious child on to the then world stage—all over India and Sri Lanka, and through sending Buddhist missionaries to many other kingdoms.

From this period on, having now externalised the *chakras* governing the religion, the need was for great Ones to appear that would develop and embody their full potency. The rest of Buddhist history therefore concerns the stages of this development. We thus have the period of the flowering of the Mahāyāna tradition, corresponding to the proper awakening of its Solar Plexus and Heart centres, and by the time the Yogācāra tradition flowered we have the awakening of its Throat centre.

The period of the Golden Age of the Buddhist philosophers and the activities of the Mahāsiddhas came about as a combination of the energies from these two *chakras*. Tantric philosophy became established as *yogins* and *yoginīs* incarnated who could reach out to develop the Ājñā centre. The establishment of Buddhism in Tibet (the 'roof of the world') and its further reach to China and Japan concerned the true beginning of awakening the 1,000 petalled lotus. Its complete awakening can, however, only happen now, after the invasion of Tibet and the diaspora of its monks into the West. This allows the *mahāmudrā* of the East and the West to manifest, and the promulgation of the Dharmakāya Way to be fully established. The opening centuries of this new millennia should produce the fruit of the expansive expression of the Head lotus.

The disciples governing the function of the seven Rays for Buddhism, plus the five that manifest the attributes of the wisdoms of the five Dhyāni Buddhas, represent the seven sacred petals and five non-sacred petals of the Heart centre. (Even though some of the disciples manifest a dual role.)

There were also sixteen great *arhats* who:

> Vowed at the time of the Parinirvāṇa to remain in the world to maintain the Dharma until the time of the Buddha Maitreya. Since then, their presence in the world has supported the Sangha and encouraged the efforts of all who seek realization. Long after the seven Patriarchs had entered nirvana, the Sixteen Great Arhats continued to appear to devoted students of the Dharma.[18]

The empowerment of these sixteen *arhats* as *Bodhisattvas* assists the Heart centre to properly awaken through the correct functioning of the two eight petalled lotus's below the diaphragm (the Diaphragm centre and Splenic centre II) that work to cleanse base *saṃskāras* and direct them to the Heart centre. The number 16 = 2 x 8 represents the way each wheel turns according to the nature of the *prāṇic* vitalisation of the eight directions, manifesting either from right to left or else the rectification from left to right. This *prāṇic* flow has an externalised expression in the movements of the various *bhikṣus* as they wander to and from various monasteries and places of seclusion to propagate the *dharma,* or to gather alms.

The number sixteen also refers to the number of petals of the Throat centre, which indicates that one of the major functions of these *arhats* is to fully empower this centre of Buddhism through their literary outpouring. We thus have the rise of the classical period of the major Buddhist philosophers.

These *arhats* are able to vow to 'remain in the world to maintain the Dharma until the time of the Buddha Maitreya' because they were spiritually younger than the seven major disciples of the Buddha and therefore closer to the humanity they have come to serve. Consequently, there are more *karmic* bonds tying them to *saṃsāra*, lengthening the time before their final liberation.

When these sixteen *arhats* are added to the six main disciples of Gautama (Śāriputra, Maudgalyāyana, Subhūti, Mahākāśyapa, Ānanda,

18 Ibid., 193.

and Upāli) then we get the number twenty-two, referring to the number of the minor *chakras* controlling the Inner Round circulation.[19] These centres can be listed:

- One at each eye.
- One at each ear.
- The Alta Major centre at the back of the head.
- One associated with the function of speech.
- One between the shoulder blades.
- One at each breast.
- The Diaphragm centre.
- One centre at the liver.
- Another at the stomach.
- The superimposed Splenic centres.
- One at each foot.
- One at each knee.
- One at each hand.
- Two Gonad centres.[20]

The Inner Round circulation was important at that stage because the qualities of the *prāṇas* they convey had to be mastered to make the later development of Buddhism possible. Each minor *chakra* is the custodian of important mental-emotional *saṃskāras,* concepts to be developed by the early exponents of the religion. All such expressions of the *dharma,* and those who incarnated to instigate them, were circulated into the Solar Plexus centre and integrated therein with further input from the *chakras* above the diaphragm, until all major aspects of the religion were formulated and further progressed. Such development is not uniform, with many diverse factors manifesting simultaneously. The more advanced Bodhisattvas would also be awakening the higher *chakras,* whilst the younger ones were still promoting the Inner Round *prāṇas.* The process parallels the way of awakening a human *nāḍī* system.

---

19 The Inner Round relates to the *prāṇic* circulation of all minor centres. The 22 minor centres are followed by 49 smaller ones, and so forth until we get to the acupuncture points. All are interrelated via *nāḍīs* of differing sizes to make the entire system.

20 See Alice A. Bailey, *Esoteric Healing,* (Lucis Publishing Co., New York, 1977), 72-73.

These *arhats* obviously had more than one incarnation in Buddhism, and thus further progressed the lineages of their dispensation this way.[21] (Rather than through the exoteric Rinpoche and Tulku system popularised in Tibet.) Different *maṇḍalas* of expression would be continuously activated by the incarnations of the *arhats*/Bodhisattvas to progressively awaken the higher *chakras* of the Buddhist ethos.

When we add the Bodhisattvas embodying the Jina wisdoms to the list then we get the number twenty-seven,[22] which refers to the triune Fires (*iḍā, piṇgalā* and *suśumṇa*) manifesting through the three major *chakras* below the diaphragm, and then to the Heart, Throat and Ājñā centres above, before being absorbed into the Head lotus to produce complete enlightenment. The Fires generate a multiplication effect at each level. Thus we have 3 x 3 (for the centres below the diaphragm) = 9 x 3 (for the centres above the diaphragm) = 27. To this one can add those embodying the seven Ray characteristics, plus the overriding energy of Gautama, making 35 = 7 x 5 potencies, relating to the complete expression of the attributes of mind (the five sense-consciousnesses) and their transformation into the corresponding wisdoms via the seven Ray attributes.

Though this numerical accounting may seem arbitrary, nevertheless it has a certain validity, and Buddhist students should note that numbers veil many hidden mysteries.

We should also note the many references of the number 500 in the accounts of these disciples:

- The five hundred disciples entrusted to Śāriputra and Maudgalyāyana by their teacher before they met the Buddha.
- The five hundred followers that Mahākāśyapa was dwelling with when the Buddha came to stay with them.
- The five hundred Śākyas that were ordained together with Ānanda six years after Gautama gained his enlightenment.
- The five hundred *arhats* that convened at the first great Council.

---

21 Another way to view the number 22 is astrologically, there being twelve signs of the zodiac and ten planetary rulers to consider.

22 Again disregarding the overlapping of function of the *arhats* concerned.

By now it should be clear that one should never take any number in Buddhist accounts literally. The number 500 is literally 5 x 100. The number 5 is the number of the sense-consciousnesses, as governed by the mind, and also of the *skandhas,* whilst the number 100 simply signifies a long duration, or of complete perfection. The number 500 therefore symbolises the duration of the processes happening within any body of manifestation where the complete powers of mind are awakened, and their eventual transmutation into the five Tathāgata wisdoms. Of necessity, this incorporates all of the gains of sense-perception and the way of transforming each associated *saṃskāra* into its equivalent wisdom attribute. The time or process of perfection needed to accomplish this is symbolised by the number 100. Thus whenever the number 500 is presented we have a symbolic representation of the externalised attributes of this process, such as in the 500 *arhats* of the first Council. When this number is doubled (representing the *iḍā* and *piṇgalā* functions) then the attributes of the 1,000 petalled Head lotus is implied, wherein this wisdom is processed. Buddhism is fundamentally a religion based upon the nature of the observations obtained from the meditative states obtained via yogic austerities. The secret of all numerological accounts can therefore be found in the deductive processes of the meditation-Mind.[23] Consequently, a vast esoteric lore is veiled in the symbolism of numbers.

Further characteristics of the Sambhogakāya Flower

First it should be noted that no Sambhogakāya Flower stands as something distinctly separate from another. Together this kingdom manifests in the form of a Heart lotus, thus they are totally integrated and group conscious. A sense of individuality however exists between them because of:

1. *Different colourings.* These manifest in terms of different Ray methods of activity engendering the various attributes of civilisation. Although groups of petals for the different Flowers have the same basic colours, there are considerable variations in their individual

23 The significance of the numbers 500 and 1,000 (etc.) are further explored in the next two volumes.

hues because of the different qualities of the abstracted mental *saṃskāras* they contain. Similarly, each person possesses different characteristics, yet they have the same essential features that distinguish them from animals.

2. *Different development of the petals.* Some petals are more awakened than others because of attributes developed by successive incarnations of the personal-I's. Where there are intellectually dull and uncaring individuals so it implies that the Will or Sacrifice and the Love-Wisdom petals of the Sambhogakāya Flower are barely unfolded. (Such Will sacrifices all phenomena for the common good by transforming base *saṃskāras*. It expresses the power to do so.) The Knowledge petals that represent the gain from basic life experiences are still awakening. The bulk of the petals are thus dormant with only the Knowledge petals in any form of activity in such people.
3. *Different forms of motion.* Depending upon the level of *saṃskāric* expression processed, so the internal motion of the petal's energies differ. There is a basic rotary motion for sluggish *prāṇas,* spiral-cyclic motion for refined *prāṇas,* and liberating forward-progressive motion for transmuted *prāṇas* vitalising the Sacrifice-Will petals.
4. *Different intensities.* The energy qualifications of the Flower's petals differ. Some possess brilliant colourations and are spinning intensely (as in the case of Bodhisattvas), and others are dull with the internal motion moving slowly.
5. *Different radiatory effects.* The Flowers change from being luminous to being vibrantly radiant, signifying enlightenment. (A mergence of the consciousness of the accomplished *yogin* with the Sambhogakāya Flower.) The *yogin's* Mind becomes the Flower, with a consequent death of the concept of an 'I'. Eventually the energies generated by the *yogin,* and those streaming in from the *dharmakāya,* are too great for the Flower to bear and a type of supernova happens upon the abstract Mental realms, spelling the end of the Sambhogakāya Flower's form. Blissful liberation ensues, and *śūnyatā* (unfettered enlightenment) becomes the normal place of residence. The process of relinquishing all *karmic* ties to the earth begins in earnest, setting the stage for eventual travel in cosmos.

The Sambhogakāya Flowers evolve as the petals awaken, like the *saṇgha* of the Buddha, which grew from the original five *yogins* to whom he gave his first sermon at Benares. The number five has much significance, as it relates to the five basic *prāṇas* incorporated as five streams of realisation that eventually develop into the Tathāgata Wisdoms for the *maṇḍala* of the entire corpus of Buddhism. Such development represents a fivefold 'perfume' breathed in by the Flowers concerned. The *prāṇas* are generated by humans producing a refined consciousness from their *dharma* practice. The links *(antaḥkaraṇas)* between the Flower and the personal-I are also governed by this number. They allow the Flower to seed its instrument's mind with the intuition and impressions that will eventually produce enlightenment. They help people to develop consciousness. The *prāṇas* manifest via a swastika of four Elements or types of *saṃskāras,* with the central hub channelling the *prāṇas* of the fifth Element. The five *prāṇas* convey the gain from the development of intelligence. Later the bonds of the limitation of the empirical mind are broken to become the seven of the awakened consciousness of Mind. The desire principle has then transformed into Love-Wisdom, and basic self will becomes the Will-to-Good, the Will to overcome *saṃsāric* impediments on the path to liberation.

The five sense perceptions organised by the intellect are basic Buddhist doctrine, but the teachings can be re-evaluated from a broader perspective:

1. *Hearing,* utilising the ear as a sense-perceptor. Hearing is the most limiting or confusing of the senses, as sound is easily mistaken or misunderstood. (Just as the physical plane is the most limiting of all the realms of perception.) The media of sound, however, can carry the sacred Word, enabling one to escape from *saṃsāric* limitations. This necessitates the ability to listen to the silent voice emanating from the innermost recesses of the Heart. The manifestation of mantra is expressed through ritualistic observance and *samādhi,* whereby 'magical creation' (the appearance of phenomena) can manifest via the *yogin's* Will. The seventh Ray of Ritualistic and Materialising power is utilised, which governs the general effects of sound throughout Nature. (Which is ruled by the cycles of Life, the seasons, day and night, lunar and solar cycles, etc.)

   The associated *prāṇa* is *apāna* and the Element is Earth.

2. *Touch or feeling* utilises the skin as a sense-perceptor. It is related to the emotions, and therefore to the energy of devotion (the sixth Ray), because touch is strongly associated with desire, and is often the result of emotional stimulation. Through the sense of touch people can contact the higher realms of perception and thus obtain an understanding of their own constitution. As we must touch before the concrete phenomena of physical objects can become real to us, so we must occultly 'touch' the matter of the other planes of perception before their nature can be ascertained.

   The eyes are easily deceived by images and mirages, the cause or purpose of sound is often confusing, and very little can be tasted or smelled. They all help to identify things, but touch is the final authority ascertaining the concrete reality of an object. Touch is strongly related to the love principle. Our sexual expression and the continuity of the species by means of touch indicates the importance of this sense. The nature of this organ of sensation is also subjectively demonstrated meditatively through the ability to contact the various domains of perception and by the psychic union of the energies of the subtle dualities (sexes) within. Both forms of union (via touch) implicate immortality. The lower form of touch produces a form of physical immortality through the genetic inheritance of offspring. The inner touch produces immortality via contact with the *dharmakāya.*

   The associated *prāṇa* is *samāna,* and the Element is Water.

3. *Sight,* utilising the eyes as a sense-perceptor, directly stimulates the image-producing faculty of the mind. Therefore it is an expression of the scientific aptitude of the fifth Ray conditioning intelligence. It facilitates the naming function, an analytical expression of the mind, thus helping to produce the correlation of ideas. Sight co-ordinates the information obtained from the other senses. Together sight and the mind guide the person in a given direction. The eyes point out the way and the body follows. The eye-mind correlation is the faculty that discriminates between the good and the bad, the light and the dark, the jungle and the path. It discerns the hidden truth. The light of the body is the eye.

   Interestingly, with the advent of scientific materialism, many of the 'dark places' of the earth (arenas of ignorance) have been lit up, symbolically seen in the lighted arenas of our civilisation at night. (Literally producing a physical form of enlightenment.) We can now see further into all directions of space and better discern the cause of things than we have ever been able to do before.

The associated *prāṇa* is *udāna,* and the Element is Fire.

4. *Taste.* When the tongue is used as a sense-perceptor it determines different taste sensations, discriminating between what is pleasing and edible and what is harmful, so that the body can be properly nourished and sustained. Such discrimination is effectively an expression of the fourth Ray of Beautifying Harmony overcoming Strife, which produces the taste of universality, the oneness of being/non-being. Universality is the effect of a high discrimination wrought from the many tribulations (taste sensations) of *saṃsāra*. First the eyes and the mind select what the person desires to eat, then it is touched to bring the food (experiential endeavour) to the mouth, and finally tasted, to see if it is nourishing, palatable. In this way a person learns to discriminate right from wrong, the real from the unreal, before the way out of the jungles of illusion into the heart of revelation can be found. One is helped by experimentation via the analytical mind. Various forms of subtlety are then determined through taste. (The intuition that is the flowering of enlightenment.)

   The person is fed via the mouth to sustain the body, physically or spiritually. Whoever is sustained from sustenance by the *tathāgatagarbha* through right discrimination and meditative practices will open the doors to liberation via the Mirror-like Wisdom, allowing integration with the All.

   Smell and taste are minor senses. In humanity they are the most underdeveloped, and are also somewhat subordinate to the sense of touch. They relate to the two higher planes that humanity rarely contact, which are associated with our faculties for intuitional and *dharmakāyic* impression. (Response to the Mirror-like Wisdom, and the Dharmadhātu Wisdom are similarly underdeveloped.)

   The associated *prāṇa* is *prāṇa*, and the Element is Air.

5. *Smell* is the most subtle and ethereal of the senses. It is universally applicable in that the odour that pervades a room is immediately

discerned by all. Unlike the other sense-perceptors it rarely needs visual (mental) impetus to assist its functioning. Therefore it is related to the highest realms of perception, to the expression of enlightened activity that surpasses the function of the mind. In a similar manner the *dharmakāya* affects all simultaneously, not just the individual or even groups of individuals. The Ray developed here is the third Ray of Mathematical Exactitude, actively manifesting the *maṇḍalas* of living expression.

An odour is carried by the wind (or air) in a similar way that the *dharmakāya* uses *śūnyatā* for its vehicle. Smell and taste are very closely interrelated and in many ways depend upon each other. Smell is taste transcendent. A subtle aroma has a direct pacifying, alleviating effect upon the mind, far more so than any of the other senses (which tend to stimulate one or other of the emotions, or the imagination). It is, however, the most limited sense in humanity. Refined perfumes help produce a meditative attitude without the medium of thought, for which reason incense is used for most religious observations and rituals. It directly translates the sensual into the divine.

The associated *prāṇa* is *vyāna* and the Element is Aether.

Though the five senses are the *raison d' etre* of the personality and its delusions, they are also the instruments of enlightenment when rightly controlled and directed. They are coordinated or synthesised by the intellect (which is viewed as the sixth sense), and all are abstracted into the rarefied consciousness of the Sambhogakāya Flower. The intellect translates sensual experiences into coded images and stores them as memory. It has a similar relationship to the Sambhogakāya Flower as that Flower has to the *dharmakāya*.

There are higher correspondences of the senses on the subtler realms. Thus we have the expressions of the various psychic powers, such as clairaudience, psychometry, clairvoyance. All levels or dimensions of being/non-being have their correspondences to the sense expressions, because they are but emanations from the five Dhyāni Buddhas which become increasingly concreted as we move closer to the physical domain. The sense-perceptors are the means whereby their wisdoms can be wrought in the formed realms.

The subjective senses stem from *chakras* that convey impressions from the dimensions of perception. (Buddhist Tantric texts organise the seven *chakras* as a grouping of five.) Comprehending the nature of these subjective senses is important because psychosomatic perceptions, psychic states and after death experiences are obtained via them, as well the insights from enlightenment. For most people such experiences are expressions of the Watery (astral) realm. The mentally polarised, however, experience directly via the realm of the mind after they have died. Such experiences can involve a hell state, or relative bliss, depending upon how the mind was utilised whilst incarnate. *Preta* and *asura*-like states are fabricated by means of astral substance.

The higher realms of perception become abstractions to the empirical mind. Each of the senses is pre-eminently related to a particular plane of perception, and therefore to the Ray that governs that plane.

	Primal Quality	Evolved Quality	Realm	Prāṇa	Element
Hearing	Limitation	Freedom	Physical (Instinct)	Apāna	Earth
Touch	Desire	Love	Emotional (Desire)	Samāna	Water
Sight	Darkness (Ignorance)	Revelation	Mental (Reason)	Udāna	Fire
Taste	Wrong discrimination	Intuition	Intuitional	Prāṇa	Air
Smell	Toxic perception	Thusness	Dharmakāya	Vyāna	Aether

Table 2. The five Senses

These five qualities are synthesised by the intellect, which is presented as a sixth sense. However, the concept of 'sixth sense' works only if one separates the five senses from the intelligence they produce. Intelligence concerns the correlated images and impressions formed in the mind as a consequence of the comingling of sense impressions at any specific time sequence. (The term 'time sequence' implies that it is impossible to determine a true distinction between one moment from the next, they simply flow into each other, as a sequence.) Thus it is best to view all five sense inputs as constituting a unity, which is intelligence. Emotional attachment, producing hatreds, spite, as well as affectionate dispositions, desire and ignorance, are the triple ever-present cause for the wheel of birth and death. By discrimination, through rightly using the mind, people first set foot on the path to enlightenment and away from the corporeal realms.

The Rays of light

The concept of *Rays of light* shall be further explained to depict basic awareness states in terms of the way that consciousness is coloured and impressions are channelled from the mind to the Sambhogakāya Flower. The eyes are the organs of vision that allow us to discern things, and hence consciously act upon what is discerned. Vision happens because we view illumined objects by means of the eye. Light counters the darkness of ignorance. We think by utilising images composed of lighted substance in the mind. Therefore, when we think, we cause consciousness to be structured in various ways, and this happens in terms of Rays of qualified light. These Rays of light have their unique hues and subhues, similarly to how visible light possesses its seven prismatic hues.[24] Similarly, consciousness functions via seven types of energy expression. When purified these are refracted through the Diamond Eye *(cintāmanī)* that is the enlightened Mind.

The five Rays of Mind earlier presented govern the expression of the Elements, which condition the *saṃskāras*, and organise them into five main groups, making a person a *mānasaputra*, a bearer of mind substance. The five groups are synthesised by the third Ray and generally govern the form of activity of the five sense-consciousnesses. We therefore have:

- Ray 3 of Mathematically Exact Activity, the Aetheric Element, smell.
- Ray 4 of Beautifying Harmony overcoming Strife, the Element Air, taste.
- Ray 5 of Scientific Reason, the Element Fire, sight.

24 The reader should therefore note that the hues for visible light and those conditioning the inner realms differ.

- Ray 6 of Devotion, the Watery Element, touch.
- Ray 7 of Ritual, Magical Endeavour, and materialising Power, the Earthy Element, hearing.

The totality of the stored and assimilated perceptions from the five senses, and the means whereby they are consciously utilised, constitutes a human personality. Similarly, the five Rays governing the expression of Nature, such as the evolution of the five kingdoms esoterically considered (mineral, plant, animal, human, and divine), are the manifest expressions of the Wisdoms of the five Dhyāni Buddhas directing their overall development. It also connotes that this action is embodied by a Divine Personality, an Avatar, the manifestation *(nirmāṇakāya)* of a 'thus gone' Tathāgata from a former aeon of evolutionary attainment. This is veiled in the concept of an Ādi (primordial) Buddha. Such an entity is needed if one wishes to properly explain the genesis of the phenomena external to a human consciousness. For the sake of philosophic brevity I call such an Entity a *Logos,* meaning the One who empowers the (mantric) Word that sustains the phenomena within which we reside.

A Logos is robed with the Rays (incorporating the five Jina Wisdoms with respect to manifest space), just as we are robed with our organs of sensation. An understanding of the higher correspondence of the function of our senses therefore provides an idea as to the manifestation of the Rays in the Body of the Lord of our earth sphere.

There are two other Rays developed in the higher stages of the evolutionary path, that together with the third Ray, govern the triads of petals of the Sambhogakāya Flower. We thus have:

- *The first Ray of Will or Sacrifice,* the prime quality that must be evoked if liberation from *māyā* is to be achieved. Without the evocation of this force enlightenment is not possible. Sacrifice, based upon wisdom, is the path of all Bodhisattvas. This Ray conditions the Sacrifice Petals of the Flower, which function during the stages of the path wherein rapid change, sacrifice and death of all aspects of the personality life occurs. This is the energy predisposing yogic austerities, and ultimately the sacrifice of the all to produce the changes that accede to *śūnyatā.*

- *Ray two of Love-Wisdom* manifests in the form of evolved *bodhicitta*, governing the central tier of petals of the Sambhogakāya Flower. This is greater than the awareness derived from the five senses. It views all outcomes from a future perspective, thus works wisely to equilibrate separative thoughts into a unity. The Sambhogakāya Flower is fundamentally an embodiment of this Ray, it is the basic emanation of all enlightened beings.
- *Ray three of Mathematically Exact Activity* governs the Knowledge tier of petals, which work to absorb the best that involvement in *saṃsāra* offers. This tier projects light to dispel the darkness of ignorance wherever it may be found within the domain of the personal-I.

One must also think in terms of these Rays of light if the *tathāgatagarbha* is to be properly understood. It possess three basic sub hues of a generally orange colouring: the Will or Sacrifice petals radiate a yellowish hue, the Love-Wisdom petals radiate an overall rose hue, and the Knowledge petals manifest an overall fiery orange hue.[25] Orange is the basic colouring of the mind, thus it is traditional for Buddhist monks to wear robes of this (saffron) colour. The colour rose is attributed to the energy of human love and devotion, and yellow indicates an intuitional or rarefied form of perception. The reddish-purple colouring of the robes worn by Tibetan monks indicates mixing rose with orange, and adding violet, indicating the importance of ritual in the religion. Yellow is also an important subsidiary colouration of the apparel. These colours consequently were not chosen randomly, but rather symbolise the demonstration of spiritual power derived from the domain of the *tathāgatagarbha*. The reddish-purple colour also has a reference to the life-giving properties of blood.

There is no separation of consciousness in the *sambhogakāya* realm; all Flowers interrelate through communal channels of thought. They manifest a collective consciousness, focussed upon one overall meditation concerning the sum of human civilisation, past, present and

---

25 Further information as to the characteristics of this subjective form is detailed in *A Treatise on Cosmic Fire* by Alice A. Bailey. Much information is presented therein specifically in relation to the nature of the appearance of its physical form, from which my account is derived.

future. Only thus can any *tathāgatagarbha* project a personal-I into formed space, incorporating all aspects of *saṃsāric* conditionings. Only thus can *karma* manifest the way that it does, for that *karma* involves the sum of the interrelated parts of the way for all personal-I's. Their interrelationships are in terms of groups and not just units. All groups are interdependent. All the more so in the realm of consciousness.

The Śūnyatā Eye and the Bodhisattva path

Because all Sambhogakāya Flowers manifest a collective *samādhi* upon the future outcome of the personal-I's they have projected into incarnation, they can weave *karma*. The future in terms of the fruition of probabilities is thus created. What the Flowers are in fact meditating upon are the images of the overview of human civilisation and its evolutionary course that are projected to their realm from a higher domain, wherein reside the Lords of Shambhala that undertake the generalised formulations. Each Flower then perceives its part in the overall schema. The personal-I's then play their part in relation to what must be achieved by the collective whole. The entire sequence of lives leading to liberation is seen in perspective by the Sambhogakāya Flowers and all possible contingencies thereto are taken into account. A paradigm *(maṇḍala)* exists for the incarnate personalities so that they can build the necessary *saṃskāras* that will produce the desired outcome (e.g., of the ability to think logically and lovingly on any issue). This produces the evolution of the wisdom developed upon the Bodhisattva path. Much evolutionary time and experimentation with many different types of personalities in all cultural situations, religions, and social standings is required.

The *tathāgatagarbha* subsequently evolves in intensity and radiance as the quality of consciousness developed by the incarnating personalities improves in clarity and scope. The process is quickened as *bodhicitta* is evoked via the eventuating spiritual will. Eventually the energy field developed is of such refinement and intensity that impressions from the *dharmakāya* via the Śūnyatā Eye can be received by the incarnate Bodhisattva. The effect from *śūnyatā* and beyond inevitably increases the motion of the petals of the Sambhogakāya Flower and it begins to strain under the weight of the energisation imparted. It becomes intensely radiatory. The Śūnyatā Eye then opens wider, allowing an increasing amount of the energy (of *tathatā)* in until the limits of the energy that can be contained by the Flower is reached. A supernova explosion in the field of consciousness ensues and the Flower is no more. The *yogin* will by now have projected links to a *dharmakāyic* form (the Monadic, or Buddha aspect) into which the essential attributes of the Flower are absorbed. It represents a greater Identification Space, a vaster field of potential Revelation, away from human consciousness and existence. This is the focus of those upon the three higher Bodhisattva stages, until a fully liberated Buddha appears and proceeds into cosmos, having transcended what the earth sphere can teach. Buddhas appear on all Ray lines, and many do not manifest a teaching dispensation whereby the masses come to know of them. There are a number of roles such ones can play in Shambhala to complete a requisite service arena. Inevitably, however, cosmos beckons.

Tathatā/Thusness is more than just a synonym for *śūnyatā*, in that it represents the expression of a 'realm beyond', the fundamental nature of a Buddha. Brown states:

> The *Ratnagotra's* first two chapters insist that *Tathatā* (Absolute Suchness) whether it be considered as *samalā* and therefore veiled by the adventitious defilements, or as *nirmalā* and manifestedly free from them, is "beyond the sphere characterized as being caused and conditioned". The text stresses: that it is incapable of being explained and is to be realised by oneself and understood "as like a thunderbolt"; that it is invisible, unutterable, and immutable; that has neither beginning, middle nor end by nature, being "a quite marvellous and unthinkable sphere"; that it is freed from all dualistic views *(prapañca)* and false discriminations *(vikalpa);* that it is unimaginable, indiscriminative, not being seen, heard, smelt, tasted or touched, and possessing no characteristic mark.[26]

The reference to *samalā* and *nirmalā* hints at *tathatā* being the central energy empowering the *tathāgatagarbha,* which must be meditated upon and 'realised by oneself and understood'. The endeavour to try to explain the *tathāgatagarbha* (as for instance presented in this

26 Brown, 75.

volume) falls far short of what is actually experienced. Nevertheless what was impossible to explain at the time of the writing of the *Ratnagotra* is now possible, with significant limitations, because the terminology now exists, aided by a scientific understanding of the nature of energy, and even of the constituency of light.

A 'thunderbolt' is a useful simile, as it implies not just the effect of instantaneous enlightenment, but also to *tathatā's* potency as a type of energy that must somehow be controlled or contained in order to be properly experienced. Therefore, much of the path to liberation concerns the methodology whereby a person develops the capability to do so. Vast is the undertaking to produce the refinement of consciousness and the etherealisation of substance that can handle the potency. However, it is in the realm of the *tathāgatagarbha* that the most potent effects are seen.

A newly liberated one has several choices to make concerning the nature or extent of the continuation of the incarnation process for the purpose of the salvation of sentient beings, as well as when to cease ties altogether with the earth to travel along any of the cosmic paths. Such a decision to cease ties is, however, academic, as the present need[27] is so great in this Kali Yuga that all liberated beings choose continued *saṃsāric* involvement as Bodhisattvas. There is, however, a point of development when what they have to offer is so abstracted that the sluggish rate of human minds is too limited to be benefitted, so the cosmic paths open for them. Here there is an exponentially expanded scope to serve other Minds.

From the 'supernova' experience until the full attainment of Buddhahood, the highest of the Bodhisattva stages are thus trod. It should be noted that the way this path is depicted in the literature falls far short of the actual realities, especially as it relates to happenings beyond the field of consciousness. Buddhists have not perceived how the process of treading this path also changes according to the way that human civilisation evolves, i.e., how Bodhisattvas adapt in skilful ways according to the changing vicissitudes of the need for every religion they incarnate into, or in society in general. The qualifications, for example, that made a seventh level Bodhisattva nearly two millennia ago (when

27 The suffering factor of all sentient beings, because of the effects of human predation against others through massed avarice, etc.

some of the *sūtras* concerning the Bodhisattva *bhūmis* were written) are not the same as today. Now considerably more is required of them.

Because future patterns of possibilities have already been achieved in the *manasic* substance generated by humanity, a Buddha or Bodhisattva can predict the future with near certainty. Such a one need only read what already exists as collective mentation of all Sambhogakāya Flowers. Or, if an individual incarnation is observed, we then have the 'individual' part of a Sambhogakāya Flower's meditation. Bodhisattvas incarnate to endeavour to make the paradigm of these meditating Flowers the objective reality. Success is not guaranteed because human free will allows new *karma* to be created by any individual, altering the hoped for outcome of the future. This happens not just for the individual, but also for the group of which he/she is a part, by the related nation, or a conglomeration of nations. The compassionate focus of any Bodhisattva can be upon any of these three levels, depending upon the Bodhisattva's attained level.

Bodhisattvas of the earlier *bhūmis* are focussed upon the spiritual development of individuals. Those on the next higher levels focus upon aberrant aspects in our social structures, religions, and political fields. They work tirelessly to produce changes for the better. Those around the seventh to the tenth levels are concerned principally with nations, religions, and civilisation as a whole. Bodhisattvas of the highest three levels also have much more esoteric considerations, such as the right education of those of the Sambhogakāya realm with the *devas* and *ḍākinīs* also being involved, and with factors proceeding from outside our earth system altogether. The entire cosmos is an integrated whole, and most of its mysteries are yet to be revealed to humanity.

The Sambhogakāya Flower's form of meditation is spontaneously a manifestation of *bodhicitta*, as each Flower is but an abstracted form of the Heart *chakra* in the process of unfolding Love-Wisdom. It also obtains impressions from the *dharmakāya*, via the Śūnyatā Eye in the centre of their forms, plus guidance from advanced Bodhisattvas. The collective meditation of those Flowers produce the background environment of the *ālayavijñāna*.

If one's mind is not comprehensively stilled and prepared for the input of the intense energies coming via the Śūnyatā Eye then disaster can occur in *chakras* who's petals do not possess the vibrancy necessary to channel the intensity of the energisation without aberration. Also, the base emotional-mental aspects of the individual will become exaggerated through undue or inappropriate stimulation. Fortunately there are safeguards, such as the fact that the way to the *śūnyatā* experience is via the Sambhogakāya Flower's Eye, which is only accomplishable in one who has a history of continuous meditation via response to *bodhicitta*. (At an advanced stage of *samādhi śūnyatā* can then be experienced directly.) Also, this necessitates a person to have built such a refined mechanism of response and associated consciousness that it is similar in vibrancy to that of the substance of the Sambhogakāya Flower. When there is near complete, or completed mergence of the two 'Minds', then meditation upon *śūnyatā* can factually begin. At the initial stages of the process such mergence is termed illumination, and when fusion is complete, then we have enlightenment. The *arhat* meditation concerns a mergence with the Sambhogakāya Flower and absorption into its consciousness for the duration of the experience to be, but is not inclusive of the process that leads to the awakening of the Śūnyatā Eye, for that is the Bodhisattva path proper.

Śūnyatā therefore is to be obtained for liberation to happen, but is not the 'ultimate', as it is not the *dharmakāya*, but reveals the *dharmakāya* to be an 'empty' but totally fulfilled, vibrant Mind that Sees omnidirectionally and multidimensionally. The term 'empty' here refers to being emptied of that which would distort the impressions received, or would glaze over the vibrancy of the images. Being totally fulfilled means that it is the product of myriad lives of evolutionary and thence meditative awakening in all fields of Life. A 'rightly completed Mind' is one that contains within its energy patterns and idea paradigms the seeds that will allow unlimited expansion from the *dharmakāya*. A vibrant Mind has such specific gravity or strength of energy associated with it that it can withstand gradients of the most potent forms of energy input from the *dharmakāya*. It is an energy input that cannot be contained in an unprepared mind. The impact of this energy upon the substance of Mind produces its radiance.

Concerning the view that *śūnyatā* is not to be considered 'absolute', Nāgārjuna states in the *Mūlamadhyamakakārikā*:

> The wise men (i.e., enlightened ones) have said that *śūnyatā* or the nature of thusness is the relinquishing of all false views. Yet it is said that those who adhere to the idea or concept of *śūnyatā* are incorrigible.[28]

In relation to this quote Brown states:

> The exponent of the *Madhyamā-pratipat* (the Middle Way) repeatedly stresses that the relativity of all conditional phenomena is itself not unconditional; to cling to relativity or *śūnyatā* as itself absolute is the most serious of errors.[29]

Kalupahana is in agreement when he states in the introduction to his translation of the *Mūlamadhyamakakārikā:*

> It is very appropriate, therefore, that Nāgārjuna decided to write a chapter on the dispositions *(saṃskāra)* after his analysis of suffering *(duḥkha)*[30]......The entire chapter is devoted to an examination of the notions of the "existent" *(bhāva),* the "non-existent" *(abhāva),* "self-nature" *(svabhāva),* etc. and the manner in which these could be avoided by adopting the conception of "emptiness" *(śūnyatā),* without allowing that notion of emptiness to be an obsession. Hence his conclusion: "The Victorious Ones have announced that emptiness is the relinquishing all views. Those who are possessed of the view of emptiness are said to be incorrigible."[31].....
>
> Many interpreters have explained "emptiness" *(śūnyatā)* as a "provisional view," thereby implying that the ultimate truth is beyond conceptualization. The foregoing analysis of the Buddha's as well as Nāgārjuna's thoughts would mean that they indeed did not recognize a "non-conceptual truth or reality." For them, there is no way in which a "truth" could be understood non-conceptually, because, as mentioned earlier, truth in its most comprehensive sense pertains to statements and thus involves conceptualization. However, conceptualizations can be comprehensive and therefore right *(samyak),* or limited and

---

28 Kenneth K. Inada, *Nāgārjuna: A Translation of his Mūlamadhyamakakārikā with an Introductory Essay,* (Hokuseido Press, Tokyo, 1970), Chapter 13, verse 8, 93.

29 Brown, 77.

30 David J. Kalupahana, *The Mūlamadhyamakakārikā of Nāgārjuna* (Motilal Banarsidass, Delhi, 1999), 48.

31 Ibid.

> confused and therefore wrong *(mithyā),* and these depend upon the amount of prejudice that has gone into the formulation of the concepts. Thus, "emptiness" is a "view," a view is not without identification, but which is identified with "the empty" *(idaṃ* śūnyaṃ*)*. It is a view that helps the individual to attain freedom from views and upholding it is the absolute or ultimate truth without any reference to "the empty" would be the last thing the Buddha or Nāgārjuna would advocate.[32]

In referring back to the opening statements of the query to the Buddha we saw that Vacchagotta represents that which comes from outside the sphere of soul-consciousness represented by the Buddha's *saṇgha*. He enquired about its true nature, but this information was denied to him, as he represented something that was transitory with respect to it. His nature was of 'coming and going'. The subjective Flower represents the collected consciousnesses of all who were enlightened (e.g., the Buddha), or facets of its permutation, thus is inclusive of his disciples. It is that which neither 'comes or goes'. It represents the sum total of their united meditative work, which can be considered the real, and only momentarily incorporates what is transitory. Having understood the nature of the transitory agent one can then discern what can be appropriately imparted and what cannot.

The Sambhogakāya Flower has ramifications in a world, solar, or cosmic evolution, as all incorporate a similar paradigm. Nothing *saṃsāric* is, however static or permanent, contrary to what is understood by the Brahmanical concept of *ātman*. The soul-form around the Buddha was born as a consequence of his initiatory activity after he gained enlightenment. The gathering of disciples around him concerned its growth from a central point, to a point within a sphere of activity, then the complete flowering of the three tiers of petals. Finally we have a maturation of free flowing mutability and activity, as there is a dynamic interrelation of all its principles. There are exchanges of ideas between various disciples, all forms of group dynamics between the various tiers of this form, and interrelated meditation experiences between whole groups of them, all perfectly coordinated by the *dhyāna* of the Buddha at the centre.

32 Ibid., 48-9.

There was an increasingly expanding maturation of this soul-form, wherein consciousness becomes more intense in the central structure. Expansion is seen in the appearance of floral sub-groupings, represented by the newly evolving sects of Buddhism, such as the Sautrāntikas, Vaibhāṣikas, the subdivisions of the Theravādin School and then the later Mahāyāna. Each sect similarly manifests as a soul-form centred around the sect's founder, and circumscribed by the energy of the originating teaching and influence of the Buddha, the over-soul. The originating structure formed by the Buddha has thus become both objectivised and subjective, with many enlightened Minds having evolved as Buddhism progressed through the ages. There is a process of a dynamically growing moving expansion, inclusive of differentiation into smaller soul-groups that are the children of the parent, as Bodhisattvas incarnate to produce their own structure and purpose. Expansion is the way forward in this realm of Mind-infused activity in the sea of consciousness that represents all human minds. In time each group will represent the petals of a larger over-soul, still abstractly presided over by the Buddha in his *parinirvāṇa*, from the realm 'beyond'. Eventually the originating Flower will follow to where the Buddha has gone, eventuating the 'death' of the manifest Buddhist form that was beheld on the earth.

The concept of no soul

It should also be queried that if the Buddha *did not categorically deny the existence of a soul,* then why did later Buddhists shoulder the karmic burden upon themselves to take *one of the extreme sides* of the argument – that there was no soul? It was a viewpoint that the *Buddha so evidently had already taken to be a wrong view* by his (seeming) non answer, that he could not side with the assertions of either school of thought; namely, that 'there is a soul', or that 'there is no soul'. In doing so the later Buddhist philosophers ended up in a philosophical quagmire (championing the assertion 'there is no soul') that the Buddha skilfully avoided by his silence. Indeed, this was effected by his wisdom of taking the Middle Way in this important question. He had thereby hoped to set Buddhists upon the right track in their line of investigations, if they had followed his example correctly and properly investigated why he was silent, and the nature of his silence in this respect. Also, what he revealed to Ānanda (indirectly, tangentially) as to what the soul was or was not should have been thoroughly investigated. This overruling of the Buddha's clear intention and instruction has led Buddhist metaphysicians into a *cul-de-sac* of opinion, circumscribing their ability to properly flower into vaster dimensions of revelation.

By taking an extreme path away from what the Buddha directly taught, the Buddhist community has erred. The consequence is of being blinded to an entire stream of revelation that they could have long ago awakened and consequently enlightened humanity with. In doing so, they have done themselves and humanity a disservice, stunting the evolutionary growth of all. The way the Buddha's example has been ignored brings with it attendant *karma* needing rectification.

The fact that this doctrine of 'no soul' *(anātman)* is a contrived doctrine of later Buddhists, and not actually what the Buddha intended, is also echoed by Wayman:

> For the purpose of this essay I read—in fact, re-read the chapter "The Doctrine of No-soul*: anatta"* in Walpole Rahula's book *What the Buddha taught.* He quoted H. von Glasenapp, "The negation of an imperishable Ātman is the common characteristic of all dogmatic systems of the Lesser as well as the Great Vehicle, and, there is, therefore, no reason to assume that Buddhist tradition which is in complete agreement on this point has deviated from the Buddha's original teaching." I must agree wholeheartedly with this statement. But those that talk this way seem [*sic*] to think it is the most important thing to say to characterize Buddhism.
>
> If this—which they call the "doctrine of no-soul"—is so important and so consistent with the Buddha's teaching, then why is it that we do not find among the passages cited by Rahula, or among the ones I have so far cited from the Pāli canon in this essay, or among any other sūtras which one might read, any dialogue of the following theoretical kind: A disciple asks the Buddha, "O Bhagavat, could you please tell me what I should *believe* about the five personal aggregates of man?" And the Buddha responds: "That is indeed a good question. You should *believe* that there is no more to man than the five aggregates; take those five aggregates away and there is nothing left; and you should *believe* that each one of those five is a non-self (or non-soul) (*anatta;* or in Sanskrit, *anātman*)." Until someone can point to such a passage in the canon, I must declare: They are promulgators of misinformation

> on Buddhism, who represent these *anātman* statements as matters to be believed in by the Buddhists; and that having believed them, they do indeed have an insight into Buddhism. Rather, what was set forth in the passage I cited, also in those which Rahula cites; and in the numerous other passages on such topics in the Pāli canon is that the Buddha was telling his disciples how they should contemplate the personal aggregates; so with right insight, "this is not mine", "I am not this", "this is not my self." In the light of the other information I have provided above, it is a reasonable conclusion that the Buddha insisted on such *anātman* contemplations, because it is a way of disengaging coarser matter from the "body made of mind." Thus, by such contemplations, one may eventually be an Arhat, etc. Whereas by simple believing that Buddhism has the doctrine of no-soul, one may have the pride of thinking one understands; but this gets one nowhere.[33]

There is an ancient esoteric axiom which states: 'that which is within is also without and that which is without is also within'. The within-without and the without-within can be viewed in terms of the dual nature of all. If you can see both the inner and the outer view simultaneously, then you can transcend the opposites as well as the 'I' concept, though the 'I' concept depends upon what you are looking at and where you are viewing from. It depends upon the fact that you are looking at something. How you view a thing determines how you define it. For example, we can ask 'is the blue pen still a blue pen when the ink has run out?' The 'I' can only see itself in relation to something else, and if 'something else' happens to be an abstract concept then this 'I' can choose to ignore it and still continue to evolve.

To identify we *must first separate* to bring about the 'self' concept in consciousness. This 'self' is a something that can identify with something else, but suppose that if one does not identify with an 'I', is one then unconscious, ignorantly (or psychically) unaware, or enlightened?

If we are ignorant then enlightenment must be obtained through identifying, by occupying our minds with certain events and 'things' before we can be freed (from names and events). Self-consciousness is, however, married to unconsciousness; one cannot identify without

33 Alex Wayman, *Untying the Knots in Buddhism* (Motilal Banarsidass, Delhi, 1997), 542-543.

starting from an unconscious state in relation to that thing and then become consciously aware of it. Therefore, what Buddhists were formerly unconscious of in relation to a soul-form they now can gain conscious awareness of. Buddhists can awaken now to a new view, a true view, a Buddha's view.

When it is said that the Buddha did not speak, then the reference is to the process of self-identification that enables one to speak, where a Buddha is considered to have transcended such identifications. Every word is an identification, activating thought processes that enquire something from somebody. In reality, the Buddha's consciousness contained all knowledge, which was apodictic and instantaneously forthcoming through an identity with some 'thing', though manifesting through the state of being internally serene and non-attached to any identification. Non-attachment produces lack of self-identification and the process is continuously refined by an aspiring one, until *śūnyatā* is obtained, and then a Buddha's *parinirvāṇa*. Much can therefore be said by such a one, but the effect is to liberate the 'selves' from attachment to all concepts of selfhood.

We can query whether all thoughts come from an unconscious[34] to a conscious state when they appear upon the horizon of awareness. This horizon can appear from a place of no thought, where there is no horizon. The horizon appears when an identification process begins to build an accumulation of thought. The concept of any enlightened being manifesting an 'unconscious state' is generally considered untenable, however, such a one possesses a state of not being conscious of everything. The reality is that despite this, any information or arena of fact can be instantaneously retrieved when needed, or pathways can be made to where needed information can be accessed.

The question of origin builds into this event-horizon many identifiable and non-identified states in consciousness, but in fact there is no separation between the two states. Therefore, the mind holds both consciousness and being unconscious of every detail of fact in its milieu. This is similar to a cell which experiences something, but does

---

34 By unconsciousness, here I refer to a condition where someone is not conscious of a thing or arena of discernment, rather than being in a mental stupor where the brain is not functioning at all.

not retain knowledge thereof. Here cells are considered as conscious units existing as part of all knowledge. There are cells with bigger storehouses of knowledge and others that represent smaller storehouses. The cell is in a state of unconsciousness on some issue, but where it dwells is fine because it functions perfectly from the perspective that it contains the seed, or seeds of further knowledge that can grow from what is stored in its regulated rhythm.[35]

Many questions, such as presented below, can then be answered.

Does an amorphous unconsciousness hold the key by which consciousness is stored? Amorphous unconsciousness to one who is unawakened can indeed hold the keys to revelation, if it contains the seeds of all past actions which are not remembered in any one life. Steps can then be taken to retrieve that which is hidden.

Does consciousness grow to overturn the bucket of unconsciousness where there is a non-satiation or identification with awareness? We know this to be a normal part of the evolutionary process that is greatly assisted through the process of right analytical deduction, and through gaining wisdom from those that have progressed into streams of greater awareness.

Is it a truism to say that consciousness can be inclusive of all, or is consciousness exclusive of unconsciousness? Obviously it is exclusive of that which it is not aware of, but how then does consciousness transform the unconsciousness and come to make it inclusive? (If it does not have awareness of its unconscious state, of the bubbles of unconsciousness—the errors of logic, distorted images, and erroneous facts that it holds and oft perceives to be true?) This can happen by the process of detailing what is and what it is not conscious of. Consciousness can only realise to what extent it is unconscious of other 'things' by identifying with those 'things' and manifesting correct analysis. The extent that *ignorance* (the principle evil in Buddhist philosophy) reigns is in direct accordance to the degree that consciousness does *not* identify with things.

The nature of what things consciousness identifies with is important, as consciousness can be aware of many things of irrelevant transiency, but ignorant of things pertaining to the real. Forms of transiency can overwhelm consciousness, therefore a proper process of selectivity is needed, as what to include as valuable and what to reject as unsatisfactory

35 This subject of cellular consciousness is explained in greater detail in Volume 4.

for the purpose of its progressive advancement to higher fields of revelation. Grasping transience to try to make it permanent leads to suffering, because of the inevitability of change. Consciousness generally reacts to this in a way to negate the suffering, which eventually produces positive outcomes. Consciousness indeed is perpetually changing. Identifying with those things that lead to release from suffering is important to most, but such identification need not be what directly makes one all-knowledgeable, though certainly wisdom can be evoked.

Wisdom is distinct from mere knowing. It includes the overview of the way the future is to manifest via the course of any proposed action of consciousness unfolding, and then takes the right steps to assist that progress beneficently. It is therefore beyond simply being not ignorant. Wisdom illumines the ignorance states of others, and from this perspective we can query what ignorance is anyway. Is enlightenment everything that ignorance is not? However, are there degrees of enlightenment, of relative states of knowledge of things, as well as being unconscious of other things? So one is enlightened when one's consciousness is inclusive of a set of 'things' that transcends the unenlightened one's set of perceptual realisations, and unenlightened with respect to other categories of things. What unenlightened person understands the contents of the mind of an enlightened one, of how many sets of 'things' such a Mind is actually inclusive of? A concept of the degree of enlightenment is important to understand, for the universe is a vast multidimensional space of milliards of 'things'.

When analysing the soul-concept, we see that the soul/Sambhogakāya Flower contains at its heart an enlightened space surrounded by tiers of increasingly unenlightened consciousness states. Each entity on any tier of this soul stands as an enlightened space in relation to an entity standing in a tier below it, i.e., a tier that has a greater materiality, but lesser intensity.

Enlightenment can thus only be considered to be so in reference to those who stand unenlightened in relation to the categories of things known by the enlightened. The unenlightened one cannot know what level of collectivised knowledge of 'things' an enlightened one possesses relative to himself or to other enlightened beings. Little more can really be said about enlightenment to the unenlightened. Of course, the Buddhist may say that the enlightened one is one that has gone beyond the categorisation of things, beyond the realm of thoughts. Indeed this may be so, but if the enlightened one is to converse or relate with an unenlightened person in any way then 'things' must be utilised to converse with and to thus interrelate. Therefore the best methods of identifying is readily used. The brain-consciousness is stimulated thereby into observing that it is different from its observations. This means that one aspect of the unit is subliminally incorporating the view of what it is yet to perceive, and another aspect is the conscious part, a 'self' which knows that there is a distinction between it and an other, or from the unconscious part, which is being revealed through the process of observation. Thus it calls its consciousness a 'self', being the mechanism to create or to cleanse *saṃskāras* and to identify with that which is not inclusive of 'itself'. It thus incorporates that which is unconscious of this 'self' to become inclusive of the not-self.

The 'self' is the conscious aspect of the person. It tries to identify with all around it (i.e., its environment) to solve the problem of duality or multiplicity, so that it can actively engage with what appears not to be itself. To do so it incorporates the myriad 'selves' (or cellular units) constituting the environment with which it interrelates, and which it considers to not be itself. However, if enlightenment is to be gained, consciousness must disassociate from what is considered 'self' and engage with a brighter spectrum of light with which it can merge, so as to make conscious all that is beyond itself. This allows identification with qualities (of a vaster cellular unit) and principles beyond the realms of form. Such an environment is indeed multidimensional and is bounded by spheres of 'finite infinities'.

This is the basis to the vows and rise to fame of a Bodhisattva, in whose consciousness the whole world is encompassed. All of the steps on the Bodhisattva's path aim to increasingly reveal the nature of this integrated complexion, which allows all in the interrelated environment to be rightly educated. They represent the integral universe that is 'not self', thus all little cellular unities are made to be consciously aware of the nature of the oneness with which the Bodhisattva has identified. Thus this environment (taken as one great cellular unit) represents the individuals and sentient lives that are helped. They are the ones that have been identified with so that they can be salvaged through enlightened action in such a way that others can be enthused by them.

To make all others conscious of the true needs of that which is not themselves is the Bodhisattva vow. It is to illuminate all with that which they were unconscious from the streams of conscious revelation concerning the true nature of things. People's consciousnesses then become inclusive of the greater environment. Thus all consciousness-links to the encompassing all become more integrated, in tune with the pulsations of the integral Heart that vivifies all cellular unities in the one organism. Cooperative sharing for the common weal, rather than aggressive competitiveness and selfish manipulation of resources, then becomes the mainstay of a civilisation. The process is perfected to remove all forms of disease bearing *prāṇas*. These links are but methods by which consciousness can divulge its purpose, through logical integration of what stems from the Buddhas who encompass all that is the outer seeming with their Love-Wisdom.

Such logic, however, appears to have been presented to the world by Buddhists in the form of a partisan sound that does not adequately take into account all that has been put forth by the other conscious minds from the rest of the human community on earth. Identifying is the way that consciousness evolves from unconscious states, therefore Buddhists need to properly identify with the rest of humanity's philosophical and educational systems, if their goal of ultimate enlightenment is to be achieved. What can be said for Buddhists, can of course also be relegated to other religious or philosophical systems. All need to be exposed to that of which they are unconscious, to be revealed in the light of consciousness, then they will see that there is no such thing as *śūnya* ('empty') other than one's views that are incorrect, distorted, or not inclusive of the whole (View). Once the 'whole view' is incorporated in a Mind, then emptiness becomes the stance of that Mind residing in the Oneness of the All.

Oṁ

6

The Sambhogakāya Flower and Dharmakāya

The Dharmakāya Flower

An analysis of the nature of the Sambhogakāya Flower will help penetrate some of the mysteries of the *dharmakāya.* The use of analogy, plus a comprehension of the nature of what is abstracted is helpful. When previously analysing the Sambhogakāya Flower it was viewed in terms of a triplicity of petals, which were described as *Sacrifice-Will, Love-Wisdom,* and *Knowledge.*

The thesis that will be posited in this chapter is that such a Flower is built in the image of what exists in the liberated realms, the *dharmakāya.* Working under directives from the *dharmakāya,* each Flower (*tathāgatagarbha*) thus becomes responsible for the *karma* of a human unit, and governs that unit's path to liberation. The *tathāgatagarbha* deals specifically with the factor of consciousness for a human unit, however, something of a similar nature must exist in the *dharmakāya* in order to explain the existence of sentience in Nature. Thus when observing the sum of Nature's domain (of which the human kingdom is a component part), something must govern its overall *karmic* determination and progressive harmony, where the sentience that is inherent in all forms is transmuted into consciousness by means of a progressive evolutionary thrust. Such an evolutionary thrust has been observed to exist by means of scientific investigation. Scientists have proven that forms have evolved from lesser species (bearing sentience) to greater species of more complex order (i.e., greater sentience). Then we have a concept of the mode where humanity has evolved within the material domain.

Those with developed inner vision view the process of evolution somewhat differently than the scientific community does. We factor in the nature of the evolution of the psyche and of the way that consciousness unfolds, taking into account the laws of *karma* and multidimensionality. The sequence of evolution is esoterically considered according to the view presented below. The term 'souls' here refers to coherent evolutionary units of either sentience, consciousness, or of superconsciousness:

> Group-souls (lesser kingdoms) → individualised souls (humanity) → liberated souls (high Bodhisattvas, Buddhas).

There are three kingdoms of Nature below the human (esoterically considered): the mineral, plant and animal. There are also three basic classes of non-Bodhisattvic human units:

a. Those that are mostly sensually focussed. The mainstay of the way they view the world is materially via their physical and desire bodies.
b. Those that fundamentally think and feel emotionally. The emotions being the glaze via which they view the sum of their interrelations with the external universe. This category includes by far the bulk of humanity.
c. The intelligentsia, the clear intelligent, self-focussed thinkers of our societies. They are mainly responsible for the present scientific materialistic aspects of our civilisation.

There are two additional classes preparatory to becoming Bodhisattvas:

1. Aspirants on the path, who are essentially scavengers of spiritual information. They learn bits of the *dharma* from various sources but cannot sustain the needed intensity of mind to achieve elevated states of awareness for other than short periods of time.
2. Probationary disciples, who are pledged to sustain the necessary ardour to achieve and to pass the tests that the development of *bodhicitta* produces on the way to liberation.

Of the ten Bodhisattva levels seven levels relate to attaining the experience of *śūnyatā*. In the three highest *bhūmis* the Bodhisattva focuses upon the *dharmakāya*. From another perspective these ten levels can be classified in terms of 3 x 3 groups, plus the last, the level of a Master of

Wisdom, which is the immediate precursor to the accomplishment of Buddhahood. The eleventh level signifies the appearance of a Buddha.

Taking the evolution of consciousness within Nature into account, including the attainment of Buddhahood and its aftermath for all upon our planet, then the nine groups listed below can be considered. This list indicates the way that the *dharmakāya* is organised with regard to the formed realms, as the method of interrelationship is similar to the way the Sambhogakāya Flower works with respect to an incarnate personality. We will therefore see three groups of petals manifesting in the form of a *Dharmakāya Flower,* constituted of petals governing the lives constituting all aspects of phenomena. Other petals then govern the expression of the suprahuman lives: liberated Bodhisattvas, the corresponding *ḍākinīs* (enlightened members of the feminine *deva* hierarchy, who embody the streams of evolution of the various kingdoms of Nature), plus the realms occupied by Buddhas.

Each of these petals therefore overshadow the overall *karmic* expression of one or other of the groups in *saṃsāra*, plus the categories of liberated beings. As such, a Dharmakāya Flower represents the manifestation of a Buddha-Field on a vaster multidimensional scale than imagined by Buddhists. (One must take into account the view that a meditating Buddha is a Lord of Compassion.) The field of compassion is the sum total of *saṃsāra* as associated with an earth sphere, plus the consequences of the gain of evolution thereon.

From this perspective we find that the denizens of the first three kingdoms of Nature would represent in their plenitude the first of the triads of petals. The kingdom of the Sambhogakāya Flower, representing the sum total of the consciousness-streams of a humanity, would similarly be expressed in the form of three of the petals (because the categorisation on its own level is triune). There would be one subsidiary petal relegated to the final process of extinguishing attachment to all aspects of consciousness and the attainment that *śūnyatā* represents.

Such Dharmakāya Flowers would be found wherever an earth or solar sphere appears. They can then alternatively be viewed as a world-Soul. (These spheres are incorporated by Logoi, being thus the *nirmāṇakāya* or externalised expression of the Dharmakāya Flower.) A 'thus gone' Buddha may find no direct placing in such a *saṃsāric* expression, but certainly His compassion necessitates the establishment of such Flowers for the salvation of the myriads still needing evolutionary perfection.

In this way the pathways to all revelation concerning any particular thing in the phenomenal world can be instantaneously found. Categories within categories of evolutionary being thus exist, coded according to line (or number), hue, resonant brilliance of the *bījas* of activity, of serene concentratedness, or of purposeful forthrightness. Everything is appropriately structured, including the pathways to the retrieval of information in a Buddha's Mind. A Dharmakāya Flower (world-Soul) is viewed below in the form of the higher transmuted correspondences to the nine petals of the Sambhogakāya Flower. The *prāṇas* earlier considered in terms of human activity now become streams of sentient and self-conscious lives, each bearing different qualities that similarly need processing and transformation.

1. The *maṇḍala* of three kingdoms below the human.
   The Knowledge—Knowledge petal.
2. The three levels of average humanity.
   The Knowledge—Love-Wisdom petal.
3. Those upon the path of aspiration, that of probation and the stream enterers who are unfolding the first Bodhisattva *bhūmi*. We must also view their correspondences in the *deva* hierarchy.
   The Knowledge—Sacrifice-Will petal.
4. The next three Bodhisattva levels wherein the aspects of the abstract levels of the Mind are explored, plus the qualities pertaining to the *tathāgatagarbha* and its realm. In conjunction with them one must add certain categories of the feminine *deva* Hierarchy that are responsible for the evolution of the kingdoms of Nature.
   The Love-Wisdom—Knowledge petal.
5. Next are three groups of Bodhisattvas whose purpose come as a consequence of the attainment of *śūnyatā*, because all aspects of consciousness has been mastered, and thus have been abstracted. The Council of Bodhisattvas govern from this level of expression. They direct the evolution of consciousness of humanity, and consequently much else related to human evolution.
   The Love-Wisdom—Love-Wisdom petal.

In the five groups so far presented we have the sum of the domain of the Sambhogakāya Flower and its concerns implicated, including the liberation of its form. This also includes the mode of genesis of that kingdom, as well as aeonic evolutionary progression. These groups represent the higher transmuted equivalents of the five sense-consciousness of a human unit. Of the remaining four, the next one equivocates to the transmuted correspondence of the empirical mind, similarly the final three with respect to the three levels of the abstract Mind. (Which thereby becomes the universal cosmic Mind, the *dharmakāya.)* By means of analogy we can also deduce that there is a transmuted correspondence to the obtaining of *śūnyatā* for the Buddhas concerned. What this means is beyond the level of consideration of this text, as no foundation has been laid for analogous (transmuted) projection of the related concepts.

6. Next, the final three Bodhisattva stages wherein the qualities of the *dharmakāya* are actively sought. Union with the *devas/ḍākinīs* is now possible. This is the true significance of the *mahāmudrā* and the *yab-yum* depicted in Tantric texts. At this level is established the base level of the domain of Shambhala and the governance of the streams of *karma* integrating our planet as an integral *maṇḍala,* a 'Self' within a vast company of similar 'Self-born' Ones in cosmos.

   The Love-Wisdom—Sacrifice-Will petal.

7. The expression of attained Buddhas when affiliated to the service potential of an earth sphere. Buddhahood is technically attained under the auspices of either of the three main Rays.[1] Gautama, for instance, attained his liberation under the auspices of the fourth Ray of Beautifying Harmony overcoming strife, which is a mirror for the higher three Rays, but the unparalleled wisdom he was noted for is an aspect of the second Ray of Love-Wisdom. Under its influence he became the heart of a major world-religion by embodying the necessary philosophical basis and wisdom to do so.

   Bodhisattvas attaining final liberation via the auspices of the *first Ray of Will or Sacrifice* do so via the path of destroying the

1 A Buddha is integrated with a similar entity as the Dharmakāya Flower, which manifests in the form of an Eye, and which I have earlier termed a Monad (meaning one, singular) that manifests as his vehicle of expression in cosmos.

lethargic and limiting forms of all that cling to *saṃsāra* when the evolutionary process demands change. They are therefore wielders of the law of *karma,* which they mete with exactitude, and often manifest in the form of world conquerors as part of their training for Buddhahood along this line. They can also manifest in the form of Wrathful Deities, there their more esoteric work is that of a Tantric destroyer of demons, the machinations of sorcerers, and all members of the dark brotherhood that actively conspire to oppose evolutionary law. They are therefore protectors of the planet from sources of evil emanating from other stellar spheres. They help direct streams of lives to their appointed destinations. Padmasambhava is an example of one who has developed under the auspices of this Ray line to Buddhahood.

A Bodhisattva attaining final liberation via the *third Ray of Mathematically Exact Activity* (which includes the Rays of Mind) does so through directing the progress of world civilisations. The course of the technological developments, scientific unfoldment, artistic, social and political life for all of humanity is seen through to its purpose so that all are accorded chances for spiritual progression according to the auspices of *karma.*

Nothing can be forced upon anyone, apart from the *karma* that they have created themselves. Therefore, every form of development along the line of learning the *dharma* must be contrived in such a way that the human units that are the targets for education will positively gain from the cultural situation they find themselves in. All religions and socio-political situations provide benefits for those that have incarnated in them for experience and to work out *karma* rightly.

A Lord of Civilisation therefore works at many angles of expression at once and is ambidextrous in the handling of all groupings of humans that constitute a civilisation or world situation. The four subsidiary departments of the Rays of Mind are worked with. It should be obvious that to change civilisation for the better takes a considerable amount of time, as human free will is inviolable, and nations, groups, as well as individuals, all display various forms of avarice and malice towards others, and they must be persuaded to develop loving kindness by whatever skilful means is available to such a one and his helpers.

There is also an interdependence between similar Shambhalic domains in our solar system, and within kindred star systems, interrelated cosmic *karma* that the great Ones within Shambhala must take into account. Many lives come and go from our planet via the rhythms of activity of this planetary Head centre.

The Sacrifice-Will—Knowledge petal.

8. The total abstraction of a Buddha into the community of similar 'thus gone' ones in cosmos. A Buddha finds his prearranged placing within a schema of developing further levels of *dharmakāyic* Insight, as part of a *maṇḍala* of expression that is inclusive of the sum total of whatever cosmos veils. Similarly, great planetary executives preside over the totality of Life upon this planet that have evolved as 'thus gone' ones from former aeons of evolution upon other globes of experience. They represent nurturing forces projecting cosmic *(dharmakāyic)* energies to all streams of Life in a planetary sphere so that all Life therein can gain access to the liberated domains.

   The Sacrifice-Will—Love-Wisdom petal.

9. The building of Buddha-spheres of activity, such as our world sphere, wherein sentient beings can evolve through the stages of evolution similar to what we observe upon the earth, for all forms of sentience to develop consciousness, and then to tread the stages of the path to liberation. This obviously involves considerable sacrificial limitation for the Buddha concerned. For our solar system it necessitated infusing the energy of *bodhicitta* (Love-Wisdom) as the mainstay of the evolutionary process. This concerns the process associated with the formation of the kingdom of the Sambhogakāya Flowers, and the gaining of enlightenment of all human aspirants.

   Such sacrifice thus concerns the limitation of an Ādi Buddha's[2] freedom of expression for the countless aeons that it takes to see through the progress of the sentient lives constituting the lesser kingdoms of Nature, through to the human stage and beyond, to final liberation for all.

   The Sacrifice-Will—Sacrifice-Will petal.

---

2 From this perspective an Ādi Buddha and his entourage can be considered a planetary Logos that has established the *maṇḍala* of a world sphere by similar methodology that *yogins* utilise *siddhis* to materialise thoughts.

It should be noted that these levels of expression concern the constitution of Shambhala, which will be the subject of the last volume of this series.

The Bodhisattva *bhūmis*

Concerning the Bodhisattva *bhūmis,* Brian Edward Brown states that:

> Essentially, they represent the various refinements in the self-explication of *Tathatā.* Suchness, in its noetic activity as *Ālayavijñāna,* having become fully self-conscious in and through the human mind's experience of the non-discriminating transcendental wisdom, delineates that immediate self-intuition in the more deliberate conceptions of that mind. Since the *Ālaya* contains the seeds *(bījas)* of perfect wisdom that assume the particular form of the *pāramitās* within the phenomenal consciousness which it grounds, the realizations of the ten *Tathatās* which "they attain" in the ten *bhūmis* are in fact the moments of its perfect, self-comprehensive elucidation.[3]

The seeds *(bījas)* of perfect wisdom contained in the *ālayavijñāna* 'that assume the particular form of the *pāramitās* within the phenomenal consciousness which it grounds' (in the world of the personal-I) are appropriately projected by the Sambhogakāya Flower. Each Flower is serenely focused upon the specifics of attaining the Bodhisattva vow in their meditations upon the world of the personal-I. Each *tathāgatagarbha* projects ideas into the consciousness of the Bodhisattva in a forthright manner to inspire such a one at impeccably timed moments of propitious *karma.* Such impressions can also come from the Council of Bodhisattvas utilising the substance of the *ālayavijñāna.*

Serene concentration is needed for the 'realizations of the ten *Tathatās'* (Bodhisattva levels), producing moments (which can also be considered as aeons) of 'perfect, self-comprehensive elucidation'. Varying degrees of revelation emanate from such focussed intent. They depend upon the level of attainment of the Bodhisattva according to the nature of the '*bījas* of activity' projected (the service work) in relation to the vicissitudes of *karmic* purpose.

---

3 Brown, xxxiv-v.

The activities of Bodhisattvas are based upon an impelling inclination to identify with higher principles; namely, with the *tathāgatagarbha* in the lower Bodhisattva *bhūmis* and *śūnyatā* or the *dharmakāya* in the higher levels. A Bodhisattva is so steeped in heuristic, teleological and metaphysical considerations by instinctively generating *bodhicitta* (producing the *pāramitās)* so direct revelation comes from either the *tathāgatagarbha* or the *dharmakāya.* The seeding process (of what are generally very subtle perceptions) proceeds without resistance from the indwelling consciousness, in contradistinction to the normal individual, who offers great resistance, because of the comparative density of obscurations.

The whorls of petals (energy levels) found in the Sambhogakāya Flowers of Bodhisattvas are so refined as to be a reflection of processes happening in the liberated realms or (planes) of being/non-being. It reflects the liberated patterns of things into the consciousness of its physical instrument via the 'seeds *(bījas)* of perfect wisdom'. (Such 'perfection' is only possible in a fully awakened state, not in the normal course of activity of a Bodhisattva's life.) This allows the enlightenment-process to be eventuated in the experience of the Bodhisattva, but also each Flower can produce eventual liberation from the constraints of its own form. It also allows a person to master all of the forces of Nature from within, by obtaining the necessary *siddhis* through the meditation process. Bodhisattvas need to draw upon the related potency from the *tathāgatagarbha,* and each of these Flowers then evoke the corresponding factor in the *dharmakāya* to produce the necessary miracles in the *māyā* of things.

The Head centre *(sahasrāra padma)* of each human unit reflects attributes of the Sambhogakāya Flower into active manifestation. The *yogin* that properly accesses the *sahasrāra* can then be liberated from illusional activity. Wisdom and eventual Buddhahood is the gain. The *sahasrāra padma* links the transformed personal-I to the *dharmakāya* because the structure of its petals facilitates sympathetic receptivity.

Another triplicity can be considered, producing a transmuted continuum from the most abstracted sources to the minute focal point (or eye) in *saṃsāra,* via the mechanism of the all-seeing Eye. Union with the All can then be visioned via profound revelation. Each level can be viewed in the form of an Eye:

a. The Dharmakāya Flower—the all, which when viewed as a unifying organism and relegated to a human unit, such a Flower is considered a 'Monad', meaning a One, integrating universal Mind into unity. In order to peer into and transform *saṃsāra* the Monad manifests in the form of an Eye that utilises its instrument, the *tathāgatagarbha/* Sambhogakāya Flower.

b. The Sambhogakāya Flower, the mediator in consciousness, absorbs attributes of the Mind of the universal One into its subtle form, when it can bear the impress. It then reflects those attributes into its instrument (the personal-I) when it has developed the serene mental countenance and luminosity of substance allowing such receptivity.

c. The Head lotus, the *nirmaṇakāyic* appearance, or focal point of the *Will* (bliss) of the *dharmakāya* and the conscious Love of the Sambhogakāya Flower. It integrates the 'one' of the personal-I, via coordinating the activities of the *chakras* and directs the impressions from the higher 'Eyes'.

From this one can gather that there are two main categories of *bījas:* those that are the seeds for differing aggregates associated with *saṃsāra*, and those existing in the form of the Impressions coming from the *dharmakāya*. (Especially at the later part of the Sambhogakāya Flower's evolution when the incarnate personality manifests via any of the higher Bodhisattva *bhūmis.)* The Sambhogakāya Flower is a repository of both, and functions accordingly. Bodhisattvas can then manifest the way that they do when reincarnating into *saṃsāra* for the purpose of rightly educating all therein as to the nature of the purpose of life. They are not totally absorbed in the *dharmakāya* as a Buddha, having not yet 'crossed over to the other shore', but nevertheless they can experience ('taste') the attributes of the universal Mind, and work to draw all separative units of consciousness to become cogniscent of that Mind by breaking all bonds of limitation to restricting forms. Consequently, the nature of this Mind is known as liberating Bliss.

Considerations of the Dharmakāya Flower continued

The Dharmakāya Flower is concerned with the manifestation and evolution of Life in cosmos, which also incorporates *saṃsāra*, whilst the

Sambhogakāya Flower is concerned with the evolution of consciousness and of its liberation. *Saṃsāra* involves the mode of the appearance of form, allowing intelligence to evolve in such a way that inevitably it masters the phenomenal world.

To properly access *dharmakāya,* one needs to attain the highest Bodhisattva *bhūmis.* With respect to the tenth *bhūmi,* Brown states that it concerns:

> The "stage of ultimate realization" and identifies the meaning and function of the Great Mirror Wisdom through which *Tathatā* knows the exact delineations of all phenomena simultaneously and without hindrance of spatial and temporal distinctions. For as *Ālayavijñāna* it is the universal storehouse which contains them as its own immanent determinations, its *bījas,* and the Great Mirror Wisdom is the self-luminosity, the perfect self-comprehension of the *Ālaya* in the entirety of those ideal determinations. If the human consciousness in and through the combined Universal Equality and Profound Contemplation Wisdoms recognized the *bījas* in their temporal projections as the phenomenal forms of mere-consciousness, the absolute consciousness (*Ālayavijñāna*), in and through the Great Mirror Wisdom recognizes them in their unmanifest, immediate inherence to itself. While the Universal Equality and Profound Contemplation Wisdoms represent the comprehensive knowledge of each particular thing in its sheer Suchness *(sarvajñāta)* as perceived by the phenomenal consciousness, the Great Mirror Wisdom is omniscience proper, the simultaneous and exhaustively detailed knowledge of all forms *(sarvākarajñāta),* including the Universal Equality, Profound Contemplation and all of the modalities of wisdom itself.[4]

This 'Great Mirror Wisdom'[5] at first manifests via the Śūnyatā Eye. After the demise of the Sambhogakāya Flower it becomes the revelation accessed via the Monadic Eye, which is but a Buddha's Eye. Within consciousness this expression is viewed as 'absolute consciousness'. *Śūnyatā* is here depicted as a mirror. At the final three *bhūmis* the Sambhogakāya Flower has been superseded by direct Identification with the Dharmakāya Flower and the Śūnyatā Eye has become the

4 Ibid., xxxv.

5 The *prajñā* of the Dhyāni Buddha Akṣobhya.

Monadic Eye. This Eye further opens as the higher *bhūmis* develop, and integrates with the Head lotus of the *nirmāṇakāya* that is the serving Bodhisattva, pouring into it ever greater revelatory streams of Bliss.

The Dharmakāya Flower consequently conditions the *ālayavijñāna,* organising its share of *bījas* so that their expression become 'its own immanent determinations'. The 'determinations' (evoking Amitābha's Discriminating Inner Wisdom) allow the 'Great Mirror Wisdom' to manifest as 'the self-luminosity, the perfect self-comprehension of the *Ālaya'* in the meditation-Mind of the Bodhisattva. Without the Monadic Eye organising and directing the *bījas* from the *ālayavijñāna* to the Mind of the Bodhisattva of the highest *bhūmis* there could be no spontaneous and effortless mirror-like wisdom. Then there is an ordered sequencing of *bījas* along a predetermined path that will produce 'perfect self-comprehension' and the attainment of Suchness, for which the *śūnyatā* experience is but the foundation. Obviously such *bījas* relate to the domains of enlightenment.

As the Bodhisattva of the lower *bhūmis* aspires upward towards the source of revelation in the *ālaya,* so then a flood of 'profound contemplative' experiences manifests via the northern direction. This is an innate and spontaneous happening because the Bodhisattva has been primed to receive them from the Śūnyatā Eye. What is herein described is a dual process, where there is a descent of impressions from above meeting the ascent of a Bodhisattva's aspiration from below; as obscuring *saṃskāras* are transformed and the Mind is conditioned to receive intense energy vectors.

It should be noted that the ten Bodhisattva stages can be viewed from two angles of perception:

1. Where *śūnyatā* still represents the goal, 'the other shore' (because the destruction of the Flower of the rebirth process still needs accomplishing). The qualities of the ten *bhūmis* are analysed with respect to this. Here *śūnyatā* is viewed as the end point of attainment, where what is known as 'great Wisdom' is an expression of the experience of *śūnyatā*. Buddhahood is here seen as a permanent residing in *śūnyatā,* there being no further attainment. Such a rather limited view is the consideration of many Buddhists.

2. Where *śūnyatā* is viewed as a mirror, in which case the three higher *bhūmi* stages represent absorption into *dharmakāya*. The *ālayavijñāna* then manifests in the form of the reflected attribute of the *dharmakāya* so that the Bodhisattva can access the supernal qualities of the wisdoms of the five Dhyāni Buddhas. These wisdoms, however, can only be explored in *dhyāna* and cannot be properly explained using words. This point of view is utilised in this thesis.

A major difference between the Sambhogakāya Flower and the Dharmakāya Flower is that the Sambhogakāya Flower is an individualised unity in relation to the evolution of a particular human consciousness-stream. The Dharmakāya Flower is not thus limited. It is the universal Mind that incorporates the sentience, consciousness, and enlightenment streams of all beings in all realms. The human unity contains the streams of sentience of the lesser kingdoms in Nature in its embrace, and is capable of attaining enlightenment through a thorough utilisation of the related experiences. The Sambhogakāya Flower is responsible for the organisation of the streams of *saṃskāras* to produce enlightenment and liberation.

The Dharmakāya Flower (here viewed as a world-Soul) is built upon a similar, though vaster patterning, wherewith all human Sambhogakāya Flowers are part of its embrace, plus the sum of the group-souls (collectivised sentience, governed by the *deva* hierarchy) of the lesser kingdoms of Nature, as well as the sum of the Bodhisattvic activities of humanity, and it extends into the universe of 'thus gone' Ones. (The above is another way of saying that such a Flower is omnipresent and omniscient with respect to the *māyā* that is our earth sphere.) Each human life-stream thus ultimately experiences what has always been, which can also be described as intrinsic Buddhahood, as the veils thereto gradually fall away. Buddhahood can thus also be viewed as Monadic (a 'One') that is inclusive of the all. Such a Buddha/Monad has its own progressive unfolding itinerary in the vast unlimited fields of service that is cosmos. Earth evolution is a tiny aspect within the Eye of its Vision. The Monadic Eye functions as part of the world-Soul until it can break free as a 'thus-gone' one and travel to a purposeful destination in cosmos.

We can now look to the prime 'limitation' of the *dharmakāya*, that it is the overriding cause for the *karma* effecting *saṃsāra* (a world sphere).

This means it is bonded to *saṃsāra*. *Saṃsāra* exists to provide the raw material for conversion into consciousness of primary mineral units through various sentience states, and through the hierarchical levels of the kingdoms of Nature as a result of evolution. It thus lays the background conditionings for the evolution of a human kingdom and the propulsion of all within *saṃsāra* towards the goal of ultimate liberation. Sentient beings thus first evolve to become humans, and later, Bodhisattvas.

This entire evolutionary process is not a product of chance, as the scientific community naively presumes. There are a vast number of interlocking factors in cosmos to make this an impossibility, for this reason some scientists have coined the term 'the anthropic cosmological principle' to account for the precision of timing of all laws that predispose the universe to lay the conditionings for the appearance of human consciousness.[6] This is indeed so because all is precisely factored in by the meditation of the primal (Ādi) Buddha who embodies the Dharmakāya Flower for an earth system, or on a vaster scale, a solar system, galaxy, or universe. All such Flowers are integrated and manifest a primary unity of great beauty in their multidimensional complexity.

Because this *dharmakāic* limitation exists, so there is the guarantee of ultimate liberation for all. This is built into the originating *karma* of the three worlds by the primordial Buddha. The *nirvāṇees* from

---

6 Gardner states, for instance:

Systematic analysis of the anthropic cosmologcal principle has, over time, revealed that the basic concept—that the universe is life-friendly—actually encompasses four separate but related subprinciples:

1. The "weak anthropic principle," which merely asserts in tautological fashion that the universe we inhabit must perforce be life-friendly since it happens to be inhabited by living observers like ourselves.

2. The "strong anthropic principle," which states that the eventual emergence of life and intelligence in the universe is actually predestined by the laws and constants of inanimate nature.

3. The counterintuitive "participatory anthropic principle," which hypothesizes, on the strength of the Copenhagen interpretation of quantum mechanics, that observer-participancy is necessary to summon the universe into existence and to give it structure.

4. The "final anthropic principle," which advances the extraordinary claim that once life has arisen anywhere on this or any other universe, its sophistication and pervasiveness will expand inexorably and exponentially until life's domain is coterminous with the boundaries of the cosmos itself.

James N. Gardner, *Biocosm*, (New Age International, New Delhi, 2006), 38-39.

such zones of limitation that enter cosmos (as a consequence of the actions of the Sacrifice of an Ādi Buddha) possess complete freedom to contemplate upon the nature of that vast Space before them, and where their compassionate activities as Buddhas best befit them to proceed. Myriads are the star systems and galaxies in the night sky. They represent identifiable objectives for the *nirvāṇees* of our earth humanity, obtained through the establishment of the pathways *(antaḥkaraṇas)* from here to there by former 'thus gone' ones. Once befitting themselves with the qualities to proceed, thence they go—to that 'further shore' of multidimensional star systems untold.

We saw that the Knowledge triad of the Dharmakāya Flower absorbs the sum total of the experiences gained from the entire evolutionary paean of our humanity. This knowledge is the gain from the Causative process (emanative *karma)* and resultant liberating *karma.* When a human kingdom appears, Knowledge is also obtained via the Dharmakāya Flower. It impresses the Sambhogakāya Flowers with the wisdom and revelations needed to be gained from beyond their realm of abstract Mind. Knowledge of the meanings, levels and orderings of the planetary and stellar spaces in cosmos are conveyed via Mind. Such awareness, however, is not the intent of the Sambhogakāya Flower. Such things as the evolutionary progress of a civilisation and all related factors of the qualities governing the associated nations, international finances, cultural situations and the *karma* governing the movements of peoples, however is. The purpose of the Sambhogakāya Flower is to fulfil the capacities of Love-Wisdom through knowledgeable pursuits and to attain the *śūnyatā* experience by awakening the Śūnyatā Eye.

Bodhisattvas of the higher *bhūmis* first identify with the lowest strata of cosmic Mind. (The abstracted, transmuted correspondence of mind.) This is concerned with separations and identifications, but on a vast transcendental scale. Such 'separations' (quotation marks used because there are no true separations in reality) are the attributes, the streams of Life, that evolve in the Womb of Nature (thus governed by the feminine principle), and hence manifest the *karma* governing *saṃsāra.* Therefore, this level is called the *ātmic*[7] *level* of the *dharmakāya.*

---

7 The term *ātma* concerns the concept of self-identity, the inner essence of Life, that which moves *('at'),* pervades or 'breathes', that which en-Souls Life. It is the domain from which the streams of evolving Life emanate, or from which they are controlled.

That group of *nirvāṇees* who are 'Contemplation-Buddhas',[8] who have gained complete liberation from consideration of being 'human' *per se,* are emanations of the *Sacrifice-Knowledge petal* of this Flower, when still orientated towards the earth, and *Sacrifice—Love-Wisdom* when orientated towards cosmos. They can be considered to represent attributes of the Throne of a liberated cosmic Entity, a Logos. They are therefore *Monadic,* because of a definable 'oneness' (via a complete, unqualified, integration with the Dharmakāya Flower), yet are universal in their expression of Awareness or Identification with the all. These Sacrifice petals exist as expressions of a strata of the *dharmakāya* beyond that concerned with gleaning the gain of the evolutionary process of human beings, but can and do work via the Sambhogakāya Flowers. The knowledge of star lore as part of a complete multidimensional *maṇḍala* of cosmos is part of what these *nirvāṇees* have assimilated into a expression of universality.

This level of the *dharmakāya* can be called *anupādaka,* for lack of a better term. *Anu* refers to the infinitesimal, and *pādaka* refers to that which is parentless, self-born. The concept of 'infinitesimal' here is that it is the start or beginning of a completely new venture—the journeying into the vastness of cosmic Space. What has been evolved through earth evolution and incorporated as Mind in such a one is small compared to what is yet to be gained by progressing through cosmos. Incarnation into earth-sphere activity was but one tiny milieu in terms of what has preceded and what is yet to come. It is 'self-born' because totally self-initiated, based upon the gains of the past evolutionary experience.

Those at this level embody Love-Wisdom because in the last resort the glue that binds the universe into a coherent process is Love, and the Wisdom is the gain through the evolutionary space that represented the womb (*garbha*) of the earth sphere. They are essentially stripped of affiliation to the past *saṃsāric* involvement, have transcended attachment to all within the earth sphere, (but wear the colouration of

8 Which is technically a translation of the term Dhyāni Buddha, but my concept here is slightly different, because a Dhyāni Buddha is conventionally represented as the embodiment of the five-fold aspect of the Mind of a Tathāgata. It denotes one or other of the five types of wisdom that such a Mind conveys. The 'Contemplation-Buddha', however, refers to one who obtained the Buddha stage upon the earth but has not moved on to cosmic spheres. The term Dhyān Chohan, a divine Being of meditation substance, can also be used to describe the nature of such a being.

what was accomplished) and have yet to learn the mysteries of what sustains the greater All of cosmos. Buddhas they are, but are spiritually dwarfed by great Beings that have aeons ago passed their point in cosmic evolution. They but represent *saṃskāras* in the *nāḍīs* of a great cosmic Logos, the Mind of which they have yet to fully comprehend.

Being cleansed of earth attachment, its attributes, and forms of knowledge (except for that which has been distilled or abstracted) leaves them with the clarity of a vast *bodhicitta* momentum, which drives them to higher cosmic goals. The nature of such consideration translates in our terminology as Love-Wisdom. Theirs is a wise beneficent absorbed Contemplation upon the good or need within the universal whole that is cosmos. Thus they travel through a *nāḍī* system to the 'Beyond'. Never-ending is this journey's quest.

Pratyekabuddhas

The term *svabhāvikakāya* refers to the highest of the bodies of a Buddha, which integrates the others into a unity. It can also be considered to emanate from the cosmic level of attainment, being the synthesis of the *trikāya*. It concerns the basic substance that a Tathāgata resides in, with which he accesses various levels of cosmos that are united by a commonality of substance. (Otherwise there would be no possibility of further travel for a Buddha.) The earlier *dharmakāyic* level still retains a tainted connection with earthy *karma*.

At this level can be seen the true esoteric basis of the idea of *pratyekabuddhas*.[9] The view here is at a transmuted level of what is normally labelled as a '*pratyekabuddha*'. These contemplative Buddhas are far more exalted than what orthodox Buddhists postulate. What was originally given to Buddhists was an exoteric doctrine, to fill in a gap of knowledge, and which logic indicated must be, as a consequence of the *arhat* doctrine, but the Buddhist mind was then not yet prepared for a deeper understanding. The esoteric doctrine has thus had to be revealed in stages.

---

9 *Pratyekabuddha*, from *prati* towards, plus *eka* one, meaning an individual Buddha, each one manifesting activity for himself, technically without concern for others. There is, however, in reality no possibility of one attaining the rank of Buddhahood thus, unless one is travelling the way of the dark brotherhood.

The reality behind the doctrine of the *pratyekabuddhas*, at the level that orthodox Buddhism views the subject is that they represent the Sambhogakāya Flowers. Such Flowers, existing upon the abstracted levels of the mind, are continuously contemplating, and being liberated from the rebirthing process, can be considered as 'Buddhas'. (The *tathāgatagarbha* is defined as the Buddha-womb.) Such contemplation manifests in three directions:

1. Upon the realms of the personal-I, when such an 'I' exists in *saṃsāra* and responds to higher principles.
2. Within the precincts of its own realm, gaining much knowledge and impressions from similar Flowers absorbed in contemplation. This must be so, as they unitedly direct the interwoven *karma* of any civilisation in the process of unfolding.
3. Upward toward the realm of *dharmakāya*, to which it turns to gain succour and revelation concerning the sum of the evolutionary direction.

With the above in mind the difference between the *arhats* and the *pratyekabuddhas* can now be considered. *Arhats* are those that have gained knowledge, or rather absorption, into the type of contemplation demonstrated by their individual Sambhogakāya Flower. They are consequently liberated from *saṃsāric* concerns for that life, but manifest an active presence in the world of human affairs.

Here *Pratyekabuddhas* are the Sambhogakāya Flowers on their own domain. Or rather, a *pratyekabuddha* is a term depicting the state that exists when the Sambhogakāya Flower is so identified with a quiescent contemplative Mind that there is no distinction in consciousness. The focus of the Flower is consequently upon *śūnyatā,* whose attributes are rapidly manifesting. They can be considered Buddhas, from the perspective that they are liberated from *karma*-forming *saṃsāric* identifications or attachments, and they are also contemplatives, because absorbed in the three modes of contemplation mentioned above. They are however far below the level of attainment of a Mānuśī ('teaching') Buddha, because they are not yet liberated from the rebirth process.

In this way the wise of the past could introduce a veiled concept of the nature of the Sambhogakāya Flower without having to spell out the full detail. That they are 'self-centred Buddhas' concerned only with their own individual liberative stance is only partially true. Concerning *pratyekabuddhas,* Coleman states:

> The term, sometimes translated in English as **'solitary realiser'** or 'self-centered, ***buddha***', indicates one who attains the state of **liberation** without relying on a teacher, following a natural pre-disposition. The ***Pratyekabuddha*** is superior to the ***Shravaka***[10] in two (or three) principal ways: 1) unlike the ***shravaka*** he accumulates merit over a hundred aeons and obtains a similitude of a ***buddha's major and minor marks***; 2) just as his own **liberation** is attained without relying on verbal transmission, he communicates with others mainly non-verbally; and 3) according to some sources, he realises the **emptiness** of the external phenomena composed of atomic particles, in addition to the **emptiness** of the individual personality, as realised by the ***shravaka***. However, according to these same sources, he fails to realise the **emptiness** of the inner mental phenomena composed of temporal moments, for which reason he is said to be realised in 'one and a half parts of **selflessness**'. The realisation of a ***pratyekabuddha*** depends not only on the **renunciation** or monastic discipline (which is undertaken by ***Shravakas***) but also on their comprehension and reversal of the **twelve links** of **dependent origination**.[11]

Sambhogakāya Flowers obviously need no teacher, as they already possess the Buddha nature, and therefore follow 'a natural disposition' to enlightenment. Because they are identical to the *tathāgatagarbha,* each Flower already possesses many of a Buddha's major and minor marks (viewed in terms of the subtle *chakra* and *nāḍī* system, as explained in chapter 3), and they persist for a vast amount of time (the symbolic 100 aeons). They also manifest communication to others non-verbally i.e., telepathically and through direct impression. Also, because of possessing the Śūnyatā Eye each Flower automatically realises the emptiness of 'the external phenomena', and of 'the individual personality', but because still imbued of *manasic* substance, theoretically it 'fails to realise the emptiness of the inner mental phenomena'. The Flower also works to reverse the effects of the 'twelve links of dependent origination' in the succession of personalities that it directs towards liberation.

---

10 In the Hīnayāna doctrine a *śrāvaka* is a hearer, a pious attendant to the Buddha. Also known as a disciple, a *chela.*

11 Coleman, *A Handbook of Tibetan Culture,* (Rider, London, 1993), 363.

Teachings had to be given of these two stages of the progress to liberation of human consciousness (of the *arhat* and *pratyekabuddha*). The two stages are then contrasted to the Bodhisattva in the Mahāyāna tradition, which espouses the true way to liberation by means of manifesting *bodhicitta*. In reality this is the only way that a human can gain enlightenment, because the *arhat* way is but temporarily for that life, and the *pratyekabuddha* is but a pseudonym, or personification, for the human soul-form existing contemplatively on its own realm, and into which the human life essence integrates after the death of the personal-I. (Though this necessitates the cleansing of the *bardo* after-death state just prior to rebirth.) It is therefore a state that can be obtained consciously, but is illusional, as a forthcoming rebirth is inevitable.

In reality, one cannot find a *pratyekabuddha* incarnate on the physical plane (except in the sense maybe of finding someone who has no obvious external teacher), though there are many active enlightened Bodhisattvas who work silently at their appointed chores without the majority around them being aware of such a gifted one being in their presence. The meditating ones may also not be on the teaching Ray (of the second Ray of Love-Wisdom), therefore upon attaining a similar Initiation status as a Mānuśī Buddha the roles of such beings will not be to manifest a major religious dispensation. They will instead manifest Bodhisattvic activity related to their own Ray department before entering *nirvāṇa* as a Tathāgata. Very few upon the physical domain may know what has eventuated, though myriads may be affected by their beneficence. Nevertheless, those existing on the inner realms with the opened Wisdom Eye, will know that a Jina has appeared and has 'gone to the other shore'. All liberated lives will bow and joyously greet this one as a consequence of a magnificent attainment. The term *pratyekabuddha* can therefore also be broadly applied to such a one, who has developed along a different Ray than that of Love-Wisdom.

The differences between the terms *arhat*, *pratyekabuddha*, Bodhisattva, Mānuśī Buddha, and Dhyāni Buddha can now be explained.

1. An *arhat* has identified with the abstract Mind, with which the world and his interrelations with it are viewed. He connects with the Sambhogakāya Flower within this Mind, and is self-absorbed in a form of mental fixation, by means of which he spends much

time and yogic austerities for the illusion of personal salvation.

2. A *pratyekabuddha* is an embodiment of the 'son of Mind' (active contemplative wisdom) in a sea of Mind. It is the Sambhogakāya Flower that is self-absorbed on its own realm, never leaving, until abstraction into *śūnyatā* causes the ending of this form of contemplation.
3. A *Bodhisattva* demonstrates the process associated with the fulfilment and then renunciation of mind. He/she constantly dynamically changes and adapts to meet continuously changing conditions in the quest for the liberation of the all. The *Bodhisattva* works with *bodhicitta* to manifest enlightenment's purpose, and will later bring the *dharmakāya* experience into active manifestation.
4. A *Mānuśī Buddha* is one who incarnates to educate all minds concerning the nature of *śūnyatā* and the *dharmakāya*, and the ramifications with respect to all aspects of the *dharma.*
5. A *Dhyāni Buddha* embodies the manifestation of the Wisdoms of the Tathātas, of which there are five differentiations, thus is a purveyor of the nature of cosmic Mind into active manifestation for all kingdoms in Nature.

Further considerations of the Dharmakāya Flower

In resuming the consideration of the *Dharmakāya Flower* I shall try to elaborate a little more concerning the nature of the three highest petals. Those existing thereupon are Lords of Sacrifice, as they have irrevocably stripped from themselves the final vestiges of attachment to earth's conditionings, and (later) within the solar system as a whole. They set the links to travel into space proper through the (cosmic) transmuted correspondence of the Śūnyatā Eye of this transcendent Flower. This level of Buddhahood may best be termed *samyaksambuddha*, 'fully and completely awakened'.

Concerning this state of Buddhahood, Paul J. Griffiths states:

> The very existence of an epithet like *samyaksambuddha* (which is sometimes coupled with the superlative 'unexcelled,' *anuttara*) suggests, though, that there is more than one kind of Buddha. For if all those to whom the title 'Buddha' was applied were thought

> to be unexcelled in their awakening, there would have been no need to develop and apply the title *samyaksambuddha*. And it is certainly the case that there is mention in the digests of awakened ones who are not *samyaksambuddha*, most often of *pratyekabuddhas* or 'individual Buddhas,' those who are awakened but who differ from *samyaksambuddhas* in that they do not perform the teaching functions of the latter, and so do not possess the same degree of salvific significance.[12]

The term *pratyekabuddhas* in the quote has been used for comparison purposes because of lack of proper distinctions between the various levels or grades of Buddhahood in Buddhism, so only the lowest 'grade' could be used to compare to the Mānuśī Buddha, and the superseding grade being termed *samyaksambuddha*. The concept of *samyaksambuddha*, however, is but a disguised form of teaching that implies there is a form of evolution also within the ranks of Buddhahood. The above list can be extended in accordance with five categories that have interrelated connection, as far as salvifical activities of an earth-like sphere that is teeming with sentient and conscious evolving lives is concerned.

1. *Pratyekabuddhas*. They are contemplatives focussed exclusively upon a specific stream of a human life within the context of the civilisations created by interrelatedness with other such contemplatives.
2. *Mānuśī Buddhas*. Buddhism teaches of a succession of these, such as Gautama, and Dīpeṅkara before him. They appear cyclically to primarily teach humanity the *dharma* (the topical need of the times for the civilisation concerned), which incorporates the need for proper emotional control and mental development in order to master the vicissitudes of *saṃsāra* through awakening the way of the Heart.
3. *Samyaksambuddhas*. They have entered cosmos upon their chosen Revelatory paths. They are trained in the ways of the emanation of cosmic Fire. (The nature and sources of the *prāṇas* that vivify the permutations of a Buddha-Mind.) With respect to this we should

12 Griffiths, 62.

note that every star system in our galaxy has its own emanatory hue and sound that distinguishes its primal evolutionary attainment from every other such source. Knowledge of the nature of the completed *maṇḍala* of all such systems constitutes the transmuted correspondence of the lore of Secret Mantra that the enlightened are privy to upon the earth.

4. *Dhyāni Buddhas.* They have gained much superlative experience from Schools of Revelation in various star systems, and having passed the necessary Initiations in cosmic schools, they then journey to an earth sphere to embody and direct the evolving Life of the associated kingdoms of Nature to liberation. They complete the *dharmakāyic maṇḍala* needed for the proper evolution of all lesser lives enthralled in *saṃsāra*. Therefore the integration of their combined substance constitutes the Dharmakāya Flowers for all, which upon our earth is termed Shambhala. They embody the seeding of mind/Mind in all that is. Thus they are the cause of the 'strong anthropic principle' that integrates everything in *saṃsāra* in terms of one universal Law that will evolve consciousness from out of the primal particles of cosmic dust, so that Buddhas eventually come to flower.
5. *The Ādi Buddha.* The great presiding, utterly accomplished Buddha, hoary with antiquity and experience, that esoterically is Guru to all Buddhas, Bodhisattvas, and Pratyekabuddhas that evolve from an earth system. He is thus the primordial One, the Source and ultimate Resolution of all.

Awakened Buddhas from past solar evolutions reside upon a higher domain than that of a Mānuśī Buddha. The highest systemic plane, *ādi,* meaning the first, beginning, the foundational start, represents dense physical incarnation for them.

The dimensions of perception

When integrating the information above with what has been presented concerning the dimensions of perception characterising our earth system, then we get seven planes of perception, each signifying a higher, subtler, transcended level of experience than the previous one. There are three concerning the realms of illusion, the three worlds of human livingness—the physical Earthy, the Watery emotional, and Fiery Mental, which culminate in the abstraction of *śūnyatā*. *Śūnyatā,* acting as a mirror, is then the middle level between the corporeal domains associated with *saṃsāra* and three liberated levels. Thus there are four planes associated with liberated being. Immediately beyond *śūnyatā* exists the plane whereon emanates the *karma* that governs the evolution of the kingdoms of Nature. (This plane is the lowest *dharmakāya* level, earlier termed *ātma*.) Then there is the Monadic level whereon are found the Buddhas of liberated Life, the second *dharmakāya* level, earlier termed *anupādaka*. Finally we have the first *dharmakāya* level whereon is enthroned the Ādi Buddha working via the Dhyāni Buddhas. (This plane of perception accordingly is termed *ādi.)*

From another perspective, we can first consider an interrelation of five planes, each demonstrating the expression of one or other of the five Elements. They are synthesised by the *third (ātmic) level* of the *dharmakāya*, where we find the emanation and resolution of all *karma* concerning the phenomenal appearance of these Elements. They therefore express the externalised qualities of the five Dhyāni Buddhas, from Vairocana to Amoghasiddhi. Above them there are two completely liberated realms of the *dharmakāya* that are not concerned with aspects of phenomena, but rather with cosmic perspectives.[13] There are also planes of revelatory awakening beyond the abovementioned seven, which are the cosmic astral, cosmic mental, etc., if we take the seven abovementioned planes to represent sub-planes of the cosmic dense physical.

Much of the information so far presented can now be integrated into a list of the dimensions of perception.

1. The Earthy *physical realm*. This is dual in its constitution, consisting of a dense part that can be touched, experienced by means of the five senses, and an etheric part which is the body of energies, consisting of the *nāḍīs* and the *chakras* (which stem from the places of intersection of several *nāḍīs)*. Because the Earthy domain reflects all of the rest in its qualities,[14] so there are three concreted planes

13 The *dharmakāya* level pertainable to earth experience is thus triune, consisting of an *āmic* level, that termed *anupādaka* (parentless), and that of *ādi* (primordial).

14 For which reason we have all of the laws known to physical science, and it is the only realm wherein Buddhas can come to be, because only here can the all be mastered.

and four etheric ones to complete its seven sub-planes. The concreted planes correspond to the three worlds of human livingness, the Earthy dense, the Watery emotional, and the Fiery mental. The etheric sub-planes correspond to the planes of liberation.

Of the *four ethers* the densest contains the minor *chakras*, known as the Inner Round, plus the major ones below the diaphragm, the Base of Spine *(mūlādhāra)*, Sacral (*svādiṣṭhana)*, and the Solar Plexus *(maṇipūra) chakras*. These *chakras* govern normal human activity and therefore the related powers are the easiest to awaken. The next, subtler ether (the third ether), contains the Throat centre *(viśuddha chakra*), which is the organ of the creative voice. The second highest of the ethers contains the Heart centre *(anāhata chakra)*. Here is derived the quality of *bodhicitta*, as well as the silent voice of the intuition with which it speaks. This substance is of a rarefied nature and only accessible to those directly upon the path to liberation. The most refined of the ethers contains the Head centre *(sahasrāra padma)* and the Ājñā centre, which can only be properly accessed by an accomplished *yogin*. They allow the expression of the highest wisdom and enlightenment within a bodily form, and the ability to see within all these dimensions of perception.

2. The Watery *emotional realm,* which constitutes the emotional and desire attributes of humans, as well as the heaven and hell states (the after-death bardo) that they incarnate into. The term 'emotional realm' is only correct as far as it refers to the conditionings established by the human kingdom. Animal sentience and *devas* also find expression here. They do not experience the human heaven/hell states, neither do they posses emotional-minds, but are connected with this substance because of involvement with humans. The term *astral* is used in reference to the quality of the substance embodying it. The term means 'starry', and refers to its (and the etheric domain's) autoluminous nature, as seen by clairvoyant vision. People's emotions are constituted of this substance, giving them auras of different colourings. There are various gradations to this substance, the grossest of which are utilised to construct the hell realms, and the subtlest in the pleasurable heaven ('god') realms of

humans in the after death state.[15]

3. The Fiery *mental realm*. This is divided into two parts, the detail of which was presented earlier:
    a. The concrete mental, representing the synthesis of the five sense-consciousness and consists of the substance of most scientific thought.
    b. The abstract or archetypal Mind, wherein reside the Sambhogakāya Flowers.
4. The Airy *buddhic realm,* of pure spiritual Reason, which derives from the experience of *śūnyatā*. Such Reason is the expression of the *dharmakāya* reflected via *śūnyatā*. The Airy Element can be considered the substance of *śūnyatā,* and *buddhi* the mechanism of comprehension of *śūnyatā*. *Buddhi* here is the term qualifying the experience obtained at the *śūnyatā-saṃsāra* nexus.
5. The Aetheric *dharmakāya realm,* the source of all individuation in the three worlds, and the related *karma*. (This can thus be called the *ātmic* realm.)

These five planes relate to the five Rays of Mind, to the experience of the five sense-perceptors, and the means of contact with the realms wherein *karma* is effected. These are synthesised by the qualities of the five Dhyāni Buddhas:

- *Vairocana*—the Dharmadhātu Wisdom, the Aetheric *ātmic* realm.
- *Akṣobhya*—the Mirror-like Wisdom, the Airy *buddhic* realm.
- *Amitābha*—the Discriminating Inner Wisdom, the Fiery *mental* realm.
- *Ratnasambhava*—the Equalising Wisdom, the Watery *astral* realm.
- *Amoghasiddhi*—the All-accomplishing Wisdom, Earthy *physical* realm.

15 Many of the terms that I have utilised here were originally conveyed in *The Secret Doctrine,* by H.P. Blavatsky, and later extended by her esoteric successor, Alice A. Bailey. Both of these women were high level Bodhisattvas who have contributed praiseworthy service (to the Western world specifically) in the excellent *dharma* found in their writings.

We should also look to the doctrine of the five *kośas* (sheaths of human consciousness). Govinda states:

> The densest and outermost of these sheaths is the physical body, built up through nutrition *(anna-maya-kośa);* the next is the subtle, fine material sheath *(prāṇa-maya-kośa),* consisting of *prāṇa,* sustained and nourished by breath, and penetrating the physical body. We may also call it the *prāṇic* or ethereal body. The next-finer sheath is our thought body *(mano-maya-kośa),* our 'personality', formed through active thought. The fourth sheath is the body of our potential consciousness *(vijñāna-maya-kośa),* which extends far beyond our active thought, by comprising the totality of our spiritual capacities.
>
> The last and finest sheath, which penetrates all previous ones, is the body of the highest, universal consciousness, nourished and sustained by exalted joy *(ānanda-maya-kośa).* It is only experienced in a state of enlightenment, or in the highest states of meditation *(dhyāna).* It corresponds in the terminology of the *Mahāyāna* to the 'Body of Inspiration' or 'Body of Bliss': the *Saṁbhoga-Kāya.*
>
> These 'sheaths', therefore are not separate layers, which one after another crystallize around a solid nucleus, but rather in the nature of mutually penetrating forms of energy, from the finest 'all-radiating', all-pervading, luminous consciousness down to the densest form of 'materialized consciousness', which appears before us as our visible physical body. The correspondingly finer or subtler sheaths penetrate, and thus contain, the grosser ones.[16]

Annamayakośa and *prāṇamayakośa* correspond to the dense and etheric part of the physical realm. There is, however, no correspondence to what I have called the emotional realm (the astral plane) above, and from a yogic perspective this is correct. This is because the astral realm is totally conditioned by human emotions and imagination, thus created by them. Only humans have heaven and hell states, and the murky realms of glamour and *māyā* they wallow in. The other kingdoms of Nature consequently do not have an astral plane *per se.* Also, the way of obtaining enlightenment consists of eliminating these emotional-mental defilements that obscure and distort vision, and which weigh down the apprehension of wisdom bright. Consequently, upon the higher

16 Govinda, *Foundations of Tibetan Mysticism,* 148.

yogic or Bodhisattvic way, the astral conditionings are diminished and then finally extinguished, leaving us with the clear luminosity of the light of the Mind. As these sheaths have been described in relation to the meditation process it is right that consideration is omitted of the attributes that the enlightened do not possess.

Another way of viewing this problem is that these Watery *prāṇas* are for the majority of people the major ones that they have developed, therefore *prāṇamayakośa* is specifically Watery-emotional, and from this perspective it relates to the second of the realms tabulated above.

It should be noted that the reference here is also to 'planes' or localities of residence for different categories of sentient beings, for *devas* and humans in the inner realms or the dense physical realm, whereas the *kośas* refer to sheaths of a human personality. The difference should be noted, but the sheaths function via the planes of perception.

Manomayakośa is described above as the mental body, specifically the intellect or lower mind.

Vijñānamayakośa corresponds to the Airy realm, termed *buddhi* above, which is what I have described as pure spiritual Reason (as the highest connotation of the meaning of *vijñāna*). This Reason is actually a fusion of the higher abstract Mind and *śūnyatā*. *Śūnyatā* is not placed as one of the *kośas* because it is said to be attributeless, technically substance free, though in fact consists of the Void Elements.

The meaning of the term *buddhi* was explained in Volume 2[17] in relation to a quote from Śantideva, where it is translated as intelligence, but it is more than that. It refers to pure insight, intuition beyond thoughts. Thus it is Airy in nature in that like the air the intuition is not contained by anything, and manifests like lightning (which passes through air) to influence consciousness. The faculty of inner knowingness here termed *buddhi* does not mentally classify, it knows the essence of what the thing represents, and instantly sees that thing as part of a composite of a complete whole and the role it plays therein. I use this term in preference to *pratyakṣa*, which is also defined as 'direct perception, intuition, spontaneity, without conceptual processes'. It essentially equates with the 'most supramundane pristine cognition', which is explained in *The Laṇkāvatāra Sūtra*. Therein there are said to be three types of

17 See Volume 2, 255 and also Volume 6, 283 for an expanded view.

pristine cognition (mundane, supramundane, and most supramundane):

> Now these three kinds [of pristine cognition respectively] generate the realisation of individual and general characteristics, the realisation of that which is created and destroyed and the realisation of that which is neither created nor ceases. The mundane pristine cognition is that of the extremists who manifestly cling to theses of being or non-being and of all ordinary childish persons. The supramundane pristine cognition is that of all pious attendants and self-centred buddhas who openly cling to thoughts which fall into individual and general characteristics. The most supramundane pristine cognition is the analytical insight of the buddhas and bodhisattvas into apparitionless reality. It is seen to be without creation or cessation, for they comprehend the selfless level of the Tathāgata who is free from theses concerning being and non-being.
>
> Furthermore, Mahāmati, that which is characterised as unattached is pristine cognition, and that which is characteristically attached to various objects is consciousness. And again, Mahāmati, that which is characterised as being produced from the triple combination [of subject, object and their interaction] is consciousness and that characterised as the essential nature which is not so produced is pristine cognition. Then again, Mahāmati, that which is characterised as not to be attained is pristine cognition, since each one's own sublime pristine cognition does not emerge as a perceptual object of realisation, [but is present] in the manner of the moon's reflection in water. On this it must be said [Ch. 3, vv. 38-9]:
>
> *The mind accrues deeds and so forth,*
> *But pristine cognition breaks them down;*
> *By discriminative awareness, too, the apparitionless*
> *Reality and powers are well obtained.*
> *It is the mind which objectifies.*[18]

The 'mundane pristine cognition' can be interpreted in terms of the exoteric rendering of *buddhi* as 'intelligence'. The 'supramundane pristine cognition' aspect of *buddhi* can be interpreted in terms of the word *pratyakṣa*. As such, 'direct perception without conceptual process' can be considered the basis to the experience of the *pratyekabuddha*.

---

18 Dudjom Rinpoche, 180-181. See also D.T. Suzuki, (trans.) *The Laṇkāvatāra Sūtra,* (Routledge and Kegan Paul, London, 1932).

Once 'intelligence' has been cleansed of its attachments to *saṃsāra*, and thereby resides in its natural state, it can act as a receptive tool whereby the *tathatā* that is the *dharmakāya* can manifest in the Mind's Eye with a view to being expressed in *saṃsāra*.

Ānannamayakośa firstly corresponds to the *ātmic* level of the *dharmakāya*. When viewed as an aspect of the Sambhogakāya Flower, then the bliss herein described is that of union or mergence of the consciousness of the *yogin* with this Flower in such a way that impressions and energisations are drawn from the *dharmakāya*.

The highest two sub-planes of the cosmic dense physical are termed:

1. *Anupādaka*, the domain of Buddhas (Dhyān Chohans), still attached to impressing Bodhisattvas upon the earth with needed revelations, and yet they also have their Eye upon the various pathways in cosmos upon which they must travel. We can also consider the Buddha aspect manifesting as the Monadic Eye of each human unit.
2. *Ādi*, the domain of Abstracting Buddhas. Here resides the Ādi Buddha, who synthesises the qualities of the five Dhyāni Buddhas, whose attributes are directed via the prismatic substance[19] of *anupādaka* to *ātma*. (*Anupādaka* diffracts the primordial Wisdom of the five Dhyāni Buddhas into manifestation via the *ātmic* realm.) Ādi embodies the qualities of the quintessential Buddha-Mind self-absorbed in its own inherent 'creative' function. It manifests aspects of cosmic Mind that are causative of the appearance of phenomena via the union of the Ādi Buddha and Consort. The Consort of the Ādi Buddha embodies the substance of all phenomena via her *devic* subordinates (the *ḍākinīs*). The five Dhyāni Buddhas are a direct expression of their union, and their wisdoms organise the substance of the dimensions of perception from *ātma* down.

The *maṇḍala* of the Dhyāni Buddhas find their embodied expression upon the *ātmic* plane, which conveys their organising purpose via the remaining planes. Vairocana, as the centre of the *maṇḍala* of the Jinas, manifests via the third of the sub-planes of the *ātmic* plane, and the remainder manifest via the lower four sub-planes. Vairocana expresses

19 This may also be described as 'the essence of consciousness, *bodhicitta*'.

the Will of the primal Mind of the Ādi Buddha to coherently impregnate every atomic unity of substance with that Mind's purpose via the Mirror-like aspect of Akṣobhhya. The manifestation of the Ādi Buddha's *vacana* (mantric sound) happens via Amitābha, and becomes the governing Law of the entire schema of manifestation. This thereby becomes the mechanism governing the exactitude of karmic law regulating the *māyā* of *saṃsāra*. The mantra is what they magnanimously broadcast to all the attributes of Nature via Ratnasambhava's Equalising Wisdom so that all aspects of life can gain the capacity to appropriately evolve toward liberation. Amoghasiddhi works with the responding patterns of the effect of this work, so that which does not meet a required standard is recycled. He helps to project the gain to *śūnyatā's* domain.

The basis to all of the lists of five, stem from this expression. The five lower planes constitute the Womb of the Mother of the World, the Consort of the Ādi Buddha.

Mastery of the emanating Sound becomes the pathway of return for prospective *nirvāṇees*. This is the esoteric doctrine that is the basis of the Secret Mantra that all *yogins* must discover, to gain liberation and the *siddhis* of mastery.

There are a series of reflections from plane to plane, until eventually Amitābha's Discriminating Inner Wisdom governs the lower mental plane. Ratnasambhava's Equalising Wisdom governs the Watery astral plane, and Amoghasiddhi's All-accomplishing Wisdom the physical plane. These three planes of perception are considered Earthy, physical,[20] from the higher perspective, hence Amoghasiddhi's energy governs their overall manifestation (despite Amitābha's rulership of the domain of mind/Mind). The *manasic* expression projected by Amitābha, however, regulates the manifold differentiations of the mineral kingdom. Here then is the esoteric validation of the Yogācāra assertion that 'all is mind/Mind', not just in terms of an expression of being found within the human mind, but also governing the externalisation of all we see in Nature.

Through the highest two realms the energies of the compassionate Meditations of Buddhas from past aeons enter our system and effect the sum total of Nature's kingdoms in accordance with the overall integration of our earth with cosmic Purpose.

---

20 The concreted sub-planes of the cosmic dense physical plane.

The seven planes are found to be the expressions of the seven Rays of light, thus:

1. Ādi—the first Ray of Will or Sacrifice.
2. Anupādaka—the second Ray of Love-Wisdom.
3. Ātmic—the third Ray of Mathematically Exact Activity.
4. Buddhi—the fourth Ray of Beautifying Harmony overcoming Strife.
5. Manas (Mind)—the fifth Ray of Scientific Reason.
6. Emotional—the sixth Ray of Devotion.
7. Dense physical—the seventh Ray of Ceremony, of Cyclic Purpose, and objective Power.

Here one can also incorporate the concept of the *lokas,*[21] where the term generally used by Buddhists is *dhātu,* meaning 'stratum, realm of being, constituent element, or part of a world construct'. Three main divisions are presented: a) *rūpadhātu* (realm of form), which refers to the physical plane, b) *kāmadhātu* (realm of desire), which refers to the realms of the desire-mind, c) *arūpadhātu* (realm of non-form), consisting of four subdivisions or 'infinities', as Kloetzli styles them.[22] These 'infinities' specifically refer to the three subdivisions of the realm of the higher abstract Mind, and also to *śūnyatā.* The *dhātus* also relate to the way of division or formation of the 1,000 petalled Lotus.

Though the fourth quality was stated to represent *śūnyatā,* it is better described as *buddhi,* being the divine Reason that mirrors the *dharmakāya,* thus is designated as *naivasañjñānāsañjñā,* 'neither consciousness nor non-consciousness'. With respect to *śūnyatā*, which is the middle of the list of seven, we can clearly see why the Noble Middle Way is what Buddhists pursue when following the way of attaining *śūnyatā* to gain liberation.

---

21 Basic information can be derived from such books as W. Randolph Kloetzli, *Buddhist Cosmology,* (Motilal Banarsidass, Delhi, 1997), 33-40, and Mathathera Narada, *The Buddha and His Teachings*, (Buddhist Publication Society, Kandy, 1973), 257.

22 W. Randolph Kloetzli, *Buddhist Cosmology, Science and Theology in the Images of Motion and Light,* (Motilal Banarsidass, Delhi, 1997), 29.

It should also be noted, that just as the lowest three realms form a triad of the three realms or worlds of human livingness *(saṃsāra),* so the higher three realms, the realms of causation are also a triad. We thus have:

1. *Ātma*, Divine Activity, the *Mother aspect,* because that which emanates from here ultimately gives birth to all of the evolving forms in *saṃsāra.*
2. *Anupādaka,* Love-Wisdom, the *Son aspect,* which is the result of the union of the Father-Mother, the expression of the *yab-yum* fusion between the Ādi-Buddha and his Consort, the evocation of the highest bliss in Tantric philosophy. It is the unifying or coherent force of the consciousness aspect (in its transformed, refined aspect), and its correspondence in all the kingdoms, exemplified as wisdom in the human kingdom.
3. *Ādi,* Will, the *Father aspect,* as this is the abstracting force that liberates as it drives all manifestation forward in terms of the overall purpose in cosmic space.

Śūnyatā is the mirror which reflects one trinity into the other, consequently it must remain spotless, unsullied, unmodified, untouched by the process. Hence the appellation 'empty'.

The *tathāgatagarbha* is also said to be triune. It consists of: 1) *dharmakāya*, 2) *tathatā*, 3) *gotra.*

Concerning the *gotra*, Brown states:

> *Gotra,* as the final term of the threefold nature *(trividha-svabhāva)* of *Tathāgatagarbha,* possesses a dual aspect. As *prakṛtistha gotra,* it is the innate germ existing since beginningless time, and as identified with *Dharmadhātu* (in the *Abhisamayālaṅkāra)* it was understood as the imperishable, permanent, unconditional and supportive ground for the realization of Buddhahood by all classes of persons; the *prakṛtistha gotra* represented as such, the unqualified assurance and validation of a universally attainable supreme enlightenment. At the same time, the germ of the Buddha is designated *samudānīta* or *paripuṣṭa gotra* as "that which has acquired the highest development." It was variously indicated that this twofold *gotra* represented the immanent, processive movement of the Absolute toward the perfect realization of itself as the unconditional Suchness of reality. Put otherwise, sentient beings could

> develop into and mature as perfect Buddhas (signifying the functional dynamic of *gotra* as *paripuṣṭa)* only because they already and always possessed the innate germ of Buddhahood (the *gotra* as *prakṛtistha).* The *Ratna* now formalizes these joint aspects of *gotra* as the germinal essence *(dhātu)* that is the cause *(hetu)* of its own self-attainment. As applied to it, this conception of *gotra* accounts for the third interpretation of *Tathāgatagarbha.* As embryo, the *garbha* is the causal essence of the *Tathāgata* (i.e. Buddhahood) within all sentient beings.[23]

The Sambhogakāya Flower can likewise be viewed directly in this fashion. I have already described the way that the Dharmakāya Flower interrelates with the Sambhogakāya Flower and of the expression of the related *bījas*. The detail of the mechanism that allows sentient beings to 'develop into and mature as perfect Buddhas (signifying the functional dynamic of '*gotra* as *paripuṣṭa')* only because they already and always possessed the innate germ of Buddhahood' shall be analysed in the next chapter. This detail of the mechanism of development has hitherto been lacking in Buddhism, but the necessity for filling the missing portion should be self-evident. *Tathatā* can be considered to be the *śūnyatā* that is the mechanism of transmission of identifications between the Dharmakāya and Sambhogakāya Flowers, whilst the *gotra* represents the sum total of all the *bījas* in the Sambhogakāya Flower. These *bījas* are of two kinds:

1. The *bījas* associated with the aggregates of the evolving I-consciousnesses. This is the *paripuṣṭa gotra* mentioned above.
2. The *bījas* emanating from the *dharmakāya*, which represents the *prakṛtistha gotra.* This then manifests the Buddha's 'processive movement of the Absolute toward the perfect realization of itself' throughout Nature.

In this dual manner, the All is served.

23 Brown, *The Buddha Nature,* 133.

7

The Ratnagotravibhāga Śāstra and the Sambhogakāya Flower

PART A
The Buddha Element

The Buddha nature

My purpose in this chapter is not to undertake an exhaustive analysis of the *Ratnagotravibhāga śāstra,*[1] which deals with many topics related to the Buddha nature. These topics consist of the three jewels (Buddha, *dharma* and *saṇgha),* the attributes of a Buddha, the *dharmakāya, svabhāvikāya,* the actual attributes of the *gotra* and enlightenment, etc. After the obeisance, the text states:

> If condensed, the body of the entire commentary [consists of] the following seven vajra points: Buddha, Dharma, the Assembly, the element, enlightenment, qualities, and then buddha activity.[2]

One may immediately discern in this list the seven Ray attributes. First, the Buddha, being the dynamic source of all that proceeds, embodies the attributes of the first Ray of Will or Power. The *dharma* represents the expression of the second Ray of Love-Wisdom. The assembly *(saṇgha)* the third Ray of Mathematically Exact Activity (when manifesting as an enlightened community). The fourth Ray of Beautifying Harmony overcoming Strife governs the Buddha element, the *tathāgatagarbha,* which is 'pure and yet has affliction'.[3]

---

1 The alternative title is *The Uttaratantra of Maitreya.*

2 Khenpo Tsultrim Gyamtso Rinpoche, trans. Rosemary Fuchs, *Buddha Nature, The Mahayana Uttaratantra Shastra with Commentary* (Snow Lion, New York, 2000), 19.

3 Ibid., 23.

The 'enlightenment' which relates to the awakening of and perfected expression of the use of the Mind, relates to mastery of the attributes of the fifth Ray of Scientific Reason. The 'qualities', such as various forms of knowingness and the 32 marks of a Buddha, represent the sixth Ray of Devotion, which here governs the nature of the manifestation of the *nāḍī* system and the attainment of *siddhis*. The qualities are said to be 'totally indivisible [and yet unapparent]'.[4] The 'buddha activity' relates to the various forms of training needed to gain enlightenment, and the consequent appearance of such a one in the minds of all, educating them in various ways as to the significance of the *dharma*. Here the seventh Ray of Ceremonial Activity and Demonstrable Power plays its role. Such activity is said to be 'spontaneous and yet without any thought'.[5]

Of these seven 'vajra points' the fourth, the Buddha element, shall herein be explained, because the related verses deal with the actual constitution and qualities of the Sambhogakāya Flower. As this Buddha element is synonymous with the *tathāgatagarbha,* the attributes of the three jewels (Buddha, *dharma* and *saṇgha)* constitute what it embodies, whilst the 'enlightenment, qualities, and then buddha activity' represent the manifest activity or *nirmāṇakāya* of this form, generated by the enlightened or enlightenment bound one that is its incarnate expression. Therefore, 'enlightenment' is what is gained upon the path, the 'qualities' represent the subtle body or mechanism of response to the outer environment, and the 'buddha action' refers to the salvifical activity of the awakened one.

The 'fourth vajra point' starts with a statement referring to the perfected body of the Buddha. It points out that all beings have the Buddha nature:

> The perfect buddhakaya is all-embracing,
> suchness cannot be differentiated,
> and all beings have the disposition.
> Thus they always have buddha nature
>
> The Buddha has said that all beings have buddha nature
> "since buddha wisdom is always present within the assembly of beings
> since this undefiled nature is free from duality,
> and since the disposition to buddhahood has been named after its fruit."[6]

---

4 Ibid.

5 Ibid.

6 Ibid. Those wishing a good detailed orthodox commentary by Jamgön Kongtrül

This statement appears pretty self-explanatory, where 'the assembly of beings' refers to 'multitudes of living beings'.[7] The 'perfect buddhakaya' refers to the *kāya* (form) of the Buddha-Mind, namely the *dharmakāya*. This undifferentiated, all-embracing Suchness manifests as the 'disposition' *(tathāgatagarbha)* that all beings possess. The term 'undifferentiated', however, in this context is curious, as the attributes of the *dharmakāya* do differentiate into the *tathāgatagarbhas,* the Sambhogakāya Flowers, that in a sense are unique to each individual, as they define the evolutionary progression ('the disposition to buddahood') of the related consciousness-stream. Nevertheless, at the heart of each *tathāgatagarbha* is *śūnyatā,* which in itself is undifferentiated. The 'fruit' then is *dharmakāya,* or *dharmatā,* and is attained via the individual paths of the individualities, the personal-I's evolving via each consciousness-stream, projected by the *tathāgatagarbha* to eventually produce this fruit.

That all beings possess the 'buddha nature', the principle of Life (divinity, the Monadic presence within), and will consequently evolve into Buddhas after an inestimably vast evolutionary process is true. However, in this long aeonic period there is a process related to the formation of the triune structure of the *tathāgatagarbha* in humans, which differs from that which drives the sentience of the lesser kingdoms of Nature. This is because humans possess intelligence, emotions, and a vastly quickened drive to know things. Consequently, there is an inevitable drive to enlightenment, and associated *saṃskāras,* that need to be processed by specialised *chakras* (such as the Head lotus, not possessed by the animal kingdom) that can accommodate the rapid pace of development and the nature of the expression of mind and its conversion to Mind. This conversion process also necessitates the appearance of a special construct upon the abstract domain of mind to process and direct the flow of the consciousness-streams of humanity, that animals do not possess and *have no need.* The *tathāgatagarbha* (Sambhogakāya Flower) thus exists to accommodate the *saṃskāras* of

Lodrö Thayé upon this and the other quotes from this text should refer to pages 117ff of this book.

7 E. Obermiller, *The Sublime Science of the Great Vehicle to Salvation, being a Manual of Buddhist Monism. The Work of Ārya Maitreya with a Commentary by Āryāsanga,* from the Journal Acta Orientalia, Vol. IX, Pars II. 111 (Apud E.J. Brill, Lugduni Batavorum, 1931), 157. In my rendition I shall compare Fuchs' translation with that of Obermiller's.

mind/Mind and the conscious quest for enlightenment. The remaining verses deal with the triune *tathāgatagarbha* as possessed by humans, and shall be analysed accordingly.

There is much concerning the aeonic subjective and phenomenal history of the various kingdoms of Nature, the evolution of such things as *devas* and *ḍākinīs,* or the process related to the multidimensional evolution of a world sphere or a cosmos, that is omitted in Buddhist philosophy, or only hinted at in the briefest terms. Such esoteric information now needs to be revealed, thus the introductory revelation of a vast 'ear-whispered' gnosis known by enlightened beings is the main purpose for the writing of this *Treatise on Mind.* The *buddhadharma* needs to progress beyond the bounds of the limitations of its exoteric doctrines. Buddhists need to better comprehend the nature and content of the enlightened Mind.

These statements are followed by ten categories for analysis of the nature of the Buddha-germ from ten viewpoints, which are elaborated as the text unfolds.

> Essence, cause, fruit, function, endowment, manifestation, phases, all-pervasiveness of suchness, unchangingness, and inseparability of the qualities should be understood as intended to describe the meaning of the absolute expanse.[8]

Obermiller elaborates this list by stating that 'the characteristics of the Germ of the Buddha is given from 10 points of view'. They are:

1. The essence of the Germ.
2. The causes (of its purification).
3. The result (of this purification).
4. The functions (of the Germ).
5. Its relations.
6. The manifestations (of the Germ in general).
7. The varieties (of the Germ) in correspondence with different states.
8. The all-pervading character (of the Absolute).
9. The unalterable character (of it).
10. The indivisible character.[9]

---

8 Rosemarie Fuchs, 23.

9 Obermiller, 158.

Armed with these headings the attributes of the *tathāgatagarbha* can now be analysed. First we have *'The essence of the Germ'*, which is:

> Just as a jewel, the sky, and water are pure
> It is by nature always free from the poisons.
> From devotion to the Dharma, from the highest wisdom,
> And from samadhi and compassion [its realization arises].[10]

The triadic aspects of the *tathāgatagarbha* are here likened to 'a jewel, the sky and water'. The jewel and the sky together represent the functions of the Śūnyatā Eye, where the jewel *(cintāmaṅī),* the diamond-Mind that is the *dharmakāya* or *dharmadhātu* manifests as the central pupil part of this Eye. The amount of the potency of Light entering the general body of the *tathāgatagarbha* is represented by the sky, the spaciousness of *ākāśa,* signifying the iris portion of the Eye. For one in *samādhi* to experience this spaciousness one must look upwards to the all-encompassing vastness of Space ('the sky'). The water here signifies the energy of enlightenment (consciousness) obtained via *samādhi* and is the *bodhicitta* expressed in the form of compassion. It quenches the thirst of all seeking the *dharma*. 'The poisons' here would have a direct reference to the three poisons at the centre of the Wheel of Life. Firstly ignorance, where the *dharmakāya* is the antidote; hatred, enmity or antagonism, where absorption in the vastness of the sky becomes the antidote; and greed, selfishness or avarice, where the developed energy of enlightened consciousness becomes the antidote.

One awakens the Śūnyatā Eye through devotion to the *dharma* and developing 'the highest wisdom', whilst *samādhi* and compassion *(bodhicitta)* develop the mirror-like wisdom allowing the wisdoms of the Jinas to be reflected by the stilled water into all aspects of phenomenal life.

Maitreya further elaborates this subject in the next verse, providing *the causes for the purification* of the *tathāgatagarbha.*

> [Wielding] power, not changing into something else,
> and being a nature that has a moistening [quality]:
> these [three] have properties corresponding
> to those of a precious gem, the sky, and water.[11]

---

10 Rosemarie Fuchs, 23.

11 Ibid.

We now observe the three main aspects of this Flower, in that it can wield power (the first Ray characteristic), it is inconvertible into anything else (the second Ray of Love-Wisdom), and has a 'moistening' quality (the effect of the third Ray of Mathematically Exact Activity). 'Moistening' refers to the ability of the *tathāgatagarbha* to work via the 'hard' Earthy substance, the lower three planes of perception (when viewed from the higher vision) that characterise *saṃsāra*. Such substance represents the crystallised attributes of mind/Mind, governed by the energies of Amitābha. This elementary substance is 'moistened' by the effects of the Watery human emotions and desire (initially seeded by the *tathāgatagarbha),* so that compassionate attributes can arise. First the defiled mind manifests *(kāma-manas* and *kliṣṭamanas).* Later, the yogic process transforms these into *bodhicitta*.

Having directed our vision to *saṃsāra* and the world of human interrelationships via the 'moistening quality' the text continues along this vein with a quick summary of the various types of individuals that have evolved therein, and of the process producing their liberation. This results in point two of the above list, the causes for the purification of the *tathāgatagarbha*.

> Enmity towards the Dharma, a view [asserting
> an existing] self, fear of samsara's suffering,
> and neglect of the welfare of fellow beings
> are the four veils of those with great desire,
> or tirthikas, shravakas, and pratyekabuddhas.
> The cause that purifies [all these veils]
> consists of the four qualities [of the path],
> which are outstanding devotion and so on.[12]

The characteristics of those that are ignorant and antagonistic towards the *buddhadharma,* those ensconced in views of selfhood, those reacting to pain and suffering, and the selfish, non-compassionate people all around, are well known and need no elucidation. The text then refers to those that do follow a spiritual path and seek enlightenment one way or other. They are symbolised by the 'tirthikas, shravakas, and pratyekabuddhas'. Little needs to be commented upon these, other than what has already been presented, as orthodox commentaries treat the

12 Ibid., 24.

subject well. The *tīrthikas* are often referred to as 'heretics', but literally mean 'the holy ones' being the followers of the Brahmanical religion, and by extension to followers of any other religion. *Śrāvakas* are pious attendants of the Buddha, referring to the Theravāda Buddhists, whilst the *pratyekabuddhas* were explained earlier.

Enmity, selfhood, fearfulness and the non-compassionate activity produce a quaternary. They refer to four attributes of the manifest form: the physical body (enmity), which must be conquered by yogic practices; the etheric substratum (conveying the *nāḍīs* and *saṃskāras* of selfhood); the emotional body, producing fears, etc; and the often cruel, calculating separative mind. They are esoterically 'the four veils of those with great desire'. The implication is that 'tirthikas, shravakas, and pratyekabuddhas' also possess subtle aspects of these veils. They, however, also implicate the completion of the septenary of manifest being.[13] They symbolise the attributes of the Knowledge, Love-Wisdom and Will or Sacrifice petals of the Sambhogakāya Flower.

The requirements of the path are explained in the next verse, which relates to point three of the above list, *'The result (of this purification)'.*

> Those whose seed is devotion towards the supreme vehicle, whose mother is analytical wisdom generating the buddha qualities, whose abode is the blissful womb of meditative stability, and whose nurse is compassion, are heirs born to succeed the Muni.[14]

These four requirements are needed to gain enlightenment. The first being great devotion, a steadfast persistence to follow the *dharma* in the face of all adversity. Many are the hindrances upon the path; obscuring *karma,* and predispositions *(saṃskāras)* from past lives and from earlier activities in this life. The obscuring *karma* refers to sudden unforseen events that offer challenges to one's life activities and *dharma* practice. Many activities from former lives often have to be karmically cleansed before the space presents itself that facilitates unreserved meditations and studies. One needs to steadfastly follow the path over the course

---

13 The higher three principles are the abstract Mind (wherein the *tathāgatagarbha* resides), *śūnyatā,* and *ātma.* Here the *tīrthikas* aspire to the abstract Mind, *śrāvakas* to *śūnyatā* and *pratyekabuddhas* to *ātma.*

14 Ibid.

of one's life, no matter the obstacles if enlightenment is to be the gain. Simultaneously, all such 'chance' happenings must be utilised as primary sources to gain wisdom from them. The reading of appropriate texts, learning from peers and one's spiritual preceptor, plus what is developed through heuristic experience are all needed to evoke wisdom.

'Meditative stability' via the yogic practices productive of *samādhi* is then needed if the 'blissful womb' that is the *tathāgatagarbha* is to be realised. This necessitates the generation of *bodhicitta* via the compassionate activity of a Bodhisattva, whence the final product is Buddhahood.

The result and function of the purification process

The *result* of this purification process can now be analysed.

> The fruit is the perfection of the qualities
> of purity, self, happiness, and permanence.
> Weariness of suffering, longing to obtain peace,
> and devotion towards this aim are the function.
>
> In brief, the fruit of these [purifying causes]
> fully divides into the remedies [for the antidotes],
> which [in their turn] counteract the four aspects
> of wrong beliefs with regard to the dharmakaya.[15]

With respect to the four qualities that are represented as the fruit, Obermiller has: 'Purity, Unity, Bliss, and Eternity',[16] where the footnote for the term 'Unity' is that it refers to *ātma-pāramitā,* where *'ātman* is to be understood in the sense of the unique essence of the Universe'.[17] Consequently, having developed the munificence of the Muni within the 'blissful womb of meditative stability', then the qualifications are seen in terms of an absolute purity of the attributes of Mind, wherein the 'unique essence', of the vastness of cosmos is perceived (thus the *dharmakāya).* This manifests in the form of Blissful experience and a permanent abode for such experience. The function thereby overcomes

15 Ibid.

16 Obermiller, 164.

17 Ibid.

the suffering experienced via involvement with *saṃsāra,* to thereby abide in the peace signified by *nirvāṇa,* producing a consequent drive to produce this end.

The next verse has reference to the 'four requirements' given two verses back, stating that these fruits divide 'into the remedies' given. Hence the product of strong devotion is absolute purity, analytical wisdom produces *ātma-pāramitā,* or *prajñāpāramitā,* the great ocean of wisdom, the Mind that is 'the essence of the Universe'. The generation of Buddha qualities produces the experience of Bliss, and *samādhi* produces a permanent abode in *nirvāṇa.* In turn these attributes counter the 'four aspects of wrong beliefs' of 'the four veils'. Their attributes are also countered by absolute purity. The false beliefs of the *tīrthikas* are counteracted by proper analytical wisdom found in the *prajñāpāramitā.* The attitudes of the *śrāvakas* are transformed by the Bliss of enlightenment, and the illusional 'peace' of the *pratyekabuddhas* is countered by a permanent abode in *nirvāṇa* after the Bodhisattva path has been followed to completion. The attributes of the *dharmakāya* and the means to residence therein have consequently been the focus in these two verses. The analysis of these attributes continues in the next verse, where the functions are elaborated.

> The [dharmakaya] is purity, since its nature is pure
> and [even] the remaining imprints are fully removed.
> It is true self, since all conceptual elaboration
> in terms of self and non-self is totally stilled.
> It is true happiness, since [even] the aggregates
> of mental nature and their causes are reversed.
> It is permanence, since the cycle of existence
> and the state beyond pain are realized as one.[18]

Though the subject begins with the theme of the *dharmakāya,* which by nature is 'pure', absolutely freed from any adventitious substance or defiling attribute, (*saṃskāras,* which here can be considered to be 'imprints'), the theme, however, quickly moves to considerations of the *tathāgatagarbha.* It is the mechanism of removing 'the remaining imprints'. Here its characteristics of *nirmalā* and *samalā tathatā,* Suchness apart from pollution and with pollution (which shall be

18 Rosemarie Fuchs, 24.

explained later) are implicated. The *tathāgatagarbha* is 'true self' because all conceptual realisations in terms of the dichotomy of 'self' and 'non-self', are not just 'stilled' but extinguished. It acts in a self-less, group-consciousness manner, and yet is responsible for the appearance of the 'selves', the personal-I's manifesting in *saṃsāra*. Obermiller here has 'It represents the Unity (of the Cosmos), the perfected Quintessence Of all Plurality, of the Individuals as well as their impersonal elements. Through the extirpation of even the non-physical elements and of their causes, it is the Supreme Bliss'.[19] Rosemarie Fuchs has 'happiness' instead of Bliss, which is incorrect, as happiness is a condition of the human emotional body and is generally quickly followed by other moods. Bliss is not thus conditioned, it is an exhilaration of the abstracted consciousness responding to intense, vibrant energies not affecting the Solar Plexus centre (wherein happiness is relegated to), but rather is an expression of the Head or Heart lotus.

Its permanence results in the fusion between *saṃsāra* (cyclic existence) and *śūnyatā* ('the state beyond pain'). This is the expression of the *śūnyatā-saṃsāra* nexus embodied by the Sambhogakāya Flower's constitution. Returning again to the *dharmakāya,* Obermiller's version states 'It is eternal (being free from the limits of both)'.[20] What should be noted here is that the Sambhogakāya Flower is the means to the realisation of the *dharmakāya* once the adventitious defilements have been removed. Note also the differences in the focus of the translations, where Obermiller's rendition is 'being free from the limits of both' and Fuch's is that they are 'realized as one'. The differences in concept are that Obermiller is referring to *dharmakāya,* whereas Fuch refers to the function of the Sambhogakāya Flower.

Having analysed the relation of the *tathāgatagarbha* to the *dharmakāya,* the focus of the text moves to those 'noble ones', the Bodhisattvas, who possessing the *tathāgatagarbha,* use it to experience *dharmakāya.*

> Their analytical wisdom has cut all self-cherishing without exception.
> Yet, cherishing beings, those possessed of compassion do not adhere to peace.

---

19 Obermiller, 173.

20 Ibid.

> Relying on understanding and compassionate love, the means to enlightenment,
> noble ones will neither [abide] in samsara nor in a [limited] nirvana.[21]

The reference in this verse is to the modes of activity of *tīrthikas, śrāvakas* and to *pratyekabuddhas*. The *tīrthikas* are still possessed of 'self-cherishing', which the Buddhist soteriology, following the *prajñāpāramitā,* decries and the Bodhisattva path eliminates. All forms of selfishness and 'selfhood' are cleansed during the early Bodhisattva stages. Those that 'adhere to peace' are the *śrāvakas,* whose methodology is superseded by Bodhisattvic activity, who rely on compassionate undertaking and true understanding of the *dharma* to gain enlightenment. Such Bodhisattvas will not abide in *saṃsāra* or in a limited *nirvāṇa,* which is the abode of the *pratyekabuddhas.* This limited *nirvāṇa* is termed *pratiṣṭhita-nirvāṇa,* which possesses dialectic thought constructs, with which the *pratyekabuddhas* interact. As the Sambhogakāya Flower can be considered a form of limited *nirvāṇa,* being the domain of pure consciousness, so then non-abiding *nirvāṇa* *(apratiṣṭhita-nirvāṇa)* is hinted at, attained by Bodhisattvas of the highest *bhūmis* after the death of this Flower's form.

The functions of the *tathāgatagarbha*

Next are presented two verses providing the reasons for the existence of the *tathāgatagarbha.*

> If the buddha element were not present,
> there would be no remorse over suffering.
> There would be no longing for nirvana,
> nor striving and devotion towards this aim.

> That with regard to existence and nirvana their respective fault and quality are seen,
> that suffering is seen as the fault of existence and happiness as the quality of nirvana,
> stems from the presence of the disposition to buddhahood. "Why so?"
> In those who are devoid of disposition, such seeing does not occur.[22]

21 Rosemarie Fuchs, 24.

22 Ibid., 25.

Detail concerning the three main effects of the absence of the *tathāgatagarbha* have been provided throughout this treatise. Intuitive perception would not exist, with no subtle internal voice producing any form of conscience. There would simply be the separative, segregative self-focussed mind dominating all activities fused with the selfish, avaricious and desire-filled attributes of the lower centres aggrandising all material resources for itself, regardless of the pain or suffering caused upon others. It simply would be insensitive to any compassionate stance, as no lessons will have been learnt from past lives, as the Sambhogakāya Flower would not exist to direct the *karma,* or consciousness-*bījas* and *saṃskāras* in a progressive manner towards enlightenment and liberation from *saṃsāra.* Nothing within the consciousness of the individual would push him/her to strive towards any other aim, other than intensifying links with pleasurable pursuits and power in *saṃsāra.*

The Buddha-germ projects images pertaining to the path into the consciousness of the personal-I linked to it, where this intuitive wisdom is the fruit of actions from past lives. It sees the problems with phenomenal existence, hence the need to strive towards liberation. Rightly viewing the causes of the factor of suffering, its antidote, as given in the Buddha's four Noble Truths and the Eightfold Path, can then be applied. Bliss (rather than mere happiness) then becomes the experience of residence in *nirvāṇa.*

Obermiller's version of this second verse more correctly provides teachings associated with the *tathāgatagarbha,* rather than 'the disposition to buddhahood', which only hints at the Buddha-germ.

> This contemplation
> Of the sufferings of Phenomenal Life and the bliss of Nirvāṇa,
> Of the defects (of the former) and the advantages (of the latter)
> Is (conditioned) by the existence of the Germ. Therefore,
> With those in whom there is no Germ, this contemplation does not exist.[23]

Also, one can say that even if this Buddha-germ existed in an individual being, but was not able to function, because of the crudeness and overly focussed materialism of the person, then such 'contemplation does not exist'. There is a long, slow process via the course of one's incarnations whereby the capacity of the *tathāgatagarbha* to influence

23 Obermiller, 176.

its instrument develops. In the latter stages of development there is a strong driving motivation to overcome all the hurdles life offers in one's quest for enlightenment. Many intuitive insights arise that stimulate the path because the links in consciousness *(antaḥkaraṇas)* with the *tathāgatagarbha* have been well established by the activities from former lives.

The relations of the *tathāgatagarbha*

These relationships are viewed in terms of similes, relating its essence to the ocean, light and gems. Hence it is a matter of deciphering these similes in the three associated verses, in order to obtain a better view as to the functions of the *tathāgatagarbha*.

> Like the great sea it holds qualities
> immeasurable, precious, and inexhaustible.
> Its essence holds indivisible properties.
> Thus [the element] is similar to a lamp.
>
> Unifying the elements of dharmakaya,
> a victor's wisdom, and great compassion,
> it is shown as being similar to the sea
> by the vessel, the gems, and the water.
>
> Clairvoyance, primordial wisdom, and absence of pollution are totally indivisible and native to the unstained abode. Thus it has properties corresponding
> to the light, heat, and colour of a lamp.[24]

Obermiller's version that corresponds to the first of these verses is:

> (The Essence of the Buddha) is like the Great Ocean
> Being the inexhaustible repository of jewels—its sublime properties;
> It is (moreover) like a light, since, by its nature
> It is endowed with properties indivisible (from it).[25]

24 Rosemarie Fuchs, 25.

25 Obermiller, 178.

From this quote we see that the pronoun 'it' of Fuchs' translation refers to the Buddha-germ, which manifests similar to 'a great sea', however, the concept of 'a great Ocean' has connotations of a vaster body of water. This 'sea' can then be considered to represent an ocean of wisdom.[26] That wisdom then is most precious, a repository of many jewels, representing the variegated aspects of that wisdom, which sheds light like a lamp. These properties are indivisible, and hence inherent within the main body or form of the *tathāgatagarbha.*

Being the embodiment of great wisdom is the major characteristic of this Flower. It represents the mechanism of the containment of the wisdom generated through many lives of experience. The quintessential aspect of this wisdom is jewel-like, an 'inexhaustible repository of jewels', which refers to the attributes of the Sacrifice-Will—Sacrifice-Will petal of this lotus, the highest and most refined of all the petals.

The next petal of the Flower, the Sacrifice-Will—Love-Wisdom petal 'is endowed with properties indivisible (from it)', being the fundamental Love-Wisdom and the power of the Will to transform *saṃsāric* allurements into wisdom vectors over a vast number of lives rayed into manifest expression. This 'vessel' of the Sacrifice-Will—Love-Wisdom petal thus collects the gain of the Bodhisattvic action, plus the precious jewel-like substance from the cosmic ocean of *dharmakāya* (via the Sacrifice-Will—Sacrifice-Will petals).

The third petal (Sacrifice-Will—Knowledge) embodies the inexhaustible knowledgeable aspects of this wisdom, that is at service for the personal-I that is striving to be enlightened. This petal stimulates the perseverance to adhere to the yogic and Bodhisattvic path through enlightening the *yogin's* Mind with necessary intuitive images and a driving energy towards liberation. (They are sacrificial in intent with respect to *saṃsāric* affiliations.) This Flower is consequently autoluminous, with an inexhaustible source of light, shedding its light in the darkness of ignorance, similar to a lamp.

The central Love-Wisdom petals of this Flower unify the 'elements of dharmakaya, a victor's wisdom, and great compassion'. This compassion

---

26 The wisdom inherent within the *tathāgatagarbha* can be considered to be likened to a sea, but when accessing the *dharmakāya* is ocean-like.

manifests as a sea or ocean of Love (the Love-Wisdom—Love-Wisdom petal of the Sambhogakāya Flower) to flood the consciousness of the incarnate personality with the impetus of Bodhisattvic virtue, from the Love-Wisdom—Knowledge petal into the Mind of the receptive Bodhisattva in the form of revelations. This Knowledge contains 'elements of dharmakaya' producing compassionate understanding. The 'victor's wisdom' then relates to the Love-Wisdom—Sacrifice-Will petal, whose purpose is to assist the personal-I to sacrifice all aspects associated with *saṃsāric* living so that liberating wisdom can be attained. The 'vessel' of the *tathāgatagarbha* then relates to the Love-Wisdom principle, and 'the gems' to the elements of the *dharmakāya* this wisdom contains, the most precious attribute embodied by this immaculate form. 'The water' manifests as the flood of compassion that emanates from this principle to assist in the transformation of an ego-bound consciousness into enlightenment. It is the Water of enlightening knowledge *(bodhicitta)* poured forth from the Love-Wisdom—Knowledge petal into the Mind of the receptive Bodhisattva or *yogin* in the form of intuitive revelations.

The attributes of the Knowledge triad of petals of this Flower are characterised by the qualities of 'Clairvoyance, primordial wisdom, and absence of pollution'. Obermiller's version of this verse is:

> (When) the state of Perfect Purity (is attained),
> One is possessed of the supernatural faculties,
> Of the Wisdom bringing about the extirpation of defilement,
> And this extirpation itself, which are indivisible.
> Therefore (the Essence of the Buddha in the aspect of the result)
> Suggests a resemblance with the rays, the heat, and the colour of a light.[27]

Clairvoyance here can be conflated with 'supernatural faculties' *(abhijñā)* and refers to the functioning of the Knowledge—Sacrifice-Will petal, which works to produce transcendental perceptions as part of the accomplishment of the *yogin* that is its instrument. (Happening at an advanced stage of development of the personal-I that the Flower has projected into manifestation.) The 'primordial wisdom' is the expression of the Knowledge—Love-Wisdom petal, which reflects

27 Obermiller, 180.

the general characteristic of the Sambhogakāya Flower, which is Love-Wisdom, into the receptive Head lotus of its instrument. The 'absence of pollution' then relates to the final, most basic of the petals, Knowledge—Knowledge. Here all knowledgeable attributes (apart from gross defilements) garnered by the reincarnating *jīvas* are absorbed and processed as part of the development of eventual wisdom.[28] This knowledge comes via the lines of the five sense-consciousnesses and the five Elements. The wisdom and will of the Sambhogakāya Flower then works to produce 'the extirpation of defilement' within the mind of the *yogin* aspiring to become enlightened.

We see, therefore, that the state of 'absence of pollution' refers to *nirmalā tathatā,* wherein *saṃsāric* defilements no longer exist. This condition manifests only at the end of the existence of the *tathāgatagarbha.* For the greatest part of the evolutionary period, however, the condition of *samalā tathatā,* suchness with defilements, persists. Though these defilements are highly refined, they are capable of being absorbed in the *tathāgatagarbha's* form as knowledgeable attributes.

The general colouring of the Sambhogakāya Flower is orange-yellow, reflecting the attributes of knowledge and wisdom, which is the colour of this 'lamp'. Its light is seen clairvoyantly by those with the inner Eye awakened, and the 'heat' is the general effect of the impact of its energies upon the *chakras,* inevitably awakening *kuṇḍalinī.*

The general manifestation of the Buddha germ

There are two verses concerned with this subject.

> Based upon the manifestation of suchness dividing
> into that of an ordinary being, that of a noble one,
> and that of a perfect buddha, He who Sees Thatness
> has explained the nature of the Victor to beings.

---

28 Gross defilements are excluded by means of the transformative process associated with the *chakras* of the associated individual. Karmic factors pertaining to the three-fold lower nature are however stored as *bījas,* as part of the constitution of the permanent atoms (mental, astral and dense) retained by the Sambhogakāya Flowers so that new *jīvas* can be reincarnated based upon their stored qualities, but are not part of its petals. See A.A. Bailey, *A Treatise on Cosmic Fire,* (Lucis Publishing Company, N.Y., 1973), 505-536 for further detail.

> [It manifests as] perverted [views in] ordinary beings,
> [as] the reversal [of these in] those who see the truth,
> and [it manifests] as it is, in an unperverted way,
> and as freedom from elaboration [in] a tathagata.[29]

The general meaning of these statements is clear enough, and warrant little commentary. Obermiller's version for the first of these quatrains provides added information.

> The Absolute manifests itself differently
> In the worldlings, the Saints, and the Supreme Buddha.
> Having perceived this, (the Lord) has declared
> That the Essence of Buddhahood exists in all that lives.[30]

With reference to this 'Essence of Buddhahood' (the *tathāgatagarbha)* the lower three Knowledge petals contain the *saṃskāras* of the ordinary, materially focussed, self-centred individual. The three central Love-Wisdom petals store the *saṃskāras* of the Bodhisattvic qualities developed by the personal-I. The three higher Sacrifice-Will petals store the *saṃskāras* pertaining to the development of the attributes of a Buddha. When the *tathāgatagarbha* projects another personal-I into incarnation then that which is stored manifests as 'perverted [views in] ordinary beings', because a new brain consciousness is developed, so the conditionings of the new life of the personality take effect. The past life has been forgotten and the environment of a new national and social identity takes hold. What is stored in a Flower's petals, plus the *bījas* in any of the three permanent atoms, slowly modify that developing consciousness via the appearing *saṃskāras.*

Also, the *tathāgatagarbha* may not yet have developed over the course of evolutionary time the characteristics relating to the higher aspects. The higher triads of petals will then exist in bud form, with only the general attribute of its inherent Love-Wisdom manifesting to direct the evolving lives. The central Śūnyatā Eye is mostly closed. The Bodhisattvic and Buddha-like qualities develop over many millennia, and the petals that can contain the associated qualities unfold slowly accordingly.

---

29 Rosemarie Fuchs, 25.

30 Obermiller, 182.

The *tathāgatagarbha's* evolution and its all-pervading character

This subject is explained in four verses.

> The unpurified, the both unpurified and purified,
> and utterly purified [phases]
> are expressed in their given order
> [by the names] "being," "bodhisattva," and "tathagata."
>
> The element as contained
> in the six topics of "essence" and so on
> is explained in the light of three phases
> by means of three names.
>
> Just as space, which is by nature free from thought,
> pervades everything,
> the undefiled expanse, which is the nature of mind,
> is all-pervading.
>
> As the general feature [of everything], it embraces [those with] faults,
> [those with] qualities, and [those in whom the qualities are] ultimate
> just as space [pervades everything] visible,
> be it of inferior, average, or supreme appearance.[31]

These verses endeavour to explain how the petals of the Flower awaken through the phases of development from newly incarnating ordinary human beings, to those that are developing Bodhisattva virtues, and finally those that are awakening the attributes of a Tathāgata, or rather, the complete resplendence of the *tathāgatagarbha*. There is a process of the petals awakening via 'the unpurified, the both unpurified and purified, and utterly purified [phases]', all manifesting via the ordering of the triads of petals, which are here designated by the names of '"being," "bodhisattva," and "tathagata"'. The six topics of '"essence" and so on' so far described, deal with this process of determining the constitution of the *tathāgatagarbha* via the rubric of the names of the three categories of the petals of this Flower.

31 Rosemarie Fuchs, 25-26.

The next verse compares space to mind, but the actual comparison is with the enlightened Mind, which, like space is 'all-pervading'. The implication with respect to the *tathāgatagarbha* is that such a Mind is a property of this Flower, as it exists upon the abstracted, rarefied strata of the mental plane. The final verse analyses the sum total of the domain of mind/Mind, where it embraces 'faults', the defilements, desire-mind, etc., generated via *saṃsāric* incarnation by the personal-I. The enlightened Mind also embraces the awakening processes engendered upon the Bodhisattva path, as well as the ultimate, or 'supreme appearance' of the *dharmakāya*. All attributes of mind/Mind can be accommodated by the *tathāgatagarbha,* until there is no more use for the existence of its form, because of the overwhelming potency of that which is 'ultimate'.

The unalterable character of the *tathāgatagarbha*

There are thirteen quatrains to this section, six of which Fuchs has combined into three verses. Of these thirteen the first verse is a summary of the general attributes of the *tathāgatagarbha,* indicating the interrelation between *nirmalā* and *samalā tathatā*. It shows that despite the adventitiousness of what is obtained via *saṃsāric* experience, the essence *(tathatā)* of the *tathāgatagarbha* remains undefiled.

> Having faults that are adventitious
> and qualities that are its nature,
> it is afterwards the same as before.
> This is dharmata ever unchanging.[32]

Fuchs here uses *dharmatā* (rather than *tathatā),* which is defined as the actual reality, the ultimate truth of phenomena (the essence of existence) and natural force of things. *Tathatā* is Suchness, the immaculate universal reality, omniscient wisdom, the essence of the *tathāgatagarbha.*

The remaining twelve verses relate to the types of attributes absorbed into the Knowledge petals of the Flower. Consequently, they concern the development of the unpurified ordinary person of the triad of characteristics earlier given related to 'being', 'the Bodhisattva' and 'the Tathāgata'.

---

32 Ibid., 26.

The next verse states:

[Though] space permeates everything,
it is never polluted, due to its subtlety.
Likewise the [dharmadhatu] in all beings
does not suffer the slightest pollution.[33]

Here the *dharmadhātu,* which Fuchs conflates with *dharmatā* and *tathatā,* is taken as the essence of the *tathāgatagarbha* ('in all beings'), which is compared to Space. Both remain undefiled, despite the pollution *(manasic* substance) that abounds in the world of the personal-I. The *dharmadhātu* is pristine cognition, the fundamental realm *(dhātu*[34]*)* of the *dharma,* hence is almost synonymous with *dharmakāya. Dharmakāya* is the body *(kāya)* of the *dharma,* whilst *dharmadhātu* is the realm upon which it resides. *Dharmatā* then manifests as the force that projects this *dharma* into manifestation via the spaciousness of the abstracted Mind. Consequently, *tathatā* becomes the mechanism of containment of that *dharma* in the form of the *tathāgatagarbha.*

The next three quatrains also express similes comparing aspects of the fundamental essence of the *tathāgatagarbha* to Space. These four similes, plus the first verse, draw our attention to the five Jina wisdoms. In these similes Space is equated with the attribute of function of mind/Mind.

Just as at all times worlds arise
and disintegrate in space,
the senses arise and disintegrate
in the uncreated expanse.

Space is never burnt by fires.
Likewise this [dharmadhatu]
is not burnt by the fires
of death, sickness, and aging.

Earth rests upon water and water upon wind.
Wind fully rests on space.

33 Ibid.

34 *Dhātu* is the 'root or base', the fundamental stratum (plane of perception), realm of being, or a constituent Element.

> Space does not rest upon any of the elements
> of wind, water, or earth.[35]

The first of the verses relates to the Mirror-like Wisdom of Akṣobhya, where *dharmatā* is reflected into the adventitious qualities in order to convert them into that which is unchanging. Being first, and not directly referring to 'space' (which here implicates one or other of the Elements), Akṣobhya's Wisdom stands here at the centre of the associated *maṇḍala* of the Jinas. His attributes therefore govern the functions of the Sambhogakāya Flower as a unit, which exists to reflect *dharmakāya* into *saṃsāra,* so that the two are equalised. Here the associated Element is Aether, the essence of Space, though the Element normally relegated to Akṣobhya is Air.

The second of the verses relates to the permeation of everything with the Dharmadhātu Wisdom of Vairocana. Accordingly, this Wisdom manifests via the eastern direction of the *maṇḍala,* being the heart of the expression of the Sambhogakāya Flower. The Element here is Air, though Vairocana's normal assignment is Aether. (Both Akṣobhya and Vairocana have complimentary functions, as is also shown by the fact that one is blue with a white radiance, and the other is white with a blue radiance.)

The third verse relates to the Discriminating Inner Wisdom of Amitābha, ruling the Fires of Mind, by means of which 'worlds' (thought-forms, ideas) 'arise and disintegrate in space'. Accordingly, within the mind the sense-consciousnesses also 'arise and disintegrate'. The western direction of outward to the field of service representing humanity is here indicated.

Though the fourth verse uses the simile of 'fires', which technically relates to the energy of the mind/Mind, its use here is relegated to that which consumes or destroys, where it is the transformative energy governing the entire life processes of 'death, sickness, and aging'. Here Ratnasambhava's Equalising Wisdom is implicated, where the effects of all such activity is inevitably 'equalised' into the Dharmadhātu Wisdom. The related direction is south, into the world of material affairs. (The Element is Water, where here this attribute relates to the flowing motion of the *prāṇas* in the *nāḍīs.)*

35 Ibid.

The fifth verse relates to Amoghasiddhi's All-accomplishing Wisdom, which relates to the yogic process that masters all of the Elements and attributes of *saṃsāric* life. Hence the terms 'space' (Fire), 'wind' (Air), 'water' (Water) and 'earth' (Earth) are used in this verse. The reference to these Elements also provides a clue that the mode of interpretation by means of the qualities of the five Jina-attributes is in order. Amoghasiddhi's direction is northwards to the realms of liberation, hence the conveyance of the *dharmakāya* into the attributes of the Elements via that of 'Space' (which 'does not rest upon any of the elements').

Having established the attributes of the five Jinas, it is natural that the way of evolution of their wisdoms via the development of the sense-consciousnesses should now be discussed. This topic is the subject of the following quatrains.

> Likewise skandhas, elements, and senses
> are based upon karma and mental poisons.
> Karma and poisons are always based
> upon improper conceptual activity.
> The improper conceptual activity
> fully abides on the purity of mind.
> Yet, the nature of the mind itself
> has no basis in all these phenomena.
>
> The skandhas, entrances, and elements
> are to be known as resembling earth.
> Karma and the mental poisons of beings
> should be envisaged as the water element.
> Improper conceptual activity is viewed
> as being similar to the element of wind.
> [Mind's] nature, as the element of space,
> Has no ground and no place of abiding.
>
> The improper conceptual activity
> rests upon the nature of the mind.
> Improper conceptual activity brings about
> all the classes of karma and mental poisons.
> From the water of karma and mental poisons
> the skandhas, entrances, and elements arise.
> As this [world] arises and disintegrates,
> they will arise and disintegrate as well.

The nature of mind as the element of space
does not [depend upon] clauses or conditions,
nor does it [depend on] a gathering of these.
It has neither arising, cessation, not abiding.

This clear and luminous nature of mind
is as changeless as space. It is not afflicted
by desire and so on, the adventitious stains,
which are sprung from incorrect thoughts.[36]

These eight quatrains, plus the earlier four, symbolise the twelve attributes or links *(nidāna)* of the turning of the Wheel of Life, Dependent Origination *(pratītyasamutpāda)*. As the subject of this wheel has been explained earlier, and will be given in greater detail in Volume 5A, I will only briefly correlate the symbolism of these twelve quatrains with the *nidānas* of Dependent Origination.

In the first verse, 'faults that are adventitious' refer to the first of the *nidānas,* that pertaining to ignorance, which is the root cause of the turning of this wheel. The 'dharmata ever unchanging' must be sought as the antidote to free oneself from continuous rebirth into it and the Six Realms. This stage is symbolised by a blind woman trying to find her way with a stick. The second *nidāna* concerns the engendering of 'karmic formations', *(saṃskāras),* which keep one bound to cyclic experiences. (The symbolism being of a potter making pots, representing thought-forms.) This relates to the gaining of pollution, tainting space. One must develop the Dharmadhātu Wisdom to be totally free from such pollution.

The third *nidāna* is symbolised by the grasping tendencies of monkeys, relating to the development of elementary consciousness *(vijñāna)*. This relates to the ability of the mind to create worlds (of thoughts, ideas) and to cause their disintegration again. The sense-consciousnesses appear and manifest their forms of activities, before they 'disintegrate in space', i.e., the Clear Light of Mind.

The fourth *nidāna* is 'name and form' *(nāma-rūpa),* whereby the thinking principle properly evolves, producing the ability to name everything it perceives in the world around it, hence the intellect develops. This is symbolised by the image of a man on boat steered by a ferryman. In the corresponding verse we have the concept of space (the abstract Mind) never being burnt by the fires of the empirical mind.

36 Ibid., 27.

The naming or identification process lasts for the duration of life; the cycles of 'death, sickness, and aging', all being designations or stages of development of the emotional mind.

The fifth *nidāna* is symbolised by the ability of consciousness to live in its own house with six windows, relating to the 'six senses' *(ṣaḍāyatana)*. The powers of the mind are now completely developed and self-consciousness rules. Consequently, the *prāṇas* of all the Elements (Air, Water, Earth and Fire) can be appropriately processed. The statements that: Earth 'rests upon' (is supported by) 'water and water upon wind', whilst 'Wind fully rests upon space' and that 'Space does not rest upon any of the elements', implicate the dimensions of perception starting from the densest (Earth) to the subtlest (Space). However, this list needs further elaboration and inclusion of the missing Elements. From this logic Space does not rest upon Air (wind), hence it refers to the higher correspondence of mind—the *dharmakāya,* the Aetheric Element. Also, the Fiery Element needs to be included, in which case Water would be supported by Fire, and Fire by Air. One can presume that the author of this text truncated the listing of the Elements here to keep the main theme of the trinities appearing throughout the text. From this perspective 'earth' relates to the attributes garnered via the Knowledge petals of the Sambhogakāya Flower, 'water' to that absorbed by the Love-Wisdom petals, and 'wind' to the attributes gained by the Sacrifice-Will petals.

The sixth *nidāna* is designated 'contact' *(sparsā)*. Here we have a pair of lovers, but not in full union. Mind (one lover) must yet fully comprehend the vicissitudes of the material domain (the other lover) that it is infatuated with. Complete comprehension of *saṃsāra* is now possible. Obermiller's rendition of the related verse states:

> In a similar manner the elements of life (classified into) groups,
> component elements, and bases of cognition.[37]
> Have their foundation in the Biotic Force[38] and Desire,
> And the latter (two) are always supported
> By the naïve appreciation (of existence).[39]

---

37 The footnotes provided by Obermilller for 'groups', is *skandhas,* for 'component elements' is *dhātu,* and for 'bases of cognition' is *āyatana.*

38 Which Obermiller explained earlier was *karma.*

39 Obermiller, 187. His footnote here being that this 'naïve appreciation' relates to 'perceiving the reality of the individual and the separate elements'.

Here then all of the categories concerning incarnation in a phenomenal body are fully integrated and functioning. They are the five *skandhas,* the five Elements, and the five sense-consciousnesses directed by *karma* and desire. Fuchs here has 'mental poisons'. The latter two are based upon 'the naïve appreciation (of existence)', here signifying intellectual ratiocination, which integrates them all into unity.

The seventh *nidāna* is 'feeling' *(vedanā),* symbolised by an arrow piercing a man's eye. Here the emotions are exemplified via the mind (as *kāma-manas).* Emotional activity driven by desire and integrated with mind produces the cyclic outpouring of *karma* (the arrow in the man's eye) which will persist governing the individual until the natural purity of mind is accomplished. We are told that 'the nature of the mind itself has no basis in all these phenomena'. Transience rules, and the suffering factor of attachment to this transience will inevitably teach the true nature of phenomena and the relationship of mind to Mind.

The eighth *nidāna* is thirst or craving *(tṛṣṇā)* for more knowledge, comprehension of why, what, wherefore, how, etc. This is symbolised by a woman serving a man a drink. The Earthy-Watery mix of *saṃskāras,* being the basis for most empirical impressions derived from the material domain, are now thoroughly experienced. In an elementary, exoteric fashion, the text relates the *skandhas*, the sense-consciousnesses and Elements to the Earth Element[40] because these factors concern the experiences gained from the material domain and interrelation with phenomena. They thus are considered Earthy, because they deal with the physical environment. 'The mental poisons' here relate to the mental-emotions *(kāma-manas),* by means of which the bulk of *karma* is created, and are much more subjective, hence the force of *karma* is considered Watery.

The ninth *nidāna* is denoted 'clinging' *(upādāna)* and is symbolised by a man or monkey gathering fruit. Here the paths in life become divergent. The person may intensify attachments to incarnate life,

---

40 See Volume 1, chapter 2, for an explanation of the *skandhas* and my usage of this term in this series. The *skandhas* include *rūpa,* the form or body; *vedanā,* perception or sensation; *saṃskāras,* aggregates of action; *samjñā* the faculty of discrimination; and *vijñāna,* revelatory knowledge. There I make a distinction between these five attributes of human existence and *saṃskāras,* which literally are the *prāṇas* conveying the consciousness-aspects of the *skandhas* through the *nāḍī* system.

the ambition for more of what is desired (the gathering of fruit), or follow the path to liberation. The corresponding verse is concerned with the higher aspects of consciousness, the fruits of life's process, viewed in terms of concepts and ideas, subtly exhorting a practitioner to eliminate 'improper conceptual activity'. These more rarefied thoughts are compared to the wind (being the Airy Element) because of their subjective fleeting nature. Those with aberrant views, no matter how subtle, need to reflect upon the Mind's nature 'as the element of space' that has 'no ground and no place of abiding'. We see, therefore, that the path to liberation is espoused for this *nidāna*.

The tenth *nidāna* is symbolised by sexual intercourse (or a pregnant woman), signifying 'becoming' *(bhāva),* the fruition of all of life's processes. Here the paths manifest either towards deep intoxication with the pleasures of *saṃsāra,* or to yogic ecstasy from the integration of wisdom and compassion. In the corresponding verse the primacy of the mind is established as the root cause of 'Improper conceptual activity' which 'brings about all of the classes of karma and mental poisons'.

The eleventh *nidāna* is symbolised by a woman giving birth *(jāti),* signifying that the gain of life's experiences are now recycled. The wheel of Dependent Origination begins again, with the gains of the former cycle projected forwards. Upon the path the symbolism refers to the way of the Bodhisattva, who can now teach many young ones. The corresponding verse states that the driving force of 'karma and mental poisons' causes the *skandhas,* etc., to arise. Consequently, as the world of sense-perception arises and then dies, so all these expressions of mind will similarly arise and die.

The twelfth *nidāna* is symbolised by a man bearing a corpse, signifying death *(maraṇa),* which sums up the final accomplishment of the entire wheel of becoming, maturity and death. Everything is an illusion. From the higher perspective there is a consequent mergence of the deceased or enlightened consciousness with the Sambhogakāya Flower. The available *karma* is absorbed and the cycle starts again. The related statement sums up the achievements of the rebirth process in terms of 'the nature of mind', where by being 'the elements of space' it consequently does not depend upon 'causes and conditions' and there is no birthing and dying. This refers to the *tathāgatagarbha* that exists within this domain of Mind. Consequently, the last of the ten points is introduced.

The indivisible character of the *tathāgatagarbha*

Four verses follow from the previous one, where the characteristics of the *tathāgatagarbha* are described in terms of Mind.

> This clear and luminous nature of mind
> is as changeless as space. It is not afflicted
> by desire, and so on, the adventitious stains, which are sprung from incorrect thoughts.
>
> It is not brought into existence
> by the water of karma, of the poisons, and so on.
> Hence it is also not consumed by the cruel fires
> of dying, falling sick, and aging.
>
> The three fires of death, sickness, and aging
> are to be understood in their given sequence
> as resembling the fire at the end of time,
> the fire of hell, and an ordinary fire.
>
> Having realized thatness, the nature of the [dharmadhatu], just as it is,
> those of understanding are released from birth, sickness, aging, and death.
> Though free from the destitution of birth and so on, they demonstrate these,
> since by their [insight] they have given rise to compassion for beings.[41]

For 'the nature of mind' Obermiller uses the phrase 'the Spiritual Essence', which is equated with 'The Essence of the Buddha',[42] hence the *tathāgatagarbha*. The Clear Light of Mind wherein the *tathāgatagarbha* resides is not afflicted by any *saṃsāric* attribute. Also, the *tathāgatagarbha,* in the form of *nirmalā tathatā,* is not born by means of them; it is not an attribute of the empirical mind, thus is not consumed by the varying types of fire related to the forms of death, cessation associated with the effects of the activity of this mind. There is, however, the state of *samalā tathatā,* the essence of the empirical gleanings obtained from *saṃsāric* activity, but they affect not the inherent purity of the *tathāgatagarbha.* Instead they become the foundation for the expression of the *dharmakāya.*

---

41 Rosemarie Fuchs, 27-28.

42 Obermiller, 188.

With respect to the personal-I, *manasic* attributes are likened to 'cruel fires', because they express the blows of *karma,* plus are an aspect of the natural order of things in *saṃsāra,* to produce sickness, ageing and death. These types of Fires (expressions of mind) are then likened to the metaphysical and eschatological concepts of 'the fire at the end of time, the fire of hell, and an ordinary fire'. For the first type of fire Obermiller's footnote states that it is 'The fire which destroys the external world *(bhājana-loka)'*.[43] The 'ending of time', or of our earth evolution, is therefore likened to the death of a physical body. This eschatological concept introduces the physiological key[44] to the concept of the nature of the evolution of phenomena and the causation of things. Sickness, which causes much emotional and physical pain, is likened to the psychic torments in the hell states, and ageing (which slowly consumes the form) is likened to an ordinary fire upon the dense physical domain. In these statements the three *lokas* of human existence are implied: the mental domain, relating to the Fire that consumes the world at the 'end of time'. Here we have an ontological concept inferring that as all things are emanations of mind/Mind, so that which causes the final ending of things is an expression of the forces of Mind. Hell states relate to the psychic astral realm (governed by the emotions) and consequently are ruled by a Watery form of Fire. Finally, there are the physical fires that consume things upon the material domain.

None of these types of transient fires affect the *tathāgatagarbha,* as it exists beyond the realm of mind that conditions *saṃsāric* phenomena. Residing upon the abstract domains of Mind, it however embodies the pure luminosity of Mind, and expresses the spaciousness of Thatness. From this stance the ordinary cycles of birth, sickness, old age and death are transcended.[45] The luminous Fire of *bodhicitta* it embodies does however give rise to the compassion of the Bodhisattva path, which concerns the next section.

---

43 Obermiller, 191.

44 This is one of the seven keys needed to be turned to gain an enlightened understanding of any sacred text. These keys are: the literal, numerical, astrological, allegorical, physiological, and esoteric forms of interpretation. For detail see my book *Karma and the Rebirth of Consciousness* (Munshiram Manoharlal, Delhi, 2006), 263-69.

45 An intense supernova that is an explosion of radiant Fire, however, does manifest at the ending of the *tathāgatagarbha's* form, when complete liberation is achieved.

The Bodhisattva, the *tathāgatagarbha* and the Heart lotus

The next twelve quatrains deal with the expression of the middle Love-Wisdom tier of petals of the *tathāgatagarbha,* as well as this lotus in general. The types of *prāṇas* it absorbs concern the way of travelling the Bodhisattva path, by means of awakening the potency of the Heart centre. As per usual, Fuchs has combined some of the quatrains, consequently, I shall number them to assist in explanation. As they relate to the Bodhisattvic activity stemming from the awakened petals of the Heart centre they can be related to the information presented in relation to Figure 2 ('The Heart centre and the zodiac'). Here we travel the way of the rectified wheel from Aries through Taurus to Pisces.

> 1) The noble ones have eradicated the suffering
> of dying, falling ill, and aging at its root,
> which is being born due to karma and poisons.
> There being no such [cause], there is no such [fruit].
>
> 2) Since they have seen reality as it is,
> they are beyond being born and so on.
> Yet, as the embodiment of compassion itself
> they display birth, illness, old age, and death.
>
> 3) After the heirs of the Victorious One
> have realized this changeless state,
> those who are blinded by ignorance
> see them being born and so forth.
> 4) That such seeing should occur is truly wonderful and amazing.
> When they have attained the field of experience of the noble,
> they show themselves as the field of experience of the children.
> Hence means and compassion of the friends of beings are supreme.
>
> 5) Though they are beyond all worldly matters,
> these [bodhisattvas] do not leave the world.
> They act for the sake of all worldly beings
> within the world, unblemished by its defects.
> 6) As a lotus will grow in the midst of water,
> not being polluted by the water's [faults],
> these [noble ones] are born in the world
> unpolluted by any worldly phenomena.

7) Viewing the accomplishment of their task,
their understanding always blazes like fire.
And they always rest evenly balanced
as meditative stability, which is peace.

8) By the power of their former [prayers]
and since they are free from all ideation,
they do not exert any deliberate effort
to lead all sentient beings to maturation.
9) These [heirs of the Victorious One] know precisely
how and by what [method] each should be trained—
through whatever teachings, form kayas, conduct,
and ways of behaviour are individually appropriate.
10) Always [acting] spontaneously and without hindrance
for sentient beings whose number is limitless as space,
such [bodhisattvas] who possess understanding
truly engage in the task of benefitting beings.

11) The way the bodhisattvas [unfold activity]
in the post-meditative phase
equals the tathagatas' [action] in the world
for being's true liberation.
12) Though this is true, indeed, whatever difference lies
between the earth and an atom or else between
[the water in] the sea and in an ox's hoofprint,
is the difference between a buddha and a bodhisattva.[46]

First the eastern petal, ruled by Aries the ram, denoted 'the Middle Path', is implicated by means of introducing the subject of 'the noble ones' (Bodhisattvas). Treading the Bodhisattva path by following Gautama's Noble Middle Way via manifesting skilful means through compassionate action awakens the attributes of the Heart centre. The Bodhisattvic purpose is not just to eradicate their own suffering, but also that of all sentient beings. This path produces liberation for all. In the consequent residence in the Suchness of being/non-being there is no cause of suffering or its fruit.

The second quatrain relates to the Taurean petal, denoted 'liberation', which allows Bodhisattvas to see 'reality as it is'. Though

46 Rosemarie Fuchs, 28-29.

the Bodhisattvas (of the higher degrees) technically need no longer incarnate, but do so because of compassionate considerations, whereby they experience the normal processes of being incarnate in a transient form. Taurus the bull relates to the attainment of wisdom, and the consequent opening of the all-seeing Eye. Such wisdom plans the rebirthing process, clothing the thought-process of the remainder of the turning of this wheel, so as to maximally produce the most beneficent effect upon the target groups with view of their final liberation from *saṃsāra.* The Eye peers far into the future so that the planned work is efficacious. *Maṇḍalas* of constructive thought are then built and energised with liberating purpose.

Next upon the wheel of the Heart centre is the petal governed by Gemini the twins. (One being immortal and the other mortal.) Here we have the dichotomy between the immortal twin, the 'heirs of the Victorious One' and the mortal one, those 'blinded by ignorance'. These blinded ones do not see the inner reality of the true nature of the Bodhisattvas (signifying the Temple of Life governed by Gemini), rather the illusionality of the phenomenal appearance. They must develop the 'calmness of mind' (the keynote of this petal) which will enable them to perceive reality, thence gain the deathlessness of the enlightened ones.

Fourth, the Cancerian petal is designated 'discerning the real'. Cancer the crab relates to the birthing process, here of the higher, enlightened vision ('such seeing should occur is truly wonderful') into the blinded ones. This comes as a consequence of meditative discipline whereby inner quietude is achieved, and 'the real' discerned. (Technically by the time the Libran petal is awakened.) The Bodhisattva path then opens up, whereby the skills can be gained to teach the 'children', the novices upon the path, the supreme way of compassion.

The fifth petal is governed by Leo the lion, who represents the self-conscious personality, thus the ego-forming tendencies of the intellectual prowess that rules the material domain of our civilisations. Consequently, this fifth verse focuses upon 'all worldly matters', which the Bodhisattvas must inevitably master. Within the constraints of the materialism they act for the sake of all, 'unblemished by its defects'. The related liberated quality is Voidness, which the Bodhisattva resides in, labouring to teach others its veracity, so that true selflessness of mind is attained, countering the major attribute developed by most people at this stage of the evolutionary process.

The sixth petal is governed by Virgo the virgin, who rules the attributes of the entire material domain. Here the lotus of consciousness-expansion has its roots in the soil of *saṃsāra* and resides in the watery muck of people's emotional nature, yet the Bodhisattva, empowered by *bodhicitta,* is not polluted by such mire. The associated liberated quality is 'comprehending it' (the Voidness associated with the previous sign) which those that are endeavouring to travel the Bodhisattva way must achieve. They undertake the process of purifying and transforming their *saṃskāras* containing *saṃsāric* defilements so that all the petals of their *chakras* awaken appropriately to shine spotlessly in the light of the spiritual sun.

The next petal is governed by Libra the balances and the quality *'samādhi',* complete absorbed contemplation upon the objective of the meditation practice. Libra, the judge and ruler of *karma,* governs the entire meditation process, thus the way of attainment for the *yogin,* and the production of 'meditative stability'. The judgemental decisions of the enlightened Libran is always 'evenly balanced', fully aware of the factors and forces needed to produce enlightenment for those they are educating. This cogent wisdom is a blaze of Fiery light able to incorporate the highest revelations. This is necessary if the Bodhisattva is to appropriately liberate people from the fields of suffering.

The eighth petal is governed by the attributes of Scorpio the scorpion and the processes producing the testings upon the path to enlightenment. For most aspirants many trials and tribulations are undertaken as they struggle to overcome their materialistic incentives and motivations. However for the Bodhisattva, with a large number of lives of achievement, the force *(vāsanā)* of their former *sādhana, dharānīs,* mantras and meditative concentration makes travelling upon the path relatively effortless. The force of compassion *(bodhicitta)* is effectively instinctual which manifests via Bodhisattvas 'to lead all sentient beings to maturation'. The inherent attribute of this petal is denoted 'not otherwise Thusness'.

Ninth is Sagittarius the archer, who fires one-pointed arrows of aspiration or revelation to achieve a foreordained goal. Bodhisattvas consequently 'know precisely how and by what [method] each should be trained', how to stimulate appropriate vision of the goal of 'error-free Thusness' (the key attribute of this petal) in those they seek to help. Apprehending the vision of what is to be achieved, the disciples of the Bodhisattva can then forthrightly set out to achieve that goal with minimal divergence.

The tenth petal is governed by the attributes of Capricorn the goat, who governs the mountain of attainment, the mount of mind/Mind that all must master if enlightenment is their goal. Upon this mount the vision of the task is clearly seen in the Thusness (the characteristics of this petal) of absolute Revelation. Consequently, the needs of all 'sentient beings whose number is limitless as space' can be discerned and spontaneously administered to. The term 'space' here implicates all aspects of Mind, the levels of *dharmakāya,* thus it includes a vast cosmic perspective, as well as the needs of the minds evolving upon our earth sphere. All are brought into one inclusive meditative absorption, that is incorporated as the meaning of the word 'Thusness'.

The eleventh verse signifies the attributes of Aquarius the water bearer, who dispenses the Waters of Life to all needy ones who thirst for the *dharma.* This relates to the manner of activity of all Bodhisattvas, and is limited only by their level of attainment *(bhūmi).* The greater the attainment, the greater the ability to quench the spiritual thirst of those that seek. This verse consequently compares the various forms of activity of Bodhisattvas with that of Buddhas, stating that the way enlightened Bodhisattvas manifest their activities equals that of Buddhas. The quality of this petal is designated 'lack of character', which has reference to Thusness that is free of all nameable attributes, as symbolised by the free-flowing energy attributed to Aquarius.

By introducing the Bodhisattva *bhūmis* here, this hints that these verses also relate to them, as Obermiller posits concerning ten of these statements.[47]

> In short the 4 kinds of the Bodhisattvas on the 10 Stages, in the state which is partly pure and partly impure, are demonstrated in these

---

47 Obermiller omits the first of the twelve verses and combines the second and third of the above verses into one, with the rest following accordingly. Thus his verses 66 and 67 correspond to verses 2, 3 and 4 from Fuchs' translation, and the remaining verses correlate accordingly.

> verses. The 4 kinds of the Bodhisattvas are:—1) He who has made the first Creative Effort (as a Saint), 2) he who exercises the activity of a Saint, 3) he who has attained the Irretrievable State, and 4) he who is separated (from Buddhahood) only by one birth. The first and second verse (66 and 67) show the perfectly pure nature of the properties of the Bodhisattva who makes the first Creative Effort (of a Saint) on the Stage of Joy, as he has (for the first time) the intuition of the Transcendental Absolute Essence which had not been perceived by him before from the outset. The third and fourth verses (68 and 69) show the same with regard to the Bodhisattva who exercises the activity (of a Saint) beginning with the Immaculate Stage and up to the Motionless, as he acts without being affected (by the defiling elements). The fifth verse (70) demonstrates the perfectly pure character of the properties of the Bodhisattva who has attained the Irretrievable State, as he, abiding on the Motionless Stage, is constantly merged in trance in order to attain Supreme Enlightenment. The sixth, the seventh and the eighth verses (71, 72 and 73) show the perfectly pure character of the properties of the Bodhisattva when he, abiding on the Stage called the Clouds of the Truth, has reached the uttermost limits of skill in fulfilling his own aim and that of others, and is separated from the attainment of the Stage of the Buddha and the Perfect Supreme Enlightenment only by one birth. [42 a. 1.] Finally, the ninth and the tenth verses (74 and 75) make known the similarity of the properties of the Bodhisattva who has finally attained his own aim and that of others, with those of the Buddha, and the difference between them.[48]

Such an exoteric doctrine concerning the nature of the Bodhisattva is too rigid a concept to be able to explain the true nature of the way that Bodhisattvas actually manifest, or of the nature of their accomplishment. Everything is much more fluid (as per the wavy lines denoting the Aquarian glyph) and governed by karmic considerations, as well as the Initiation level the Bodhisattva has attained. The last two volumes of this *Treatise on Mind* will endeavour to explain the Initiation process, as well as the way the Council of Bodhisattvas are structured in relation to Shambhala. This concerns organisation of the Ray Ashrams of the Masters of Wisdom (the most senior members of this Council). The true nature of this Council has been veiled in the *buddhadharma,* and can now

48 Obermiller, 201-202.

be revealed in conjunction with this esoteric view of the *tathāgatagarbha* and of the detailed explanation of the activity of the *chakras.*

The twelfth quatrain is governed by the attributes of Pisces the fishes, signifying the ending of the cycle of attainment, and also of bondage between a higher directing principle and that which represents embodied form. Such bondage is here indicated by the 'difference between a buddha and a bodhisattva', where the vastness of a Buddha's attainment compared to that of a Bodhisattva is shown via two similes. Obermiller has 'Like the great Earth and a grain of sand, Or like the ocean and (a pool of water) Left in a foot-print of a bull'.[49] The nature of these differences depends upon the degree of attainment (Initiation status) of the Bodhisattva concerned. The comparative differences can therefore only be truly known by those that have attained high Initiations, such as the author of this *śastra,* and cannot really be conveyed to the uninitiated. Their comprehension will be like that of a 'pool of water' left 'in a foot-print of a bull' compared to an ocean.

The imagery of a bull is purposely used because it hearkens that a certain wisdom has been attained (as symbolised by the attributes of Taurus) by the lesser Initiated, and more materialistically so by the non-Initiated.

There is however a link between the Council of Bodhisattvas and the Buddha, as these great Bodhisattvas were formerly his disciples, and subjectively the relationship persists. The quality attributed to this petal of the Heart lotus is 'without extremes', signifying that despite the perceived 'extremes', as noted in this verse, there is a subjective unity, and that all ultimately become Buddhas. All move together as one body of an organism, as seen from the vast perspective of a Logoic Mind, which is inclusive of a Buddha-Mind.

The *dharmakāya* and the *tathāgatagarbha*

Now is presented twelve quatrains dealing with the *dharmakāya* as a state of perfect purification. The quatrains relate to attributes that are responsible for empowering the Sacrifice-Will petals of the Sambhogakāya Flower, and directly pertain to the awakening and qualities of the twelve main petals of the Head lotus (*sahasrāra padma*).

49 Obermiller, 201.

This is the third level of the attributes governing the *tathāgatagarbha,* earlier designated as "'being", "bodhisattva", and "tathagata"'. I shall again number the quatrains for easier explanation.

> 1) [The dharmakaya] does not change into something else, since it has inexhaustible properties.
> It is the refuge of beings, since [it protects them] without any limit of time, until the final end.
> It is always free from duality, since it is foreign to all ideation.
> It is also an indestructible state, since its nature is uncreated.
>
> 2) It is not born, and it does no die.
> It suffers no harm and does not age
> since it is permanent and steadfast,
> the state of peace and immutability.
>
> 3) It is not [even] born in a body of mental nature,
> since it is permanent. Steadfast it does not die,
> not [even] through the death and transmigration
> that constitute an inconceivable transformation.
> 4) Since it is peace, it does not [even] suffer harm
> from illness caused by subtle karmic imprints.
> Since it is immutable, there is not [even] aging
> induced by compositional factors free from stain.
>
> 5) [Combining] sentences from the foregoing
> two by two, the uncreated expanse should be known
> [as possessing] in the same sequence
> the attributes of being permanent and so forth.
>
> 6) Since it is endowed with inexhaustible qualities, [the dharmakaya]
> is unchangingness itself and thus [has] the attribute of permanence.
> Equaling the uttermost end it is refuge itself
> and thus [holds] the attribute of steadfastness.
> 7) Since absence of thought is its nature, it is dharmata
> free from duality and thus [has] the attribute of peace.
> Hosting uncreated qualities, it is immutability itself
> and thus [possesses] the attributes of indestructibility.

8) Why is it the dharmakaya, the tathagata,
the noble truth, and the absolute nirvana?
Its qualities are inseparable, like the sun and its rays.
Thus other than buddhahood there is no nirvana.

9) Since the unpolluted expanse has, put briefly,
four different types of meaning,
it should be known in terms of four synonyms:
the dharmakaya and so forth.

10) Buddha qualities are indivisible.
The disposition is attained as it is.
The true state is [always] free from fickleness and deceit.
Since beginningless time the nature has been peace itself.

11) Direct perfect enlightenment [with regard to] all aspects,
and abandonment of the stains along with their imprints
[are called] buddha and nirvana respectively.
In truth, these are not two different things.

12) Liberation is distinguished by indivisibility
from qualities present in all their aspects:
innumerable, inconceivable, and unpolluted.
Such liberation is [also called] "tathagata."[50]

Very little can be said about the Head centre at this stage because of the complexity of the subject. Detail concerning the nature of just one major petal is provided in chapter 7 of Volume 5A. The twelve main petals shall be relegated to the twelve signs of the zodiac, as with the Heart lotus, and indeed convey the true import of the energies of these signs when properly interpreted. I shall, however, only briefly integrate the symbolism concerning the main attributes of these petals to the information presented in the twelve quatrains.

As the subject matter is the *dharmakāya,* hence dealing with abstractions, the true import of the verses will be known only to the enlightened. The correlation to the signs of the zodiac start with Capricorn, which in this brief enumeration allows placing the attributes

50 Rosemarie Fuchs, 29-30.

of these twelve verses upon the wheel of the Head lotus. From this it is possible to discern the types of *saṃskāras* that are the focus of the twelve main petals and which are processed to produce the *dharmakāyic* characteristics indicated.

Beginning with the subject of the *dharmakāya,* and hence the attribute ascertained via the northernmost petal of the thousand petalled lotus, we are told that it is unchangeable and inexhaustible. This necessitates the entire *sahasrāra padma* to be awakened (in all of its five levels) and receptive to the impress from *dharmakāya.* This northern petal is then the directive agent to the vastness of *dharmakāya.* There is no need for thought-constructs, simply an originating query, and in its limitless expanse of 'Knowingness' (ruled by Capricorn the goat, embodying the sum of the mountain of mind/Mind), the associated revelations will be seen. It is 'indestructible' because it is the experience of the vastness of cosmos, the Thusness thereof.

Next we are told that because it is 'permanent and steadfast', absolutely immutable and peaceful, it 'is not born, and it does not die'. These attributes are symbolised by the mutable bands of energy symbolising Aquarius, which pours forth the Waters of steadfast Revelation into the serene Mind-Space attained via this petal of the Head lotus. It lacks the characteristics of *saṃsāra.*

The third petal is that governed by the characteristics of Pisces the fishes, which ends the cycles of activity with *saṃsāra* (of 'death and transmigration'), producing 'an inconceivable transformation' of experience into cosmic perception. (The Waters of cosmic space.) The form body is no longer a consideration (the bond thereto has been broken), hence there are 'no extremes', simply an absorption into the vast permanence of the All. Therein new projections *(antaḥkaraṇas)* are made to various destinations (Buddha or stellar-spheres) wherein the requisite revelations are to be obtained.

Next is the easternmost petal, formerly relegated 'the Middle Path', as governed by Aries the ram. The various forms of the will (governed by the Arian impetus), generated by the *yogin,* the Will-to-Love, the Will-of-Love and Divine Will[51] formerly projected via the Life cycles of the turning of the wheel of Life, of the zodiac, have overcome all

51 See Volume 4, pages 202-221.

negative *saṃskāras* that produce sickness, disease and death. There is only the tranquil dynamic Will perceiving the vastness of the Heart that is the governing All, which 'is peace' *(śūnyatā).*

The fifth petal is governed by the attributes of Taurus the bull, hence of immaculate wisdom, and the awakened all-seeing Eye. Liberation is the keyword. Here the fifth verse informs us that we must combine the sentences of the previous phrases (Obermiller has 'words'[52]). The implication here is of an internal dialogue (within the *dharmakāya)* of what type of Thought-construct is needed to produce a given end. Hence any of the characteristics already provided can be combined to produce the outcome. (Similar to the Buddha after his *nirvāṇa* under the *bodhi* tree determining whether to give his revelations to the world or not.) Taurus clothes the Divine Thought. This petal consequently directs the Eye (Ājñā centre) to produce the image of what must be. The concept of 'two by two' here also implies duality, esoterically the projection of impressions from the *dharmakāya* (words, sentences) into manifestation (minds in *saṃsāra),* in accord with Bodhisattvic activity.

Sixth, the petal governed by the attributes of Gemini the twins, who rule the Temple of Life, accessed by the two paths *(iḍā* and *piṇgalā),* which in this case represent the twins holding hands in service to enter this temple. In this verse the *iḍā (manasic)* quality, as the foundation of the inexhaustible *dharmakāya,* is characterised by the 'unchangingness', thus the attribute of permanence. That which was formerly quite changeable (the 'mortal brother'), the intellectual *(iḍā)* aspect and the myriad thought permutations of the personal-I, has been transformed into the wisdom characteristics of the *dharmakāya.* The *piṇgalā* characteristics evolved into an ocean-like compassion, which now has 'the attributes of steadfastness'. These characteristics then are what this petal floods the *nāḍīs*[53] of manifestation with. The associated petal of the Heart centre is designated 'calmness of mind', which must be attained if *dharmakāya* is to be realised.

The next petal is governed by the characteristics of Cancer the crab, the polar opposite of Capricorn. Normally, Cancer represents the open

52 'Here two words and the following two (Are explained) by two and again by two, respectively, Making known, in regard of the Absolute Essence, The meaning of "Eternal" and the rest'. Obermiller, 204.

53 The *nāḍī* system and blood stream are also ruled by the sign Gemini.

gate into incarnation, but here it represents the doorway to liberated space. This doorway is constructed once the mind frees itself from chattering thought and dialectics. The duality of 'self' and 'other' does not exist in the serene space of absorption in *dharmatā* that comes as a consequence of transforming the attributes of manifestation (the destructable) associated with incarnation, thus is indestructible. From this Cancerian position the process of transformation of *saṃsāric* attributes begins to eventually reach the heights of *dharmakāyic* revelation associated with the sign Capricorn. Thereby one 'discerns the real'.

The eighth petal is governed by the sign Leo the lion, the sign of the self-conscious, intelligent and hence enquiring personality. For this reason the corresponding eighth verse begins with a question, which the personal-I is expected to answer once the necessary yogic disciplines and meditations are undertaken successfully. The four subjects that are the objects of this query need to be meditated upon, producing internal revelations that bypass the active critically deductive mind. The differences between these four topics will then be considered expressions of each other, 'like the sun and its rays'. The *dharmakāya* is the nature of a Buddha's Mind, hence 'the noble truth' is consequently taught, and 'absolute nirvana' is the space within which such a noble One resides, to travel to far distant *dharmakāyic* shores within cosmos. The reference here to a sun and its rays also relates to the sign Leo, as the sun is both its esoteric and exoteric ruler. The attribute of Voidness (the elimination of the concept of 'self') is the assignment of the corresponding petal of the Heart centre.

The ninth petal is the seat of Virgo the virgin, thus the sum total of material space, as governed by the attributes of the mind/Mind that rules the appearance of all phenomena. The associated quality of this petal of the Heart centre is 'comprehending it', meaning the use of the Mind to comprehend the nature of this appearing phenomena plus its relation to Voidness. Once mastered and transmuted this material substance becomes 'the unpolluted expanse' (of cosmos), comprehension of which is given birth to via this sign. Hence the ontology, the true nature of the four synonyms given above become thoroughly experienced.

Such realisations come as a consequence of the *samādhi* manifested in the petal ruled by the next sign, Libra the balances, which governs the faculty of meditation. Such *samādhi,* being error-free, by overcoming 'fickleness and deceit', reaches out to the far reaches of the cosmic ocean (*dharmakāya*). In relation to this Obermiller's rendition is valuable, where translating the *dharmakāya* as 'the Cosmical Body', he states:

> (It is the Cosmical Body, since)
> The properties of the Buddha are indivisible (manifesting themselves in all that exists).
> (It is the Buddha)—
> Because the Germ has developed in him into the Absolute.
> (It is the Highest Truth), being neither error nor illusion,
> (And it is Nirvāṇa), being by nature quiescent from the outset.[54]

Here we are reminded that the focus of these verses relate to the attributes of the 'Germ', the *tathāgatagarbha,* or rather, the means whereby the attributes of enlightenment can be incorporated into the Sacrifice-Will petals of this Flower, as well as being accommodated by the Head lotus. 'Since beginningless time' this Buddha-germ 'has been peace itself', since it resides in the abstracted domains beyond the whirlwind of *saṃsāric* activity.

The eleventh petal is ruled by Scorpio the scorpion, which is concerned with the testings associated with the cleansing of untoward *karma* and the thorough refinement of *saṃskāras.* (The 'abandonment of the stains along with their imprints'.) 'Perfect enlightenment' is the gain, the making of a Buddha and his residence in *nirvāṇa.* This petal of the Head lotus consequently projects *prāṇas* to the centres below the diaphragm (Splenic centres I and II) with the aim of the total conversion and transmutation of the manifesting *prāṇas* so that complete enlightenment is possible. A Buddha is thereby wrought out of this transformed substance. When transmuted, this substance establishes residence in the higher, transcendental dimensions of perception *(nirvāṇa)* wherein a Buddha resides. One must take into account that the *saṃskāras* represent the consciousness-attributes that a person resides in. They determine the characteristics of consciousness that are expressed as people's total psyche. Their transformed and transmuted attributes become the *dharmakāya* that is the Mind of a Buddha. The related quality of the Heart centre is 'not otherwise thusness'.

54 Obermiller, 205-206.

Finally we have the Sagittarian petal, who fires the arrows of sure-sighted direction to achieve the intended goal or target. (The *dharmakāya* represented by the next, Capricornian petal.) In this case it is 'liberation', which is 'distinguished by indivisibility from qualities present in all their aspects'. Such unqualified liberation, which combines the two truths into unity ('error-free thusness'), is then the Tathāgata. (At first in the form of the *tathāgatagarbha,* and later even liberation from that sublime form.)

The Parable of the Painting

Having analysed the Head lotus and the Heart centre with respect to the attributes of the Sambhogakāya Flower, it now remains to consider the rest of the body of manifestation, the general *chakra* system. This is illustrated by the parable of the painting.

> Suppose some painters mastered their craft,
> each with respect to a different [part of the body],
> so that whichever part one would know how to do,
> he would not succeed without any other part.
> Then the king, the ruler of the country,
> hands them a canvas and gives the order:
> 'You all together paint my image on this!'
> Having heard this [order] from the [king]
> they carefully take up their painting work.
> While they are well immersed in the task,
> one among them leaves for another country.
> Since they are incomplete
> due to his travel abroad,
> their painting in all its parts
> does not get fully perfected.
> Thus the example is given.[55]

The symbolism of a painting is used because it depicts the colourings and form of whatever the artists (here representing the *chakras)* intend to portray. Each painter is a specialist in only part of the body, and all are needed for the complete view. Similarly, the *chakras* are only

55 Rosemarie Fuchs, 31.

responsible for the arenas of the body they are situated in and deal with the colourations *(prāṇas)* of that area and arena for which they are the custodians. However, they also have direct relations to other *chakras* via the *nāḍī* system, in a similar manner that the painters need to work together. The king (the centrally integrating Head lotus, or else the *tathāgatagarbha)* gives an order for the *chakras* to paint an image of the complete integrated view, relating therefore to the course of enlightenment. To gain enlightenment all of the component parts of the *nāḍī* system must work in perfect accord manifesting their various specialities. No matter how well the other 'artists' do their job, if one aspect of the integrated view is left incomplete (going to another country) then the image of the 'king', the enlightenment-principle, cannot be fulfilled. Enlightenment therefore necessitates the mastery of the potency of all the *chakras* and their effects.

Enlightenment is also the result of group effort and group service work, where all Bodhisattvas (painters) are engrossed in their various specialised roles to paint the complete picture of the task of enlightening any nation or civilisation. This is the way that the *dharma* (the painting) is spread by the council of Bodhisattvas (the *saṇgha)* under the directives of a central enlightening principle, the king/Buddha.

This process of gaining enlightenment is elaborated in the verses composing the remainder of this section.

> Who are the painters [parts of the image]?
> They are generosity, morality, patience, and so on.
> Emptiness endowed with all supreme aspects
> is described as being in the form [of the king].
>
> Illuminating, radiating, and purifying,
> and inseparable from each other, analytical wisdom,
> primordial wisdom, and total liberation
> correspond to the light, rays, and orb of the sun.
>
> One will therefore not attain nirvana
> without attaining the state of buddhahood.
> Just as one could not see the sun
> if one were to eliminate its light and its rays.

In this way the nature of the Victorious One
is expressed [by] the 'Tenfold Presentation'.[56]

Here another interpretation of the painters of parts of the image is revealed, namely the *pāramitās,* the transcendental virtues. Normally six of these are presented, though sometimes seven or ten. Ten are here indicated by the final statement 'is expressed [by] the "Tenfold Presentation"', though this presentation also has other connotations. The *pāramitās* are needed to be expressed to perfection if the potencies of the *chakras* are to be fully awakened on the path to enlightenment.

I shall only list the *pāramitās* here, as they are explained elsewhere, and they are a well known topic amongst Buddhists. 1) generosity (*dāna-pāramitā*) producing self-sacrifice, 2) moral discipline (*śīla pāramitā*), producing all-embracing Love, 3) patience (*kṣānti pāramitā*), eliminating intolerance, 4) diligent effort (*vīrya pāramitā*), producing the steadfast path to enlightenment, 5) meditation (*dhyāna pāramitā*), producing the realisation of the immaculate nature of Mind, 6) wisdom (*prajñāpāramitā*), producing complete enlightenment. If ten are required, then to the above six can be added 7) skilful means *(upāya),* 8) prayer or aspiration *(praṇidhāna),* 9) power to rightly act *(bala),* and 10) pristine cognition *(jñāna).*

Following these wisdoms together produce the experience of Emptiness 'endowed with all supreme aspects'. They therefore produce the highest of attainments, the complete 'picture of the king', all of the *chakras* in the *nāḍī* system fully awakened and active. Their qualities illuminate the mind/Mind, purify the defilements and transform *saṃskāras,* thereby producing the natural radiance of the Clear Mind. The attributes of this Mind then manifest in terms of three characteristics of *dharmakāya;* 'analytical wisdom', when relating to things pertaining to *saṃsāra,* 'primordial wisdom' when residing in its own natural state, and 'total liberation' (unfettered *nirvāṇa)* when travelling the far reaches of cosmos. The triads of attributes are then said to correspond to 'light, rays, and orb of the sun'. Here then we are again reminded of the three tiers of petals of the Sambhogakāya

56 Ibid., 31-32.

Flower, where 'light, rays, and orb of the sun' relate to the general characteristics of its form as observed by clairvoyant vision. Here the attributes of the Knowledge petals are indicated. The 'Illuminating, radiating, and purifying' attributes relate to the attributes of the three Love-Wisdom petals, whilst 'analytical wisdom, primordial wisdom, and total liberation' relate to the three Sacrifice-Will petals, when obtaining impressions via the Śūnyatā Eye, producing the eventual demise of this Flower's form as the energies passing through this Eye become too great for the Flower to bear, hence producing 'total liberation'. This step is then necessary to attain Buddhahood.

The 'Tenfold Presentation' can therefore refer to these nine petals, plus that associated with the Śūnyatā Eye. It can also refer to the painters as Bodhisattvas, each embodying one or other of the ten *pāramitās,* or else the usual six plus emptiness, 'all supreme aspects' and manifesting in the form of a king (of wisdom), all as attributes of the Buddha-germ. The 'king' (in the form of the *tathāgatagarbha)* is then 'Illuminating, radiating, and purifying', manifesting 'analytical wisdom, primordial wisdom, and total liberation', corresponding to 'the light, rays, and orb of the sun'. As Bodhisattvas, the 'painters' also evolve via the ten Bodhisattva stages whilst manifesting their spiritual powers.

Next is presented a series of nine examples illustrating the characteristics of the *tathāgatagarbha,* which shall be the subject of chapter 7B.

7

The Ratnagotravibhāga Śāstra and the Sambhogakāya Flower

PART B
Nine illustrations characterising the *tathāgatagarbha*

The levels of perception

In this chapter the triadic aspects of the *tathāgatagarbha* presented in the *Ratnagotravibhāga śāstra* shall be analysed through an examination of nine similes. The information is idealised and as such has a reference to the nine main petals of the Sambhogakāya Flower. A quote from Brian Edward Brown is a useful supplement to what was earlier said in chapter 7A concerning the *tathāgatagarbha* in all beings. He states that the *Ratnagotravibhāga* provides the meaning of the *tathāgatagarbha* 'in a trio of synonymous phrases'.[1] We thus have 3 x 3 meanings or qualities to consider:

> The first set is somewhat obscure and becomes clear only in the light of the two other triplicate combinations. It can be said that all beings are possessed of the Buddha-embryo since they are all equally included in the Buddha's Wisdom, because their inherent "immaculateness" is non-dual by nature, and because the result of that innate purity becomes manifest "on the germ *(gotra)* of the Buddha." There follows immediately the second parallel expression specifying the same intent as the first. Accordingly, all living beings are possessed of the embryo because of the universal penetration of all things by the Buddha's Body, because Suchness *(Tathatā)* is of undifferentiated nature, and because the germ *(gotra)* of the Buddha exists in all living beings. The third set of the coincident definitions states that due to the penetration of

1 Brian Edward Brown, *The Buddha Nature,* (Motilal Banarsidass, Delhi, 2004), 56.

> the Absolute Body *(Dharmakāya)* into all living beings, and because the Tathāgata is the Absolute Reality or Suchness *(Tathatā)* and is therefore the "undifferentiated whole," and finally, since the germ of the Tathāgata *(Tathāgatagotra)* exists in every living being, it may be said that all animate beings are possessed of the embryo of the Tathāgata *(sarvasattvās tathāgatagarbhāḥ).*[2]

In chapter 7A I noted that though these reasons for the existence of a Buddha-embryo is true for all sentient beings, nevertheless there is a distinction between the existence of a *tathāgatagarbha* for a human kingdom and the direct expression of the Monadic Presence (the Buddha-essence) incorporated in and directing animal sentience en-masse via various streams of the categories of lives in Nature, and also via the agency of the *deva* kingdom. Such technicalities have not yet been established in Buddhist eschatology and are avoided in the texts. Nevertheless, the esoteric doctrine can now cogently be established. In short, humans possess a specialised Soul-form, a *gotra,* which is needed to process the *saṃskāras* of mind/Mind, which animals do not possess and have no need, neither can they consciously work to gain liberation. The *tathāgatagarbha* is also needed to process the evolutionary development of each individualised consciousness-stream via a sequence of rebirths that inevitably will produce liberation. *Devas* and *ḍākinīs* on the other hand, play a similar role with directing the streams of animal sentience towards their 'liberation', namely becoming members of a human kingdom via the necessary formation of the structure of the Sambhogakāya Flower. This Flower can then process the consequent evolution of human consciousness.

Rūpa, kāma and *arūpalokas*

The various *lokas*[3] (levels) of the Abhidharma *cakravāla* (world system) should be briefly explained. Three realms are depicted: *rūpaloka*, the formed realms, comprised of eighteen 'heavenly' states of corporeal

---

2 Ibid.

3 Alternatively, *dhātu,* meaning 'root or base', fundamental stratum, realm of being, constituent Element, or part of a world construct. It comprises the categories of classes of all manifested things.

existence without desire, grouped according to four zones of meditation; the *kāmaloka* or desire realm, with six levels, and the *arūpaloka*, or the formless realm, with four *dhyāna* (meditation) levels.

Kāmaloka consists of the sum of the world of human desire, of the body of cravings and sense-contact with the phenomenal world. Hence we have the input from the five sense-consciousnesses plus the collating intellect. This desire body is also seeded with *kliṣṭamanas*. One could make a case that the six 'heavens' associated with the *kāmaloka* relate to the six petals of the Sacral centre (which governs the field of desire in the body) and their extensions into the *nāḍī* system. The four *rūpaloka* zones then embody the attributes of the four petals of the Solar Plexus centre governed by the incoming and outgoing *iḍā* and *piṇgalā nāḍīs,* leaving six petals free that interrelate *prāṇas* with the Inner Round of minor *chakras*.[4] (These six petals then process the *prāṇas* groupings of six, or of their constituent triads, of this *loka.)* The four 'heavens' of the *arūpaloka* then relate to the incoming and outgoing *iḍā* and *piṇgalā nāḍīs* to the Heart or Throat centres, depending upon the type of qualities one would attribute to these formless zones (viewed from the standpoint of the centres below the diaphragm).

The four *rūpaloka* zones of meditation (forms of meditative concentration or awareness) can be considered to refer to the four sub-planes of the concrete mental realms. The eighteen subsidiary states are classified according to the gains from the perceptions of the 'six sense-consciousnesses', the related sense organs, and objects of perception. These attributes are then exoterically reflected in the domain of the mind. The eighteen 'heavens' are philosophically divided into three groups of three (each therefore dealing with the *prāṇas* of body, speech and mind, the corporeal physical and mental attributes) for these three levels. The final of the four 'heavens' consists of nine such subdivisions, thus dealing with the more subjective attributes of 'body, speech and mind' as derived from the lower triads.[5]

These four 'heavens' are more esoterically viewed in terms of mental-emotional *saṃskāras* that are distilled into the four levels of progressively

4 See Volume 5A, chapter 5, for detail on this subdivision of the Solar Plexus centre.

5 See Adrian Snodgrass, *The Symbolism of the Stupa* (Motilal Barnasidass, 1992), 131, for a diagram illustrating these 'heavens'.

refined substance of the mind. They deal with processing the Elements of Earth, Water, Fire and Air as subdivisions of the Fiery Element. Cleansing, refining and transmuting the import of the dross of these *saṃskāras* by a *yogin* produces the 'heavens' of the four meditation stages.

From a different perspective one could also observe the sum of the formed nature of the human equipment of response. This is the instrument through which the meditating one functions and experiences, consisting of the dense physical form, the etheric body (incorporating the *nāḍī* system), the Watery astral body and the Fiery empirical mind. All associated factors and forces together constitute the aggregates and mind, the qualities of the personal-I, upon which the worthy one meditates.

The *arūpaloka* (the 'four meditative absorptive' states) relate to the three higher abstracted realms of consciousness, signifying the higher Mind, where the three main tiers of the Sambhogakāya Flower are found, plus that associated with the three central bud-like petals prior to abstraction into *śūnyatā*. We therefore have the *śūnyatā-saṃsāra* nexus, which represents the highest of the four *arūpaloka* 'heavens'. The three other levels are:

a. *Dharmatā,* which conditions the Sacrifice (or Will[6]) petals, which are built of the substance of the most refined sub-plane of the abstract Mind. *Dharmatā* projects the *dharmakāya* into manifestation via the activity of these petals. Inevitably when what is knowable awakens in consciousness the condition termed ignorance is overcome. This is the purpose of the driving force causing the appearance of successive incarnations of personal-I's. They experience phenomena by means of sense-perceptions, but inevitably must transcend that process to directly experience the *dharmakāya.* As a consequence, all *saṃsāric* allurements are mastered when the lower sense contacts are sacrificed via the higher guiding impulses. With the force of *dharmatā* the Sacrifice petals of the Sambhogakāya Flower organise the long aeonic process related to the quest for knowledge and its liberating outcome.

These petals are situated upon the second highest of the four *arūpaloka* levels, which is designated *ākiñcanya*, the 'realm of

6 These petals manifest both as sacrificial intent, and also convey the energy of the will. They can thus be thought of as sacrificial will. For convenience they shall be labelled as Sacrifice petals throughout the text.

nothingness'. This is so designated because here the conceptual processes have been cleansed, with the remainder being the Clear Light of Mind in a quiescent state.

b. *Tathatā*[7] conditions the Love-Wisdom petals. This is the general conditioning qualification of the entire Flower. The principle of desire *(kāma)* and clinging that causes human beings to appropriate things for the pleasure of their concept of 'self' is initially seeded via these petals. Thus are caused the delusions of attachment and greed, the afflictions of mind *(kliṣṭamanas)* which must be overcome if love and wisdom are to be gained. The process of overcoming such attributes eventually awakens *bodhicitta. Bodhicitta* is the energy expressive of *tathatā,* with which the fabric of the Sambhogakāya Flower is constructed.

   The Love-Wisdom petals are situated upon the second of the four *arūpadhātu* levels (or the middle of the triad of the abstract Mind),[8] which is designated *vijñānānantya*, 'infinity of intellect', because here consciousness is abstracted and freed from all considerations of form. (Except when another personal-I is to incarnate.) The unit of consciousness resides within the ocean of consciousness that is the *ālayavijñāna,* and the naturalness of its own expression is infinite in its scope. The joyous emanation of consciousness on its own natural sphere of involvement demonstrates as *bodhicitta*, the compassionate-Mind, because such emanation is seeded from the prismatic ground of *tathatā.*

c. The *ālayavijñāna* conditions the Knowledge petals, which seeds the development of the intellect, with its separative and discriminative capabilities. From the lower mind comes knowledgeable pursuits, as

7 Brown states concerning *Tathatā* (Ibid., 58-59) that: 'Suchness is not only the unilateral "immaculateness" existing in all beings, the undifferentiated universal reality, but may, by affiliation, be characterised as omniscient wisdom. At this point in the analysis, such a reference is no more than suggested, and will only be further defined in the tenth chapter treating the transformation of *Samalā Tathatā* (Suchness mingled with pollution) into *Nirmalā Tathatā* (Suchness apart from pollution). But here is the nascent indication of Absolute Suchness *(Tathatā),* not statically conceived as latent and neutral entitative reality, but as dynamically operative and efficient permeation. This concept gains immediate reinforcement through the final term of the threefold equality, "the germ of the Tathāgata" (*Tathāgata-gotra*)'.

8 This is a generalisation. In effect the Flower moves from the lower *arūpadhātu* to this level as the attributes of these Love petals are developed.

well as criticisms and hatreds that afflict human beings. Eventually the mind creates the scaffolding of the illumination that produces the highest wisdom.

The lowest of the *arūpadhātus, ākāśānantya*, the 'infinity of space', manifests here, referring to the space that is discovered once the mind is freed from considerations of form.

The Six Realms and planetary evolution

Having established the foundation for comprehending the origination of ignorance, greed and hatred, the three poisons can be placed in the centre of the wheel of rebirth governing the Six Realms. They are symbolised in the form of a red cock (passionate desire and attachment), green snake (hatred, critical attitudes), and a black hog (ignorance). Each animal bites the other's tail, indicating the cyclic interrelatedness of all things in *saṃsāra*. The purpose for the existence of all the realms conditioned by the wheel of rebirth is for the denizens therein to gain eventual freedom from the respective limitations through developing wisdom. The wheels of each domain turn according to the precepts of a higher law that drives all to liberation. All are really expressions of the human condition (their mental-emotional constitution) in one way or another, and therefore find their foundation in the purpose of the rebirthing principle.

Briefly put, and observing the theory of the Six Realms as it presently stands, we can say that of the six *karmic* states, that of the *gods* is seeded by the *bījas* from the *dharmakāya*. The *dharmakāya* also emanates the *bījas* of *saṃsāra*, from whence we get the animal kingdom as the highest below the human. The means to salvation from this state is to obtain knowledgeable experiences.

Tathatā is the liberating heart of the realm of the *asuras/titans,* with their jealous and war-like disposition. Its lowest reflex is the realm of the *pretas*, who suffer the *karma* of extreme desire which is but an expression of *kliṣṭamanas*. The means of salvation from these realms is the development of *bodhicitta*, the thought of compassion.

Ālayavijñāna conditions the consciousness states of the human kingdom. There it helps to develop the illumination, the bright wisdom, that enables people to avoid *saṃsāric* ensnarements. It also contains the *bījas* of the hell-like states caused by plotting, planning, and scheming (i.e., using *kāma-manas*) against others with hate and manifest cruelty. Their way to salvation is to master all of the Six Realms by means of awakening the Heart's Mind.

The above is also indicated by Tsongkhapa in his *Commentary on the Yogācāra Doctrine of Mind,* as translated by Gareth Sparham:

> If one says that such appearances [of hell to humans] are visible to the sense-consciousness of those sentient beings, but that they are not the same as appearances visible to their *ālaya-vijñāna,* we answer that both of these appearances of the five objects to the sense-consciousness [i.e., the appearance of hell to humans and of the human realm to hell-beings] are also beheld by the *ālaya-vijñāna.*[9]

The actual ordering in the *Wheel of Life* (Tib. *srid-pa'i-khor-lo)* puts the three relatively pleasurable realms (gods, titans, humans) at the top of the *maṇḍala* and the more unfavourable states are placed below them. In Tantric terms this symbolises the division between that which is above the diaphragm (the more liberated states of being, containing the Heart, Throat, and Head centres) and that below, representing the Solar Plexus, Splenic and Sacral/Base of Spine centres. The Head lotus corresponds to the realm of the gods, the Heart centre to the human world, the Throat centre, to the realm of the *asuras*, the Solar Plexus centre to the animal realm, the Splenic centre to the realm of the *pretas*, and the Sacral/Base centres to the hell states. The aberrations of the *prāṇas* associated with these *chakras* cause the attributes ascribed to those ensconced in these realms. Effectively, however, all such aberrations are generated in centres below the diaphragm, with the *prāṇic* effects being carried through to the centres above. The abovementioned *chakras* present the major synthesising or abstracting centres for the wholesome *prāṇas* of the entities comprising the various realms (i.e., their place of storage), before transiting into the next higher level of expression for them.

The information presented earlier concerning the minor *chakras* (where both the Head and Heart centres also act to abstract *prāṇas*) concerns the zones of cleansing, i.e., experiencing the *karma* of the residents of the Six Realms. In the account below, the view shall be from the perspective of these residents representing certain planetary forces, rather than the Bardo experiences of humans.

---

9 Gareth Sparham, *Ocean of Eloquence.* (Sri Satguru, Delhi, 1995), 56.

The 'gods' experience *karma* in the outer tiers of petals in the Head lotus, and manifest an enlightened stance as they move towards the centre of the 1,000 petals.

Humans cleanse *karma* by way of the Heart centre. It represents the mode of evolution that develops wisdom via the driving force of *bodhicitta.* The Heart centre acts as a minor *chakra* up to the time of aspiration, and then treading the Bodhisattva path. Until then the Solar Plexus centre is dominant, awakening and invigorating the 'self' concept to override liberating considerations, whereas the purpose of the Heart centre is the production of selflessness.

From an esoteric perspective, taking the nature of *planetary evolution* into account, we see that humans evolve into 'gods', taking a 'god' here to represent an advanced component of a Buddha-Field.[10] Ultimately, it relates to one who has evolved far on the road of becoming an Ādi Buddha. This is the inevitable result of developing the qualities of being able to manifest in a 'god' realm.

Asuras (taking the term here to represent certain planetary conditioning or formative forces, *devas,* units of intelligent creative life[11]) evolve into *ḍākinīs.* (Entities that govern the disposition of karmic law upon our planet.) To do this they must master the complete qualities of Mind as they travel from the planetary twelve petalled Splenic centre to the Throat centre.

Pretas (lesser *devas* embodying the human emotions) evolve into the *devas* of the higher orders.[12] To do so they must evoke the qualities to manifest the full functions of the dual Splenic centre. Thereby they learn to properly vitalise all phenomenal life.

Animals evolve into humans. To do this they must travel from the minor centres of the Inner Round to the Solar Plexus centre. There are many cycles of rebirthings within Nature's kingdoms that are concerned with the in and outbreathing of the airs that vitalise all of the minor *chakras* in turn. They qualify the sum of the sentience of the animal

---

10 Vol. 5A, pages 146-69, has a different esoteric perspective on the symbolism of these realms.

11 From this perspective they are not 'jealous' of the gods, but rather control the karmic direction of human jealousy, and all kindred *kāma-manasic* attributes. In reality the denizens of the Six Realms are constituted by humans with their emotional-mental conditioning, plus the devic entities that embody the substance of their sheaths.

12 That is, members of the angelic kingdom.

kingdom causing them to progressively evolve. The Solar Plexus centre then becomes the centre wherein the self-will of a human is developed, thereby the concept of individual 'self'. This concept is one of the distinguishing factors between the human and animal kingdoms.

The residents of the *hells* evolve into enlightened beings through the cleansing of *karma.* They do this through the human development of positive control and transmutation of the qualities that sent them into the hell realms. They thereby become masters of yoga as they manifest the channels from the lower Splenic centre to the Sacral and Base of Spine centres, and then to the Head lotus. Enlightenment thereby ensues.

The outline presented above is also a view that concerns the analysis of differing types of *prāṇas* conveyed within the *nāḍīs.* This view helps to integrate the main elements of the philosophy of the nature of the manifestation of phenomena through the appearance of what can be termed a 'self', taking both *deva* and human evolution into account.

The nine major petals of the Sambhogakāya Flower

The three groups of three petals to the Sambhogakāya Flower's form, which exist upon the three higher, abstracted, mental realms can now be further analysed, as presented via the symbolism of the *Uttaratantra śastra.*

The three Knowledge petals

The Knowledge petals are concerned specifically with understanding the nature of things associated with *saṃsāric* activity.

a. The *Knowledge–Knowledge* petal.

   The phrase from Brown: 'all beings are possessed of the Buddha-embryo since they are all equally included in the Buddha's Wisdom' refers to the Sambhogakāya Flower as a unit, but in the lowest reflex a Buddha's Wisdom is an expression of knowledge of the material world. Each Sambhogakāya Flower is prearranged in its genesis by the originating Buddha (Monad), out of whose meditation-substance the *tathāgatagarbha* was constructed.

   The construction of such a form is necessary because this primeval Buddha can descend no further into embodied space than the second *dharmakāyic* level *(anupādaka).* Consequently, a form was constructed at the junction between *saṃsāra* and liberated space *(śūnyatā)* for compassionate reasons. Its purpose is to effect the liberation of the elementary lives imprisoned as the substance of *saṃsāra* by means of the formation of a vehicle of mind/Mind that would produce the necessary transformations and transmutations. This form is the *tathāgatagarbha,* and its instruments, the personal-I's that incarnate into the *māyā* and that transform base substance (signified by primeval ignorance) via the evolutionary process of first evolving mind and then its conversion into Mind. This is an outline of a vast eschatological ontology yet to be fully revealed.

The most basic petal of the Sambhogakāya Flower, the Knowledge—Knowledge petal, is at first vitalised with *prāṇas* derived from empirical observations, because the pursuit of knowledge in each personal-I is the beginning of the evolution of a Buddha's Wisdom. Consequently, each personal-I is rayed into *saṃsāra* to gain experience of the manifold vicissitudes of its phenomena, and the meaning of it all. The 'Buddha-embryo' thus incorporates via the Knowledge—Knowledge petal the understandings concerning phenomena gleaned from unfolding civilisations as gained by the succession of personal-I's that incarnate into them. Progressive streams of gained awareness then become the *bījas* in the embryo that work towards future enlightening activity. Consequently, the *bījas* concerned with the general *prāṇic* circulation of the average person are stored here, with their mental-emotional interactions right up to, and including, the awakening and functioning of the *manasic* output of the Throat centre, producing the foundation of wisdom.

b. The *Knowledge—Love-Wisdom* petal.

This petal is implicated by the phrase from Brown: 'because their inherent "immaculateness" is non-dual by nature'. Knowledge that becomes translated into Love-Wisdom is the driving force evolving a Buddha's wisdom. This energy clarifies the personal-I's mind to awaken *bodhicitta,* which works to unify the all into the One. It causes the drive towards liberation, which is 'non-dual', the correct way for consciousness to proceed. This petal processes the initial development of compassionate concepts, thus inevitably the role a Bodhisattva plays in the scheme of things in order to follow the Bodhisattva Path. The 'immaculateness' of the *buddhadharma* can then be understood.

Here the *bījas* associated with the minor *chakras* and those that will inevitably control the activity of the Solar Plexus centre are stored. They must be refined over time to express attributes of the Heart.

c. The *Knowledge–Sacrifice-Will* petal.

The associated phrase concerns the result of the progress towards liberation. Thus the 'innate purity [of consciousness] becomes manifest "on the germ *(gotra)* of the Buddha"'. This petal helps cause the sacrifice of all knowledgeable attachments to *saṃsāra,* which defile or debase the clarity of Mind. Thus it sweeps away the defilements of wrong thought processes. The detachment process produces the most refined type of consciousness, the Clear Mind that expresses the purpose of this petal. The revelations incorporate dispassionate considerations in relation to *saṃsāra.* They remove the obstacles of all forms of defiled mind through the force of the innate purity of consciousness of this petal. Here an inherent link to the *dharmakāya* is established, that all Sacrifice petals further engender, which makes an incarnate individual sacrifice all attributes of phenomena to reach that goal. Sound yogic logic is established, producing the elimination of the obstacles to enlightenment. The teaching value of pain and suffering, and necessary relinquishments over time become known. The way knowledge works within itself is comprehended, rather than the direct expression of embracive wisdom. The furtherance of knowledge necessitates struggle and effort in order to remove obstacles to higher realisations.

Here are stored the *bījas* that are responsible for the yogic control of the Sacral and Base of Spine centres and their relation to the Throat and Head centres. The pathways to the awakening of *kuṇḍalinī* can thereby be established. This necessitates the manifestation of the 'innate purity [of consciousness]' right through to the lowest centre of our psychic constitution.

The three Love-Wisdom petals

The second triad concerns the major qualities embodied by the Sambhogakāya Flower. This Flower is a vehicle of Love first and foremost, existing to transform the levels of desire-mind of the incarnate personality by impregnating the individual with *bodhicitta*. These petals embody the attributes that universally penetrate 'all things'. The *tathāgatagarbha* thereby manifests as a body of sacrificial love impregnated with wisdom. Therefore the actual compassionate substance of the Meditation-Mind of a Buddha is specifically imbued here, thus into the *tathāgatagarbha* as a unit. The Flowers work in conjunction with the compassionate doctrines from an externalised Tathāgata to produce liberation from *saṃsāra* over a huge expanse of evolutionary time.

a. The *Love-Wisdom—Sacrifice-Will* petal, assists in the 'universal penetration of all things by the Buddha's Body', as this petal wields intense liberating energies needed to be withstood by consciousness. They stimulate aspiration to Buddhahood. This penetration is a limitation (of the Buddha-Mind) and hence sacrifice on its own accord. For the *Knowledge—Knowledge* petal the statement presented is that 'all beings are possessed of the Buddha-embryo since they are all *equally included* in the Buddha's Wisdom'. Virtually the same words are given for the *Love-Wisdom—Sacrifice-Will petal,* but the emphasis is 'the universal penetration of all things'. This wisdom is not just included, but penetrates. This has reference to the *dharmakāya's* potency reaching right down into *saṃsāra*, to penetrate all with *bodhicitta*, and hence effect their eventual liberation from the formed realms. Thus the sacrificial potency of Love-Wisdom does not just affect the Flower, but penetrates and changes the brain consciousness of the incarnated personal-I's to manifest Buddha-like activity over evolutionary time.

   The *bījas* producing the complete awakening of the twelve petals of the rectified wheel, and thus of treading the Bodhisattva *bhūmis* to liberation are stored here. The *bījas* from this petal will eventually control the dynamics of the Splenic centres for the elimination of coarse *prāṇas* in the *nāḍīs* out of the system altogether. Thus we have the experience of the cleansing of *karma* and the transformation of *saṃskāras* by a *yogin*.

b. The *Love-Wisdom–Love-Wisdom* petal. This quality manifests because 'Suchness *(tathatā)* is of undifferentiated nature'. This phrase refers to the natural state or conditioning of the germ on its own realm, with emphasis of the value of the principle of Love (Suchness) of and in itself. By engendering Love-Wisdom all phenomena is brought to the undifferentiated state of Suchness, producing experience of the pure all-embracive Love of the cosmic magnet of Oneness. With respect to the *Knowledge–Love-Wisdom* petal we saw that its 'Immaculateness' refers to the quality of that petal, and of what a person's consciousness must develop to experience it. The term undifferentiated, in contradistinction, refers to all *saṃsāric* things that were formerly differentiated, and the processes of Love-Wisdom that strips them of their forms of separateness (a fundamental property of the mind), producing a unity, or integration into an undifferentiated interdependent whole. This ultimately is the basis of experiencing *śūnyatā*.

Here are stored *bījas* causing the rectification of the wheel of the Heart centre, and thus the way of treading the first set of the Bodhisattva *bhūmis*. These petals store attributes of the Suchness *(tathatā)* that manifest as the principle of Love as a downpour of energy (received inwards through meditation), allowing the meditator to experience its undifferentiated nature.

c. The *Love-Wisdom–Knowledge* petal, denoted by the phrase: 'the germ *(gotra)* of the Buddha manifests actively in all living beings'. This petal sets into motion the *bījas* producing the awakening of enlightened perception, the generation of compassionate attributes within the mind of the personal-I. The effect produces wisdom through knowledgeable activity. When delineated by Love, the germ of consciousness will incorporate a sound reasoning as to the nature and purpose of compassionate action (*bodhicitta*). Revelation for the need to aspire towards liberation consequently manifests. Such loving intelligence is the gift of the *gotra* to all.

The *bījas* (of the energy of Love-Wisdom) work upon the knowledgeable attributes of consciousness by the inherent or intrinsic nature of the qualities of this petal in a similar way as yeast upon dough. The Solar Plexus centre and its relation to the Heart centre is the focus of activity for this petal.

The three Sacrifice petals.

Sacrifice involves the elimination of all things *saṃsāric* that do not relate to the quest for enlightenment, and which hinder one's ability to serve all sentient beings.

a. The *Sacrifice-Will—Sacrifice-Will* petal, which is concerned with 'the penetration of the Absolute Body *(dharmakāya)* into all living beings'. The mechanism here concerns the slow infusion into substance of the principle of Mind, producing an aeonic conversion into *dharmakāya* of the threefold substance (body, speech and mind) that each human unit incarnates into and appropriates for that and each succeeding life. Incomprehensible is the vast duration of time and the sacrifice needed by this 'man-plant' to produce the transformation in the soil of *saṃsāra* so that 'all animate beings are possessed of the embryo of the Tathāgata'.

   Upon the path of return, when a *yogin* appears that is capable of producing the *siddhis* of transformation, then the outpouring of the potency of the *dharmakāya* manifests into the quiescent Mind of the attained Bodhisattva-*yogin*. This concerns the complete awakening of the 1,000 petalled lotus, thus causing enlightenment. It involves mastering the testings associated with the path of Initiation, the process of awakening these petals by mastering *saṃsāra*.

   With the coursing of the Fiery Element through the petals of the Head lotus the *arhat* form of meditation is completed. When the Airy Element gains dominance then the higher Bodhisattva *bhūmis* are trodden and *śūnyatā* is revealed. When the Aetheric Element is expressed then the *dharmakāya* is the experience of the fully awakened One.

b. The *Sacrifice-Will—Love-Wisdom* petal, and the phrases: 'the Tathāgata is the Absolute Reality or Suchness *(Tathatā)* and is therefore the undifferentiated whole', and 'all animate beings are possessed of the embryo of the Tathāgata'. The knowledge gained from *saṃsāric* activity is driven by the wisdom and sacrificial activity of the incarnate personality to eliminate all allurements and attachments, so that the higher Bodhisattva *bhūmis* can be persued. This will eventually produce the sacrifice of the Flower's form through conscious identification with the all and the increasing

Revelation of the Suchness that the opening Śūnyatā Eye affords.

Here the *bījas* associated with the Ājñā centre are fully activated, to open this Eye of Wisdom, and the inner petals of the Heart in the Head. The substance of the mind, and its interrelation with 'all animate beings' are thereby integrated with the essence of the Buddha-germ. The *tathāgatagarbha* becomes integrated, 'at-oned' as the Mind of the incarnate personality.

c. The *Sacrifice-Will–Knowledge* petal. The pertinent quote is: 'it may be said that all animate beings are possessed of the embryo of the Tathāgata'. This statement is in the form of a deduction evoking Mind. This petal works to eliminate forms of attachment to outmoded ideas in the consciousness of the personal-I, so that consciousness can remain steady in the Clear Light for further revelation that will come from the opening Śūnyatā Eye. Looking inward, that Eye will perceive how all beings are infused with integral Life via the Meditation-Mind of a primordial Buddha, who sustains the *maṇḍala* of all that evolves in our earth sphere so that all units of *manasic* limitation can be brought to Buddhahood. The focus therefore is upon Shambhala and what can be gleaned from its domain. Therein the liberated Lives are continuously meditating on how to best direct the streams of life to revelation of that *maṇḍala* of Life as part of the Mind-space that is *dharmakāya*. For the lesser evolved species of life right environmental conditionings are needed. For humans the appearance of a civilisation and appropriate doctrines related to the development of compassionate understanding are needed. Though the principle of Life, or 'Buddha-germ' is present in all entities (otherwise there would be no progressive evolutionary process), only in humans has this *gotra* expanded in the form of the Sambhogakāya Flower, to accommodate the process of the development of mind and the accumulation of knowledge. Such knowledgeable bits of information grow into vast compendiums of ideas, concepts and revelations concerning the nature of phenomena, cosmos, and eschatology.

All knowledge must eventually be refined and made pertinent to enlightenment's quest, which is the purpose of these Sacrifice petals to achieve in the mind of the yogically inspired one. Here the *bījas* associated with the complete awakening of the Throat centre and the ability to command the mantras governing all *saṃsāric* permutations by way of the Element Fire can be accessed. This produces complete *manasic* control. The *saṃskāras* of the innermost tier of the Head lotus are governed by this petal.

This Sacrifice triad is basically concerned with the effect of the liberating qualities coming from the *dharmakāya* that manifest via the Sambhogakāya Flower into the mind/Mind of the receptive personal-I. Its energies work upon and through the Flower and the Head lotus in such a way that all of the *bījas* of mind are eventually cleansed of defilements and brought to the level of abstraction that *nirmalā tathatā* represents. The means whereby this is accomplished is here styled 'sacrifice', because this is the effect of the manifesting potency of the I-consciousnesses working in the mind of the person. Aspects of what is deemed real in the phenomenal world must be sacrificed to gain the liberated states pertaining to the *dharmakāya*. The Will-of-Love must be utilised in order to achieve this.

The first petal of this triad absorbs the attributes of the *dharmakāya,* which seeds all Sambhogakāya Flowers with the efflorescence from a Buddha's Wisdom. All Flowers are thus indeed Buddha-embryos. This fact guarantees eventual liberation from *saṃsāra*. Those ensconced within the wheels of *saṃsāra* must evoke the energies of will and sacrifice to do so.

The second of the Sacrifice petals embodies the sacrificial nature of love. Suchness is thus expressed in the form of sacrificial Love, which is non-dual, and therefore one-pointed, leading only to liberation, to the oneness of the *dharmakāya*. This then is the nature of *tathatā*.

The third of the Sacrifice petals refers to the way consciousness is expressed via the seeds in the Flower. Consciousness then comes under the auspices of the *bījas* of sacrificial knowledge, i.e., of the way that right knowledge is utilised to bring about liberation of consciousness from attachment to things that are ephemeral. As one becomes non-attached to the associated defilements, so the 'innate purity' of the germ becomes evident, as it admits nothing that is defiled.

The Sambhogakāya Flower and the Ratnagotravibhāga

The nine similes concerning the nature of the progression of enlightenment via the awakening of the petals of this Flower can now be analysed. The similies present a more detailed symbolic account of the qualities of these nine petals in terms of their mode of expression in the realms of form. I shall continue in sequence with Fuchs' translation, supplemented by Obermiller's and Brown's where useful. First an overview of these nine similes is presented.

> This [tathagatagarbha] abides within the shroud of the afflictions,
> as should be understood through [the following nine] examples:
>
> Just like a buddha is a decaying lotus, honey amidst bees,
> a grain in its husk, gold in filth, a treasure underground,
> a shoot and so on sprouting from a little fruit,
> a statue of the Victorious One in a tattered rag,
> a ruler of mankind in a destitute woman's womb,
> and a precious image under [a layer of] clay,
> this [buddha] element abides within all sentient beings, obscured by
> the defilement of the adventitious poisons.
>
> The defilements correspond to the lotus,
> the insects, the husk, the filth, the earth,
> the fruit, the tattered rag, the pregnant woman
> direly vexed with burning suffering, and the clay.
> The buddha, the honey, the grain, the gold,
> the treasure, the nyagrodha tree, the precious statue,
> the continents' supreme ruler, and the precious image
> are similar to the supreme undefiled element.[13]

In the first statement we are told that the *tathāgatagarbha* 'abides within the shroud of the afflictions', where this 'shroud' represents the corporeal form, which is a good representation of our physical bodies. Literally they are corpses, constituting of the defilements garnered via *saṃsāric* activity. The 'location' of the Sambhogakāya Flower therefore is within this 'shroud', however, one must look inwards to the abstract domain of Mind. The attributes of the nine petals are then summarised, which shall later be analysed in depth. Their qualities are not known by the empirical mind because of the obscurations therein by the 'adventitious poisons'. Consequently, these 'poisons' *(saṃskāras, kleśas)* must be eliminated by means of transformation of their adventitious attributes and transmutation by means of yogic methodology, if the undefiled *tathāgatagarbha* is to be experienced.

13 Rosemarie Fuchs, 32.

Having outlined these examples, the text then presents the nature of the obscurations of the human persona, of the pollutions of the human mind *(samalā tathatā)* preventing experience of the *tathāgatagarbha*. Obermiller states in his footnotes that 'the lotus' illustrates desire, 'insects' (Obermiller's version is 'bees') refers to hatred, 'the husk' refers to infatuation, 'the filth' to the '3 Sources of Evil in a developed state,'[14] 'the ground', or 'earth' refers to illusion (ignorance), 'the fruit', to the obscurations eliminated by the intuition, 'the tattered rag', to the obscurations eliminated by concentrating the mind. With respect to 'the pregnant woman direly vexed with burning suffering' Obermiller states that the symbolism relates to 'the Obscurations on the 1st seven Stages of the Bodhisattva'.[15] For 'the clay', where Obermiller has 'dust', he states that it refers to 'the Obscurations on the 3 last stages'.[16] Here then is implied not only the obscurations but also the mechanism of their unveiling or elimination by means of travelling the Bodhisattva path.

The text then refers to the undefiled elements *(nirmalā tathatā)* of the *tathāgatagarbha*. The meaning of the nine illustrations shall be explained in the following section concerning the nine similes. 'The nyagrodha tree' is a mighty tree that can be considered to represent the entire *nāḍī* system. With the *chakras,* the *nāḍīs* are an expression of a plant or tree (with its branches and flowers) of a human unit, extended to include the petals of the Sambhogakāya Flower.

1. The Sacrifice-Will—Sacrifice-Will petal

With respect to this we are given the simile of 'a decaying lotus'.

> Seeing that in the calyx of an ugly-colored lotus
> a tathagata dwells ablaze with a thousand marks,
> a man endowed with the immaculate divine vision
> takes it from the shroud of the water-born's petals.
>
> Likewise the Sugata with his buddha eye perceives his own true state even in those

---

14 Obermiller, 213.

15 Ibid.

16 Ibid.

who must abide in the hell of the direst pain.
Endowed with compassion itself, which is unobscured and endures to the final end,
he relieves them from their obscurations.

Once his divine eye sees the Sugata abiding within the closed ugly lotus, the man cuts the petals. Seeing the perfect buddha nature within beings, obscured by the shroud of desire, hatred, and the other mental poisons, the Muni does likewise and through his compassion defeats their veils.[17]

Brown's commentary:

the ugly withered lotus flowers symbolizing the defilements, while the essence of the Tathāgata (*Tathāgatadhātu* which is equivalent to *Tathāgatagarbha)* is compared to the presence of the apparitional Buddha resplendently abiding within the petals[18]....The lotus flower, appearing at first delightful but soon withering and turning foul, represents the dormant state of desire *(rāgānuśayalakṣaṇa-kleśa)* found in all worldly persons who are however freed from actual desire. This defilement causes the forces which account for the motionless state, and give rise to the material and immaterial sphere *(rūpārūpyadhātu).* It can only be removed by the supermundane wisdom *(lokottarajñāna).*[19]

As the concern here is with the highest and most sublime of the petals of the Sambhogakāya Flower, so the description also symbolises the Flower as a whole. The text thus begins with an image of a lotus flower, pointing out esoterically exactly to what is being referred. The symbolism presents an overview of the groups of the Sambhogakāya Flowers of humanity, in terms of 'ugly withered lotus flowers' (using Brown's depiction). The lotus is an apt symbol for all *chakras,* which the Sambhogakāya Flower can also be considered to be upon a subtler level of expression. The term 'ugly' indicates the paucity of qualities possessed by the Flowers at first. Much sacrificial Will must be evoked, knowledgeable attributes, Love and wisdom developed before the full beauty and radiance of the

17 Fuchs, 32-33.

18 Brown, 125.

19 Ibid., 128.

Sambhogakāya Flower is seen. Nevertheless, the resplendent beauty of a Tathāgata resides at the centre, shielded by the three bud petals.

Very little of the quality of sacrifice is evidenced by the Eye of the seer in the Flowers of average humanity, right up to the beginning of the Bodhisattva *bhūmis*. The incarnate personal-I's are far too avaricious and desirous of pleasurable and sensual things (defilements). The Sacrifice petals cannot develop much under these conditions. The *bījas* that they contain coming from the material realms for the greater part of the evolutionary journey lack in vibrancy. The petals are closed around the central bud because their inherent qualities have not yet been developed, hence the term 'ugly'. This Sacrifice petal is awakened only at the end of the evolutionary spiral, on the higher stages of the Bodhisattva path.

The Tathāgata that 'dwells ablaze with a thousand marks' refers to the awakened Head lotus, with its symbolic 1,000 petals. The implication here is that only when this petal is vibrant and functioning can the 1,000 petalled lotus be awakened appropriately so that the Buddha attributes (the *dharmakāya)* it is designed to embody can be revealed. By then all of the petals of the Sambhogakāya Flower are awakened, with the Śūnyatā Eye opened and receptive to impressions from the *dharmakāya,* which floods the Head lotus with relevant revelations. The *dharmakāya* feeds the activity of the petals as a whole via the Sacrifice petals and their correspondence in the Head lotus. (Effectively the three innermost tiers of petals out of the five tiers.)

The entire evolutionary history of the individual can then be viewed, as stored in the constitution of the Sambhogakāya Flower, and reflected in the petals of the Head lotus. The awakened Eye will then perceive one's 'own true state', as well as visioning one's past lives, right to sojourn in hell states if need be, or observe the karmic history of others. To awaken this, the highest of all the petals, necessitates travelling the higher Bodhisattva *bhūmis,* hence developing the compassionate activity to relieve others from the causes of their sufferings.

Obermiller's rendering of the phrase 'the man cuts the petals', is: 'rents asunder the petals (in order to release him)'[20], which refers to the ultimate liberation of the Flower's form (undertaking the fourth

20 Obermiller, 214.

Initiation), producing residence in *śūnyatā,* which is the next step of the Bodhisattva's path to Buddhahood.

The Sacrifice petals can be counted as a triad, or else as a pentad:

The three direct Sacrifice petals, plus the Love-Wisdom—Sacrifice-Will, and the Knowledge—Sacrifice-Will petals.

There are similarly five Love-Wisdom petals and five Knowledge petals. This makes an arrangement of 3 x 5 groups of petals. Such an arrangement is necessary in order to convey the qualities of the five Dhyāni Buddhas, plus the transmuted correspondences of the five *skandhas*, the five *prāṇas* via the three levels of expression associated with the three worlds of human perception. There is also an affiliation with all triads, e.g., the three worlds of human perception, mental, astral and physical; body, speech and mind.

The five Sacrifice petals convey the qualities of the five Dhyāni Buddhas into the formed realms. The five Knowledge petals convey the transmuted qualities of the *saṃskāras* into the *dharmakāya*. The five Love-Wisdom petals convey the gain of the wisdom developed during the vast number of lives that the Sambhogakāya Flower has sown. Love (compassion) is inherent to the Flower, and its petals are organised to compassionately project many personal-I's into manifestation so that the 'little lives' comprising the lesser kingdoms in Nature can be salvaged and turned into 'man-plants'. The Love-Wisdom petals are also telepathically integrated with all groups of Sambhogakāya Flowers. Integrating all this activity into a unity, the Śūnyatā Eye at the heart of each Flower, represents the *saṃsāra-śūnyatā* nexus. It consists of *manasic* substance (Clear Light) of such refinement that it can withstand the dynamic destructive (transmutative) energy of *śūnyatā,* and yet help sustain a form that allows *saṃsāra* to be experienced in full. The 'dormant state of desire' can then lead to the most intense forms of self-identification and yet represent all that must be sacrificed over a vast time expanse (taking innumerable lives into account), if enlightenment is to be obtained.

Obermiller's translation of the text is illuminating.

97. Suspose, in a lotus flower of ugly form,
The Buddha, shining with a thousand marks of beauty, were abiding,

And a man possessed of immaculate divine sight[21] would perceive him.
And draw him out from the petals of the water-born lotus;
98. In the same way the Lord perceives with his sight of a Buddha[22]
His own essence even in those that abide in the lowest of hells,
And, endowed with the uttermost Commiseration, free from impediments,
Delivers the living beings from the Obscurations.
99. Just as a person possessed of divine sight
Sees in an ugly lotus flower with folded leaves
The Buddha who abides in its interior,
And rends asunder the petals (in order to release him),
In the same way the Lord perceives the Essence of the Supreme Buddha,
Existing in all that lives, but obscured by lust, hatred and other coverings of defilement,
And, full of mercy, vanquishes these Obscurations.[23]

The three major parts to this section refer to the way that the Sacrifice-Will—Sacrifice-Will petal functions with respect to the other petals. They present an explanation of the qualities and mode of activity of the nine petals in general, with the Sacrifice-Will—Sacrifice-Will petal governing the overall purpose of the *tathāgatagarbha,* and thus of each of the petals. Consequently, these three verses present a brief summary of the qualities of each of the nine petals in turn, plus their direction of the *bījas* activating the main *chakras* in the body of the personal-I.

Verse 97 presents an overview of the work (purpose) concerning the *chakras* in the Head and Throat. Verse 98 presents an overview of the purpose relating to the Heart centre and its relation to the Splenic centres. Verse 99 presents an overview of the way the Sambhogakāya Flower works with the centres below the diaphragm and the Inner Round group of *chakras.*

To summarise, the Sacrifice-Will—Sacrifice-Will petal represents the place of abstraction for all wilful *saṃskāras* generated by the

21 Obermiller, footnote, 214, *Divya-cakṣuḥ.*

22 Ibid. *Buddha-cakṣuḥ.*

23 Ibid. See also, E. Obermiller, Ed. H. S. Prasad, *The Uttaratantra of Maitreya,* (Sri Satguru Publications, Delhi, 1997), 344.

Flower-Personality combination, facilitating their conversion into the qualities of the *dharmakāya*. The Sacrifice-Will—Love-Wisdom petal abstracts consciousness preparatory to its absorption into *śūnyatā*. The Sacrifice-Will—Knowledge petal clarifies the *bījas* of the *ālayavijñāna*.

The *first* statement regarding this 'lotus flower of ugly form' asks us to suppose that the 'Buddha, shining with a thousand marks of beauty, were abiding' in it. This refers to the functioning of the *Sacrifice-Will—Sacrifice-Will* petal, where only the sacrifice of all aspects of phenomena can reveal the purest essence of a Buddha, whilst the '1,000 marks of beauty' refers to the 1,000 petalled lotus *(sahasrāra padma),* which a Buddha perfectly utilises to express his wisdom. The utilisation of will and sacrifice causes each petal to be cleansed of defilements, and transforms all impediments into wisdom-attributes. This happens as the energies of this petal increasingly manifest via the Head lotus, causing the Buddha to 'shine' with 'a thousand marks of beauty', signifying the radiance of the Head lotus that is revealed at the latter stages of the process and attainment of enlightenment.

Only by walking the sacrificial path of a well-accomplished *yogin* can this Head lotus be awakened, with the help of the Sacrifice petals of the Sambhogakāya Flower. Then enlightenment (Buddhahood, also referring to the resplendence of the manifest fully revealed *dharma*) appears via the Jewel in the Heart of the Lotus. The evocation of the energies of this Sacrifice-Will—Sacrifice-Will petal (which has its roots directly implanted in the *dharmakāya*) is the only way of removing the obscurations preventing the appearance of these 'marks of beauty'. The process awakens the *bījas (saṃskāras* of past life attainment) of all former accomplishments, when each of the 1,000 petals of the Head lotus reveal their content. They can then be expanded upon and cleansed of impediments.

The Head lotus is designed to accommodate the potencies of all three major tiers of the Sambhogakāya Flower. The Heart centre integrates the sacrificial potency with love and wisdom, whilst the centres below the diaphragm are primarily receptive to impressions from the Knowledge petals, until the quest for enlightenment is actively pursued by the incarnate personality. The evocation of the energies from the Sacrifice petals produces the transmutation of the substance of the sheaths and the will to overcome obstacles. Development of the Love-Wisdom petals produces the quest for enlightenment. The unfoldment of the Knowledge petals lay the foundation for the development of the five Jina wisdoms.

The *second* statement is: 'And a man possessed of immaculate divine sight *(divya-cakṣuḥ)* would perceive him'. This refers to the main function of the *Sacrifice-Will—Love-Wisdom petal,* which overshadows the accomplished *yogin* and endows him with sacrificial *bījas* and the wisdom to overcome all allurements to enlightenment. The 'divine sight' is incurred by the opening of 'the third eye', the Ājñā centre, which when awakened will allow the *yogin* to see whatever he wills in the three realms and in the liberated domains. The Will aspect pierces the veils or obstacles to perception, the Love assures the universality of the vision, and the wisdom perceives its veracity in terms of all Knowledgeable realisations. When the Head lotus is awakened the *dharmakāyic* view also becomes accessible. The interrelation between the *yogin* and Flower is via the consciousness link *(antaḥkaraṇa)* that the *yogin* has projected to the Sambhogakāya Flower. This differs to the Life link *(sūtrātmā)* that is attached to the evolving personality via the Heart centre at birth. The mechanism of anchorage also involves the pineal and pituitary glands (the externalisations of the Head and Ājñā centres).

The Ājñā and Head centres function as an integral unity, allowing the Sambhogakāya Flower (or accomplished *yogin)* to simultaneously vision both toward the *dharmakāya* and the realm of the personal-I. This means that the succession of lives associated with the form can be continuously monitored in accord with the *dharmakāyic* purpose.

The *third* statement is: 'And draw him out from the petals of the water-born lotus'. Here 'the water-born lotus' refers to the Solar Plexus centre, which governs the emanation of the Watery Element. It can also refer generally to the *chakra* system in the body, which grows from out of the Watery-Earthy environment. The Solar Plexus centre is the central dynamo for this system until the Fires of mind gain dominance upon the yogic path. The Throat centre (working in conjunction with the Heart) then draws the consciousness principle from out of the Waters. This centre, as previously stated, is directed by the *Sacrifice-Will—Knowledge petal,* which stores the *bījas* governing the awakening of the *chakras* associated with the development of the Fires of mind/Mind. Thus it causes the elimination of all Watery considerations. One's emotional concerns and attachments to all forms of the lower *siddhis* (associated with the Solar Plexus centre) thus become sacrificed through the impetus of this petal of the Sambhogakāya Flower.

The Solar Plexus centre is also the place where the 'self' concept is generated. This third statement therefore has reference to the process whereby thinking of everything in terms of the little 'self' becomes annihilated through right esoteric knowledge and through yogic practice. The 'self' must sacrifice everything that is dear to its world of interrelationships to be truly selfless. As it does so knowledge of Secret Mantra enters into consciousness. The Throat centre then manifests its complete potential in the resplendent silence of the Heart's Mind.

Verse 98 refers to the *purpose* of the *Love-Wisdom* petals as directed by the corresponding Sacrifice petals.

The *fourth* statement, which refers to the purpose of the *Love-Wisdom—Knowledge petal*, is: 'In the same way the Lord perceives with his sight of a Buddha *(buddha-cakṣuḥ).* His own essence even in those that abide in the lowest of hells *(avici)'.*

The concept of 'sight' directly concerns the domain of the mind, thus the evocation of its powers to discern and esoterically see. The perception therefore relates to visioning 'like a Buddha', i.e., with compassionate insight into the mind of the personal-I, no matter where consciousness may be temporarily residing, even if that be 'the lowest of hells'. No matter how debased the human unit may be, or of the density of the *saṃskāras* and *karma* that weigh down the individual, we will still find the presence of the *tathāgatagarbha* guiding that consciousness-stream. The inherent Love-Wisdom of the *tathāgatagarbha* will inevitably drive that consciousness-stream toward eventual liberation from the thraldom of *karma*.

This relates to the ability to master the Solar Plexus centre, which is the cause of the experience of hell states, and all forms of psychosomatic conditions because it governs the potency of the 'self' concept and the related Watery emotional thinking. Once mastered, this centre is also the mainstay of the lesser *siddhis,* clairvoyance, clairaudience, etc., to which the *'buddha-cakṣuḥ'* refers, when directed to the centres below the diaphragm.

The Flower utilises this Wisdom to oversee the *karma* of the personal-I right through to the experiences in hell if need be, and it takes much love if the personal-I manifests forms of sorcery, where the process of cleansing *karma* may continue for aeons. The information presented is that the Flower can gain an overview of the entire course of the evolutionary attainment of the *santāna*[24] of personalities that must be rayed down into manifestation until final liberation is achieved. This involves seeding the mind of the individuals with rightly sequenced information and images, whenever the mind is receptive to them, so that the types of actions producing the necessity of experiencing emotional hell states are eventually eliminated.

The *fifth* statement is: 'endowed with the uttermost Commiseration, free from impediments', which refers to the pure expression of the *Love-Wisdom—Love-Wisdom petal* of the Flower. Being constituted of the *saṃskāras* of intensified Love, it is naturally 'freed from impediments'. This pure expressed Love manifests in the form of compassion for the sufferings of the personalities experiencing the tribulations fuelled by self will. They are cleansed by the effects of the *karma* that they must go through. The pain and suffering one experiences, when cause to effect is understood, inevitably produces commiserations for the suffering others undergo. The *bījas* of compassionate concern are absorbed by this petal. From it also emanates the compassionate force *(bodhicitta)* that engenders kindness, charity and solicitude for others. Inevitably the Bodhisattva Path is trod. Only the purest form of Love and Wisdom can rightly express *bodhicitta,* which manifests as a law for the perfection of all. This petal consequently controls the process concerning the rectification of the wheel of the Heart centre. The *saṃskāras* of the incarnate personality will be expressed in such a way that they will unerringly produce the crises associated with 'turning about in the seat of consciousness', which is the effect of the awakening of *bodhicitta.*

The *sixth* statement is: 'Delivers the living beings from Obscurations'. This refers to the purpose of the *Love-Wisdom—Sacrifice-Will petal* wherein the *bījas* of aspirational perception are stored that will allow the personal-I to recognise and understand the nature of the obscurations

---

24 *Santāna,* flow or river (of consciousness).

preventing the final goal to liberation. This concerns the *saṃskāras* evoked through turning the rectified wheel of the Heart centre. It prepares the way for the complete experience of Thusness via the Sacrifice petals in general and the opening of the Śūnyatā Eye for the revelation of the *dharmakāya*. Love sacrifices all for this end.

The energy of sacrifice then manifests below the diaphragm of the personal-I via the *Splenic centres,* which refine and transform available *saṃskāras,* eliminating those no longer viable to the system, and redirecting all *prāṇas* in the body according to their merit. Only the most refined and subtlest of energies can reside in the domain of the Heart centre (above the diaphragm). Attributes of mind/Mind are directed via the Throat centre, but all *prāṇas* not productive of enlightenment must be sacrificed within the crucible of Life in the Splenic centres. They are refined and transformed until they meet the requirements for the Heart centre's expression. The *prāṇas* too gross for normal healthy functioning are dispensed into the Eighth Sphere (the equivalent to the hell zone in the body) and expelled.

The seventh to ninth statements refer to the *purpose* of the *Knowledge petals.*

The seventh statement is: 'Just as a person possessed of divine sight, Sees in an ugly lotus Flower with folded leaves, the Buddha who abides in its interior, And rends asunder the petals (in order to release him)'. This refers to the *Knowledge—Sacrifice-Will petal,* which utilises the most forceful form of energy to 'rent asunder' (awaken) the petals of the *chakras* in order to release the hidden Buddha nature (the jewel in the heart of the lotus) in each of them. This force is needed because the Sambhogakāya Flower needs to reach down to the densest substance to influence the struggling personal-I to do right. It works to awaken the *chakras* from above down or from within without. *Manasic prāṇas* derived from the sense-consciousnesses and contact with the material domain must be refined to produce attributes of the Clear Light of Mind.

From the perspective of the *chakra* system, the 'ugly lotus Flower with folded leaves' at first refers to the Solar Plexus centre (the *maṇipūra chakra*) of the average person, from whence emanates the most selfish, avaricious, self-centred *saṃskāras.* All emotional attachments to material things are produced. When the *bījas* of these *saṃskāras* are expressed in the Knowledge petals of the Sambhogakāya Flower, then similarly we can view a relatively ugly flower, compared to the later resplendence that will be seen when more loving qualities are developed. Later the focus moves to the Sacral and Base of Spine centres, as they must be yogically prepared for the liberation of *kuṇḍalinī*. The entire field of desire must then be tackled by the activation of the Throat centre's Fiery energies to dry out all Watery dispositions. The liberation of *kuṇḍalinī* and its right direction will reveal the Buddha residing at the heart of each *chakra* and awaken the crowning glory of the Head lotus.

The process of awakening the *chakras* in right sequence to eventually make a Buddha out of the personal-I's is a millennium long activity. Fiery sacrificial *bījas* must be developed through right knowledge, activity, and aspiration to liberate one from emotional thraldom.

The eighth statement is: 'In the same way the Lord perceives the Essence of the Supreme Buddha, Existing in all lives, but obscured by lust, hatred and other coverings of defilement'. This statement refers to the *Knowledge—Love-Wisdom petal.* This petal is therefore concerned with the ability of the Flower to wisely control the karmic flow of the sum of its incarnate personality. Diseases, sickness, well-being and the effects of people's mental-emotional expressions all have to be appropriately regulated to produce the desired effects in the consciousness of the 'I'. It thus concerns the way the Buddha *gotra* perceives the lives embodied as the incarnate form, the little units of mind governing the manifestation of the organs, etc. It then works to project the sum of each little cellular sentience of the form towards collectivised liberation. Without this collective or overall loving control and conversion of the little lives that manifest in the form of the *saṃskāras* of 'lust, hatred and other coverings of defilement' the *karma* conditioning the form could not manifest, neither could the personal-I reign in the myriad wild horses of emotions that it generates.

Here the *prāṇas* from the sum of the Inner Round series of *chakras* must be consciously and appropriately dealt with. These *chakras* embody the attributes experienced via the sum of the body's organs ('all lives') and by extension their correspondences throughout Nature's kingdoms.

The ninth statement is: 'And full of mercy, vanquishes these Obscurations', which consequently concerns the *Knowledge—Knowledge petal* of the Sambhogakāya Flower. The implication is that once the complete weight of right knowledge is gained after millenniums of incarnated existence, the personality-Sambhogakāya Flower duo finally vanquish these obscurations with the help of 'mercy', i.e., compassion for the suffering ones. Such mercy has been gained at a great price, of much suffering and thence the understanding of the nature and purpose of suffering, as per the Four Noble Truths, and by following the path to liberation. All this is eventuated whilst the personal-I exists in a physical body, wherein these obscurations must finally be vanquished. The Flower does not do this, but it has the capacity to seed knowledge of how to do so via the *bījas* that it has stored in the Knowledge petals. All of the *saṃskāras* of mind incorporated in the general *nāḍī* system are consequently utilised and must be controlled to produce the eventual triumph over all the obscurations.

It should be noted that for each of the petals governed by the general gist of the Sacrifice petals we are presented with the mode of removal of defilements of obscurations from the realm of the personality, as this is the way of sacrifice.

2. The Sacrifice-Will—Love-Wisdom petal

Continuing with Obermiller's translation we see that this section constitutes verses 100-102 of the text. The three verses depict a triune sub-expression of this petal.

100. Suppose some honey were encircled by a swarm of bees,
And a skilful person, desirous to obtain this honey,
Would perceive it and, by using clever means,
Would separate the honey from the swarm.

101. Similarly, the Greatest of Sages with his vision of Omniscience,
Sees this fundamental essence, resembling honey,
And brings about the complete removal
Of the Obscurations that are like the bees.

102. A man who is desirous of obtaining honey
Hidden by thousands and millions of bees,
Removes the latter and disposes of the honey as he wishes.
[47b. 1.] The undefiled Spirit that exists in the living beings is like the honey,

> The defiling forces are like the bees,
> And the Lord who is skilful in vanquishing them
> Is like the man (that obtains the honey).[25]

The Sacrifice-Will—Love-Wisdom petal qualifies the fundamental energy embodying the Flower, likened to honey, in terms of the Love that sacrifices itself to follow the purpose of the Dharmakāya Way to conclusion. The honey is the sweet, nourishing energy *(bodhicitta)* that feeds the enlightened person via the 1,000 petalled lotus (where the wisdom aspect is exemplified) and the Heart centre (where the love aspect is exemplified). This Sacrifice-Will—Love-Wisdom petal is thus a directing agent for the expression of *bodhicitta,* the force of enlightenment, the 'immaculate wisdom'. This petal conveys the Suchness of *tathatā* (here allegorised as honey) to help liberate the enlightenment-bound *yogin.*

The honey bees (signifying thought-elements of the mind) might have the capacity to sting (signifying hatred, the conveyance of poison), but they are also bringers of the nectar from which they fabricate the honey, 'the Essence of the Buddha'. This means that the type of obscurations that the bees represent are converted to enlightenment-factors via the bee's digestive process (higher thought processes). The bees therefore can also 'sting' the obscurations (that they convey) to death. In this guise they become part of a *yogin's* arsenal (in the form of intense one-pointed thought forms, *dhāraṇis)* to quickly overcome *saṃsāric* impediments.

Hatred is the opposite to the energy of Love, into which it must be transmuted. Hatred, or critical attitudes of mind, are exemplified in a bee's sting because they represent destructive qualities manifesting through abuse of the intensity of the energies that emanate from this Sacrifice petal to the personal-I. The aspirant must persistently work to transform this forceful tendency, and all of its lesser offshoots, such as irritation. We thus have the entire evolutionary progress of the transformation of *saṃskāras* of destructive attributes into the corresponding most beneficent ones. Inevitably a form of enmity is developed against the attributes of *saṃsāra* by the Bodhisattva, who vows to never cease striving until all sentient beings have been liberated

25 Ibid., 215.

from it. His inspiration and empowerment comes from the impetus of the energies and the *bījas* of this Sacrifice petal.

Verse 100 refers to the Will or Power aspect, where the Sacrifice-Will—Love-Wisdom petal works to separate the honey from the swarm of empirical thought-forms of the incarnate 'I'. It extracts the essence (or essential meaning) from the thought structure of the person, leaving the rest of the *bījas* of *karma* to be cleansed by the activities of the future.

The perception of the honey implicates the utilisation of the Eye (or eyes of the *chakras*—the eyes being the central jewel in the hearts of each lotus), controlled by the Sacrifice-Will—Love-Wisdom petal. The honey is Love-Wisdom, the essence of enlightenment, encircled by obscuring thought-forms and desire impulses. This 'essence' represents the *tathāgatagarbha's* qualities in general. The fundamental energy qualification is *bodhicitta,* here likened to 'honey', a 'sweet' nourishing energy that is food for the one on the path of enlightenment.

'A skilful person' is the Bodhisattva, who under impetus from the qualities of this petal, awakens his/her Eye (the Ājñā centre) to obtain perception of the higher way of the *dharmakāya*. 'Clever means' are used to separate the honey from the swarm of mental impressions. Consequently, this petal is activated when a Bodhisattva appears from the progress of the personal-I's that form the *santāna* of the aeonic meditation of the Flower. The energy from this petal then stages the Initiation testings producing the lower Bodhisattva *bhūmis*.

The Bodhisattva's vow is but a manifestation of sacrificial Love. Thus purpose unfolds as the *bījas* stored in this petal are activated so as to ripen particular types of *karma* and the necessary energisations. From this perspective the 'swarm of bees' represents the type of *bījas* the Flower embodies, which the Bodhisattva must carefully distinguish by using 'clever means' in order to release their liberating energy that feeds the entire Bodhisattvic career. Each *bīja*/bee has the capacity to sting with aspects of *karma*. For the Bodhisattva, the objective is not to avoid the 'stings' of *karma*, but rather to rightfully experience them via a compassionate process that will cleanse the type of poison associated with them. The *karma* is expressed as group *karma,* with the Bodhisattva as the centre of a field of liberating expression.

In verse 101 the 'greatest of sages' is a Buddha, who embodies the qualities of the most idealised aspect of this Sacrifice-Will—Love-

Wisdom petal. The 'vision of omniscience' (Fuchs has 'his eye of omniscience'[26]) reminds us that this petal of the Sambhogakāya Flower governs the process of awakening the Ājñā centre, which when fully awakened produces such vision in the seer. The ability to utilise the Ājñā centre is given in this second sublist of the Sacrifice-Will—Love-Wisdom petal because the Love-Wisdom aspect is exemplified, which must be fully developed for this centre to awaken. It necessitates the right combination of sacrificial Will, Love, and Wisdom by the meditating *yogin,* if the left hand path is to be avoided.

What is also implied here is that this energy of Love that produces sacrifice in the material world comes via a Buddha's *dharma.* He is Love-Wisdom and works to produce sacrificial acts by those involved in *saṃsāra.* The effect is via energisation of the Love-Wisdom and Sacrifice petals of each individual's Sambhogakāya Flower. Once the *yogin* has properly heeded the wise instructions from the highest source then the complete removal of the bee-like obscurations is possible. This involves sacrificial activity that rides *saṃskāras* through to their transmutation, and thus liberation.

The 'fundamental essence' that resembles honey refers to that aspect of the *dharmakāya* that the Sacrifice petals can command. That our vision must be oriented to this level of experience is denoted by the fact that we are directed to the vision of the Buddha. (The hint being to emulate his attributes.) By residing in the *dharmakāya* the *yogin* is thereby able to produce the complete removal of the thoughts that obscure the Clear Light of the pristine Mind.

Verse 102 refers to the application of the attributes of knowledge of this particular petal. Such knowledge reveals the vast stores of knowledgeable images stored in the Mind (symbolised by 'thousands and millions of bees'), which being in the form of *prajñā,* 'removes the latter and disposes of the honey as he wishes'. Thus is the wisdom of the sages expressed.

This relates to the world of the aspirant on the path, who is the 'man who is desirous of obtaining honey'. He must utilise right knowledge to walk the way of love, for which he ultimately sacrifices himself when heeding the instructions of a Buddha. The principle of Love (from the Buddha-*gotra*) descends upon the aspiring personal-I, awakening his

---

26 Fuchs, 33.

heart with the thoughts of *bodhicitta* arising. Thus the Bodhisattva Path is properly instigated. The love of (right) knowledge eventually produces thoughts of loving sacrifice (wisdom) as the higher Way is gleaned in the aspirant's mind.

The 'millions of bees' signify the many *saṃskāras* developed by the personality vehicles throughout the millennium as they aspire towards right knowledge gleaned from their material involvement with *saṃsāra*. This is then rightly directed by means of the guiding principle of Love-Wisdom from the *gotra*. The bees become the *bījas* that manifest in time and space. Their removal happens when each personal-I cleanses the many aspects of the *karma* (and consequently *saṃskāras*) preventing the finer aspects of the path from manifesting. The path thus opens as the personality eliminates the grosser desires, emotions and forms of attachments to material things that formerly captivated his/her earlier incarnations.

Once these defilements are cleansed from the incarnatory repertoire then access to the sweet honey of love is gained, which can be disposed of as wished to benefit all sentient beings. This entire course of events is directed via the general impetus coming from the Sacrifice-Will—Love-Wisdom petal. This is the 'undefiled Spirit that exists in the living beings'. It is 'undefiled' because not tainted by means of the rebirthing process, but gains instead from the *dharmakāya* to ensure that the entire process eventually leads the developing personal-I's on to Buddhahood. The honey manifests as the *dharma* that directs that way, whilst as stated, the 'defiling forces' represent the *saṃskāras* developed by the various personal-I's as they evolve throughout space-time.

Each of the three remaining phrases to verse 102 implicate one of the three aspects of the *tathāgatagarbha,* viewed as Sacrifice, Love-Wisdom and knowledgeable Activity. 'The undefiled Spirit' that is like honey refers to the abstracted Sacrifice aspect of the *tathāgatagarbha*. It is undefiled, because its purpose forges the link with the *dharmakāya*. The Love and Wisdom of this petal of the *tathāgatagarbha* works to uncover and remove the 'defiling forces'. The Lord that is 'like the man (that obtains the honey)' refers to the Knowledge principle of the Flower that works via the personal-I to gather valuable impressions from *saṃsāra*.

We are also informed that it is 'the Lord', i.e., the Buddha *gotra* itself, that is 'skilful in vanquishing them'. The energy and impressions that produce the vanquishing of the *saṃskāras* thus come from above and beyond the world of the personality, who must respond to them via internal yogic meditation and alignment to the Flower. The *yogin* then obtains the honey. Thus in these few words the entire story is told concerning the method to gain enlightenment.

The five Sacrifice-Will, Love-Wisdom, and Knowledge petals

The five *Sacrifice petals* anchor the qualities of *dharmakāya* into the Sambhogakāya Flower in accordance with its evolved capacity to withstand or contain the immaculateness of the related qualities and energies. All attributes concerned *(prāṇas, saṃskāras, bījas)* manifest in the most refined, clarified form that is possible to be contained by consciousness. Viewed in terms of the Elements and the corresponding wisdoms of the Dhyāni Buddhas, their energies manifest through the Sacrifice petals in the following manner.

- *Sacrifice-Will—Sacrifice-Will petal,* the Dhyāni Buddha is Vairocana, the Dharmadhātu Wisdom and the Element is Aether.
- *Sacrifice-Will—Love-Wisdom petal,* the Dhyāni Buddha is Akṣobhya, the Mirror-like Wisdom and the Element is Air.[27]
- *Sacrifice-Will—Knowledge petal,* the Dhyāni Buddha is Amitābha, the Discriminating Inner Wisdom and the Element is Fire.
- *Love-Wisdom—Sacrifice-Will petal,* the Dhyāni Buddha is Ratnasambhava, the Equalising Wisdom and the Element is Water.
- *Knowledge—Sacrifice-Will petal,* the Dhyāni Buddha is Amoghasiddhi, the All-accomplishing Wisdom and the Element is Earth.

Consequently, the *symbol* associated with the Sacrifice petals is the *vajra* of the combined action of the Dhyāni Buddhas, or rather of the *viśvavajra,* that indicates the immutable power projected in four directions. It relates to the dynamism of liberation.

27 I have assigned the Elements attributed to the Jinas to be equable to the types of wisdoms each one embodies. Hence the attribution (the point of view) is different to that given in various Buddhist texts. The rationale of my view compared to that attributed in the *Bardo Thödol* (the normal view) is given in chapter six of Volume 5A.

Regarding the five *Love-Wisdom petals* the emphasis is *tathatā*, the Suchness of things, as an expression of the wisdoms derived from the transmuted qualities of the *prāṇas*. Consequently we have the attributes developed by the Bodhisattvas, and symbolised by the eight *mahābodhisattvas* presented in the texts, with their accompanying *ḍākinīs*. They accompany the Dhyāni Buddhas. The *mahābodhisattvas* and Consorts are presented in pairs around the Buddhas of the four cardinal positions. A great deal of their more esoteric work consists in helping to seed the wisdom aspect of the Sambhogakāya flowers of humanity. They stimulate the evolutionary growth of these petals either directly, or else indirectly through fostering wisdom in people. Information concerning the organisation of these great Bodhisattvas shall be introduced in Volume 4 and shall be elaborated in Volume 7. They can be viewed as heads of the Council of Bodhisattvas, the Hierarchy of Light and Love. The energies of the Mahābodhisattvas help effect the awakening of the petals via the symbolism of the Jinas as shown below.

Amoghasiddhi, representing the Element Earth, manifests in the *northern* position of the *maṇḍala* of the Dhyāni Buddhas, where north is the direction upward toward the higher spheres of enlightenment. This northern orientation is from the viewpoint of having reoriented one's focus of consciousness from material involvement to that of liberation. The Bodhisattvas associated with him are Vajrapāṇi (north) and Samantabhadra (northwest). Their Consorts are Nrityā and Mālā respectively.[28] The Elements are Air and Earth. The *Love-Wisdom—Sacrifice-Will petal* corresponds to this northern direction of Amoghasiddhi with respect to the Love-Wisdom petals as a unit. Here the will is utilised to master all aspects of phenomena to produce Amoghasiddhi's All-accomplishing Wisdom. Amoghasiddhi's potency directs all experiences upward to realms sublime after converting them into the qualities utilisable by an enlightened Being. The Earthy defilements must become transmuted into their most subjective Airy counterparts through the sacrificial potency of Love. The Equalising Wisdom of Ratnasambhava of the *Sacrifice* pentad also works to harmonise all impressions coming to the Love-Wisdom petals in general on their upward way to be absorbed into the *dharmakāya*

28 The information concerning the *mahābodhisattvas* are derived from the book *Secret Doctrines of the Tibetan Books of the Dead* by Detlef Ingo Lauf, (Shambhala, Boston, 1989). The detail can be found from page 114ff.

experience. Consequently, Ratnasambhava's potency generally qualifies the expression of the Love-Wisdom petals. Amoghasiddhi's transformative potency governs the general expression of the Sacrifice petals, whilst Amitābha's rulership of the Fires of Mind governs the expression of the Knowledge petals.

The *eastern* direction is attributed to Akṣobhya. This is the way inward to the Heart of Life, to the complete expression of *bodhicitta*, which is carried lightning-like through the Airy Element. This way of inward contemplation produces the spaciousness associated with this Element. The Bodhisattvas associated with him are Kśitigarbha (east) and Mañjuśrī (northeast). Their Consorts are Lāsyā and Ālokā respectfully. The *Love-Wisdom—Love-Wisdom petal* is identified with this *eastern* direction. The Elements are Fire and Air. Here the Fiery consciousness principle must be converted into the Airy Love-Wisdom normally associated with the eastern direction. Fuelled by the Airy principle the Fiery quality burns most intensely and transmutes all impurities into the luminescent *bodhicitta*. The Airy quality pertains to the Love part and the Fiery to the Wisdom part of the dual Love-Wisdom aspect.

The *southern* direction of downward to material involvement is attributed to Ratnasambhava and the Element Water, because from this Element (governing the emotions and desire) the major defilements are precipitated. This concerns the glazes that consciousness works through in order to produce actions in the manifest realms. The majority of human actions are sustained by desire until the enlightenment-path is trod as a consequence of experiencing the Equalising Wisdom from Ratnasambhava. (The emotions are 'equalised' with the unificatory energy of Love.) The Bodhisattvas associated with him are Ākāśagarbha (south), and Maitreya (southeast). Their Consorts are Dhūpā and Puśpā respectfully. The *Knowledge—Love-Wisdom petal* is identified with the *southern* direction. The Elements are Earth and Water. Here all of the gross *saṃsāric* experiences are melded together (equalised) in the crucible of the enlightenment experience to produce the philosopher's stone. *Bodhicitta* is then the Airy-Watery[29] elixir that is added to the Earthy mineral that represents our *saṃskāras* in the material domain, where right knowledge must be wrought to produce enlightenment.

29 The Element Water here is abstracted, pure Love as a liberating energy.

The *western* direction is attributed to Amitābha. This direction represents the outward meditation toward the field of human interrelations and of the way of service thereto through the medium of human consciousness. Consequently the Element is Fire, by means of which consciousness is expressed. The Bodhisattvas associated with him are Avalokiteśvara[30] (west) and Nivaraṇa-viṣkambhin (southwest). Their Consorts are Gitā and Ghandhā. The *Love-Wisdom–Knowledge petal* is identified with this *western* direction. The Elements are Water and Fire. Right knowledge and discriminative wisdom must transform all Watery emotional and devotional qualities into their highest forms of aspiration, and the ability to vision the real.

The *Sacrifice-Will–Love-Wisdom petal* governed by Vairocana expresses the Dharmadhātu Wisdom reflected by Akṣobhya, which becomes mirrored to the four directions and translated into the qualities of the eight accompanying Bodhisattvas. The Element is Aether-Air.

The *symbol* of the Love-Wisdom Petals is the *eight spoked wheel* of spacious direction of the manifestation of wisdom, as embodied by the eight *mahābodhisattvas,* signifying the qualities needed to be gained in treading the Eightfold Path and the form of the wisdoms derived from them.

The emphasis of the *five Knowledge petals* are the *bījas* obtained from *saṃsāra* concerning the nature of phenomena and consciousness volitions. The gross consciousness-volitions of desire, envy, lust, etc., must be transformed into their corresponding harmless and virtuous correspondences before they are acceptable to the Sambhogakāya Flower. This is done with the assistance of the actions of the protectors or guardians of the *dharma,* the five wrathful Herukas. Lauf describes their appearance thus:

> On the eighth day (the first day of the wrathful deities) there appears in the centre of the lotus cakra the Heruka of Buddha Vairocana in the form of the smoke-colored dPal-chan Buddha-Heruka with his white Ḍākinī, Buddha-Krodheśvarī. The central Heruka has three faces, six arms, and four legs. The right face is white, the middle smoke black, and the left red. In his right hands he carries a long-handed axe, a

30 In Volume 4 of this series it will be explained that Avalokiteśvara also symbolises the qualities of the Sambhogakāya Flower.

> flaming sword, and the wheel of the teachings; in his left, a kapāla, a ploughshare, and a bell. This wrathful Heruka is an emanation of Buddha Vairocana, manifesting himself in a terrifying flaming form.
>
> His retinue then appears at the four cosmic directions, one of the remaining Buddha-Herukas on each day, as emanations of the peaceful meditation-Buddhas. They are the dark blue Vajra-Heruka with the Ḍākinī, Vajra-Krodheśvarī in the east, the yellow Ratna-Heruka with his Ḍākinī, Ratna-Krodheśvarī in the south, the red Padma-Heruka with the Ḍākinī, Padma-Krodheśvarī in the west, and finally the green Karma-Heruka with his Ḍākinī, Karma-Krodheśvarī in the north. All Herukas have three heads, six arms, and four legs and are adorned with the tantric buddha-crown of skulls and with skull-necklaces. These five Herukas in their terrifying numinosity vehemently set upon the "five poisons," with their seemingly ineradicable roots in ignorance, hatred, pride, passion, and envy.[31]

It should also be noted that the last of the Sacrifice petals, the *Knowledge—Sacrifice-Will petal* is an effect of the expression of the All-accomplishing Wisdom of Amoghasiddhi. This governs the sum of the qualities derived from *saṃsāra* and their transmutation into the corresponding wisdoms. His energy is necessary if *saṃsāra* is to be totally and irrevocably mastered. Also, if everything gained from incarnation is to be appropriately transformed into the appropriate awareness, then the work of Amitābha is also necessitated. Thus the qualities of Amitābha-Amoghasiddhi together help transform the *bīja* seeds in the Knowledge petals. In a similar manner, Akṣobhya-Ratnasambhava are the overseeing Dhyāni Buddhas for the Love-Wisdom petals. Vairocana-Amoghasiddhi are the overriding or synthesising Dhyāni Buddhas of the Sacrifice petals. Vairocana here can also be considered part of an identifying couplet with the Ādi Buddha.

With respect to the *Sacrifice-Will—Knowledge petal* the ruling Dhyāni Buddha is Amitābha, whose Discriminating Inner Wisdom governs the overall expression of these five Knowledge petals. His wisdom is thereby responsible for the assimilation of the fires of consciousness into the *dharmakāya*. The Fiery flames surrounding each of the Herukas, and within which they dance, is his specific quality.

---

31 Detlef Ingo Lauf, *Secret Doctrines of the Tibetan Books of the Dead*, (Shambhala, Boston, 1989), 145-146.

Each of the *prāṇas* of the Herukas therefore manifest a predominant transformative Fire. The energies associated with the Wrathful Deities work via the Head lotus. Detail concerning the transformation of *saṃskāras* in the body by means of these Herukas shall be provided in Volume 5A on the *Bardo Thödol*, consequently the subject need only be mentioned here. The Heruka assigned to Amitābha is Buddha-Heruka, with his Consort Buddha-Krodheśvarī, an emanation of Vairocana. The Element is Aether-Fire, the Prāṇa is *vyāna.*[32] The other petals are:

- The *Love-Wisdom—Knowledge petal* is governed by the energy of Vajra-Heruka and his Consort Vajra-Krodheśvarī, an emanation of Vajrasattva-Akṣobhya. The Element is Air-Fire, the Prāṇa is *prāṇa.*
- The *Knowledge—Sacrifice-Will petal* is governed by the energy of Padma-Heruka and his Consort Padma-Krodheśvarī, an emanation of Amitābha. The Element is Fire-Fire, the Prāṇa is *udāna.*
- The *Knowledge—Love-Wisdom petal* is governed by the energy of Ratna-Heruka and his Consort Ratna-Krodheśvarī, an emanation of Ratnasambhava. The Element is Water-Fire, the Prāṇa is *samāna.*
- The *Knowledge—Knowledge petal* is governed by the energy of Karma-Heruka and his Consort Karma-Krodheśvarī, an emanation of Amoghasiddhi. The Element is Earth-Fire, the Prāṇa is *apāna.*

The *symbol* for this group of petals is the moving *swastika,* which turns the Wheel of Life onwards in time and space garnering knowledge. The teachings from *The Uttaratantra of Maitreya* can now continue.

3. The Sacrifice-Will—Knowledge petal

Obermiller's translation runs thus:

103. The kernel of a fruit covered by a husk
Cannot be enjoyed by any man. Therefore
They who are desirous of eating it and the like
Extract it from the husk (that hides it).

---

32 Concerning the Prāṇas, the subject of the *vāyus,* the five winds which course through the *nāḍī* system, is introduced. The *vāyus* are here relegated to five main *nāḍīs,* or energy directions in the system, as controlled by one or other of the five main *chakras.* This subject shall be explained more fully in the later volumes.

104. In a similar way the (Essence of the) Buddha
Exists in the living beings, mingled with defilement,
And as long as it is not free from the contact with the stains of the passions,
It cannot perform the acts of the Buddha in the 3 Spheres.

105. The kernel of a grain of rice, of buckwheat or barley, unextracted from its husk and covered with bristles
And not duly prepared, cannot become sweet food enjoyed by man.
Similar is the Body of the Lord of the elements,
Existing in the living beings and undelivered from the coverings of defilement,
It does not grant to the living brings affected by the passions
The delightful flavour of the Truth.[33]

First we must analyse the kernel of fruit covered by a husk. This refers to the *gotra*, which is 'covered' by a skin of ideas and images of all types formulated by the knowledgeable pursuits of humanity throughout the ages. (The content of the mental plane within which it resides.) The sum of humanity's thoughts and desires, cultural mores, philosophies and religions (etc.) are implied here. Together they coalesce in the form of this 'husk'. All of humanity have contributed to its formation because they have collectively produced the images and forms of knowledge of the civilisations that we have laboured through.

The petals of the Sambhogakāya Flower also represent this 'husk', and 'the kernel' is the jewel in the heart of the lotus, which I have termed the Śūnyatā Eye. The entire Flower's growth emanates from this Eye and is sustained by its protective petals through the progress of time, from incarnation to incarnation of the personal-I's. The darkness of ignorance is overcome through the development of the right qualities of knowledge, and all such knowledge is synthesised in the five Knowledge petals of the Sambhogakāya Flower. In the concept of a husk or sheath surrounding a pure kernel there is thus the idea of incarnation. The link from the Sambhogakāya Flower anchors itself in the Head centre, the kernel of the personal-I, giving the ability to gain the enlightenment implicit in the Flower. The husk here represents the *saṃskāras* and *skandhas* that must be cleansed by the evolving consciousness.

33 Obermiller, 345-346.

The statement, however, is that they 'cannot be enjoyed by any man'.[34] In other words, not everyone at first has the capacity to pluck the sum of the collectivisation at will to get to the kernel. The husk must be rightfully removed in layers. There are very few that develop the capacity to sacrifice their own desires to remove the layers of relative truths and untruths, to get to the foundational source of all truth and ideas. The way of sacrifice is only developed upon the Bodhisattva path. All of the Sacrifice petals are directly concerned with treading the Bodhisattva *bhūmis*, of which there are three groups of three (3 x 3) plus an integrating one. From another perspective the five Sacrifice petals help develop the five pairs of the *bhūmis*. The Love-Wisdom—Sacrifice-Will petal and the Knowledge—Sacrifice-Will petal, however, are more directly concerned with establishing the environment of a Bodhisattva's Mind. They produce the 'entering of the stream' by the attainment of the right qualifications, first in the field where knowledge reigns supreme, and then in the field of Love.

Concerning the three main Sacrifice petals, an important concept is incorporated in the 'poisons'[35] that become the keywords of what sustains incarnated life and which are sacrificed upon the path to liberated Life. As earlier stated they are: *hatred,* overcome by the Sacrifice-Will—Sacrifice-Will petal, *desire,* overcome by the Sacrifice-Will—Love-Wisdom petal, and *ignorance,* overcome by the Sacrifice-Will—Knowledge petal. They are the seed causes of all wanderings in *saṃsāra,* and their qualities are found in the centre of the Wheel of Life (*srid-pa'i-khor-lo*). Govinda styles them greed, hate and delusion, and states:

> These three basic motives or root-causes *(hetu)* of unenlightened existence form the nave of the wheel of rebirths and are depicted in the form of three animals, symbolizing greed, hatred and delusion: a red cock stands for passionate desire and attachment *(rāga; Tib.: ḥdod-chags);* a green snake is the embodiment of hatred, enmity and aversion (*dveṣa; Tib.: źe-sdaṅ),* the qualities that poison our life; and a black hog symbolizes the darkness of ignorance and ego-delusion *(moha; Tib.: gti-mug),* the blind urge, that drives beings round and round in the unending cycle of births and deaths.

34 Fuchs, 33, has 'not fit to be eaten by man'.

35 Fuchs, 33: '[The nature of] the Victorious One, which is present within beings [but] mixed with the defilement of the poisons'.

> The three animals are biting each other's tails and are linked in such a way that they too form a circle, because greed, hatred, and delusion condition each other and are inseparably connected. They are the ultimate consequences of ignorance *(avidyā; Tib.: ma-rig)* concerning the true nature of things, on account of which we regard transient things as permanent, and unreal things as real and desirable.[36]

The entire course of the evolutionary journey is postulated here, starting from being 'buried' into these three root causes of perpetual rebirths, to the eventual transmutation of their qualities into their respective enlightenment-consciousnesses. What must be overcome through the use of sacrifice in the later stages is the self will, which robes the individual in husks of desire. (Self will is but an intensified form of personal desire.) Self will feeds the carnal person with the objects of desire. It creates the strands of *karma* whereby the rebirth process follows. The Will-to-Love must be developed in its place if liberation from these *karmic* strands is to eventuate. As the higher supplanting will is evoked so the qualities of these Sacrifice petals are developed and the person begins to acquiesce to *tathatā* and the totally transcendental qualities of the *dharmakāya.* Therein is expressed the qualities of the Dhyāni Buddhas. Such will produces the austere meditation of a *yogin,* which likewise drove the Buddha away from his pleasure palace to practice extreme forms of yogic disciplines.

This Sacrifice-Will—Knowledge petal of the Sambhogakāya Flower controls the functioning of the *Throat centre* and its equivalent in the Head centre (the Throat in the Head). The Throat centre is wherein the Fires of mind/Mind are awakened and controlled. Here, therefore, *bījas* of all types of images and thought impulses in the mind are rightly directed to produce liberating wisdom. All limiting, circumscribed, self-centred thought-forms are then eliminated or transformed into more wholesome fare for the abstract Mind, by means of the activity of this petal. This then sets the keynote for the interpretation of the three verses of this section.

The concept of 'hatred' with respect to the Sacrifice-Will—Sacrifice-Will petal implicates the complete elimination of all tendencies to the left hand path in yogic practices. It also relates to the complete transformation and transmutation of the attributes of *saṃsāra* (which are yogically

36 Govinda, 238.

'hated'). The strongest disciplining will is used to control the awakening *siddhis* so that they do not pervert into untoward consequences. The mastery of this energy awakens the complete Head centre.

The principle of desire-attachment to all pleasurable and desirous things, even of the beauteous images obtained through religious observations, and the awakening of euphoric sensations developed through the lower *siddhis* must be abandoned if the higher *siddhis* of *dharmakāyic* bliss is to be obtained. Many are the *yogins* that have fallen to wayward psychic impressions and distorted images that feed subtle forms of the ego rather than cultivate the true compassionate dispassion that produces liberation (from the 'self' concept). This is the objective of the Sacrifice-Will—Love-Wisdom petal to achieve via vitalising the petals of the Heart in the Head centre.[37] Wish-fulfilling images feeding subtle personal desires and glamour are other allurements fed by our brothers of dark countenance that must be discerned and converted into selflessness. They are but forms of psychic seduction and must be resisted sternly by all seeking genuine enlightenment.

This Sacrifice-Will—Knowledge petal is principally concerned with overcoming all vestiges of ignorance by providing impeccable rationale in the Clear Light of Mind. This petal is therefore directly concerned with the qualities attained by the Bodhisattva that strives to attain the first three of the *bhūmis*, which involve the right use of attained knowledge in the three worlds. The other petals lay the proper foundation for the eventual attainment of the advanced stages of the Bodhisattva Path.

The nature of the Sacrifice-Will—Knowledge petal of the Flower thus assists such a one to so refine the layers of accumulated knowledge from the husk so as to obtain the kernel of truth that lies at the heart of any line of investigation. The process of the accumulation of knowledge, causing the formation of the husk, and then its transformation, through right sacrificial activity, takes many millennia of evolutionary development for the personal-I's concerned.

We can see that the Throat centre's ability to control the Fires of mind/Mind in their most sacrificial aspect (and therefore the most refined or intense aspect of Fire) is specifically developed by means

37 See Volume 5A, chapter 7, for a detailed explanation of the Heart in the Head, the Throat in the Head and Solar Plexus in the Head centre.

of this petal. Pure logic is utilised to counteract wrong or erroneous thoughts and beliefs, thus layer after layer of the husk is removed until the pure kernel of truth remains.

Verse 104 refers specifically to the development of the wisdom aspect of this sacrificial Mind. Therefore it is focussed upon the nature of the kernel itself, which is pure sacrificial Love-Wisdom. We are thus told that 'in a similar way the (Essence of the Buddha) exists in the living beings, mingled with defilement'. This Buddha-essence is identifiable with the sacrifice aspect of this petal because that is the way of the attainment of Buddhahood, whilst the defilement with which it is mingled refers to the knowledge part of the petal. Knowledge must be converted to sacrificial wisdom over the course of time. Next we have a negatively phrased passage informing us that 'as long as it is not free from contact with the stains of the passions' then it 'cannot perform the acts of the Buddha in the 3 Spheres'. 'The stains of the passions' obviously refers to the nature of the *saṃskāras* of the desire-mind.

A stain refers to the surfacing of something with a colour of a different type that was there originally, or to taint one's integrity with guilt, vice, or corruption. It esoterically refers to a flow of the associated *saṃskāras* manifested via a number of lives. This then colours, or rather stains the pure hues of the Flower with the auric emanations of the *saṃskāras*. The specific type of stains referred to here are of 'the passions' (i.e., of one's emotions) that are the full expression of the desire-mind manifested in the realms of form. We therefore have an aeonic history implied whereby the personal-I's persistently colour their lives with such stains. The added information is provided, that as long as they do so, the Flower ('it') cannot project the sacrificial aspect of the Buddha quality into the personality world to cause the 'acts of the Buddha' to manifest. This is not just in the physical domain, but in the 'three spheres'—in the psychic and mental realms as well. Therefore, before the Sacrifice aspect of this petal can be activated we must wait for the 'turning about in the seat of consciousness' of a personal-I. Only then can the thoughts of compassion stream into consciousness whereby the Buddha nature can gain the upper hand to rightly cleanse *saṃskāras*.

Verse 105 deals with the mechanism whereby the sacrifice-knowledge aspect from the Flower (i.e., what manifests the 'acts of a

Buddha' in the realms of mind) can influence the lives of the incarnating personal-I's. This refers to awakening the attributes of Mind within the petals of the Head centre, the 1,000 petalled lotus. There are three major tiers of petals to this crown *chakra:*

1. The central tier—the Throat in the Head, concerned with the development of the sacrificial aspects of an enlightened Mind. This tier is actually triune, making five tiers to the Head lotus in all. This is essential, otherwise the five *prāṇic* emanations (Wisdoms) from the Dhyāni Buddhas could not influence the individual. The Throat tier is governed by the qualities of the Dhyāni Buddha Amoghasiddhi, whose All-accomplishing Wisdom is gained through the complete mastery of *saṃsāra* by means of the development of Mind. Its *prāṇas* are directed principally to the *Sacrifice-Will—Knowledge petal* of the Sambhogakāya Flower. (Verse number 99, when analysed correctly.) This concerns the beginning of the process of yogic mastery of mind and its transformation into Mind. It necessitates the discovery of Secret Mantra coupled with the unfoldment of the petals of the Throat tier in the Head lotus.
2. The middle tier, the Heart in the Head, governed by the *Sacrifice-Will—Love-Wisdom* petal of the Sambhogakāya Flower. This tier is concerned with the development of the qualities of *bodhicitta* and of wisdom. Consequently, it is the main avenue and conduit of *prāṇas* to the Sambhogakāya Flower, as *bodhicitta* is its main embodying energy, whose general qualities are governed by Ratnasambhava's Wisdom. The 'honey' to be gathered in verse number 102 represents the main energy directed by this tier of petals.
3. The outermost tier that is denoted 'the Solar Plexus in the Head' in Volume 5A consists of by far the greatest number of petals. It reaps the sum of knowledgeable attributes from *saṃsāric* involvement. Overall it processes the *prāṇas* absorbed by all of the remaining petals of the Sambhogakāya Flower, except the Sacrifice-Will—Sacrifice-Will petal. Amitābha's Wisdom rules the development of this tier of Head centre petals. The petals refine *prāṇas* before they are passed on to the inner tier. Verse 105 provides a general summary of the attributes developed by this outermost tier.

In verse 105 we are first presented with three types of grains to which this germ of the Buddha (in its three attributes) can be likened. The grains are of increasing coarseness, from rice, the most refined, hardest to produce and tastiest of the three, to buckwheat, coarser, but still delectable, and finally we have barley, covered with bristles, which is also used as a feed for stock. They consequently relate to the three major tiers of petals of the Head Lotus, the rice to the inner Throat in the Head tier, the buckwheat to the Heart in the Head tier and the barley to the Solar Plexus in the Head tier. Each kernel (referring to the innate triune essence of the *tathāgatagarbha*) is said to be 'unextracted from its husk', and 'covered with bristles' (the *samalā tathatā* condition), which has a reference to the hair of an incarnate individual, thus esoterically to the *nāḍīs* stemming from the tiers of the 1,000 petalled lotus. However, instead of being protective in nature (which the bristles are to the kernel) they extract information *(prāṇas)* from the lower centres. They can also symbolise the *antaḥkaraṇas* projected to the Sambhogakāya Flower by the personal-I.

Each type of grain needs to be cleansed of its husk and properly prepared to be the 'sweat food enjoyed by man'. The first stage of such preparation is that the bristles that can cause discomfort if swallowed, and that have no nutrition, must be eliminated. Here they symbolise the *saṃsāric* activities carried out by the incarnate personal-I's that do not contribute, or are antithetical, to gaining enlightenment. (Erroneous forms of activity, however, inevitably do contribute to the progress of wisdom by inadvertently teaching us what not to do.) This is similar to the bristles acting as a dispersal mechanism, allowing the seed to be carried by the wind, to propagate new fields of activity, new realms of knowledge. The husk symbolises the sum of the *saṃskāras* contained within the personal-I's persona and which must be dealt with appropriately. This characterises much of the type of activity of the outer Solar Plexus tier of the Head lotus.

The 'sweat food' refers to what the Sambhogakāya Flower extracts from the manifold activities of the personal-I via the Head Lotus that has been properly prepared (by cooking for instance, the mixing with other ingredients from the realm of enlightened being) so that it can be consumed, 'enjoyed by man'. Here the term 'man' refers to the

Flower's consciousness and what is consequently offered to humanity for its further progress. What is offered is the driving force behind the activities of a Bodhisattva. The Bodhisattva (the 'man') utilises the gain of all former knowledgeable pursuits and sacrifices them at the altar of human beneficence.

Next is the statement 'Similar is the Body of the Lord of the elements'.[38] The 'Lord of the elements' can refer to the Sambhogakāya Flower, and the 'Body' of this Lord to the personal-I, wherein the Elements, or qualities *(saṃskāras* and *skandhas)* are contained in a bodily form. We are thus asked to look to the reflection of the Flower in the body, namely the Head lotus, wherein consciousness is centred. We are told that this also is 'undelivered from the coverings of defilement'. This means that the person has yet to tread the yogic path to mastery whereby the defilements can be uncovered. (Similar to removing one's clothing to reveal the naked truth as to what lies underneath). The Flower stands revealed via the agency of the awakened Head lotus.

This Head lotus 'does not grant to the living being affected by the passions' the ability to see clearly the 'delightful flavour of the Truth' if *saṃskāras* are not worked upon by means of yogic processes. It should be noted that the former phrase concerning the 'coverings of defilement' implicates the mental *saṃskāras* which act as wrappings of mental substance, preventing clear vision or conception of the truth. The next phrase concerning those afflicted by 'the passions' refers to the emotional *saṃskāras*, which prevent clear perceptions of truth. They occlude mental impressions via their turbulent nature. The phrase 'the delightful flavour of the Truth' therefore refers directly to the effects upon consciousness that can 'taste' (signifying a subtle discernment of information) all higher impressions so as to directly experience truth. We thus have the development of the intuitive faculties, conferred by *bodhicitta* via awakening the Heart centre,[39] from which the truth can definitely be ascertained.

Note that the seven Ray attributes are veiled by the list given in this verse. We thus have:

---

38 Fuchs (page 34) has the statement 'Lord of Qualities'.

39 Note that both the Heart and Head centres have twelve main petals. They are needed for the complete conveyance of the energy of *bodhicitta*.

1. The *'kernels'* refer to the first Ray of Will or Power (manifesting via each of the three groups of petals of the Flower), as they are intrinsic to the *gotra* and will grow according to prearranged pathways.
2. The *'sweat food'* refers to the second Ray of Love-Wisdom, as this food is the emanation of the *buddhadharma* itself.
3. The *'Lord of the elements'* refers to the third Ray of Mathematically Exact Activity, as here the *gotra* is made active within the lives of the personal-I's that must eventually evolve the Buddha nature.
4. That which is *'existing in living beings'* can be considered the *gotra*, or else *śūnyatā*. In either case we observe the principle that will produce harmony in the midst of *saṃsāric* strife (the fourth Ray). It refers also to the Heart centre sustaining the Life of all living things. Without a heart pumping the Blood *(prāṇa)* of Life no living being could exist. This *chakra* is the fourth (or middle one) of the seven.
5. The *'covering of defilement'* refers to the various aspects of mind, and thus to the application of consciousness, which relates to the fifth Ray of Scientific Reasoning.
6. The *'passions'* refer to the emotions, and therefore have reference to the sixth Ray of Devotion, which is but a heightened emotion.
7. The *'delightful flavour of Truth'* relates to the seventh Ray of Ceremonial or Cyclic activity and manifest Power, as such truth is wrought through physical plane involvement via cyclic *saṃsāric* activity to produce its consequent mastery.

4. The Love-Wisdom—Sacrifice-Will petal

Verses 106-109 of Obermiller's translation relate to the *Love-Wisdom—Sacrifice-Will petal.*

106. Suppose that the gold belonging to a certain man
Were, at the time of his departure, cast into a place filled with impurities.
Being of an indestructible nature, this gold
Would remain there for many hundreds of years.

107. Then a god possessed of pure divine vision
Would see it there and say to men:—
The gold which is to be found here, this highest of precious things,
I shall purify and return to its precious form.

108. In a like way the Lord perceives the true virtues of the living beings
Sunk amidst the passions that are like impurities,
And, in order to wash off this dirt of Desire,
Lets the rain of the Highest Doctrine descend on all that lives.

109. Just as a god, seeing gold falling into a pit of impurities,
Would zealously show it to men in its beautiful nature in order to gladden them,
In a like way the Lord sees in the living beings
The jewel of the Supreme Buddha fallen amidst the great impurities of the passions,
And shows the Doctrine in order to purify it.[40]

Verse 106 refers directly to the energy of the Flower as an aspect of (Divine) Love. This energy is the 'gold belonging to a certain man'. A golden colour (golden-orange) is the general hue or radiance of the Flower, specifically once the Love-Wisdom petals have been properly activated. (It stands thus as a golden sun.) It should be emphasised that we are observing energy states whenever such qualities as 'love' is expressed. Energy of one form or other is all there is, which becomes quantified by consciousness to produce the forms of consciousness-attributes, such as are here being described.

This gold symbolises the pure nature and high value of the teachings and is the colour that qualifies the Heart centre, thus the *bodhicitta* associated with it.[41] Only a Bodhisattva in the process of becoming a Buddha, the embodiment of Love-Wisdom, can fully mine and refine this principle of Love from out of the mire ('rotting refuse'[42]) of *saṃsāra*. The quality of the petal indicated by this verse is that of Love-Wisdom—Sacrifice-Will. It concerns the right sacrificial expression of the wisdom (gold) gleaned from aeons of knowledgeable pursuits directed towards self aggrandisement (dirt). Only through wisdom can one glean the precious gold hidden in the mire and rain down the cleansing, purifying energies of Love, 'the Highest Doctrine' upon others so that they too can abstract what is precious amongst the filth.

40 Obermiller, 216-217.

41 This is one colouration of this energy, intense blue is another, depending upon the mode of its expression.

42 Fuchs translation (p. 34) is 'the gold he owned fell into a place filled with rotting refuse'.

The rain analogy relates to the downpour of purifying energies *(bodhicitta)* from this Love-Wisdom—Sacrifice-Will petal via the Head lotus to the centres below the diaphragm. (Hence literally the energies pour from a high place to the 'ground'.) There the dirt of the Earthy-Watery *saṃskāras* are to be cleansed of their gross impurities by means of the action of the Splenic centres.

Those that are receptive to the energies from this petal thus must manifest the skilful use of *bodhicitta* (from where this energy is derived), which in the form of Love-Wisdom, teaches all sentient beings the right and wrong things to do on the path to liberation. This is precisely the function of the Buddha here, who pours forth 'the rain of sacred Dharma',[43] which comes from above to cleanse the defilements below.

The phrase 'a certain man' can refer to the Sambhogakāya Flower, or of a particular personal-I. The 'gold' then being the wisdom extracted from *saṃsāric* mire by the various incarnations of the personal-I. When each individual disincarnates ('the time of his departure') then all of the *saṃskāras* generated return to the general pool of past life accumulations. The resultant *bījas* of all types of propensities constitute the impurities that fill this mind-space (*ālayavijñāna*), which is wherein the wisdom-gold is placed. The wisdom content of all the *saṃskāras* is indestructible because it is incorporated in context into the *tathāgatagarbha.*

The phrase 'at the time of his departure' can refer to the interlude between incarnations, wherein the Flower 'departs' from one personal-I and then projects the gold of its radiance into the Head lotus of the succeeding 'I'. This makes the Head lotus and the rest of the *chakra* system 'the place filled with impurities', as *saṃskāras* from previous lives are evoked for the new set of experiences. The gold which is the spiritual Love and Wisdom of the Flower is of an indestructible nature and will remain for the symbolic 'many hundreds of years'.[44] We know the personality will not live that long on the physical realm, but consciousness persists, which eventually becomes imbued with the Flower's radiance, as it transforms the consciousness to evolve *bodhicitta*, by manifesting or emulating the qualities of the Flower.

43 Fuchs, 34.

44 The sum of the cycles of incarnatory experience until Buddhahood (evolutionary perfection) is reached.

The 'gold' may remain in *bīja* form for a vast amount of time before being extracted and refined from the mire of knowledgeable things. This then is the background to an understanding of the way that knowledge is transformed into wisdom, which is a vast undertaking. In a sense, this number of years expresses the sacrifice of the aeons of time by the Flower, as it waits for the fruits of that which it has seeded in *saṃsāra* to ultimately germinate into golden sacrificial wisdom bright. This process awakens the rectified wheel of the Heart *chakra*, which this particular petal of the Sambhogakāya Flower controls.

From this perspective the 'time of departure' refers to entering into *śūnyatā* by the *yogin* absorbed in *dhyāna* with the fruit of his attainment, the gold, being left behind in the *ālayavijñāna* (which is the 'place filled with impurities'). The many hundreds of years then refers to the timeless nature of the *samādhi,* and indicates that the wisdom principle would be regained upon awakening from such meditation.

The 'god possessed of pure divine vision' in verse 107 represents the consciousness of the Sambhogakāya Flower, which here directs its Eye away from the *dharmakāya* into the human world via the *Love-Wisdom—Sacrifice-Will petal.* (Thus its vision represents the purest intent to Love.) It has projected its essence into the 1,000 petals of the Head centre of the personal-I, wherein the essence has become 'the highest of precious things'. This is what is sought by the *yogin* in deep meditation. Once such a *yogin* has appeared from the stream of the personal-I's then the Flower can wisely work to purify the defilements via this petal, and return the spiritual gold 'to its precious form'. 'Gold' then becomes the philosopher's stone. It is in the nature of the energy of the sacrificial aspect of Love to work ardently to cleanse the muddy auric and murky *saṃskāric* colourings of the defilements with the radiance of the golden honeyed energy. These energies can then work from within-without. The *yogin* draws upon them to effect his *prāṇic* cleansings upon the upward way, and to gain the *siddhis* producing an occult vision allowing conscious work upon the transmutation of all gross qualities associated with the threefold form.

The *Love-Wisdom—Sacrifice-Will petal* works directly via the petal of purest Love (the *Love-Wisdom—Love-Wisdom petal)* to express its purpose in the manifest world. Verse 108 deals with this combination, as only the deepest Love allows perception of 'the true virtues of the living beings'. It necessitates being able to peer deep into the Heart centre, to determine what extent Buddha-like qualities have been developed.

For such a meditation to be effective the Sambhogakāya Flower must be able to discern the strength of the Love of general humanity, not just that of the individual personal-I to which it is responsive. This is necessary if the activities borne of Love are to wisely manifest, as the patterns of Humanity's true needs must be understood. This information can then be projected into the Mind of the Bodhisattva that manifests as the Flower's incarnate expression to help awaken the Heart centres of all humanity. In this way what is truly needed can be rightly given through skilful means.

The prime effect of this meditation upon the Heart centre works to compassionately cleanse the Watery *piṅgalā* stream of the consciousness-aspect of humanity.[45] This refers to cleansing 'the passions that are like impurities' and the 'dirt of desire'. 'Passions' can refer to the higher passions, akin to aspiration, and a fervent wish to do right (but not yet having developed sufficient comprehension of how to rightly act), as well as forms of obsessions to sensuality and pleasurable things. For the *yogin* all forms of passions, being emotions, are 'impurities'. Desire is here identified with 'dirt' because such desire is always for *saṃsāric* allurements. Fuchs gives us 'sunken in the filth-like mental poisons' upon which is poured the 'rain of sacred Dharma' to 'purify the muddiness of their afflictions',[46] which more correctly depicts the Watery nature of the attribute of desire-emotions (the 'afflictions'), which when mixed with the 'dirt' of physical plane attachments and activities produces muddied *saṃskāras* needing purifying.

Pure Love, the purest outflow of the *dharma*, manifests as an Airy-Fiery purificatory force when working to cleanse and transform the Watery *prāṇas*. This Airy-Fiery energy is effectively the way that the highly energetic Waters of cosmic Love[47] (of a Buddha) 'rains' down 'the Highest Doctrine' upon the human units needing its outpouring. This 'Doctrine' is in fact the Dharmakāya Way directed by means of the

45 The focus here is along the second Ray line of the 2, 4, 6 Rays, rather than the mind line *per se* (the 1, 3, 5, 7 Rays).

46 Fuchs, 34.

47 These Waters represent a higher transcendental, transmuted version of the Watery Element that governs human emotions via the substance of the astral plane. (The plane is explained in Volume 4.)

Sacrifice-Will and Love petals of the Sambhogakāya Flower to the world via the awakened Bodhisattva that can express the energies. The teachings feed the minds of those willing to cleanse their *nāḍīs* from defilements.

The mechanism of cleansing the impurities and 'the muddiness of their afflictions' is given in verse 109, which relates to the functioning of the superimposed *Splenic centres*. This is the 'pit of impurities' into which the gold falls. Here a 'pit' is likened to a *chakra* because a pit can be considered a storage device (e.g., of types of *prāṇas*) and is normally circular in nature. The impurities being the grosser *saṃskāras* that are channelled to the Splenic centre to be refined and recycled through the *nāḍīs*. The 'gold' being the energy that effects their purification and transformation.

The 'god' zealously showing people the 'beautiful nature' of the gold in 'order to gladden them' refers to the qualities of the Sambhogakāya Flower emanating via the Heart centre and projecting the golden energy to the highest (twelve petalled) Splenic centre, which then effects the necessary purification of *prāṇas*. The 'gladdened', purified *prāṇas* are then circulated throughout the *nāḍīs*, vitalising all with golden energies. Thus the body is sustained and kept healthy.

The second part of verse 109 concerns the work of the superimposed eight-petalled Splenic centre and represents the powerhouse for cleansing the most muddied *prāṇas*. It deals with the process of rejecting unnecessary, putrid *prāṇas* ('the great impurities of the passions'). Here the proper white *dharma* must be obeyed and actively followed if the grosser *saṃskāras* are to be transmuted, allowing cleaner *prāṇas* to flow through the *nāḍīs*. It is essential that the sacrificial energies of Love and wisdom are utilised to cleanse impurities from the system. Only the purest Love can rightly combat the evil doing of people. Compassion is needed for the duration that people manifest muddied action, the right educational activity made manifest so that people learn what not to do. This necessitates working from the precincts of the Heart centre. The Bodhisattva path ensues.

5. The Love-Wisdom—Love-Wisdom petal

The verses from *The Uttaratantra of Maitreya*, translated by Obermiller relating to the *Love-Wisdom—Love-Wisdom petal* are numbered 110-112:

110. Suppose in a poor man's house, deep under the ground,
An inexhaustible treasure were concealed.
The man would know nothing about it,
And the treasure itself could not say to him
That it is to be found here in this place.

111. Similar to this is the treasures contained in the Spirit,
The Immaculate Essence which neither diminishes nor increases;
The living beings that know nothing about it
Constantly experience manifold suffering that is like poverty.

112. As a treasure of jewels concealed in a poor man's house
Does not make it known to that man,—
I, the treasure am here, — and the man does not know about it, —
Such is the treasure of the Highest Truth abiding in the dwelling place of the Spirit,
And the living being possessed of it are like beggars;
In order to secure for them this treasure
The Sage makes his apparition in the world.[48]

We can now analyse the heart of the Sambhogakāya Flower's form and purpose. At the beginning stages of evolution this is likened to 'the poor man's house'. The 'house' here is the Flower whose petals must yet gain the 'Tathāgata's priceless treasure of jewels', which is structured to contain it. The heart of the Flower, the Śūnyatā Eye, contains this 'treasure' obtained from 'above', but the form of the Flower must also exhume treasure (wisdom) from the 'ground'. The phrase 'under the ground' refers to *saṃsāra* wherein the personal-I's incarnate to develop wisdom via compassionate activity, representing the radiance of the 'jewels' that vivify the petals of the *chakras* of a person. The jewel-like qualities of the various wisdoms must be extracted from the dirt of *saṃsāra* and made radiant via the *chakras* that are conditioned to embody the qualities. The attributes are then absorbed by the Sambhogakāya Flower.

The 'inexhaustible treasure' thus refers to the ineffable *dharma* that is equated with the expression of compassionate understanding (Love) and the accompanying wisdom. The greatest treasure is concealed as

48 Obermiller, 347.

the jewel in the heart of each *chakra*, ranging from the Base of Spine to the Head centre. These 'jewels' are aligned in the *suṣumṇā nāḍī* and integrated by the Sambhogakāya Flower. The 'ground' here being the substance into which consciousness incarnates, the deepest part of which psychically is the Base of Spine centre *(mūlādhāra chakra)*. The principle of Love, however, is seeded in the Heart centre. No matter how deeply the principle may be buried in the most base of humans the evolutionary process will ascertain that inevitably this treasure will be revealed. This is possible because this process is governed by the Sambhogakāya Flower for each human unit. The Lords of Life (advanced Bodhisattvas and *ḍākinīs)* existing on the Dharmakāyic realms also assist in the development of its foundation in all kingdoms of Nature. The entire Bodhisattvic purpose ensures a process of gradual revelation of the treasure. Thus the Heart centre is gradually awakened.

For the greatest part of the evolutionary journey, however, 'the man' who occupies this house of the human form will know nothing about the treasure because the Sambhogakāya Flower cannot speak to him to reveal its whereabouts. This is because the person is too engrossed with gross desire, focussed upon outer sense indulgences and pleasurable pursuits. The noises of this world are far too deafening to hear the subtleties of the silent voice of the Heart speaking. For this 'the ears to hear' the cries of the suffering ones need to be developed. *Bodhicitta* consequently cannot yet resoundingly speak. Still, the subtle processes of the Flower will work for epochs upon the incarnated personal-I's, as need demands, until the 'I' learns to reject the clashing sounds of the external noises by seeking the meditative peace of the way of the Heart's Mind unfolding. Therein instructions can be heard as how best to treat the ephemera all around. The Clear Light of Mind is experienced, 'which is free from defilement. Nothing is to be added and nothing is to be removed'.[49]

It has already been posited that the *arhat* experience concerns conscious absorption into the Sambhogakāya Flower, which contemplates much upon the conditions concerning its own realm and upon *saṃsāra*. Eventually such contemplation causes one who has previously chosen an *arhat's* form of meditation to take rebirth upon the Bodhisattva path

49 Fuchs, 34.

so that a Tathāgata's body of Love-Wisdom and Mind can be obtained. The most priceless treasures of the *dharma* are contained within these Love-Wisdom petals of the Flower.

The *Love-Wisdom—Love-Wisdom petal* is spoken of in the form of 'the Dharma's treasure',[50] being 'the Highest Truth abiding in the dwelling-place of the Spirit'. Love-Wisdom is 'The Immaculate Essence which neither diminishes nor increases'. As Love-Wisdom is on both sides of the expression signifying this petal, there is no way for this petal to expresses itself other than in the form of Love-Wisdom. It can neither diminish or increase. This is true enough, but what is implied here is the nature of the energy of *bodhicitta* and the effect of the revelation of its qualities in the Minds of those that express it. It means that Love suffices unto itself. All that a person does when travelling along the path is to eliminate the layers of obscuration between his/her consciousness-muck and the Love that is already fully established, evolved and placed there by means of the inherent Flower which has seeded all of the *chakras* with its presence. As the obscurations are eliminated by means of wisdom (and yogic will) the principle of Love is increasingly revealed and the Bodhisattva Path is trod to Buddhahood. The 'Immaculate Essence' of the principle of Love, therefore, is simply revealed for what it is as the person unfolds the compassionate way by following the Bodhisattva path.

The 'living beings that know nothing about it' (of the true nature of Love, hence of the Bodhisattva way) will as a consequence constantly 'experience manifold suffering'. Only the path of Love and its application as wisdom leads one out of the trap of the suffering of *karma*-engendered activities. A lack of manifestation of Love is indeed poverty of the spirit. Such poverty concerns the non-revelation of the treasures contained at the heart of any of the *chakras* wherein this Love is veiled in the seven distinct ways (of the Rays) yet to be properly awakened by the person. The ensuing enlightenment makes one very wealthy indeed.

Verse 112 deals with the general qualities of the Heart centre (the *anāhata chakra),* because this *chakra* holds the power of the collectivised jewels of Love in its grasp. It represents an open door to *śūnyatā*. In this respect *śūnyatā* is but the way of Love revealed as the

50 Fuchs, 35.

Heart of all that is and will be. Is this definition too difficult to bear for the discriminative mind, or can it grasp the way that Love lays all bare, so that which is void of all attributes is revealed through the elimination of the attributes of mind? All has been fused into oneness (where there is no real distinction between this or that). Oneness is a close approximation or description of such a Love. When this petal is awakened and functioning via one's meditations then the *śūnyatā* experience is possible, as this experience must come via the Śūnyatā Eye at the heart of the Flower.

It is also in the nature of *śūnyatā* to 'not make itself known to that man', it has not the ability to speak and say 'I, the treasure am here'. However, the Flower can do this. It can reveal the way and indicate the nature of that which is to be experienced. This is 'the treasure of the Highest Truth abiding in the dwelling place of the Spirit' (the Heart centre, and specifically the Love-Wisdom petals of the Flower). At first living beings that are possessed of it are like beggars because they can only receive the goodness and associated wisdom derived from its expression in small doses. Only as the higher Bodhisattva *bhūmis* are attained do they actually become 'wealthy', able to dispense some of these riches to others. Thereby the sage with a fully awakened Heart centre 'makes his apparition in this world'. The term 'apparition' informs us that all is truly phenomenal, even the appearance of the sage.

6. The Love-Wisdom—Knowledge petal

From Obermiller's translation the verses relating to the *Love-Wisdom—Knowledge petal* are numbered 113-115:

113 The germ of the seed, contained in the fruit
Of the Mango-tree and the like, is of an imperishable nature,
And through cultivation of the ground, water and other (agencies),
Gradually attains the form of a lordly tree.

114. In a like way the Sublime Absolute Essence
Is concealed under the coverings of the fruit
Of a living being's ignorance and the like,
(But) on the foundation of this and that form of virtue,
It gradually assumes the character of the King of Sages.

115. Conditioned by water, the light of the sun,

> By air, soil, time, and space,
> From the rind of the Mango's and Palmyra's fruit
> There springs forth a tree;
> Like that the Germ of the seed of the Buddha,
> Concealed in the peal of the fruit of a living being's passions,
> Can thrive when the Highest Truth is revealed by this and that condition.[51]

The *Love-Wisdom—Knowledge petal* represents the active expression of the Love that must grow fruit, like a 'tree' bearing the Head lotus of the incarnate personality in the form of all knowable things. The tree of revelation that is chosen here (verse 113) is that of the 'Mango-tree and the like'. A mango tree grows to a large size and bears many delicious fruits, of a yellow-orange colour within the general green of the activity of Nature. This colouration is likened to the nature of the form of activity of this Love-Wisdom—Knowledge petal within the world of the personal-I. The germ, the Love principle, is however of 'an imperishable nature', for the fruits of Love are imperishable and produce the attainment of Buddhahood. The knowledge part refers to the propagation of the fruit all over the tree that anyone can pick and eat. It is that which grows.

This is the tree of 'the Highest Truth' appearing from the defilement covered seed. This refers to the fact that the seed of *bodhi* planted in the personal-I gradually grows through the accumulation of many knowledgeable things in the field of right giving and service to the whole. The seed has not only grown the trunk of the *dharma*, but many branches of wisdom as well, and various layers of leaves and floral offerings to greet the bewildered ones in *saṃsāra*'s domain. With the accumulation of knowledge of how to rightly Love, so also the Knowledge petals of the Sambhogakāya Flower have grown to begin to embrace the qualities of the transcendental truth of a Tathāgata. The *bījas* of such knowledge can be rayed down into the successive appearing personal-I's to facilitate growth to enlightenment in any life, and to act as a store of realisable wisdom upon which each 'I' can draw in the quest to rightly educate others.

---

51 Obermiller, 217-218.

The phrase 'through cultivation of the ground, water and other (agencies)' refers to the development of right knowledge along the path of Love/*bodhicitta* gleaned by the personalities that evolve in the formed realms. The water refers to the emotional input of this development, and the 'other agencies' refer to the sum of the *karma* and *saṃskāras* that must also play their part in the right education of the person concerned. Fuchs has 'earth, water, and other [conditions]',[52] which refer to the Elements constituting the *saṃskāras*. The Flower thus seeds the person with the qualities to rightfully develop knowledge and wisdom upon the road of Love. The personal-I 'attains the form of the lordly tree' as a consequence. This tree refers to the tree of Initiation into the mysteries of being/non-being, which is the *bodhi* tree that the Buddha sat under to gain his enlightenment. Each person develops his own version of such a tree. Another interpretation is that the intricate *nāḍī* system within the body can be considered to be in the form of a tree.

Verse 114 directs us first to the *gotra*/Flower, specifically to the way that it reflects the qualities of the *dharmakāya,* which is veiled in the words, 'the Sublime Absolute Essence'. Ultimately the knowledgeable attributes gained from *saṃsāra*'s domain in conjunction with Love-Wisdom are needed to develop the Dharmakāya Way; whereas Love-Wisdom progressed to its conclusion leads to *śūnyatā*.

At first knowledge can contain 'ignorance and the like', but later revelatory understanding clarifies this. Here we have an indication as to the interrelation between the Knowledge—Love-Wisdom petal and the Love-Wisdom—Knowledge petal, the qualities of which are evolved within the mind of the person. Right knowledge seeds the personality with the understanding of all things concerning *saṃsāra*. When Love-Wisdom is incorporated then *bodhicitta* is awakened, so that ultimately the *dharmakāya* can be gleaned. This entire path is thus 'concealed under the coverings of the fruit'. The objective is to conquer a 'being's ignorance and the like', to convert ignorance into revelation by means of the application of the right quantity and quality of golden-orange light. This is expressed as wisdom when Love is engendered via the developing mind. Such accomplishment is by means of gaining 'this and that form of virtue' to counter the spiritual squalor that ignorance

52 Fuchs, 35.

fosters. The resultant following of the Dharmakāya Way then allows the appearance of 'the King of sages', a fully realised Buddha, from amongst the ranks of humanity.

Verse 115 directs our vision to the functioning of the *chakras* below the diaphragm, to the world of the self-willed personality and his/her emotional conditionings. We have the functions of the *Splenic centres* implied and their relation to the Solar Plexus centre. This centre (the *maṇipūra chakra)* is most important at this stage of development and becomes the focus for all activity. It is the 'abdominal brain', the powerhouse of the Watery circulation controlling the expression of the emotional-mind. Here all *bījas* associated with the personality are accommodated and processed, as previously explained. Eventually the will must be evoked to overcome all *saṃsāric* impediments along the road leading to *dharmakāya.* The verse thus starts with the major conditionings influencing this arena of activity, starting with that of Water (the emotions/desire), which is the major Element that circulates through the *nāḍīs* of this lower way. Next we have 'the light of the sun',[53] which refers directly to the emanatory *prāṇas* from the Heart centre. They serve to rectify the personality oriented *prāṇas* into those of wisdom and Love. Having analysed the major Watery influences below the diaphragm the list then moves to the remaining Elements and the *bījas* that are seeded to help in nurturing positive life within *saṃsāra,* 'air, soil, time, and space'.

- Soil—the *prāṇas* of the Earthy Element.
- Water—the *prāṇas* of the Watery Element.
- Time—the *prāṇas* of the Fiery Element, as time is an aspect of consciousness, which is governed by this Element.
- Air—the *prāṇas* of the Airy Element.
- Space—the *prāṇas* of the Aetheric Element.

The phrase 'the light of the sun' needs further explanation, because it would normally be relegated as an aspect of the Airy Element, as this Element is equated with the Love principle, *śūnyatā*, and *bodhicitta.* They are all veiled by the sun. The sun stands for the sum of the

53 Esoterically, the Heart centre is symbolised by the sun, and the Solar Plexus centre by the moon.

Sambhogakāya Flower and the nature of its qualities, of the way it works with respect to the evolving personal-I's, feeding them with the radiance and the energy of Life that sustains their integral being. Both are sources of the light that conquers darkness. Within the body, however, three 'suns' can be visualised:

a. *The Central Spiritual Sun*—the 1,000 petalled Head lotus, responsible for vitalising the personal-I with the invigorating quality of the consciousness that is borne.

b. *The Heart of the Sun*—the Heart centre responsible for vitalising the personal-I with the energy of *bodhicitta.*

c. *The Physical Sun*—the Sacral centre, responsible for vitalising the entire body with *prāṇas* that produce physical well being.

These suns[54] are symbolically responsible for vitalising the various forms of trees. There are actually three trees veiled by the text, each to be nourished by one or other of the three suns:

a. The *Mango tree,* which gives forth luscious golden yellow fruit. This symbolises the energies and qualities of the *piṇgalā nāḍī.* It is directly vitalised by the Heart of the Sun. This tree has its roots in the Solar Plexus centre and is sustained by nourishing Waters and the Airy qualities of *bodhicitta.*

b. The *Palmyra tree.* This palm is noted for its hard resistant wood, fronds, and sugar-rich sap. Thus it symbolises the qualities of the active aspects of the *iḍā nāḍī.* It has its roots in the soil of *saṃsāra* via the Sacral centre, as it is sustained by the field of desire producing knowledgeable attributes via the five senses. It is vitalised by the physical Sun.[55]

c. That relating to the phrase 'There springs forth a tree', which refers to the *nāḍī* system extending from the *suṣumṇā nāḍī* in the central spinal column. This is the Tree of Life, allowing Initiation into the mysteries of being/non-being, vitalised by the Central Spiritual

54 There are higher interpretations of these 'suns', such as the central spiritual sun referring to Monadic Life, the Heart of the sun to the Sambhogakāya Flower, and the physical sun to the Head lotus.

55 Rather than the Palmyra, Fuchs has 'the fruit of a banana'. Ibid., 35.

Sun. It has its roots in the Base of Spine centre and projects up to the Sambhogakāya Flower, and is sustained by the Fires of the *ālayavijñāna*. Ultimately, the *nāḍīs* extend all the way to the *dharmakāya*. Its flowers are all of the *chakras* in the body.

This *suṣumṇā* 'tree' then metaphorically 'springs forth' from 'the rind', the hard, tough exterior portion of 'the Mango's and Palmyra's fruit'. The 'fruit' having reference to the energies of the Love-Wisdom—Knowledge petal (symbolically the Mango) and the Knowledge—Love-Wisdom petal (symbolically the fruit of the Palmyra tree). The 'rind' therefore refers to that which is projected into manifestation in the form of the *saṃskāras* contained by, or associated with, the *iḍā* and *piṅgalā nāḍīs*. From this perspective there would be two lots of air, water, soil, time, and space conditionings to consider.

The qualities of the *suṣumṇā nāḍī* manifests like 'the germ of the seed of the Buddha, concealed in the peal of the fruit of a living being's passions'. It, however, thrives 'when the highest Truth is revealed by this and that condition'. These conditions refer to the attributes that become manifest upon the highest Tantras perfected by the accomplished *yogin*. 'This and that condition' can therefore refer to *prāṇas* within the *iḍā* and *piṅgalā nāḍīs*. These *nāḍīs* manifest an integral unity with the *suṣumṇā nāḍī*, making the three-fold cord running up the spinal column, uniting the Base of Spine *chakra* and the Head Lotus with living Fire.

7. The Knowledge—Sacrifice-Will Petal

The last of the triads of the Sambhogakāya Flower, which govern the Knowledge attributes, can now be analysed. They are normally the most developed in a human unit because directly related to the experiences gained by means of the five sense-perceptors. This concerns the accumulation of all the lives of consciousness-gains in the field of learning; first knowledge for knowledge's sake (the Knowledge—Knowledge Petal), then the love of knowledge placed in the service of family, community, the nation, and later for the all. Finally, there is the sacrifice of redundant or erroneous knowledge by the religiously or altruistically inclined who are willing to suffer martyrdom, verbal animosity, and slanderous hostility and malice, for what they know to be right and true.

The continuing verses (numbers 116-118) from Obermiller's translation relate to the *Knowledge—Sacrifice-Will petal.*

116. Suppose the image of the Lord made of precious jewels
Were covered by a tattered foul-smelling garment,
And a god travelling that way would see it
And, in order to free it (from that covering),
Would explain the meaning of its abiding on the path
To the people that are met with there.
117. In a like way the Buddha perceives his own Essence
As it exists even in animals,
Covered by the various forms of defilement which are beginningless,
And, in order to release it, shows the means (of deliverance).
118. As the precious image of the Buddha covered by a foul-smelling garment
Is seen by a god with divine vision who shows it to men in order to release it,
In the same way the Lord perceives, even in the beasts,
The Germ covered by the tattered garment of defilement.
And abiding on the path of worldly existence, —
And expounds his Doctrine in order to deliver it.[56]

The concept of 'tattered foul-smelling garment' indicates the fact that the sacrificial qualities (the *saṃskāras* of the Sacrifice petals), and the related energy of spiritual Will, are the hardest things to achieve during the course of human evolution. They are antithetical to normal human avaricious, self-seeking activities. Consequently, the 'garment' of the *saṃskāras* with which the Knowledge-Sacrifice petal must deal for the most part of the evolutionary history of the incarnate personal-I's is 'tattered', threadbare. True sacrificial activity of the 'I' rarely manifests, except at the end of the evolutionary process. It is 'tattered' in relation to the easier to relate to Love-Wisdom qualities, and even more substantial knowledgeable factors. It is easier to follow the patterns established in the cultural norm of one's religion or society than to go against it (when inconsistencies or errors are found therein). One can still be a loving being in following the cultural norm, but the highest form of Love is

56 Obermiller, 218-219.

sacrificial in nature, and the people that develop this form of Love are Bodhisattvas. Such ones are consequently rare.

The 'tatteredness' relates also to the nature of the intellect from whence knowledge is derived, as compared to the Love principle (which is given the qualities of 'honey', 'inexhausatable treasures', or 'the flesh of fruit').

All of the 'precious jewels' constituting the 'image of the Lord' are made up of the revelations gained as a consequence of the myriad little acts of sacrifice that inevitably produce the Bodhisattva Path. The greater the number of precious jewels there are the greater the accomplishment of the sage or Bodhisattva concerned. The *bījas* contained in this Knowledge—Sacrifice-Will petal are thus constituted of the sacrifice of all irrelevant knowledge accrued from former lives of attainment and which no longer serve a useful function. Until this is accomplished the 'garment' (taking the sum of the Knowledge petals into account) is 'foul-smelling' with the covering *(samalā tathatā)* of the mental-emotional impurities. The concept of 'smelling' relates to the absorption of *prāṇas* (which are esoterically conveyed in the Air) by the Flower,[57] whilst the term 'foul' relates to their type of energy qualification.

Each sacrifice of a past attainment, or attachment to something ephemeral, means a step forward upon the spiral of evolution and thus constitutes a jewel stored within the constitution of this petal of the Flower. An interpretation of 'the image of the Lord' here is the image of the Sambhogakāya Flower as a whole, which takes the attributes of a Buddha for the personal-I.

This 'tattered foul-smelling garment' thus represents the Watery attributes of mind, within which the Flower is normally ensconced. More specifically however it represents the *nāḍīs* of the incarnate individual. It is 'foul-smelling' because that is the way that the mental-emotional *prāṇas* are perceived by the Sambhogakāya Flower (or liberated one) that abstracts the essences or perfumes of what is gained through the experience of repeated incarnations. The foul quality expresses the person's normal gross passions and desires. The putrefaction factor is produced by many uselessly repeated actions in the murky swamp of *saṃsāra*. The word 'tattered' as representing the mental *saṃskāras*

57 Such attributes are then stored in *bīja* form.

of the individual has already been given. We saw that the levels of knowledge are not complete along any line of investigation, with many lacunae of wrong knowledge and plain ignorance. The 'garment of the mind' of the average individual is perceived thus by a seer. There is also much to be sacrificed, but little willingness to do so, as the individual concerned is usually attached to little shreds of knowledge, as if these were the most valuable things in the world.

How to assist such a one to eliminate such tatters of understanding, and to move on to new fresh garments, is a difficult thing for any passing 'god' (an awakened sage or seer) to do. Such sages are indeed 'gods' to the average person, because their garments are radiant, composed of the most brilliant colours, containing many jewels, and are complete in every detail.

The phrase 'travelling that way' indicates that such a 'god'/sage is also travelling in *saṃsāric* realms. When an accomplished one sees another person with a 'tattered garment', yet at the same time seeing hidden within the potential for much sacrificial action by virtue of what has been accrued in the Knowledge—Sacrifice-Will petal of that person's Flower, then the sage will deem the person worthy of education. He/she will try to assist the removal of the tattered garment because the person has the capacity in that life to do so. Thus the 'meaning of the abiding of the path' can be explained to all such well destined aspirants.

Verse 117 informs us that in a similar way a Buddha (in the form of the Lord of Nature) is not just concerned with liberating the essential Life of individual humans, but also of every sentient being, because the *gotra* is hidden in all that is evolving human awareness states. Animal Life too must therefore be helped on their evolutionary road to intelligent awareness. In fact, all Life is 'covered by the various forms of defilements which are beginningless'. The term 'beginningless' here means since before the foundations of time, i.e., before time was even reckoned (by human minds that could do so). Enlightened beings are concerned with the sum of the evolutionary process throughout Nature, and liberated ones have been actively working with the group evolution of the lesser kingdoms even before there was an appearance of the present human kingdom to appreciate things with their minds.

When the liberated one looks occultly to the fabric of Nature, it is likewise seen tattered, incomplete, with many aspects, designs and colours not yet woven into it, and with some streams of evolution having progressed far along their paths and others still at the beginning, thus making a more substantial, but somewhat tattered appearance of the wove of the fabric. A difference between this type of garment and that constituting the human experience is that the human one is also 'foul smelling' because of human involvement with passions, desires, hatreds, spites, cupidity, avarice, etc. These are qualities which the denizens of the lesser kingdoms do not possess.

All such activity also comes under the general auspices of the Knowledge petals, because knowledge is what the animal kingdom is learning to attain, as well as elementary love via the generation of strong affection (as found in dogs, for instance). Fostering such attributes is then the 'means of deliverance' for the animal kingdom.

When one can clearly look at these garments with the 'divine vision' then they are seen to reveal the 'essence of the Tathāgata', as this sacrifice quality is clearly the essence or most highly distilled efflorescence of the entire evolutionary journeying. It is related to the qualities that must be developed if the secrets to the door of *dharmakāya* is to be opened. The 'divine vision' is developed and clarified upon the yogic path, the Vajrayāna, which clearly involves and brings the concept of sacrifice to its highest level. The 'vision' is not just through the Ājñā centre but also via all of the awakened *chakras*. This necessitates the removal of all forms of defilements, which is only accomplished through the highest sacrifices of time, thoughts and activity to produce the most refined energy states; the most transmuted, clarified types of *manasic saṃskāras* possible for the Flowers[58] to hold.

In verse 118 we are immediately brought to view the Sambhogakāya Flower (the 'precious image of a Buddha') within the human form (the 'foul-smelling garment' covering this 'image'). This is seen by a god (or sage) with 'divine vision' (i.e., with the Ājñā centre awakened), who shows it to those who can properly cleanse *saṃskāras* and thereby reveal the *tathāgatagarbha*, the enlightenment-principle from within the form. A Buddha works similarly to effect the liberation of those in bondage and capable of demonstrating the teachings.

58 All of the *chakras* are implied here, including the Sambhogakāya Flower.

This verse consequently directs our perception to the Throat centre (*viśuddha chakra*). This centre must be developed by 'the beasts' (the animal kingdom) if they are to gain their evolutionary step forward and enter the human kingdom by way of the development of mind, as the Throat centre governs this aspect within humanity. The ability of the Throat centre to awaken the Fires at the Base of Spine centre by humans is also implied, once the 'beastly passions' are controlled by the rightly focussed *yogin*. This can then awaken the Ājñā centre producing the vision that reveals the *tathāgatagarbha*. This perspective incorporates the combination of the Sacrifice-Will—Knowledge and the Knowledge—Sacrifice-Will interrelation of the Flower.

The phrase 'the beasts' here thus does not just refer to members of the animal kingdom, but also to those human units that are beastly in nature, who do not effectively use their minds in any intelligent fashion, but rely instead almost entirely upon their lower base sensual and desire natures.

Once rudimentary intelligence is awakened in a new humanity then they will abide upon 'the path of worldly existence' wherein sages expound the doctrine to them by using the Throat centre and the associated organs of speech. Our analysis here is thus the processes associated with the genesis of a human kingdom. Without the development of intelligent functions such education is impossible. The sacrificial function of knowledgeable sages therefore manifests for the entire duration of the evolution of intelligence by an animal kingdom, and then bringing that evolution to conclusion in humans. At first the doctrine to be expounded is simple, basic teachings about how to manifest properly upon the physical plane, basic social mores, religious custom and ritual. Later, more sophisticated doctrines can be expounded, concerning what pertains to engendering the forces of the Heart. Every form of teaching is only appropriate at the right time for proper comprehension for the (limited) truths contained within them.

8. The Knowledge—Love-Wisdom petal

Brown's commentary for this eighth simile is valuable:

> The eighth illustration from the *Tathāgatagarbhasūtra* uses the image of a pregnant, abandoned woman to symbolize the defilements, while the essence of the Tathāgata is portrayed as a future emperor, now in

> the form of the embryonal elements. Thinking that she is alone and wretched, the woman, reduced to living in an orphanage, unknowingly bears the glory of royalty within her[59]...The defilement remaining in the impure stage of the Bodhisattva *(aśuddhabhūmigata-kleśa)*, tainting those Bodhisattvas who haven't reached ultimate perfection *(aniṣṭhāgatabodhisattva)* is symbolized by the royal embryo within the abandoned woman. This defilement is the enemy to the wisdom attained on the first seven stages of the Bodhisattva, and can be removed only by the wisdom obtained through the practice of the eighth, ninth and tenth stages *(aṣṭamyādibhūmitrayabhāvanā-jñāna)*.[60]

This petal is responsible for the development of the base level of all Bodhisattva activity because through the development of its attributes the principle of Love, *bodhicitta* is first awakened. The yet to be Bodhisattva is the future emperor in the woman's womb. The woman here refers not only to the ideal mother of a physical human child, but also to Mother Nature, i.e., the bearer of the Womb within which all sentient beings find scope for evolutionary attainment. This particular petal can also be considered the Bodhisattva-womb, where the woman refers to the associated *bījas* rayed into manifestation that will eventually Flower into the capacity of the one that serves others. This necessitates gaining right knowledge, such as of the Four Noble Truths, through regular *saṃsāric* activity. Without the development of Love-Wisdom no Bodhisattvic activity is possible. Therefore, the illustration relating to this petal focuses upon the basis to the genesis of a Bodhisattva which emphasises the purpose of the entire Flower.

Consequently, all of the higher petals are awakened specifically by the stages *(bhūmi)* developed by Bodhisattvas. The Knowledge—Knowledge petal is concerned with the background processes leading to the attainment of the first *bhūmi*.[61] The Knowledge—Love-Wisdom petal is concerned

---

59 Brown, 126.

60 Ibid., 129.

61 In the book *The Bodhisattva Doctrine in Buddhist Sanskrit Literature* Har Dayal states that a *bodhisattva* enters his first Stage immediately after the production of the "'Thought of Enlightenment'. He rejoices exceedingly, as he remembers the teaching of the Buddha and thinks of the discipline of the *bodhisattvas*. He realizes that he has now risen above the life of the foolish common people and is also delivered from the fear of unhappy rebirths. He feels that he is the refuge of all creatures. He is not

with generating the general base characteristics of the *bodhicitta* needed to be borne by all Bodhisattvas. The Knowledge—Sacrifice-Will petal produces the sacrifice of the forms of perception that does not relate to gaining wisdom. The result is knowledge of the attainment of the Bodhisattva path. The remaining petals relate to the qualities gained by Bodhisattvas up to the seventh *bhūmi* and residence in *śūnyatā*.

The above is one way of analysing the ten stages of the Bodhisattva path, wherein *śūnyatā* is seen as the final goal. If we look to the higher level of interpretation, as outlined in this text, wherein the *dharmakāya* is the goal, then the Sambhogakāya Flower relates to the development of seven of the Bodhisattva *bhūmis*, whilst the highest three are beyond the capacity of the Flower to convey. The Bodhisattvas will then have travelled through the Śūnyatā Eye to the 'other shore' of *śūnyatā*. But the final severance from all earthly (*karmic*) ties necessitates travelling the higher *bhūmis*.

The lowest two of the petals of the Sambhogakāya Flower therefore relate firstly to the development of the qualities that allows one to properly cognise what *saṃsāra* is all about, so that the foundation for its mastery or transcendence is built. This happens predominantly in the Knowledge—Knowledge petal. The second, Knowledge—Love-Wisdom petal, lays the foundation for understanding and experiencing the *bodhicitta* that drives a Bodhisattva on to fulfilment, which is only an embryo in the womb of this beggar woman. The foundational experiences are developed and the person finally enters the stream of the Bodhisattva path, to finally become the fully crowned emperor of Love-Wisdom in the highest stages. On a higher spiral, the Love-Wisdom—Knowledge petal continues the theme of developing Bodhisattvic qualities, whilst the Love-Wisdom—Sacrifice-Will petal works to inundate Bodhisattvic qualities into the personality by way of seeding the *bījas* of *bodhicitta*. The Sacrifice-Will—Love-Wisdom petal seeds the sacrificial Will that produces the higher Bodhisattva stages.

It should be emphasised that the petals do not develop evenly, consequently neither do the Bodhisattvas. Thus there are really no

---

troubled by the five fears that embitter the lives of other men". The qualities presented continue for some length in the text. From Har Dayal, *The Bodhisattva Doctrine in Buddhist Sanskrit Literature*, (Motilal Banarsidass, Delhi, 1975), 284-285.

Bodhisattvas that are purely at one stage or at another, for they have generally developed more of one quality belonging to one stage than to another stage, which qualifies them as of this or that level. To be at any particular level they have to have mastered more than two thirds of the qualifications associated with that level.

In Obermiller's translation the attributes of the *Knowledge—Love-Wisdom petal* relate to verses 119-121.

> 119. Suppose a woman of miserable appearance and helpless
> Were abiding in a place without shelter and protection,
> And, bearing in her womb the glory of royalty,
> Would not know that the Lord (who could protect her) were in her own body.
>
> 120. The birth in this world is like the house without shelter,
> And the impure living beings are like that pregnant woman;
> The immaculate Germ through which one is protected
> Is like (the king) abiding in the womb.
>
> 121. As a woman of ugly appearance, covered with a foul-smelling garment
> Experiences the greatest suffering in a place without shelter,
> Though the Lord of the Earth abides in her own womb;
> In a like way the living beings whose spirit is helpless,
> Though the protection exists within themselves,
> Abide amidst sufferings, their minds being troubled by the passions.[62]

This Knowledge—Love-Wisdom petal is the womb of *bodhicitta*, the principle that emanates the 'glory of royalty'. 'Royalty' here referring to high spiritual achievement. Right knowledge in *saṃsāra* sets the conditionings for the awakening of Love in a person through learning not to attach oneself to ephemeral things. The incremental birthing of forms of right attachment, which is the basis to the Love principle, can then occur. The symbolism concerning the woman that bears this principle in her womb is more complicated than what superficially appears, and can be interpreted upon three levels.

a. Mother Nature, within whose womb all sentient beings learn the principles of group interrelations as part of their basic instinct to knowledge. According to normal human eyes Nature is quite beautiful, with all of its greens, the brown earths, and the multihued

62 Obermiller, 219.

flowers to brighten up the scenery. However, from a yogic view, it is 'of miserable appearance' because the principle of mind has not yet been developed therein. (Omitting here the factor of the human kingdom.) Without the manifestation of intelligence, Love cannot be known, understood, or properly expressed. Nature progresses along a prearranged plan, guided by the Love and wisdom of the greater luminaries that have long passed the human stage of the attainment of knowledge. The 'miserable appearance' defines what must yet be developed. Nature is 'helpless' in the face of human predation. This is obvious to us in this age of mass industrialisation and exploitation of Nature's reserves for the manufacture of the consumer items that people so much desire. The urban spread and the exploitation of forests for paper and timber products, the mass overgrazing by livestock and rapacious mining, has caused immense destruction upon the formerly pristine natural habitats of the earth.

b. The Knowledge—Love-Wisdom petal of the Flower, from which the *bījas* of the understandings of the Love principle can be rayed. If we take the 'miserable woman' as Nature then the 'Immaculate Germ' is the Sambhogakāya Flower, likened to a king in her womb. It is accordingly protected as part of the evolutionary process governing all kingdoms in Nature. There are no elements or avaricious human minds upon its realm to ravage it. There is only ordered serenity and the most refined streams of consciousness. Therefore, there is no need for 'shelter or protection'.

c. That born 'in this world' that is 'like the house without shelter' is the consciousness-principle of a human being, which exists as a 'womb' wherein understanding of the nature of *bodhicitta* can sprout and grow. The womb of a woman also represents the naval area, which constitutes a fusion of the Sacral and Solar Plexus energies vitalising all of the minor centres. These centres effectively garner the experiences derived from the forces of Nature via which 'the experience of direst suffering'[63] ensues. The Sacral centre provides the (desire) energies and substance for the growth of the child and the Solar Plexus centre the Waters that form its basic (emotional) environment. The sum of the Inner Round grouping

63 Fuchs, 36.

of *chakras* condition all of the *prāṇas* that govern the activities of consciousness-growth within this womb (of mind/Mind). In the text, therefore, we have the woman who bears 'in her womb the glory of royalty' because the compassionate Mind can develop from her and slowly mature from the stage of the aspirant to the fully awakened Buddha. From this perspective the 'womb' represents the *tathāgatagarbha,* which is the 'protector' that 'resides within their own [minds]'.[64]

The most trite level of interpretation is to take the womb to refer to that of an ordinary human mother. If done so then the last sentence of verse 119 would refer to this interpretation, for she 'would not know that the Lord (who could protect her) were in her own body'. This Lord is the awakening compassionate understanding emanating from her Heart centre (via the *tathāgatagarbha)* to flood the self-focussed waters of the Solar Plexus centre with unselfish and unifying conditionings. This Lord also embodies the consciousness-aspect manifesting via the 1,000 petalled lotus that grows within the matrix of the womb. The purpose is to learn how to live properly therein so that wisdom is evoked, when coupled with the Love aspect. What is therefore born from the womb is the fully developed child of Love-Wisdom, which can then grow into the realised Buddha. This Love-Wisdom *(bodhicitta)* is the true Lord that can protect her, for only it can guide her through the snares of *saṃsāric* affiliation.

Verse 120 continues in the vein presented above, where we implicitly take into account the three levels of interpretation given.

The phrase 'The birth in this world is like the house without shelter' refers to point (c) above, the womb of the consciousness-principle of a human being. All consciousness-bearing human units are born to the world that is to them like 'a house without shelter' because their *saṃskāras* offer no respite from the vicissitudes of *saṃsāra*. As long as

64 Ibid. The verse given is: 'A ruler of the earth dwells in the womb of a woman who has an unpleasant appearance and whose body is dressed in dirty clothes. Nevertheless she has [to abide] in a poorhouse and undergo the experience of direst suffering. Likewise, beings deem themselves unsheltered though a protector resides within their own [minds]. Thus they have to abide in the ground of suffering, their minds being unpeaceful under the predominating drive of mental poisons'.

they remain attached to *saṃsāric* allurements there will be no shelter from suffering and assault from all aspects of life. Residence in the house of their physical bodies and personalities assures this.

The next sentence, 'the impure living beings are like that pregnant woman' refers to point (a) above, to the womb of mother Nature. Each sentient being evolves the principle or germ of knowledge and Love that is the *tathāgatagarbha,* symbolised as being contained in the womb of a pregnant human. It is just a question of undergoing the evolutionary process, as ordained by the Lords of Nature.[65]

'The Immaculate Germ', the Buddha-*gotra*, 'through which one is protected', here refers to the Knowledge—Love-Wisdom petal of the Sambhogakāya Flower. This Flower protects by overshadowing the evolving personality with its beneficence, and by raying into the personality the *bījas* of the next evolutionary attainment to be mastered on the long eventful road of developing wisdom with view of Buddhahood. The Flower rains down the immaculate treasures of the spirit into the receptive personality at exactly the right time when needed for spiritual advancement. Thus protection is provided throughout the long progression of successive lives until liberation is eventually attained.

A king is one who is crowned, therefore this term symbolises the mental principle (consciousness) which is stored by means of the Crown *chakra*, the 1,000 petalled lotus. This king *(raja)* of *chakras* directly awakens to the *dharmakāya* as a course of its natural progress along the road of the development of Love-Wisdom. Thus the potential of the Dharmakāya Way is what abides in this womb.

The 'woman of ugly appearance, covered with foul-smelling garments' in Verse 121 concerns the 'trite level of interpretation', where as explained, such garments refer to the periodic vehicles of the body, the psychic (astral) form, and the mind. The putrid 'foul-smelling' nature relates to the *prāṇas* coursing through the *nāḍīs* of the average being. This woman is ugly because she has not yet developed the *bodhicitta* that will brighten up and cleanse her aura from its murky constitution.

The verse also focuses specifically upon the conditionings associated with the expression of the minor centres and the activity of

65 There are *gotras* for groups of sentient streams of Life, collectivised as 'group-Souls'.

the Sacral centre (the *svādiṣṭhāna chakra*). This centre is concerned with human interrelationships of all types, specifically that form of physical attractiveness that incorporates forms of bonding that all people experience as a basis to their sex lives (and which produces the embryo in the womb of the mother). Those who learn to develop family and social relationships in a charitable manner begin the process of awakening *bodhicitta*. The Sacral centre is vivified by the Knowledge—Love-Wisdom petal of the Flower when the main purpose of the desire principle and attractiveness to form is to express loving action in the person.

This 'woman' (the personality) 'experiences the greatest suffering in a place without shelter' because 'shelter' here refers to the realm of the Flower (as explained above), and she is 'without shelter' when she is not responsive to the subtle impressions (the silent Voice of the 'ear-whispered truths') coming from the Sambhogakāya Flower. This happens because the average person is so addicted to gross passions, sensuality, and cravings for pleasures of all types that any higher impressions are blotted out by the noises of *saṃsāric* identification. Not listening to such impressions engenders further *karmic* experiences that must be cleansed through pain and suffering. If the person can listen then the process of fixing up *karmic* misdeeds would ensue.

Those who have developed some wisdom know that suffering comes because of the strength of attachment to things that are ephemeral, such as the sex experience producing all types of human relationships. Nothing in *saṃsāra* is lasting, therefore we have the suffering that teaches one to not be attached or to generate forms of desire that lead to attachment.

The 'place without shelter' also refers to *saṃsāra*, because here one can find no shelter from the manifestation of one's own passions and desires, as everything concerning it is ephemeral, and will be destroyed inevitably. This will happen according to the strength of the vitality one contains and the nature of the associated *karma*. Everything in the material world has its use-by date and such a date affords no proper shelter for any of us. This use-by date terminates all expressions of desires, emotions, mentality and physical posturing of various types of ambition in this world.

The 'Lord of the Earth' then refers to one that has gained mastery of the physical plane, i.e., a fully enlightened being. The phrase 'though the Lord of the Earth abides in her own womb' therefore refers to the fact that though this person has the capacity to gain enlightenment, she experiences great suffering because she cannot attain such an enlightened state in that particular life.

The phrase 'living beings whose spirit is helpless' can refer to the average mass of human beings who likewise do not possess the ability to become enlightened in that life. It can also refer to all sentient beings, for they cannot gain enlightenment until they have evolved to become humans. 'The protection' then is the *gotra* that exists within all. As a consequence, all beings experience suffering of one sort or another, and (specifically) humans, whose minds are 'troubled by the passions'. There is a long evolutionary history from the mindless state of a sentient being to the development of the manifestation of the passions, and then the ability to control them in such a way that people become 'Lords of the Earth', masters of *saṃsāra* in its entirety.

These passions are specifically conveyed in the Inner Round series of *chakras* and are often an offshoot of the energies from the Sacral centre. Consequently, mastery of this centre is the true beginning of the yogic path. It is a major reason why the *yogins* of the past practised celibacy as a prelude to the awakening of the fires within their Base *chakras*, as the Base of Spine and Sacral centres form a functioning unity. The phrase 'the Lord of the Earth' therefore also refers specifically to one who has mastered the qualities of the Base of Spine/Sacral centre duo, as the Earthy Element is controlled via their petals. The entire path of *yoga* is therefore implied by this phrase.

9. The Knowledge–Knowledge petal

The *Knowledge–Knowledge petal* is concerned principally with the most basic skills that need to be developed to survive *saṃsāra*. This concerns the development of the basic forms of knowledge that allow a society to exist. This petal, therefore, is unfolded via the activities that most people manifest. The rise of modern mass education, science and technology, as well as sophisticated philosophies and religions acceded to, has assisted many to awaken the higher petals of the Sambhogakāya Flower.

Obermiller's translation relating to the *Knowledge–Knowledge petal* in *The Uttaratantra of Maitreya* are the verses numbered 122-124.

122. Suppose a great statue of melted gold from within,
And from without covered by mud and dust that hides (the gold),
Were seen by some, who, knowing its nature,
Would remove the outward cover in order to purify the gold within;
123. In a like way the Buddha perceives
That the Essence is pure and radiant and that the stains,
Are only occasional (and not real),
And leads (the living beings) to Supreme Enlightenment
Which purifies from all the Obscurations
The living beings resembling jewel-mines.
124. Just as a statue wrought of pure, shining gold and
covered by earth [49b. 1.]
Is seen by one who, knowing its true nature, removes the earth,—
In the same way the Omniscient perceives
The quiescent Spirit which is like gold,
And, by touching the Doctrine, produces a chisel
Through which he removes all the Obscurations.[66]

In this account the essence of the Tathāgata is depicted materially in terms of a golden statue covered in 'mud and dust'. Fuchs' version for verse 122 is:

An artistically well-designed image of peaceful appearance,
which has been cast in gold and is [still] inside [its mold],
externally has the nature of clay. Experts, upon seeing this,
will clear away the outer layer and cleanse the gold therein'.[67]

What is hinted at with the symbolism of mud or clay surrounding the statue is an observation of those *saṃskāras* that relate to the physical appearance of a normal person. The concern, therefore, is specifically with the consciousness of the form, of the Earthy images the personal-I develops via sense-contact and utilising the substance of the mind *(cittaprakṛti).* Without such development wisdom cannot be obtained, nor the understanding as to why the Bodhisattva path should be trod.

Also, the five *skandhas* are implied by means of an 'artistically well-designed image', which we can presume to be of human form,

66 Obermiller, 219-220.

67 Fuchs, 36.

consisting of the torso, head, two arms and two feet. Specifically the *rūpa-skandha* is implied, which includes everything concerning corporeality, including all past concepts relating to the body, and of its interrelationship with the phenomenal appearance of things. This includes the sense organs, the objects of the senses, plus the sense-consciousnesses developed via them.

What should be emphasised when observing phenomena is that the *skandhas* are mainly developed and perfected under the jurisprudence of the five Knowledge petals. The Love-Wisdom petals on the other hand are developed by compassionate insight, philosophical and religious understandings and devotion to noble ideals. Finally, all defilements are cleansed and transmuted into their respective five Tathāgata Wisdoms via the activity of the Sacrifice petals.

It is hard to eliminate empirical concepts and considerations incorporated around subtle impressions of an 'I', hence we have the *arhat dhyāna*. Such meditation is too engrossed in contemplation upon a pre-established formula of the nature of enlightenment, the consequent attachment prevents true liberation. A concretised image of what 'a Buddha' is engrosses such a meditator. Images of what a Buddha may or may not be must vanish, if the *arhat* meditation is to be transcended. The concept of a 'clay mould' surrounding a golden Tathāgata form hints at such a meditation. The Knowledge petals of the Sambhogakāya Flower also manifest the higher interpretation of the symbolism of a Buddha image, around which the sum of the human personality (the 'clay mould') is constructed. Indeed, the Knowledgeable attributes of the Flower must first be sought in enlightenment's quest. The experience of the *ālayavijñāna* content of the Sambhogakāya Flower can then manifest. The attributes of the Love-Wisdom petals must also be fully developed, to produce the unfoldment of the Bodhisattva Path. Inevitably a meditator must finally relinquish (sacrifice) imagery of all forms, be they those that take on the attributes of the *sambhogakāya* aspect of Buddhas or Bodhisattvas, as depicted in Buddhist art, or that of the Sambhogakāya Flower, to finally fully enter into *śūnyatā*. Then the higher identifications with *dharmakāya* become possible.

Verse 122 speaks of 'melted gold from within', which refers to the basic energies that sustain the person, as coming from the Heart Lotus, and which is concerned with general *prāṇic* vitality and well being. The statue also symbolises the image formed within the Personal-I's mind by the Sambhogakāya Flower of what is to be done for that life. It therefore awakens a wise perception of one's placing in the social environment. Such images are normally strongly delineated, as they concern a person's awakening interrelation with those around him/her; the developed congenial social mores, habits, and customs of any society, to which the person adheres. These images can be considered golden (at this stage of development) because they constitute the necessary way forward. Later the images of dissatisfaction with the status quo manifest, producing a need to seek out enlightenment. Therefore this 'statue' (as it is not specifically mentioned as an image of a Buddha, so it can represent anything) is by nature of beautiful appearance to the perceiver, if the mores of the society in which he/she resides is agreeable, or if visions manifest as to the way ahead towards a liberating spiritual goal.

The statue is covered by the mud and dust of normal human emotions and selfishness that are developed in the earlier stages of human evolution. *Saṃsāra* is intensely alluring and is really all that one at first knows as a fact in life. First a tribal or social consciousness is developed, and later a strong self-centred personal focus upon the 'I' or 'me' is experienced, when the mind develops sufficiently to segregate the unit from the tribe. Then the strongest attachments to materialism manifest, such as is found in our societies today. The image formed by the Flower of what to do and of how to be is thus well hidden, because of the superimposition of muddied images of what a self-centred one represents to him/herself. Such an image is then asserted in the face of the desires and image-making tendencies of those around.

Within all societies there are some that develop a more sophisticated understanding as to the nature of attachment and of the errors of too much self-focus, of ugly avaricious activities. Inevitably, they must also 'remove the covering' of *saṃsāric* murk by purifying 'the gold within'. This purification necessitates changing one's self-image into more refined states of consciousness, whereby wholesome, loving, social attributes are developed. It means, therefore, the development of the qualities inherent within the other petals of the Sambhogakāya Flower, with their more radiant auric colourings. This is another meaning of the purification of the internal gold.

Verse 123 brings our vision away from the realm of the personality to that of the Flower, which stands in the guise of a Buddha that perceives that 'the Essence (of living beings) is pure and radiant'. This essence is the energy that is emanated from the Flower. When one attains its standpoint upon the abstracted realms of the Mind then one knows that 'the stains are only occasional and not real'. This is because the energies and mental-images that develop obscuring stains incarnating in and out of *saṃsāra* within the consciousness-stream are relatively fleeting compared to the aeonic life-span of the Flower. Inevitably a personal-I will evolve who will gradually remove, purify or transmute the stains.

The *tathāgatagarbha* meditates upon the entire sequence of lives from the beginning (covering many epochs of evolutionary time, where the most coarse *saṃskāras* are engendered) to the ending, when it can lead 'the living beings' to 'supreme enlightenment'. The entire course of the sacrificial Love of this Flower is to purify all obscurations, leaving only the jewels and gold in the end. We then have auras resembling 'jewel-mines' produced by the Bodhisattvas amongst humanity.

Verses 122, 123 and 124 are concerned with the qualities of the Knowledge tier of petals, because they deal firstly with the mental-emotional (mainly Watery-Earthy) covering of 'clay', and then with the concept of perception 'like the way the Buddha perceives', and consequently the use of the 'chisel' of the perceptive Mind determined to remove all of the obscurations (of mind). When a personality develops basic loving attributes, then both the Knowledge—Knowledge and Knowledge—Love-Wisdom petals are developed simultaneously. Later, as a personal-I awakens sacrifice attributes, e.g., in war, where one may sacrifice one's life for the good of the nation or tribe, then the Knowledge—Sacrifice-Will petal awakens.

Verse 122 concerns the activity aspect of the mind, where knowledge is developed concerning the true nature of the covering of mud or clay around the golden image (of the Flower) and the need to remove it. This relates to the development of the *iḍā nāḍī* stream of *saṃskāras,* which produces the unfoldment of all the Knowledge petals of the Flower.

Verse 123 includes the awakening of the more Watery aspects of desire-emotion-affection within each expressed personality in the flow of the stains, which are 'only occasional', adventitious. Consequently, they can be purified into 'jewel-mines', thus manifesting attributes such as devotion, aspiration, and Love. Here the development of the *piṇgalā nāḍī* stream of *saṃskāras* is implied. We thus have the development of the qualities of the Knowledge—Love-Wisdom petal, and later the Love-Wisdom—Knowledge petal. Then aspects of the Love-Wisdom—Sacrifice-Will petal are awakened when the highest forms of loving sacrifice are engendered. This process is normally facilitated by following the fields of religious development.

Verse 124 consequently includes the unfoldment of the qualities of the Knowledge—Sacrifice-Will petal, from whence is projected the power of the symbolic chisel that can be used to help remove all obscurations by one who knows the 'true nature' of the covering clay. All forms of erroneous knowledge must be uncovered by 'the Omniscient' so that the 'quiescent Spirit which is like gold' can be revealed and the *dharma* taught. The *suṣumṇā nāḍī* stream awakened by the accomplished *yogin* is here implied. Only such a one can chisel away at the defilements to reveal the flawless image (of the *tathāgatagarbha)* made from 'shimmering gold'.[68] The unpolluted *nirmalā tathatā* aspect of the Flower manifests in the form of a sympathetic ideation from the Sacrifice petals. The resultant 'quiescent Spirit' represents a *samādhi* wherein the *dharmakāya* is revealed.

In this verse we are first informed that the 'one' (the Flower) who, knowing the true nature of the 'statue wrought of pure, shining gold' (the highest form of Love), works to remove the 'earth' (*karma*, *kleśas,* and *saṃskāras*) covering it. The Flower thus projects the image of what is to be (the 'statue') in the *yogin's* mind and together they work to make it so.

The general quality of the Flower is presented in the term 'the Omniscient', because of the high level of attainment achieved once the Sacrifice petals are developed. Also the Sacrifice petals open the direct door to the *dharmakāya*, which indeed is omniscient. The development of a 'quiescent Spirit' within the mind of a personal-I allows such a one (a *yogin* or Bodhisattva) to listen to the subtle silent Voice from the Flower, the internal Buddha. We are told that this quiescence is 'like gold', signifying the expression of *bodhicitta*. This then allows the *tathāgatagarbha* to 'teach the doctrine', thereby reminding the reader that though this doctrine comes forth from the *ālayavijñāna*, it is the *dharma* derived from the *dharmakāya*.

68 Fuchs, 37.

Once the doctrine is listened to and appropriate response is made then 'a chisel' can be produced, constituting the sacrificial Mind that can remove all obscurations to enlightenment. The hard substances (gross *saṃskāras)* are removed, allowing the development of the attributes of the five Dhyāni Buddhas as the qualities of the various Sacrifice petals are gradually revealed.

The meaning of the examples

The main section dealing with the major attributes of the Sambhogakāya Flower petals has now concluded. Consequently, the 'meaning of all these examples' which summarise the preceding concerning the Sambhogakāya Flower shall be briefly analysed. The next three verses are styled in terms of the three principle *nāḍīs*, which represent the three ways the Flower communicates with the personality.

The meaning of all these examples is in short as follows:—

125. Within a lotus, amidst a swarm of bees,
Within the husk of a fruit, impurities, and the ground,
Within a seed, within a tattered garment,
The womb of a woman, and the covering of the earth,
respectively,

126 Like the Buddha, like honey, like the kernel of a fruit,
Like gold, like a treasure, and like a tree,
Like a precious image, like the sovereign
Of the Universe, and like a golden statue, —

127. The Immaculate Essence of the Spirit in the living beings
Is unaffected by the coverings of defilement;
As such it exists eternally,
Being spoken of as having no beginning.[69]

Verse 125 presents nine statements qualified by the concept of 'within'. They thus implicate what is intrinsic ('within') to the Flower, hence to the *piṅgalā* outpouring of consciousness, which is Love *(bodhicitta).* The *nāḍīs* are vivified from the Love-Wisdom petals of the Flower which finds their focal point in the Heart *chakra.* The awakening of these *prāṇas* happen upon the Bodhisattva path.

69 Obermiller, 220.

We saw that the phrase 'within a lotus' refers to evoking the qualities of the Sacrifice-Will—Sacrifice-Will petal. That which exists 'amidst a swarm of bees' refers to the evocation of the qualities of the Sacrifice-Will—Love-Wisdom petal. That which exists 'within the husk of a fruit' refers to the evocation of the qualities of the Sacrifice-Will—Knowledge petal. That which exists within 'a place filled with impurities' refers to the evocation of the qualities of the Love-Wisdom—Sacrifice-Will petal. That which is contained 'under the ground' refers to the evocation of the qualities of the Love-Wisdom—Love-Wisdom petal of the Flower. That which is veiled 'within a seed' refers to the evocation of the qualities of the Love-Wisdom—Knowledge petal of the Flower. That which is within 'a tattered garment' refers to the evocation of the Knowledge—Sacrifice-Will petal. That which is 'within the womb of a woman' refers to the evocation of the qualities from the Knowledge—Love-Wisdom petal of the Flower. Finally, we have the evocation of the qualities of the Knowledge—Knowledge petal in the statement 'within the covering of earth'. Corresponding to these petals there are the nine major stages of overcoming allurements before one can gain enlightenment, which will be explained later.

Verse 126 presents nine statements preceded with the word 'like', of that which manifests 'in the imitation of', and consequently is conceived of in the mind. This relates to the activity or *iḍā nāḍī* stream wherein all attributes of mind become fully developed. The concern is therefore the awakening and projection of the qualities of the Knowledge petals to the personality. The focal point of this activity is at first via the Solar Plexus centre and later the Throat centre. Here the objects of comparison are presented. That which is 'like the Buddha' refers to the Sacrifice-Will—Sacrifice-Will petal. That which is 'like honey' refers to the Sacrifice-Will—Love-Wisdom petal. The which is 'like a kernel of fruit' relates to the Sacrifice-Will—Knowledge petal. The colouring of the Love-Wisdom—Sacrifice-Will petal is 'like gold'. The qualities of the Love-Wisdom—Love-Wisdom petal can be likened to the storage of inexhaustible 'treasure'. The growth of the enlightenment-'tree' is like the manifestation of the Love-Wisdom—Knowledge petal. A 'precious image' is like the Knowledge—Sacrifice-Will petal in its effect upon consciousness. The 'sovereign of the Universe' is like the Knowledge—Love-Wisdom petal, for this universe is material in nature, as is knowledge itself. Finally, 'a golden statue' is like the

Knowledge–Knowledge petal. Knowledge of its own accord creates images of all types, but when related to that which can be absorbed into the petals of this Flower, the images must be made golden.

Verse 127 speaks of 'the Immaculate Essence of the Spirit', which relates to the *suṣumṇā nāḍī.* This *nāḍī* draws upon the energies of the Sacrifice petals of the Flower and finds its anchorage within the Head lotus. The evocation of this *nāḍī* happens properly upon the higher Bodhisattva *bhūmis* and is needed for Buddhahood. It is unaffected by the defilements, manifesting only the type of energies that will quickly eliminate or transmute the last of them. The abstracted, or distilled essence flowing in this *nāḍī* 'exists eternally', as it is that which has been transformed into the Dharmakāya Way. This is the Way that 'is spoken of', i.e., presented in the form of information that minds can understand and interpret, 'as having no beginning'. There is no beginning because of the limitation of the mind[70] to comprehend the nature of the genesis of this 'distilled essence' because such an essence has existed prior to the appearance of phenomena and the evolution of forms. It existed before the beginning of things. Its ending can be conceived as the limit of what consciousness can comprehend. Whatever consciousness cannot fathom is then 'the end'. The essence, however, persists as the *dharmadhātu,* which transcends consciousness.

Fuchs presents a slightly different viewpoint.

> The lotus, the bees, the husk, the filth,
> the earth, the skin of the fruit, the tattered rag,
> the woman's womb, and the shroud of clay
> [exemplify the defilements], while [the pure nature]
> is like the buddha, the honey, the kernel, the gold,
> the treasure, the great tree, the precious statue,
> the universal monarch, and the golden image.
> It is said that the shroud of the mental poisons
> [which causes the veils] of the element of beings,
> has no connection with it since beginingless time,
> while the nature of mind, which is devoid of stains,
> [has been present within them] since beginingless time.[71]

---

70 Which is conditioned by 'comings and goings', beginnings and endings.

71 Fuchs, 37.

In this extract the distinction between *nirmalā* and *samalā tathatā,* Suchness apart from pollution and with pollution, that conditions the *tathāgatagarbha* is exemplified. 'The nature of mind' here refers to the abstract domain of Mind wherein resides the *tathāgatagarbha.* The phrase 'the shroud of the mental poisons [which causes the veils] of the element of beings, has no connection with it since beginingless time' is correct from the point of view that 'the pure nature' is untainted, but incorrect from the view that the defilements, once purified, become attributes of this 'pure nature'. The 'nine aspects of defilement' from Fuchs' translation are shown below.

> The nine aspects of defilement: desire, aversion,
> and mental blindness, their fierce active state,
> the remaining imprints [of unknowing], the defilements to be abandoned in the paths of seeing and meditation, and the defilements based on the impure levels
> and pure levels respectively, are fully taught
> by the shroud of the lotus and the other examples. [When] classified, the shroud of the secondary poisons
> is beyond any end. But when it is comprised concisely, the nine defilements of desire and the other afflictions are well explained in the given order by the nine similes
> of the shroud of the lotus and the subsequent examples.[72]

Obermiller's version is far more illuminating:

128. Passion, hatred, infatuation,
Their outburst in a violent form,
The force of Transcendental Illusion,
The defilement that is extirpated by intuition,
And that removed by transic meditation,
The stains relating to the impure,
And to the pure Stages (of the Bodhisattva).
129. These 9 forms (of defilement) are illustrated
By the example of the petals of the lotus and the rest;
But all coverings of defilement
In their variety extend beyond millions and millions.
130. These 9 forms of defilement, Passion and the rest,

72 Ibid.

Being taken in short, respectively,
Are illustrated by 9 examples,—
That of the coverings of a lotus and the rest.[73]

These defilements can be relegated to the work of the nine 'petals of the lotus' of the Sambhogakāya Flower in seeding the existence of the personal-I and the development of the consciousness-stream. They indicate the main afflictions that are first engendered by the effects of their energies in *saṃsāra,* and later of their cleansing. Utilising Obermiller's version we see that passion (or desire) is first seeded by the Knowledge—Knowledge petal via the activity of the Sacral centre that it awakens in a personal-I so that *saṃsāric* activity can begin by means of attachment to the phenomena desired. From this the sense-consciousnesses can garner knowledgeable bits of information concerning that phenomena. Such seeding happened at the primeval beginning of the consciousness-stream, the *santāna* governing the individual. Each such cycle is recapitulated in childhood. The Sacral centre controls the flow of the general *prāṇic* circulation, as the *iḍā* and *piṅgalā nāḍīs* stem from its petals. In Obermiller's commentary each of the defilements are depicted as a 'dormant residue'[74] *(anuśaya),* indicating that they are residues (*bījas*) from previous actions (incarnations of the personal-I's) stored via the petals of the respective Flower.

Hatred (aversion) is then a quality where the antidote is contained in the Knowledge—Love-Wisdom petal, when compassionate understanding begins to flood the consciousness of the personal-I. (This happens as part of the evolutionary trend of the consciousness-stream.) In doing so the attributes of the minor *chakras* begin to be dominated by the forces from the Heart centre. At first animosity manifests concerning other's activities, philosophies, religions, politics, etc., based upon an inflated concept of one's own self-worth and related opinions. Later a more wholesome understanding as to the nature of phenomena produces an aversion to attachments to the causes of pain and suffering.

Infatuation or 'mental blindness' is an expression of the Love-Wisdom—Knowledge petal, as it principally vitalises the Solar Plexus

73 Obermiller, 221-223.

74 Ibid., 221.

centre, which feeds the emotions of the personal-I. The resultant desire or emotional-mind *(kāma-manas)* is rampant for a great number of lives. Therein, however, lies the foundation to eventually awakening the loving, compassionate attributes that is the hallmark of the Bodhisattva. The entire *piṇgalā nāḍī* qualities are engendered over time, once an individual learns the hard lessons in life that curb emotional thought (the source of 'mental blindness') into more compassionate fare.

The phrase 'Their outburst in a violent form' relates to the will energies manifesting via the Knowledge—Sacrifice-Will petal in relation to attachments concerning one's lifestyle in the material world. The ideas of the empirical mind are intensified with the potency derived from the Base of Spine centre that support the activities of the major *chakras* below the diaphragm. The attributes of the Love-Wisdom—Knowledge petal precedes those of the Sacrifice-Will—Knowledge petal in the listing because the qualities of the Solar Plexus centre dominates the activities of most people. The true sacrificial intent that produces the renunciation of material and mental-emotional activities, in order to follow the path to enlightenment, comes after the lessons of unbridled emotionality have been learnt.

'The force of Transcendental Illusion' relates to the Love-Wisdom—Love-Wisdom petal. This force is referred to by Obermiller as *vāsanā,* which is the driving force of *karma* and consciousness that projects *saṃskāras* to the surface of experiential activity. The subtlest possible *saṃskāras* are implied here, as is equable with the attributes of this petal, whose purpose is to awaken the potency of the Heart centre in the personal-I. Fuchs calls them 'the remaining imprints [of unknowing]', and Obermiller 'Transcendental Illusion', signifying the last (psychic) veils obscuring true awakened vision.

The focus of the remaining phrases is upon the Sacrifice petals, whose function is to direct *vāsanā* in order to purify and transform *saṃskāras.* First is the Love-Wisdom—Sacrifice-Will petal, whose concern is the 'defilement that is extirpated by intuition' (seeded impressions) as it works via the Heart centre (the source of the intuition) to project its *prāṇas* to the Splenic centres. There the major transformative battles occur, once the personal-I is ready to so project yogic Will. Fuchs' version is that they are the 'defilements to be abandoned in the paths of seeing'.

Next is the Sacrifice-Will—Knowledge petal, which awakens the powers of the Throat centre, thus the ability to utilise Secret Mantra to overcome impediments and to direct the objective of meditation to its conclusion. Obermiller's version here is that it relates to the defilements being 'removed by transic meditation', where his footnote states 'that which is to be removed on the Paths of Illumination and Concentrated Trance'.[75] Fuchs simply states that these defilements are removed by the path of meditation.

The final two statements relate to the impurities removed upon the Bodhisattva *bhūmis,* translated by Obermiller as 'The stains relating to the impure, And to the pure Stages (of the Bodhisattva)', and by Fuchs as 'the defilements based on the impure levels and the pure levels respectively'. These defilements are collectivised in terms of the seven lower Bodhisattva stages and the higher three in the exoteric doctrine. Similarly esoterically, but there are aspects of the higher three stages still needing refining post the *ālayavijñāna* enlightenment. Here the Sacrifice-Will—Love-Wisdom and the Sacrifice-Will—Sacrifice-Will petals are implied, whose purpose is to assist the complete awakening of the Ājñā and Head centres.

We are then informed that though these nine defilements are illustrated concerning 'the petals of the lotus', there are, however, a vast number of defilements that 'the shroud', the incarnate personality, must deal with. Nevertheless these nine illustrations aptly symbolise the main categories of 'the secondary poisons'.

The next verse, quoting Fuchs:

> These defilements cause in their given sequence
> the four impurities of children, the impurity of arhats,
> the two impurity of followers of the path of training,
> and the two impurities of those with understanding.[76]

The 'children' here refer to spiritual children, namely, ordinary people that eventually develop stirrings towards enlightenment. The defilements develop and begin to be mastered and transformed as the attributes of the first four petals of the Sambhogakāya Flower awaken. They must

75 Ibid.

76 Fuchs, 37.

be eliminated for the complete radiance of these petals to shine. The impurity developed by *arhats* relates to the inability of those following this path of meditation to awaken the pure essence of the Love-Wisdom—Love-Wisdom petal, hence the compassionate understanding that is the basis to the Bodhisattva Path. The impurities developed are cleansed by those entering the stream of the *bhūmis* of the Bodhisattva path as the attributes of the next two petals (the Love-Wisdom—Sacrifice-Will, and the Sacrifice-Will—Love-Wisdom petals) are awakened. The final two impurities are eliminated by the Bodhisattvas of the higher degrees as the highest of the Sacrifice petals are awakened.

Next follow nine quatrains (using Fuchs' rendition) detailing the points of the above verse.

> When a lotus [just] born from the mud
> appears to [a beholder], it delights his mind.
> Yet later it changes and becomes undelightful.
> The joy born from desire is similar to this.
>
> Bees, when extremely agitated,
> will fiercely use their stings.
> Similarly, hatred, once arisen,
> brings suffering to the heart.
>
> The kernel of rice and so on
> is obscured by its outer husk.
> Likewise the vision of the [true] meaning
> is obscured by the eggshell of ignorance.
> Filth is repugnant.
> Being the cause for those bound up with greed
> to indulge in sense pleasures,
> the active state [of the poisons] resembles it.
>
> When wealth is hidden, one is ignorant of it
> and therefore does not obtain the treasure.
> Likewise self-sprung [wisdom] is veiled in arhats
> by the ground of remaining imprints of ignorance.
>
> As by gradual growth from bud to shoot
> the skins of the seed are cut,

the vision of thatness averts
[the stains] to be abandoned by seeing.

Through their junction with the noble path
they have overcome the essential part of the transitory collection.
What their wisdom must abandon [on] the path of meditation
is explained as being similar to tattered rags.

The stains based on the seven [impure] levels
resemble the defilements of the shrouding womb.
Concept-free primordial wisdom [is released]
like the mature [prince] from the womb's confine.

The defilements connected with the three [pure] levels
should be known as being similar to the layer of clay.
They must be overcome by the vajra-like samadhi
of [those] who are the embodiment of greatness.[77]

These verses deal with the stains and obscurations, starting from the order previously analysed, however, the defilements manifest in the form of a mirror-like image of what has transpired so far, thus the deepest obscurations are coupled to the most refined of the petals. That relating to the development of the highest attribute, 'the vajra-like samadhi' hence is coupled to the most basic petal, the Knowledge—Knowledge petal. The reason being that this point of view is in terms of the meditation-Mind enacted in the Head lotus. As the Knowledge—Knowledge petal is closely interlinked with this lotus by means of consciousness-links *(antaḥkaraṇas)* to it, so it becomes an extension of it.

From the view of the Head lotus, therefore, the defilements are reflected downwards into the corporeal body, with increasing layers of filth and mud as the meditating one digs deeper into the lower centres, the psychosomatic constitution of the *nāḍī* system and the *kleśas* (defilements, afflictive, dissident emotions) conveyed by the *saṃskāras.* The hardest attributes to conquer, requiring the most intense will and the longest evolutionary time to overcome, relate to the mud of the Watery desire-mind. Hence the lotus grown from this mud is that of

77 Fuchs, 38-39.

the Sacral centre. 'Sensual passion'[78] dies as a consequence of sickness, old age, and upon the yogic path. When the *kleśas* contain attributes of hatred and aversion then the view shifts to the Solar Plexus centre and its extension to the minor *chakras,* such as the Stomach centre wherein the *saṃskāras* of hatred (the emotional proclivity to sting like a bee) are stored and processed. Similarly, the obstacles of ignorance, indulgence in sexual pleasures and greed, avarice, etc., are all attributes processed by the centres below the diaphragm: the Solar Plexus, Stomach, Liver, and Sacral centres, and appropriately processed by the Splenic centres.

The first four quatrains therefore relate to the deepest illusions and most intense forms of mire, far away from the sacrificial and wisely compassionate attributes needed to be developed to replace them (associated with the attributes of the Sacrifice-Will petals of the *tathāgatagarbha).* Average humanity need to master the allurement of these poisons, and evoke some sacrificial Will to oppose and convert them, if the path to liberation is to be trod. Similarly they must learn the meaning of compassionate considerations.

When such Will is evoked (to transform base *saṃskāras),* then firstly the *arhat* path is normally discovered (the subject of the fifth quatrain). The hidden wealth (of the Flower) is sought in a self-seeking form of liberation. Many forms of ignorance are conquered, but still there is the remaining 'imprints of ignorance'. They are conquered by the 'gradual growth' from the bud of wisdom (the nucleus of the Flower and its petals) producing the Bodhisattva Path. The Flower sends streams of revelations to awaken the many petals of the Head lotus. The 'skins of the seed' are then cut, referring to the piercing of the dimensions of perception from the lowest (of the three-fold personality), being the subtle etheric double, the Watery astral sheath, and the empirical mind and the highest level of the abstract Mind. The 'seed' here represents the *bīja* of enlightenment, the focus of the Śūnyatā Eye, from which the 'vision of thatness' is viewed. The *kleśas* or stains are then clearly seen in the meditation and what needs to be removed determined. The 'seed' is also that of *kuṇḍalinī* stored at the juncture between the Sacral and Base of Spine centres. The correct yogic actions set the task of fully awakening it and all of the *chakras* upon enlightenment's quest.

78 Utilising Obermiller's version here, from verse 132: 'But later (when it withers) it no more excites joy. Similar to it is the delight of sensual passion'.

The meditation upon the 'noble path' intensifies whilst residing in a *yogin's* 'tattered rags', symbolising the remnants of attachment to *saṃsāra*. The potency of the Knowledge-Sacrifice petal is evoked to awaken *kuṇḍalinī*, and the Fires directed throughout the *nāḍīs*, empowering the Head centre with its crowning achievement. The Bodhisattva Path has been followed to the seventh level[79] (producing the *ālayavijñāna* enlightenment), and 'concept-free wisdom' (Obermiller has 'non-dialectical wisdom' *nirvikalpaka-jñāna*[80]), is gained. 'A glorious King'—of Mind,[81] crowned with 1,000 marks of wisdom, has now evolved from the Buddha-womb.

The final quatrain relates to the attainment of the three highest Bodhisattva levels, governing complete mastery of *saṃsāra* (the 'layer of clay'), which is overcome by means of following the *vajrayāna* ('vajra-like samadhi'[82]).

The *dharmakāya* and the *tathāgatagarbha*

The following statements from Fuchs' translation summarise the *dharmakāya* and the *tathāgatagarbha*.

> Thus desire and the further of the nine defilements
> correspond to the lotus and the following examples.
>
> Its nature unifying three aspects, the element has properties
> that correspond to those of the Buddha and the other similes.
>
> Its nature is dharmakaya, suchness,
> and also the disposition. These are to be
> known by the [first] three examples,
> the [fourth] one, and the [following] five.

---

79 The number seven also hints at the completion of the various septenaries governing manifestation, such as the seven *chakras*, Rays and sheaths.

80 Obermiller, 225.

81 Though Fuchs here states 'the mature [prince] from the womb's confine', the earlier version of what is in the woman's womb is: 'the woman bearing [a king] in her womb'. A king is more appropriate because it refers to the fully awakened (crowned) Head centre.

82 Obermiller has 'the diamond-cutter', the 'most sublime' form of 'concentrated trance', 225.

> The dharmakaya is to be known [in] two aspects.
> These are the utterly unsustained dharmadhatu
> and the cause conducive to its [realization],
> which is teaching in the deep and manifold way.[83]

Here we are told that the triune nature of the *tathāgatagarbha* has properties that 'correspond to those of the Buddha and the other similes'. Therefore the three bodies of a Buddha are hinted at, which can be correlated in their qualities (though in a reified way) to the three groups of petals of the *tathāgatagarbha.* Thus the *dharmakāya* relates to the Sacrifice-Will petals, the *sambhogakāya* to the Love-Wisdom petals, and the *nirmāṇakāya* to the Knowledge petals. We are then told that its 'nature is dharmakaya, suchness, and also the disposition', where Suchness is also viewed as the *dharmadhātu.* (Obermiller has: Its nature is that of the Cosmical Body, Of the Absolute, and the lineage of the Buddha.[84]) The *dharmakāya* then relates to the three main Sacrifice-Will petals, Suchness to the gold associated with the Sacrifice-Will—Love-Wisdom petal (and the Love-Wisdom petals in general) and 'the lineage' or 'disposition' to the attributes of the remaining five petals where the focus is knowledgeable pursuits for the establishment of wisdom.

The significance of the number five here is that it relates to the qualities of the five Dhyāni Buddhas ('the lineage of the Buddha'), where the Love-Wisdom—Love-Wisdom petal contains the 'inexhaustible treasure' signifying the Dharmadhātu Wisdom of Vairocana. The Love-Wisdom—Knowledge petal reflects the attributes of the 'treasure' into the Knowledge petals in the form of the Mirror-like Wisdom of Akṣobhya. The Knowledge—Sacrifice-Will petal utilises the 'treasure' to mould the 'image of the Victorious One' in the form of the All-accomplishing Wisdom of Amoghasiddhi. The Knowledge—Love-Wisdom petal then 'holds in her womb a glorious king' of the *dharma,* which is consequently born in the phenomenal realms in the form of the Equalising Wisdom of Ratnasambhava. Finally, the Discriminating Inner Wisdom of Amitābha, in the guise of the Knowledge—Knowledge

83 Fuchs, 39.

84 Obermiller, 226.

petal, expertly 'removes the layers of clay' from the precious Buddha image of the incarnate awakened personal-I.[85]

The text now presents a dissertation on the nature of the *dharmakāya,* which is said to be known in its two aspects. The first is that of the 'utterly unsustained dharmadhatu', where as earlier stated, the *dharmadhātu* is pristine cognition, the fundamental realm *(dhātu)* of the *dharma.* The second is 'the cause conducive to its [realization]', which in Obermiller's translation is the *dharmadhātu's* 'natural outflow, the Word Which speaks of the profound (Highest Truth) And (of the elements of the Empirical World) in their variety'.[86] This second interpretation then represents the mode of manifestation of the *tathāgatagarbha.*

The text then continues, relating the *dharmakāya* to the petals of the Sambhogakāya Flower, even though there is nothing in the phenomenal domain to which the absolute body of the *dharma* can really be compared, with the closest being the attributes of a Buddha and the *tathāgatagarbha.*

> [The dharmakaya] being beyond the worldly,
> no example for it can be found in the world.
> Therefore the element and the Tathagata
> are explained as being [slightly] similar.
> Teaching in the deep and subtle way
> is like the single taste of honey,
> while teaching through the various aspects
> resembles grain in its variety of husks.
>
> Since the nature is unchanging,
> full of virtue, and utterly pure,
> suchness is said to correspond
> to the shape and color of gold.

85 This is one way of relating the attributes of the Sambhogakāya Flower to the Jina wisdoms. The list found in Volume 5 incorporates the five Knowledge petals, because knowledge derived from *saṃsāric* turmoil is what is converted to the Jina wisdoms. The difference being that here pure Love-Wisdom is the focus of being the Dharmadhātu Wisdom, whereas in the later listing Sacrificial intent is emphasised, which produces the conversion of knowledge into the Jina wisdoms on all levels of expression.

86 Obermiller, 226.

Similar to the treasure and the fruit of a tree,
the disposition is to be known in two aspects,
as it has existed [as] the nature since beginningless time
and has become supreme [through] right cultivation.[87]

The first two quatrains present the three Sacrifice petals, likening their qualities to the phenomenal expression of the *dharmakāya* in the symbolism of 'the Tathagata', then to 'the single taste of honey', and finally 'its variety of husks' (whereby the various aspects of the *dharma* are taught). The teaching of this *dharma* then manifests 'in the deep and subtle way'. (Obermiller has 'The Teaching of the profound and subtle Doctrine'.[88])

The next quatrain presents the symbolism of the Love-Wisdom—Sacrifice-Will petal in relation to the *dharmakāya* in the words 'the nature is unchanging, full of virtue, and utterly pure'. The *dharmakāya* also extends into the Love-Wisdom—Love-Wisdom petal in the form of Suchness that manifests as 'the shape and color of gold'. Suchness was equated with the *dharmadhātu* earlier, whereas here we see that it relates to the purest compassionate wisdom, which literally sustains the evolutionary expression of any form.

The imagery of the next quatrain extends our vision to 'the treasure and the fruit of a tree' (the Love-Wisdom—Love-Wisdom, and Love-Wisdom—Knowledge petals), and informs us that 'the disposition', the domain of the *tathāgatagarbha,* is 'to be known in two aspects' (Love-Wisdom and Knowledge), which have always existed and 'has become supreme [through] right cultivation'. The reference therefore is to the myriads of incarnations that have evolved the Bodhisattva virtues leading to Buddhahood. Obermiller's version (verse 148) is more illuminating:

Being like a treasure and like (the germ of) a tree in a seed,
The source (of Buddhahood) is known to be of 2 kinds,—
The Fundamental that exists without beginning,
And that which undergoes the highest process of development.[89]

87 Fuchs, 39-40.

88 Obermiller, 227.

89 Obermiller, 229.

Here the 'Fundamental that exists without beginning' can be considered the Love or compassionate aspect (the Heart of the *dharmadhātu),* whilst knowledge has been generated, like a seed developing into a tree. Also, as it is processed to its highest level of development (utilising the will to overcome *saṃskāras),* and integrated with love, it manifests as wisdom. Here then is the source of Buddhahood.

The theme of the Buddha bodies *(trikāya)* as evolved via the *tathāgatagarbha* is continued in the following verses:

> The attainment of the three kayas of a buddha
> is seen to stem from the twofold disposition.
> By the first aspect there is the first [kaya],
> through the second there are the latter two.
>
> The beautiful svabhavikakaya
> is like the statue of a precious material,
> since [it exists] naturally, is not created,
> and is a treasure of gem-like qualities.
> Wielding the sublime majesty of the Great Dharma,
> the sambhaga[kaya] resembles the Chakravartin.
> Being of the nature of a [mere] representation,
> the nirmana[kaya] is similar to the golden image.[90]

The first quatrain simply informs us that the *dharmakāya* stems from the refinement of Love-Wisdom (necessitating the expression of will and sacrifice to do so). The next four lines teach that the right application of knowledge, as it evolves into Love-Wisdom, lays the foundation for the expression of the *sambhogakāya* (the subtle apparitional body of a Buddha)[91] and the *nirmāṇakāya,* the phenomenal appearance in the world of human interrelationships.

Next we are introduced to the concept of the *svabhāvikāya* (or *svabhāvikakāya),* the Self-born fourth body of a Buddha, the body of absolute existence, which integrates the three other *kāyas*. If the

90 Fuchs, 40.

91 It should be noted that this *sambhogakāya* form differs from the Sambhogakāya Flower, in that the first is self-created upon the inner dimensions of perception by a liberated Bodhisattva or Buddha, the second exists for the purpose of leading a 'man' *(mānasaputra,* mind-bearing form) to liberation over a vast duration of time.

dharmakāya is 'being beyond the worldly, no example for it can be found', how much more so the *svabhāvikāya?* It is literally the absolute body of a Buddha as it exists in cosmos and integrated with all other Buddha-forms. Nevertheless, the author of the *Uttaratantra Śastra* tries, by using a simile that compares it to an unwrought, uncreated precious statue that is a repository of all precious transcendental virtues of compassionate wisdom. That which wields 'the sublime majesty of the Great Dharma' relates to the *dharmakāya,* whilst the *sambhogakāya* is likened to a universal king *(cakravartin,* who normally holds seven [wish-fulfilling] jewels used to help his kingdom in the best manner possible.) The *nirmāṇakāya* that is incorporated as part of the manifestation of the *svabhāvikāya* is likened to 'a golden image'. As this image also relates to the Knowledge—Knowledge petal, which earlier was stated to be practically integrated with the Head lotus, so then the nature of the *nirmāṇakāya* becomes evident via the integration between the Flower and the Head lotus. (For the first seven *Bodhisattva bhūmis.*)

Having introduced the Knowledge—Knowledge petal, the next three quatrains summarise the main characteristics of the three groups of petals of the Sambhogakāya Flower by way of conclusion concerning what has been said regarding the *tathāgatagarbha.*

> This truth of the Self-Sprung Ones
> is to be realized through faith.
> The orb of the sun blazes with light,
> [but] is not seen by the blind.
>
> Nothing whatsoever is to be removed.
> Not the slightest thing is to be added.
> Truly looking at truth, truth is seen.
> When seen, this is complete liberation.
>
> The element is empty of the adventitious [stains],
> which are featured by their total separateness.
> But it is not empty of the matchless properties,
> which are featured by their total inseperability.[92]

92 Fuchs, 40.

The reference to the blaze of the sun refers to the luminosity of the Knowledge petals (being the most 'corporeal' aspect of the Flower) and thus to the general appearance of the *tathāgatagarbha* to clairvoyants. Faith here refers to complete trust or confidence in the doctrine that the Buddhas exist and that the *dharma* taught by them concerning the way to liberation is correct. Similarly with the doctrine concerning the existence of the *tathāgatagarbha,* the golden luminosity of the truth, likened to the blaze of the sun. Those who are blind cannot see the sun, likewise those that are blinded by *saṃsāra* or dogma will not see the *tathāgatagarbha.* Consequently, once faith is there the steps must be taken to open the eyes, hence the mind must be developed to rightly cognise so that the 'truth of the Self-Sprung Ones' can be recognised and followed.

The next verse relates to the Love-Wisdom petals of the Flower, to which, once wisdom is developed, nothing can be added or removed, as compassion (Love) then drives one to truly see truth via direct transcendental perception *(pratyakṣa).* This is the Heart's perception directly speaking. When the Heart centre is awakened complete liberation ensues.

The third verse presents the attributes of the Sacrifice-Will petals, which are 'empty of the adventitious [stains]'. The force of the sacrificial will eliminates these defilements in the *nāḍī* system and must be evoked by the *yogin* to be liberated from *saṃsāra.* Because there is a 'separateness' (a void or emptiness) between these stains and the Sacrifice petals, it means that these petals manifest Buddha-like properties. They are literally mechanisms of identifying with the *dharmakāya.*

Reasons for presenting the *tathāgatagarbha* doctrine

This section concerning the fourth *vajra* point concludes with some miscellaneous teachings.

> [The sutras of the second turning of the wheel of Dharma] state in numerous places
> that all knowable [phenomena] are in all ways empty like a cloud, a dream, or an illusion.
> Why is it then, that in [the sutras of the third turning of the wheel of Dharma]
> the Buddha, having said this, declared that buddha nature is present within beings?[93]

93 Fuchs, 40.

We are first presented with an observation concerning the differences presented in the *buddhadharma* of two doctrinal dispensations (turnings of the *dharma* wheel). These differences manifest as a consequence of new teachings concerning the existence of the *tathāgatagarbha* during the third turning of the wheel (presenting the Mahāyāna doctrines[94]). The reason given for the necessity of presenting these teachings are provided in the next verse, and elaborated in the remaining verses.

> With regard to faintheartedness, contempt for inferior beings,
> perceiving the untrue, disparaging the true nature,
> and exceeding self-cherishing, he said this to persuade those
> who have any of these five to abandon their defects.[95]

Faintheartedness concerns lack of faith, fearfulness, being easily daunted concerning the spiritual path, or in fact to overcome the many obstacles in life. Here the necessary energies from the Sacral centre (the source of *prāṇic* vitality) is not evoked in order to empower the person to accomplish the task at hand.

Contempt relates to the development of the scornful, prideful attitudes that denigrate and deride others because of a lack of compassionate development. The Heart centre is blocked from manifesting any input in the person's life.

Perceiving untruths and taking them as facts relates to the desire-mind impulses governed by the Solar Plexus centre, preventing clear logical thought.

The materialistic attitudes of the concrete-minded ones (empiricists) sometimes produces agnostic, but more often nihilistic or antagonistic attitudes concerning all religious beliefs and practices. Thereby the true nature of things, hence the path to Buddhahood, is denigrated. The related *chakra* is the Throat centre, governing the outpouring of the empirical mind.

Finally, we have the exceedingly self-focussed activities ('self-cherishing') of the average avaricious and worldly individual, whose every activity is centred around the aggrandisement of the little 'I' that

94 The first turning is considered the *śravakayāna,* the vehicle of the disciples ('hearers') of the Buddha. The second being the Hīnayāna, where the concept of the Pratyekabuddha (or *arhat* path) is espoused.

95 Ibid., 40-41.

is made to be the centre of the universe. Here the sum of the Head lotus comes into play, where every thought-impulse builds this empire of the 'I'.

In relation to these five *chakra* families (where the Base of Spine and Sacral centres are viewed as a unity, as well as the Ājñā and Head centres) all of the other afflictions governing the human conditioning fall into place.

We are then told that the teaching concerning the *tathāgatagarbha* was given to the world in order to help offset the evil-doing concerning these five conditions. This teaching necessitates comprehension of the meaning of Life, overcoming ignorance, control of mental-emotional energies, and eliminating the I-concept in relation to the development of compassionate understanding that emanates from the Sambhogakāya Flower.

The text now proceeds with a more detailed explanation, which is more or less self explanatory.

> The final truth is in every respect
> devoid of anything compounded.
> The poisons, karma, and their product
> are said to be like a cloud and so on.
>
> The mental poisons are like a cloud.
> Karma resembles a dream experience.
> The skandhas produced by the poisons and karma
> are similar to an illusion or a deceptive apparition.[96]

The poisons and related *karma,* everything phenomenal, is illusional. The final (ultimate) truth (emptiness), is void of all of these. We are then presented with a triad concerning the type of phenomena dealt with upon the path to liberation. In continuing with the theme of the *tathāgatagarbha* this triad therefore relates to the three groups of petals. First we are told the 'mental poisons are like a cloud'. Such poisons are 'like a cloud' of thought forms, hence they mainly have to be cleansed by cogent thinking, utilising the energies from the Knowledge petals. The focus is awakening the potency of the Throat centre. The poisons, however, are primarily generated in the centres below the diaphragm, which thereby have to be mastered.

---

96 Ibid., 41.

The statement 'Karma resembles a dream experience', relates to the fact that the effects of the karmic play all around us is phantasmagorical, illusory, like 'a dream experience'. This force manifests primarily via the subtle psychic constitution and works upon transgressions of body, speech and mind. It is cleansed by the compassionate energies from the Love-Wisdom petals acting via the Heart centre as it awakens.

The five *skandhas* relate to the sum of the five-fold personality. They must be purified and the gross attributes transformed by the energies from the Sacrifice-Will petals in conjunction with the awakening of the Head lotus. The sum of the body of manifestation is involved in this process of liberation of energies and enlightenment, hence it is said the *skandhas* are 'produced by the poisons and karma'. Illusions 'or a deceptive apparition' are images formed in the mind, or that which forms phenomenally, like a mirage or a magical construct, but which have no real substantiality. The entire phenomenal world can be viewed thus.

The final teachings of this *vajra* point are presented below, revolving around the concept of *bodhicitta,* which is the main energy embodied by the Flower.

> For the time being it was thus expounded.
> Additionally in this unsurpassable continuity
> it was taught: "The element is present,"
> so that the five evils would be abandoned.
> As long as they have not heard this,
> bodhicitta will not be born in those
> whose minds are feeble and fainthearted,
> stirred by the evil of self-contempt.
> Having engendered [a little] bodhicitta,
> some proudly imagine: "I am supreme!"
> Towards those who have not developed it
> they are imbued with notions of inferiority.
> In those who entertain such thoughts,
> true understanding will not arise.
> They hold the untrue [to be true]
> and thus will not realize the truth.
> Being artificially produced and adventitious
> these faults of beings are not truly [existent].
> In truth these evils do not exist as self,

but exist as the qualities by nature pure.
While they hold the evils, which are untrue, [to be true]
and disparage the true qualities, [denying their presence,]
even those of understanding will not attain the love
that perceives the similarity of oneself and others.[97]

We are told that the teachings of the earlier and later period (the third turning of the wheel) manifested concerning the *tathāgatagarbha* so that the abovementioned five poisons could be eliminated. The text then states that if people did not know this teaching then *bodhicitta* would not 'be born in those whose minds are feeble and fainthearted', or fearful (full of 'self-contempt'). They need to be taught that all beings have the Buddha *gotra,* hence the capacity to eventually become Buddhas, if only they strive to awaken *bodhicitta,* thereby overcoming their feeblemindedness. However, even when a little *bodhicitta* is awakened, it can nevertheless stimulate pride when they compare themselves to others. Pride is the slayer of the real, the inflator of the illusional concept of 'self' (which is the antithesis to compassionate thought), hence must especially be carefully observed and eliminated at its root. Compassionate considerations must be continuously developed for those struggling under the weight of illusions and defilements, rather than forms of contempt.

Because the attachments are by nature adventitious and illusional they have no lasting value. They are only imputed as valuable. Only the wisdom derived from compassionate actions is true and of lasting value. One must eliminate all forms of conceit and truly comprehend the good in all to awaken *bodhicitta* in them, thereby producing the equalising wisdom developed by all who walk the Bodhisattva Path. Knowing that the Buddha-*gotra* is therefore of the greatest joy, because all have the capacity to be compassionate and consequently gain liberation.

Once one has heard this, joy will be born.
Respect as towards the Buddha, analytical wisdom,
primordial wisdom, and great love will arise.
Through the arising of these five qualities,
one is rid of the faults and sees similarity.
[By realizing] the absence of defects and the presence of qualities,

97 Ibid.

> and through love, [seeing] the equality of oneself and [all] beings,
> buddhahood will be quickly attained.[98]

Great 'joy is born' as a consequence of overcoming faintheartedness and the other poisons. Respect for the Buddha and his *dharma* is gained through overcoming contempt to inferiors. Analytical wisdom is the antidote to belief in falsehoods. Receptivity to the 'primordial wisdom' of the *tathāgatagarbha* is the antidote to nihilism, and belittling the *dharma.* 'Great love' (literally boundless compassion) overcomes self-cherishing with compassion for the sufferings of all. In addition to this, 'analytical wisdom' is the keynote attribute developed via the Knowledge petals of the Sambhogakāya Flower. 'Primordial wisdom' is the inherent attribute of the Love-Wisdom petals of this Flower, plus being its overriding quality. 'Great love' then is the expression of the Sacrifice-Will petals of the Flower, causing the compassionate acts of the Bodhisattva.

Buddhahood is the supreme achievement for all sentient beings via the existence of the *tathāgatagarbha.* That is the joy of the knowingness of all Bodhisattvas on the path.

Oṁ svāhā!

98 Ibid., 41-42.

Bibliography

Bailey, Alice A. *A Treatise on Cosmic Fire.* New York: Lucis Publishing Company, 1973.

——. *Esoteric Astrology* London: Lucis Publishing Company, 1968.

——. *Esoteric Healing* London: Lucis Publishing Company, 1977.

Balsys, Bodo. *A Treatise on Mind, Volume 1* Sydney: Universal Dharma Publishing, 2016.

——. *A Treatise on Mind, Volume 2* Sydney: Universal Dharma Publishing, 2016.

——. *A Treatise on Mind, Volume 4* Sydney: Universal Dharma Publishing, 2015.

——. *A Treatise on Mind, Volume 5a* Sydney: Universal Dharma Publishing, 2015.

——. *A Treatise on Mind, Volume 5b* Sydney: Universal Dharma Publishing, 2015.

——. *A Treatise on Mind, Volume 6* Sydney: Universal Dharma Publishing, 2014.

——. *Karma and the Rebirth of Consciousness.* Delhi: Munshiram Manoharlal, 2006.

Blavatsky, H.P. *The Secret Doctrine. Vol. 1.* Adyar: Theosophical Publishing House, 1971.

Brown, Brian Edward. *The Buddha Nature.* India: Motilal Banarsidass, 1991.

Coleman, G. *A Handbook of Tibetan Culture.* London: Rider, 1993.

Dayal, Har. *The Bodhisattva Doctrine in Buddhist Sanskrit Literature.* Delhi: Motilal Banarsidass, 1975.

Dorje, Gyurme. Trans. *The Tibetan Book of the Dead: The Great Liberation by Hearing in the Intermediate States.* London: Penguin Books, 2005.

Dudjom Rinpoche. *The Nyingma School of Tibetan Buddhism.* Translated by Gyurme Dorje and Matthew Kapstein. Boston: Wisdom, 1991.

Evans-Wentz, W.Y. *The Tibetan Book of the Dead.* London: Oxford University Press, 1960.

——. *Tibetan Yoga and Secret Doctrines.* London: Oxford University Press, 1958.

——. *Tibet's Great Yogi, Milarepa.* London: Oxford University Press, 1972.

Gardiner, James N. *Biocosm.* New Delhi: New Age International, 2006.

Getty, Alice. *Gods of Northern Buddhism.* Oxford: Oxford University Press, 1928.

Govinda, Lama Anagarika. *Foundations of Tibetan Mysticism.* London: Century Paperbacks, 1987.

Guenther, Herbert. V. *The Royal Song of Saraha.* Berkeley: Shambhala, 1973.

——. *Buddhist Philosophy in Theory and Practice.* Berkeley: Shambhala, 1971.

Gyamtso Rinpoche, Khenpo Tsultrim. Trans. and Fuchs, Rosemary *Buddha Nature, The Mahayana Uttaratantra Shastra with Commentary.* New York: Snow Lion, 2000.

Gyatso, Tenzin and Hopkins, Jeffrey. *Kālachakra Tantra: Rite of Initiation.* Boston: Wisdom Publications, 1991.

Inada, Kenneth K. *The Mūlamadhyamakakārikā of Nāgārjuna with an Introductory Essay.* Tokyo: Hokuseido Press, 1970.

Kalupahana, D.J. Trans. *Mūlamadhyamakakārikā of Nāgārjuna. The Philosophy of the Middle Way.* Delhi: Motilal Banarsidass, 1999.

Kholsa, Sarla. *The Historical Evolution of the Buddha Legend.* New Delhi: Intellectual Publishing House, 1989.

Kloetzli, W. Randolph. *Buddhist Cosmology, Science and Theology in the Images of Motion and Light.* Delhi: Motilal Banarsidass, 1997.

Lauf, Detlef Ingo. *Secret Doctrines of the Tibetan Books of the Dead.* Boston: Shambhala, 1989.

Narada, Mathathera. *The Buddha and His Teachings.* Kandy: Buddhist Publication Society, 1973.

Obermiller, E. *The Sublime Science of the Great Vehicle to Salvation, being a Manual of Buddhist Monism. The Work of Ārya Maitreya with a Commentary by Āryāsangha* from the Journal Acta Orientalia, Vol. IX. 1931.

Obermiller, E. Ed. and Prasad, H.S. *The Uttaratantra of Maitreya.* Delhi: Sri Satguru Publications, 1997.

Pettit, John W. *Mipham's Beacon of Certainty.* Boston: Wisdom, 1999.

Prashad, Brahmchari Sital. *A Comparative Study of Jainism and Buddhism.* Delhi: Sri Satguru Publications, 2nd Ed, 1982.

Rhys Davids, Mrs. Trans. *Samyutta Nikaya.* London: Pali Text Society, 1950.

——. Trans. *Nidānakatha* (Buddist Birth Stories). From the Fousboll's edition of the Pali Text. Varanasi: Indological Book House, 1973.

Snellgrove, David. *Indo-Tibetan Buddhism.* Boston: Shambhala, 2002.

Snodgrass, Adrian. *The Symbolism of the Stupa.* Delhi: Motilal Banarsidass, 1992.

Sparham, Gareth. *Ocean of Eloquence, Tsong-kha-pa's Commentary on the Yogācāra Doctrine of Mind.* Delhi: Sri Satguru, 1995.

Stcherbatsky, Theodore. *The Central Conception of Buddhism.* Delhi: Motilal Baranasidass, 1994.

Suzuki, Daisetz Teitaro. *The Lankavatara Sutra.* London: Routledge & Kegan Paul Ltd, 1973.

——. *Studies in The Lankavatara Sutra.* London: Routledge & Kegan Paul Ltd, 1975.

Tarthang Tulku. Ed. *The Crystal Mirror, Vol. VI.* Berkeley: Dharma Publishing, 1984.

Wayman, Alex. *Untying the Knots in Buddhism, Selected Essays.* Delhi: Motilal Banarsidass, 1997.

Index

doctrine, 348
experience, 263
explained, 351–352
impurities of, 498
meditation, 321
path, 500, 508
sixteen, 304–306
Arrow/s, 93–94, 96
Arūpadhātu, 363, 415
Arūpaloka, 413, 414
Aryan cycle, 266, 267
Aśoka, 288, 297, 302, 303
Aspirants, 333
Aṣṭadiśas, 33, 34
Astral body, 356, 414, 500
Astral plane, 358–359, 362, 462
Astral realm, 357
Asuras, explained, 200
Ati yoga, 17
Atlantean cycle, 266, 267
Atlantis, sinking of, 267
Ātma, 346, 355, 364, 372
Ātman, 276, 323, 373
denial of, 277–279
explained, 277
Ātma-pāramitā, 373, 374
Ātmic plane, 361, 363
realm, 357, 361
Atyanta-śūnyatā, 243, 246
Aura
healing effect, 126
radiatory, 183
Auric fields, 258–259
Avalokiteśvara, 128, 133, 447
Avatar, 65, 315
Avici, 435
Avidyā, 452
Āyatana, 45, 162, 205, 389
Āyuṣmat, 15–16, 251

B

Bala, 409
Bardo states, 122, 202, 220
Beasts, symbolism, 477
Beingness, 268
Bhājana-loka, 393
Bhāva, 42, 58, 322, 391
Bhikṣus, 304
Bhumispraśamudra, 12
Bīja/s, 95, 114, 258, 289, 292, 339, 342, 365, 381, 416, 420, 421, 423, 461, 468, 470
and the past, 253
of activity, 335
of compassion, 436
of mind, 426
sequencing of, 343
two categories of, 341
Black hog, 11, 245, 416, 451
Black magician, 4–5
Blind spots, 255–256
Bliss, 374
vs happiness, 375
Blood and prāṇa, 75
Bodhicitta, 64, 79, 84, 107, 121, 126, 133, 136, 150, 155, 156, 157, 160, 178, 182, 186, 189, 190, 192, 197, 198, 206, 211, 212, 234, 243, 260, 262, 281, 288, 291, 300, 316, 317, 320, 321, 333, 338, 340, 351, 352, 356, 361, 370, 371, 373, 380, 397, 415, 416, 418, 420, 422, 423, 436, 440, 443, 446, 455, 457, 459, 466, 469, 470, 471, 478, 479, 490, 491, 510
and honey, 441
and tension, 96
and the Heart centre, 46
awakening of, 511
evolution of, 263
generation of, 188
luminous Fire, 393
womb of, 480–484
Bodhisattva Path, 65, 143, 221, 228, 230, 251, 393, 394–400, 418, 421, 436, 443, 453, 466, 474, 487, 498, 511
and Śūnyatā Eye, 317–321
generation of, 500
to 7th level, 501

Bodhisattva/s, 82, 84, 106, 147, 168, 351, 457
 activity of, 159, 160
 and Aquarian service, 134–135
 and bodhicitta, 133
 and karma, 5
 and meditation, 65
 and Scorpio, 63
 and service, 74
 and tathāgata, 375–376
 and Thusness, 135
 and Western direction, 182
 as light bearers, 107
 bhūmis, 52, 119, 124–137, 136, 140, 155, 159, 241, 265, 293, 318, 319–320, 333–336, 339–341, 342–344, 346–347, 376, 422, 423, 424, 430, 441, 451, 453, 467, 478–480, 493, 497, 501–503, 506
  and Cancer, 109, 124
  definition, 124
  explained, 398–399
 Council of, 16, 51, 98, 122, 129, 137, 155, 180, 267, 335, 339, 399, 400, 445
 development of, 126
 directive agency of, 149
 explained, 352
 fame of, 330
 planetary, 120
 ten stages, 124–137
 vow/s, 237, 331, 441
 wisdom of, 36
Bodhisattvic virtue, 380
Bodhi, seed of, 468
Bodhi tree, 404, 469
Body secret, 221, 222
Body, speech and mind, 238–239, 250
Brahmans (500), 301
Breathing process, 190
Bristles, symbolism, 456
Buddha bodies, three, 220–223
Buddha-cakṣuḥ, 432, 435
Buddhadharma, 286, 458
Buddha element, 367
Buddha-embryo, 411, 412, 420
Buddha-essence, 454
Buddha-Fields, 158, 264, 271, 418
 manifestation of, 334
Buddha-germ, 115, 377, 379, 406, 410, 425
 ten viewpoints of, 369
Buddha-gotra, 442, 511
Buddha-Heruka, 449
Buddhahood, 130
Buddha-Krodheśvarī, 447, 449
Buddha-Mind, 43, 135, 161, 261, 287, 353, 361, 400, 422
 and Bodhisattvas, 265
 and mantric syllable, 29
 limitations of, 264
Buddha nature, 368, 458
Buddha qualities, 374
Buddha/s, 15, 46, 212, 279, 281, 282, 283, 291, 298, 323, 366, 400
 and Love-Wisdom, 442
 and Māra, 8–12
 and the Rays, 318
 as over-soul, 324
 aura of, 215
 definitions of, 270–271
 disciples of, 280–283
 in cosmos, 338
 Mānuśī, 349, 351, 352–353, 354
 not speaking, 327
 three bodies, 502
 thus gone, 334–335
Buddha-spheres, 338
Buddha's Wisdom, 419, 420, 422, 426
Buddha Vairocana, 447
Buddha-womb, 295, 349, 501
Buddhi, 357, 359, 360, 363
Buddhic realm, 357
Buddhism
 18 schools, 301
 corpus of, 299

Bud petals, 288, 293, 430
Bull of desire, 112

C

Caduceus staff, 116
Cakravāla, 412
Cakravartin, 506
Calmness of mind, 88, 110, 135, 138, 150, 154, 163
Catuṣkoṭikā, 269
Cellular units
 and 'selves', 330
Central channel, 218
Central Spiritual Sun, 106, 471–472
Chakra
 Ājña centre, 44, 112, 116, 153, 164, 168–170, 196, 216, 227, 285, 287, 288, 292, 299, 300, 303, 306, 356, 404, 425, 434, 441, 442, 476, 477, 497
  petals of, 154–155
 Alta Major centre, 305
 Base of Spine centre, 39, 112, 136, 154, 161, 164, 168, 180, 201, 220, 227, 267, 286, 288, 297, 302–303, 356, 417, 419, 421, 438, 465, 472, 477, 485, 496, 500
 combined Splenic centres, 107, 159, 164, 168, 183–185, 220, 285, 406, 418, 432, 437, 460, 463, 470, 496, 500
 Diaphragm centre, 97, 165–166, 166, 168, 177–178, 180, 186–197, 220, 304, 305
  and preta realm, 200
  as pump, 195
 families, 509
 Gonad centre/s, 201, 220
  left, 203
  right, 206
 Head centre, 11, 13, 32, 43, 66, 67, 114, 117, 128, 132, 134, 144, 148, 150, 152–153, 157, 164, 170, 178, 180, 185, 186, 188, 189, 196, 199, 204, 208, 212, 216, 217, 219, 220, 226, 227, 244, 247, 248, 249, 251, 282, 283, 286, 287, 288, 292, 294, 297, 299, 300, 301, 303, 306, 307, 341, 343, 356, 363, 368, 381, 395, 400, 402–404, 406, 417, 418, 419, 421, 424, 426, 430, 432, 433, 434, 438, 440, 449, 450, 452, 453, 455, 456, 457, 460, 461, 471, 472, 482, 483, 497, 499, 500, 501, 509, 510
  and Ājñā centre, 155
  and brain's perceptions, 193–194
  and Dependent Origination, 36
  and dharmakāya, 340
  considerations of, 151–161
  levels of awakening, 158–159
  planetary, 122, 132, 338
 Heart centre, 25, 39, 44, 46–52, 53, 59, 66–67, 70, 76, 84, 106, 107, 115, 117, 134, 140, 141, 142–143, 146, 150, 151–152, 154, 155, 156, 160, 164, 168–169, 170–171, 173, 174, 176, 178, 187–189, 197, 203, 206, 208, 209, 210, 216, 217, 219, 220, 225, 226, 227, 231, 242, 245, 253, 262, 263, 267, 268, 285, 287, 288, 300, 302, 303, 306, 320, 356, 375, 394–400, 402, 404, 413, 417, 418, 423, 432, 433, 436, 437, 440, 457, 458, 461, 462, 463, 465, 466, 470, 471, 482, 491, 495, 496, 507, 508, 510
  and Dependent Origination, 37
  and dharmatā, 260
  and eastern direction, 190
  and Liver centre, 191
  and Middle Path, 215
  and Splenic centre, 166
  Arian petal, 144, 165, 171

astrology of, 51–59
awakening, 184–185
in the Head, 46, 51, 106, 151–152, 156, 168, 207, 263, 289, 425, 453, 455, 456
non-sacred petals, 55, 56, 138, 160, 163, 232, 304
prāṇas from, 192
reversed wheel, 48–52
sacred petals, 55, 144–150, 304
Scorpio petal, 87
Taurean petal, 56, 97, 142, 186–187
thinking with, 35
vajra of, 297
Virgoan petal, 87
Liver centre, 169, 176–177, 189, 190, 191, 220, 225, 267, 500
Lung centre/s, 186, 196
and yogic breathing, 189
left, 188, 189
right, 192, 196
Maṇipūra. *See* Solar Plexus
Naval Centre, 210
Sacral centre, 39, 112, 136, 154, 161, 164, 166, 168, 169, 189, 201, 204, 205, 220, 224, 225, 227, 267, 286, 288, 302–303, 356, 413, 417, 419, 421, 438, 471, 481, 484, 485, 495, 500
and vitality, 508
Sahasrāra padma. *See* Head centre
Shoulder Blade centre, 186–187, 189, 193, 196
Solar Plexus centre, 10, 106, 108, 129, 136, 143, 154, 155, 156–157, 161, 164, 165, 166, 168, 169, 177, 189, 190, 197, 208, 217, 219, 220, 227, 234, 242, 243, 245, 267, 285, 287, 288, 302, 303, 305, 356, 375, 413, 417, 418, 419, 421, 423, 434–435, 437, 470, 471, 481, 482, 492, 495–496, 508
Airy prāṇas, 175
and 80 minor marks, 217
and animals, 194
and kleśas, 500
as synthesising centre, 195
iḍā attributes, 224
in the Head, 170, 298, 453, 455, 456
petals of, 223–227
Watery, 226
Splenic centre I, 48, 107, 143, 160, 163, 165, 168, 173, 176, 180, 184, 186, 187, 192, 195, 197, 201, 204, 205, 206, 209, 223, 225, 226, 230–238, 417, 418
and asura realm, 200
and Heart centre, 166, 171–172
and saṃskāras, 198
Aquarian petal, 231, 245
Arian petal, 172, 231, 232–233, 234, 248
Cancerian petal, 235, 244, 249
Capricornian petal, 231–232, 245
Gemini petal, 236, 244
Leonine petal, 235, 244
Libran petal, 234, 244
petals of, 170–179, 231–236
Piscean petal, 231, 245
prāṇas from, 188
Sagittarian petal, 232
Scorpionic petal, 233
Taurean petal, 236, 244, 248
Virgoan petal, 234, 244
Splenic centre II, 163, 165, 169, 171–175, 179, 183, 184, 187, 189, 197–211, 207, 234, 304
and animal realm, 200
and Gonad centres, 201
and preta realm, 200
and Six Realms, 198–199
and transforming prāṇas, 203–208
eight spokes, 201

empowerment of, 203
idā prānas, 174–175
northern petals, 207
pingalā prānas, 172–174
Watery-Earthy prāṇas, 188
Stomach centre, 169, 178–179, 188–189, 190, 191, 220, 224, 267
and hatred, 500
and Heart centre, 194–195
attributes, 193
Throat centre, 44, 52, 144, 154, 164–165, 168, 185, 186, 191, 193, 204, 207–208, 208, 210, 216, 220, 224, 227, 232, 245, 267, 285, 287, 288, 301, 303, 304, 306, 356, 413, 417, 418, 420, 421, 425, 432, 434–435, 437, 438, 452, 453, 477, 492, 497, 508, 509
and 32 marks, 217
and dark path, 169
and Dependent Origination, 32–38
and Taurus, 111
attributes of, 244–245
in the Head, 170, 298, 452, 453, 455, 456
sixteen petals of, 39–44, 219, 229
Viśuddha. *See* Throat centre
Chakras, 281
and emotions, 194
and physical organism, 193–194
and the senses, 313
as eyes, 255, 441
awakening of, 155
below the diaphragm, 470
explained, 205
minor, listed, 305
science of, 184
the Inner Round, 161, 163, 181, 183, 188, 190, 195, 197, 198, 204, 226, 229, 288, 302, 305, 356, 413, 418, 432, 438, 481, 485
Chakra system, 407–410, 437
and Middle Path, 168–169
Chakra wheels
motion of, 184–185
Character, lack of, 89
Chenrizigs Padmapani, 296
Children, symbolism, 497
Chisel, symbolism, 490, 491
Cintāmaṅī, 370
Cittaprakṛti, 486
Clairvoyance, 176, 380
Clarification, 31
and Clear Light, 27–28
and syllables, 30
and the two truths, 29
as Void, 26
four directions, 23–25
Clay, 489
Clay mould, symbolism, 487
Clear Light, 19, 21, 55, 56, 92–93, 117, 122, 130, 136, 149, 153, 158, 175, 177, 179, 194, 215, 227, 233, 236, 239, 247, 249, 256, 258, 260, 294, 296, 388, 392, 415, 425, 431, 437, 442, 453, 465
Clear Mind, 189, 409, 421
Clinging, 42, 232
Colour, 22, 31
and mantra, 20
Compassion, 142
Competitiveness, 262
Consciousness (vijñāna), 40, 57
Constellations (twelve), 51
Contact (sparśa), 41, 57
Contemplation-Buddhas, 347, 348
Copenhagen interpretation, 345
Cosmic astral, 355
Cosmic astral ocean, 142
Cosmic Fire, 353
Cosmic Love, 462
Cosmic magnet, 212
Cosmic mental, 355
Cosmic Mind, 131, 133, 148, 159, 336, 346
Cosmic Paths, 123, 131, 319
Cosmic Waters, 97, 107, 148, 159
Cosmic whole, 273

Cow Goddesses, 113
Crab, symbolism, 69–70
Craving, 233
Craving (tṛṣṇā), 42, 58, 80–81
Creative imagination, 30, 36
  and mantra, 25
Crises
  points of, 96, 116
  signs of, 66
Cross
  cardinal, 25, 71, 108, 118, 132, 146, 147
  eight-armed, 180–182
  fixed, 72, 73, 118, 128, 132, 149, 150, 240
  mutable, 25, 72, 73, 118, 150

D

Ḍākinī/s, 3, 320, 334, 336, 361, 369, 412, 418, 445, 465
Dalai Lama (13th), 50
Dāna, 230
Dāna-pāramitā, 228, 409
Dark brotherhood, 1–2, 5–6, 12, 14, 16, 123, 262, 337, 348
Darkness
  as ignorance, 97
  Lords of, 1–2
Death (jaramaraṇa), 58
Death Māra, 16
Deduction, methods of, 274
Defilement
  nine aspects of, 494–497
  symbolism, 458
Deity Yoga, 77
Demons
  and Vajrapāṇi, 13
Dependent Origination, 31–39, 48, 56, 59, 69, 74, 76, 80, 82, 86, 128, 138, 166, 222–223, 225, 230–238, 269, 388, 391
  and Heart centre, 37, 47
  and Secret Mantra, 34
  and syllables, 32
  and the zodiac, 52–58
  and Throat centre, 40–44
  and Virgo, 52, 103
  and voidness, 55
  as Void, 42–43
Desert symbolism, 254
Desire, 451
  as dirt, 462
  battlefield of, 85, 181
Destiny's action, 45, 203, 204, 207, 208
Deva hierarchy, 334, 335, 344
Deva/s, 3, 199, 320, 336, 356, 359, 369, 418
  and mantra, 19
  kingdom, 412
Devotion, 214
Dhāraṇīs, 29, 135, 189, 440
Dharma, 385
  eye of, 299
Dharmadhātu, 243, 245, 364, 370, 493, 502, 504
  definition, 385
  explained, 503
  Heart of, 505
  Wisdom, 260, 261, 388
Dharmakāya, 13, 49, 66, 92, 96, 102, 104, 108, 110, 118, 122, 130, 134, 135, 136, 139, 140, 147, 151, 152, 153, 155, 156, 158, 165, 167, 170, 180, 194, 213, 214, 216, 220, 222, 226, 227, 229, 238, 244, 246, 248, 250, 255, 258, 260, 263, 265, 266, 271, 272, 275, 279, 282, 285, 286, 288, 290, 291, 292, 308, 310, 312, 317, 320, 340, 341, 346, 349, 352, 361, 363, 364, 368, 373, 374, 375, 379, 384, 385, 387, 389, 392, 398, 404, 405, 406, 409, 412, 414, 416, 421, 424, 425, 431, 434, 441, 448, 452, 461, 469, 472, 476, 483, 487, 502
  and central Spiritual Sun, 106
  and cosmic Waters, 97, 157
  and dharmatā, 260
  and Head centre, 403–407
  and pure Reason, 28

and Sacrifice-Will petals, 442, 490
and svabhāvikāya, 506
and the Sambhogakāya Flower, 289
and the tathāgatagarbha, 400–407
as Cosmic Mind, 131, 336
ātmic level, 361
dissertation on, 503–507
experience, 215
levels, 355
limitation of, 344–345
mysteries of, 332–334
organisation of, 334–338
second level, 142
teachings, 287
'ultimate', 321
view from, 257
Dharmakāya Eye, 293
Dharmakāya Flower, 332–338, 341, 341–348
and a Buddha, 336
and Dhyāni Buddhas, 354
elaborated, 352–365
Dharmakāya realm, 357
Dharmakāya Way, 34, 122, 152, 168, 173, 214, 215, 287, 303, 440, 462, 469, 470, 483, 493
and Cancer, 109
and Head centre, 185
iḍā path, 169
suṣumṇā path, 169–170
Dharma/s, 25, 46, 64, 213, 276
explained, 227
verities of, 250
white, 2, 5
Dharma's treasure, 466
Dharmatā, 122, 150, 260, 263, 268, 368, 384, 386, 405, 414
definition, 385
Dharma wheel, 508
Dhātu, 45, 162, 204, 365, 389, 503
definition, 385, 412
explained, 363
Dhītika, 284, 300–301
Dhūpā, 446
Dhyāna, 222, 223, 237, 280, 289, 323, 413
Dhyāna-pāramitā, 243, 409
Dhyān Chohan/s, 347, 361
Dhyāni Buddhas, 17, 43, 44, 138, 213, 221–222, 232, 245, 260, 262, 296, 304, 312, 315, 344, 351, 355, 431, 491, 502
Akṣobhya, 3, 44, 142, 148, 150, 151, 153, 168, 170, 173, 210, 213, 222, 246, 293, 342, 357, 362, 386, 444, 446, 447, 448, 449, 502
and Vajrapāṇi, 21
Amitābha, 44, 141, 149, 153, 168, 170, 209, 210, 214, 221, 233, 246, 293, 295–296, 343, 357, 362, 371, 386, 444, 446, 447, 448, 449, 455, 502
Amoghasiddhi, 13, 43, 141, 148, 157, 159, 170, 209, 210, 214–215, 221, 233, 246, 294, 357, 362, 387, 444, 445, 446, 448, 449, 455, 502
Consorts of, 169
explained, 347, 352, 354
maṇḍala of, 169, 361
Ratnasambhava, 44, 142, 147, 168, 170, 209, 214, 221, 233, 246, 262, 294, 357, 362, 386, 444, 445–446, 446, 448, 449, 455, 502
Vairocana, 43, 142, 148, 150, 168, 170, 210, 213, 233, 246, 293, 296, 357, 361–362, 386, 444, 447, 448, 449, 502
Wisdoms of, 385
Diamond-cutter, 262, 501
Diamond Eye, 314
Dīpeṅkara, 353
Discursive thought, 179, 231
Discussion, 31
Divine Love, 145
Divine Thought, 404
Divine vision, 476

Divine Will, 212, 403
Divine Word, 111
Divya-cakṣuḥ, 432, 434
dPal-chan Buddha-Heruka, 447
Duḥkha, 322
Dveṣa, 451
Dweller on the threshold, 91, 107

E

Earth, The, 145
Earth touching gesture, 9, 12
Earthy domain, 355–356
Earthy substance, 371
Education, right, 101
Eighteen heavens, 413
Eighteen schools, 288
Eightfold Path, 38, 54, 59, 60–66, 95, 377, 447
Eighth Sphere, 199, 200, 204, 267, 437
Eight spoked wheel, 447
Elders, 280
Electric Fire, 118
Elements
  Aether, 14, 20, 29, 219, 238, 312, 314, 386, 389, 424, 444, 470
  Aether-Fire, 449
  Aetheric, 229
  Air, 14, 20, 29, 44, 59, 130, 140, 170, 230, 238, 311, 314, 357, 386, 391, 424, 444, 445, 446, 470, 474
  Air-Fire, 449
  Earth, 20, 43, 59, 77, 79, 126, 138, 139, 141, 147, 173, 201, 209, 229, 230, 238, 309, 315, 390, 444, 445, 446, 470, 485
  Earth-Fire, 449
  Fire, 20, 59, 79, 105, 118, 170, 201, 203, 219, 227, 230, 232, 238, 311, 314, 389, 414, 424, 444, 446, 453, 470
  Fire-Fire, 449
  five, 13, 139, 170, 213, 293, 355
  Void, 28, 29, 30, 67, 127, 141, 144, 171, 260, 359
    explained, 259
  Water, 20, 44, 59, 73, 86, 128, 142, 147, 170, 201, 219, 220, 229, 238, 302, 310, 315, 386, 434, 444, 446, 447, 462, 470
    action of, 118
    drying of, 209
    explained, 125, 156
  Water-Fire, 449
  winds, 13
Elephant, symbolism, 10
Emotional realm, 356
Emotions, mastery of, 125
Emptiness, 253–255, 263, 264
Enlightened view, 257
Enlightenment
  and the will, 212
  degrees of, 329–330
  drive to, 368
  four requirements, 372, 374
  gaining of, 330
  germ of, 120
  right completed, 217
Enlightenment-tree, 492
Equinoxes, 58, 133
Equipoise, 31
  and meditation, 21
Esoteric Astrology, 50–51
Esoteric view, 49
Essence, distilled, 493
Eternalism, 176
Etheric body, 19, 137, 414
Etheric double, 500
Evil forces, 1–6
Evil spirits, 2, 12, 14
Evil weeds, 125
Evolution, cycles, 266
Eye
  all-seeing, 25, 56, 76, 113, 129, 134, 143, 148, 153, 160–161, 189, 245, 300, 340, 396, 404
    and Taurus, 112
    as Ājña centre, 116
  and Clear Light, 256

and impediments, 255
of consciousness-void, 258
of the bull, 56
of Wisdom, 351, 425
symbolism, 370
various higher, 340–341

F

Feeling, 234
Feet, symbolism, 119
Fire, blaze of, 158
Fire-mist, 226
Fires, 393
and Throat centre, 32
of mind, 204, 208
of Mind, 386, 446
First Council, 287, 306–307
Five Tathāgata Wisdoms, 143
Forbearance, 241, 242
Foul-smelling, symbolism, 474
Four-Cornered Proof, 47, 48
Four ethers, 356
Four heavens, 413–414
Four Noble Truths, 61, 104, 270, 377, 439, 478
Fourth Council, 288
Four veils, 371, 372, 374
Free will, 320
Fruit, 373–374

G

Gandharvas, 3
Garbha, 279–280, 292, 347, 365
Garuḍa, 13
Gautama, 218, 283, 284, 285, 293, 336
Ghandhā, 447
Ghosts, 2, 12, 15
Gitā, 447
Gods as sages, 475
Golden Age, 303
Golden image, 489, 506
Golden statue, 492
Gold, symbolism, 459, 488, 490, 492, 504
Goodwill, 195, 197, 212
Gotra, 291, 364, 365, 411, 412, 421, 423, 450, 485
Grains, symbolism, 456
Grasping (upādāna), 42, 58
Great Gate, 252
Great love, 512
Green snake, 11, 245, 416, 451
Guṇas, 11
Guruparamparā, 126

H

Hands, symbolism, 74
Hathor, 113
Hatred, 440, 451, 495, 500
Head centre of Buddhism, 298
Heart of Life, 105, 137, 145, 446
Heart of the Sun, 106, 471
Heart's energy, 194
Heart's Mind, 465
Hell states, 393, 435
Hell zone, 199
Hermit crab, symbolism, 69
Heruka Consorts, 171
Heruka guardians, 128
Herukas, 170–171, 448–450
Buddha, 447, 448
Hetu, 365, 451
Hexagram, symbolism, 103
Hierarchy of Light, 267, 445
Hīnayāna śūnyatā, 263
Hindering demons, 2, 12, 14–15
Hiṅgalācī, 302
Holy of Holies and śūnyatā, 75
Honey bees, symbolism, 440, 441, 442, 443, 492
Honey, symbolism, 440–441, 442, 443, 444, 504
Horizon of awareness, 327
HRĪḤ, 210
Hūṁ, 209, 297
Husk, symbolism, 450–451, 456, 504
Hydra, 10, 60, 161

I

I-consciousness, 68, 105
Identity, 275
Ignorance, 40, 57, 328, 451
    as darkness, 97
    conquering of, 500
    elimination of, 49, 59
Illumination, 321
Illusion, transcendental, 496
Imagination, 36
Immortal brother, 136, 137, 172
Indriya, 45, 162, 204
Initiate
    fifth degree, 131
    in Capricorn, 91
Initiation, 119, 123, 132, 133, 134, 145, 146, 159
    1st, 126
    2nd, 128, 129
    3rd, 129
    4th, 431
    mount of, 59, 147
    path of, 137, 147, 148, 182
    tree of, 469
Initiation process, 399
Initiation status, 400
Inner giving, 230
Inner hearing, 157
Inner sun, 256
Intellect
    and Dependent Origination, 41
    and the senses, 313
Intensity, 281
Intuition, 311
Intuitive perception, 377
Īśvarī, 223

J

Jāti, 391
Jewel in the Heart, 296, 433, 437, 450, 465
Jina Wisdoms. *See* Dhyāni Buddhas
Jīva, 183, 186, 188, 289
Jñāna, 409
Judge
    activity of, 100
    qualities of, 98–99
Judgement day, 118
Jungle, symbolism, 67–68
Jupiter, 121, 123, 145, 148, 149

K

Kali Yuga, 319
Kāma, 415
Kāmadhātu, 363
Kāma-manas, 149, 170, 179, 223, 371, 390, 417, 418, 496
Kapilvastu, 8
Karma, 14, 15, 21, 38, 42, 47, 48, 49, 54, 55, 62, 67, 71–72, 73, 78, 84, 87, 99, 116, 120, 127, 134, 144, 146, 159, 161, 175, 201, 203, 204, 207, 231, 234, 237, 278, 296, 333, 337, 339, 344, 346, 348, 355, 372, 377, 390, 391, 393, 397, 406, 416, 422, 435, 438, 441, 452, 469, 484, 496, 509
    and a Buddha, 270–271
    and bodhicitta, 263
    and Capricorn, 90
    and chakras, 154
    and Dependent Origination, 35
    and destiny's action, 197
    and Leo, 106
    and Libra, 52, 102, 108, 145
    and Logos, 269
    and Sambhogakāya Flower, 317
    and śūnyatā, 262
    and testings, 128
    and the Eye, 255
    and the judge, 100
    as a dream, 510
    bubbles of, 258
    cleansing of, 436
    conjoined, 80, 113
    cosmic, 338
    elimination of, 208, 241–242
    future, 199
    mount of, 83–84

national / group, 53, 86, 102, 131
of self-volition, 82, 89, 104, 131
of Six Realms, 417–419
of wrong view, 325
originating, 345
rectification of, 90, 129, 184
streams of, 156
Wheel of, 273–274
Karma-formations, 87, 198, 207
Karma-Heruka, 448, 449
Karma-Krodheśvarī, 448, 449
Karmic law, 362
Kāya, 368
Kernel/s, symbolism, 450, 458
Kingdoms of Nature
and dharmakāya Flower, 334
King, symbolism, 483
Kleśa/s, 7, 238, 427, 499, 500
Kliṣṭamanas, 156, 190, 201, 225, 371, 413, 415, 416
refinement of, 208
Knowledge, 291
Knowledge-Holding Deities, 210
Kośas, 358, 359
Krodeśvarī, 146
Kṛṣṇa, 284, 301–302
Kṣānti, 231, 237
Kṣānti pāramitā, 409
Kśitigarbha, 446
Kuṇḍalinī, 12, 39, 111, 161, 180, 201, 207, 219, 220, 227, 297, 381, 421, 438, 500, 501
as serpent power, 13

L

Lāsyā, 446
Laws, cruel, 99
Laws of Life, 98
Leagues
250, symbolism, 10
nine, symbolism, 10
twelve, symbolism, 9–10
Left hand path, 133, 155, 169, 452
Legislators and karma, 100
Lemurian development, 266, 267
Letters explained, 19–20, 22, 30
Liberation (vimokṣa), 45, 46, 88, 186
Life, 288
and nirvāṇa, 271
energy, 190
principle of, 151
Light
and wisdom, 261
generation of, 69
Light of Life, 92
Lion's mane, symbolism, 126
Lion's roar, 106
Lipikas (karmic Scribes), 109
Logoic Mind, 400
Logoic One, 265
Logos/Logoi, 142, 258, 264, 266, 268, 334, 348
and 'emptiness', 268
and śūnyatā, 269
explained, 315
planetary, 338
Lokas, 178, 204, 214, 363, 393, 412–413
kāmaloka, 206, 413
rūpaloka, 206, 412–413
Lokottarajñāna, 429
Lord, image of, 474
Lord of Civilisation, 337
Lord of Compassion, 296, 334
Lord of karma, 147
Lord of Nature, 475
Lord of the Earth, 484–485
Lords of Life, 465
Lords of Sacrifice, 352
Lotus flower, symbolism, 281–282
Love, flood of, 107
Love-Wisdom, 142, 144, 147, 148, 149, 156, 161, 168, 170, 212, 213, 225, 282, 289, 291, 300, 309, 316, 320, 331, 336, 338, 346, 347, 348, 351, 371, 379, 380, 420, 423, 441, 442, 443, 446, 459, 466, 469, 473, 478, 482, 503, 505
and Pisces, 82

M

Madhyamaka, 129
Madhyamā-pratipat, 322
Mādhyamika, 150
Magadha, 299, 300
Mahābodhisattvas, 445, 447
Mahākāśyapa, 283, 284, 287, 293, 297, 304, 306
Mahāmudrā, 111, 117, 148, 287, 303, 336
Mahārājas, four, 109
Mahāsudarśaṇa, 284, 302–303
Mahāyāna doctrines, 286, 294
Mahāyāna ideal, 263
Mahāyāna tradition, 303
Maitreya, 107, 137, 304, 370, 446
Maitrī, 239, 240
Major marks (32), 217–220, 218, 219, 220, 350, 367
Mālā, 445
Malevolent forces, 14
Manas, 203, 229, 239, 363
Mānasaputra, 505
Manasic attributes, 393
Manasic Fires, 301
Maṇḍala, 18, 251–252, 275
  and mantra, 30
  mode of manifestation, 22–26
  of a 'soul', 279
  of Love-Wisdom, 80
Maṇḍalic palaces, 268
Maṇḍalic plan, 296
Mango tree, symbolism, 468, 471–472
Maṇi, 296
Mañjuśrī, 86, 117, 446
Manomayakośa, 359–360
Manovijñāna, 222, 223, 224
Mantra
  construct of, 28–29
  definition, 18–19, 18–20
  Void, 30
Mantrapiṭaka definition, 17
Mantrayāna, 77
Manvantara, 266
Maraṇa, 43, 391
Māra/s, 2, 6–11, 16, 30, 31, 117
  Adhipati, 6
  and prāṇa, 7
  and skandhas, 6
  and Solar Plexus centre, 10
  Antāgu, 6
  daughters of, 9, 11–12
  defeat of, 20
  dual aspects of, 12
  five, 6–7
  hosts of (Mārabalam), 5, 8, 9
  Kaṇha, 6
  Maccu, 6
  Manuci, 6
  Pamattabandu, 6
  Ten-fold army (Daśabala), 7, 8–10
  Vāsavatti, 6
  Yakṣa, 6
Marijuana smokers, 99–101
Marpa, 5
Mars, 78, 85, 116–117, 145, 149, 150, 159, 160
Master/s of Wisdom, 131, 147, 399
Mātṛpadma, 103
Maudgalyāyana, 280, 284, 285, 287, 294, 304, 306
  and subjective power, 283
Māyā, 53, 56, 75, 125, 138, 141, 218, 258, 273, 420
  causes of, 137
  fields of, 96
Meditation (dhyāna), 62
  and bhūmis, 127
  five steps of, 53–54
Meditation-Mind, 54, 62, 422, 425, 499
  and Thusness, 135
Mediumship, 121, 123
Mental blindness, 496
Mental plane, 362
Mental poisons, 509
Mental realm, 357

Mercury, 74, 103, 109–110, 111, 112, 115, 116, 116–117, 145, 149
Merit, 221
Middle Path, 45, 46, 88, 115, 116, 129, 135, 136, 144, 146, 159, 162–165, 166, 169, 177, 178, 184, 185, 215, 224, 226, 227, 231, 233, 236, 251, 253, 259, 262, 322, 324, 395, 403
    and chakras, 168–169
    and Libra, 102
    wheel of, 163
    zodiacal signs of, 170–179
Milarepa, 5
mind
    attributes of, 239
    monkey, 41
    straying, 17, 21
Mind
    abstract, 21, 66, 258, 266, 283, 289, 292, 296, 346, 351, 359, 363, 372, 385, 388, 415, 452, 500
    archetypal, 357
    attributes of, 251
    Calm-abiding, 278
    clear light of, 21, 130, 149, 175, 179, 194, 215, 227, 233, 236, 239, 247, 388, 392, 415, 437, 442, 453, 465
    diamond, 95
    enlightened, 384
    equipoised, 18
    Heart's, 76, 91, 159, 185, 209
    higher, 414
    mountain of, 147
    son of, 352
    tension of, 167
    universal, 141, 149, 161, 178, 341, 344
Mind's Eye, 153, 256
Minor marks (80), 217–220, 218, 219, 220, 350
Mipham, 261
Mirror Wisdom, 342
Miserable woman, symbolism, 481
Mithraic religion, 113
Mithyā, 323
Moha, 451
Moistening, symbolism, 371
Monad, 26, 293, 336, 341, 344, 419, 471
Monadic Eye, 271, 343, 344, 361
Monadic Form, 318
Monadic presence, 136, 347, 368
Moon, 68–69, 145
Mortal brother, 136, 137, 172
Mother Nature, 480–481
Mother of the World, 12, 362
Mudrā/s, 80, 167
Mud, symbolism, 486, 488, 489, 499–500

N

Nāḍīs, 219, 257, 372
    and chakras, 355
    and etheric body, 19
    and physical form, 71–161
    and pillars of temple, 75
    and spiral eights, 132
    iḍā, 11, 12, 115, 144, 153, 154, 178, 219, 220, 224–225, 229, 236, 244, 251, 287, 298, 404, 413, 471, 472, 489, 492, 495
        and Leo, 105
    piṅgalā, 11, 12, 110, 115, 143, 160, 219, 220, 225, 229, 236, 243, 251, 287, 298–299, 404, 413, 462, 471, 472, 490, 495, 496
    suṣumṇā, 11, 12, 116, 121, 144, 178, 219, 220, 227, 471, 472, 490, 493
Nāḍī system, 53, 121, 137, 154, 161, 168, 173, 180, 218, 219, 253, 285, 367, 390, 408, 409, 413, 414, 469, 499, 507
    and Heart centre, 262
    as tree, 428
    of cosmos, 348
Nāgārjuna, 93, 288, 321, 322
Nāgas (serpents), 13
Nairātmya, 277

Naivasañjñānāsañjñā, 363
Nāma-rūpa, 235, 388
Name, 19–21, 30
and 'self', 21
Nature, womb of, 70
Neptune, 145
Neurons, 194
New Age, 270
Nexus, 28
śūnyatā-saṃsāra (saṃsāra-śūnyatā), 22, 27, 33, 34, 56, 173, 215, 289, 292, 357, 375, 414, 431
and Gemini, 75
Nidāna/s, 41, 231, 232, 388–391
Nihilism, 175–176
Nine months of gestation, 60
Nirmalā tathatā, 151, 291, 318, 374, 381, 392, 415, 426, 428, 490, 494
Nirmāṇakāya, 44, 134, 185, 220, 223, 225, 243, 249, 283, 288, 315, 334, 367, 502, 505, 506
and speech, 222
teachings, 244
Nirvāṇa, 250, 259–260, 271, 374, 406
abode in, 374
limited, 376
non-abiding, 376
seven Ray aspects, 247–248
subplanes of, 270
unfettered, 409
Nirvāṇee explained, 131
Nirvāṇees, 345–348, 362
Nirvāṇī. *See* nirvāṇee
Nirvikalpaka-jñāna, 501
Nivaraṇa-viṣkambhin, 447
Noble Middle Way, 363, 395
No soul doctrine, 324–327
Nrityā, 445
Number 5, 309
Number 7, 501
Number 9, 60
Number 10
as a multiplier, 10–11
Number 15, 207
Number 16, 304
Number 22, 306
Number 27, 306
Number 35, 306
Number 100, 307
Number 500, 306–307
Number 777, 185
Number 2000, 300
Nyingma tradition, 17, 150, 261

O

Objective realms, 206
Oṁ, 207, 296
Oṁ, Āḥ, Hūṁ, 209–210
Oṁ Maṇi Padme Hūṁ, 296
One Thousand marks, 433
Outer giving, 229–231
Over-soul, 324

P

Padma family, 153
Padma-Heruka, 448, 449
Padma-Krodheśvarī, 448, 449
Padmasambhava, 13, 337
Padme, explained, 297
Painters, symbolism, 408–410
Pairs of opposites, 109–111
Pāli canon, 325–326
Palmyra tree, 471, 472
Paramārtha, 221, 222, 228
Pāramitās, 230, 232, 339, 340, 410
eight, 246
explained, 409
six, 228–252
Parinirvāṇa, 214, 264, 265, 283, 285, 287, 324, 327
Paripuṣṭa gotra, 364, 365
Passion, 500
Patriarch
1st, 284, 297
2nd, 285, 297
3rd, 283, 285, 299
4th, 300
5th, 300
6th, 301
7th, 302

Perception, dimensions of, 355–360, 500
Perfection
of Forbearance, 239–240
of Giving, 228, 237
of Insight, 238, 246
of Meditation, 243
of Morality, 237, 238
of Power, 237, 246
of Skilful Means, 246
of Striving, 240–241, 243
Permanent atoms, 382
Phenomena, co-actively produced, 81
Philosopher's stone, 461
Phur ba, 209
Physical plane, 362
Physical realm, 355–356, 357
Physical Sun, 471
Physiological key, 393
Piṭaka, 17
Planetary evolution, 418
Planetary Fire, 118
Pluto, 145, 148, 156
Prajñā, 169, 218, 281, 294, 442
Prajñāpāramitā, 150, 232, 236, 243, 247, 249, 284, 285, 288, 293, 294, 300, 374, 376, 409
definition, 237
feminine, 246
Prakritya-saṃkliṣṭa, 291
Prakṛti, 268
Prakṛtistha gotra, 364, 365
Pralaya, 119
Prāṇamayakośa, 358, 359–360
Prāṇa/s, 5, 52, 191, 219, 266, 309
Aetheric, 53, 171
Airy, 54, 196, 200
and karma, 102
and physical spleen, 202
apāna, 309, 449
Earthy, 54, 205
Fiery, 54, 111, 174, 199, 208
iḍā, 155, 157, 169, 189, 190, 193, 207, 287
kāma-manasic, 190, 267
manasic, 188
piṅgalā, 155, 157, 168, 169, 176–177, 190, 196, 207, 287
prāṇa, 311, 449
refinement of, 107
rejection of, 48
samāna, 310, 449
smoky, 9
suṣumṇā, 157, 161
two types, 229
udāna, 311, 449
vyāna, 312, 449
Watery, 54, 142, 198, 199, 207, 359
Will-Sacrifice, 286
zodiacal, 70
Praṇidhāna, 409
Prapañca, 318
Prasajyapratiṣedha, 261
Prāsaṅgika-Mādhyamika, 150
Pratiṣṭhita-nirvāṇa, 376
Pratītyasamutpāda. *See* Dependent Origination
Pratyakṣa, 360, 507
explained, 359
Pratyekabuddha/s, 351, 360, 372, 374, 376, 508
explained, 348–352, 352–353
orthodox explanation, 350
Pravṛttivijñāna, 41
Prayogamārga, 218
Precious jewels, symbolism, 474
Pretas, 200
Pride, 68, 511
Primordial wisdom, 512
Pristine cognition, 360
Probationary disciples, 333
Psychic sensitivity, 123
Pure Land School, 295
Purification process, 191–192
Puśpā, 446

R

Radiance, explained, 321

Rāga, 451
Rāgagṛha, 283
Rākśasas, 14
Ram, symbolism, 78
Ratna, 365
Ratna-Heruka, 448, 449
Ratna-Krodheśvarī, 448, 449
Ray Ashrams, 399
Ray aspects/qualities, 233
1st ray, 20, 77, 103, 112, 113, 122, 123, 144–145, 146, 148–149, 158–159, 167, 212, 233, 234, 247, 284, 315, 336, 363, 366, 371, 458
2nd ray, 20, 120, 123, 144–146, 148–149, 159–160, 167, 233, 236, 247, 285, 300, 316, 336, 351, 363, 366, 371, 458
and the Buddha, 212
3rd ray, 20, 103, 144–145, 146–147, 152–153, 167, 213, 248, 285, 314, 315, 316, 337, 363, 366, 458
and smell, 312
4th ray, 20, 109, 116, 117, 144, 149, 151–152, 159–160, 167, 213, 236, 248, 285, 314, 336, 363, 366, 458
and taste, 311
5th ray, 20, 144, 149, 153–155, 167, 214, 235, 248, 285, 314, 363, 367, 458
and sight, 310
6th ray, 22, 116, 144, 149, 157, 159–160, 167, 214, 248, 285, 315, 363, 367, 458
and touch, 310
7th ray, 22, 144, 146, 148–149, 155, 156–157, 167, 214, 235, 248, 286, 315, 363, 367, 458
and hearing, 309
of Buddha's disciples, 284–286, 304
seven rays, 55, 306, 366, 457–458
and enlightenment, 211–215
and liberation, 167
and light, 56
Rays of Light, 144, 314–317
Rays of Mind, 146, 232, 234, 314, 337, 357
Rays of Nature, 315
Real, the, 45, 46, 186, 188, 205
discerning, 54, 88, 108, 138, 165–166
Rebirth (jāti), 42, 58
Rectified wheel, 49, 88–123
Red cock, 11, 245, 416, 451
Reversed wheel
and zodiac, 66–88
of Heart centre, 48–52
Right hand path, 4, 7, 133, 155, 169
Rind, symbolism, 472
Royalty, symbolism, 480
Rūpadhātu, 363
Rūpārūpyadhātu, 429
Rūpa-skandha, 487

S

Sacrifice, way of, 451
Sacrifice-Will, 290, 291
Sacrificial Love, 489
Ṣaḍāyatana, 57, 235, 389
Sādhana, 75, 158, 207
Śākyamuni, 286
Śākyas, 306
Samādhi, 16–18, 45, 46, 54, 76, 88, 97–98, 111, 122, 158, 240, 242, 252, 309, 397
and comprehension, 102, 104
and karmic formations, 101
and Libra, 103, 116
and prāṇas, 13
and Sambhogakāya Flower, 317
mastery of, 53
yogin's, 48
Samalā tathatā, 291, 295, 318, 374, 381, 392, 415, 428, 456, 474, 494
explained, 291
Samantabhadra, 146, 445

Śamatha, 53, 56, 76, 137, 139, 163, 173
Sambhogakāya, 220, 223, 288, 502, 505
  and speech, 222
  of a Buddha, 271
  realm, 295
  teachings, 243
Sambhogakāya Flower, 24, 36, 51, 76, 81, 96, 106, 108, 110, 111, 115, 120, 121, 122, 124, 129, 135, 136, 157, 159, 181, 183, 199, 221, 249, 268, 288–292, 292, 295, 296, 323, 329, 351, 352, 361, 365
  and Akṣobhya, 386
  and ālayavijñāna, 487
  and bodhicitta, 320
  and compassion, 291
  and dharmakāya Flower, 332–348
  and Jina Wisdoms, 503
  and karma, 317
  and pratyekabuddhas, 349–352
  and Ratnagotravibhāga Śāstra, 366–410, 411–512
  and Rays, 315–316
  and 'self', 26–27
  and the 'dweller', 91
  and the future, 320
  as lion, 139
  as transforming agent, 265
  characteristics of, 280–288, 307–313
  death of, 130, 308, 317–319
  dharmakāyic revelation, 375
  five levels of, 293–294
  heart of, 464
  Knowledge--Knowledge petal, 381, 419–420, 422, 438–439, 449, 478, 479, 485–491, 492, 493, 499, 502, 506
    and passion, 495
  Knowledge--Love-Wisdom petal, 380, 420–421, 423, 438, 446, 449, 469, 477–485, 489, 490, 492, 502
    and hatred, 495
    and the Sacral centre, 484
  Knowledge petals, 282–283, 286, 293, 308, 316, 372, 384, 389, 410, 415, 431, 433, 434, 447, 450, 476, 487, 502, 507, 509, 512
    purpose of, 437–439
  Knowledge--Sacrifice-Will petal, 380, 421–422, 437, 444, 448, 449, 451, 472–477, 479, 489, 490, 492, 496, 501, 502
  links to, 170
  Love-Wisdom--Knowledge petal, 380, 423, 435, 447, 449, 467–472, 490, 492, 496, 502, 504
    and mental blindness, 495–496
  Love-Wisdom--Love-Wisdom petal, 423, 436, 446, 461, 463–467, 492, 496, 498, 502, 504
  Love-Wisdom petals, 282–283, 286, 294, 308, 316, 372, 379–380, 389, 394–400, 410, 415, 422–423, 431, 433–434, 445, 446, 487, 491, 502, 507, 510, 512
    purpose of, 435
    symbol of, 447
  Love-Wisdom--Sacrifice-Will petal, 380, 422, 436, 444, 445, 451, 458–463, 479, 490, 492, 496, 498, 504
  nine major petals, 419–426
  principle nāḍīs of, 491
  purpose of, 368–369
  Sacrifice-Will--Knowledge petal, 379, 425, 433, 434, 444, 448, 449–458, 451, 477, 492, 496, 497
  Sacrifice-Will--Love-Wisdom petal, 379, 424, 433, 434, 439–444, 444, 447, 451, 453, 455, 479, 492, 497, 498, 502
  Sacrifice-Will petals, 286, 294, 308, 315, 316, 372, 389, 400,

406, 410, 414, 424–426, 426, 430, 431, 444–449, 451, 452, 487, 490, 496, 500, 502, 507, 510, 512
- and dharmakāya, 504
- symbol of, 444

Sacrifice-Will--Sacrifice-Will petal, 379, 424, 428–439, 444, 451, 452, 455, 492, 497

Sampannakrama, 218

Saṃsāra, 272, 416
- and a soul, 279
- and dharmakāya, 108
- and mantras, 19
- and śūnyatā, 262
- as thought construct, 30
- mastery of, 233
- swamp of, 282

Saṃskāras, 47, 51, 80, 82, 87, 106, 126, 192, 204, 228, 260, 266, 281, 302, 322, 344, 388, 390, 496
- and Dependent Origination, 40
- and evil spirits, 14
- and māyā, 137
- and Splenic centre I, 198
- and the Sambhogakāya Flower, 289
- animal-like, 190
- as 'bees', 443
- as imprints, 374
- as objects of focus, 259
- as stains, 454
- Fiery, 14
- habitual, 274
- kāma-manasic, 197
- karma-forming, 192
- manasic, 476
- mastery of, 232
- mental, 262
- overcoming, 86
- refinement of, 171, 189, 190
- stream of, 263
- superficial, 178
- transformation of, 267, 295
- Watery, 14, 295

Saṃskṛta-dharmas, 227

Samudānīta, 364

Saṃvṛti, 218, 221, 222

Samyak, 322

Samyaksambuddha, 352–354

Śāṇavāsika, 283, 284, 285, 294, 299–300

Saṇgha, 281, 284, 285, 287, 293, 294, 297, 300, 301, 309, 323, 366, 367, 408

Santāna, 441, 495
- definition, 436

Śantideva, 359

Śāradvatīputra, 2, 15–16, 17, 216, 217, 221, 228, 243, 251

Saraha, 93

Śāriputra, 280, 283, 284, 285, 287, 294, 304, 306
- and Abhidharma, 282

Sarvākarajñāta, 342

Sat, 17

Saturn, 83, 90, 91, 145, 146
- Lord of karma, 147

Sautrāntika-Mādhyamika, 150

Sautrāntikas, 324

Sceptre-javelin, 11

Scorpion, symbolism, 63

Secret folk, 2–3, 13, 15

Secret Mantra, 23, 24, 28, 30, 36, 44, 94, 129, 147, 148, 156, 207, 220, 245, 354, 362, 455, 497
- and Dependent Origination, 34
- and Heart centre, 25, 46, 48
- and syllables, 29
- power of, 17–18

Seeing, paths of, 496

Self concept, 326, 330
- and Void, 26, 27–28

Self will, 452

Sensations (nāma-rūpa), 41, 57, 69, 74

Sense perceptions
- hearing, 139, 230, 309
- sight, 139, 230, 310–311
- smell, 138, 229, 311–312

taste, 138, 206, 230, 311
touch, 138–139, 208, 229, 310
Serpents, 116
Seven Patriarchs, 284, 286, 297–304
Seven planes, 363
Sexual forces, 110
Sexual function, 203
Shambhala, 94, 122, 130, 157, 318, 336, 338, 339, 354, 399, 425
and dharmakāya, 140
attainment of, 132
Lords of, 317
Shape, 31
and mantra, 20–21
Siddha, 4, 19
birth of, 201
Siddhis, 14, 112, 220, 237, 285, 340, 362, 367, 424
and mantra, 18–19
awakening of, 161
consideration of, 4
higher, 36, 121, 453
minor, 44, 129, 155, 169, 227, 435, 453
Śīla pāramitā, 409
Silence, 280
teaching of, 277–279
Sinful Māra/s, 14, 23, 29
six heavens, 413
Six Realms, 40, 198–199, 200, 201, 245, 270, 416–419
animal realm, 198, 200, 417
asura realm, 198, 200, 313, 416, 417, 418
god realm, 199, 417, 418
hell realms, 198, 417, 419
human realm, 198, 417
preta realm, 198, 200, 207, 313, 416, 417, 418
Sixteen consonants, 218
Sixteen delights, 218, 219
Skandha/s, 45, 162, 238, 289, 389, 391, 486, 510
and Splenic centre II, 203
explained, 390
rūpa, 238, 239
samjñā, 239
saṃskāras, 239
vedanā, 238
vijñāna, 239
Watery, 204
Skilful means, 63, 230
Skull cup, 156
Sky, symbolism, 370
Soil, symbolism, 470
Solar Fire, 105, 118
Solar light, 105
Sorcerer, 4, 6, 14
Soul-concept, 329
Soul-form/s, 267, 280, 281, 324, 327, 412
and the Buddha, 323
nine petals to, 282
Soul/s, 333
denial of, 277–279
functions of, 279
Sound, explained, 19–20
Space, 387, 389
Sparsā, 234, 389
Speech, 221, 222, 225, 239, 249
organs of, 32
Sphinx, 175
Spiral eights, 132
Spirit, Essence of, 493
Spiritual Knowledge, 281, 289
Spiritual Love, 281
Spiritual Power, 281
Spiritual Reason, 357, 359
Spiritual Sacrifice, 289
Spiritual teacher (ācārya), 107
Spiritual Will, 289
Spleen, 202, 204
Śrāvaka/s, 252, 374, 376
explained, 350, 372
Śravakayāna, 508
Stains, 454, 499–501, 507
Statue, 488
Strong anthropic principle, 354
Subhūti, 283, 284, 285, 293, 304
Substance (prakṛti), 103

Suchness (sarvajñāta), 342, 423, 502, 504
Sukhāvati, 295–296
Sun, 145
and prāṇa, 106
light of, 470–471
symbolism, 507
Śūnya, 331
Śūnyatā, 19, 25, 45, 46, 53, 80, 83, 88, 105, 114, 120, 123, 129, 135, 151, 168, 170, 172, 216, 227, 238, 242, 255, 269, 272, 283, 288, 292, 293, 318, 321, 327, 334, 335, 343–344, 349, 355, 357, 359, 363, 364, 365, 372, 404, 420, 424, 431, 461, 469
and Aries, 115
and attributes, 190
and clarification, 26
and compassion, 122
and eighth bhūmi, 130
and Nyingma tradition, 261
and subjective death, 157
and the mind's Void, 260–261
and the Sambhogakāya Flower, 289
as 'absolute', 321–322
as base for saṃsāra, 262–263
as mirror, 261–262, 342
as way of love, 466–467
concepts of, 271
containment of, 286
effect of, 317
five characteristics of, 259–263
four gates to, 47, 71, 108
Hīnayāna, 261
magnitude of, 185
obscuration of, 254
two characteristics, 262
veil of, 140
Śūnyatā Eye, 112, 121, 122, 124, 151, 183, 286, 292–294, 296, 321, 342, 343, 346, 350, 352, 382, 410, 425, 430, 431, 437, 450, 464, 467, 479, 500
and Bodhisattva path, 317–321
and diamond-Mind, 370
and Thusness, 136
Suṣumṇā, 244
Sūtras, 17, 282, 297
Mahāyāna, 298
Sūtrātmā, 120, 121, 434
Sūtrayāna, 251
Svabhāva, 291, 322
Svabhāvikakāya, 153, 348, 505–506
Svabhāvikāya, 366, 505–506
Svalakṣaṇa, 32, 39
Swastika, 449
Sweat food, symbolism, 456–457, 458
Swerving spirits (vināyaka), 2, 12, 15
Syllables, 40
and imagination, 36
explained, 32–33
Sympathetic joy, 237

T

Tantrapiṭaka, 23
Tantrayāna, 17
Tantricism, 286, 288, 293, 303
Tapas, 207
Tārā, 104
Tathāgata, 26, 55, 227, 247, 249, 293, 300, 315, 351, 365, 383, 407, 424, 430, 468
attributes of, 216–217
essence of, 486
sambhogakāya of, 221, 243
womb of, 279
Tathāgata-embryo, 291
Tathāgatagarbha, 103, 115, 117, 121, 129, 151, 155, 157, 163, 214, 221, 263, 265, 267, 269, 275, 279, 284, 291, 292, 294, 295, 311, 318, 319, 332, 335, 339, 340, 349, 350, 366, 367, 380, 410, 419, 422, 428, 435, 443, 460, 476, 489, 490, 494, 503, 504. *See also* Sambhogakāya Flower
3 x 3 meanings, 411–412
and Buddhahood, 512

and Heart of the Sun, 106
and Mind, 392–393
and nine similies, 411
and rebirth, 382
and stalking lion, 118
and Śūnyatā Eye, 370
and the dharmakāya, 400–407
and Virgo, 104
and Wisdom, 379
appearance of, 507
as sun, 105–106
as true self, 375
as womb, 482, 483
attributes of, 280–288, 384–391
awakening of, 383–384
colourations of, 316
construction of, 420
evolution of, 317
flowering of, 182
Individualisation of, 266
purification of, 371–373
reasons for existence, 368–369, 376–378, 509
relationships of, 378–381
three main aspects, 371
triune, 364, 502
Tathāgata-gotra, 415
Tathāgata's eye, 216
Tattered robe, symbolism, 284–285, 473–475, 501
Telepathy, 194
Tension, 94–96
sparks of, 96
Thaṅ-ka, 210
Theravāda, 284
Theravādin, 324
Third Council, 288, 294
Third Eye, 154
Thought-bubbles, 263–267
Three jewels, 367
Three poisons, 370
symbolism, 451
Three worlds, 354–355
Thus gone ones, 116, 344, 346
Thusness (tathatā), 45, 46, 54, 88, 90, 91, 104, 131, 140, 142, 150, 153, 158, 161, 213, 215, 216, 257, 265, 291, 297, 318, 339, 342, 361, 364, 365, 384, 398, 403, 411, 416, 437, 440, 445, 452
3 forms of, 135
and Aquarius, 89
definition, 385, 415
distinct from Voidness, 167
error-free, 46, 55, 88, 92, 135, 139, 142, 151, 152, 398
not otherwise, 46, 88, 96–97, 102, 142, 143–144, 397
potency of, 319
Tīrthikas, 374, 376
explained, 372
Treasure, symbolism, 492
Tree
fruit of, 504
symbolism, 428
Tree of Life, 471
Trikāya, 104, 348, 505
Tripiṭaka, 282, 283, 285, 298
Trividhasvabhāva, 291, 364
Tṛṣṇā, 233, 390
Truth
conventional, 29
flavour of, 457–458
Highest, 467, 468
relative, 269
relativity of, 268–275
ultimate, 32, 268, 272, 509
and clarification, 29
Tukhāra, 301
Two extremes, 172–173
Two truths, 37, 407

U

Ugly, symbolism, 429, 437–438
Universal king, 506
Upādāna, 232, 390
Upagupta, 284, 300
Upāli, 284, 286, 294, 305
and the vinaya, 283
Upāya, 218, 409

Upāya-pāramitā, 228, 246
Upekṣā, 238
Uranus, 145, 146, 149, 155

V

Vacana, 43, 222
Vacchagotta, 276, 277, 278, 279, 323
Vaibhāṣikas, 324
Vajradhara, 3, 17
Vajra (dorje), 3, 13, 14, 17, 18, 109, 247, 252, 444
Vajra family, 153
Vajra-Heruka, 448, 449
Vajrakīla, 209
Vajra-Krodheśvarī, 448, 449
Vajra-like samadhi, 499
Vajra-mind, 20
Vajra of the Heart, 209, 211
Vajrapāṇi, 2–3, 7, 15, 16, 22, 23, 216, 217, 218, 219, 221, 228, 236, 243, 246, 251, 252, 445
  and Akṣobhya, 21
  and mantras, 20
  and secret folk, 2, 12–15
  explained, 13
Vajra points, 366, 367
  fourth, 367, 507, 510
Vajrasattva, 148, 151, 210, 449
  and mantra, 17
  explained, 17
Vajrayāna, 17, 18, 148, 248, 251, 287, 476
Vajrayāna path, 13
Vāsanā, 81, 130, 159, 214, 258, 259, 397, 496
Vāyu/s, 218, 219, 449
Vedanā, 41, 58, 78, 234, 390
Venus, 87, 110, 111, 113, 145, 146
Vijñāna, 236, 359, 388, 390
Vijñānamayakośa, 359
Vijñānānantya, 415
Vikalpa, 318
Vinaya, 15, 17, 283
  teachings, 283
Vināyaka, 15
Vipassanā, 53, 166, 240, 242, 280
Virgin-Mother, 59
Vīrya, 237
Vīrya pāramitā, 409
Viśuddha. *See* Throat centre
Viśvavajra, 444
Vital body, 201
Void, 22, 53, 54, 67, 119, 155, 257, 265, 275, 286
  and mantras, 24
  and saṃsāra, 48
  as a force, 254
Void Elements, 28, 29, 30, 67, 127, 140, 141, 144, 171, 260, 359
  explained, 259
Voidness, 45, 46, 105, 139, 163, 172, 177, 244, 246, 405
  and Leo, 54
  distinct from Thusness, 167
  transcendent, 246
Vulcan, 112–113, 145, 149

W

Waters of Life, 110, 131, 133, 141
Water, symbolism, 370, 470
Watery thought, 175
Wheel of Dharma, 164
Wheel of Life, 11, 417, 449, 451
  and Libra, 101–102
  reversal, 73
White brotherhood, 12
White magicians, 4
Will and Sagittarius, 84
Will-of-love, 212, 213, 403
Will-Sacrifice, 292
Will-to-enlightenment, 281
Will-to-good, 113, 174
Will-to-liberate, 114
Will-to-love, 403, 452
Wisdom, 329
  and śūnyatā, 260
  Dharmadhātu, 311
  Mirror-like, 311
Woman, ugly, 483
Womb of Nature, 346

Womb, symbolism, 478–479, 480–482, 492, 501
Women, ordination of, 298
Words, 19–20, 22, 30
World-Soul, 280, 334, 335, 344
Wrathful Deities, 128, 156, 337, 449

Y

Yab-yum, 336
Yakṣas, 299, 302
Yakṣinīs, 302
Yin-yang (yab-yum), 70, 109, 263
Yogācāra doctrine, 150
Yogācāra-Mādhyamika, 150
Yogācāra tradition, 288
Yoga of the Inner Fire, 210
Yogic breathing, 189
Yogin, universe of, 3
Yugas, 266

Z

Zodiac, 9–10
  Air signs, 59, 110
  and Dependent Origination, 52–58
  and pairs of opposites, 109–111
  Aquarius the water bearer, 58, 59, 72, 81, 82–83, 84, 88–90, 110, 117, 123, 132, 133, 134, 135, 144–145, 149, 150, 153–155, 158–159, 161, 178–179, 232, 233, 250, 398, 403
    and Eightfold Path, 64–65
    and field of service, 141
    and light, 104
    and ninth bhūmi, 130–131
    and śūnyatā, 95
    and Void, 136
    as Airy petal, 141
    glyph, 399
  Aries the ram, 56, 57, 59, 77–79, 81, 88, 105, 108, 114–119, 116, 117, 130, 132, 134, 135, 143, 144–147, 156, 158–159, 165, 166–167, 171–172, 176, 232, 244–245, 395, 403
    and Dependent Origination, 56
    and Eightfold Path, 61
    and samādhi, 158
    and seventh bhūmi, 129
    glyph for, 114
  Cancer the crab, 54, 55, 57, 59, 68–73, 88, 91, 92, 99, 107–109, 117, 133, 134, 141, 145, 147, 153, 161, 173–174, 396, 404–405
    and aspiration, 71
    and first bhūmi, 124–125, 126
    and instinctual consciousness, 70
    and touch, 138–139, 140
    and Watery Element, 73
    and yin-yang, 109
    objective of, 107
  Capricorn the goat, 58, 59, 60, 62, 66, 71, 83–84, 84, 86, 88, 90–91, 92, 93, 99, 108, 109, 114, 117, 119, 129, 133, 134, 140, 142, 144–148, 150, 152–153, 158–159, 161, 177–178, 232, 233, 250, 398, 402–403, 405, 407
    and enlightenment, 90
    and I-Concept, 83
    and tenth bhūmi, 131
  Earth signs, 53, 59, 77, 114
  Fire signs, 59, 68, 79, 105, 118
  Gemini the twins, 53, 57, 59, 72, 73–76, 84, 88, 94, 95, 98, 103, 109–111, 117, 136–137, 140, 142, 145, 150, 154, 160, 172–173, 235, 249, 396, 404
    and bhūmis, 132
    and Calmness of mind, 135
    and causes of māyā, 75
    and Eightfold Path, 61–62
    and śamatha, 56
    and taste, 138, 139–140
  Leo the lion, 54, 55, 57, 59, 62, 66, 67, 72, 87–88, 88, 90, 99, 105–107, 107, 115, 117, 118, 132, 136, 141, 145, 149, 155, 158,

161, 174, 249, 396, 405
and I-concept, 68
and nirmāṇakāya, 134
and second bhūmi, 126
and self-consciousness, 70
and self-mastery, 105
and sight, 139, 140
Libra the balances, 52, 53, 54, 58, 59, 62, 66, 67, 79, 81, 85, 86–88, 88, 97–102, 102, 108, 110, 111, 115, 116, 118–119, 132, 133, 135, 137, 143, 144–146, 146, 158, 159, 161, 163, 175–176, 249, 397, 405–406
and fourth bhūmi, 127
and karma, 56, 75
and meditation, 87
and samādhi, 55, 116
as judge, 98–101
wheel of the law, 175
Pisces the fishes, 58, 59, 65–66, 72–73, 78, 79, 80–82, 82, 88, 95, 107, 117, 119–124, 132, 135, 141, 144–145, 148, 150, 154, 156–157, 159, 161, 179, 233, 250, 400, 403
and Bodhisattvas, 134
and cycles of time, 81
and eighth bhūmi, 130
glyph of, 121, 130, 157
rectification of wheel, 191
Sagittarius the archer, 58, 59, 72, 74, 84–85, 88, 92–94, 99, 105, 113, 117, 118, 137, 139–140, 142, 144–145, 150, 151–152, 158–159, 160–161, 177, 232, 245, 397, 407
and ambition, 92
and bhūmis, 132
and Eightfold Path, 64
and error-free Thusness, 135
arrows, 250
Mind and mantra, 94
Scorpio the scorpion, 58, 59, 70–71, 76, 85–86, 88, 92, 96–97, 104, 107, 113, 117, 119, 127, 133, 134, 135, 142–143, 144–145, 149, 158, 159–161, 176–177, 232, 236, 245, 249, 397, 406
and bhūmis, 136
and Eightfold Path, 63–64
and fifth bhūmi, 128
and power testing, 72, 90
and sting, 99
and Thusness, 56
Taurus the bull, 53, 57, 59, 72, 76–79, 88, 110, 111–114, 127, 133, 134, 135, 142–143, 145, 148–149, 159–161, 171–172, 396, 400, 404
and Eightfold Path, 61
and sixth bhūmi, 129
and smell, 138
and wisdom, 56
twelve signs of, 47–59, 402–407
Virgo the virgin, 52–53, 54, 55, 57, 66, 67, 71, 72, 81, 88, 92, 95, 102–104, 114, 120, 132, 133, 145, 148–149, 150, 159, 161, 163, 174–175, 249, 397, 405
and hearing, 139, 141
and the Eightfold Path, 59–66
and third bhūmi, 127
and time, 103
as mother, 59–61, 117, 156
womb, 148
Water signs, 59, 80
wheel of, 58–59

About the Author

BODO BALSYS is the founder of The School of Esoteric Sciences. He is an author of many books on subjects centred on Buddhism and the Esoteric Sciences, a meditation teacher, poet, artist, spiritual scientist and healer. He has studied extensively across multiple traditions including Esoteric Science, Buddhism, Christianity, Esoteric Healing, Western Science, Art, Politics and History. His advanced esoteric insights, gained through decades of meditative contemplation, enable him to provide a rich understanding of the spiritual pathway toward enlightenment, healing and service.

Bodo's teachings can be accessed via the School of Esoteric Science's website:
http://universaldharma.com

For any other enquiries, please email
sangha@universaldharma.com

About Universal Dharma Publishing

Universal Dharma Publishing is a not for profit publisher. Our aim is make innovative, original and esoteric spiritual teachings accessible to all who genuinely aspire to awaken and serve humanity. The books published aim in part to provide an esoteric interpretation of the meaning of Buddhist *dharma* with view of reformation of the way people perceive the meaning of the related teachings. Hopefully then Buddhism can more effectively serve its principal function as a vehicle for enlightenment, and further prosper into the future. A further aim is to provide the next level of exposition of the esoteric doctrines to be revealed to humanity following on the wisdom tradition pioneered by H.P. Blavatsky and A.A. Bailey.

Cover Design by
Angie O'Sullivan & Kylie Smith

www.ingramcontent.com/pod-product-compliance
Lightning Source LLC
Chambersburg PA
CBHW020632300426
44112CB00007B/91
* 9 7 8 0 9 9 2 3 5 6 8 2 8 *